ANGLO-AMERICAN RELATIONS AT THE PARIS PEACE CONFERENCE OF 1919

Anglo-American Relations

at the

Paris Peace Conference

of 1919

BY

SETH P. TILLMAN

PRINCETON, NEW JERSEY

PRINCETON UNIVERSITY PRESS

1961

Publication of this book
has been aided by the Ford Foundation program
to support publication,
through university presses, of work in the
humanities and social sciences.

✧

Printed in the United States of America
by Princeton University Press
Princeton, New Jersey

TO MY PARENTS

PREFACE

For perhaps the only time in modern history, an effort was made in 1919 to end a general war with a peace settlement which would apply principles of justice to victors and vanquished alike so as to prevent the recurrence of conflict. The states uniquely endowed by historical traditions and national interests to lead the world in this great task were Great Britain and the United States. Having long since solved their own internal problems of creating ordered societies under the rule of law, and being politically, territorially, and economically satisfied nations with no substantial positive ambitions to be derived from the peace, the English-speaking powers shared a vital interest in creating a new system of world order which would guarantee the perpetuation of their own happy state. They undertook to serve this interest by the application on a world scale of their own principles of ordered society and peaceful redress of grievances, and by the generalization, insofar as possible, of political, territorial, and economic satisfaction among all nations.

For the most part, the British and American delegations to the Paris Peace Conference of 1919 worked together with reasonable harmony for the achievement of common objectives. But there were issues over which the English-speaking powers were at direct odds and others over which secondary factors and obligations to third powers brought them into conflict with each other. The fullest measure of Anglo-American cooperation was achieved in those aspects of the peace settlement which involved measures for the maintenance of permanent peace, as distinguished from the immediate settling of accounts with the defeated enemy states. At no time, however, did the English-speaking powers identify their community of interests to the point of pursuing acknowledged common objectives by a coherent common strategy. It is the purpose of the present study to examine the patterns of cooperation and conflict between the United States and the British Empire in the various issues dealt with at the Paris Peace Conference, in the hope that the tracing of these strands will add another chapter to the still incomplete story of the peace settlement of 1919.

ACKNOWLEDGMENTS

I AM deeply indebted to a number of persons for invaluable assistance and counsel in the preparation of this book. Professor Ruhl J. Bartlett of the Fletcher School of Law and Diplomacy, who directed the doctoral dissertation on which this work is based, gave generously of his great knowledge and wisdom in the field of American diplomatic history, guiding me in every phase of research and writing, suggesting points of significance, and restraining me, on occasion, from excesses of judgment. Professor Albert H. Imlah of the Fletcher School of Law and Diplomacy gave invaluable guidance in British and European diplomatic history, assisted me with his authoritative knowledge of the complex economic and financial aspects of the Peace Conference, and suggested many improvements of writing style. Professor Arthur S. Link, distinguished historian and biographer of Woodrow Wilson, read the manuscript and offered many valuable comments and criticisms. Professor Norman J. Padelford, my former teacher and present colleague at the Massachusetts Institute of Technology, gave me counsel and encouragement throughout the preparation of the work, which I deeply appreciate. I am obligated to Mrs. Woodrow Wilson for permission to use the Woodrow Wilson papers and to Professor Charles Seymour for permission to use the papers of Colonel Edward Mandell House, Sir William Wiseman, and William H. Buckler. I am also much in the debt of Miss Dorothy Fox, Mrs. Rachel Lewis and the staff of the Edwin Ginn Library at the Fletcher School.

A very special debt of gratitude is owed to my sister, Mrs. Ruth T. Rubin, who gave prodigiously of her time and talent in the typing and editing of the earlier drafts. Miss Marion Polk lent cheerful and very efficient assistance in the typing of the final draft. The staff of the Princeton University Press have been most kind and helpful in the preparation of the manuscript for publication. Mrs. James Holly Hanford of the Press edited the text with painstaking care and a fine eye for detail and improvements of style. I alone am responsible for any errors in fact or judgment or other shortcomings of the book.

SETH P. TILLMAN

April 15, 1961

CONTENTS

ANGLO-AMERICAN RELATIONS AT
THE PARIS PEACE CONFERENCE
OF 1919

CHAPTER 1

THE EVOLUTION OF ANGLO-AMERICAN
WAR AIMS, 1917-1918

MORE by coincidence than by design, the war aims of Great Britain and the United States developed along closely parallel lines during the period of American belligerency in World War I. The emergence of common war aims between the two English-speaking democracies is readily understood against the background of political values deeply rooted in the Anglo-American past. But at no time in the course of the war did the heads of the two Governments undertake a joint declaration of common purpose. Reluctantly drawn from a century of isolation, the United States remained distrustful of its British associate and formulated an American program for peace while Great Britain formulated a parallel but separate program.

In the course of the war a significant measure of Anglo-American communication and cooperation developed between officials of the second rank and between private citizens interested in the creation of a league of nations.[1] There developed also a high degree of cooperation between the United States and the European Allies on the practical level of military and economic measures for the successful prosecution of the war. But on the highest level of government there remained a residue of distrust which was never fully dispelled in the course of the war or during the Peace Conference. It is the purpose of the present chapter to examine the double phenomenon of essentially common Anglo-American war aims separately formulated in 1917 and 1918.

I. *American and British Peace Objectives during the Final Stage of American Neutrality, December 1916—April 1917*

Relations between the Wilson Administration and the newly installed British Government of Lloyd George and Balfour got off to a bad start in December 1916. Distressed by the fall of the

[1] See Chapter 4.

[3]

Liberal Government of Asquith and Grey at a time when President Wilson was contemplating an appeal to all belligerents for a negotiated peace, Colonel House, the President's trusted adviser, predicted that the Lloyd George group would base their policy on a "knock-out blow," destroying any possibility of an early peace.[2] Wilson proceeded, nevertheless, with his plans for a peace appeal. Before he could issue it, however, the German Government asked the United States to convey a proposal for immediate peace negotiations to the Allied Powers.[3] The American Ambassador to Great Britain, Walter Hines Page, conveyed the German proposal but emphasized America's disassociation from it.[4]

Despite House's fear that an immediate appeal by Wilson for a negotiated peace would offend the militant Lloyd George Government and would appear to be in collusion with the German offer,[5] President Wilson issued his note to all the belligerents on December 18. Emphasizing that his approach was in no way associated with the overture of the Central Powers, the President appealed to the belligerents to state their views on *terms* for ending the war and *arrangements* for securing the peace. The President noted that both sides had stated common objectives in general terms, and he offered to serve in a mediating capacity. The note affirmed also the willingness of the United States to participate fully in "ultimate arrangements" for the maintenance of permanent peace.[6]

[2] House to Wilson, December 3, 1916, Charles Seymour, ed., *The Intimate Papers of Colonel House* (4 Vols., Boston and New York: Houghton Mifflin Company, 1926-1928), Vol. 2, p. 397.

[3] Chancellor Bethmann Hollweg to the American Chargé in Berlin, December 12, 1916, Edward Parkes, ed., *British and Foreign State Papers, 1916* (London: His Majesty's Stationery Office, 1920), pp. 496-497; Great Britain, Parliament, *Papers by Command*, 1916, Miscellaneous No. 38.

[4] Burton J. Hendrick, *The Life and Letters of Walter H. Page* (3 Vols., Garden City, New York: Doubleday, Page and Company, 1922-1925), Vol. 2, pp. 201-203.

[5] Seymour, ed., *Intimate Papers*, Vol. 2, pp. 398, 404.

[6] Department of State, *Papers Relating to the Foreign Relations of the United States*, 1916, Supplement, *The World War* (Washington: United States Government Printing Office, 1929), pp. 97-99, hereafter referred to as *Foreign Relations*; Ray Stannard Baker and William E. Dodd, eds., *The Public Papers of Woodrow Wilson* (6 Vols., New York and London: Harper & Brothers, Publishers, 1925-1927), *The New Democracy*, Vol. 2, pp. 402-406; James Brown Scott, ed., *Official Statements of War Aims and Peace Proposals, December 1916 to November 1918* (Washington: Carnegie Endowment for International Peace, 1921), pp. 12-15; Parkes, ed., *State Papers, 1916*, pp. 600-603.

President Wilson's assertion that all the belligerents had declared common general objectives was received in England with dismay and outrage as implying that the war aims of the Entente and the Central Powers were on the same moral level. The London press condemned the assertion as insulting.[7] Ambassador Page found Lord Robert Cecil, a leader in the Anglo-American league movement, deeply aggrieved. "The President," said Cecil, "has seemed to pass judgment on the Allied cause by putting it on the same level as the German. I am deeply hurt."[8]

The Entente Powers rejected the German proposals out of hand,[9] but in that winter of bleak reverses on the western front the American overture was not to be so lightly dismissed. Representatives of the Entente Governments met in London on December 25 to consider a reply to Wilson.[10] Their formal reply, on January 10, 1917, paid tribute to the sentiments inspiring the American note and endorsed the project for the creation of a league of nations, but asserted, nonetheless, the determination of the Allies to achieve a peace based on just reparation, restitution, and guarantees against Austro-German aggression. The Entente, in short, insisted upon a peace of victory.[11] The British Government supplemented the formal Allied reply to the United States with a communication from Foreign Secretary Balfour frankly declaring that the English people "do not believe peace can be durable if it be not based on the success of the Allied cause."[12]

Although President Wilson was not unmoved by the January

[7] Armin Rappaport, *The British Press and Wilsonian Neutrality* (Stanford, California: Stanford University Press, 1951), p. 118.

[8] Hendrick, *Walter H. Page*, Vol. 2, pp. 207-211.

[9] Parkes, ed., *State Papers, 1916*, pp. 497-500; *Cmd.* 8467, 1917, Miscellaneous No. 4.

[10] David Lloyd George, *The Truth about the Peace Treaties* (2 Vols., London: Victor Gollancz, Ltd., 1938), Vol. 1, pp. 53-58.

[11] *Foreign Relations, 1917*, Supplement 1, *The World War* (Washington: United States Government Printing Office, 1931), pp. 6-8; Parkes, ed., *State Papers, 1917-1918* (London: His Majesty's Stationery Office, 1921), pp. 603-606; *Cmd.* 8468, 1917, Miscellaneous No. 5; Scott, ed., *War Aims and Peace Proposals*, pp. 35-38. See also H. W. V. Temperley, ed., *A History of the Conference of Paris* (6 Vols., London: Henry Frowde and Hodder and Stoughton, 1920-1924), Vol. 1, pp. 171-173.

[12] Ambassador Spring-Rice to Secretary of State Lansing, January 13, 1917, *Foreign Relations, 1917*, Supplement 1, pp. 17-21; Parkes, ed., *State Papers, 1917-1918*, pp. 606-610; Scott, ed., *War Aims and Peace Proposals*, pp. 45-49.

replies, he was by no means ready to accept the Balfour proposition that a just peace could result only from the victory of the Entente. In a notable address to the Senate on January 22, 1917, the President set forth the conditions under which the United States would adhere to a league for peace. "There must be," he asserted, "not a balance of power, but a community of power; not organized rivalries, but an organized common peace." Such a peace could only be a "peace without victory," for victory means humiliation and duress. "Only a peace between equals can last." The peace, said the President, must be based on the principle of self-determination of peoples, and it must vindicate the principles of freedom of the seas and limitations of armaments. These, he affirmed, were "American principles" and "the principles and policies of forward looking men and women everywhere. . . ."[13]

Wilson's pronouncement evoked two distinct reactions in England: intense but private expressions of displeasure on the part of Government spokesmen and warm enthusiasm on the part of the Liberal and Labour radicals. Ambassador Page, who had received a copy of the speech in advance, warned that, by putting both sides in the war on the same moral level, it would give great offense.[14] To Lloyd George, the "peace without victory" speech evidenced the President's "detachment from realities." "To the Allies," wrote Lloyd George, "the speech was an offense —to the Germans a jest."[15] Colonel House reported an interview with Sir William Wiseman in New York: the Allies "consider it inconsistent for us to want to let Germany go free from punishment for breaking the very rules we wish to lay down for the future."[16] A substantial body of English radicals, on the other hand, who dissented from the official view of the war held by the Liberal and Labour parties, found themselves in close agreement with President Wilson. The call for "peace without victory" seemed to them to symbolize the joint hopes of Anglo-American

[13] *Foreign Relations, 1917*, Supplement 1, pp. 24-29; Parkes, ed., *State Papers, 1917-1918*, pp. 874-879; Baker and Dodd, eds., *Public Papers, The New Democracy*, Vol. 2, pp. 407-414; Scott, ed., *War Aims and Peace Proposals*, pp. 49-55.

[14] Hendrick, *Walter H. Page*, Vol. 2, pp. 213-214.

[15] David Lloyd George, *War Memoirs of David Lloyd George* (6 Vols., Boston: Little, Brown and Company, 1933-1937), Vol. 3, p. 525.

[16] Seymour, ed., *Intimate Papers*, Vol. 2, pp. 420-421.

liberalism. In the course of the war and in the Peace Conference, Wilson continued to enjoy the warm support of the English radicals.[17]

Nor indeed was Lloyd George, despite his propensity for bellicose fulminations, in basic disagreement with the President's ultimate objectives. William H. Buckler, Special Agent attached to the American Embassy in London and an astute observer of British affairs, reported an unofficial intimation by the Prime Minister that he hoped for American entry into the war not only for military reasons but also because of the moderating influence which the United States would exert on the postwar demands of Britain's continental allies. Lloyd George, in short, wanted both a crushing victory and an American sedative for its probable consequences.[18]

At this juncture, German policy was bringing about a profound alteration in official American attitudes and in Anglo-American relations. Germany declared unrestricted submarine warfare on January 31 and on February 3 the United States severed diplomatic relations. Wilson proclaimed the policy of armed neutrality on February 26 and by April the inevitable provocations had occurred which brought the United States into war.[19]

Wilson delivered his war message to Congress on April 2, 1917. Calling for a "partnership of democratic nations," the President declared that "the world must be made safe for democracy." The United States, he said, would fight for a "universal dominion of right by such a concert of free peoples as shall bring peace and safety to all nations and make the world itself at last free."[20]

[17] Laurence W. Martin, *Peace without Victory* (New Haven: Yale University Press, 1958), p. vii. This excellent study traces the unique wartime relationship between Wilson and the English radicals and its effects upon public policy. For a critical study of the *official* view of the English Liberals and the Liberal press toward the war, see Irene Cooper Willis, *England's Holy War* (New York: Alfred A. Knopf, 1928).

[18] Buckler to House, March 10, 1917, William H. Buckler Papers, Sterling Library, Yale University. Buckler engaged in an unofficial correspondence with Colonel House from 1916 to 1919, reporting on many matters of significance for Anglo-American relations, but especially on the views of prominent British liberals and radicals, with whom he had many personal, and of course unofficial, connections.

[19] Samuel Flagg Bemis, *A Diplomatic History of the United States* (4th edn., New York: Henry Holt and Company, 1955), pp. 611-615.

[20] Baker and Dodd, *Public Papers, War and Peace*, Vol. 1, pp. 6-16; Parkes,

The entry of the United States into the war on a resounding note of idealism guaranteed Germany's ultimate defeat—both military and moral. It was Wilson's call for a revolution in American foreign policy and in the international relations of all countries.[21]

As the United States entered the war, Sir William Wiseman, who was then in the United States, dispatched to London a memorandum on American attitudes: "The sentiment of the country would be strongly against joining the Allies by any formal treaty. Subconsciously they feel themselves to be arbitrators rather than allies." There remains, Wiseman wrote, a mistrust of Great Britain, inherited from the days of the Revolution, which makes it more likely that America will clash with England than with any of the other Allies. President Wilson reviewed the memorandum and pronounced it an "accurate summary."[22]

II. *The Pattern of Anglo-American Wartime Cooperation*

Justly or not, the personalities of the American Ambassador in London and the British Ambassador in Washington precluded the possibility of close Anglo-American wartime cooperation through normal diplomatic channels.

Walter Hines Page had been so outspoken in his sympathy for Britain and in his criticisms of American neutrality that the President and the Department of State placed little confidence in him, regarding him as being in the British pocket.[23] President Wilson was far from restrained in his opinion, referring to Page on one occasion as the "damnedest fool we ever appointed."[24]

---

ed., *State Papers, 1917-1918*, pp. 913-921; Scott, ed., *War Aims and Peace Proposals*, pp. 85-93.

[21] On the significance and implications of the war message, see: Ray Stannard Baker, *Woodrow Wilson: Life and Letters* (8 Vols., Garden City, New York: Doubleday, Doran and Company, Inc., 1927-1939), pp. 508-516; Francesco Nitti, *The Wreck of Europe* (Indianapolis: The Bobbs-Merrill Company, Inc., 1922), p. 32; Robert Endicott Osgood, *Ideals and Self-Interest in America's Foreign Relations* (Chicago: The University of Chicago Press, 1953), p. 257.

[22] Seymour, ed., *Intimate Papers*, Vol. 3, pp. 30-32.

[23] Sir Arthur Willert, *The Road to Safety* (London: Derek Verschoyle, Ltd., 1952), p. 58.

[24] Josephus Daniels, *The Wilson Era* (Chapel Hill: The University of North

Sir Cecil Spring-Rice, the British Ambassador to Washington, had only the most formal relations with Wilson. As a junior member of the British Embassy before 1913, he had established close ties with Theodore Roosevelt and the Republicans, which he maintained as Ambassador, causing him to be highly suspect to the Democratic Administration. Moreover, Spring-Rice resented what he considered Wilson's pretensions of moral superiority. He defined his own status in Washington most succinctly when he wrote that the President "practically never sees Ambassadors, and when he does, he exchanges no ideas with them."[25]

The necessary coordination of the Anglo-American war efforts turned out, in any case, to be of such scope that it could not be executed through normal diplomatic channels. It was brought about through a series of special British missions to the United States, while a pattern of the most intimate and informal Anglo-American communication developed between Colonel House and Sir William Wiseman. At no time, so far as is known, was any consideration given to a kind of "summit" relationship between Wilson and Lloyd George, or even between Lansing and Balfour, such as existed between Roosevelt and Churchill in World War II. Nor was such a relationship possible, given the personalities and positions of the two heads of government and their foreign ministers.

On the initiative of Lloyd George, a British mission, led by Foreign Secretary Balfour, was sent to the United States within a few weeks of the American declaration of war. Although the purpose of the Balfour mission was to promote wartime cooperation and to stimulate Anglo-American good will, there was some discussion of war aims, particularly with regard to the secret treaties among the European Allies. In a conversation on April 28, Balfour revealed to Colonel House the contents of the secret treaties regarding Italy and Asia Minor but, according to House, said nothing of those concerning the Far East.[26] Balfour and

---

Carolina Press, 1946), p. 623. On Wilson's attitude toward Page, see also Hendrick, *Walter H. Page*, Vol. 2, pp. 346-348.

[25] Stephen Gwynn, ed., *The Letters and Friendships of Sir Cecil Spring-Rice* (2 Vols., Boston and New York: Houghton Mifflin Company, 1929), Vol. 2, pp. 428-429; Beckles Willson, *Friendly Relations (1791-1930)* (Boston: Little, Brown and Company, 1934), pp. 313-324; Willert, *The Road to Safety*, pp. 49-53.

[26] Seymour, ed., *Intimate Papers*, Vol. 3, pp. 44-46. For an excellent study of

House dined with President Wilson at the White House on April 30. After dinner, in the President's study, Balfour repeated for the President the account of the secret treaties involving Italy and the Near East which he had given to House.[27] In compliance with a suggestion made by House at this meeting, Balfour, on May 18, 1917, sent Wilson copies of the Treaty of London, the Sykes-Picot Agreement, the Allied Notes of March-April 1915, and the Treaty of Bucharest. In his cover letter, Balfour expressed doubt that the documents would "add much to the knowledge which you already possess."[28] In a letter to the President dated January 31, 1918, Balfour elaborated his personal thoughts on the Treaty of London, in reply, he said, to the President's solicitation of these views through Sir William Wiseman.[29]

In the light of the evidence, it is difficult to credit Wilson's assertion to the Senate Committee on Foreign Relations in the summer of 1919 that he knew absolutely nothing of the existence of the secret treaties before going to Paris.[30] Although the British Foreign Office found it difficult to refute Wilson's testimony,[31] the evidence is convincing that Wilson was in fact informed of the secret treaties in the spring of 1917, and certainly before the Peace Conference. Neither Balfour nor Lloyd George, however, charged the President with anything more than a loss of memory

---

the significance of the wartime secret treaties among the Entente Powers, see W. W. Gottleib, *Studies in Secret Diplomacy during the First World War* (London: George Allen and Unwin, Ltd., 1957).

[27] Seymour, ed., *Intimate Papers*, Vol. 3, pp. 47-49; Blanche E. C. Dugdale, *Arthur James Balfour* (2 Vols., New York: G. P. Putnam's Sons, 1937), Vol. 2, pp. 145-146. See also Arthur Walworth, *Woodrow Wilson* (2 Vols., New York, London, Toronto: Longmans, Green and Company, 1958), Vol. 2, *World Prophet*, pp. 130-131.

[28] Baker, *Wilson: Life and Letters*, Vol. 7, pp. 74-75; Walworth, *Wilson*, Vol. 2, p. 13, n.7.

[29] Balfour to Wilson, January 31, 1918, Edward M. House Papers, Sterling Library, Yale University.

[30] United States Senate, *Report of the Conference between Members of the Senate Committee on Foreign Relations and the President of the United States, at the White House, August 19, 1919. Treaty of Peace with Germany*, 66th Congress, First Session, Senate, Document No. 76 (Washington: United States Government Printing Office, 1919), pp. 22, 29.

[31] No record could be found in the Foreign Office in August 1919 as to exactly what documents had been sent to President Wilson. Curzon to Balfour, August 25, 1919, E. L. Woodward and Rohan Butler, eds., *Documents on British Foreign Policy, 1919-1939*, First Series (8 Vols., London: His Majesty's Stationery Office, 1947-1958), Vol. 5, pp. 992-993.

attributable to the impaired state of his health in the summer of 1919.[32]

Balfour, it must be noted, was not altogether accurate in asserting about the White House meeting of April 30, 1917: "There were no secrets between us then or afterwards, on any of the many subjects that came up for discussion."[33] For there is no evidence that Balfour discussed with either Wilson or House in 1917 the Anglo-French agreements with Japan concerning German colonies in the Pacific and rights in the Chinese province of Shantung.[34]

The somewhat arid historical debate as to the veracity of Wilson and Balfour in regard to the secret treaties seems, therefore, to be resolved as follows: Balfour informed House and Wilson as to the general character of the secret treaties involving Europe and the Near East in April 1917, and sent copies of these documents in May, which Wilson probably saw but may not have read; Balfour did not, apparently, reveal the agreements on the Far East; Wilson seems to have been mistaken, probably due to faulty memory, in asserting to the Senate Committee on Foreign Relations that he had no knowledge of the secret treaties before going to the Paris Peace Conference. It is also possible that in his testimony to the Senate Committee on Foreign Relations the President meant that he had received no *official* information as to the secret treaties.

The Balfour Mission was a considerable success in its avowed purpose of stimulating Anglo-American good will. Balfour addressed a joint session of the two houses of Congress—the first Englishman to do so—and was very warmly received, while President Wilson applauded from the gallery.[35] Public distrust of Great Britain seems to have been decidedly diminished as a result of the Balfour visit, while official relations became distinctly more cordial. Spring-Rice reported that the visit had

[32] Dugdale, *Balfour*, Vol. 2, pp. 145-146; Lloyd George, *War Memoirs*, Vol. 3, p. 550.

[33] Arthur James Balfour, *Retrospect* (Boston and New York: Houghton Mifflin Company, 1930), p. 243.

[34] Seymour, ed., *Intimate Papers*, Vol. 3, p. 45; Baker, *Wilson: Life and Letters*, Vol. 7, pp. 74-75; Herbert Hoover, *The Ordeal of Woodrow Wilson* (New York, Toronto, London: McGraw-Hill Book Company, Inc., 1958), pp. 79-80.

[35] Dugdale, *Balfour*, Vol. 2, pp. 147-150; Willert, *The Road to Safety*, p. 76.

created "an entirely new atmosphere in Anglo-American relations,"[36] and Polk advised Page that Wilson and Balfour had got
on together "tremendously."[37]

At President Wilson's suggestion, Balfour assigned Sir William
Wiseman to remain in Washington as British Intelligence Officer,
in fact to serve as a special link between the United States Government and the British Foreign Office. Wiseman had first come
to the United States in 1915 and had long since become the chosen
British intimate of both the President and Colonel House.[38]
Wilson encouraged a very intimate relationship between House
and Wiseman in order to foster a frank Anglo-American relationship not possible between official departments of government.[39]
House and Wiseman occupied apartments in the same building
on East 53rd Street in New York, where they spent hours together
daily and from which House maintained a private telephone line
to the White House and Wiseman cabled by a private code to
the Foreign Office in London.[40] A pattern of communication thus
developed whereby Balfour could communicate privately with
President Wilson and receive a response within a few hours. The
apartment building on East 53rd Street, and the House-Wiseman
relationship, became the "nerve center" of Anglo-American wartime cooperation. Even the President opened his door and his
mind to the self-possessed and unemotional Wiseman, using him
fully as a liaison agent.[41]

House and Wiseman, highly congenial to each other, became
life-long friends. "No one," wrote House to Lloyd George, "knows
the American viewpoint better than Wiseman. He has my entire
confidence and his good sense and discretion have been of more
value to the two Governments than I can tell you."[42] House

[36] Spring-Rice to (probably) Cecil, May 18, 1917, Gwynn, ed., *Spring-Rice*,
Vol. 2, p. 400.
[37] Polk to Page, May 25, 1917, Hendrick, *Walter H. Page*, Vol. 2, pp. 263-264.
See also Charles Seymour, "War-Time Relations of America and Great Britain,"
The Atlantic Monthly, Vol. 133, No. 5 (May 1924), pp. 669-677.
[38] Willert, *The Road to Safety*, pp. 1-16, 81.
[39] Seymour, ed., *Intimate Papers*, Vol. 3, pp. 64-65.
[40] House Diary, Vol. 13, February 15, 1918, House Papers.
[41] Seymour, "War-Time Relations," *The Atlantic Monthly*, Vol. 133, pp. 674-
676; Seymour, ed., *Intimate Papers*, Vol. 3, p. 65; Willert, *The Road to Safety*,
pp. 61-66.
[42] House to Lloyd George, July 15, 1917, House Papers.

even recommended to the President, during the Peace Conference, that he award the Distinguished Service Medal to Wiseman.[43]

The Balfour Mission to Washington was followed in 1917 by missions led by Lord Northcliffe and Lord Reading for purposes of coordinating specific aspects of the Anglo-American war effort.[44] Lord Northcliffe remained in the United States from June to November 1917 as head of the British War Mission. He had no diplomatic status, lived in New York, and concentrated on problems of shipping, food, and munitions. He engaged, however, in extensive propaganda activities through the press and public appearances and achieved a considerable measure of mass publicity.[45] Lord Reading came to the United States in September 1917 to deal with inter-Allied problems of supply and finance. His conversations with Secretary of the Treasury McAdoo paved the way for the establishment of an inter-Allied financial council to coordinate Allied war purchases in the United States. Reading strongly urged an American war mission to Europe, which resulted in House's trip to London and Paris late in 1917.[46] Reading returned to England with Lord Northcliffe in November 1917.

Anglo-American wartime cooperation was not without certain stresses. Wilson seems to have entertained a vague mistrust of the British Government, observing on one occasion that they did not "stand put,"[47] complaining on another of the lack of imagination of the British Admiralty.[48] Lloyd George, on the other hand, regarded American preparations in 1917 for a vigorous prosecution of the war as inexplicably slow and regarded President Wilson as "not cut out for a great War Minister."[49] On the whole, however, a system of cooperation and consultation

---

[43] House to Wilson, April 25, 1919, Woodrow Wilson Papers, Library of Congress, Washington, D.C., Series 8-A.

[44] These missions dealt largely with technical problems of food, shipping, petroleum, aeronautical supplies, etc. See Colonel W. G. Lyddon, *British War Missions to the United States, 1914-1918* (London, New York, Toronto: Oxford University Press, 1938).

[45] Seymour, ed., *Intimate Papers*, Vol. 3, pp. 84-86; Willert, *The Road to Safety*, pp. 95-115.

[46] Concerning the House mission, see Section IV below.

[47] House Diary, Vol. 13, May 17, 1918, House Papers.

[48] See Wilson's address to Officers of the Atlantic Fleet, Baker and Dodd, eds., *Public Papers, War and Peace*, Vol. 1, pp. 82-87; Daniels, *The Wilson Era*, pp. 43-45.

[49] Lloyd George, *War Memoirs*, Vol. 5, pp. 394-395, 450-451.

evolved in 1917, focused on the informal relationship between House and Wiseman, and to a lesser extent on the special British war missions to the United States. The official diplomatic channels, largely because of personality factors, were in great measure ignored. What is perhaps of greatest significance, in its implications for Anglo-American relations at the Peace Conference, is the failure of Wilson and Lloyd George to develop, indeed, so far as is known, even to consider, a kind of personal "summit" relationship.

III. *Anglo-American War Aims, April-December 1917*

The entry of the United States into the war terminated President Wilson's role as a mediator but it did not alter his basic objective or even his essential methods. The President's objective was still a peace of justice and reconciliation; his methods were still those of a spokesman of mankind standing apart from and above the ambitions and passions of the European "Associates."[50]

President Wilson became the mind and voice of the Western Powers. To the British, his addresses had a special appeal, partly, of course, because they were delivered in English, but essentially because their content and texture of thought had an English setting. Wilson the southern Presbyterian had much of the New England Puritan and the English Whig in his composition. The Wilsonian pronouncements contributed to a temporary but genuine spiritual union between the English and American peoples.[51] This effect in Anglo-American relations issues from the fact that Wilson chose to couch his pronouncements in terms of universal values and a new world order, although the objective of world peace and a world order under the rule of law could as well have been framed in terms of the national interests of so satisfied a country as the United States. Wilson's public pronouncements were all but devoid of references to the strategic impact which a German victory would have on the United States. He did not neglect problems of American strategic interest but consciously subordinated them to the ideal values with which they so fully

[50] See Arthur S. Link, *Wilson the Diplomatist* (Baltimore: The Johns Hopkins Press, 1957), pp. 97-98.
[51] See R. B. Mowat, *The American Entente* (London: Edward Arnold and Company, 1939), pp. 181-182.

harmonized, and thereby became the spokesman not only of the United States but of the entire democratic world.[52]

On June 14, 1917, Flag Day, President Wilson delivered an address embodying a slashing attack on the "military masters of Germany" and warning against a premature peace, emphasizing that the Allied and Associated Powers had no quarrel with the German *people*.[53] The Flag Day speech set off a flurry of alarm among the English radicals, who regarded it, rightly, as a departure from "peace without victory" and feared that Wilson had been caught up in the war fever. Their disenchantment with the President was to prove brief, however, as the President's subsequent pronouncements reassured these dissident Englishmen of the common objectives which he shared with them.[54]

The British Government proclaimed its full identification with the war aims pronounced by Wilson. In an address at Glasgow on June 29, 1917, Lloyd George laid down some of the specifics of these war aims as he conceived them: Germany must pay indemnities; Mesopotamia must never be restored to the "blasting tyranny of the Turk"; Germany's colonies would be disposed of at the peace conference in accordance with the wishes of the inhabitants.[55] In London on July 21, Lloyd George took up the theme of Wilson's Flag Day speech, declaring that the Allies could readily make peace with a "free Germany," but not with a Germany dominated by autocracy.[56] Foreign Secretary Balfour, in a speech to the House of Commons on July 30, called for a peace which "commends itself to the conscience of America and Great Britain . . . the only two [countries] which have no selfish European interests to serve. . . ."[57]

Despite this harmony, indeed seeming coordination, of British and American declarations, Wilson remained suspicious. He

[52] Concerning the relationship between American interests and Wilson's espousal of the universal values of democracy, see Charles Seymour, *American Diplomacy during the World War* (Baltimore: The Johns Hopkins Press, 1934), p. 255; Osgood, *Ideals and Self-Interest*, pp. 174-177; George Creel, *The War, the World and Wilson* (New York and London: Harper and Brothers Publishers, 1920), p. 124.

[53] *Foreign Relations, 1917*, Supplement 2 (2 Vols., Washington: United States Government Printing Office, 1932), Vol. 1, pp. 96-100.

[54] Martin, *Peace without Victory*, pp. 136-141.

[55] Scott, ed., *War Aims and Peace Proposals*, pp. 107-114.

[56] *ibid.*, pp. 117-120.   [57] *ibid.*, pp. 122-128.

wrote to House on July 21: ". . . England and France have not the same views with regard to peace that we have by any means. When the war is over we can force them to our way of thinking, because by that time they will, among other things, be financially in our hands; but we cannot force them now and any attempt to speak for them or to speak our common mind would bring on disagreements which would inevitably come to the surface in public. . . ."[58]

Sir William Wiseman pointed to the absence of mutual understanding between Great Britain and the United States in a memorandum written for the British Government in August 1917. Although the war aims of the two nations were probably the same, wrote Wiseman, and the President believed in the special political virtues of the Anglo-Saxon race, there was nevertheless a lingering historical mistrust of Great Britain among the American people dating from the Revolution, by contrast with their historical sympathy with France. As to the prospects of Anglo-American cooperation at the peace conference, Wiseman wrote: "America would never for a moment admit that she is prepared to follow the lead of England, but it is nevertheless true that unconsciously she is holding on to British traditions and would more readily accept the British than any other point of view, always provided no suggestion escaped that England was guiding or leading the foreign policies of the United States."[59]

On August 1, 1917, the Pope addressed the belligerents, suggesting peace on the basis of complete restoration of all territories and arrangements for disarmament and international arbitration.[60] The Papal peace offer was automatically suspect to the Allied and Associated Powers because of the rather cordial relations which existed between the Vatican and Berlin and Vienna, where, in fact, the press was generally sympathetic to the Papal offer.[61] Wilson decided on a stern reply to the Vatican, rejecting a settlement based on the *status quo ante bellum* and flatly refusing to

[58] Baker, *Wilson: Life and Letters*, Vol. 7, p. 43, n.3.
[59] Memorandum on Anglo-American Relations, August 1917, Sir William Wiseman Papers, Sterling Library, Yale University.
[60] *Foreign Relations, 1917*, Supplement 2, Vol. 1, pp. 162-164; Parkes, ed., *State Papers*, 1917-1918, pp. 576-579; *Cmd.* 261, 1919, Miscellaneous No. 7.
[61] Kent Forster, *The Failures of Peace* (Washington: American Council on Public Affairs, 1941), pp. 129-134.

deal with the "morally bankrupt" Imperial German Government.[62] House cabled the substance of Wilson's views to Balfour, who replied with an assertion of his "fullest sympathy" for the President's position.[63] Lloyd George and Balfour left it to President Wilson to reply officially, confident that his views were in accord with their own.[64]

The President's reply to the Pope firmly rejected a peace based on the *status quo ante bellum,* a condition, said Wilson, which would foster the renewal of the Imperial German Government's power and policy. Emphasizing again the theme of Allied friendliness toward the German people, the message asserted that the word of the present German rulers could not be counted upon to sustain the guarantees essential to a lasting peace.[65] Wilson's stern rejection of the Papal offer was wholeheartedly endorsed by the British Government.[66]

Despite continuing evidences of harmony between the war aims of Britain and the United States, Wilson remained doubtful as to the true objectives of Britain and the Allies. He wrote to House on September 2 that he thought the time had come to seek to ascertain systematically the specific objectives of all the Allies for the peace settlement, "in order that we may formulate our own position either for or against them and begin to gather the influence we wish to employ. . . ." The President went on to suggest that Colonel House gather a group of experts to collect materials for formulating an American program.[67] Wilson further discussed the idea of an organization of experts with Secretary Lansing and on September 19 wrote again to House giving him a free hand to undertake a program of preparing data for the peace conference. There came thus into being "the

[62] Wilson to House, August 16, 1917, Baker, *Wilson: Life and Letters,* Vol. 8, pp. 218-219.

[63] Balfour to House, August 22, 1916, Seymour, ed., *Intimate Papers,* Vol. 3, pp. 155-156.

[64] Lloyd George, *War Memoirs,* Vol. 4, pp. 283-284.

[65] *Foreign Relations, 1917,* Supplement 2, Vol. 1, pp. 178-179; Baker and Dodd, eds., *Public Papers, War and Peace,* Vol. 1, pp. 93-95; Scott, ed., *War Aims and Peace Proposals,* pp. 133-135.

[66] Page to Lansing, August 30, 1917, *Foreign Relations, 1917,* Supplement 2, Vol. 1, p. 181.

[67] Wilson to House, September 2, 1917, Seymour, ed., *Intimate Papers,* Vol. 3, pp. 168-169; Seymour, *American Diplomacy during the World War,* p. 278.

Inquiry," an organization designed not only to prepare an American peace program but to study Allied aims as well and to prepare plans for coping with them where they conflicted with American aims.[68]

House began at once to gather scholars from the various social sciences. Sidney Edward Mezes of the City College of New York was appointed director of the Inquiry; David Hunter Miller was selected as treasurer and legal expert; Walter Lippmann as secretary, interpreter of policy, and liaison agent to House; Professor Archibald Coolidge of Harvard as authority on Eastern European history; Dr. Isaiah Bowman, Director of the American Geographical Society, as Chief Territorial Expert and Executive Officer; George Louis Beer as expert on Anglo-American relations and colonial policy. Other members of the Inquiry staff were Professor Allyn A. Young of Cornell on economics, Dean Charles H. Haskins of the Harvard Graduate School on French eastern frontiers, R. H. Lord of Harvard on Poland, Charles Seymour of Yale on Austria-Hungary, and many other distinguished academicians.[69] The Inquiry established its headquarters in the building of the American Geographical Society in New York and set to work gathering data for the peace conference. The bulk of its work dealt with proposed frontiers in Central Europe and the Near East. By late fall of 1917, the Inquiry was submitting its first reports.[70]

In December 1918, the Inquiry went as a body to Paris, where its members served as experts on committees dealing with boundaries, reparations, international law and organization, and other problems, providing the statesmen with the objective data and advice on which claims for the justice of the treaties must so largely rest. Sir William Wiseman in 1928 recalled the work of the Inquiry as one of the most important historical services of

---

[68] Seymour, ed., *Intimate Papers*, Vol. 3, pp. 169-170; Seymour, *American Diplomacy during the World War*, pp. 278-279.

[69] Sidney Edward Mezes, "Preparations for Peace," *What Really Happened at Paris* (Edward Mandell House and Charles Seymour, eds., New York: Charles Scribner's Sons, 1921), p. 1; James T. Shotwell, *At the Paris Peace Conference* (New York: The Macmillan Company, 1937), pp. 3-10.

[70] Mezes, "Preparations for Peace," *What Really Happened at Paris* (House and Seymour, eds.), pp. 5-8. See also initial reports submitted, *Foreign Relations, 1919, The Paris Conference* (13 Vols., Washington: United States Government Printing Office, 1942-1947), Vol. 1, pp. 14-16, 17-21, 34-39.

the American nation to the world, "a fine example of a difficult task, well accomplished and most modestly."[71]

British spokesmen continued to express unbounded enthusiasm for Wilson's pronouncements on war aims. In a "private and personal" letter to the President, the Prime Minister expressed his great appreciation of Wilson's speeches as major contributions to human freedom.[72] General Smuts of South Africa contributed another voice to the harmony of Anglo-American pronouncements on war aims. "There is one great dominant war aim," he declared on October 25, 1917, "the end of militarism, of standing armies, of all this threat which like a dark cloud is hanging over our fate. . . ."[73]

American suspicions remained unassuaged while the British and French Governments confined their statements of war aims to general declarations of virtuous intent and support of Wilsonian principles. In the wake of the Bolshevik Revolution and Russian demands for a peace of "no indemnities and no aggression," Colonel House in London found it "useless" to attempt to extract from the British and French specific renunciations of imperialist intent.[74]

On December 4, 1917, President Wilson asked Congress for a declaration of war on Austria-Hungary, and in so doing, made another major statement of war aims. It would be a "premature peace," said the President, if it came before militarism had been crushed, but the democracies must not imitate the wrongs of their enemies. "The wrongs," said Wilson, "the very deep wrongs, committed in this war will have to be righted. That of course. But they cannot and must not be righted by the commission of

[71] Memorandum of June 5, 1928, Seymour, ed., *Intimate Papers*, pp. 170-172. The documents of the Inquiry are distributed through the Paris Peace Conference collection of the National Archives. A representative group of documents of the Inquiry, known at the Peace Conference as the Intelligence Section, illustrating its organization and operating procedure, may be found in: Department of State, American Commission to Negotiate Peace, 1918-1919, 184/83.

[72] Lloyd George to Wilson, September 20, 1917 (received); Lloyd George, *War Memoirs*, Vol. 4, pp. 518-524; Baker, *Wilson: Life and Letters*, Vol: 7, p. 277, n.1.

[73] Sarah Gertrude Millin, *General Smuts* (2 Vols., London: Faber and Faber, Ltd., 1936), Vol. 2, p. 100.

[74] House Diary, November 16, 1917, Seymour, ed., *Intimate Papers*, Vol. 3, p. 233.

similar wrongs against Germany and her Allies." "As always," said the President, "the right will prove to be the expedient. . . ."[75] Congress declared war on Austria-Hungary on December 7. Quite understandably, the speech of December 4 was received in England with the most enthusiastic approval and satisfaction.[76]

Late in 1917, there was a brief revival of discussion in England of "peace without victory." Lord Lansdowne, Foreign Secretary under Lord Salisbury and author of the Entente Cordiale of 1904, made a statement of striking similarity to President Wilson's peace note of December 1916 and speech of January 22, 1917. Noting that *all belligerents* agreed on the need for a permanent system of peaceful settlement of international disputes, Lansdowne argued that steps should be taken for immediate termination of the war on terms short of victory.[77] The London press shouted down the Lansdowne proposals.[78] Lloyd George dismissed them with contempt, asserting his agreement with Wilson's speech of December 4 and declaring there could be "no half-way house between victory and defeat."[79] There is no recorded reaction on the part of President Wilson to Lansdowne's "peace without victory" proposal. In the wake of his statements from April to December, there can be little doubt as to what his reaction would have been.

Lloyd George, stung by charges that he never said anything which "travelled in the same direction as President Wilson," made a major pronouncement on war aims before the House of Commons on December 20. Repeating the principles of his Glasgow speech of June, the Prime Minister called also for permanent guarantees of peace based on such equitable conditions that no nation would *wish* to disturb them. Such guarantees, Lloyd George emphasized, could only be realized upon the achievement of complete victory.[80]

[75] Baker and Dodd eds., *Public Papers, War and Peace*, Vol. 1, pp. 128-139; Scott, ed., *War Aims and Peace Proposals*, pp. 193-202.

[76] Page to Lansing, December 6, 1917, *Foreign Relations, 1917*, Supplement 2, Vol. 1, p. 455.

[77] G. Lowes Dickinson, ed., *Documents and Statements Relating to Peace Proposals and War Aims* (December 1916—November 1918) (London: George Allen and Unwin, Ltd., 1919), pp. 84-89.

[78] Page to Lansing, November 30, 1917, *Foreign Relations, 1917*, Supplement 2, Vol. 1, pp. 327-328.

[79] Speech of December 14, 1917, Scott, ed., *War Aims and Peace Proposals*, pp. 210-215.

[80] Scott, ed., *War Aims and Peace Proposals*, pp. 216-220.

By the end of 1917, there existed the closest apparent harmony between Britain and the United States on war aims. So at least it would seem from a comparison of the public pronouncements of the President and the Prime Minister. But while England extended to America a hand of eager intimacy, President Wilson remained distrustfully aloof and sometimes, it would seem, gratuitously distrustful. An incident which occurred at the end of the year, of no great importance in itself, illustrates this anomaly of Anglo-American relations.

It had occurred to Walter Hines Page in 1917 that the cause of Anglo-American friendship would be well served if Americans of distinction would come to Britain to talk about American goals and ideals. The British Government enthusiastically took up this proposal and extended an invitation to former President Taft to engage in a lecture tour in Great Britain. Taft accepted.[81] On December 12, Taft called upon the President and found him unalterably opposed to the proposed visit. He did not wish the United States to seem in any way involved with British policy, he told Taft. There were divergencies of purpose, and there were also features of British policy of which he heartily disapproved. "There are too many Englishmen in this country and in Washington now," said the President, "and I have asked the British Ambassador to have some of them sent home." Taft advised the President that the speaking tour had been suggested by Ambassador Page and Wilson countered: "Page is really an Englishman and I have to discount whatever he says about the situation in Great Britain."[82]

The Taft speaking tour was of course cancelled. The President subsequently told Wiseman that he generally disapproved of Anglo-American exchanges of speakers, lest there be generated an artificial entente, which he did not consider to be a sound basis for Anglo-American relations.[83] Wilson's position suggests perhaps not so much an anti-British attitude as an excessive zeal to avoid sullying his hands with a special connection of un-

[81] Hendrick, *Walter H. Page*, Vol. 2, pp. 345-346.

[82] House Diary, Vol. 13, January 3, 1918, House Papers; Hendrick, *Walter H. Page*, Vol. 2, pp. 346-348; Baker, *Wilson: Life and Letters*, Vol. 7, p. 407. See also Wilson's letter to George Creel, January 16, 1918, reiterating his opposition to all projects for Anglo-American speaking tours, *ibid.*, p. 473.

[83] "Notes on an Interview with the President," January 23, 1918, Wiseman Papers.

proved moral purity, and perhaps also a personal mistrust of William Howard Taft.

IV. Anglo-American Military Cooperation: the Supreme War Council

More than once in the course of 1917 the British Government indicated that it would welcome American participation in Allied conferences on policy and strategy.[84] At first President Wilson was unwilling, refusing, for instance, to send a representative to the Allied War Conference in Paris in July.[85] Lord Reading and Sir William Wiseman, at the urging of Lloyd George, strongly recommended to Wilson and House that at least a special war mission be sent to Europe. Wiseman wrote to House on September 26 arguing the necessity of a war mission and permanent machinery of cooperation. "I believe," wrote Wiseman, "the greatest asset Germany has today is the 3,000 miles that separates (sic) London from Washington. . . ."[86]

Wilson agreed in early October that a war mission was desirable and he designated Colonel House to head it. House and his mission, which included Rear Admiral W. S. Benson, Army Chief of Staff Tasker H. Bliss, and Assistant Secretary of the Treasury Oscar T. Crosley, landed in Plymouth, England, on November 7.[87] It was understood that the American Mission would participate only in a *war conference* and not engage in any discussion of peace terms.[88]

On the very day of House's arrival in England, Lloyd George and the French and Italian Premiers, meeting at Rapallo in the wake of the Italian military disaster at Caporetto and the Bolshevik Revolution in Russia, established as urgently needed a Supreme War Council to coordinate Allied strategy.[89] The British Govern-

[84] See (e.g.) Page to Lansing, July 2, 1917, *Foreign Relations, 1917*, Supplement 2, Vol. 1, p. 114; Page to Lansing, July 18, 1917, *ibid.*, p. 131; Spring-Rice to Lansing, July 21, 1917, *ibid.*, p. 142.

[85] Polk to Page, July 20, 1917, *Foreign Relations, 1917*, Supplement 2, Vol. 1, p. 138.

[86] Wiseman to House, September 26, 1917, House Papers; Willert, *The Road to Safety*, pp. 124-130.

[87] Seymour, ed., *Intimate Papers*, Vol. 3, pp. 196-197, 207-209.

[88] Lansing to Page, November 7, 1917, *Foreign Relations, 1917*, Supplement 2, Vol. 1, pp. 295-296.

[89] Lloyd George, *War Memoirs*, Vol. 4, pp. 550-551; F. S. Marston, *The*

ment informed the United States of the creation of the new agency,[90] and President Wilson promptly authorized Colonel House and General Bliss to participate in its first meeting.[91] Wilson became strongly enthusiastic for military cooperation while remaining reticent about cooperating in any inter-Allied *policy* bodies. "Take the whip hand," he cabled House in November. "We not only accede to the plan for a unified conduct of the war but insist upon it. . . ."[92]

Eighteen Allied and Associated Powers attended an Inter-Allied Conference which convened on November 29 in Paris. The newly formed Supreme War Council, with British, French, Italian, and American representation, convened at Versailles on December 1. House and Bliss were overridden in proposing that the Supreme War Council act as a purely military council of the chiefs of staff. At Lloyd George's insistence, the Council was placed under the political control of the Prime Ministers and Foreign Ministers, with the military representatives separated and subordinated in a purely advisory role. The American military adviser selected General Bliss; the British, General Sir Henry Wilson.[93]

The Supreme War Council, sitting at Versailles became a high policy body although the United States refused to maintain a permanent political representative and denied the right of the Council to raise postwar political questions.[94] In February 1918, Wilson sternly reminded the Allies that he had agreed to the creation of the Supreme War Council only as an agency to coordinate problems of supply and strategy.[95] Lloyd George and Wilson thus had strikingly different concepts of the proper function of the Supreme War Council. Its ultimate value was prob-

---

Peace Conference of 1919 (London, New York, Toronto: Oxford University Press, 1944), pp. 3-9; Lord Maurice Hankey, *Diplomacy by Conference* (London: Ernest Benn, Ltd., 1946), pp. 22-24.

[90] British Embassy Memorandum to the Department of State, November 12, 1917, *Foreign Relations, 1917*, Supplement 2, Vol. 1, pp. 306-307.

[91] Wilson to House, November 16, 1917, *Foreign Relations, 1917*, Supplement 2, Vol. 1, p. 308; Seymour, ed., *Intimate Papers*, Vol. 3, pp. 220-221.

[92] Baker, *Wilson: Life and Letters*, Vol. 7, p. 358.

[93] Seymour, ed., *Intimate Papers*, Vol. 3, pp. 248-264.

[94] See Howard P. Whidden, Jr., "Why Allied Unity Failed in 1918-19," *Foreign Policy Reports*, Vol. 18, No. 23 (February 15, 1943), p. 301.

[95] Lansing to American Ambassadors in London, Paris, and Rome, February 18, 1918, *Foreign Relations, 1918*, Supplement 1, *The World War* (2 Vols., Washington: United States Government Printing Office, 1933), Vol. 1, p. 125.

ably as the high policy body which Lloyd George fostered rather than as a purely military organ. So, at least, thought the American military representative, General Bliss.[96]

Sir Cecil Spring-Rice was suddenly recalled from Washington in January 1918. In his final interview with President Wilson on January 3, the President indicated that he would welcome a "statement of moderate and unaggressive character" by the Allies, one that would belie all suspicion of aggression and conquest.[97] Spring-Rice died in Ottawa on his way home. He was replaced in Washington by the able and popular Lord Reading, Chief Justice of England, who remained until the spring of 1919. Reading found himself mainly occupied with the task of supervising the British missions which swarmed over Washington in 1918. Reading himself had little contact with Wilson or Lansing, depending for personal relationships on Sir William Wiseman.[98]

The working relationships among Wilson, House, Wiseman, and Reading made for good Anglo-American relations in 1918. Good relations were also fostered by distance. There were no wartime meetings and no trans-Atlantic telephone to bring together Wilson and Lloyd George. As the Paris Peace Conference was to demonstrate, their personalities were mutually antagonistic, rendering impossible the kind of personal understanding which existed between Roosevelt and Churchill in World War II.

V. *The Fourteen Points*

One of the objectives of House's mission to Europe in late 1917 was to induce the Allies to issue a joint statement of liberal war aims as a counter to the ringing declarations of the Russian Bolsheviks. At House's request, Wiseman sounded out Lloyd George, who insisted that the aims of the Allies had already been fully enunciated. At the Inter-Allied Conference in Paris, Lloyd

---

[96] See the Final Report of General Bliss to the Secretary of State, February 6, 1920, Frederick Palmer, *Bliss, Peacemaker—The Life and Letters of General Tasker Howard Bliss* (New York: Dodd, Mead and Company, 1934), p. 237. Concerning General Bliss's role on the Supreme War Council, see *ibid.*, pp. 237-252.

[97] Spring-Rice to Balfour, January 4, 1918, Gwynn, ed., *Spring-Rice*, Vol. 2, pp. 422-425; Willson, *Friendly Relations*, pp. 326-327.

[98] *ibid.*, p. 329; Willert, *The Road to Safety*, pp. 137-142.

George and Clemenceau were unwilling to issue a joint manifesto, arguing that in the wake of the Caporetto disaster in Italy and the Bolshevik Revolution and military collapse in Russia, even to hint at a peace offer would imply the recognition of possible defeat. Lloyd George was, in any case, probably too deeply committed to the English conservatives to consider a liberal restatement of war aims.[99]

The failure to secure Allied agreement to a *joint* statement of war aims was the genesis of the Fourteen Points. When House, upon arriving home, reported to Wilson the unwillingness of the Allies to join in a declaration of liberal intent, the President determined to make a unilateral pronouncement and instructed House to have the Inquiry gather appropriate statistics and materials for a major address.[100] House had consulted with English and continental radicals while in Europe and was convinced that such a statement would receive wide public support in Europe.[101] Page too reported a widespread desire for "some summary that the man in the street and the man in the trenches can understand."[102] The Inquiry thereupon set to work gathering facts and statistics and produced a complete program consisting of recommendations for a liberal declaration and specific territorial proposals. House delivered this document to the President on January 4, 1918.[103] Wilson, in consultation with Colonel House, carefully reviewed the Inquiry proposals and proceeded to formulate his manifesto.[104]

The only integral part of the President's projected declaration which seemed likely to arouse British objections was the principle of the freedom of the seas. Wilson at first framed a declaration of absolute freedom of the seas as Point 2 but then expressed some doubts as to what the British reaction would be. House, by

[99] *ibid.*, p. 134; Seymour, ed., *Intimate Papers*, Vol. 3, pp. 278-284; Seymour, *American Diplomacy during the World War*, pp. 281-282.

[100] Seymour, ed., *Intimate Papers*, Vol. 3, pp. 285-286, 316-319; Seymour, *American Diplomacy during the World War*, pp. 282-284.

[101] Martin, *Peace without Victory*, pp. 150-151.

[102] Page to Wilson, December 22, 1917, Hendrick, *Walter H. Page*, Vol. 3, p. 413.

[103] Report by the Inquiry, "War Aims and Peace Terms," prepared by S. E. Mezes, David Hunter Miller, and Walter Lippmann, January 1918, Ray Stannard Baker, *Woodrow Wilson and World Settlement* (3 Vols., Garden City, New York, Doubleday, Page and Company, 1922), Vol. 3, pp. 23-41.

[104] Seymour, ed., *Intimate Papers*, Vol. 3, pp. 322-330.

his own account, suggested that any British objections would be met by adding that "the seas might be closed by international action in order to enforce international covenants." Wilson seized upon this and, with minor changes, it became incorporated into the final Point 2.[105] House, of course, was quite wrong. The British objected in the strongest possible terms to Point 2 and finally refused their assent to it as part of the Pre-Armistice Agreement.[106]

Wilson was now anxious to put out his manifesto before Lloyd George and Clemenceau could forestall him. He typed out a cable which was dispatched to Lloyd George on January 5, stating his intent to speak on war aims and expressing his hope that no inconsistent utterances would occur.[107]

For some time the pressures for a broad declaration had been mounting on the Prime Minister. The Russian Bolsheviks had published the secret treaties in November, successfully arousing certain opposition spokesmen in the Allied countries. In addition, House had belabored Lloyd George in London and at the Paris Conference. Most decisive, probably, were the domestic pressures of the English radicals and the trade unions, who were insistently demanding a declaration of liberal and moderate war aims.[108] The Government, moreover, was in deadlock with the trade unions over problems of manpower. Lloyd George decided, therefore, to enlist their cooperation by inviting them to participate in a discussion of war aims. He had a detailed statement prepared and endorsed officially by the Cabinet and unofficially by the Liberal Opposition leaders, Asquith and Grey, and by the representatives of the Dominions in London. The Prime Minister met in conference with the Trade Unions Congress in Caxton Hall in London on January 5, 1918.[109]

Lloyd George's speech of January 5, 1918, was the most significant British statement of objectives of the war. It was elaborate and precise and moderate in tone, in marked contrast to the

[105] House Diary, January 5, 1918, Seymour, ed., *Intimate Papers*, Vol. 3, p. 327.
[106] See Chapter 2, Section 11.
[107] House to Balfour, January 5, 1918, Seymour, ed., *Intimate Papers*, Vol. 3, p. 339; Walworth, *Wilson*, Vol. 2, p. 150.
[108] Baker, *Wilson and World Settlement*, Vol. 1, pp. 38-39; Martin, *Peace without Victory*, pp. 154-156.
[109] Lloyd George, *War Memoirs*, Vol. 5, pp. 38-40.

strident self-confidence of the last official statement, Balfour's reply to Wilson of January 16, 1917.[110] Declaring that the Allied and Associated Powers did not wish to destroy Germany or the German people, nor Austria or Turkey, the Prime Minister asserted that in order to secure a just and stable peace in Europe, "government with the consent of the governed must be the basis of any territorial settlement in this war." The first requirement was the complete restoration of Belgium, and of Serbia, Montenegro, and the occupied parts of France, Italy, and Roumania, with "reparation for injustice done. . . ." Alsace-Lorraine must be restored to France, a "sore which has poisoned peace for half a century." As to Russia, Lloyd George hoped that she would continue to fight as a democracy, but if the Bolshevik leaders acted independently of the Allies, he said, they could not help Russia. "Russia," he declared, "can only be saved by her own people." The Prime Minister called for an independent Poland "comprising all those genuinely Polish elements who desired to form a part of it. . . ." For the peoples of Austria-Hungary, there must be "genuine self-government on true democratic principles. . . ." The Italians were entitled to "union with those of their own race and tongue." As to the Ottoman Empire, Lloyd George favored the integrity of national Turkey, but the straits must be internationalized, and Arabia, Armenia, Mesopotamia, Palestine, and Syria were entitled to a "recognition of their separate national condition." The German colonies should be placed "at the disposal of a conference whose decisions must have primary regard to the wishes and interests of the native inhabitants of such colonies," the principle of self-determination being "as applicable in their cases as in those of occupied European territories." Finally, there must also be "reparations for injuries done in violation of international law." And a great effort must be made "to establish by some international organization an alternative to war as a means of settling international disputes." In conclusion, Lloyd George enunciated three fundamental conditions of a just peace: the sanctity of treaties, a territorial settlement based on the principle of self-determination, and "some international organization to

[110] See G. P. Gooch, "British War Aims, 1914-1919," *The Quarterly Review*, Vol. 280, No. 556 (April 1943), pp. 172-174.

limit the burden of armaments and diminish the probability of war."[111]

Balfour at once cabled House the contents of Lloyd George's speech. The statement was the result of consultations with labor and Parliament leaders, Balfour explained, and there had been no time to consult the Allies. Balfour expressed his certainty that the statement was fully in accord with the President's previous utterances, and indicated that a further statement by the President would be welcomed.[112] House immediately called back his heartiest congratulations to Lloyd George.[113]

President Wilson, on the other hand, was far from pleased by Lloyd George's enunciation of a peace program so nearly identical with his own, and he considered calling his own speech off.[114] House counseled that Lloyd George's statement, evidencing a broad area of Anglo-American agreement, made the President's speech even more advisable and Wilson went ahead with his plan. It is clear, however, that Lloyd George's speech of January 5 and Wilson's of January 8 were drafted absolutely independently. Wilson's address had been drafted before he knew of Lloyd George's, and he made no changes after reading Lloyd George's speech.[115] It may also be that what was said was of less importance than by whom it was said, that the world reputations of the Prime Minister and the President were such that only from the rostrum of the latter could a statement of ideals resound with such sincerity as to win the mind and heart of the world.[116]

Wilson delivered his address on January 8, 1918, before a joint session of Congress. The President paid tribute to the "admirable candor" and "admirable spirit" of Lloyd George's speech of January 5. Speaking first of Russia, he expressed the wish that America might be able to assist the Russian people to achieve "their utmost hope of liberty and ordered peace." Asserting that the

---

[111] *Foreign Relations, 1918*, Supplement 1, Vol. 1, pp. 4-12; Lloyd George, *War Memoirs*, Vol. 5, pp. 63-73; Scott, ed., *War Aims and Peace Proposals*, pp. 225-233.

[112] Balfour to House, January 5, 1918, Seymour, ed., *Intimate Papers*, Vol. 3, pp. 340-341; Baker, *Wilson: Life and Letters*, Vol. 7, pp. 452-453.

[113] House to Lloyd George, January 6, 1918, House Papers.

[114] Seymour, ed., *Intimate Papers*, Vol. 3, p. 341.

[115] *ibid.*, pp. 325-330, 341; Seymour, *American Diplomacy during the World War*, p. 288.

[116] See Silas Bent McKinley, *Woodrow Wilson* (New York: Frederick A. Praeger, 1957), p. 216.

day of "secret covenants" was past and renouncing all selfish objectives, Wilson declared the recognition of America that "unless justice be done to others, it will not be done to us." He then set forth his program in fourteen points: Point 1 called for "open covenants of peace, openly arrived at"; Point 2 for "absolute freedom of navigation upon the seas, outside territorial waters, alike in peace and in war, except as the seas may be closed in whole or in part by international action for the enforcement of international covenants." Point 3 called for removal of economic barriers and establishment of equality of trade conditions; Point 4 for reduction of national armaments "to the lowest point consistent with domestic safety"; Point 5 for an "impartial adjustment of all colonial claims," based on the principle that "the interests of the populations concerned must have equal weight with the equitable claims of the governments whose title is to be determined." Point 6 laid down a policy of nonintervention in Russia and proffered to Russia a "sincere welcome into the society of free nations under institutions of her own choosing" as well as any "assistance" which she might desire. Point 7 required the evacuation and restoration of Belgium, while Point 8 made similar provision for France, as well as for the righting of the wrong of 1871 in regard to Alsace-Lorraine, "which has unsettled the peace of the world for nearly fifty years. . . ." Point 9 called for readjustment of Italian frontiers "along clearly recognizable lines of nationality"; Point 10 for the "freest opportunity of autonomous development" for the peoples of Austria-Hungary; Point 11 for the restoration of Roumania, Serbia, and Montenegro. Point 12 called for a "secure sovereignty" of the Turkish portions of the Ottoman Empire but an "absolutely unmolested opportunity of autonomous development" for the non-Turkish nationalities and the internationalization of the Straits. Point 13 required an independent Poland composed of "indisputably Polish populations," with "free and secure access to the sea. . . ." Point 14, by far the most important in President Wilson's mind, stated: "A general association of nations must be formed under specific covenants for the purpose of affording mutual guarantees of political independence and territorial integrity to great and small states alike." Underlying the entire program, Wilson concluded, was the principle of "justice to all peoples and nationalities, and their right to live on equal terms of liberty and safety with one another, whether they be strong or weak."[117]

The reception to the President's speech, at home and abroad, was enormously favorable. The English press, reported Page, received the speech with the "most appreciative and laudatory editorials," expressing doubt only on the issue of freedom of the seas.[118] The British Embassy informed Wilson of the enthusiasm with which Lloyd George and Balfour received his speech, and the President responded with an expression of deep gratification at finding his program "so entirely consistent with the program set forth by Mr. Lloyd George. . . ."[119] In his *War Memoirs*, however, Lloyd George comments on the Fourteen Points with distinct coolness and surprising brevity: "This declaration, which subsequently played such an important part at the Armistice and the Peace Conference, was not regarded by any of the Allies as being at variance on vital matters, except in respect of the freedom of the seas, with their own declarations—although we never formally accepted them, and they constituted no part of the official policy of the Alliance."[120]

While the reaction of Lloyd George was thus less than enthusiastic, English radicals received the Fourteen Points with virtually nothing but praise. The radicals received Lloyd George's speech with approval but expressed far greater enthusiasm for Wilson's. Wilson now reasserted his leadership of English radicalism with greater success than at any time since January 1917, and radical activity was thereafter dedicated to the vigorous enlistment of British and Allied support for the President's program.[121]

French reaction to the two speeches varied on official and unofficial levels. Significantly, Clemenceau sent a telegram of congratulation to Lloyd George,[122] but not to President Wilson.

---

[117] Baker and Dodd, eds., *Public Papers, War and Peace*, Vol. 1, pp. 155-162; Parkes, ed., *State Papers*, 1917-1918, pp. 950-955; Scott, ed., *War Aims and Peace Proposals*, pp. 234-239; *Foreign Relations, 1918*, Supplement 1, Vol. 1, pp. 12-17.
[118] Page to Lansing, January 10, 1918, *ibid.*, pp. 17-18. See also Seymour, *American Diplomacy during the World War*, pp. 290-291.
[119] Baker, *Wilson: Life and Letters*, Vol. 7, p. 475.
[120] Lloyd George, *War Memoirs*, Vol. 5, p. 42.
[121] Martin, *Peace without Victory*, pp. 158-162. See also Seymour, *American Diplomacy during the World War*, p. 295.
[122] Clemenceau to Lloyd George, January 6, 1918, Scott, ed., *War Aims and Peace Proposals*, p. 233.

French public interest, however, focused on the Fourteen Points, which eclipsed the pronouncement of Lloyd George. [123]

These major declarations of war aims by the President and the Prime Minister did, in fact, set forth remarkably similar programs. Generally, they agreed on the principles of self-determination and equal justice under the law. Specifically, they agreed on the territorial restoration of Belgium, Alsace-Lorraine and the occupied regions of France, Italian irredentist territories and the Balkan states, on the revival of national Poland, nonintervention in Russia, and autonomy for the Austro-Hungarian nationalities, on respect for the integrity of Turkey but self-determination for the Arabs and Armenians, on the principles by which Germany's colonies would be dealt with, and, finally, on the need for an international organization to keep peace.

The close similarity in concept and detail between these major pronouncements by the President and the Prime Minister is perhaps attributable to the fact that Lloyd George's speech was substantially written not by himself but by Lord Robert Cecil, who more than any major British official shared President Wilson's point of view. Wiseman told House that Lloyd George's speech was almost identical with a memorandum which had been prepared by Cecil after consultation with Wiseman, confirming House in his view that neither the style nor the substance of the speech of January 5 were those of Lloyd George.[124]

There were four notable points of difference between the two speeches. First, Lloyd George laid far heavier stress than did Wilson on *reparations*, which were to constitute a major area of Anglo-American controversy at the Paris Peace Conference. Second, Lloyd George made no mention of open covenants or of the lowering of trade barriers, as Wilson did in Points 1 and 3 respectively. Third, Wilson called for *freedom of the seas*, a principle to which Great Britain was to object most vehemently in the pre-Armistice negotiations but which evaporated as an issue at Paris. Finally, Lloyd George expressed approval of the project for a league of nations without special emphasis while Wilson made

---

[123] George Bernard Noble, *Policies and Opinions at Paris, 1919* (New York: The Macmillan Company, 1935), p. 30.

[124] House Diary, January 19, 1918, House Papers. The Wiseman Papers contain a draft statement on war aims by Cecil, dated January 3, 1918, which is almost identical with Lloyd George's speech of January 5.

it the heart of his program—but at the Peace Conference Britain gave effective and unwavering support to Wilson in the creation of the Covenant. The fundamental difference between the two speeches was not in content but in tone: Lloyd George somehow made liberalism and justice seem practical and expedient, while Wilson, expressing virtually the same principles, appealed to the noblest ideals and the conscience of mankind.

Why, it may be asked, with war aims and concepts of the peace so similar in principle and details, was not a joint Anglo-American program enunciated? Wilson, it will be recalled, had asked for a joint manifesto, but Lloyd George and Clemenceau had refused it. Lloyd George spoke in January primarily in response to domestic pressures. Moreover, the personalities of the President and the Prime Minister were such as to repel identity of action— there was, it seems, a mutual diffidence between Lloyd George, the practical politician, and Wilson, the self-appointed but world-accepted spokesman of mankind. Nor was there, in 1918, any working concept—certainly not in America—of an Anglo-American entente as the vital core of world democracy and a just peace. America, in 1918, was scarcely emergent from a century of isolation and distrust of the old mother country. The Anglo-American idea was not to be born until another world war had devastated mankind—too late, by then, to realize the fullest measure of its promise and its opportunity. Thus it occurred that the two most significant statements of war aims during World War I were, though practically identical in content, separately formulated and separately pronounced.

VI. *Anglo-American War Aims,* *February-November 1918*

On February 11, 1918, responding to Austro-German reactions to the Fourteen Points, President Wilson again went before a joint session of Congress to spell out further his program for peace. Building his speech around self-determination as an "imperative principle of action," the President set forth four principles to be applied: first, that each part of the peace settlement must be based upon the "essential justice of that particular case . . ."; second, that "peoples and provinces are not to be bartered about from sovereignty as if they were chattels . . ."; but that, third, "every territorial settlement involved in this war must be made in the interest and for the benefit of the populations concerned . . ."; and fourth, that "all well defined national aspirations shall be accorded the utmost satisfaction that can be accorded them without introducing new or perpetuating old elements of discord and antagonism. . . ."[125] Foreign Secretary Balfour found nothing in Wilson's four principles that was "novel or paradoxical" and he perfunctorily endorsed them.[126] The liberal press in Britain warmly endorsed the President's statement, while the pro-Government organs were either silent or cool.[127]

Confronted in early 1918 with the Russian surrender of Brest-Litovsk and the success of German arms on the western front, President Wilson altered the tone of his pronouncements, giving up the seemingly fruitless appeals to the German people against their militarist rulers for a new emphasis on the relentlessness of Allied determination. Speaking at Baltimore on April 6, the President denounced the peace imposed at Brest-Litovsk by the military rulers of Germany and proclaimed that only one response was possible: "force, force to the utmost, force without stint or limit, the righteous and triumphant force which shall make right the law of the world and cast every selfish dominion down in the dust."[128] The speech was received by the British Government with gratitude and appreciation.[129]

"Force without stint or limit!"—on its face, a remarkable evolution from the "peace without victory" of January 1917. The paradox of Wilson's conversion from advocacy of a negotiated peace to a determination to fight to a complete victory has been much commented upon and much criticized. Perhaps it can be better understood when it is realized that Wilson was never a pacifist, that his only unvarying *objective* was a peace of justice based on

---

[125] Baker and Dodd, eds., *Public Papers, War and Peace*, Vol. 1, pp. 177-184; *Foreign Relations, 1918*, Supplement 1, Vol. 1, pp. 108-113; Scott, ed., *War Aims and Peace Proposals*, pp. 265-271.

[126] Balfour in the House of Commons, February 27, 1918, *ibid.*, p. 287.

[127] Buckler to House, February 13, 1918, Buckler Papers.

[128] Baker and Dodd, eds., *Public Papers, War and Peace*, Vol. 1, pp. 198-202; *Foreign Relations, 1918*, Supplement 1, Vol. 1, pp. 200-203; Scott, ed., *War Aims and Peace Proposals*, pp. 309-312.

[129] Page to Lansing, April 10, 1918, *Foreign Relations, 1918*, Supplement 1, Vol. 1, p. 205.

permanent guarantees. The *method* of achieving it, by compromise, by negotiation, by victory, was always secondary, to be determined pragmatically. To the Convention of the American Federation of Labor in November 1917 the President had said: ". . . What I am opposed to is not the feeling of the pacifists but their stupidity. My heart is with them, but my mind has a contempt for them. I want peace, but I know how to get it, and they do not."[130]

' President Wilson's next major address was delivered at Mount Vernon on July 4, 1918. Proclaiming "no compromise," Wilson set forth the ends for which the Allies were fighting: first, the destruction of "every arbitrary power" that can threaten the peace of the world; second, the settlement of all questions on the basis of free consent of the people concerned; third, the consent of all nations to be bound in their relations "by the same principles of honor and of respect for the common law of civilized society that govern the individual citizens of all modern states in their relations with one another . . ."; fourth, the establishment of an organization of peace to make certain that the "combined power of free nations will check every invasion of right" and afford a "tribunal of opinion to which all must submit. . . ." "What we seek," the President summarized, "is the reign of law, based upon the consent of the governed and sustained by the organized opinion of mankind."[131]

Wilson received reports that Lloyd George had laughed and Clemenceau had sneered at the Mount Vernon reference to a league of peace. The validity of these reports may be questioned, but the President was apparently impressed. "Yes," he is reported to have said, "I know that Europe is still governed by the same reactionary forces which controlled this country until a few years ago. But I am satisfied that if necessary I can reach the people of Europe over the heads of their rulers."[132] The President's rather testy attitude in the summer of 1918 was a cause of anxiety among British officials and Wiseman found it necessary to reassure them that Wilson was not fundamentally anti-British. But even Sir

---

[130] Baker and Dodd, eds., *Public Papers, War and Peace*, Vol. 1, p. 120.

[131] *ibid.*, pp. 231-235; *Foreign Relations, 1918*, Supplement 1, Vol. 1, pp. 268-271; Scott, ed., *War Aims and Peace Proposals*, pp. 349-352.

[132] Walworth, *Wilson*, Vol. 2, p. 175.

William conceded that the President was a "most difficult person to deal with."[133]

Whatever the reactions of Allied officials, Wilson's speeches were indeed having effect on the peoples of Europe. His words, by July of 1918, were eagerly heard by a war-weary world, and, with the tide of battle turning in France, they were beginning to find their long-sought mark on the peoples and rulers of the Central Powers.[134]

On August 1, 1918, Walter Hines Page, due to failing health, submitted to the President his resignation as Ambassador to Britain.[135] The departure of the wartime Ambassador evoked a chorus of praise for him in England. Balfour said later to an American friend: "I loved that man. I almost wept when he left England."[136] Page, the tireless advocate of Anglo-American amity, returned to his home in North Carolina, where he died on December 21, 1918, at the age of sixty-three.

He was succeeded in London by John William Davis, hitherto President Wilson's Solicitor-General, who arrived in London in December 1918 when Anglo-American amity was at its pre-Conference peak. This cordiality continued until the conflicts of the Paris Peace Conference caused official relations between the American Ambassador and the British Government to revert to the traditional formality which had prevailed before the war. Davis remained in London until the Wilson Administration left office in 1921.[137]

By September 1918 the outcome of the war was no longer in doubt and Lloyd George again proclaimed the necessity of complete victory. Calling for a league of nations with real power, the Prime Minister warned that a league established while militarist power survived would be a "league of fox and geese." The only sure foundation for a league, he reiterated, was complete victory.[138]

[133] Wiseman to Reading, September 5, 1918, Wiseman Papers.
[134] See Temperley, ed., *A History of the Peace Conference of Paris*, Vol. 1, pp. 198-199.
[135] Page to Wilson, August 1, 1918, Hendrick, *Walter H. Page*, Vol. 2, pp. 393-395; Wilson to Page, August 24, 1918, *ibid.*, p. 396.
[136] Beckles Willson, *America's Ambassadors to England (1785-1928)* (London: John Murray, 1928), pp. 460-462.
[137] Willson, *America's Ambassadors to England*, pp. 463-469.
[138] Speech of September 12, 1918, Scott, ed., *War Aims and Peace Proposals*, pp. 381, 383.

In September, Colonel House suggested to the President another attempt to negotiate with the Allies a basic agreement on war aims. The President declined to do this but decided himself to make another major statement and to invite the Allies to accede.[139]

In his speech of September 27, 1918, President Wilson rejected any compromise with the Central Powers and called for a permanent peace secured by payment of the price of "impartial justice in every item of the settlement, no matter whose interest is crossed . . . ," and fulfilled by the "indispensable instrumentality" of a league of nations as the "most essential part" of the peace settlement. The President then set forth five "particulars" of a just peace: first, "impartial justice" must involve "no discrimination between those to whom we wish to be just and those to whom we do not wish to be just"; second, no "special or separate interest" can override the "common interest of all"; third, there can be "no leagues or alliances" within the "general and common family of the League of Nations"; fourth, no selfish economic combinations within the League and no economic boycotts except as a disciplinary instrument invoked by the League; and fifth, all international agreements and treaties "must be made known in their entirety to the rest of the world." The United States, Wilson concluded, would "assume its full share of responsibility for the maintenance of the common covenants. . . ."[140]

No official approval was given to this significant statement by Great Britain or any of the Allied Governments, but the unofficial response in England was enthusiastic. Lord Robert Cecil declared it "the finest description of our war aims yet uttered. . . ."[141] The English radical supporters of President Wilson, among whom misgivings had arisen during his summer-long silence, were once again reassured as to his intentions and rehabilitated to his leadership.[142] Lloyd George lauded the "five particulars" as setting out a uniquely Anglo-American attitude,

---

[139] Seymour, ed., *Intimate Papers*, Vol. 4, pp. 64-66.

[140] Baker and Dodd, eds., *Public Papers, War and Peace*, Vol. 1, pp. 253-261; *Foreign Relations, 1918*, Supplement 1, Vol. 1, pp. 316-321; Scott, ed., *War Aims and Peace Proposals*, pp. 399-405.

[141] Cecil to House, September 28, 1918, Seymour, ed., *Intimate Papers*, Vol. 4, p. 72.

[142] Martin, *Peace without Victory*, pp. 181-182.

entirely different from that of traditional "power diplomacy," toward the problems of war and peace.[143]

In a speech to the leaders of the Liberal Party on November 12, 1918, the day after the signing of the Armistice, Lloyd George warned against allowing any spirit of revenge and greed to override the "fundamental principles of righteousness." Declaring a league of nations an "absolute essential to permanent peace," the Prime Minister promised: "We shall go to the Peace Conference to guarantee that the League of Nations is a reality."[144] President Wilson sent an expression of "sincere admiration" for Lloyd George's address. "It is delightful," said the President, "to be made aware of such community of thought and counsel in approaching the high and difficult task now awaiting us."[145] Lloyd George cabled back his thanks, expressing his certainty that "the ideals of our two countries in regard to international reconstruction are fundamentally the same. . . ."[146]

As the war ended, Anglo-American war aims and peace proposals had evolved to a point of ostensible outward harmony. In the final months of the war, such pronouncements were virtually the monopoly of President Wilson. Lloyd George made no further major statements after his address of January 5, 1918, while Wilson made at least three more speeches of significance. The evolution of war aims thus became essentially a matter of Wilsonian utterances and Allied reactions. While each of Wilson's statements received expressions of approval in England from both Government and private sources, at no time prior to November 1918 was there any *official* acceptance of Wilson's program as the program of the Allies.

From the time of America's entry into the war, Wilson's eloquence and idealism placed him increasingly in command of the shaping of Allied objectives in the war. Unofficially, at least, he became the world spokesman of the free nations. To the end, however, the President remained suspicious that the Allied Powers harbored imperialist ambitions and were paying only lip service to his program.

[143] Lloyd George, *War Memoirs*, Vol. 6, pp. 231-232.
[144] Scott, ed., *War Aims and Peace Proposals*, p. 472.
[145] *Foreign Relations, 1919, The Paris Peace Conference*, Vol. 1, pp. 3-4.
[146] *ibid.*, p. 5.

These suspicions, so far as Great Britain was concerned, were largely unfounded. Wilson's program, in its general principles and in most of its particulars, was also the program of England. There were differences in emphasis: Lloyd George spoke more of reparations and less of a league of nations; but the only fundamental difference was over the issue of freedom of the seas, and a ready solution to this problem, as Wilson was to recognize at the Paris Peace Conference, lay at hand in the very project for a league of nations.

Factors ranging from the personalities of Wilson and Lloyd George, and perhaps the misconceptions that each had of the other, to the historical antipathy of America for Europe thwarted the possibility of a unified Anglo-American peace program. Great Britain and the United States each quite separately formulated and separately pronounced identical objectives, never coming together to add the weight of unity in explicit agreement to their common purposes. It can only be speculated as to whether a common Anglo-American program would have significantly altered the course of the Peace Conference and made for a better peace. It seems clear, however, that the failure of the English-speaking powers to avow their unity of purpose was due, not to a conflict of interests, but to the failure to identify the fact that they shared a community of interests with respect to the issues they now faced and that these issues far transcended past differences, idle rumors, or personal predilections and vanities.

CHAPTER 2

FROM THE PRE-ARMISTICE AGREEMENT TO THE OPENING OF THE PEACE CONFERENCE

THE negotiations of October and November 1918, which led to the Armistice of November 11, generated the first major controversy between Great Britain and the United States. When the German Government approached Wilson for peace on the basis of the Fourteen Points, their content was suddenly of vital significance. For the British, the focus of concern was Wilson's Point 2, the Freedom of the Seas. This issue brought America's historic interest in the wartime rights of neutral ships into direct collision with Great Britain's equally cardinal strategic dependence on sea power for the strangulation of a continental enemy by blockade. The result of this conflict of historic interests was a bruising diplomatic clash between the English-speaking powers in the pre-Armistice negotiations.

In the two months between the pre-Armistice negotiations and the convening of the Peace Conference in Paris, the American President and the British Prime Minister prepared their positions for the making of the peace. Generally, Wilson concentrated on the refinement and definition of his principles, while Lloyd George maneuvered to create for himself a position of tactical advantage. Both leaders were involved deeply in domestic politics during this period. Wilson's party, in spite of an appeal by the President for party support, suffered an off-year election defeat which ultimately had disastrous effects on the peace settlement. Lloyd George and his Government called a general election immediately after the Armistice, and endorsed candidates won a smashing victory at the polls on issues which, as will be presently shown, had consequences only less disastrous than the defeat of the Democrats in America. A visit by the President to Great Britain in December 1918 scarcely advanced the cause of Anglo-American amity or the prospect of Anglo-American co-operation at the Peace Conference.

I. *Wilson's Negotiations with Germany and the Attitude of Great Britain, October 1918*

In September 1918, the Central Powers crumbled. Prince Max of Baden, the German Chancellor, appealed to President Wilson on October 4, asking specifically for peace on the basis of the Fourteen Points.[1] Although the Allied Premiers were left officially uninformed of the negotiations thus inaugurated between Germany and the United States, unofficially they were kept fully informed by French Intelligence, which in fact had intercepted Prince Max's note to President Wilson of October 4. Convening in Paris on October 5 as the Supreme War Council, Lloyd George, Clemenceau, and Orlando reached prompt agreement on their general requirements for an armistice, and on October 7 they referred consideration of specific terms to the military and naval representatives at Versailles, who began immediately to draw up specifications. General Bliss, who was without instructions, did not at first participate.[2]

Wilson received Prince Max's note on October 6. On the 7th, he received Sir Eric Geddes, First Lord of the Admiralty and head of the British Naval Mission in the United States, who asked Wilson for an interpretation of "freedom of the seas." Geddes reported to Lloyd George that the President's views were "obviously unformed" but that his intention seemed to be to press for acceptance of the principle that no single member of the league of nations might use naval power against a belliger-

[1] Swiss Chargé Oederlin to President Wilson, October 4, 1918, Department of State, *Papers Relating to the Foreign Relations of the United States, 1918*, Supplement 1, *The World War* (2 Vols., Washington: United States Government Printing Office, 1933), Vol. 1, pp. 337-338; hereafter referred to as *Foreign Relations*. Peace notes referred to in the present chapter will be cited from this source. Other convenient collections of the correspondence leading to the Armistice are found in: Edward Parkes, ed., *British and Foreign State Papers, 1917-1918* (London: His Majesty's Stationery Office, 1921), pp. 641-651; Alma Luckau, *The German Delegation at the Paris Peace Conference* (New York: Columbia University Press, 1941), pp. 3-26, 140-147; James Brown Scott, ed., *Official Statements of War Aims and Peace Proposals, December 1916 to November 1918* (Washington: Carnegie Endowment for International Peace, 1921), pp. 414-457, passim.

[2] Harry R. Rudin, *Armistice, 1918* (New Haven: Yale University Press, 1944), pp. 89-96. The present chapter relies heavily on this monograph, which contains an excellent detailed discussion of the negotiation of the Pre-Armistice Agreement.

ent state without the consent of the league.[3] On the same day, Lloyd George approached Frazier, the American diplomatic liaison officer at the Supreme War Council, and inquired anxiously as to whether the President had yet responded to the German note, urging that the President send Colonel House over as quickly as possible.[4]

Wilson replied to the German note on October 8, asking whether Germany accepted the Fourteen Points and the principles set forth in his subsequent addresses with the understanding that it remained only to negotiate the details of application. The President's reply further insisted on the evacuation of the occupied regions and asked whether the Chancellor spoke for the German people or only for the military leaders of the war.[5]

Meeting on the evening of October 9 to discuss the President's note, the Allied Premiers reacted with alarm and anger at Wilson's apparent intention to engage in bilateral negotiations with the German Government. Clemenceau wished to ignore Wilson's reply to the Germans but Lloyd George insisted successfully on the dispatch of a joint note to the President. The Allied note protested that Wilson's condition of evacuation of invaded territories was in itself inadequate, that the enemy would be permitted to reform his lines, and urged that the military experts should fix the terms of an armistice.[6] In another note, sent later the same evening, the Allied Premiers pleaded that a representative possessing the full confidence of the United States Government be sent to Europe.[7]

The second German note was received in Washington on October 14. It agreed to the requirements of Wilson's note of October 8 and assured the President of the representative character of

[3] Geddes to Lloyd George, October 13, 1918, Sir William Wiseman Papers, Sterling Library, Yale University; David Lloyd George, *War Memoirs of David Lloyd George* (6 Vols., Boston: Little, Brown and Company, 1933-1937), Vol. 6, pp. 260-261; Ray Stannard Baker, *Woodrow Wilson: Life and Letters* (8 Vols., Garden City, New York: Doubleday, Doran and Company, Inc., 1927-1939), Vol. 8, p. 456.

[4] Frazier to Lansing, October 7, 1918, *Foreign Relations, 1918*, Supplement 1, Vol. 1, pp. 344-345.

[5] Lansing to Oederlin, October 8, 1918, *ibid.*, p. 343.

[6] Frazier to Lansing, October 9, 1918, *ibid.*, p. 353.

[7] *ibid.*, pp. 353-354. See Rudin, *Armistice, 1918*, pp. 106-108; Lloyd George, *War Memoirs*, Vol. 6, pp. 254-255.

the German Government.[8] While this note was in transmission, Lloyd George, now back in London, held a luncheon conference to discuss these developments with his political and military advisers. The diary of General Sir Henry Wilson provides a vivid impression of the attitudes expressed in this meeting toward Wilson's peace negotiations: ". . . . As regards Wilson, we agreed that we would wire to say that he must make it clear to the Boches that his fourteen points (with which we do not agree) were not a basis for an armistice, which is what the Boches pretend they are. As regards the Press, we agreed that they should be told that Wilson is acting on his own, that the War is *not* over, that the fourteen points are *not* an armistice, and that an armistice is *not* a peace. It was a very interesting afternoon. Everyone angry and contemptuous of Wilson."[9]

President Wilson dispatched his second note to Germany on October 14. It informed the German Government that the terms of an armistice would be determined by the Allied military advisers and that they must guarantee Allied military supremacy. Submarine warfare and spoliation of evacuated areas must cease and guarantees must be given of the destruction of "arbitrary power."[10] On the same day, the British Government was informed that Colonel House was to be sent to Europe at once as the President's special representative.[11] Sir Eric Geddes wired Lloyd George that the President recognized that the time had come for negotiations with the Allies.[12]

While Wilson thus stiffened his terms for Germany and complied with the Allied request for an American representative, the British and French continued to feel that Wilson had usurped more authority to negotiate the end of the war than American

[8] Oederlin to Lansing, October 14, 1918, *Foreign Relations, 1918*, Supplement 1, Vol. 1, pp. 357-358.

[9] Major-General Sir C. E. Callwell, *Field Marshal Sir Henry Wilson* (2 Vols., London, Toronto, Melbourne, Sydney: Cassell and Company, Ltd., 1927), Vol. 2, p. 136. The account by Sir Henry Wilson may perhaps not reflect the view of the British Government with full accuracy. His diary is replete with hostile references to President Wilson and to the League of Nations.

[10] Lansing to Oederlin, October 14, 1918, *Foreign Relations 1918*, Supplement 1, Vol. 1, pp. 358-359.

[11] Lansing to Laughlin (American Chargé in London), October 14, 1918, *ibid.*, p. 361.

[12] Lloyd George, *War Memoirs*, Vol. 6, p. 260.

efforts had earned. Laughlin, the American Chargé d'Affaires, reported from London the existence of "grave doubts" as to the Fourteen Points, especially the freedom of the seas,[13] while Sir Henry Wilson fulminated against the President as a "super-Gladstone—and a dangerous visionary at that."[14]

Wilson at this time was meditating on the whole range of issues rendered urgent by the sudden prospect of peace, and he opened his mind to Sir William Wiseman, especially in regard to the question of British sea power and the freedom of the seas. In an interview with Sir William on October 16, the President said that he recognized that the British Navy in the past had served as a sort of world police force, a role which the British people had never abused and one which he himself would be content to leave with them. But many nations, Wilson continued, chafed under British naval predominance and, indeed, he felt, the "deepest cause of the present war" was Germany's unjust jealousy of the British Navy. Wiseman was left with the impression that the President recognized that the introduction of the submarine as an instrument of naval warfare created the necessity to revise international maritime law and that the President was seeking a way by which the British Navy might be used as an instrument of the league of nations.[15]

The third German note to Wilson, received on October 22, accepted determination of armistice terms by the Allied military, announced the cessation of submarine warfare, and insisted that the new Government of Prince Max was representative of the people and responsible to the Reichstag.[16] The British Cabinet, with this latest German note already known to them, held a long meeting on October 21, which resulted in the dispatch to the President of a telegram, labeled "Very Urgent," warning that the Germans were seeking a conditional Armistice which would allow them to retreat to strong frontier positions and ap-

[13] Laughlin to Lansing, October 15, 1918, *Foreign Relations, 1918*, Supplement 1, Vol. 1, pp. 365-367.

[14] Callwell, *Sir Henry Wilson*, Vol. 2, p. 137.

[15] "Notes on an Interview with the President at the White House," October 16, 1918, Wiseman Papers.

[16] Oederlin to Lansing, October 22, 1918, *Foreign Relations, 1918*, Supplement 1, Vol. 1, pp. 379-381.

pealing to Wilson to make no commitments without consulting the Allies.[17]

Wilson was by this time quite ready to consult the Allies. He dispatched his third note to Germany on October 23, agreeing to submit his correspondence with the German Government to the Allies with the recommendation that the military representatives undertake the preparation of armistice terms, although he still questioned the representative character of the German Government.[18] On the same day, the correspondence between Wilson and the German Government was transmitted to the Allied capitals with an inquiry as to whether the Allies were prepared to formulate an armistice on its terms.[19]

The British Government was immediately mollified. On October 24, Lloyd George expressed to the Cabinet his full approval of Wilson's final note to Germany.[20] The fear of the British Government that the President would usurp the prerogatives of the coalition in the making of peace and allow himself to be duped by the Germans in the bargain was fully dispelled by Wilson's adroit conduct of the negotiations with Germany. Even so ardent an enthusiast for power diplomacy as Winston Churchill conceded that Wilson had dealt with the suppliant Germans "in the strongest manner," using the weapon of delay with "masterly skill."[21]

II. *The Anglo-American Conflict over the "Freedom of the Seas" at the Inter-Allied Conference of October 29-November 4; The Armistice of November 11, 1918*

Colonel House, who arrived in Paris on October 26 to represent the President in the pre-Armistice negotiations with the Allies, regarded it as the primary object of his mission to secure

[17] Baker, *Wilson: Life and Letters*, Vol. 8, p. 501.

[18] Lansing to Oederlin, October 23, 1918, *Foreign Relations, 1918*, Supplement 1, Vol. 1, pp. 381-383.

[19] Lansing to Allied Ambassadors in Washington, October 23, 1918, *ibid.*, p. 383. See also H. W. V. Temperley, ed., *A History of the Peace Conference of Paris* (6 Vols., London: Henry Frowde and Hodder and Stoughton, 1920-1924), Vol. 1, pp. 130-133.

[20] Lloyd George, *War Memoirs*, Vol. 6, p. 272.

[21] Winston S. Churchill, *The Aftermath*, Vol. 4 of *The World Crisis, 1918-1928* (New York: Charles Scribner's Sons, 1929), p. 99. See also Rudin, *Armistice, 1918*, p. 399.

explicit acceptance of President Wilson's principles as the basis of peace. He took little part in the discussion of specific military and naval terms.[22] His first step was to arrange for an interpretative commentary on the Fourteen Points to be used in explaining their meaning and implications to Lloyd George and Clemenceau. The resulting Cobb-Lippmann Memorandum, which Wilson approved as a satisfactory but "merely illustrative" interpretation,[23] was used frequently by House in the negotiations with Lloyd George and Clemenceau.[24]

The Cobb-Lippmann Memorandum interpreted the crucial Point 2 on freedom of the seas as referring to navigation under three conditions: general peace, during which absolute freedom of the seas would prevail; general war, involving peace enforcement action by the league of nations, in which case complete nonintercourse with an aggressor state would be enforced; limited war, involving no breach of international covenants, in which case the historic rights of neutral vessels under international law would be fully respected by belligerents.[25]

The British Government and Admiralty were anything but reassured by this definition of the clause on the freedom of the seas. To British statesmen and naval authorities, the implication of Point 2 seemed to be the transfer from Great Britain to an untested international organization of the power to enforce a blockade such as had sapped the power of Germany, virtually prohibiting the offensive use of British sea power and largely nullifying the strategic position of England in relation to the continent.[26]

Colonel House conferred on October 28 with Sir William Wiseman, who told him that the British Cabinet was in rebellion against Point 2. House replied sternly that the United States and the world would no more readily submit to British domina-

[22] Charles Seymour, ed., *The Intimate Papers of Colonel House* (4 Vols., Boston & New York: Houghton Mifflin Company, 1926-1928), Vol. 4, p. 150.

[23] Wilson to House, October 30, 1918, *Foreign Relations, 1918*, Supplement 1, Vol. 1, p. 421.

[24] Seymour, ed., *Intimate Papers*, Vol. 4, pp. 152-154. See also Thomas A. Bailey, *Woodrow Wilson and the Lost Peace* (New York: The Macmillan Company, 1944), p. 44.

[25] Seymour, ed., *Intimate Papers*, Vol. 4, p. 193.

[26] Harold and Margaret Sprout, *Toward a New Order of Sea Power, 1918-1922* (2nd edn., Princeton: Princeton University Press, 1946), pp. 60-61; Churchill, *The Aftermath*, p. 103.

tion of the seas than to German mastery on land. If challenged, he warned, the United States would build a greater army and navy.[27]

The Allied Premiers and Foreign Ministers and Colonel House convened on October 29 in the first of several sessions in which many harsh words and threats were exchanged between the British and American representatives over the issue of freedom of the seas. The final agreement reached, which made possible the Pre-Armistice Agreement of November 5, 1918, was effected by an ostensible compromise on Point 2 which was in fact a virtual acceptance by the United States of the British position.[28]

At the outset of the Inter-Allied Conference, Lloyd George struck a posture of unbending hostility to the freedom of the seas. At a luncheon meeting with House on October 29, the Prime Minister said that Britain could not accept a peace including the principle of Point 2 as it stood, and insisted that a specific reservation be made in any armistice agreement with Germany since the Allies would otherwise be committed to the Fourteen Points in their entirety.[29] In the formal meeting on the same day, Lloyd George bluntly rejected Point 2, asserting that its implementation during the war would have nullified the blockade and insisting that a league of nations would have to be "thoroughly established and proved" before any decision on freedom of the seas could be reached. House warned that if Point 2 were not accepted the United States might be compelled to build a great navy to protect its maritime commerce and might, in any future war, find itself in sympathy with the "weaker naval power."[30]

The discussion became more heated as Clemenceau and Son-

[27] House Diary, October 28, 1918, Seymour, ed., *Intimate Papers*, Vol. 4, pp. 159-160.

[28] Generally excellent brief accounts of the Inter-Allied Conference of October 29-November 4, besides the indispensable material in the *Intimate Papers*, may be found in: Rudin, *Armistice, 1918*, pp. 266-284, and Charles Seymour, *American Diplomacy during the World War* (Baltimore: The Johns Hopkins Press, 1934), pp. 366-400, both drawing heavily on the *Intimate Papers*. The House Papers in the Sterling Library at Yale University contain a set of the official British minutes of this Conference.

[29] House to Lansing, October 29, 1918, Seymour, ed., *Intimate Papers*, Vol. 4, pp. 160-161; Churchill, *The Aftermath*, p. 102.

[30] David Lloyd George, *The Truth about the Peace Treaties* (2 Vols., London: Victor Gollancz, Ltd., 1938), Vol. 1, p. 77; Seymour, ed., *Intimate Papers*, Vol. 4, pp. 163-164.

nino, the Italian Foreign Minister, supported Lloyd George in resisting the demand for a blanket endorsement of the Fourteen Points. If the Allies refused to accept the Fourteen Points, House threatened, the President would have no recourse but to tell the Germans that his conditions were rejected by the Allies. "The question would then arise," said House, "whether America would not have to take up these questions directly with Germany and Austria." Clemenceau demanded to know if this meant that the United States would consider a separate peace. "It might," replied House. Lloyd George remained adamant in the face of this threat. "If the United States made a separate peace," he averred, "we would be sorry, but we could not give up the blockade, the power which enabled us to live . . . we will fight on." The meeting was adjourned upon its being agreed that each of the Allies would draw up its reservations to the Fourteen Points for discussion the next day.[31]

House cabled the events of October 29 to Wilson,[32] who on the same day had cabled a stern message to House demanding Allied acceptance of the Fourteen Points: ". . . It is the Fourteen Points that Germany has accepted. England cannot dispense with our friendship in the future and the other Allies cannot without our assistance get their rights as against England. If it is the purpose of the Allied statesmen to nullify my influence, force the purpose boldly to the surface and let me speak of it to all the world as I shall. . . ."[33]

In another cable on October 30, the President stated bluntly: ". . . I cannot consent to take part in the negotiation of a peace which does not include freedom of the seas. . . ."[34] Lloyd George regarded Wilson's threat of an appeal to Allied public opinion as an "unloaded blunderbuss," since, he perceived, the dangers

---

[31] Lloyd George, *The Truth about the Peace Treaties*, Vol. 1, pp. 77-78; Seymour, ed., *Intimate Papers*, Vol. 4, pp. 165-167; Stephen Bonsal, *Unfinished Business* (Garden City, New York: Doubleday, Doran and Company, Inc., 1944), pp. 1-2.

[32] House to Wilson, October 30, 1918, *Foreign Relations, 1918*, Supplement 1, Vol. 1, pp. 421-423.

[33] Wilson to House, October 29, 1918, *Foreign Relations, 1919, The Paris Peace Conference* (13 Vols., Washington: United States Government Printing Office, 1942-1947), Vol. 1, p. 285; Baker, *Wilson: Life and Letters*, Vol. 8, p. 529.

[34] Wilson to House, October 30, 1918, *Foreign Relations, 1918*, Supplement 1, Vol. 1, p. 423; Baker, *Wilson: Life and Letters*, Vol. 8, p. 533.

of public sentiment in Britain and France derived not from resistance to a liberal peace but from "exactly the opposite direction."[35]

Despite these threats and fulminations, House focused his efforts
on the British, recognizing that however vehemently they objected
to Point 2, it was only Point 2 to which they objected, while
France and Italy might raise many issues.[36] On the morning of
October 30, Lloyd George presented a draft memorandum which
made reservations only on the freedom of the seas and on reparations. House threatened that if there were many objections the
President would submit to Congress the issue of continuing the
war or not on the Allied terms, adding a specific threat to England that its policy might lead to a great naval building program
by the United States.[37]

Other matters were dealt with in the sessions from October
30 to November 3. An Italian attempt to include a reservation
on Point 9 in regard to Italian territorial expansion was disposed
of with the explanation that the Italian claims were concerned
with Austria-Hungary and not with Germany, and a Belgian
objection to the commercial nondiscrimination of Point 3 was
brushed aside. Agreement was reached defining the requirements
for restoration of invaded territories as encompassing "all damage done to the civilian populations of the Allies and their property by the aggression of Germany by land, by sea and from
the air."[38]

There remained the seemingly irreconcilable positions of the
English-speaking powers on the freedom of the seas. In his
memoirs, Lloyd George asserts that Great Britain was prepared
to go on with the war without the United States rather than
give up the right of naval blockade which he believed Point 2
to require.[39] In a gesture combining conciliation and threat,

[35] Lloyd George, *The Truth about the Peace Treaties*, Vol. 1, pp. 82-83.

[36] Seymour, ed., *Intimate Papers*, Vol. 4, pp. 167-168.

[37] House to Wilson, October 30, 1918, *Foreign Relations, 1918*, Supplement 1,
Vol. 1, pp. 423-427; Seymour, ed., *Intimate Papers*, Vol. 4, pp. 170-171; Bonsal,
Unfinished Business, pp. 2-3.

[38] Seymour, ed., *Intimate Papers*, Vol. 4, pp. 172-178; Lloyd George, *The Truth
about the Treaties*, Vol. 1, pp. 78-81; André Tardieu, *The Truth about the Treaty*
(Indianapolis: The Bobbs-Merrill Company, Inc., 1921), pp. 70-71.

[39] Lloyd George, *The Truth about the Treaties*, Vol. 2, p. 81.

Wilson cabled House on October 31: "I fully and sympathetically recognize the exceptional position and necessities of Great Britain with regard to the use of the seas for defense. . . ." The freedom of the seas, Wilson conceded, required "careful definition," but the principle must be accepted, or the President would go to Congress, "who confidentially will have no sympathy whatever with spending American lives for British naval control. . . ."[40]

The reservation of the Allies to the freedom of the seas, drafted by the British, objected that Point 2 was "open to various interpretations, some of which they could not accept," and reserved "complete freedom" on the subject should it arise at the Peace Conference.[41] House spent most of his time outside the formal conference sessions in vain efforts to induce the British to modify their stand. In a conference with Sir William Wiseman on November 1, he warned that unless British concessions on the freedom of the seas were forthcoming, "all hope of Anglo-Saxon unity would be at an end. . . ." The United States, he said, could not yield the principle for which it had gone to war with England in 1812 and with Germany in 1917. He feared that if Lloyd George persisted in his attitude, "there would be greater feelings against Great Britain at the end of the war than there had been since our Civil War. . . ."[42]

The tension between the United States and Great Britain reached formidable proportions. Wilson cabled that unless Point 2 was explicitly accepted, the British could "count on the certainty of our using our present equipment to build up the strongest navy that our resources permit . . . ,"[43] while Lloyd George staunchly insisted that Great Britain would "spend her last guinea to keep a navy superior to that of the United States or any other power. . . ."[44]

House, who had counseled a most rigorous definition of the freedom of the seas when the President was drafting the Four-

---

[40] Wilson to House, October 31, 1918, *Foreign Relations, 1918*, Supplement 1, Vol. 1, pp. 427-428; Baker, *Wilson: Life and Letters*, Vol. 8, pp. 537-539.

[41] Seymour, ed., *Intimate Papers*, Vol. 4, p. 170; Churchill, *The Aftermath*, pp. 106-107.

[42] House Diary, November 1, 1918, Seymour, ed., *Intimate Papers*, Vol. 4, pp. 179-180.

[43] Wilson to House, November 4, 1918, *ibid.*, p. 179.

[44] House Diary, November 4, 1918, *ibid.*, pp. 180-181.

teen Points,[45] now made a major concession to the British. Convinced that the entire peace depended upon a solid foundation of Anglo-American cooperation, he ceased to insist that the principle of freedom of the seas must be then and there recognized and required only that the British reservation, *which he was prepared to accept,* must not exclude full and free discussion of the issue at the Peace Conference.[46] Clearly, this was the major "break" which made agreement possible.

The deadlock was broken at the formal meeting of November 3. House again vainly assured Lloyd George that the President did not propose to alter the international law of blockade but only insisted upon the principle of freedom of the seas. "It's no good saying I accept the principle," replied the Prime Minister. "It would only mean that in a week's time a new Prime Minister would be here who would say that he could not accept this principle. . . ."[47] Lloyd George was, however, willing to *discuss* the issue at the Peace Conference and, at House's request, agreed to state this willingness in writing.[48]

That very evening, House received the following letter from Lloyd George: "I write to confirm the statement I made in the course of our talk this afternoon at your house when I told you that 'We were quite willing to discuss the freedom of the seas in the light of the new conditions which have arisen in the course of the present war.' In our judgment this most important subject can only be dealt with satisfactorily through the freest debate and the most liberal exchange of views. . . ."[49]

The issue was thus settled on the basis of a major American concession on an issue which, in the strongest possible terms, had been declared to be beyond compromise. The Supreme War Council, on November 4, formally approved a memorandum to President Wilson accepting a peace based on the Fourteen Points and subsequent addresses, with the two agreed provisos, one defining the meaning of reparations and the other reserving the

[45] House Diary, January 9, 1918, House Papers.
[46] See Seymour, ed., *Intimate Papers,* Vol. 4, pp. 181-182.
[47] *ibid.,* pp. 182-184.
[48] House to Lansing, November 3, 1918, *Foreign Relations, 1918,* Supplement 1, Vol. 1, pp. 455-456; Seymour, ed., *Intimate Papers,* Vol. 4, p. 184.
[49] Lloyd George to House, November 3, 1918, *Foreign Relations, 1918,* Supplement 1, Vol. 1, p. 456; Seymour, ed., *Intimate Papers,* Vol. 4, pp. 184-185.

right of "complete freedom" to discuss the principle of Point 2 at the Peace Conference. The phrasing of the letter was identical with the original draft submitted by Lloyd George. Although the American concession had been great, the principles of the Fourteen Points and subsequent addresses were, with the two reservations, thus legally and morally accepted as the basis of the Armistice and the treaty of peace.[50]

Undoubtedly, the winning of Allied agreement to make peace on the President's terms was a major achievement. Colonel House exulted in the outcome of the Inter-Allied Conference as a signal triumph for American diplomacy.[51] But over whom was the victory won? Except for the British objection to Point 2, the resistance of the Allies had not been formidable. The objections of Italy and Belgium were overcome with ease, while the French insistence on a definition of reparation was not unacceptable to the United States. Only on the issue of Point 2 did House encounter strong opposition, and on this the British had their way, yielding only the sop of a promise to *discuss* a principle which they had explicitly rejected. The principle of freedom of the seas under international law, for which the United States had gone to war, as enlarged by Wilson to "absolute" freedom of the seas, was thus virtually abandoned before the Peace Conference convened. Lloyd George regarded his letter to House of November 3 as a face-saving device for President Wilson, and he felt certain, quite correctly as it turned out, that "nothing more would be heard of the subject."[52] At least as far as Point 2 was concerned, Winston Churchill was quite right in scoffing at House's claim of triumph as "naive."[53]

The Anglo-American controversy over Point 2 should not obscure the position of Great Britain on the other thirteen points. On these there was virtual agreement, for the British and American programs were essentially parallel. Lloyd George's statement of January 5, 1918, it will be recalled, differed in few respects and more in tone than in content from the Fourteen

[50] House to Lansing, November 4, 1918, *Foreign Relations, 1918*, Supplement 1, Vol. 1, pp. 461-462; Seymour, ed., *Intimate Papers*, Vol. 4, p. 187; Temperley, ed., *A History of the Peace Conference of Paris*, Vol. 1, p. 383.

[51] Seymour, ed., *Intimate Papers*, Vol. 4, p. 188.

[52] Lloyd George, *The Truth about the Treaties*, Vol. 1, p. 85.

[53] Churchill, *The Aftermath*, p. 109.

Points.[54] Lloyd George's assertion that Wilson's peace program was almost identical with his own was irrefutable.[55] The agreement of the Allied and Associated Powers to make peace on the basis of President Wilson's principles is, therefore, hardly to be classed as a victory over Great Britain, or even over the continental Allies. It was rather a triumph of enlightened and moral statesmanship over the discredited and amoral principles of the past.

The military and naval terms of the Armistice were drawn up by the military advisers of the Allied and Associated Powers, who deliberated at Versailles while the statesmen were engaged in the debate over the Fourteen Points.[56] The terms they proposed for Germany were formally approved by the Supreme War Council on November 4 and communicated to President Wilson.[57]

President Wilson promptly accepted the terms of the proposed Pre-Armistice Agreement, including the two Allied reservations, and on November 5 Lansing dispatched to Germany the note which became the legal contract between victors and vanquished binding them to a peace based on President Wilson's principles. The note advised Germany of the agreement of the Allies to make peace on the basis of the Fourteen Points and Wilson's subsequent addresses, with the reservation on the freedom of the seas and the interpretation of compensation for damage. Germany was informed that Marshal Foch was authorized to receive accredited representatives for the purpose of communicating the military terms of an armistice.[58]

At this juncture, a minor but sharp outcry arose as to the status of the British Dominions in the negotiation of peace. In a letter to *The Times* of London, Prime Minister Hughes of Australia

[54] See Chapter I, Section IV.

[55] See Lloyd George, *The Truth about the Treaties*, Vol. I, pp. 86-91.

[56] The drafting of the military and naval terms is excellently summarized in Rudin, *Armistice, 1918*, pp. 285-319. See also Seymour, ed., *Intimate Papers*, Vol. 4, pp. 114-137; Tardieu, *The Truth about the Treaty*, pp. 68-70.

[57] House to Wilson, November 4, 1918, *Foreign Relations, 1918*, Supplement I, Vol. I, pp. 463-468.

[58] Lansing to the Swiss Minister, Sulzer, November 5, 1918, *ibid.*, pp. 468-469. For a precise definition of the documents—speeches and correspondence—legally embodied in the Pre-Armistice Agreement, see Temperley, ed., *A History of the Peace Conference of Paris*, Vol. I, pp. 386-388.

protested against the armistice terms, which the British Government had accepted without consulting the Dominions. Specifically, Hughes objected to Point 3 on commercial nondiscrimination and Point 5 in regard to the German colonies in the Pacific. The Dominions, he complained, had fully participated in the policy discussion of the Imperial War Cabinet, and ". . . most certainly Dr. Wilson's Fourteen Points were never agreed to, they were not even specifically discussed."[59] Generally, the other Dominions did not support Hughes's protest, but General Smuts of South Africa publicly called attention to the fact that Canada and Australia had suffered heavier war losses than the United States.[60] The flurry of Dominion discontent in November foreshadowed more significant clashes with the United States at the Peace Conference, especially over the issue of the German colonies and especially between Wilson and the obstreperous Hughes.

The English radicals who had so warmly supported President Wilson during the war bestirred themselves to new heights of enthusiasm over his success in winning Allied agreement to the Fourteen Points as the basis of peace. They were not, however, in Wilson's pocket and never had been. They had developed meticulous standards during the war years, and when the exigencies of Peace Conference diplomacy later compelled Wilson to accept terms that fell short of these, the English radicals went into opposition, becoming articulate participants in the postwar revisionist movement.[61]

The Armistice with Germany was signed on November 11, 1918. Although Germany accepted virtually all of the terms that the Allied and Associated Powers had drafted, it was not an unconditional surrender, because the Pre-Armistice Agreement contracted the victors, both legally and morally, to a peace settlement based on President Wilson's principles. The Pre-Armistice Agreement was a literal embodiment of American principles and a practical embodiment of British principles as set forth dur-

[59] Consul-General Skinner (London) to Lansing, November 9, 1918, *Foreign Relations, 1918*, Supplement 1, Vol. 1, pp. 490-491.

[60] Temperley, ed., *A History of the Peace Conference of Paris*, Vol. 6, pp. 343-344.

[61] Lawrence W. Martin, *Peace without Victory* (New Haven: Yale University Press, 1958), pp. 189, 195, 207-208.

ing the war. The manner in which these principles were subsequently implemented was accordingly a moral test of the adherence of the English-speaking peoples to their own professed articles of belief.

III. *Politics and Preparations for the Peace Conference in the United States, November 1918*

A shaky interparty truce in the United States on issues relating to the war and its termination was brought to an end when, on October 24, 1918, President Wilson typed out a partisan appeal to the American people. "I would not send it out," counseled Mrs. Wilson. "It is not a dignified thing to do." "That is what I thought at first," the President replied, "but it is too late now. I have told them I would do it."[62] The President's appeal was issued at the urgent request of his party in order to counter the contention of Republican candidates for Congress that they had fully supported the President's peace aims and that he, therefore, was as willing to see Republicans as Democrats elected to Congress. The statement called upon the American people, if they approved of the President's leadership, to return Democratic majorities to the Senate and the House of Representatives in the Congressional elections on November 5. "The return of a Republican majority to either House of the Congress," said the President, "would . . . certainly be interpreted on the other side of the water as a repudiation of my leadership."[63]

The statement gave rise to an immediate outcry against the President's use of the "national" issue of war and peace for party advantage and led to a long-range historical debate as to the wisdom of the appeal. Undoubtedly, Wilson's prestige at home and abroad was damaged by the Republican victory of November 5, by his own definition an expression of disapproval of his leadership. But was the President's own definition of the meaning of the election valid? Colonel House thought the partisan appeal an egregious error.[64] So astute a Democratic politician as Alben W.

[62] Edith Bolling Wilson to Ray Stannard Baker, Baker, *Wilson: Life and Letters*, Vol. 8, p. 510.

[63] Ray Stannard Baker and William E. Dodd, eds., *The Public Papers of Woodrow Wilson* (6 Vols., New York and London: Harper & Brothers, Publishers, 1925-1927), *War and Peace*, Vol. 1, pp. 286-288.

[64] House Diary, October 25, 1918, House Papers.

Barkley of Kentucky believed that the appeal was Wilson's one great political mistake, that if he had asked for a "cooperative Congress" regardless of party, he might have got the Democratic Congress he desired.[65] It has also been suggested, however, that the appeal, instead of contributing to the Democratic defeat, actually prevented greater losses than were suffered.[66]

It is, moreover, not likely that a nonpartisan appeal would have produced Republican supporters of the President's program who could have overridden the hostile attitude of the Republican leadership. The crucial issue was party control of the organization of the Senate, especially of the Committee on Foreign Relations. The President believed in party government and party responsibility and saw no transcendent virtue in a bipartisan approach to policy. In view of the performance of the Republican Senate in the course of 1919, it is difficult to challenge absolutely the wisdom of the President's partisan approach or, specifically, of his appeal of October 24, 1918.[67]

The "repudiation" of Wilson's leadership in the Congressional election was, in fact, more apparent than real, but the appearance itself was sufficient to weaken the position of the President vis-à-vis his European colleagues. The election resulted in only a small Republican majority in the House of Representatives and a bare majority in the Senate. But for the seating of the Republican Truman Newberry of Michigan, who was subsequently indicted for illegal campaign expenditures and compelled to resign his seat, the Senate would have been tied and the Vice President could have resolved the tie for Democratic control. The election, therefore, can hardly be regarded as a Republican victory or a Democratic defeat of any proportions, nor a repudiation of the leadership of

[65] The University of Chicago in cooperation with the Woodrow Wilson Foundation, Lectures and Seminar at the University of Chicago, January 30-February 3, 1956, in Celebration of the *Centennial of Woodrow Wilson, 1856-1956*, Central Theme: *Freedom for Man: A World Safe for Mankind*, p. 69.

[66] See Bailey, *Wilson and the Lost Peace*, p. 62; Dana Frank Fleming, *The United States and the League of Nations, 1918-1920* (New York and London: G. P. Putnam's Sons, 1932), pp. 51-52.

[67] For opinions generally sustaining this view, see: Arthur S. Link, *Wilson the Diplomatist* (Baltimore: The Johns Hopkins Press, 1957), p. 28; Josephus Daniels, *The Wilson Era* (Chapel Hill: The University of North Carolina Press, 1946), p. 307; Silas Bent McKinley, *Woodrow Wilson* (New York: Frederick A. Praeger, 1957), p. 230.

the President, whose tenure was not at issue. The President's position at the Peace Conference, nevertheless, was undoubtedly weakened by the ostensible electoral repudiation, especially by contrast with the massive votes of confidence won by Lloyd George and Clemenceau. In Lloyd George's view, the President came to Europe to represent the United States "discredited by the universal knowledge that he was no longer the authentic spokesman of its opinions, or the real accredited interpreter of its policy."[68]

Sir William Wiseman counseled his Government to adopt a more realistic view of the significance of the American Congressional elections. He advised British officials to avoid in public pronouncements too fulsome flattery of Wilson and to stress British good will toward all American parties, while emphasizing his opinion that the President as "Foreign Minister" retained the support of the great majority of the American people.[69] In a memorandum on American policy Wiseman reminded the British Government that the President alone, and not the Republican leaders, could speak for the United States. Wiseman urged against courting Republican support for British policies because, he pointed out, in any dispute with a foreign country the American people always rallied behind the President. The American people, Wiseman wrote, had been taught to regard Britain as a "nation of imperialists, who want to boss the whole world," but he felt that there was a growing awareness not only that Britain and America would emerge from the war as the only remaining Great Powers but that the British and American peoples "believe in the same things and follow the same ideals."[70]

A minor Anglo-American discord arose in the pre-Conference period over the question of where the Peace Conference should be held. Wilson and Lloyd George were at first in agreement that it should be on neutral rather than French soil. On October 28, Wilson cabled House, then attending the Inter-Allied Conference in Paris, that he preferred Lausanne to Paris, "care being taken not to choose a place where either German or English influence

[68] Lloyd George, *The Truth about the Peace Treaties*, Vol. I, pp. 155-156.
[69] Wiseman to ? (name of recipient in code), November 25, 1918, Wiseman Papers.
[70] "The Attitude of the United States and of President Wilson towards the Peace Conference," undated memorandum, Wiseman Papers.

would be strong."[71] At the conference of Allied Premiers on October 29, Lloyd George and Colonel House presented a united front for a conference on neutral soil against Clemenceau's demand for Paris.[72] This apparent Anglo-American understanding was broken when President Wilson suddenly reversed himself and came out for Paris, contending that Switzerland was "saturated with every poisonous element and open to every hostile influence in Europe."[73] House reluctantly supported the President's new position in the Allied Conference on November 9,[74] and proceeded to overcome Lloyd George's opposition by inducing Lord North-cliffe, the British press magnate, to come out strongly for Paris in an editorial in *The Times*.[75] Thus deprived of American support for a neutral site, the British Government reluctantly agreed to a peace conference to be held in Paris.[76] Lloyd George, who had personally favored Geneva, regarded the choice of Paris, with its charged atmosphere, as regrettable, but Great Britain, he felt, could not hold out for a neutral site without American support.[77] Whether in fact the holding of the Peace Conference in "shell-shocked" Paris contributed to the harshness of the peace treaties is problematical. It is difficult to believe that the French would have struck a more liberal posture on security, or the British on reparations, at Geneva or Lausanne.

The decision of President Wilson to attend the Peace Conference in person was received with misgivings by the British and French Governments and by various American officials. Before the decision was made, Lloyd George had questioned Sir William Wiseman closely as to the President's intentions, making it clear that he wanted no "conquering hero" from America, which had done

[71] Wilson to House, October 28, 1918, *Foreign Relations, 1919, The Paris Peace Conference*, Vol. 1, p. 119; Baker, *Wilson: Life and Letters*, Vol. 8, p. 524.
[72] House Diary, October 29, 1918, Seymour, ed., *Intimate Papers*, Vol. 4, p. 217. See also Bonsal, *Unfinished Business*, pp. 8-9.
[73] Wilson to House, November 7, 1918, *Foreign Relations, 1919, The Paris Peace Conference*, Vol. 1, p. 121; Seymour, ed., *Intimate Papers*, Vol. 4, p. 218; Baker, *Wilson: Life and Letters*, Vol. 8, p. 560.
[74] Seymour, ed., *Intimate Papers*, Vol. 4, pp. 218-219.
[75] Bonsal, *Unfinished Business*, p. 9.
[76] House to Lansing, November 20, 1918, *Foreign Relations, 1919, The Paris Peace Conference*, Vol. 1, p. 124; Seymour, ed., *Intimate Papers*, Vol. 4, p. 220. See also F. S. Marston, *The Peace Conference of 1919* (London, New York, Toronto: Oxford University Press, 1944), pp. 38-39.
[77] Lloyd George, *The Truth about the Peace Treaties*, Vol. 1, pp. 147-148.

so little fighting, to impose his will on the diplomats of Europe.[78] Colonel House also questioned the advisability of the President going to Paris, doubting his ability as a negotiator *inter pares*. He cabled the President from Paris that the opinion of Americans there was "practically unanimous," that Presidential participation beyond the preliminaries of the Peace Conference would involve a "loss of dignity and your commanding position," and that French and British diplomats, including Sir William Wiseman, fully shared this opinion.[79] House further reported a message from Clemenceau to Lloyd George opposing Wilson's presence on the ground that, unlike themselves, he was a head of state.[80] Wilson replied angrily to House his belief that the British and French wished to "pocket" him, "for fear I might there lead the weaker nations against them." "The fact that I am head of the state," the President asserted, "is of no practical consequence."[81] On November 18, it was officially announced that the President would sail for France immediately after the opening of Congress. The announcement said that the President would probably not remain throughout the sessions of the formal Peace Conference, his purpose being to deal only with the "greater outlines" of the treaty.[82]

The decision of the President to attend the Peace Conference has been much condemned. Former President Theodore Roosevelt, who had either forgotten or suppressed his understanding of the Constitution, proclaimed that Wilson had "no authority whatever to speak for the American people at this time."[83] Secretary of State Lansing was "surprised and disturbed."[84] Harold Nicolson wrote that the presence of President Wilson in Paris constituted an "historical disaster of the first magnitude," and, with remarka-

[78] Sir Arthur Willert, *The Road to Safety* (London: Derek Verschoyle, Ltd., 1952), p. 161.

[79] House to Wilson, November 14, 1918, *Foreign Relations, 1919, The Paris Peace Conference*, Vol. 1, pp. 130-131; Seymour, ed., *Intimate Papers*, Vol. 4, pp. 212-213.

[80] House to Wilson, November 15, 1918, *Foreign Relations, 1919, The Paris Peace Conference*, Vol. 1, pp. 131-132; Lloyd George, *The Truth about the Peace Treaties*, Vol. 1, pp. 148-149.

[81] Wilson to House, November 16, 1918, *Foreign Relations, 1919, The Paris Peace Conference*, Vol. 1, pp. 134-135; Seymour, ed., *Intimate Papers*, Vol. 4, pp. 213-214.

[82] Baker and Dodd, eds., *Public Papers, War and Peace*, Vol. 1, p. 305.

[83] Bailey, *Wilson and the Lost Peace*, p. 72.

[84] Robert Lansing, *The Peace Negotiations* (Boston and New York: Houghton Mifflin Company, 1921), p. 15.

ble ignorance of the American Constitution, that his presence without a committee appointed by the Senate was constitutionally open to question.[85]

A close study of the battles fought at Paris tends to refute these views. If anything, the President secured far more of his program by personal participation than could have been secured through Colonel House, who was prone to compromise, or Secretary Lansing, who was largely not in sympathy with that program. Wilson went to Paris as the acknowledged moral spokesman of the democratic world. It is difficult to believe that he could more effectively have conducted his struggle for a league of nations and a peace of impartial justice by remote control. Long after the Peace Conference, General Smuts said: "There are some who think Wilson should not have come to Paris at all. I don't agree with them. Only Wilson could have put through the League and did. He was the one statesman who had the power and the vision. . . ."[86]

Further controversy, immediate and historical, was generated by Wilson's selection of an American delegation consisting of, besides himself, Colonel House, Secretary Lansing, General Tasker Bliss, and the career diplomat Henry White, passing over such prominent Republican supporters of his program as former President Taft and former Secretary of State Elihu Root. White, the only Republican on the delegation, was not a prominent figure in his party. In Lloyd George's view, the President's choice of commissioners evidenced a purely partisan desire to make the peace a "Democratic triumph."[87] Although it seems clear in retrospect that the President would have served his own cause well by leading a bipartisan delegation to Paris, it must be remembered that the extent and intensity of subsequent Republican opposition to the President's peace program was by no means obvious in the autumn of 1918. Indeed in December 1918, the politically astute Joe Tumulty was sending Wilson soothing assurances of dwindling Republican opposition and unanimous support in the country for a league of nations.[88]

[85] Harold Nicolson, *Peacemaking 1919* (Boston and New York: Houghton Mifflin Company, 1933), pp. 71, 73.

[86] Sarah Gertrude Millin, *General Smuts* (2 Vols., London: Faber and Faber, Ltd., 1936), Vol. 2, p. 173.

[87] Lloyd George, *The Truth about the Peace Treaties*, Vol. 1, pp. 155-156.

[88] Tumulty to Wilson, December 9, 1918; Tumulty to Wilson, December 21, 1918; Woodrow Wilson Papers, Series 8-A.

IV. *Wilson and the London Conference of December 1-3, 1918; the Voyage of the "George Washington"*

In the first days of December, a formal meeting of Allied Premiers and Foreign Ministers was held in London. Colonel House was ill in Paris, and the United States was therefore unrepresented. At the outset, Marshal Foch confronted Lloyd George for the first time with the French program for a military frontier at the Rhine and the detachment of the Rhenish provinces from Germany. Lloyd George demanded to know how these plans could be reconciled with the Fourteen Points and asked whether Foch did not fear a reverse of Alsace-Lorraine leading to a new war of revenge. Foch thought that these difficulties could be overcome. On December 2, the Allied leaders agreed to set up an Inter-Allied Commission on Reparations and Indemnities for the purpose of examining the capacity of Germany to pay. It was further agreed that a demand should be made to Holland to hand over the former German Emperor and the Crown Prince to be brought to trial before an Allied tribunal on charges of criminal responsibility for the war and for breaches of international law committed by German forces.[89] The Conference agreed on December 3, at the insistence of Balfour, that all of its conclusions were provisional, subject to the approval of President Wilson.[90]

The London Conference probably contributed to Wilson's considerable distrust of his prospective colleagues. House dispatched a full report of the Conference to Wilson, suggesting that all references to "indemnity" be eliminated from the Allied agreements.[91] Wilson cabled back to House from the "George Washington" that it was imperative that the Allied resolutions of December 2 be suspended until he arrived in Paris.[92]

Sailing for France aboard the U.S.S. "George Washington," Woodrow Wilson thought deeply and spoke freely about a wide range of problems of the peace, revealing both the profound con-

[89] Lloyd George, *The Truth about the Peace Treaties*, Vol. 1, pp. 132-145.
[90] Miller to House, December 3, 1918, David Hunter Miller, *My Diary at the Conference of Paris*, privately printed (21 Vols., New York: Appeal Printing Company, 1924), Vol. 1, p. 33; *Foreign Relations, 1919, The Paris Peace Conference*, Vol. 1, p. 339.
[91] House to Wilson, December 6, 1918, *ibid.*, pp. 340-342.
[92] Wilson to House, December 8, 1918, *ibid.*, p. 343.

viction underlying his professed principles and his deep distrust of the motives and objectives of the European Allies, including Great Britain.

On December 10, the President summoned the members of the Inquiry and set forth his views on the impending problems of the Peace Conference. Dr. Isaiah Bowman recorded this significant interview. The American delegation, said the President, would be the "only disinterested people" at the Peace Conference, dealing with men who "did not represent their own people." Unless the Conference followed the will of the peoples instead of the leaders, he said, there would soon occur "another breakup of the world, and when such a breakup came, it would not be a war but a cataclysm." The President spoke of the league of nations as guaranteeing political independence and territorial integrity, "plus later alteration of terms and alteration of boundaries if it could be shown that injustice had been done or that conditions had changed." The league would provide both "elasticity and security," the very opposite of balance of power politics. The Conference, in short, must take an "entirely new course of action." Turning to specific questions, the President set forth his views on how the league council would function. Germany's colonies, he said, should become the common property of the league, administered by small powers as trustees. The "poison of Bolshevism," Wilson contended, was a "protest against the way in which the world has worked." It was therefore essential to fight for a new world order, "agreeably if we can, disagreeably if necessary." In conclusion, the President expressed his hope that the experts would feel free to bring critical problems to his attention: "Tell me what's right and I'll fight for it; give me a guaranteed position."[93]

Wilson also revealed aboard the "George Washington" his deep distrust of British sea power. "Militarism," said the President, "is no different on sea than it is on land." He rejected any proposals for the British and American navies acting together as a world sea patrol as "militaristic propaganda." Referring to British vio-

[93] Notes taken by Dr. Isaiah Bowman, December 10, 1918. This memorandum may be found in: James T. Shotwell, *At the Paris Peace Conference* (New York: The Macmillan Company, 1937), pp. 73-78; Seymour, ed., *Intimate Papers*, Vol. 4, pp. 280-283; David Hunter Miller, *The Drafting of the Covenant* (2 Vols., New York, London: G. P. Putnam's Sons, 1928), Vol. 1, pp. 41-44; Miller, *Diary*, Vol. 1, pp. 370-373.

lations of American neutral rights, the President declared that if he had not been convinced that Germany was the "scourge of the world," he would have been "ready then and there to have it out with Great Britain on that point."[94]

V. Lloyd George and the "Khaki" Election, December 1918

While Wilson engaged in his reflections aboard the "George Washington," Lloyd George, with all his vast energy and resourcefulness, was undertaking to win a popular mandate for his Coalition Government to carry to the Peace Conference. The election, coming at the close of the greatest war in England's history, generated an outburst of public passions which the Government did little, if anything, to restrain. The result was an overwhelming but largely Pyrrhic victory for the Government. At the Peace Conference, Lloyd George was to find himself, at least on the issue of reparations, much more the prisoner of the irresponsible promises made by his associates in the campaign than the democratic politician liberated from pressures by a broad mandate from his electorate.[95]

The Coalition Government, headed by Lloyd George and Bonar Law, won a smashing victory. Of the 540 Coalition candidates for the House of Commons, only 14 were defeated, giving the Government an immense majority of 526 out of 707 seats.

The Liberal Party was torn asunder by the election. Outside the Coalition, the Asquith-Grey Liberals, who had dominated British policy from 1906 to 1916, and in whose circle Wilsonian ideas had generally found their most cordial reception, ceased to be a major factor in British politics. The demise of the British Liberal Party undoubtedly weakened the prospects of an Anglo-American program of moderation at the Peace Conference, for Lloyd George,

[94] Records of Charles Swem in the Princeton University Library. Quoted in Arthur Walworth, *Woodrow Wilson* (2 Vols., New York, London, Toronto: Longmans, Green and Company, 1958), Vol. 2, *World Prophet*, p. 217.

[95] A generally excellent account and analysis of the British election of December, 1918, and its effects upon the Peace Conference and the Treaty of Versailles, is found in R. B. McCallum, *Public Opinion and the Last Peace* (London, New York, Toronto: Oxford University Press, 1944), pp. 27-60. McCallum argues that the criticisms of this election have been greatly overstated, that Lloyd George himself was moderate, and that there would have been jingoistic pressures even if this campaign had not occurred.

though himself a Liberal, was rendered highly vulnerable to the nationalistic pressures of his predominantly Conservative coalition.

British public opinion was unquestionably in an abnormal condition during the electoral campaign. While the liberal press in Great Britain was reporting a "slump in idealism" in December 1918,[96] an American Embassy official told David Hunter Miller that British public opinion was in a condition of nerves bordering on hysteria due to the war, its end, and the election.[97]

Although the Coalition exploited the nervous state of mind of the electorate with irresponsible promises of astronomical reparations and "hanging the Kaiser," the personal responsibility of Lloyd George for these excesses is at least open to question. In his memoirs, Lloyd George vigorously denies that he made irresponsible promises during the campaign. The core of his electoral program, he asserts, was disarmament and the league of nations, a program to "make Britain a fit country for heroes to live in." Lloyd George dismisses the charge that his Government promised to impose huge indemnities and "hang the Kaiser" as false and slanderous. He personally referred to reparations only once, he says, and called for the prosecution, not the "hanging," of the Kaiser.[98]

While the personal charges against Lloyd George are not altogether spurious, it seems clear that they have been somewhat overstated. In his early campaign speeches, the Prime Minister made an honest effort to restrain exorbitant public expectations, carefully qualifying reparations demands by the requirement that Germany must pay "to the limit of her capacity." As the campaign progressed, Lloyd George gave way somewhat, but not altogether, to the mounting pressures of mob sentiment and press jingoism. In a major address at Bristol on December 11, Lloyd George had before him a report on German capacity to pay prepared by a special committee of financiers for the Imperial War Cabinet

[96] Ray Stannard Baker, *Woodrow Wilson and World Settlement* (3 Vols., Garden City, New York: Doubleday, Page and Company, 1922), Vol. 1, pp. 84-87.

[97] Miller to House, December 3, 1918, *Foreign Relations, 1919, The Paris Peace Conference*, Vol. 1, p. 337; Miller, *Diary*, Vol. 1, p. 28.

[98] Lloyd George, *The Truth about the Peace Treaties*, Vol. 1, pp. 162-163, 177-178. For Lloyd George's detailed defense of his position on reparations in the campaign, see *ibid.*, pp. 436-473; see also David Lloyd George, *The Truth about Reparations and War Debts* (Garden City, New York: Doubleday, Doran and Company, Inc., 1932), pp. 14-16.

calling for the payment of total war costs in the sum of $200 billion. The Prime Minister neither used nor referred to this report. In his speech, he explained the doubts of financial experts as to German capacity but emphasized that Germany must "pay to the utmost limit of her capacity." Proclaiming the "absolute right" of the Allies to demand war costs, Lloyd George warned that the exacting of payment must be "in such a way that it does not do more harm to the country that receives it than to the country which is paying it." But the first consideration must be "the interests of the people upon whom Germany has made war, and not the interests of the German people who have been guilty of this crime against humanity."[99]

Thus did Lloyd George seek to have the best of two worlds, undertaking to satisfy the vindictive demands of his electorate without specifically promising what they demanded. Although he uttered no single sentence promising vast reparations and showed commendable restraint in suppressing the report of the financial experts, the tone of the Bristol speech was such as to satisfy irresponsible demands. Generally, the Prime Minister was inclined to shout the popular demands and to whisper the qualifications. And certainly he did too little to dispel the illusions which were liberally sowed by his associates in the campaign. At least technically, however, his protestations of moderate intent must be credited. His real error was perhaps in underrating his own prestige and power in the hour of victory. Instead of bending with popular passion and seeking to evade its impact, he might have elevated British public opinion to an ethical level compatible with his own genuine moderation.[100]

Regardless of the innocence or culpability of Lloyd George for the excesses of the campaign, it is clear that the "Khaki" election did the cause of Anglo-American cooperation no good. It eclipsed the Liberal and Labour elements which had been so receptive to Wilson's program and returned to Westminster a jingo Com-

[99] Lloyd George, *The Truth about the Peace Treaties*, Vol. 1, pp. 458-467; Frank Owen, *Tempestuous Journey—Lloyd George: His Life and Times* (London: Hutchinson and Company, Ltd., 1954), p. 501; Churchill, *The Aftermath*, p. 37.

[100] See Thomas Jones, *Lloyd George* (Cambridge: Harvard University Press, 1951), pp. 160, 163; McCallum, *Public Opinion and the Last Peace*, pp. 48-49; Bailey, *Wilson and the Lost Peace*, pp. 243-245.

mons which was to thwart any possibility of a united Anglo-American front for a conservative reparations settlement.[101]

VI. *President Wilson's Visit to England, December 1918*

Soon after his arrival in France, President Wilson crossed the Channel to pay an official visit to Great Britain. The prospect of a Presidential visit to England had arisen almost as soon as Wilson announced that he would go to Europe. In early December, he had received many invitations from local officials and private organizations in Great Britain.[102] Lloyd George personally had desired a visit, hoping thereby to ascertain the President's real attitude toward Great Britain. The Prime Minister had been disturbed by the paucity of warm or generous allusions to England in the President's public pronouncements and hoped that a Presidential visit would help to dispel the apparent mistrust.[103] Wilson was greeted with a tumultuous popular reception in London, equal to the delirious welcome which he had received in Paris, and he and Mrs. Wilson were received in splendor at Buckingham Palace.

Despite these official amenities, Lloyd George, for one, found Wilson's demeanor little to his liking. At a state dinner at Buckingham Palace, His Majesty toasted American arms and the President spoke eloquently of the "great moral tide running in the hearts of men," but offended Lloyd George by failing to pay tribute to the gallantry of the British Armed Forces. Lloyd George asked Lord Reading to suggest delicately to the President that he rectify this by some cordial reference in his speech at the Guildhall next day. The word was passed to Wilson, who complied with a sparse reference to Allied gallantry.[104]

Wilson made a number of public appearances. At the Guildhall on December 28, he declared himself delighted to have found how identical were the objectives of the leaders of Britain and the

[101] See Chapter 9. See also: McCallum, *Public Opinion and the Last Peace*, p. 42; Nicolson, *Peacemaking 1919*, pp. 19-20; A. G. Gardiner, "The Prospects of Anglo-American Friendship," *Foreign Affairs*, Vol. 5, No. 1 (October 1926), p. 9.
[102] Woodrow Wilson Papers, Library of Congress, Washington, D.C., Series 8-A.
[103] Lloyd George, *The Truth about the Peace Treaties*, Vol. 1, pp. 156-157.
[104] *ibid.*, pp. 180-183; H. C. F. Bell, *Woodrow Wilson and the People* (Garden City, New York: Doubleday, Doran and Company, Inc., 1945), p. 277.

United States, "how our thought was always that the key to the peace was the guarantee of the peace, not the items of it. . . ."[105] On December 29, the President spoke in the church at Carlisle of which his grandfather had been minister. ". . . I believe," he said, "that as this war has drawn the nations temporarily together in a combination of physical force, we shall now be drawn together in a combination of moral force that will be irresistible."[106] At Manchester on December 30, President Wilson spoke of a "pulse of sympathy" and a "theme of common interest" between the English and American peoples. The United States, Wilson said, was not interested in European politics but in the "partnership of right between America and Europe." He did not expect every item of the peace to be satisfactory but anticipated the creation of the "machinery of readjustment, in order that we may have the machinery of good will and friendship."[107]

Wilson's private contacts with the British leadership were limited. Lord Robert Cecil, who probably more than any other British official sympathized with the President's program, hoped to engage in a serious exchange of views with the President, but succeeded only in engaging Wilson in a brief conversation during the reception at Buckingham Palace. Greatly disappointed, Cecil went to Paris in January 1919 without knowing very much of what was in Wilson's mind.[108]

In an apparently chance conversation at Buckingham Palace with a minor British official, the President did reveal his thoughts, with remarkable candor, on the bases of Anglo-American relations: "You must not speak of us who come over here as cousins, still less as brothers; we are neither. Neither must you think of us as Anglo-Saxons, for that term can no longer be rightly applied to the people of the United States. Nor must too much importance in this connection be attached to the fact that English is our common language. . . . No, there are only two things which can establish and maintain closer relations between your country and mine: they are community of ideals and of interests."[109]

---

[105] Baker and Dodd, eds., *Public Papers, War and Peace*, Vol. 1, pp. 341-342.
[106] *ibid.*, pp. 349-350.
[107] *ibid.*, pp. 352-354.
[108] Viscount Cecil, *A Great Experiment* (New York: Oxford University Press, 1941), p. 63.
[109] Frank Worthington, Deputy Chief Censor of the War Office, "Statement

The President conferred privately with Lloyd George and Balfour in a meeting at 10 Downing Street. According to Lloyd George's account of this meeting, he and Balfour readily agreed that the league of nations should be the first subject dealt with by the Peace Conference, and Wilson offered no objection to the Prime Minister's proposal that the question of the freedom of the seas be deferred for consideration after the setting up of the league. There was general harmony in the discussion of the disarmament of Germany and the problem of Russia. As to the Near East, the President was cool to Balfour's proposal of an American mandate over Constantinople. On the matter of the German colonies, the President resisted Lloyd George's demand that those conquered by the Dominions should not be placed under league of nations mandates. Lloyd George found Wilson stiffer on the question of indemnity than on any other issue. He found the President distinctly anti-Italian and anti-Japanese, but in basic agreement with the British in opposing French schemes for the Rhineland.[110]

The Imperial War Cabinet reacted unfavorably to Lloyd George's report of his talk with the President. Prime Minister Hughes of Australia thought that Wilson wished to dictate how the world was to be governed. Lord Curzon thought that, although the future of the world depended largely on Anglo-American cooperation, it might be necessary on some issues for Lloyd George to work in alliance with Clemenceau if the President persisted in his present line. Only Sir Robert Borden of Canada and Lord Robert Cecil emphasized the necessity and prospect of close Anglo-American collaboration, even on the issues of colonies and the indemnity. Borden warned that Canada would not support an Imperial policy of cooperation with any European nation against the United States. Cecil argued for a close Anglo-American understanding and the league of nations as the best guarantees of a stable peace. The Cabinet, according to Lloyd George, registered a generally bad impression of his meeting with Wilson, being most impressed with the view of Prime Minister Hughes.[111]

Made by President Wilson to Me on the Evening of Saturday, the 28th December, 1918," House Papers.

[110] Lloyd George, *The Truth about the Peace Treaties*, Vol. 1, pp. 184-194.

[111] *ibid.*, pp. 194-201.

Wilson, for his part, was not favorably impressed by the British leadership. He told House, upon returning to France, that he thought he could more easily get on with Lloyd George than with Balfour—if he could trust "The Little Man."[112]

The visit of President Wilson to England probably constituted a net loss for the prospect of Anglo-American collaboration. The personalities of the President and the Prime Minister were far from mutually attractive and the President did not come into close contact with those British officials, like Lord Robert Cecil, who strongly supported his program. While British officials on the whole were markedly suspicious of parts of Wilson's program, his attitude toward the British Empire, and of the President personally, Wilson, in turn, apparently saw little value in a special bond between the English-speaking peoples. He was distrustful of British sea power and unsympathetic to the concept of a close identity of strategic interest in Anglo-American control of the Atlantic. The President's thoughts at this time were focused on the role of the English-speaking democracies in a moral union of *all* peoples, in a "partnership of right" dedicated to the perpetuation of peace and justice under the rule of law.

[112] House Diary, December 31, 1918, House Papers.

CHAPTER 3

THE OPENING OF THE PEACE CONFERENCE AND THE ANGLO-AMERICAN CONTROVERSY OVER COLONIAL CLAIMS AND THE MANDATE PRINCIPLE

IN THE course of the Paris Peace Conference, there developed a closer working relationship between the British and American delegations than between any other delegations. It was a natural alliance between men who spoke the same language and thought in terms of the same broad political and moral frame of reference. At its best, it was an alliance based on common sense and common interest, pragmatism, moderation, and moral purpose. Almost as a matter of course, the English-speaking delegations detected the natural affinity of their thought processes and the equally natural barrier between their own and Latin minds. Organizational and procedural differences arose between the British and American delegations over such issues as the role of the British Dominions and the publicity of the proceedings of the Peace Conference. They were generally, however, in accord on problems of procedure, especially as to the primary role which the President demanded for the league of nations. The working alliance of British and American delegations reached its fullest fruition on the level just below the summit, between such figures as Colonel House and Lord Robert Cecil, and on the level of consultation among experts and specialists, who labored harmoniously to gather the raw data out of which their chiefs might strive to forge a peace of justice.

One of the sharpest and most significant clashes between the United States and the British Empire arose at the outset of the Peace Conference when the demands of the British Dominions for the annexation of former German colonies came into direct conflict with the determination of President Wilson to apply a new principle of international trusteeship to the colonial settlement. The principle itself was as much British as American in origin but the Dominions frankly demanded that their own territorial ambitions be excepted from its application. The issue did not involve a direct clash between the United States and the

United Kingdom, for the latter accepted the trusteeship principle without qualification as to itself. Great Britain, however, adopted the cause of the Dominions as its own and the United States found itself opposed by a united British Empire. The unity of the Empire was not such as to prevent varieties of approach toward a settlement by its members. While Australia, represented by Prime Minister Hughes, was adamant in its demands, the United Kingdom, and especially Canada, which like Britain fully accepted the mandate principle and had no direct interests at stake, undertook to appease the United States without taxing Imperial unity. The final solution was the invention of General Smuts of South Africa, who successfully devised a compromise which satisfied the ambitions of the Dominions, including his own South Africa, while preserving the trusteeship principle to which he, as well as President Wilson, was dedicated. Perhaps the most significant long-range result of the mandates controversy and its resolution, from the point of view of the United States, was the acquisition by Japan of the German islands of the North Pacific, lying athwart the strategic communications routes between the United States and its possessions in the Western Pacific.

I. *Wilson, Lloyd George, and Other Personalities*

Like most men of great and complex character, Woodrow Wilson has been the subject of fascinated study by his contemporaries and by historians. Perhaps the only valid generalization that can be made about his character is that it was deep and complex.[1] Brought up in the southern Presbyterian Church, Wilson was a man who believed in the existence of universal law. He believed that it was incumbent upon men and upon nations to comply with that law, not as a matter of option, but as an in-

[1] The observance of the Woodrow Wilson centennial in 1956 called forth a wide variety of comments and assessments of Woodrow Wilson the man, the politician, and the statesman. See, e.g., the following collections of essays by historians and public figures published in observance of the centennial: The University of Chicago in cooperation with the Woodrow Wilson Foundation, Lectures and Seminar at the University of Chicago, January 30-February 3, 1956, in Celebration of the *Centennial of Woodrow Wilson*, 1856-1956, Central Theme: *Freedom for Man: A World Safe for Mankind; Confluence*, Vol. 5, Nos. 3 and 4 (Autumn 1956 and Winter 1957), *Woodrow Wilson and the Problems of Liberalism; The Virginia Quarterly Review*, Vol. 32, No. 4 (Autumn 1956), Centennial Number, *Woodrow Wilson*, 1856-1924.

escapable duty. What others saw as intransigence in Wilson was in fact helplessness before the injunctions of universal law. Like Gladstone, whom he greatly admired, Wilson was a practicing Christian statesman. Although he was ostensibly cold and austere, the President in fact had a warm and emotional nature and a reservoir of wit and humor that provided him with great resiliency. When he lay ill with influenza during the crisis of the Peace Conference and Tumulty warned him not to tax his constitution, the President wrote back: "Constitution? Why man, I'm already living on my by-laws." The unhappy side of Wilson's character was moral arrogance. Like most men of unwavering faith in transcendental laws, he was capable of an egotistical self-righteousness which called forth contempt and anger from his associates. He tended to equate political opposition with personal antagonism and he doubted the integrity of a man who disagreed with him.[2]

The President's character included one special bond with England, not to be confused with any special affection for the British nation. He had a kind of mystic faith in the superiority of Anglo-Saxon institutions and regarded American history as an extension of English history. From this faith sprang an implicit belief in an Anglo-Saxon mission to serve mankind.[3]

Besides Colonel House, the other members of the American Commission to Negotiate Peace played insignificant roles in the making of the peace. Colonel House, who for a time enjoyed the full confidence and affection of the President, was a powerful and influential figure at the Peace Conference and, on the American side, the principal architect of Anglo-American cooperation. His geniality, diplomatic skill, and willingness to compromise were at times extremely useful complements to the President's firm adherence to principle, although these very talents, zealously exercised, led to the ultimate loss of Wilson's confidence. Secretary of State Lansing, as his own writings indicate, was little trusted by the President and had little faith in his program.[4] General Bliss,

[2] See Gerald W. Johnson, "Wilson the Man," *Virginia Quarterly Review*, Vol. 32, No. 4 (Autumn 1956), pp. 496-505; Virginius Dabney, "The Human Side of Woodrow Wilson," *ibid.*, pp. 508-523; Arthur S. Link, "A Portrait of Wilson," *ibid.*, pp. 531-540; Raymond B. Fosdick, "Personal Recollections of Woodrow Wilson," University of Chicago, *Centennial of Woodrow Wilson*, pp. 3-4.

[3] See John Morton Blum, *Woodrow Wilson and the Politics of Morality* (Boston, Toronto: Little, Brown and Company, 1956), pp. 9-17.

[4] See Robert Lansing, *The Peace Negotiations* (Boston and New York:

who had had considerable experience in dealing with the Allies, was simply not "used." He saw the President in personal interviews only five times in the course of the Peace Conference.[5] Henry White was in the same position. His cherished hope to serve as mediator between Wilson and the Republicans was not realized.[6]

In contrast with the widely divergent assessments of Woodrow Wilson, there has been little dissent from the commonly accepted portrait of David Lloyd George as a man who was genial, charming, intuitive, garrulous, politically astute, amazingly flexible, and utterly free of deeply held convictions. The Prime Minister had all the delicate intuition for human relations that the President lacked. He was extraordinarily representative of postwar Britain, reflecting all the doubts, perplexities, and contradictions of the British people in a time of historical transition. That Lloyd George was an opportunist, a man of shifts and expedients, is beyond doubt. He was unreliable and changed his mind under the pressures of parliamentary and public opinion with a dexterity that baffled and disgusted the American President. His own instincts were for moderation and decency, but he was able, under pressure, to conquer his conscience. His mercurial shrewdness of political judgment compensated in great measure for a remarkable ignorance of continental politics. It is not adequate, however, to define Lloyd George's character as only "flexible" or "mercurial." His mind was perceptive and adroit and his instinctive sympathy for human suffering was quite genuine. He was malicious at times but never cruel or vindictive.[7]

Unlike the American Commission, the British Empire delegation consisted of a number of powerful and influential men. Lloyd

---

Houghton Mifflin Company, 1921), and *The Big Four and Others of the Peace Conference* (Boston and New York: Houghton Mifflin Company, 1921).

[5] Frederick Palmer, *Bliss, Peacemaker—The Life and Letters of General Tasker Howard Bliss* (New York: Dodd, Mead and Company, 1934), p. 363.

[6] Allan Nevins, *Henry White: Thirty Years of American Diplomacy* (New York and London: Harper & Brothers, Publishers, 1930), p. 356.

[7] See A. L. Kennedy, *Old Diplomacy and New* (London: John Murray, 1922), pp. 282-283; Thomas Jones, *Lloyd George* (Cambridge: Harvard University Press, 1951), pp. 168ff.; Lansing, *The Big Four and Others of the Peace Conference*, pp. 77-87; Karl Friedrich Nowak, *Versailles* (London: Victor Gollancz, Ltd., 1928), p. 91; Edith Bolling Wilson, *My Memoir* (Indianapolis, New York: The Bobbs-Merrill Company, Inc., 1936), p. 233; Herbert Hoover, *America's First Crusade* (New York: Charles Scribner's Sons, 1942), p. 31.

George's principal colleague was of course Foreign Secretary Balfour, whose diplomatic tact and intellectual powers were complementary to the Prime Minister's talents and a decided asset to Anglo-American relations.[8] At least one member of the British delegation, Prime Minister Hughes of Australia, was pure anathema to President Wilson. For Lord Robert Cecil and General Smuts, the President had an esteem and affection that surely exceeded his regard for any of his American colleagues except Colonel House.

It is probably not possible for two men of such strikingly different temperament as Wilson and Lloyd George to strike a genuine intellectual comradeship or even a personal relationship of great warmth. The elements of mistrust were built into their characters, especially that of Wilson. But the man of principle and the man of common sense are often on common ground when abstractions are translated into practical problems. Thus it occurred that on most of the substantive issues of the Peace Conference the President and the Prime Minister were on the same side, although they sometimes took pains to explain that they had arrived there by different routes. Generally, Wilson and Lloyd George were the exponents of justice and liberalism at the Paris Peace Conference. If Wilson was more dedicated to justice, Lloyd George was probably more dedicated to liberalism.

Lloyd George has provided posterity with an extremely clear picture of his views on Woodrow Wilson. To the British Prime Minister, President Wilson was a man who soared "in the clouds of serene rhetoric," shunning the unpleasant realities that "diverted him from his foregone conclusions." Lloyd George saw the President as a "most extraordinary compound" of visionary, partisan, and idealist, a man of petty personal rancors and a "bigoted sectarian," whose greatest weakness, among many others, was his "pervasive suspiciousness." Nevertheless, Lloyd George contends, he was himself much more in sympathy with Wilson's ideas and program than with those of Clemenceau.[9]

Colonel House was unquestionably the British favorite. Lloyd

[8] See, generally, Blanche E. C. Dugdale, *Arthur James Balfour* (2 Vols., New York: G. P. Putnam's Sons, 1937).

[9] David Lloyd George, *The Truth about the Peace Treaties* (2 Vols., London: Victor Gollancz, Ltd., 1938), Vol. I, pp. 221-222, 229-231, 234, 244.

George found him a highly congenial associate, with a "well-balanced but not a powerful mind."[10] Foreign Secretary Balfour strongly admired House. The President, Balfour writes with revealingly faint praise, always seemed an "interesting talker and quite without pose," but with Colonel House the Foreign Secretary was on terms of "intimacy and friendship," finding him "always resourceful and always with unruffled temper."[11]

II. *Anglo-American Problems Relating to the Organization and Procedure of the Peace Conference*

American preparations for the Peace Conference were both grand in scope and carefully structured in detail. The President had spelled out in the Fourteen Points and other major pronouncements an extremely clear and coherent set of principles that defined the grand design and many of the specific objectives of the American peace program. Within this context of defined objectives, the experts of the Inquiry—historians, economists, geographers, statisticians, and ethnologists—labored to gather the concrete data through which the President's principles might be translated into the articles of a definitive treaty of peace. This was the "new diplomacy" which America brought to Paris, the basis for an honest attempt at dispassionate implementation of general principles of justice.[12]

The experts of the Inquiry who came to Paris as the Intelligence Section were given direct advisory access to the American Commissioners and served as actual negotiators on inter-Allied commissions. Early in January, a skeleton draft treaty of peace was submitted by David Hunter Miller and James Brown Scott.[13] On January 21, the Inquiry submitted its tentative report and recommendations for the territorial, economic, and labor clauses of the

---

[10] *ibid.*, p. 245.

[11] Arthur James Balfour, *Retrospect* (Boston and New York: Houghton Mifflin Company, 1930), p. 244.

[12] See Ray Stannard Baker, *Woodrow Wilson and World Settlement* (3 Vols., Garden City, New York: Doubleday, Page and Company, 1922), Vol. 1, pp. 108-113. See also H.W.V. Temperley, ed., *A History of the Peace Conference of Paris* (6 Vols., London: Henry Frowde and Hodder and Stoughton, 1920-1924), Vol. 1, pp. 239-240.

[13] Department of State, *Papers Relating to the Foreign Relations of the United States, 1919, The Paris Peace Conference* (13 Vols., Washington: United States Government Printing Office, 1942-1947), Vol. 1, pp. 298-324, 329-332; hereafter referred to as *Foreign Relations*.

treaty.[14] On February 13, the Inquiry submitted recommendations on questions of the colonial settlement, the Far East, Persia, and inner Asia.[15]

British preparations for the Peace Conference had also been long underway. In 1917, the Foreign Office had set up an organization which proceeded to prepare handbooks on the geography, history, and economic conditions of all parts of the world likely to come under consideration. The program of this British body was essentially similar to that of the Inquiry. Its monographs were published in 1920 under the title of "Peace Handbooks." Both the British and American experts focused their preparatory efforts on substantive issues, giving little advance attention to problems of Peace Conference procedure.[16]

Virtually nothing, in fact, was decided as to organization and procedure before the opening of the Peace Conference. Some informal Anglo-American consultations took place between David Hunter Miller and Sir William Wiseman,[17] but these apparently came to nothing. The only formal scheme of procedure worked out in advance of the Peace Conference was prepared by the French Government and delivered to the State Department on November 29, 1918.[18] The French plan called for the settlement of the immediate issues of the war first and the relegation of the league of nations to later consideration, and, incidentally, for the sweeping away of all of the wartime secret agreements.[19] David Hunter Miller, having consulted with Sir William Tyrrell and Sir Eyre Crowe in London, advised that no program of procedure be accepted in advance of the Peace Conference,[20] and President Wilson rejected the French scheme.

Both Wilson and Lloyd George were far more interested in the

[14] Department of State, American Commission to Negotiate Peace, Paris, 1918-1919, 185.112/1; David Hunter Miller, *My Diary at the Conference of Paris*, privately printed (21 Vols., New York: Appeal Printing Company, 1924), Vol. 4, pp. 212-281.

[15] Woodrow Wilson Papers, Library of Congress, Washington, D.C., Series 8-A; see also James T. Shotwell, *At the Paris Peace Conference* (New York: The Macmillan Company, 1937), pp. 15-17, 90.

[16] Temperley, ed., *A History of the Peace Conference of Paris*, Vol. 1, p. 240; Shotwell, *At the Paris Peace Conference*, pp. 14, 29-30.

[17] Miller, *Diary*, Vol. 1, pp. 10, 12-13, 30.

[18] Jusserand to Lansing, November 29, 1918, *Foreign Relations, 1919, The Paris Peace Conference*, Vol. 1, pp. 365-371.

[19] *Foreign Relations, 1919, The Paris Peace Conference*, Vol. 1, pp. 344-352; Baker, *Wilson and World Settlement*, Vol. 3, pp. 56-63.

[20] Miller to House, December 6, 1918, Miller, *Diary*, Vol. 1, p. 36.

early achievement of their substantive policy objectives than in the formulation of a logically structured plan of procedure. At the outset of the Peace Conference, President Wilson proposed that the league of nations be considered first but that generally the order of discussion be prepared "from time to time." Lloyd George agreed and Clemenceau's insistence on a formal structure was thus overridden.[21] André Tardieu, the author of the French plan, attributed its rejection to the "instinctive repugnance of the Anglo-Saxons to the systematized constructions of the Latin mind."[22]

The question of whether to deal first with European or colonial problems was raised in the Supreme Council on January 23. Lloyd George, eager to realize quickly the ambitions of the British Dominions, argued that European problems were too complicated for immediate solution, whereas colonial problems were less involved and could be promptly disposed of. President Wilson replied that the world's unrest arose from conditions in Europe and that for this reason a European solution was most urgent. The issue was passed over with an agreement that the Secretary General of the Peace Conference would invite all powers with territorial claims to submit their claims within ten days.[23]

The Plenary Session of the Peace Conference on January 25 established the principal special commissions, including those on the league of nations and reparations,[24] and soon thereafter the Council of Ten took to setting up joint committees of experts on territorial problems with instructions to report directly to the Conference rather than to their national delegations. A pattern of informal consultations quickly developed among the British and American members of the various expert commissions. Harold Nicolson and other members of the British delegation concerned with southeastern Europe, for instance, conferred frequently with

[21] Council of Ten, January 13, 1919, 4 p.m., *Foreign Relations, 1919, The Paris Peace Conference*, Vol. 3, pp. 536-537; F. S. Marston, *The Peace Conference of 1919* (London, New York, Toronto: Oxford University Press, 1944), pp. 71-72.

[22] André Tardieu, *The Truth about the Treaty* (Indianapolis: The Bobbs-Merrill Company, Inc., 1921), p. 91. See also Marston, *The Peace Conference of 1919*, pp. 69-71.

[23] Council of Ten, January 23, 1919, 10:30 a.m., *Foreign Relations, 1919, The Paris Peace Conference*, Vol. 3, pp. 699-700. See also Paul Birdsall, *Versailles Twenty Years After* (London: George Allen and Unwin, Ltd., 1941), pp. 59-60.

[24] Second Plenary Session, January 25, 1919, *Foreign Relations, 1919, The Paris Peace Conference*, Vol. 3, pp. 178-201.

Charles Seymour, Clive Day, and other members of the Inquiry. Meeting quietly in Maxim's in order not to wound French and Italian sensibilities, the Anglo-American experts worked out proposed frontiers for the new states of southeastern Europe. The habit of frank discussion, established early between the British and American experts, survived throughout the Peace Conference.[25]

Colonel House's relationships with Sir William Wiseman and other prominent Englishmen continued to serve as a special Anglo-American link. At least in the early stage of the Peace Conference, House conferred with Wiseman almost daily. "He is invaluable," House wrote in his diary.[26] "He keeps me in touch with everything going on at the British headquarters and prepares me in advance for difficulties, and in this way they are usually overcome before they actually arise."[27] House also exercised considerable influence with Lord Northcliffe. No one, House told Wiseman, did more from day to day to assist the American point of view.[28]

In its first week of meetings, the Council of Ten discussed the working relationship to be established between the great powers and the lesser Allies.[29] Within this context, a minor controversy arose between Great Britain and the United States as to the representation of the British Dominions. It had been agreed in the Imperial War Cabinet in December 1918 that the Dominions and India should have the same representation as the small powers and that, in addition, one member of the British delegation of five commissioners should be selected from a rotating panel of the Dominion Prime Ministers, depending upon the subject under consideration.[30] In the Council of Ten on January 12, Lloyd George demanded two representatives for each of the Dominions and India, the same as for the lesser Allies, and one for Newfoundland, in addition to their representation on the British

[25] Harold Nicolson, *Peacemaking 1919* (Boston and New York: Houghton Mifflin Company, 1933), pp. 105-107, 223-232, 257.

[26] House Diary, January 26, 1919, Edward M. House Papers, Sterling Library, Yale University.

[27] *ibid.*, February 1, 1919.

[28] Wiseman Diary, January 17, 1919, Sir William Wiseman Papers, Sterling Library, Yale University.

[29] Marston, *The Peace Conference of 1919*, pp. 57-61.

[30] Lloyd George, *The Truth about the Peace Treaties*, Vol. 1, pp. 204-209.

Empire delegation. Lloyd George cited the war effort of the Dominions, calling attention to the fact that Australia had suffered more war dead than the United States. President Wilson, fearing the reaction of the small states to such double representation for the Dominions, argued against separate representation and insisted that the Dominion representatives be incorporated into the British delegation. Lloyd George pressed his case and the President countered with the observation that other states would have no such "backers and sponsors" as the Dominions would have in the five representatives of Great Britain. He would, however, accept one representative for each of the Dominions.[31]

The issue was easily resolved. Lloyd George explained to the Dominion Prime Ministers, who convened in some alarm on the morning of January 13, that the President did not oppose their representation as such but contested only the number of representatives.[32] Later in the day in the Council of Ten, Wilson assured Lloyd George that he did not oppose separate representation for the Dominions but wished only to remove any causes for jealousy among the lesser states. He now proposed two representatives each for Canada, South Africa, Australia, and India, and one for New Zealand, but no separate representation for Newfoundland. Lloyd George agreed to this proposal and the Council accepted the arrangement as settled. The President offered to submit this plan to the Plenary Conference.[33] The result of this agreement was that the Dominions secured representation both in their own sovereign capacities and as part of the British Empire delegation, a position far stronger than that of the other small powers.[34]

The reason for Wilson's brief resistance followed by his ready accommodation to the desire of the Dominions for separate representation is not readily assessed. Perhaps his initial opposition was as much motivated by fear of the reaction of American

---

[31] Council of Ten, January 12, 1919, 2:30 p.m., *Foreign Relations, 1919, The Paris Peace Conference,* Vol. 3, pp. 483-487; Lloyd George, *The Truth about the Peace Treaties,* Vol. 1, p. 216; Marston, *The Peace Conference of 1919,* pp. 62-63.

[32] Henry Borden, ed., *Robert Laird Borden: His Memoirs* (2 Vols., New York: The Macmillan Company, 1938), Vol. 2, p. 899.

[33] Council of Ten, January 13, 1919, 4 p.m., *Foreign Relations, 1919, The Paris Peace Conference,* Vol. 3, pp. 532-533.

[34] Marston, *The Peace Conference of 1919,* p. 63; Temperley, ed., *A History of the Peace Conference of Paris,* Vol. 6, pp. 344-345.

public opinion as by his stated fear of small power jealousy. But the President's resistance was brief and his accommodation gracious. Perhaps he perceived that the strategic and political interests of the overseas Dominions, especially Canada, with its close American ties, were essentially parallel to the interests of the United States.

The first of Wilson's Fourteen Points called for "open covenants of peace, openly arrived at." The practical meaning of "open diplomacy," as some, including Wilson himself at times, have quite misleadingly called it, was tested at the outset of the Peace Conference, calling forth an Anglo-American difference as to the *degree* to which it should be implemented, while the French would have preferred not to implement it at all. The demands of the press, "ambassadors of public opinion" numbering some five hundred newsmen at the height of the Conference, placed the peacemakers in an extremely awkward position, threatening to enslave them to the turbulent nationalist feelings which their own wartime propaganda had so successfully aroused.[35] Wilson never intended that there should be no private diplomatic discussions. He had written to Lansing soon after announcing the Fourteen Points: ". . . certainly when I pronounced for open diplomacy I meant not that there should be no private discussions of delicate matters, but that no secret agreement of any sort should be entered into and that all international relations, when fixed, should be open, aboveboard, and explicit."[36]

The question of publicity was raised in the Supreme Council on January 15. It was readily agreed that all information for the press as to the daily proceedings of the Council of Ten would be channeled through a special committee of the Great Powers and that no other information as to the daily proceedings would be released. President Wilson proposed that the Plenary Conference, at least, be given full publicity and that the press be allowed

[35] Baker, *Wilson and World Settlement*, Vol. I, pp. 116-121; George Bernard Noble, *Policies and Opinions at Paris, 1919* (New York: The Macmillan Company, 1935), p. vi.

[36] Wilson to Lansing, March 12, 1918, Ray Stannard Baker and William E. Dodd, eds., *The Public Papers of Woodrow Wilson* (6 Vols., New York and London: Harper & Brothers, Publishers, 1925-1927), *War and Peace*, Vol. I, p. 192.

to attend its sessions. Lloyd George feared that the presence of reporters would serve only to inspire the delegates to interminable and meaningless oratory. Clemenceau, Balfour, and Baron Sonnino supported Lloyd George's position, and President Wilson said he would not press the point.[37] Wilson successfully resisted a French proposal for censorship of information transmitted by cable. The President also suggested that the press be asked to pledge voluntary restraint in the release of information that might hamper the negotiations.[38]

Wilson and Lloyd George stood together in resisting a proposal put forth by Clemenceau on January 16 for the creation of a "political committee" of the Great Powers to "correct false news and guide public opinion in the right direction." Wilson expressed his doubt that the American public would be satisfied with anything short of "complete publicity." Lloyd George favored the issuance of a general *warning* to the press against believing unauthorized reports and an *appeal* to the public to understand that differences in the course of negotiation were transitory. The President strongly supported Lloyd George's proposal, and Clemenceau's plan for a controlled flow of news was rejected. It was agreed that each government's press officer would explain to reporters the difficulties of providing information on debates in progress while assuring them that they would be kept informed of results achieved.[39] Great Britain and the United States, while agreeing to restrictions on publicity, here rejected out of hand the French proposal for actual censorship, preferring to rely—here as on many other issues—on the voluntarist principle.

In accordance with the decision of January 16, a press committee composed of Ray Stannard Baker, Lord Riddell, and Captain Pueux met with the reporters and explained the need for secrecy and appealed for restraint. The British correspondents

[37] Council of Ten, January 15, 1919, 10:30 a.m., *Foreign Relations, 1919, The Paris Peace Conference*, Vol. 3, pp. 543-545, 550-552; Baker, *Wilson and World Settlement*, Vol. 1, p. 143.

[38] Council of Ten, January 15, 1919, 4:30 p.m., *Foreign Relations, 1919, The Paris Peace Conference*, Vol. 3, pp. 562-564; Baker, *Wilson and World Settlement*, Vol. 1, pp. 144-145.

[39] Council of Ten, January 16, 1919, 10:30 a.m., *Foreign Relations, 1919, The Paris Peace Conference*, Vol. 3, pp. 578-580; Baker, *Wilson and World Settlement*, Vol. 1, pp. 146-149.

were understanding of the difficulties involved but the Americans were adamant, demanding complete publicity.[40]

In the Council of Ten on January 17, Wilson urged again that the press be admitted to the Plenary Sessions. Balfour thought that such admittance would be a hollow privilege since few matters of importance would be dealt with in these meetings. Lloyd George agreed reluctantly to the President's proposal, emphasizing his fear of a "peace settled by public clamor."[41] The Council agreed on a communication to the press, drafted by Lloyd George, explaining the need for secret meetings of the Supreme Council but promising that the press would generally be admitted to Plenary Sessions, the right being reserved, however, to hold even these in camera.[42]

The agreed arrangement on publicity came closer, in practice, to meeting Lloyd George's specifications than those of the President. The arrangement served, in Lloyd George's opinion, to keep public opinion informed while avoiding the daily reports which would so arouse public opinion as to make compromise seem like surrender.[43] Wilson was certainly mistaken in believing that he had won "complete publicity for the real conferences."[44] As Balfour predicted, the Plenary Sessions turned out to be little more than ceremonial occasions. As the Peace Conference progressed, the principal negotiations were more and more removed from the public view and finally lodged in the secret Council of Four. In any case, the press and American public opinion were not made aware of the President's fight for publicity, and the President was widely accused of having betrayed the principle of "open diplomacy."

On the issue of *historical*, as distinguished from immediate, publicity, positions were curiously reversed. When, at the end of the main stage of the Peace Conference, the British secretary, Sir Maurice Hankey, asked for instructions concerning the disposi-

[40] *ibid.*, pp. 148-149.
[41] Council of Ten, January 17, 1919, 10:30 a.m., *Foreign Relations, 1919, The Paris Peace Conference*, Vol. 3, pp. 595-599; Baker, *Wilson and World Settlement*, Vol. 1, p. 150.
[42] Council of Ten, January 17, 1919, 3:00 p.m., *Foreign Relations, 1919, The Paris Peace Conference*, Vol. 3, pp. 609-611. See also Temperley, ed., *A History of the Peace Conference of Paris*, Vol. 1, pp. 255-256.
[43] Lloyd George, *The Truth about the Peace Treaties*, Vol. 1, pp. 218-219.
[44] Wilson to Tumulty, January 20, 1919, Wilson Papers, Series 8-A.

tion of his *procès-verbaux* of the Supreme Council, Wilson argued strongly against the release of what he considered to be private and unofficial conversations. Clemenceau thought that the minutes could not be treated as private property, while Lloyd George foresaw the possibility of having to refer to them against domestic political attacks.[45] The American State Department, as it turned out, was the first to publish these minutes, while the British archives have not yet been opened to this point.

The presence of two English-speaking Great Powers at the Paris Peace Conference accounted for a revolution in 1919 against the hitherto unchallenged position of French as the universal language of diplomacy. The initiative for elevating the English language to a position of diplomatic equality with French was taken by the United States, a newcomer to the councils of world diplomacy, while the British were more reluctant to tamper with tradition.[46] Under prodding from Colonel House, the British Government agreed in November 1918 to take a positive stand for the equal status of English.[47]

This issue was joined in the Supreme Council on January 15. Lloyd George argued that the 100 million people of America and the 350 million of the British Empire were entitled to coequal status for English as an official language of the treaty. President Wilson pointed out that English was the accepted diplomatic language of the Pacific. Clemenceau retorted with a defense of tradition and the "extreme precision" of the French language, suggesting with exquisite Gallic logic that all texts of the treaty might be regarded as *official* while the French text should be taken as *authoritative* in cases of disputes as to interpretation.[48] Wilson argued that the precedents for the use of French as the language of diplomacy were purely European, but that now the nations were embarked upon a new era of world diplomacy. Lloyd George suggested that English and French both be accepted

[45] Council of Four, June 28, 1919, 5 p.m., *Foreign Relations, 1919, The Paris Peace Conference*, Vol. 6, pp. 752-755.

[46] Marston, *The Peace Conference of 1919*, p. 65.

[47] House to Wilson, November 24, 1918, *Foreign Relations, 1919, The Paris Peace Conference*, Vol. 1, p. 171; House to Wilson, November 27, 1918, *ibid.*, pp. 173-174.

[48] Council of Ten, January 15, 1919, 10:30 a.m., *ibid.*, Vol. 3, pp. 553-556.

as official, with disputes over interpretation to be referred to the league of nations. Pichon appealed to his colleagues not to deprive France of this "ancient prerogative." Wilson said that he would yield if he listened "only to his sentiments," but "the work of this Conference concerned the future and not the past." Balfour pointed out that in the United States treaties were concluded by the Senate, and "it was clear that that body must ask for an English text."[49]

The issue was resolved in April. Pressed by the Drafting Committee for a decision, the Council of Three decided that English and French would be the two official languages of the peace treaties.[50]

The structural organization of the Peace Conference, it is generally agreed, was something less than a model of efficiency. The Council of Ten, in which all significant decisions except those concerning the league of nations were made from January to March, was essentially a continuation of the Supreme War Council, which in turn had been closely modeled on the British War Cabinet. The Council of Ten proved unwieldy for confidential negotiation and its effectiveness was constantly undermined by leakages of its proceedings to the French press.[51]

The Council of Ten established expert commissions on territorial problems not directly affecting the Great Powers. Far more than their French and Italian colleagues, Wilson and Lloyd George put faith in the reports of the expert commissions, which were instructed to delineate frontiers on the basis of nonpolitical considerations, principally on the basis of national and ethnographic

[49] Council of Ten, January 15, 1919, 4:30 p.m., *ibid.*, pp. 557-561. See also: Baker, *Wilson and World Settlement*, Vol. 1, pp. 202-206; Temperley, ed., *A History of the Peace Conference of Paris*, Vol. 1, p. 253; Marston, *The Peace Conference of 1919*, pp. 65-66.

[50] Council of Four, April 25, 1919, 6:30 p.m., *Foreign Relations, 1919, The Paris Peace Conference*, Vol. 5, pp. 244-245. See also Baker, *Wilson and World Settlement*, Vol. 1, pp. 207-209; Temperley, ed., *A History of the Peace Conference of Paris*, Vol. 1, p. 254.

[51] Marston, *The Peace Conference of 1919*, pp. 97-110, 229; Lord Hankey, *Diplomacy by Conference* (London: Ernest Benn, Ltd., 1946), pp. 26-28; Temperley, ed., *A History of the Peace Conference of Paris*, Vol. 1, pp. 249-250; Clive Day, "The Atmosphere and Organization of the Peace Conference," *What Really Happened at Paris* (Edward Mandell House and Charles Seymour, eds., New York: Charles Scribner's Sons, 1921), pp. 16-25.

groupings. Most of the reports of the territorial commissions were accepted without question by the Supreme Council.[52] The "objective" judgments of the territorial commissions provided criteria for decisions on frontiers which were especially welcome to the English-speaking powers, who, with no territorial ambitions of their own, had nonetheless a vital interest in stable territorial settlements which would not pose threats to the future peace of the world.

On Lloyd George's initiative, but with the full compliance of Wilson and Clemenceau, the regular sessions of the Council of Ten were terminated on March 24 and thereafter the heads of governments met as a Council of Four.[53] The Council of Four did the main work of drafting the German treaty, exploiting the advantages of secrecy and intimacy in order to solve the most difficult problems. For several weeks the Four met alone except for the interpreter, Paul Mantoux. Late in April, Maurice Hankey was admitted as secretary.[54] The Foreign Ministers met simultaneously as a Council of Five, dealing primarily with economic questions and the reports of the territorial commissions. But the fundamental work was done and the overriding decisions made in the secret Council of Four.[55]

Almost as an afterthought, it was agreed that the treaty with Germany was to constitute an imposed rather than a negotiated peace. The Council of Four decided in April that Germany might submit counterproposals to the draft treaty in writing but that

[52] Marston, *The Peace Conference of 1919*, pp. 111-123; Clive Day, "The Atmosphere and Organization of the Peace Conference," *What Really Happened at Paris* (House and Seymour, eds.), pp. 25-30; Charles Homer Haskins and Robert Howard Lord, *Some Problems of the Peace Conference* (Cambridge: Harvard University Press, 1920), pp. 28-31.

[53] Paul Mantoux, *Les Délibérations du Conseil des Quatre* (2 Vols., Paris: Éditions du Centre National de la Recherche Scientifique, 1955), Vol. 1, p. 13; Marston, *The Peace Conference of 1919*, pp. 161-164.

[54] Hankey kept the official minutes for the British delegation both in the Council of Ten and the Council of Four, providing copies also for the American delegation. Except for the period from January 12 to January 22, 1919, no separate minutes were kept by the American delegation. See *Foreign Relations, 1919, The Paris Peace Conference*, Vol. 3, p. 468.

[55] Hankey, *Diplomacy by Conference*, pp. 28-29, 36; Marston, *The Peace Conference of 1919*, pp. 165-174; Clive Day, "The Atmosphere and Organization of the Peace Conference," *What Really Happened at Paris* (House and Seymour, eds.), pp. 33-36; Tardieu, *The Truth about the Treaty*, pp. 101-104.

there would be no oral discussions.[56] Neither British nor American statesmen objected to this significant decision. Lloyd George held it to be justified by the extreme urgency of an early settlement, the appearance of a dictated peace being the lesser evil under the circumstances.[57] Wilson's ready assent to the imposition of the treaty without oral negotiations marked a complete reversal of his position before the Peace Conference when he had opposed even the discussion of peace terms before the enemy had stated his case and favored German participation in the constitution of the league of nations.[58]

In summary, there was essential harmony between the British and American delegations as to problems of the organization and procedure of the Peace Conference. Both had come to Paris elaborately prepared to deal with substantive issues but little concerned with problems of formal organization. Rejecting an elaborate plan of procedure, the English-speaking powers preferred and imposed a flexible and pragmatic approach, with the result that the principal organs and decision-making procedures of the Peace Conference evolved *ad hoc* with neither plan nor logic. Great Britain and the United States found the use of expert territorial commissions especially congenial to their interests, and British and American experts worked together in close and informal harmony. The chief differences between the two nations were over the issues of Dominion representation and secret diplomacy, and neither of these was fundamental, both being differences in degree rather than principle.

III. *Anglo-American Origins of the Mandate Principle*

In Liberal and Labour circles in Great Britain, the idea of international responsibility for the tutelage of backward peoples had been long in vogue before the Paris Peace Conference. As early as 1915, Liberal and Labour advocates were calling for

[56] Council of Four, April 26, 1919, 12:15 p.m., *Foreign Relations, 1919, The Paris Peace Conference*, Vol. 5, p. 293; Marston, *The Peace Conference of 1919*, p. 189; Baker, *Wilson and World Settlement*, Vol. 1, pp. 174-175.

[57] Lloyd George, *The Truth about the Peace Treaties*, Vol. 1, pp. 150-152.

[58] These views were expressed to Sir William Wiseman. "Notes on an Interview with the President at the White House," October 16, 1918, Wiseman Papers.

equality of economic opportunity in the colonial areas of the world. In April 1916, Philip Kerr, later Lloyd George's personal secretary, called for a system of tutelage of backward peoples by advanced peoples acting as "trustees for all mankind." The Labour Party took up the cause of trusteeship in 1917, and in February 1918, the Inter-Allied Labour and Socialist Conference pronounced for international trusteeships under a league of nations. In 1918, the Labour Party became the leading advocate of the trusteeship movement.[59]

Both Wilson and Lloyd George implied support for the trusteeship principle in their pronouncements on war aims. President Wilson's Point 5 called for an "impartial adjustment of all colonial claims," based on the principle that "the interests of the populations concerned must have equal weight with the equitable claims of the governments whose title is to be determined." In his address of January 5, 1918, Lloyd George declared that the German colonies should be placed "at the disposal of a conference whose decisions must have primary regard to the wishes and interests of the native inhabitants of such colonies," the principle of self-determination being "as applicable in their cases as those of occupied European territories."[60] Besides implying the removal of all colonial areas from Germany, these pronouncements, especially that of Lloyd George, strongly implied a principle of international responsibility for the well-being and protection from exploitation of at least some of the world's non-self-governing peoples.

The Cobb-Lippmann Memorandum, drawn up in October 1918, in explanation of the Fourteen Points and approved by President Wilson, defined Point 5 as follows: "It would seem as if the principle involved in this proposition is that a colonial power acts not as owner of its colonies, but as trustee for the natives and for the interests of the society of nations, that the terms on which the colonial administration is conducted are a matter of international concern and may legitimately be the subject of inter-

[59] Henry R. Winkler, *The League of Nations Movement in Great Britain, 1914-1919* (New Brunswick, New Jersey: Rutgers University Press, 1952), pp. 199-222; Ernest B. Haas, "The Reconciliation of Conflicting Colonial Policy Aims: Acceptance of the League of Nations Mandate System," *International Organization*, Vol. 6, No. 4 (November 1952), pp. 522-523.

[60] See Chapter I, Section v.

national inquiry and that the peace conference may, therefore, write a code of colonial conduct binding upon all colonial powers."[61]

The trusteeship principle was unquestionably in the President's mind during the pre-Conference period. He told Sir William Wiseman that while he had little faith in international administration for the German colonies and was absolutely opposed to their restoration to Germany, he favored administration by single states "in trust." "In trust for whom?" Wiseman asked. "Well, for the league of nations, for instance," Wilson replied.[62] Aboard the "George Washington," the President said that the German colonies "should be declared the common property of the league of nations and administered by small nations."[63]

Lloyd George expressed qualified sympathy with the trusteeship principle in a conversation with Colonel House on October 29, 1918. He told House that he hoped the United States could serve as trustee for the German East African colonies. He insisted, however, that Southwest Africa must go to the Union of South Africa and the German Pacific islands south of the equator to Australia, or he would face a "revolution" in these Dominions. House was left with the feeling that Great Britain wanted the United States to accept something "so they might more freely take what they desire."[64]

The disposition of the conquered German colonies was thoroughly discussed in the Imperial War Cabinet in November 1918, it being taken for granted that none would be restored to Germany. Great Britain herself and Canada wanted no additional territory and were ready and eager to entrust some of the German possessions to an American mandate, but the representatives of Australia, New Zealand, and South Africa made it clear that

[61] Charles Seymour, ed., *The Intimate Papers of Colonel House* (4 Vols., Boston and New York: Houghton Mifflin Company, 1926-1928), Vol. 4, p. 195.

[62] Sir William Wiseman, "Notes on an Interview with the President at the White House," October 16, 1918, Wiseman Papers.

[63] Notes taken by Isaiah Bowman, December 10, 1918, Shotwell, *At the Paris Peace Conference*, p. 77; Seymour, ed., *Intimate Papers*, Vol. 4, pp. 281-282. See Herbert Hoover, *The Ordeal of Woodrow Wilson* (New York, Toronto, London: McGraw-Hill Book Company, Inc., 1958), pp. 222-223.

[64] House to Wilson, October 30, 1918, *Foreign Relations, 1919, The Paris Peace Conference*, Vol. 1, p. 407.

they would not give up the conquered German territories. Sir Robert Borden, naturally more sensitive to the state of Anglo-American relations than any of his Imperial colleagues, suggested that it would be unwise for the British Empire to acquire vast new territories while the United States undertook no new responsibilities. He feared that Anglo-American relations would be damaged if German, Irish, and other anti-British groups in the United States could point to extensive British aggrandizement. Lloyd George observed that the question was not one of annexations but of "assuming a responsibility." Lord Milner emphasized the desirability of American mandates on the ground that the acquisition of such responsibility by the United States would create a bond of union between the United States and the British Empire. It was agreed that Lloyd George would sound out President Wilson as to the prospects of American acceptance of mandatory responsibility. The Imperial War Cabinet, according to Lloyd George, unanimously accepted the mandate principle for the German colonies, *except* for Southwest Africa and the islands of the Pacific.[65]

On December 16, 1918, General Smuts proposed a plan for a league of nations entitled "The League of Nations: A Practical Suggestion."[66] Almost a third of Smut's tract was devoted to a scheme for mandates under the league of nations, to be applied to "territories formerly belonging to Russia, Austria-Hungary, and Turkey." The plan called for the application of the principle of self-determination to states and territories according to the stage of their development and went on to elaborate a scheme of graded mandates under the trusteeship of the league. Authority would not be exercised directly by the league but by individual states, "subject to the supervision and ultimate control of the league." The Smuts scheme did not envision mandatory status for the German colonies in Africa and the Pacific. Noting that these areas were "inhabited by barbarians" for whom self-determination in the European sense was "impracticable," the plan

[65] Lloyd George, *The Truth about the Peace Treaties*, Vol. I, pp. 114-123. See also Frank Owen, *Tempestuous Journey—Lloyd George: His Life and Times* (London: Hutchinson and Company Ltd., 1954), pp. 530-532.
[66] See Chapter 4, Section III.

implied the annexation of such areas by the British Dominions.[67] The Smuts proposal of December 16 was the most elaborate articulation of the mandate principle up to that time and it commended itself highly to President Wilson, except for the exclusion of the territories coveted by the Dominions.

The British Dominions, in short, accepted the mandate principle, but not for themselves. Lunching with Lord Riddell on December 22, General Botha of South Africa said: "We must hold East Africa because of its dominating position. The Americans do not understand that. The situation must be explained to Wilson."[68] Prime Minister Hughes of Australia took up the cry far less gently, indulging in violent invective in the Imperial War Cabinet against Wilson's reported opposition to Australia's claims in the Pacific.[69]

Upon arriving in Paris, President Wilson proceeded to define the mandate principle in detail. He had added it to his latest draft covenant of the league of nations, envisioning the league as "residuary trustee" for the German and Turkish Empires.[70] Wilson incorporated the mandate principle into his first and second Paris draft covenants,[71] using the language of the Smuts plan but making two significant changes: the omission of Russian territories and the inclusion of the German colonies.[72] At the urging of Premier Orlando of Italy, Wilson removed the Austro-Hungarian succession states from the application of the mandate principle and his third Paris draft applied it only to the German and Turkish Empires.[73]

The position of the United States in the mounting controversy over colonies and mandates was based unambiguously on adherence to a principle, while Great Britain found herself caught between her own acceptance of that principle and her desire for

[67] David Hunter Miller, *The Drafting of the Covenant* (2 Vols., New York, London: G. P. Putnam's Sons, 1928), Vol. 1, pp. 30-36, Vol. 2, pp. 27-35. See also Lloyd George, *The Truth about the Peace Treaties*, Vol. 1, pp. 623-625.

[68] *Lord Riddell's Intimate Diary of the Peace Conference and After, 1918-1923* (New York: Reynal and Hitchcock, Inc., 1934), pp. 5-6.

[69] Borden's Diary, December 30, 1918, Borden, ed., *Robert Laird Borden: His Memoirs*, Vol. 2, p. 889.

[70] Seymour, ed., *Intimate Papers*, Vol. 4, pp. 283-284.

[71] See Chapter 4, Section IV.

[72] Miller, *The Drafting of the Covenant*, Vol. 1, pp. 101-102.

[73] *ibid.*, p. 102. See Chapter 4, Section IV.

good relations with the United States on the one hand, and the necessity to support the Dominions on the other. Aside from a sentimental interest in Armenia and the desire to prevent the establishment of hostile naval bases in the Pacific, the United States had no concrete interests at stake. But having adopted the principle of international trusteeship, President Wilson under-took with great vigor to compel its application in opposition to what the Dominions conceived to be their vital interests. The British Government was in a most uncomfortable position. It had no interests at stake in regard to annexations as distinguished from mandates in Africa and the Pacific; it was committed to the mandate principle; and it very much wanted a good under-standing with the United States. On the other hand, the Domin-ions were adamant in their demands and if Great Britain were to have adopted a position of unqualified support of the man-date principle, the unity of the Imperial family would surely have been shattered.

IV. *The Mandates Controversy in the Council of Ten*

The disposition of the German colonies was the first major substantive issue dealt with by the Peace Conference. On January 23, it had been agreed that all delegations with territorial claims would submit them within ten days.[74] The claims of the Domin-ions were ready on the next day and the Council of Ten was compelled to deal with them first. With almost no discussion, the Supreme Council agreed in its first discussion of the issue that no colonies would be restored to Germany.[75]

Lloyd George and his Imperial colleagues launched the discus-sion of mandates. Rejecting direct administration by a league of nations as unfeasible, Lloyd George proposed that mandates be accorded to single nations who would be responsible to the league to maintain the paramount interests of the natives and equality of commercial access. Such a mandatory system, said

[74] Council of Ten, January 23, 1919, 10:30 a.m., *Foreign Relations, 1919, The Paris Peace Conference*, Vol. 3, pp. 699-700.

[75] Council of Ten, January 24, 1919, 3 p.m., *ibid.*, p. 718; Ray Stannard Baker, *Woodrow Wilson and World Settlement* (3 Vols., Garden City, New York: Doubleday, Page and Company, 1922), Vol. 1, p. 255; Birdsall, *Versailles Twenty Years After*, pp. 59-60.

Lloyd George, would be virtually a codification of British colonial policy. Lloyd George wished, however, to except the territories captured by the British Dominions: German Southwest Africa should be annexed by the Union of South Africa, New Guinea by Australia, and German Samoa by New Zealand. The Dominion representatives then stated their pleas. Hughes argued the vital strategic importance of New Guinea for the defense of Australia. Smuts claimed Southwest Africa on the ground of its contiguity to the Union and the disadvantages of administrative separation. Massey claimed the strategic importance of German Samoa for New Zealand. Borden, who had no claims to make for Canada, endorsed the arguments of his colleagues.[76] The French, Italians, and Japanese were unsympathetic to the mandate principle but took little part in the discussion. Only the Japanese had a vital stake in the issue, and they were content to let the British Empire present the case for annexations.[77]

President Wilson explained his concept of the mandatory system in the Council of Ten on January 27. Citing the case of Southwest Africa as an appropriate mandate for the Union of South Africa, the President said that the "fundamental idea" of the system would be that "the world was acting as trustee through a mandatory" and would exercise this responsibility "until the day when the true wishes of the inhabitants could be ascertained." If the Union of South Africa hoped for annexation of the mandate territory, it was up to the Union "to make it so attractive that Southwest Africa would come into the Union of their own free will." Challenging Australia's claim of strategic necessity for the annexation of New Guinea, Wilson said that the Australian position was "based on a fundamental lack of faith in the league of nations." Any nation threatening a mandatory power, he said, would be an "outlaw." There could, therefore, be no danger to New Guinea, or any mandatory, "because all the other nations would be pledged, with the United States in the lead, to take up arms for the mandatory." Australia might

[76] Council of Ten, January 24, 1919, 3 p.m., *Foreign Relations, 1919, The Paris Peace Conference*, Vol. 3, pp. 719-728; Lloyd George, *The Truth about the Peace Treaties*, Vol. I, pp. 517-523; Baker, *Wilson and World Settlement*, Vol. I, pp. 257-258; Birdsall, *Versailles Twenty Years After*, pp. 60-62.
[77] See Section v below.

well become the mandatory power for New Guinea, the President concluded. "But if the process of annexation went on, the league of nations would be discredited from the beginning."[78]

The Dominion Prime Ministers vigorously contested the President's views. General Botha insisted that Southwest Africa was naturally "part and parcel" of the Union and that the league was a fledgling and untested organization on which to rely. Prime Minister Hughes questioned the general validity of the mandate system, asserting the right of Australia to annex New Guinea on the grounds of geographical proximity and Australian sacrifices in the war. Lloyd George stated his agreement with the "principle" of mandates, but its "practical application," he thought, should be carefully considered by the experts. President Wilson retorted that it was not an area appropriate for experts: "A new regime was about to be established."[79]

The conflict became acrimonious in the Supreme Council on January 28. Lloyd George proclaimed his acceptance of the mandate principle as to territories captured by the forces of the United Kingdom. He regarded the Dominion claims, however, as a "special case" and he hoped that President Wilson would "look into it again." Prime Minister Massey recited the case of New Zealand, inquiring irrelevantly whether President Washington would have agreed to a system of mandates over the unsettled lands of America after the Revolution. Simon, the French Minister of Colonies, expressed his strong preference for annexations. President Wilson observed that the discussion so far had been "a negation in detail—one case at a time—of the whole principle of mandatories." The President thought that the discussion had reached a point "where it looked as if their roads diverged." Balfour and Lloyd George insisted that Great Britain supported the general principle but was concerned only with practical details. The President retorted that the two ideas of mandates and annexations were "radically different." Noting that France, Japan, and the Dominions all insisted upon annexations, Wilson ob-

[78] Council of Ten, January 27, 1919, 3 p.m., *Foreign Relations, 1919, The Paris Peace Conference*, Vol. 3, pp. 741-743; Baker, *Wilson and World Settlement*, Vol. 1, pp. 261-262.

[79] Council of Ten, January 27, 1919, 3 p.m., *Foreign Relations, 1919, The Paris Peace Conference*, Vol. 3, pp. 743-748; Baker, *Wilson and World Settlement*, Vol. 1, p. 267.

served that the only acceptance of the mandate principle was by Great Britain as to territories occupied by British troops. "This was an important exception," said the President, "but it appeared to be the only exception to the rejection of the idea of trusteeships on the part of the league of nations." He feared that the league would be reduced to a "laughing stock." Orlando and Clemenceau expressed sympathy with the mandate principle but agreed with the British that certain exceptions were justified. Lloyd George expressed the hope that Wilson would not insist upon postponing the selection of mandatories until after the league of nations was set up, but the President insisted that colonial questions could wait until the more urgent European questions were settled. He feared that an immediate distribution of mandates would appear to the world a "mere distribution of the spoils."[80]

The deadlock now seemed to be unbreakable and tempers were aroused. Lloyd George convened the Imperial War Cabinet on January 29 and implored the Dominion Prime Ministers not to wreck the Peace Conference. Hughes haggled and Lloyd George lost his temper, telling Hughes that he had fought Australia's battle for three days but he was not going to quarrel with the United States for the Solomon Islands. Botha was conciliatory and Borden helped to restrain Hughes and Massey. Only after a heated session did Lloyd George secure agreement on a resolution to be presented to the Council the following day.[81]

The resolution to which Lloyd George secured the consent of the Dominions on the 29th was written by General Smuts. It proposed that the German and Turkish colonies not be restored but be entrusted to the tutelage of "advanced nations" as a "sacred trust of civilization." The essence of Smuts's compromise lay in the proposition that the character of mandates should differ according to stages of development, geography, and economic conditions. Smuts devised three categories of mandates: the first, consisting of the territories severed from the Turkish

[80] Council of Ten, January 28, 1919, 4 p.m., *Foreign Relations, 1919, The Paris Peace Conference*, Vol. 3, pp. 749-771; Lloyd George, *The Truth about the Peace Treaties*, Vol. 1, pp. 530-538; Baker, *Wilson and World Settlement*, Vol. 1, pp. 268-271. See also Birdsall, *Versailles Twenty Years After*, pp. 62-65.
[81] Lloyd George, *The Truth about the Peace Treaties*, Vol. 1, p. 538; Borden's Diary, January 29, 1919, Borden, ed., *Borden's Memoirs*, Vol. 2, p. 906.

Empire, were deemed to have reached a stage of development where their independence could be "provisionally recognized subject to the rendering of administrative advice and assistance" by a mandatory power until they were ready to stand alone; the second, consisting of former German possessions in Central Africa, were regarded as being at such a stage that the mandatory should be responsible for administration, subject to conditions guaranteeing the prohibition of the slave trade, traffic in arms and liquor, and militarization; the third category, consisting of such territories as Southwest Africa and the islands of the South Pacific, were, "owing to the sparseness of their populations, or their small size, or their remoteness from the centers of civilization," to be "administered under the laws of the mandatory state as integral portions thereof," subject to the same safeguards as the mandates of the second category. States holding mandates of any of the three categories were to be required to submit annual reports to the league of nations.[82]

President Wilson saw the Smuts plan on January 29 and his immediate reaction was one of guarded approval. He could accept the scheme, he noted, "if the interpretation in practice were to come from General Smuts. . . . My difficulty is with the demands of men like Hughes and the certain difficulties with Japan. The latter loom large." Colonel House thought the Smuts proposal a "fair compromise."[83]

The Smuts formula, almost without change, became the final decision of the Supreme Council, and, with minor alterations, it became Article 22 of the Covenant of the League of Nations. Agreement was not reached, however, until after another session of the Council of Ten which generated an Anglo-American exchange even more acrimonious than that of January 28. The discussion in the Council of Ten on January 30 was, according to Lloyd George, "the only unpleasant episode of the whole

[82] The Smuts resolution on mandates may be found in: Miller, *The Drafting of the Covenant*, Vol. 1, pp. 109-110; *Foreign Relations, 1919, The Paris Peace Conference*, Vol. 3, pp. 795-796; Lloyd George, *The Truth about the Peace Treaties*, Vol. 1, pp. 538-541. See also Birdsall, *Versailles Twenty Years After*, pp. 66-67.

[83] Pencil notes in the margin of House's copy of the Smuts plan, House Papers.

Congress."[84] The President, for the first time, lost his temper with the British in this session. Colonel House commented that if he had been in the President's place, he "should have congratulated them over their willingness to meet us more than halfway."[85]

At this critical meeting, Lloyd George submitted the Smuts plan, emphasizing that it had been accepted by the Dominions even though it did not represent their "real views." Hughes indicated his grudging assent. President Wilson said that Lloyd George's resolution was "very gratifying" and he accepted it as a "precursor of agreement." But it did not, said Wilson, constitute a "rock foundation," because the league was not yet established and it was impossible to reach a decision before its creation. Lloyd George declared that the President's statement "filled him with despair." Only with the greatest difficulty, he pleaded, had the Dominions been brought to accept the Smuts resolution, and he asked that it be provisionally adopted subject to reconsideration when the Covenant was formulated. Wilson agreed to accept the Smuts scheme as a purely provisional arrangement, subject to reconsideration when the full scheme of the league was drawn up. Hughes was not satisfied. The "*de facto* League of Nations," he insisted, was in this very room, and it should act as the "executive of the future League of Nations" and apportion the mandates at once.[86]

Between the morning and afternoon sessions of January 30, Sir Robert Borden, whose chief concern was Anglo-American accord, played the peacemaker. He urged moderation on Massey and Hughes and explained to President Wilson Lloyd George's difficulties with the Dominions, pointing out that he could neither control their policies nor fail to support them.[87]

An extremely acrid discussion took place in the afternoon session of the Council as Hughes and Massey relentlessly pressed their demands for immediate distribution of mandates. Wilson

---

[84] Lloyd George, *The Truth about the Peace Treaties*, Vol. 1, p. 541.

[85] Seymour, ed., *Intimate Papers*, Vol. 4, p. 299.

[86] Council of Ten, January 30, 1919, 11 a.m., *Foreign Relations, 1919, The Paris Peace Conference*, Vol. 3, pp. 785-794; Miller, *The Drafting of the Covenant*, Vol. 2, pp. 194-202; Baker, *Wilson and World Settlement*, Vol. 1, pp. 272-274.

[87] G. P. de T. Glazebrook, *Canada at the Paris Peace Conference* (London, Toronto, New York: Oxford University Press, 1942), pp. 90-92.

finally demanded to know whether New Zealand and Australia had "presented an ultimatum to the Conference." Did their agreement to the Smuts plan, he asked, depend upon the annexation of New Guinea and Samoa? Massey said that it did not. Hughes launched forth on another matter and the President sharply interrupted to ask whether Mr. Hughes had heard his question. One of the Australian secretaries hastened to explain that Mr. Hughes's electrical hearing apparatus had failed to function,[88] and Wilson repeated his question. Hughes replied that President Wilson had "put it fairly well." He had agreed, he said, to the clause of the Smuts plan defining the third category of mandates only with the greatest reluctance and he would not go beyond that. General Botha made a conciliatory speech, explaining to Wilson the extreme difficulty with which Lloyd George had won the assent of the Dominions to his resolution and appealing to the President to support Lloyd George's position. Massey assured Wilson that no threat had been intended and Lloyd George appealed once again for the acceptance of his resolution as a "provisional decision subject to revision."[89]

The issue thereupon moved rapidly toward agreement. Since the President had already accepted the Smuts plan as a provisional agreement, the only question remaining was when the mandates would be apportioned. Lloyd George favored definite apportionments at once, but President Wilson insisted that if the United States was to share the burden of mandates, he must first have an opportunity to explain the necessity to the American people. At the President's suggestion, it was agreed that the military advisers of the Supreme War Council would submit recommendations for the temporary occupation and control of the mandate areas.[90]

[88] Stephen Bonsal, *Unfinished Business* (Garden City, New York: Doubleday, Doran and Company, Inc., 1944), p. 42.

[89] Council of Ten, January 30, 1919, 3:30 p.m., *Foreign Relations, 1919, The Paris Peace Conference*, Vol. 3, pp. 797-802; Miller, *The Drafting of the Covenant*, Vol. 2, pp. 206-215; Lloyd George, *The Truth about the Peace Treaties*, Vol. 1, pp. 542-546. Lloyd George comments that Wilson was "ruffled and irritable" in this session and "hectoring" and "dictatorial" toward the Dominion Prime Ministers. *ibid.*, p. 542.

[90] Council of Ten, January 30, 1919, 3:30 p.m., *Foreign Relations, 1919, The Paris Peace Conference*, Vol. 3, pp. 805-807; Miller, *The Drafting of the Covenant*, Vol. 2, pp. 220-226; Lloyd George, *The Truth about the Peace Treaties*, Vol. 1, p. 546. See also Birdsall, *Versailles Twenty Years After*, pp. 68-73.

The Anglo-American mandates crisis was thus brought to a solution on the basis of the Smuts compromise. Implicitly, Wilson had agreed that the Dominions would receive as mandates of the third category the territories they had wished to annex. This amounted to the substance of annexation but the President secured universal assent to the trusteeship principle from unwilling states which were in military occupation of the territories concerned. After the meeting of January 30, Wilson told Miller that the resolution did not go as far as he had hoped, but that his chief anxiety was not the concessions to the Dominions but the prospect of *Japanese* control of the islands of the North Pacific.[91] On the whole, President Wilson achieved a notable victory, establishing a principle of tremendous importance. The trusteeship idea foreshadowed the eventual demise of colonialism, not only in the mandate areas but throughout the world. The mandate principle, though more British than American in conception, was successfully implemented in 1919 almost entirely because of the forceful and effective advocacy of President Wilson.[92]

The tacit agreement on the apportionment of the mandates was made explicit in May 1919. Lloyd George raised the issue and Wilson said that it was to all intents settled: third-class mandates would be accorded to the Union of South Africa for German Southwest Africa, to Australia for New Guinea, to New Zealand for German Samoa. Wilson would not agree to *formal* apportionment until after the signing of the treaty, lest it give the appearance of a "division of the spoils being simultaneous with the peace,"[93] but informally, the apportionment of the mandates was agreed to on May 7.[94]

The short, sharp conflict between the United States and the British Empire left no deep scars, nor did it impair the cooperation of the English-speaking powers on subsequent issues of the Peace Conference. There would appear to be several reasons for

[91] Miller, *Diary*, Vol. 1, pp. 99-100.
[92] For an excellent brief discussion of the mandates controversy, its resolution and significance, set in historical perspective, see Ernest B. Haas, "The Reconciliation of Conflicting Colonial Policy Aims: Acceptance of the League of Nations Mandate System," *International Organization*, Vol. 6, No. 4 (November 1952), pp. 521-536.
[93] Council of Four, May 5, 1919, 11 a.m., *Foreign Relations, 1919, The Paris Peace Conference*, Vol. 5, pp. 472-473.
[94] Council of Four, May 7, 1919, 4:15 p.m., *ibid.*, pp. 507-508.

this. First, the issue was the first substantive matter dealt with by the Peace Conference and it was settled quickly. Secondly, Great Britain, which held by conquest much of the territory at issue, early accepted the mandate principle—the only Great Power besides the United States to do so. It was bound, however, to maintain Imperial unity, and was extremely grateful for a compromise acceptable to both the United States and the Dominions. Lloyd George handled this difficult matter with great skill, not least in his reliance on Borden and Smuts to bridge the gulf. Thirdly, the compromise itself was genuinely satisfactory to both sides, satisfying the ambitions of the Dominions without greatly impairing Wilson's trusteeship principle. Finally, the issue was quickly superseded by attention to the drafting of the Covenant of the League—in which Great Britain and the United States achieved their highest point of harmony of the entire Peace Conference.

V. *Japan and the Islands of the North Pacific*

By its largely successful advocacy of its own claims in the Pacific, the British Empire almost automatically secured for Japan the islands to which it laid claim, for it would have been quite impossible to dispose of the demands of the Dominions in one way and the quite similar demands of Japan in another.

In January 1917, Great Britain had asked for Japanese naval support in the Mediterranean, which Japan agreed to provide only on condition of a British promise of support at the Peace Conference for Japanese claims to the German islands in the Pacific north of the equator and to the German rights in the Chinese province of Shantung. The British Government had agreed to these conditions, and Japan in turn agreed to support British claims to the German Pacific islands south of the equator. These agreements were embodied in an Anglo-Japanese exchange of notes in February 1917 and in similar notes with France and Russia.[95]

[95] British Ambassador at Tokyo to Japanese Minister of Foreign Affairs, February 16, 1917, Carnegie Endowment for International Peace, John V. A. MacMurray, ed., *Treaties and Agreements with and concerning China, 1894-1919* (2 Vols., New York: Oxford University Press, 1921), Vol. 2, pp. 1167-1168; Japanese Minister of Foreign Affairs to British Ambassador, February 21, 1917, *ibid.*, p. 1168; E. L. Woodward and Rohan Butler, eds., *Documents on British Foreign Policy, 1919-1939*, First Series (8 Vols., London: His Majesty's Stationery Office, 1947-1958), Vol. 6, p. 563. See also Russell H. Fifield, *Woodrow*

President Wilson, and especially his naval advisers, were greatly disturbed by the prospect of Japanese acquisition of the North Pacific islands because of their strategic position astride the American communications route to the Philippines. In December 1918, American naval officers had taken such alarm at the prospect of Japanese acquisition of the islands that they had advised that American strategic interests absolutely required the acquisition by the United States of the Marshalls, the Carolines, and the Marianas and that Japan should be appeased by allowing her a free hand on the continent of Asia.[96] President Wilson was not driven to such extremes in the discussion of mandates in the Council of Ten, but Lloyd George found the President's attitude "strongly anti-Japanese."[97]

In view of the commitment of Britain and France to support the Japanese claims and the demands of Australia and New Zealand for annexation of the South Pacific islands, the Japanese strategy was to leave it to the Allies to press for annexation, which could not exclude Japan, while focusing her own efforts on her other principal objectives.[98] Baron Makino, one of the Japanese representatives, presented the claims of Japan to the Council of Ten on January 27, demanding the unconditional cession of all German rights in Shantung as well as all of the German islands in the Pacific north of the equator.[99] In the discussion on January 28, Baron Makino and his colleague Viscount Chinda remained silent while Lloyd George appealed on behalf of the Dominions for annexations instead of mandates. The resolution of the mandates controversy on January 30 was accepted by the Japanese delegates, and Japan ultimately received the North Pacific islands as mandates of the third category under the Smuts plan, to be "administered under the laws of the mandatory state as integral

---

Wilson and the Far East (New York: Thomas Y. Crowell Company, 1952), pp. 53-54.

[96] Secretary of the Navy Daniels to Wilson, December 3, 1918, Memorandum by the General Board of the Department of the Navy, Wilson Papers, Series 8-A.

[97] Lloyd George, *The Truth about the Peace Treaties*, Vol. 1, p. 188. Lloyd George does not discuss Far Eastern questions as such in his memoirs, making only incidental comments on the Japanese claims at Paris.

[98] Fifield, *Wilson and the Far East*, p. 122.

[99] Council of Ten, January 27, 1919, 3 p.m., *Foreign Relations, 1919, The Paris Peace Conference*, Vol. 3, pp. 738-740.

portions thereof." The Japanese thus secured the substance of their ambitions in the North Pacific without effort as a by-product of the Anglo-American mandates controversy.[100]

President Wilson was, as he told David Hunter Miller, more disturbed by the prospect of Japanese acquisition of the Pacific islands than by any other consequence of the mandates settlement, but he offered no significant resistance to these particular Japanese claims in the Council of Ten and apparently accepted the outcome with resignation. The reasons for this would appear to be several. First, and probably most important, was the utter inconsistency that would have been involved in attempting to deny mandates of the third category to Japan in the North Pacific while conceding them to Australia and New Zealand in the South Pacific. Secondly, Japan was in possession of the islands and probably could not have been dislodged by means short of military force. Thirdly, despite the strategic importance of these islands to the United States and the urgings of his naval advisers, Wilson was apparently far more concerned to curb Japanese expansion on the Asian mainland than in the Pacific. Finally, on this issue, as on that of Japanese aspirations in China, Britain and France were absolutely committed, whatever their unofficial preferences, to support the claims of Japan.[101]

[100] See Section IV above.
[101] See Chapter 12, Section IV.

CHAPTER 4

THE COVENANT OF THE LEAGUE OF NATIONS:
AN ANGLO-AMERICAN DOCUMENT

THE idea of an international organization to subject international relations to the rule of law quite naturally found its most congenial reception in the English-speaking democracies, whose own legally ordered societies constituted prototypes which seemed eminently suitable for international application. Considerations of interest, justice, and experience commended the idea of an international legal order to the English-speaking peoples above all others. Alone among the Great Powers, Great Britain and the United States had found it possible in the nineteenth century to resolve many of their conflicts of interest by resort to legal instrumentalities. Why could this approach not be universalized and applied to all nations?

Although the underlying concept can be traced at least as far back as the Middle Ages, the immediate origins of the League of Nations were predominantly English and American. During the period of American belligerency in the war, many schemes and proposals for a league for peace were formulated by private citizens in both England and America and these unofficial league movements came into increasingly close touch with each other. On the official level, the British Government took the lead in formulating specific plans while President Wilson, for essentially tactical reasons, declined until the final months of the war to consider a specific formulation. The British Government unquestionably made the principal contributions of draftsmanship, while Wilson's contributions were those of broad conception and forceful advocacy.

In the month of January 1919, a series of British and American drafts for the Covenant of the League of Nations were devised and revised in a milieu of significant and intensive communication between British and American statesmen. Now at last, President Wilson was ready to translate the principles of a new world order into a practical instrument and the result was the most fruitful collaboration between Britain and America of the entire

Peace Conference. The different emphases of British and American concepts of international organization were synthesized into a single document which became the working basis of discussion in the Commission on the League of Nations.

The proceedings of the League Commission were dominated by President Wilson and Lord Robert Cecil. The conflicts that occurred were almost without exception between Anglo-American and French concepts of the League, and equally without exception, the Anglo-American views prevailed. The result was the creation of a constitution for a society of nations based on Anglo-American principles of voluntarism and equal justice under law.

I. *The Emergence of Official and Unofficial Proposals in Great Britain and the United States for a League of Nations*

In the autumn of 1914, President Wilson and Colonel House considered a scheme for the welding of the states of North and South America into a closer union. In a conversation on December 16, 1914, Wilson and House drafted a clause for the proposed pan-American pact calling for mutual guarantees of political independence under republican forms of government and mutual guarantees of territorial integrity. The proposed pact was not realized, but this clause became the inspiration of Article 10 of the Covenant of the League of Nations. It was agreed between Wilson and House that the pan-American plan could serve as a model for European application when peace was restored.[1]

The foremost British advocate of a league for peace during the first years of the war was Sir Edward Grey, the Foreign Secretary. Grey was profoundly influenced in his thinking about international organization by the failure of his own efforts to preserve peace in the summer of 1914. The chaos of telegrams frantically exchanged among the chancelleries of Europe at that time had persuaded Grey that if the Concert of Europe had had some established machinery of obligatory consultation, war might have been prevented.[2] He wrote to House in 1915: ". . . . If neutral

---

[1] Charles Seymour, ed., *The Intimate Papers of Colonel House* (4 Vols., Boston and New York: Houghton Mifflin Company, 1926-1928), Vol. 1, pp. 208-210.

[2] See David Hunter Miller, "The Making of the League of Nations," *What*

nations and the opinion of the world generally had been sufficiently alert to say that they would side against the party that refused a Conference, war might have been avoided. Peace in future years, after this war is over, seems to me to depend greatly upon whether the world takes this lesson to heart sufficiently to decide promptly if ever such a crisis occurs again."[3]

Grey looked to the United States for leadership in the formulation of plans for permanent peace. Early in 1915 he expressed to House his hope that at the end of the war the United States would participate in some form of general guarantee for world peace,[4] and on another occasion he predicted that if the United States should enter the war, it would exercise preponderant influence upon the formulation of plans for the preservation of permanent peace.[5]

The British came to conceive of a league of nations as an enlarged and improved Concert, but Wilson thought of it as a universalized application of the Monroe Doctrine, which he regarded as a partnership of American states for the advancement of democracy in world affairs. Grey's thinking was empirical in terms of European experience, a latter-day effort to bring in the new world to redress the balance of the old. Wilson's conception was universal and idealist, generalizing the Monroe Doctrine as he conceived it into a world moral order. Though logically incompatible, these two views were not mutually exclusive.[6]

Despite these early expressions of official sentiment, until late in the war the most vigorous advocates of a society of nations were not government officials but groups of private citizens. The league movement during the war, though widespread, reached significant proportions only in England and America. Study groups interested in international organization were formed—in the United States under former President Taft and President A. Lawrence

---

Really Happened at Paris (Edward Mandell House and Charles Seymour, eds., New York: Charles Scribner's Sons, 1921), p. 401.

[3] Grey to House, July 14, 1915, Seymour, ed., *Intimate Papers*, Vol. 2, pp. 55-56.

[4] Interview on February 9, 1915, *ibid.*, Vol. 1, p. 363.

[5] Grey to House, June 6, 1915, *ibid.*, Vol. 2, p. 54.

[6] See Alfred Zimmern, *The League of Nations and the Rule of Law, 1918-1935* (2nd edn., London: Macmillan and Company, Ltd., 1945), pp. 216-217; Edward H. Buehrig, *Woodrow Wilson and the Balance of Power* (Bloomington: Indiana University Press, 1955), pp. 273-274.

Lowell of Harvard, in Great Britain under Lord Bryce and the Fabian Society. In 1915, league advocates organized the League to Enforce Peace in the United States and the League of Nations Society in Great Britain. The dominant concern of both of these organizations was "to prevent the next war."[7]

The unofficial league groups in both Britain and the United States conducted vigorous educational campaigns during the course of the war and developed increasingly close contacts with each other. Between 1914 and 1920, the League to Enforce Peace provided the principal organized support for the league movement in America.[8] In 1918, another society, the League of Free Nations Association, was organized, and in November 1918, the two American groups issued a joint statement of their principles under the title of a "Victory Program."[9] The British League of Nations Society issued abundant promotional literature and kept in constant contact with the American League to Enforce Peace. In 1918, a group of Parliamentary Liberals formed the League of Free Nations Association, and in October 1918, the two British groups merged as the League of Nations Union. The Union propagandized actively until the Peace Conference, publishing many propaganda pamphlets in support of a league.[10] The correspondence of Theodore Marburg, a leading member of the League to Enforce Peace, with Lord Bryce and other English league advocates richly illustrates the harmony of purpose and close cooperation between the private league movements in England and America.[11]

President Wilson was greatly impressed with Sir Edward Grey's letters to Colonel House, which ceaselessly expressed the view that a stable peace must be based on a permanent international organi-

[7] Zimmern, *The League of Nations and the Rule of Law*, pp. 161-162; F. P. Walters, *A History of the League of Nations* (2 Vols., London, New York, Toronto: Oxford University Press, 1952), Vol. 1, p. 18. See generally Ruhl J. Bartlett, *The League to Enforce Peace* (Chapel Hill: The University of North Carolina Press, 1944) and Henry R. Winkler, *The League of Nations Movement in Great Britain, 1914-1919* (New Brunswick, New Jersey: Rutgers University Press, 1952).

[8] Bartlett, *The League to Enforce Peace*, p. v.

[9] *ibid.*, pp. 111-112, 220-222.

[10] Winkler, *The League of Nations Movement in Great Britain*, pp. 52-56, 70-81.

[11] See, e.g., John H. Latané, ed., *Development of the League of Nations Idea* (2 Vols., New York: The Macmillan Company, 1932), Vol. 1, pp. 59, 83-85, 98, 100-101, 157-158, 294-295.

zation. The President asked House to advise him on a speech he was to deliver to the League to Enforce Peace on May 27, 1916, "as if you were seeking to make the proposal as nearly what you deem Grey and his colleagues to have agreed upon in principle. . . ."[12]

Wilson's speech of May 27, 1916, to the League to Enforce Peace constituted a proposal for a revolution in American foreign policy.[13] Stating that at the end of the war the United States would be as much concerned as the belligerents with arrangements for permanent peace, the President asserted, in the form of three principles, the fundamental beliefs of America: the right of self-determination, equality of rights between great and small powers, and the right of the world to be free from military aggression. The United States, Wilson declared, "is willing to become a partner in any feasible association of nations formed in order to realize these objects and make them secure against violation." If the United States were to suggest peace, the President asserted, an indispensable part of it would be a "universal association of nations" to maintain the freedom of the seas and provide a "virtual guarantee of territorial integrity and political independence."[14]

The attitude of British and Allied statesmen toward this significant pronouncement was surprisingly negative. Virtually ignoring the revolutionary proposal of the speech, the British expressed annoyance with an incidental phrase concerning the war, "with its causes and objects we are not concerned," regarding this as placing the Allies on the same moral plane as Germany.[15] Sir Edward Grey complained of the President's failure to define the freedom of the seas.[16]

The President reasserted, in a Memorial Day Address,[17] his willingness to join a "disentangling alliance" for peace, and the private advocates of a league took encouragement to seek official

[12] Wilson to House, May 18, 1916, Seymour, ed., *Intimate Papers*, Vol. 4, p. 3.
[13] See Bartlett, *The League to Enforce Peace*, p. 51; Harley Notter, *The Origins of the Foreign Policy of Woodrow Wilson* (Baltimore: The Johns Hopkins Press, 1937), p. 521.
[14] Ray Stannard Baker and William E. Dodd, eds., *The Public Papers of Woodrow Wilson* (6 Vols., New York and London: Harper & Brothers, Publishers, 1925-1927), *The New Democracy*, Vol. 2, pp. 184-188.
[15] Page to House, June 2, 1916, Seymour, ed., *Intimate Papers*, Vol. 2, p. 302.
[16] Seymour, ed., *Intimate Papers*, Vol. 2, pp. 302-303.
[17] Speech at Arlington National Cemetery, May 30, 1916, Baker and Dodd, eds., *Public Papers, The New Democracy*, Vol. 2, pp. 191-196.

endorsement of a specific program. Wilson, however, emphatically rejected a proposal for the introduction of a Congressional resolution endorsing the program of the League to Enforce Peace.[18] The President firmly refused to sanction the formulation of a precise program lest it provide a focus for opposition, but in subsequent speeches in 1916, he reiterated his conviction that the United States should join a league for the maintenance of peace.[19]

In late 1916 and early 1917, the league movement began to win official sanction in Great Britain as well as in the United States. In the autumn of 1916, Lord Robert Cecil submitted to the Cabinet a memorandum on plans to prevent the recurrence of war. The essence of the plan was a proposed requirement of obligatory consultations between parties to a dispute before resorting to war, a requirement conceived with reference to the efforts of Sir Edward Grey in 1914. Cecil regarded this scheme as the "earliest British germ of the Covenant."[20] The first official acceptance by the Entente Powers of the project for a league of nations came in the Allied reply of January 11, 1917, to President Wilson's peace proposal of the previous month.[21] Though thus committed to the league, Balfour, who had replaced Grey as Foreign Secretary when Lloyd George's cabinet was formed in 1916, was as reluctant as President Wilson to formulate specific plans, although he encouraged private contacts between English and American league advocates.[22] Balfour granted a brief interview to Theodore Marburg during his mission to the United States in the spring of 1917 but refused any specific commitment to the program of the League to Enforce Peace.[23] General Smuts, in an address to the League of Nations Society in London on May 14, 1917, joined the league movement, declaring enthusiastic support for President Wilson's proposals. Smuts remained thereafter one of the leading proponents of the proposed league.[24]

[18] Taft to Marburg, June 6, 1916, Latané, ed., *Development of the League of Nations Idea*, Vol. 1, p. 123.

[19] Baker and Dodd, eds., *Public Papers, The New Democracy*, Vol. 2, pp. 360, 381-382.

[20] Viscount Cecil, *A Great Experiment* (New York: Oxford University Press, 1941), pp. 47, 353-357.

[21] See Chapter 1, Section 1.

[22] Balfour to Marburg, February 12, 1917, Latané, ed., *Development of the League of Nations Idea*, Vol. 1, pp. 268-269.

[23] Marburg to E. H. Short, May 18, 1917, *ibid.*, pp. 303-305.

[24] Sarah Gertrude Millin, *General Smuts* (2 Vols., London: Faber and Faber, Ltd., 1936), Vol. 2, pp. 82-86.

To a limited extent, the league of nations movement was fostered during the war by the experience of the Allied and Associated Powers with the functional international organs of wartime cooperation. The war provided the Allied and Associated Powers with much practical experience in dealing through international agencies with such problems as shipping, the maintenance of supplies of food and raw materials, and the coordination of military strategy. The Supreme War Council, for instance, under Marshal Foch, was virtually an international cabinet for the conduct of the war and it evolved into the Supreme Council of the Peace Conference.

The pivot of Anglo-American cooperation was the Allied Maritime Transport Council, constituted at British suggestion by the Inter-Allied Conference at Paris in November 1917 for the purpose of coordinating Allied tonnage allocations. This body, which sat in London, was composed of two representatives of ministerial rank from each of the four Great Powers. The Allied Maritime Transport Executive served as a permanent office and staff. The operation of the Allied Maritime Transport Council shifted gradually from cooperation by national representatives toward international administration. The association of the United States, though always somewhat tentative and provisional, had reached the point by the time of the Armistice where specific actions by the United States were frequently altered to comply with the proposals of the Council. Executive control of national shipping, however, remained with the member governments, and the Armistice came before the international principle could be fully realized. The Allied Maritime Transport Council influenced, coordinated, and supplemented national policies, but it remained an advisory rather than an executive body.[25]

The functional international organization of the war was confined to special tasks where cooperation was urgent and its promise as a nucleus for postwar international organization was not realized. President Wilson specifically opposed the conversion of the wartime machinery into organs of the league. He rejected as impracticable, for instance, a proposal by Theodore Marburg that

[25] J. A. Salter, *Allied Shipping Control* (Oxford: The Clarendon Press, 1921), pp. 151-155, 175-176, 231; Zimmern, *The League of Nations and the Rule of Law*, pp. 146-148; Howard P. Whidden, Jr., "Why Allied Unity Failed," *Foreign Policy Reports*, Vol. 18, No. 23 (February 15, 1943), p. 302.

steps be taken to develop the Supreme War Council into a "rudi-
mentary league of nations."[26] The British, with their affinity for
building upon existing institutions, were far more inclined to
utilize the wartime agencies as a nucleus of world organization
than was President Wilson, whose concern with the forging of
a "new order" directed his thoughts toward unformed schemes.
One British statesman, for example, extolled the functional approach as making internationalism "an instinctive necessity instead of an ideal program."[27] But the Covenant of the League of
Nations as it finally emerged was more the creature of American
idealism than of British empiricism.

II. *Proposals for the League of Nations and Early British and American Drafts of a Covenant, 1917-1918*

In late 1917 and early 1918, President Wilson promoted the *idea*
of a league for peace with ever increasing emphasis but firmly
resisted British proposals, both official and unofficial, for Anglo-
American cooperation in the formulation of a specific scheme.
Lord Robert Cecil suggested in September 1917 that commissions
be set up in England and America to study existing plans and
make further plans for a league of nations.[28] Wilson rejected this
proposal, fearing a premature crystallization of opinion. The
organization of peace, he believed, would have to be worked out
by democratic processes among the nations, and since these processes would inevitably involve many mutual accommodations, the
President wished to encourage public consideration of the problems and principles of international order but not to crystallize
public thought around specific blueprints which would almost
certainly have to undergo many alterations.[29] Early in 1918, Lord
Bryce proposed the creation of an Anglo-American committee to
"put the plan into a practicable definite shape. . . ."[30] Marburg

[26] Marburg to Wilson, August 6, 1918, Wilson to Marburg, August 8, 1918,
Latané, ed., *Development of the League of Nations Idea*, Vol. 2, pp. 504-506.
[27] Lord Eustace Percy to Wiseman, September 3, 1918, Sir William Wiseman Papers, Sterling Library, Yale University.
[28] Cecil to House, September 3, 1917, Seymour, ed., *Intimate Papers*, Vol. 4,
pp. 6-7.
[29] Bartlett, *The League to Enforce Peace*, p. 90.
[30] Bryce to Marburg, February 1, 1918, Latané, ed., *Development of the
League of Nations Idea*, Vol. 1, pp. 403-404.

forwarded this proposal to Wilson, who replied that while the principle was "easy to adhere to," the consideration of a formal constitution would arouse "all sorts of jealousies" which "ought not now to be added to other matters of delicacy."[31]

Both Wilson and Lloyd George included the league of nations in their war aims pronouncements of January 1918. The President strongly reinforced his advocacy of the principle of a league of nations in Point 14, which he was to make the very heart of his program. In his speech of January 5, 1918, Lloyd George included a general endorsement, albeit without great emphasis, of the principle of international organization.[32]

The first official British proposal, the Phillimore Report, was adopted by the War Cabinet in March 1918. The Phillimore plan was the product of a committee of three historians and three Foreign Office officials under the chairmanship of Lord Phillimore, an international lawyer and former Lord Justice of the Court of Appeal. The committee had been appointed by Lloyd George in January 1917 at the suggestion of Lord Robert Cecil.[33] The Phillimore Report, the first draft scheme of a league of nations prepared under official auspices, reviewed and rejected sixteenth and seventeenth century schemes of European confederation under a supranational authority and asserted the only feasible method of international organization to be "cooperation or possibly a treaty of alliance. . . ." The draft scheme contained four parts: Articles 1 and 2, dealing with the avoidance of war, provided for the submission of all disputes to arbitration or conciliation before resort to war, with all members becoming *ipso facto* at war with a violator; Articles 3 to 12 defined procedures for the pacific settlement of disputes; Articles 13 to 17 dealt with relations between members and nonmembers of the proposed alliance; Article 18 declared the convention of alliance to supersede all previous and inconsistent treaties.[34]

[31] Wilson to Marburg, March 8, 1918, *ibid.*, p. 415.

[32] See Chapter 1, Section v.

[33] David Lloyd George, *The Truth about the Peace Treaties* (2 Vols., London: Victor Gollancz, Ltd., 1938), Vol. 1, pp. 605-607; Cecil, *A Great Experiment*, pp. 60-61; Winkler, *The League of Nations Movement in Great Britain*, pp. 233-234.

[34] David Hunter Miller, *The Drafting of the Covenant* (2 Vols., New York, London: G. P. Putnam's Sons, 1928), Vol. 1, pp. 3-10, Vol. 2, pp. 3-6; Ray Stannard Baker, *Woodrow Wilson and World Settlement* (3 Vols., Garden

On the other side of the Atlantic, Wilson maintained his opposition to the formulation of specific plans for a league of nations. On the very day that the Phillimore Report was submitted to the British War Cabinet, he fulminated against the "folly of these League to Enforce Peace butters-in" for insisting upon an immediate discussion of a constitution for the league.[35] "My own conviction," Wilson wrote to House on March 22, "is that the administrative constitution of the League must *grow* and not be made; that we must begin with solemn covenants, covering mutual guarantees of political independence and territorial integrity . . . but that the method of carrying these mutual pledges out should be left to develop of itself, case by case. . . ."[36]

The Phillimore Report was transmitted to the Allied and Associated Governments. Cecil suggested that an Anglo-American exchange of views take place before the publication of the scheme. Wilson expressed the hope that it would not be published and House advised Cecil that for the present the United States was interested in considering only the general nature of the league.[37]

The French Government, too, was moving in this matter. A committee under Léon Bourgeois, appointed by the French Government in July 1917, reported a plan for the league on June 8, 1918. The French scheme, going far beyond the Phillimore Report, called for an International Council empowered to apply diplomatic, economic, and military sanctions. Military measures were to be applied through an international force.[38] The French plan, which more closely resembles the Charter of the United Nations than the final Covenant of the League, was opposed with equal

---

City, New York: Doubleday, Page and Company, 1922), Vol. 1, pp. 215-217, Vol. 3, pp. 67-68; Lloyd George, *The Truth about the Peace Treaties*, Vol. 1, pp. 608-609. See also Zimmern, *The League of Nations and the Rule of Law*, pp. 180-186.

[35] Wilson to House, March 20, 1918, Ray Stannard Baker, *Woodrow Wilson: Life and Letters* (8 Vols., Garden City, New York: Doubleday, Doran and Company, Inc., 1927-1939), Vol. 8, p. 38.

[36] Wilson to House, March 22, 1918, *ibid.*, p. 44; Seymour, ed., *Intimate Papers*, Vol. 4, p. 16.

[37] *ibid.*, p. 17; Lloyd George, *The Truth about the Peace Treaties*, Vol. 1, pp. 609-610.

[38] Miller, *The Drafting of the Covenant*, Vol. 1, pp. 10-11, Vol. 2, pp. 238-246; Lloyd George, *The Truth about the Peace Treaties*, Vol. 1, pp. 611-616. See also Zimmern, *The League of Nations and the Rule of Law*, pp. 187-188.

firmness in the League Commission of the Peace Conference by President Wilson and Lord Robert Cecil.[39]

Taking account of the British and French league plans put forth in 1918 as against Wilson's refusal to consider a specific constitution, Lloyd George in his memoirs assails the "unjust legend" that Wilson imposed the League of Nations on the unwilling Allies. The British and French alone, Lloyd George contends, labored for practical plans during the war, and "the Covenant was in substance the outcome of their joint efforts."[40] The facts on which Lloyd George bases his assertion of substantial Anglo-French responsibility for the Covenant are unassailable. The assertion itself, however, is unsound. Wilson's title to the fatherhood of the League rests not on creation but on the influence of his advocacy, on the fact that of the most convinced believers in the idea of a peaceful community of nations, he was by far the most politically influential, and that of the influential statesmen of his day, he was the most ardent and effective protagonist of the league ideal.[41]

By the summer of 1918, President Wilson was ready to consider the drafting of a constitution for a league of nations. On July 8, he asked House to undertake a revision of the Phillimore draft. With the assistance of David Hunter Miller and the advice of Sir William Wiseman, House drew up a scheme on July 13 and 14.[42] In his letter of transmission to Wilson, House explained that his plan had been drafted without reference to the Phillimore plan but that he had then compared the two documents and incorporated several of the Phillimore articles into his own scheme.[43]

The House draft was elaborate and detailed. The first three articles, which House considered to be the "keystone of the arch," laid down principles of national honor and ethics. Article 5, which declared any war or threat of war to be "a matter of concern to the League of Nations, and to the Powers members thereof," became the core of Article 11 of the final Covenant. Article 10 provided for an international court with jurisdiction over disputes relating

---

[39] See Section VI below.

[40] Lloyd George, *The Truth about the Peace Treaties*, Vol. 1, p. 635.

[41] See William E. Rappard, *The Quest for Peace* (Cambridge: Harvard University Press, 1940), p. 59.

[42] Seymour, ed., *Intimate Papers*, Vol. 4, pp. 21-23.

[43] House to Wilson, July 14, 1918, *ibid.*, pp. 24-25; Baker, *Wilson: Life and Letters*, Vol. 8, p. 279.

to treaties, Article 13 for compulsory arbitration of all other disputes not settled by diplomacy. Article 14 provided for economic sanctions and Article 15 for measures of blockade against violators of awards under Articles 10 and 13. Article 20 provided for a mutual guarantee of territorial integrity and political independence, subject to a defined procedure of peaceful change in the face of altered conditions. Although it added to the Phillimore plan the mutual guarantee article while retaining the requirement of compulsory arbitration, the House plan eliminated the provision for *ipso facto* war against a violator, providing for blockade as the strongest sanction.[44]

Cecil raised certain objections to the House plan. He wrote to House commending it but he questioned the efficacy of the code of ethics, insisting that "some form of coercion" was needed. Cecil opposed the mutual guarantee of territorial integrity, asserting that the sanctity of treaties should be guaranteed, but not territory as such.[45] House forwarded Cecil's letter to Wilson with the observation, apparently about Cecil's opposition to the mutual guarantee, that Cecil's proposals would "make the League an innocuous affair and leave the world where it is now. . . ."[46]

Wilson himself worked over the House draft and made major revisions. He struck out the proposed international court and restored military force as a sanction in addition to economic measures and blockade. Wilson retained the qualified mutual guarantee of political independence and territorial integrity.[47]

Wilson conferred with Wiseman and House on the league in mid-August at the latter's home in Magnolia, Massachusetts. The President explained his alterations of the House draft and in a

[44] Miller, *The Drafting of the Covenant*, Vol. 1, pp. 12-15, Vol. 2, pp. 7-11; Seymour, ed., *Intimate Papers*, Vol. 4, pp. 28-35; Baker, *Wilson and World Settlement*, Vol. 1, pp. 218-222, Vol. 3, pp. 81-87; Department of State, *Papers Relating to the Foreign Relations of the United States, 1919, The Paris Peace Conference* (13 Vols., Washington: United States Government Printing Office, 1942-1947), Vol. 1, pp. 497-501; hereafter referred to as *Foreign Relations*. See also Zimmern, *The League of Nations and the Rule of Law*, pp. 221-230.
[45] Cecil to House, July 22, 1918, Seymour, ed., *Intimate Papers*, Vol. 4, pp. 39-42.
[46] House to Wilson, August 9, 1918, Baker, *Wilson: Life and Letters*, Vol. 8, p. 328.
[47] Miller, *The Drafting of the Covenant*, Vol. 1, pp. 15-17, Vol. 2, pp. 12-15; Baker, *Wilson and World Settlement*, Vol. 1, pp. 222-223, Vol. 3, pp. 88-93; *Foreign Relations, 1919, The Paris Peace Conference*, Vol. 1, pp. 501-505.

long private conversation with Wiseman expressed dissatisfaction with the Phillimore plan. "It has no teeth," he said. "I read it to the last page hoping to find something definite but I could not." Wilson also reiterated his opposition to public discussion of a specific scheme, which he thought would aggravate anti-British feeling in the United States, and refused to consider the appointment of a joint Anglo-American committee, although he was quite willing, he said, to discuss the league with any representative whom the British Government might choose to send.[48] At Wilson's request, Wiseman cabled the Foreign Office advising that the Phillimore plan not be published.[49] Lord Robert Cecil reluctantly deferred to the President's wish and agreed not to publish the Phillimore Report, expressing doubt, however, as to whether the President "realizes the immense difficulties there will be in the way of establishing a league of nations."[50] Wilson remained confirmed in his decision not to focus public attention on a specific plan until the end of the war.

III. *Pre-Conference Ideas and Proposals, November-December 1918*

President Wilson was preoccupied in the autumn of 1918 with the immediate problems of the ending of the war and the negotiation of the Armistice. He formulated no further specific league proposals before going to Paris. In the British Empire, however, significant ideas and proposals were formulated during this period, the most important being the "Practical Suggestion" of General Smuts in December 1918.

The British Foreign Office produced a memorandum in November embodying its conception of a league of nations. The focus of the plan was a conference system inspired by the experience of the Supreme War Council and the British Imperial Conference, a "standing interstate Conference" of Great Powers with a permanent secretariat. The proposal called for a general guarantee of peace, prohibiting resort to war even after the use of

[48] Wiseman to Lord Reading, August 16, 1918, Wiseman Papers.
[49] Seymour, ed., *Intimate Papers*, Vol. 4, pp. 48-50, 52-54; Sir Arthur Willert, *The Road to Safety* (London: Derek Verschoyle, Ltd., 1952), pp. 151-153.
[50] Cecil to Wiseman, conveyed to Wilson by House, September 13, 1918, Baker, *Wilson: Life and Letters*, Vol. 8, p. 399.

procedures of peaceful settlement, but no specific guarantee of political independence and territorial integrity. The plan seems in essence to have meant an improved Concert system, reflecting the impact on British thought of Sir Edward Grey's unsuccessful attempt to invoke the unstructured Concert of Europe in 1914. Cecil used this memorandum as the basis of his own subsequent proposals, omitting, however, the guarantee of peace.[51]

Both British and American officials rejected the French proposal for an international force and general staff. Sir Eyre Crowe and Sir William Tyrrell, consulting on the league with David Hunter Miller, dismissed the French scheme as fantastic.[52] Henry White, after a confidential talk with Wilson and Lansing aboard the "George Washington," assured Senator Lodge that Wilson would not assent to "any organization of that league whereby our army and navy would be placed under the orders of a combination of powers, or any orders but our own."[53]

On December 16, 1918, General Smuts issued a treatise entitled "The League of Nations: A Practical Suggestion," which contained a significant new plan for a league of nations. Smuts conceived of the league as more than an instrument for the punishment of aggression. It was to be the successor to the shattered old order of Europe, an "ever visible working organ of the polity of civilization." The league, in Smuts's view, would also form the basis of a binding link between the United States and the British Empire. It would "bring America to our side in the policies of the future. . . ."[54]

The Smuts plan was an extensive revision of the Phillimore proposal, reinforcing the idea of the Foreign Office memorandum of November that the league was to be not a superstate but a permanent conference of independent states. Article 1 set forth the proposition, highly congenial to President Wilson, that the establishment of the league was the primary and basic task of the Peace

[51] Zimmern, *The League of Nations and the Rule of Law*, pp. 191-209. Concerning the Cecil plan, see Chapter 4, Section IV below.

[52] David Hunter Miller, *My Diary at the Conference of Paris*, privately printed (21 Vols., New York: Appeal Printing Company, 1924), Vol. 1, p. 33.

[53] White to Lodge, December 24, 1918, Allan Nevins, *Henry White: Thirty Years of American Diplomacy* (New York and London: Harper & Brothers, Publishers, 1930), pp. 361-362.

[54] Millin, *General Smuts*, Vol. 2, pp. 168-171.

Conference. Articles 2 to 9 were devoted to the elaboration of the mandate principle.[55] Articles 10 to 14, dealing with the organization and constitution of the league, called for the creation of a "General Conference" and an "Executive Committee" composed of the Great Powers and a rotating panel of small states. Articles 15 to 17, concerned with disarmament, provided for the abolition of conscription and the nationalization of munitions industries. Articles 18 to 21, dealing with the settlement of disputes, were directly taken over from the Phillimore plan. The Smuts plan omitted the guarantee of peace of the Foreign Office memorandum, leaving open, like the Phillimore plan, a gap for war after the exhaustion of procedures of inquiry and delay. Nor did the plan contain the mutual guarantee of political independence and territorial integrity of the House and Wilson drafts.[56]

A critical memorandum on the Smuts plan was submitted to the American delegation at the Peace Conference by David Hunter Miller and James Brown Scott. The preoccupation of the plan with Europe and its application of the mandates clauses to Russian territories were criticized, the latter as implying massive intervention in Russia. The powers of the "Executive Committee" were held to be too loosely defined and the failure to mention navies in the disarmament clauses was criticized. Finally, it was contended that the provision for *ipso facto* war against a violator of procedures of peaceful settlement was, under the United States Constitution, incompatible with the sole power of Congress to declare war.[57]

A memorandum submitted to President Wilson by Secretary of State Lansing on December 23 had also contested the constitutionality and the wisdom of the binding obligation to use force contained in the British drafts. Lansing recommended that all sanctions involving force and the mutual guarantee, which he held to be meaningless without coercion, be removed. He sub-

[55] See Chapter 3, Section III.
[56] Miller, *The Drafting of the Covenant*, Vol. 1, pp. 34-37, Vol. 2, pp. 23-60. See also Zimmern, *The League of Nations and the Rule of Law*, pp. 210-215; Millin, *General Smuts*, Vol. 2, pp. 179-187; J. C. Smuts, *Jan Christian Smuts* (New York: William Morrow and Company, Inc., 1952), pp. 196-201; Lloyd George, *The Truth about the Peace Treaties*, Vol. 1, pp. 619-628.
[57] "Summary Observations on the Smuts Memorandum of December 16, 1918," by D. H. Miller and J. B. Scott, January 13, 1919, Miller, *Diary*, Vol. 3, pp. 239-240.

mitted draft clauses calling for a simple negative obligation on the part of league members *not* to violate the political independence or territorial integrity of other states. The strongest sanction against violators, under the Lansing scheme, would be a breach of relations. Lansing received no reply or acknowledgment from the President for the memorandum of December 23.[58] The Lansing plan, sharply at variance with the main stream of both British and American thinking, was never seriously considered by the framers of the Covenant.

The Imperial War Cabinet met on the eve of Christmas 1918 to review the position of the British Empire in regard to proposals for a league of nations. Lloyd George and others emphasized the central importance of provisions for disarmament, without which, in their view, the league would be a sham. Lloyd George further suggested the utility of such organs as the Supreme War Council and the Imperial War Cabinet itself as models for the structure of the proposed organization. Of the entire Cabinet, only Prime Minister Hughes of Australia indicated basic distrust of the league idea.[59] House reported to Wilson that the British Cabinet was prepared to support him on the league "almost to the extent of letting you write the covenants of it yourself."[60]

On the eve of the Paris Peace Conference, British and American thought was significantly focused on the project for a league of nations. British concepts were largely conditioned by the events of the past, especially the events of July 1914 when the unstructured Concert of Europe had disintegrated, and by the practical experience of the Allied and Associated Powers with the machinery of wartime cooperation. American thought, dominated by President Wilson, was more oriented to the *principles* of world organization than to specific schemes and precedents. The constitution of a league of peace, Wilson believed, could be drafted only when the principles of justice on which it was to rest were established and accepted as a moral frame of reference for a new order of international relations. The difference between the British and American approaches to the league idea turned out to be secondary

---

[58] Robert Lansing, *The Peace Negotiations* (Boston and New York: Houghton Mifflin Company, 1921), pp. 50-54, 58-62, 67-68.

[59] Lloyd George, *The Truth about the Peace Treaties*, Vol. I, pp. 628-635.

[60] House to Wilson, December 25, 1918, Woodrow Wilson Papers, Library of Congress, Washington, D.C., Series 8-A.

in importance to the basic unity of purpose of the two great democracies. The Covenant drawn up at Paris in 1919 was in its essence a practical synthesis of Anglo-American ideas for a new world order.

IV. *Anglo-American Drafts and Negotiations and the Unification of Policy, January 1919*

President Wilson's second draft covenant, or first Paris draft, was completed on January 10. It contained significant changes from his first draft, based largely on the Smuts plan of December 16, 1918, with which he had been greatly impressed. Smuts's plan for a Council, or "Executive Committee," appeared as Article 2 of Wilson's new draft, his plan for the abolition of conscription as Article 4. The greatest changes from Wilson's draft of the previous summer were in the methods of settlement of disputes. Abandoning his original scheme for general obligatory arbitration, Wilson now adopted as Articles 5 and 6 the provisions of Articles 18 to 21 of the Smuts plan, providing for the reference of Council disputes either to arbitration or to the Council and the sanction of *ipso facto* war against violators of this procedure. These provisions, in fact, derived from the Phillimore plan. Wilson added to his plan a series of "Supplementary Agreements," several constituting an adaptation of Smuts's mandates system and others dealing with humane conditions of labor and equality of treatment for racial and national minorities. The plan retained as Article 3 the mutual guarantee of political independence and territorial integrity of Wilson's earlier draft.[61]

President Wilson's first Paris draft was not well received by his American colleagues. David Hunter Miller pronounced it "very poor" and, apparently with reference to the sanction of *ipso facto* war, clearly unconstitutional.[62] In a detailed commentary, Miller averred that the plan unconsciously adopted the British Empire point of view, "which looks for protection by the United States against the future without a thought of changing or improving the past." Miller feared also that the abolition of conscription

[61] Miller, *The Drafting of the Covenant*, Vol. 1, p. 40, Vol. 2, pp. 65-93; Baker, *Woodrow Wilson and World Settlement*, Vol. 1, pp. 225-229, Vol. 3, pp. 94-110. See also Seymour, ed., *Intimate Papers*, Vol. 4, pp. 286-287.
[62] Miller's Diary, January 11, 1919, Miller, *Diary*, Vol. 1, p. 72.

would leave the British fleet supreme in the world.[63] Secretary Lansing thought the President's plan "entirely out of harmony with American ideals, policies, and traditions." Lansing specifically objected to the potential use of force to back the mutual guarantee and to the primacy of the Great Powers which he considered to be implicit in the plan.[64]

The outstanding English contributor to the drafting of the Covenant was Lord Robert Cecil, who was the special adviser to the British delegation on questions relating to the league of nations. Through the month of January he worked over the various draft covenants and engaged in frequent consultations with Wilson, House, and Miller. On January 14, Cecil put forth a draft of his own based substantially on the Phillimore plan. The chief innovation of Cecil's plan was its limitation of membership in the Council to Great Powers, eliminating the minority of small power members provided for in the Smuts proposal.[65]

President Wilson's second Paris draft was completed on January 20. It incorporated certain changes proposed by General Bliss in a memorandum submitted on January 14,[66] including a stipulation that the mutual guarantee of Article 3 would apply "as against external aggression." In deference to Miller's assertion that a commitment to war *ipso facto* by the United States would be an unconstitutional incursion upon the power of Congress to declare war, Article 6 of the first Paris draft was altered in the second to read that a Covenant-breaking state "shall thereby *ipso facto* be deemed to have committed an act of war against all the members of the League. . . ." Several new "Supplementary Agreements" were added, including a pledge against religious discrimination, an affirmation of the principle of freedom of the seas, a declaration against secret treaties, and a prohibition of economic discrimination.[67]

---

[63] Miller's Comment on Wilson's First Paris Draft, January 14, 1919, Miller, *Diary*, Vol. 3, pp. 258-261.

[64] Robert Lansing, *The Peace Negotiations* (Boston and New York: Houghton Mifflin Company, 1921), pp. 81-82.

[65] Miller, *The Drafting of the Covenant*, Vol. 1, p. 38, Vol. 2, pp. 61-64.

[66] *ibid.*, Vol. 2, pp. 94-97; Baker, *Wilson and World Settlement*, Vol. 3, pp. 111-116.

[67] Miller, *The Drafting of the Covenant*, Vol. 1, pp. 48-50, Vol. 2, pp. 98-105. Baker omits the text of this draft, confusing it with Wilson's third Paris draft, which he reproduces. Baker, *Wilson and World Settlement*, Vol. 3, pp. 117-129.

Neither the Smuts plan nor the Cecil proposal of January 14 was, strictly, an official proposal of the British Government. On the same day that Wilson completed his second Paris draft, Cecil released the official British draft. As in Cecil's draft of the 14th, the Council was to consist only of Great Powers. The draft provided for separate representation in the league for the Dominions and India. The provisions for peaceful settlement of disputes were essentially those of the Phillimore plan, which had also been adopted in the Smuts plan and the two Paris drafts of President Wilson, and the sanctions of economic boycott, blockade, and *ipso facto* war were as in the Phillimore plan. A new proposal in the Cecil plan (one which Wilson had stricken from Colonel House's plan of the previous summer) was for the establishment of a permanent court of international justice. Cecil adopted Wilson's guarantee of territorial integrity in altered terms, omitting the guarantee of political independence and providing for recommendations of peaceful change by the league, the rejection of which by the parties concerned would release the other members from the obligation of guarantee.[68]

The Cecil and Wilson drafts of January 20 were in most respects similar and an attempt was immediately undertaken to formulate a single Anglo-American draft. Colonel House being ill, David Hunter Miller began discussions with Lord Robert Cecil on January 21 at the Hotel Majestic, the headquarters of the British delegation.[69] Miller criticized two features of the British draft. First, he feared that the provision authorizing the league to recommend boundary changes would tend to legalize dangerous agitations in Eastern Europe. Cecil maintained that treaties should not be made immutable and a general provision for the periodic revision of treaties was agreed upon. Secondly, Miller objected to the advance commitment to *ipso facto* war and Cecil agreed to its replacement by the wording of Article 6 of Wilson's draft of January 20. Cecil, in turn, objected to Wilson's inclusion of small powers on the Council, contending that a league, to be effective, would have to be run by the Great Powers. Cecil argued further

[68] Miller, *The Drafting of the Covenant*, Vol. 1, pp. 50-52, Vol. 2, pp. 106-116; Baker, *Wilson and World Settlement*, Vol. 1, pp. 231-232, Vol. 3, pp. 130-143.

[69] Seymour, ed., *Intimate Papers*, Vol. 4, pp. 287-288; Miller, *The Drafting of the Covenant*, Vol. 1, p. 52.

for the separate representation in the League of the Dominions.[70]

Meanwhile, President Wilson acted to secure the inclusion of the league as an integral part of the treaty of peace. Cecil readily lent his support and prepared a resolution for the Plenary Session, which Wilson endorsed.[71] Cecil's draft resolution, calling for the creation of a league of nations as an "integral part of the general treaty of peace" and the appointment of a committee to draft a constitution, was endorsed by the Council of Ten on January 22. Over the opposition of President Wilson, who feared that a large committee would be unmanageable, Lloyd George and Clemenceau successfully insisted that the resolution provide for small power representation on the League Commission.[72] Wilson accepted this condition readily enough. There is no evidence that Lloyd George and Clemenceau, as charged by Ray Stannard Baker,[73] were engaged in a plot to relegate the league to an unwieldy commission packed with small powers.

President Wilson introduced the league resolution to the Plenary Session of January 25. "Settlements may be temporary," said the President in his speech, "but the actions of the nations in the interests of peace and justice must be permanent. We can set up permanent processes." The league, he declared, would be the "keystone of the arch." Lloyd George rose to second the resolution, stating "how emphatically the people of the British Empire are behind this proposal." Other speeches of endorsement were made and the resolution making the League of Nations an "integral part of the general treaty of peace" and establishing the League of Nations Commission was unanimously adopted.[74]

On January 27, Miller, having reviewed all the British proposals and incorporated some of their provisions into Wilson's second Paris draft, conferred at length with Cecil. They came to agreement on all but a few questions, notably Wilson's freedom

[70] ibid., pp. 52-55; Miller's Diary, January 21, 24-25, 1919, Miller, Diary, Vol. 1, pp. 86-87, 89-91.

[71] Seymour, ed., Intimate Papers, Vol. 4, pp. 289-290.

[72] Council of Ten, January 22, 1919, 3 p.m., Foreign Relations, 1919, The Paris Peace Conference, Vol. 3, pp. 677-682.

[73] Baker, Wilson and World Settlement, Vol. 1, p. 242.

[74] Second Plenary Session, January 25, 1919, Foreign Relations, 1919, The Paris Peace Conference, Vol. 3, pp. 178-187, 201; Miller, The Drafting of the Covenant, Vol. 2, pp. 156-164; Baker, Wilson and World Settlement, Vol. 1, pp. 239-248; Seymour, ed., Intimate Papers, Vol. 4, pp. 290-291.

of the seas and economic equality clauses and Cecil's proposal for an international court of justice, which were reserved. This Cecil-Miller draft, a revision of the President's, contained two significant concessions to the British: separate representation of the Dominions in the League and a Council limited to Great Powers and only such others as they might choose to add.[75]

President Wilson, House, Miller, Cecil, and Smuts convened at the Hotel Crillon on the evening of January 31 and engaged in a candid general discussion of the differences between Wilson's second Paris draft and the British draft of January 20. Wilson agreed to Dominion representation and, dropping at last his curious antilegalism, to Cecil's proposal for an international court. The issue of small power representation in the Council was not discussed at this meeting. It was agreed that Miller would meet on the next day with the British legal adviser, Cecil Hurst, to formulate a single Anglo-American draft, referring any questions found impossible of adjustment to Cecil and House.[76]

Meeting on February 1 and 2, Miller and Hurst produced a draft which was a synthesis of elements from Wilson's second Paris draft, the official British draft, the Cecil-Miller draft, and the agreements reached in the open discussion of the evening of January 31. Articles 1 to 5 of the Hurst-Miller draft defined the structure of an Assembly and a Council of Great Powers. Article 7 provided for an unqualified guarantee of territorial integrity and political independence, dropping, at Hurst's suggestion, the qualification for alterations of the *status quo*. This article was ultimately adopted without change as Article 10 of the Covenant. Article 12 provided for the establishment of a permanent court of international justice. Article 14 defined sanctions, including force, adopting the wording of Wilson's draft of January 20 defining a breach of covenant as an *ipso facto* act of war against all members of the League. Article 17 defined mandates. The freedom of the seas and certain other proposals which had been reserved in the Cecil-Miller draft were dropped.[77]

[75] Miller, *The Drafting of the Covenant*, Vol. 1, pp. 55-57, 61-64, Vol. 2, pp. 131-141.

[76] *ibid.*, Vol. 1, pp. 65-67; House Diary, January 31, 1919, Seymour, ed., *Intimate Papers*, Vol. 4, pp. 299-300.

[77] Miller, *The Drafting of the Covenant*, Vol. 1, pp. 67-71, Vol. 2, pp. 231-237; Baker, *Wilson and World Settlement*, Vol. 3, pp. 144-151.

Miller delivered the new draft to House on February 2. Wilson and House went over it and the President was dissatisfied, objecting that too much had been taken out. The President asked House and Miller to recast his own second Paris draft with some adaptations from the Hurst-Miller draft.[78]

President Wilson's third Paris draft was completed on February 3. It reverted to a Council including small powers and made other less important changes in the Hurst-Miller draft. Wilson accepted in this draft the dropping of the qualification from the mutual guarantee article as in the Hurst-Miller draft. The President now proposed that this, rather than the Hurst-Miller draft, serve as the basis of discussion in the Commission on the League of Nations.[79]

On the morning of February 3, the day of the first meeting of the League Commission, Cecil received the message that Wilson had decided to scrap the Hurst-Miller draft and present his own plan. Greatly disturbed, Cecil feared that Wilson aspired to dictate a covenant to the Commission.[80] Wiseman called House and informed him of Cecil's agitation. House thereupon telephoned the President and warned him that it would be a mistake to alienate Cecil, who more than anyone else in the British Government was devoted to the League of Nations. Cecil hurried over to the Hotel Crillon and Wilson, Cecil, and House met in the latter's study before the Commission met. Under the importunities of Cecil and House, the President yielded, agreeing to the Hurst-Miller draft as the basis of discussion.[81] House sent Miller in haste to obtain copies of the Hurst-Miller draft, and when he returned, the President asked him to distribute them to the members of the Commission.[82] In agreeing to the Hurst-Miller draft at the last moment, Wilson was making a sacrifice that hurt. Clearly, he recognized that Lord Robert Cecil was an ally to be valued.

Anglo-American differences over the Covenant of the League

[78] Seymour, ed., *Intimate Papers*, Vol. 4, pp. 300-301; Miller's Diary, February 2, 1919, Miller, *Diary*, Vol. 1, p. 105.
[79] Miller, *The Drafting of the Covenant*, Vol. 1, pp. 72-74, Vol. 2, pp. 145-154; Baker, *Wilson and World Settlement*, Vol. 3, pp. 117-129; Seymour, ed., *Intimate Papers*, Vol. 4, p. 301.
[80] Cecil, *A Great Experiment*, p. 69.
[81] House Diary, February 3, 1919, Seymour, ed., *Intimate Papers*, Vol. 4, pp. 302-303; Cecil, *A Great Experiment*, p. 69.
[82] Miller's Diary, February 3, 1919, Miller, *Diary*, Vol. 1, p. 106.

of Nations were thus accommodated before the League Commission ever convened. The month of January was a period of extremely close and frank collaboration between equally dedicated British and American officials. Aside from the small imbroglio over the Hurst-Miller draft, the relatively minor differences between the British and American drafts were adjusted in an atmosphere of common purpose and personal harmony.

V. *Anglo-American Issues in the League of Nations Commission, February 3-11, 1919*

The further refinement of the Covenant of the League of Nations was also essentially an Anglo-American project. The proceedings of the League Commission were for the most part dominated by the British and American representatives, perhaps because to them above all others it seemed that the guarantee rather than the items of the peace was the central issue of the Peace Conference. The French played a conspicuous but decidedly secondary role in the drafting of the Covenant, securing in the final Covenant only one of their major proposals, the military advisory committee of Article 9.

The League Commission operated with exemplary speed and efficiency. Ten meetings were held over a period of eleven days. Starting with fifteen members, the Commission was increased to nineteen as of the fourth meeting without impairment to the smoothness of its proceedings. Within the broader harmony was the nucleus of Anglo-American cooperation. Sitting to the left of President Wilson, who presided, were House and then Cecil and Smuts, with whom Wilson and House frequently consulted. The meetings were greatly dominated by the President, and second to him in influence was Cecil. To Wilson, these proceedings were the most congenial of his tasks at the Peace Conference, calling for the capacities which he clearly had—clarity of thought, imagination, courage, and persuasive rhetoric.

At the first meeting of the League Commission, agreement was readily secured to use the Hurst-Miller draft as the basis of discussion although the French and Italians introduced plans of their own.[83]

---

[83] League of Nations Commission, First Meeting, February 3, 1919, 2:30 p.m., Miller, *The Drafting of the Covenant*, Vol. 2, p. 231. The English minutes of all of the meetings are reproduced *ibid.*, as Document 19, pp. 229-394. A useful

Attention focused in the second and third meetings on Article 3 of the Hurst-Miller draft, which provided for a Council of Great Powers. Almost all of the representatives demanded small power representation, which, though included in all of Wilson's drafts, had been stricken from the Hurst-Miller draft in deference to Cecil. Confronted with almost unanimous opposition, Cecil yielded, agreeing to consider a redraft of the article at the next meeting.[84] An informal gathering in Colonel House's offices on the morning of February 5 agreed to a redraft calling for two small powers on the Council.[85] In the Commission meeting that evening, Cecil staunchly resisted the demand for more than two small powers, and Wilson supported him to the extent of assuring the small powers that they would derive full protection from the mutual guarantee provision even though they had only two representatives on the Council. Agreement was reached on a new draft of the article on small power representation, but the number of small power representatives was left open.[86] The number was finally fixed at four, leaving the Great Powers a majority of one.[87]

Article 6 of the Hurst-Miller draft, which defined conditions of admission to the League, was accepted at the meeting of February 5. President Wilson was somewhat dubious about India but agreed to its eligibility along with the Dominions.[88] "No one seems to have thought," wrote House in his diary, "that the British in a general conference of the League of Nations will have six votes. . . . As far as I am concerned, I shall not bring it up. . . .

---

breakdown of the Covenant, with relevant extracts from the minutes attached to each article, may be found in Florence Wilson, *The Origins of the League Covenant* (London: The Hogarth Press, 1928), pp. 17-107.

[84] League Commission, Second Meeting, February 4, 1919, 8:30 p.m., Miller, *The Drafting of the Covenant*, Vol. 2, pp. 257-258. See also *ibid.*, Vol. 1, pp. 137-138; Stephen Bonsal, *Unfinished Business* (Garden City, New York: Doubleday, Doran and Company, Inc., 1944), p. 25.

[85] Miller, *The Drafting of the Covenant*, Vol. 1, p. 154.

[86] League of Nations Commission, Third Meeting, February 5, 1919, 8:30 p.m., Miller, *The Drafting of the Covenant*, Vol. 2, pp. 259-260. See also *ibid.*, Vol. 1, pp. 160-163; Bonsal, *Unfinished Business*, p. 26.

[87] League of Nations Commission, Ninth Meeting, February 13, 1919, 10:30 a.m., Miller, *The Drafting of the Covenant*, Vol. 2, pp. 301-302.

[88] League of Nations Commission, Third Meeting, February 5, 1919, 8:30 p.m., *ibid.*, Vol. 1, pp. 164-167.

If Great Britain can stand giving her Dominions representation in the League, no one should object."[89]

At its fourth meeting, the Commission considered Article 7 of the Hurst-Miller draft, which became Article 10 of the Covenant, and which to President Wilson was the very heart of the League system. Article 7 of the Hurst-Miller draft read: "The High Contracting Parties undertake to respect and preserve as against external aggression the territorial integrity and existing political independence of all States members of the League." At President Wilson's suggestion, a clause was added providing that the Council would "advise the plan and the means by which this obligation shall be fulfilled." Cecil was opposed to the guarantee and proposed to reduce the article to innocuousness by striking the clause: "and preserve as against external aggression." He also favored a provision allowing for periodical revisions of international obligations, which had been stricken from the draft at the behest of Cecil Hurst. With the support of Premier Orlando of Italy, Wilson insisted upon the guarantee and the article was accepted. Cecil's proposal for a provision for periodic revisions led ultimately to the insertion of Article 19, the "peaceful change" article, into the final Covenant. Several other articles were adopted without significant controversy at this meeting, including the ultimate Article 11 deeming any war to be a matter of concern to the League and its members, and the article, so dear to Cecil, providing for the establishment of a permanent court of international justice.[90]

The difference between Wilson and Cecil over the ultimate Article 10 was not sharp but it suggests a significant difference in emphasis between Great Britain and the United States as to the basic operating principles of the Covenant. Cecil thought that the mutual guarantee "seemed to crystallize for all time the actual position which then existed" and agreed to it only in connection with the provisions for peaceful change of the ultimate Article 19.[91] To President Wilson, Article 10 was a guarantee of the

[89] House Diary, February 5, 1919, Seymour, ed., *Intimate Papers*, Vol. 4, pp. 311-312.

[90] League of Nations Commission, Fourth Meeting, February 6, 1919, 8:30 p.m., Miller, *The Drafting of the Covenant*, Vol. 2, pp. 264-268, Vol. 1, pp. 169-170.

[91] Cecil, *A Great Experiment*, pp. 77, 96.

"land titles of the world," indispensable to an ordered society of mankind.[92] Article 10, said the President, was the "backbone of the whole Covenant," without which the League would be "hardly more than an influential debating society."[93] The article, in short, represented the guarantee which is the *sine qua non* of any valid system of collective security, an obligation inherent in membership, flowing directly from the Covenant, and not dependent upon the decisions of any organ of the League.

The British delegates on February 7 suggested certain amendments to the Hurst-Miller draft, including a proposed new article which read: "The Body of Delegates shall make provision for the periodic revision of treaties which have become obsolete and of international conditions, the continuance of which may endanger the peace of the world."[94] Miller urged that it be made explicit that such action for revision of treaties would be only by recommendation, since a binding decision made by the League, even by unanimous vote, would be unconstitutional for the United States.[95] Accordingly, in the meeting of the League Commission on February 11, President Wilson proposed a new wording of the British amendment: "It shall be the right of the Body of Delegates from time to time to advise the reconsideration by the States, members of the League, of treaties which have become inapplicable, and of international conditions, the continuance of which may endanger the peace of the world." This greatly watered-down substitute was adopted and, in slightly revised form, became Article 19 of the final Covenant.[96]

The League of Nations was thus endowed with purely hortatory powers to encourage peaceful change, leaving a premium on the guarantee of the *status quo* implicit in Article 10. The British draft article, though ostensibly stronger, in fact would have given

[92] Speech at Coeur d'Alene, Idaho, September 12, 1919, Baker and Dodd, eds., *The Public Papers of Woodrow Wilson, War and Peace*, Vol. 2, p. 141.

[93] Report of the Conference between Members of the Senate Committee on Foreign Relations and the President of the United States, at the White House, August 19, 1919, *Treaty of Peace with Germany*, 66th Congress, First Session, Senate, Document No. 76 (Washington: United States Government Printing Office, 1919), p. 6.

[94] Miller, *The Drafting of the Covenant*, Vol. 2, p. 556.

[95] Memorandum of February 9, 1919, for Colonel House, Miller, *Diary*, Vol. 5, pp. 196-197.

[96] League of Nations Commission, Eighth Meeting, February 11, 1919, 10:30 a.m., Miller, *The Drafting of the Covenant*, Vol. 2, pp. 288-289.

the League no power to compel peaceful change because of the requirement of unanimity in the Assembly. The substitution of Wilson's draft was designed merely to render the article compatible with the American Constitution. Article 19 was undoubtedly an extremely weak vehicle for peaceful change and the League itself has been much criticized as an instrument wedded to the *status quo*. It can be argued, however, that law itself, with its preservatory function, is wedded to the *status quo*, and that the Covenant was no more so than is any legal instrumentality by its very nature. The drafting of Articles 10 and 19 constituted an honest Anglo-American effort to devise the best possible synthesis of stability and orderly change that the circumstances of the time would allow.[97]

The Articles dealing with settlement of disputes by the League Council and the application of sanctions (Articles 15 and 16 of the final Covenant) were adopted by the League of Nations Commission without serious controversy. Wilson and Cecil successfully resisted a Belgian-French proposal that members be bound not to go to war against a state complying with the recommendations of a *majority* of the Council as to a dispute. Article 15 of the Covenant thus retained the Hurst-Miller provision that such recommendations, to be binding, must be reported by a unanimous vote of Council, except for the parties to the dispute.[98]

The provisions for settlement of disputes, contained in Articles 12 to 16 of the final Covenant, were essentially of British inspiration, deriving from the Phillimore Report. The objective, inspired largely by the conviction of Sir Edward Grey that the existence of obligatory machinery of consultation might have prevented war in 1914, was to enforce *delay* and an *attempt* at peaceful settlement before resort to war. The restriction of enforcement of Council recommendations to an obligation not to go to war with a party complying with a unanimous report was based on the British conviction, shared by the United States, that it was

[97] For a good brief discussion of the drafting of Article 19, much more critical than the view herein set forth, see Lincoln P. Bloomfield, *Evolution or Revolution* (Cambridge: Harvard University Press, 1957), pp. 23-31.

[98] League of Nations Commission, Fifth Meeting, February 7, 1919, 8:30 p.m., Miller, *The Drafting of the Covenant*, Vol. 2, pp. 269-270; Eighth Meeting, February 10, 1919, 10:30 a.m., *ibid.*, p. 282. See also *ibid.*, Vol. 1, pp. 180, 192-195.

unacceptable to compel the parties to a dispute to accept a solution dictated by the League Council. It was felt that a sufficient measure of coercion was contained in the economic and military sanctions of Article 16 to be applied against states going to war in breach of their covenants.[99]

The mandates article was adopted by the Commission without serious controversy, the basic issue having been settled by the Council of Ten on January 30.[100] Orlando and Bourgeois objected to the elaborate definition of territories in the draft presented by General Smuts, but Wilson and Cecil successfully defended the British draft, accepting only minor changes. The Commission agreed to the creation of a permanent commission to receive the annual reports of mandatory powers and to advise the Council on all matters relating to mandates.[101]

The amendments to the Hurst-Miller draft presented by the British representatives on February 7 contained a proposed article on amendments to the Covenant which read: "Amendments to the constitution and functions of the League can be made by a unanimous vote of the Executive Council confirmed by a majority of the Body of Delegates."[102] Miller argued that this was unconstitutional for the United States, the Covenant being a treaty and therefore subject to amendment only by ratification by the executive with the consent of the Senate.[103] President Wilson therefore proposed a new text declaring that amendments "will take effect when ratified by the States whose representatives compose the Executive Council together with a three-fourths majority of the States whose representatives compose the Body of Delegates." This text was accepted in the eighth meeting of the League Commission and, with revisions in nomenclature, became Article 26 of the final Covenant.[104]

---

[99] See Cecil, *A Great Experiment*, pp. 73-76.

[100] See Chapter 3, Section IV.

[101] League of Nations Commission, Sixth Meeting, February 8, 1919, 10:30 a.m., Miller, *The Drafting of the Covenant*, Vol. 2, pp. 272-275. See also Bonsal, *Unfinished Business*, pp. 34-35.

[102] Miller, *The Drafting of the Covenant*, Vol. 2, p. 555.

[103] Memorandum of February 9, Miller, *Diary*, Vol. 5, pp. 196-197.

[104] League of Nations Commission, Eighth Meeting, February 11, 1919, 10:30 a.m., Miller, *The Drafting of the Covenant*, Vol. 2, p. 290, Vol. 1, pp. 203-204.

The structure of the Covenant was essentially completed by the eighth meeting of the League Commission. Built upon the carefully devised Hurst-Miller draft, that structure was with few exceptions the embodiment of Anglo-American ideas and proposals. The chief British contribution was the procedures for peaceful settlement of disputes and the system of sanctions contained in Articles 12 to 16 of the final Covenant. These largely voluntary provisions, derived from the Phillimore plan and inspired by the collapse of the Concert of Europe in 1914, were readily adopted by President Wilson in his early drafts and secured by Anglo-American efforts in the League Commission against the Franco-Belgian desire for more compulsory procedures. The fundamental American contribution was the principle of collective security asserted in Article 10, which was perhaps the President's only personal contribution to the wording of the Covenant. The British were distinctly reserved as to this principle, fearing its vagueness and its implied sanctification of the *status quo*, but in deference to the President they accepted it as an integral part of the Anglo-American program.[105]

VI. *Anglo-American versus French Principles in the League of Nations Commission, February 11-13; The Covenant of February 14, 1919*

The basic divergence within the League of Nations Commission came to the fore in the final three February meetings. It was a conflict between the French concept of a military League with rigidly defined powers of compulsion and the Anglo-American concept of an organization of sovereign states designed to promote flexible procedures of voluntary accommodation with measures of compulsion to be used only as a last resort.

On February 11, Léon Bourgeois, one of the French representatives on the League Commission, launched an assault on the disarmament article of the Hurst-Miller draft. This article was little more than an invitation to national disarmament. It endorsed the principle of disarmament to the lowest point consistent with domestic safety and the necessities of international enforce-

[105] See Rappard, *The Quest for Peace*, pp. 107-124.

ment action and stated that the League Council should formulate plans for the reduction of armaments and inquire into the feasibility of the abolition of conscription.[106] Bourgeois proposed to alter this article to give the Council authority to *determine* the level of armaments permissible to each state and to "fix the conditions under which the permanent existence and organization of an international force may be assured," due regard being given to the risks of "geographic situation" in determining the number of troops to be allowed to a state. President Wilson retorted sharply that such controls would be generally unacceptable and, for the United States, unconstitutional as well. The creation of an international army, the President declared, would create the appearance of "substituting international militarism for national militarism." Bourgeois pressed his demand, arguing that his plan was not for a standing international army but for some system for rapid organization of national contingents against an aggressor. Cecil said that the French proposal departed from the British conception of the League, but that he might consider a less stringent arrangement such as the creation of a permanent committee to advise the League on military questions. Wilson assured Bourgeois that the League would provide security to its members, but safety, he said, would rest ultimately on the good faith of the nations who belonged to the League. "When danger comes," the President said, "we too will come, and we will help you, but you must trust us. We must all depend on our mutual good faith."[107]

The entire Covenant, including the French amendments, was now turned over to a drafting committee, where Larnaude revived the French proposals for endowing the League with binding military powers. His nerves apparently frayed by the importunities of the French, Cecil delivered a stern lecture to M. Larnaude on the positions of America and Great Britain in relation to Europe. The United States, said Cecil, could well afford to remain aloof from European affairs and to a lesser extent, this was also true of Great Britain. The support offered through the

---

[106] Miller, *The Drafting of the Covenant*, Vol. 2, p. 233.

[107] League of Nations Commission, Eighth Meeting, February 11, 1919, 10:30 a.m., Miller, *The Drafting of the Covenant*, Vol. 2, pp. 292-297. See also Seymour, ed., *Intimate Papers*, Vol. 4, pp. 307, 313; Cecil, *A Great Experiment*, p. 78; Birdsall, *Versailles Twenty Years After*, pp. 121-132.

League of Nations, Cecil declared, was "practically a present to France," and if France rejected this "gift" because more was not offered, the alternative would be an alliance between Great Britain and the United States.[108]

The French proposals were disposed of at the final February meeting of the League of Nations Commission. President Wilson was absent and Cecil presided. The French now proposed to append to Article 9 of the Hurst-Miller draft (Article 11 of the final Covenant), which declared any war or threat of war to be a matter of concern to the League and its members,[109] a provision for the creation of a permanent body to plan and prepare a military and naval program by which the Covenant would be enforced. Cecil observed that this amounted to a proposal for an international general staff and he flatly rejected it. After a lengthy debate, the French amendments were voted on and defeated. As a sop, the French were conceded Cecil's earlier suggestion of a permanent commission to advise the Council on military affairs, and this became Article 9 of the final Covenant.[110]

A number of other matters were disposed of with dispatch on February 13 and Cecil declared the Covenant adopted by the Commission on the League of Nations.[111]

The Anglo-American concept of the League was thus preserved against the attempt of the French to create a centralized executive authority with powers to control national armaments and mobilize an international force. The Covenant as adopted by the League of Nations Commission was instead based on the widest diffusion of authority among voluntarily affiliated sovereign states. While the Anglo-American concept depended upon force as an ultimate sanction, it was confidently expected that the power of public opinion and democratic good faith would usually obviate the need for stronger sanctions. Implicit in this conception of

[108] Miller's Diary, February 12, 1919, Miller, *Diary*, Vol. 1, pp. 119-120. See also Bonsal, *Unfinished Business*, p. 30.

[109] Miller, *The Drafting of the Covenant*, Vol. 2, pp. 233-234.

[110] League of Nations Commission, Tenth Meeting, February 13, 1919, 3:30 p.m., *ibid.*, pp. 317-321. See also Zimmern, *The League of Nations and the Rule of Law, 1918-1935*, pp. 252-255.

[111] League of Nations Commission, Tenth Meeting, February 13, 1919, 3:30 p.m., Miller, *The Drafting of the Covenant*, Vol. 2, pp. 321-326. The Covenant as adopted by the League Commission on February 13 may be found *ibid.*, pp. 327-335, and in Baker, *Wilson and World Settlement*, Vol. 3, pp. 163-173.

the League was the twin belief that public opinion was bound to prevail and that public opinion was the voice of reason.[112] If this assumption was invalid, the League might not have succeeded even if an honest attempt had been made in the years after 1919 to implement the principles of Woodrow Wilson and Lord Robert Cecil.

To Wilson and to Cecil, the ultimate basis of obligation under the League was not legal but moral. Article 10, Wilson told the Senate Committee on Foreign Relations, was binding "in conscience only, not in law." But a moral obligation, he asserted, "is superior to a legal obligation, and . . . has a greater binding force. . . ."[113] Lord Robert Cecil shared this faith. "I am prepared to say," he said in 1923, "that the State is an individual, a moral individual, and is subject as such to the moral law."[114] The harmony of moral conviction between Wilson and Cecil had perhaps as much to do with the success of Anglo-American cooperation in the framing of the Covenant as the harmony of national interests between the United States and Great Britain.

The text of the completed Covenant was received by the Plenary Session of the Peace Conference of February 14. President Wilson read the report of the Commission on the League of Nations and described the character of the Covenant. Its primary dependence, he said, was on the "moral force of the public opinion of the world." "Armed force is in the background in this program," the President affirmed, "but it is in the background, and if the moral force of the world will not suffice, the physical force of the world shall. But that is the last resort. . . ." Wilson explained the machinery of the League as simple and flexible. "A living thing is born . . . ," he said. "It is a definite guarantee of peace." The Covenant, Wilson concluded, was "a practical document and a humane document. There is a pulse of sympathy in it. There is a compulsion of conscience throughout it. It is practical, and yet it is intended to purify, to rectify, to elevate." Cecil spoke for the British Empire. He explained the Covenant

---

[112] See Edward Hallett Carr, *The Twenty Years' Crisis, 1919-1939* (London: Macmillan and Company, Ltd., 1956), pp. 34-35.

[113] Conference of August 19, 1919, *Treaty of Peace with Germany*, pp. 6, 19.

[114] Lord Robert Cecil, *The League of Nations, Its Moral Basis*, The Essex Hall Lecture, 1923, Christianity and World Problems: Pamphlet No. 4 (New York: George H. Doran Company, 1924), p. 5.

as based on two precepts: first, that "no nation shall go to war with any other nation until every other possible means of settling the dispute shall have been fully and fairly tried"; second, that, "under no circumstances, shall any nation seek forcibly to disturb the territorial settlement to be arrived at as the consequence of this peace or to interfere with the political independence of any of the States in the world."[115]

This was Wilson's greatest hour, the time of triumph for a practical idealist, presenting to the world "a living thing," a document both "practical" and "humane." The League was the practical instrument which would secure the values of America—peace, democracy, and the rule of law. These were the interests of America and they could only be secured for her if they were secured for all others at the same time.

Riding home by car after the plenary session, the President said to Mrs. Wilson: "This is our first real step forward, for I now realize, more than ever before, that once established, the League can arbitrate and correct mistakes which are inevitable in the treaty we are trying to make at this time . . . one by one the mistakes can be brought to the League for readjustment, and the League will act as a permanent clearinghouse where every nation can come, the small as well as the great."[116]

[115] Plenary Session, February 14, 1919, *Foreign Relations, 1919, The Paris Peace Conference*, Vol. 3, pp. 209-217; Miller, *The Drafting of the Covenant*, Vol. 2, pp. 560-567.

[116] Edith Bolling Wilson, *My Memoir* (Indianapolis, New York: The Bobbs-Merrill Company, Inc., 1938), p. 239.

CHAPTER 5

ANGLO-AMERICAN POLICY AND THE
RUSSIAN REVOLUTION, 1919

No problem that came before the Paris Peace Conference confronted Anglo-American statesmen with greater dilemmas of policy than that of the Russian Revolution. The peacemakers were torn, on the one hand, by revulsion for Bolshevik principles and practices and, on the other, by the desire to apply their own principles of self-determination and nonintervention. Impelled, moreover, by a strong distaste for a further large-scale military operation, they made several unsuccessful efforts in the course of 1919 to cope with the threat to their nascent system of world peace and order posed by the Russian civil war and by the aggressive dynamism of Bolshevik ideology. British and American statesmen, equally sincere in their desire to assist Russia and equally unwilling to intervene against the Bolsheviks, cast about for means of either coming to terms with them or finding a viable democratic force to which they might lend moral and material assistance. Lloyd George, who had said in his war aims speech of January 5, 1918, that Russia "can only be saved by her own people," adhered to that attitude throughout the Peace Conference. Wilson, whose Point 6 had promised to Russia a "sincere welcome into the society of free nations under institutions of her own choosing," found no one to welcome and no such institutions.[1] Only the British Secretary of State for War, Winston Churchill, called for a positive policy to destroy Bolshevism, but Wilson and Lloyd George rejected his militarist proposals. In the course of 1919, one effort after another to forge an effective Russian policy ended in failure. At the end of the year, Great Britain and the United States abandoned their efforts to influence events in Russia, leaving the Bolsheviks to complete unimpeded the forging of a new totalitarian empire.

[1] See Chapter 1, Section v.

I. *The Decision against Intervention and the Abortive Proposal for a Conference with the Russian Factions at Prinkipo*

Although American forces were landed in Siberia in 1918 and British forces were established at Murmansk, neither government intended or used its forces for intervention in Russia's civil war. Their mission was to guard stores of Allied war material lest they fall into German hands, to assist a Czech legion fighting eastward across Siberia, and, for the American forces, to keep a watchful eye on the mistrusted Japanese in Siberia. The official view of the United States Government in 1918 toward military intervention was that it "would add to the present sad confusion in Russia rather than cure it, injure her rather than help her. . . ." The United States therefore, would not take part in any intervention or sanction it in principle.[2] The British Government favored a large-scale American-Japanese intervention in Siberia, but for the purpose of distracting German forces from the western front and not for any purpose of interfering in Russian affairs. Indeed, Balfour contended the opposite, that such intervention would confer on the Russian people the "most signal service to be imagined," making it possible for them to settle their own affairs.[3] President Wilson described his Russian policy as being essentially similar to his Mexican policy. "I believe in letting them work out their own salvation," he said, "even though they wallow in anarchy for a while. . . ."[4]

The Inter-Allied Conference at London in December 1918 discussed the possibility of Bolshevik representation at the Peace Conference. Balfour and Clemenceau were opposed, but Lloyd George, with the support of Sir Robert Borden, expressed the view that the Bolsheviks had the support of the majority of the Russian people and therefore should be represented at Paris. It

[2] Aide-Memoire, Lansing to Allied Ambassadors, July 17, 1918, Department of State, *Papers Relating to the Foreign Relations of the United States, 1918, Russia* (3 Vols., Washington: United States Government Printing Office, 1931-1932), Vol. 2, pp. 288-289; hereafter referred to as *Foreign Relations*.

[3] Balfour to Reading, for the State Department, July 29, 1918, *ibid.*, pp. 315-317.

[4] Sir William Wiseman, "Notes on an Interview with the President at the White House," October 16, 1918. Sir William Wiseman Papers, Sterling Library, Yale University.

was agreed that no decision would be made until the United States was consulted.[5]

The problem of Russia was further considered in the Imperial War Cabinet on December 31, 1918. Winston Churchill argued strongly for joint action in Russia by the Great Powers, with or without American participation, expressing his conviction that a free election held under Allied auspices would sweep away Bolshevism. Lloyd George opposed military intervention as too formidable an undertaking and one which public opinion would not support. Lloyd George also feared that foreign troops would actually drive the people to rally behind the Bolsheviks. The "one sure method of establishing Bolshevism in Russia," he contended, was "to attempt to suppress it by foreign troops."[6]

Britain and the United States thus went to the Peace Conference with established policies of nonintervention in Russia's civil strife. The question that remained to be settled as the Peace Conference convened was how, if at all, the contending Russian factions would be represented before the world peace congress. Generally, Anglo-American statesmanship favored some form of communication with the Russian parties, including the Bolsheviks. It was only when the effort to establish such contact had failed that some half-hearted attention was given to the possibility of assisting the anti-Bolshevik forces within Russia.

The Peace Conference at the outset excluded Russia from official participation. The French Foreign Minister, Pichon, suggested to the Council of Ten on January 12 that various Russian individuals then in Paris, self-proclaimed representatives of diverse factions, be allowed to express their views unofficially to the Peace Conference. Lloyd George was opposed to hearing these individuals, who, he said, represented "every opinion except the prevalent opinion in Russia." President Wilson remained silent in this discussion. It was agreed that Russia itself would not be represented at the Peace Conference but that the Russians in Paris, such as Prince Lvov and the wartime Foreign Minister Sazonov, might supply memoranda or be personally interviewed.[7]

[5] David Lloyd George, *The Truth about the Peace Treaties* (2 Vols., London: Victor Gollancz, Ltd., 1938), Vol. I, pp. 321-323.

[6] *ibid.*, pp. 325-328.

[7] Council of Ten, January 12, 1919, 4 p.m., *Foreign Relations, 1919, The Paris Peace Conference* (13 Vols., Washington: United States Government Printing

Lloyd George proposed a Russian policy to the Supreme Council on January 16. He favored an effort to promote a truce in the civil war, whereupon all of the factions, including the Bolsheviks, could be invited to Paris, where the Allies might assist them in resolving their differences. Noting that Bolshevism appeared to be stronger than ever, Lloyd George pointed out that three possible policies were open to the Peace Conference: (1) they might intervene to destroy Bolshevism—Britain, however, would not undertake to set Russia in order by force; (2) they might try to insulate Bolshevism behind a *cordon sanitaire*—which would starve the Russian people; (3) or they might pursue the policy he suggested of inviting the Russian factions to make a truce and send representatives to Paris.

President Wilson strongly endorsed Lloyd George's views. "There was certainly a latent force behind Bolshevism," he said, "which attracted as much sympathy as its more brutal aspects caused general disgust." Bolshevism, Wilson said, was rooted in the genuine grievances of the workers against the capitalist classes. Neither British nor American troops would fight in Russia, the President asserted, "because they feared their efforts would lead to the restoration of the old order, which was even more disastrous than the present one." Bolshevism would be strengthened by the threat of intervention, said the President. He therefore favored Lloyd George's proposal as the "only suggestion that led anywhere."[8]

President Wilson was increasingly disposed to be conciliatory toward the Bolsheviks. He had received overtures from them in December 1918, assuring him of their acceptance of his peace program.[9] He received reports from William Buckler, who was engaged in confidential conversations in Stockholm with Maxim Litvinov, that the Soviet Government was anxious for peace and willing to compromise on all issues. Their conciliatory attitude was

Office, 1942-1947), Vol. 3, pp. 490-491. The extracted minutes of the Supreme Council relevant to Russia may also be found along with other documents, in *Foreign Relations, 1919, Russia* (Washington: United States Government Printing Office, 1937).

[8] Council of Ten, January 16, 1919, 10:30 a.m., *Foreign Relations 1919, The Paris Peace Conference*, Vol. 3, pp. 581-584; Lloyd George, *The Truth about the Peace Treaties*, Vol. 1, pp. 330-337.

[9] Litvinov to Wilson, December 24, 1918, Woodrow Wilson Papers, Library of Congress, Washington, D.C., Series 8-A.

unquestionable, Buckler reported, and they were prepared to cease at once all propaganda activities abroad. The Bolsheviks, according to Buckler, recognized that there was no possibility of revolution in western Europe, and they were prepared to support the League of Nations.[10]

On January 21, President Wilson reaffirmed his view that negotiations should be undertaken. Since Clemenceau was opposed to the presence of Bolshevik representatives in Paris, Wilson suggested that the Russian factions be invited to confer with the Allied and Associated Powers at some other place. Such a conference, Wilson asserted, would undermine the moral argument of the Bolsheviks as to alleged Allied imperialism and might set off a reaction against them. Lloyd George and Balfour enthusiastically endorsed the President's proposal. Clemenceau feared a Bolshevik trap and Baron Sonnino of Italy dissented altogether, calling for the dispatch of Allied volunteers to fight the Bolsheviks. It was nevertheless agreed that President Wilson would draft an invitation to all of the Russian factions to make a truce and participate in a conference with the Allies to discuss means of restoring peace and order in Russia.[11]

The Council of Ten adopted and dispatched Wilson's draft invitation on the next day. It stated the desire of the Allies to help the Russian people and assured them that the Allies would not interfere in their affairs or aid a counterrevolution: "They recognize the revolution without reservation. . . ." The document invited "every organized group that is now exercising, or attempting to exercise, political authority or military control" in Russia to send representatives to a conference with the Allies in the Princes Islands in the Sea of Marmara on February 15, provided that these groups first entered into a truce and ceased all military activities.[12]

---

[10] William H. Buckler, "Notes on Russia and Meeting with Litvinov, Stockholm," William H. Buckler Papers, Sterling Library, Yale University; Council of Ten, January 21, 1919, 10:30 a.m., *Foreign Relations, 1919, The Paris Peace Conference*, Vol. 3, pp. 643-646; Lloyd George, *The Truth about the Peace Treaties*, Vol. 1, pp. 342-343. Concerning the Buckler mission, see also *Foreign Relations, 1919, Russia*, pp. 15-18.

[11] Council of Ten, January 21, 1919, 3 p.m., *Foreign Relations, 1919, The Paris Peace Conference*, Vol. 3, pp. 647-653; Lloyd George, *The Truth about the Peace Treaties*, Vol. 1, pp. 353-363.

[12] Council of Ten, January 22, 1919, 3 p.m., *Foreign Relations, 1919, The Paris Peace Conference*, Vol. 3, pp. 676-677; Lloyd George, *The Truth about the Peace Treaties*, Vol. 1, pp. 364-366.

The proposed conference at Prinkipo in the Princes Islands quickly collapsed due to the intransigence of the Russian factions. The Bolsheviks accepted the invitation, lavishly expressing their desire to purchase peace at great sacrifice. They were prepared, they replied, to recognize the financial obligations of Russia, to grant raw materials concessions, and to pledge noninterference in the affairs of other states.[13] The representatives of the anti-Bolshevik groups in Paris, however, in the name of the "unified" governments of Siberia, Archangel, and southern Russia, declared their willingness to accept Allied collaboration in the internal pacification of Russia but absolutely refused to negotiate with the Bolsheviks.[14]

The collapse of the Prinkipo proposal marked the end of the first stage of the efforts of the Peace Conference to cope with the complex Russian problem. Wilson and Lloyd George had put forth the proposal hoping to bring peace to Russia and perhaps to undermine Bolshevism by a clear demonstration of the good faith and generous intent of the Peace Conference. Anglo-American statesmanship was to move, after the Prinkipo failure, from one dead end to another.

II. *Churchill's February Proposals and Anglo-American Refusal to Intervene; the Bullitt Mission to Russia*

Winston Churchill, the newly appointed British Secretary of State for War, appeared before the Supreme Council on February 14 as the representative of the British Cabinet. Lloyd George at this time was absent in London. Churchill inquired whether some substitute was to be devised for the Prinkipo conference. President Wilson said that he had only two clear opinions in regard to Russia: that Allied forces were doing no sort of good there and that they should be promptly withdrawn. Wilson hoped, he said, for some form of contact with the Bolsheviks, not for the sake of a rapprochement, but in order to gain "clear information." Churchill argued that withdrawal would mean the certain destruction of all anti-Bolshevik forces in Russia, and if this were to happen, he said,

[13] Tchicherin, Commissar of Foreign Affairs, to the Peace Conference, February 4, 1919, *Foreign Relations, 1919, Russia*, pp. 39-42.
[14] Russian Embassy in Paris to the Secretariat-General of the Peace Conference, February 12, 1919, *ibid.*, pp. 53-54.

"an interminable vista of violence and misery was all that remained for the whole of Russia." In the ensuing debate, Churchill argued for the dispatch of volunteers and military equipment to assist the anti-Bolshevik forces. The President replied that such aid might be used to bolster reactionaries and that the continued presence of Allied forces would only defer the evil consequences for Russia. Churchill pressed the Council for a decision, asking whether they would undertake to arm the anti-Bolsheviks if all hope for a conference faded. The President was hesitant, saying only that he would "cast in his lot with the rest." No decision was reached and the President left that day for America.[15]

With Wilson and Lloyd George away, Churchill pressed his demand for intervention in Russia. In the Supreme Council on February 15, he accused the Allies of temporizing while friendly armies were disintegrating in Russia. He proposed a telegram to the Bolsheviks demanding a cease-fire within ten days to be followed by a conference. In addition, Churchill suggested that an Allied Council for Russian Affairs be established to provide "continuity of policy, unity of purpose and control." If no conference were to materialize, this Council should formulate a "definite military policy" to be enforced against the Bolsheviks. Clemenceau and Sonnino endorsed Churchill's proposal for a council to formulate a Russian policy, but Lansing thought that its formation should await "consultation" and House feared the alienation of peoples east of the Rhine "unless tact were used." Balfour was opposed to abandoning the Prinkipo plan. He favored a message to the Bolsheviks to the effect that there would be no negotiations unless they accepted a cease-fire. It was agreed that such a message should be dispatched, but both the message and Churchill's plan for a Council for Russian Affairs were postponed for consideration on February 17. In fact, the Churchill plan was not discussed again in the Supreme Council.[16]

[15] Council of Ten, February 14, 1919, 6:30 p.m., *Foreign Relations, 1919, The Paris Peace Conference*, Vol. 3, pp. 1041-1044; Winston S. Churchill, *The Aftermath*, Vol. 4 of *The World Crisis*, 1918-1928 (New York: Charles Scribner's Sons, 1929), pp. 173-174.

[16] Council of Ten, February 15, 1919, 3 p.m., *Foreign Relations, 1919, The Paris Peace Conference*, Vol. 4, pp. 13-21. The Churchill proposals were again deferred in the discussion of February 17 and thus apparently laid to rest by tacit agreement. *ibid.*, p. 28.

Lloyd George quickly repudiated Churchill's military proposals. British policy, he told Churchill, was to supply equipment to anti-Bolshevik forces only if every effort at peaceful settlement should fail.[17] In a letter to Philip Kerr on February 19, the Prime Minister reasserted his unalterable opposition to military intervention in Russia but indicated that military equipment might be provided to anti-Bolshevik forces to enable them to hold areas, and only those areas, which were genuinely opposed to Bolshevik rule. The Allies should work on the principle, said Lloyd George, that "Russia must save herself."[18] In subsequent months, Lloyd George attempted to base British assistance to the anti-Bolshevik forces on three conditions: that there must be no effort to conquer Bolshevik Russia; that support would be given only as long as the people were clearly anti-Bolshevik; that there would be no restoration of the Tsarist regime.[19]

President Wilson reacted to the Churchill proposals with no less alarm than Lloyd George. From the U.S.S. "George Washington," he cabled the American commissioners in Paris: "Greatly surprised by Churchill's Russian suggestion. . . . It would be fatal to be led further into the Russian chaos."[20] He instructed House that under no circumstances would the United States join a military operation in Russia and expressed surprise that Churchill had even been permitted to bring his proposals to Paris.[21] The President was promptly reassured that "Churchill's project is dead and there is little danger that it will be revived again by the Conference."[22]

In the face of strong opposition by Wilson and Lloyd George, the Churchill proposals were quietly buried. In March, he again warned the Prime Minister of the mounting military disintegration of the anti-Bolshevik forces in Russia, attributing it to the

[17] Frank Owen, *Tempestuous Journey—Lloyd George: His Life and Times* (London: Hutchinson and Company, Ltd., 1954), p. 512; Churchill, *The Aftermath*, pp. 175-176. See also *Lord Riddell's Intimate Diary of the Peace Conference and After, 1918-1923* (New York: Reynal and Hitchcock, Inc., 1934), pp. 162-163.

[18] Lloyd George to Kerr, February 19, 1919, Lloyd George, *The Truth about the Peace Treaties*, Vol. 1, pp. 375-377.

[19] Lloyd George, *The Truth about the Peace Treaties*, Vol. 1, pp. 382-383.

[20] Wilson to American Commission to Negotiate Peace, February 19, 1919, *Foreign Relations, 1919, Russia*, p. 72.

[21] Wilson to House, February 20, 1919, Wilson Papers, Series 8-A.

[22] American Commission to Negotiate Peace to Polk (Acting Secretary of State) for Wilson, February 23, 1919, *Foreign Relations, 1919, Russia*, p. 73.

lack of an Allied policy and the failure to provide effective support for their armies.[23]

Meanwhile, the American Commissioners undertook a new project for an approach to the Bolsheviks. William C. Bullitt, a young member of the American delegation, was instructed by Secretary Lansing on February 18 to "proceed to Russia, for the purpose of studying conditions, political and economic, therein for the benefit of the American Commissioners. . . ."[24] According to Bullitt, House and Lansing instructed him to seek from the Bolsheviks an exact statement of the terms on which they would agree to a cease-fire and House further authorized him to indicate to the Bolsheviks that if they accepted an armistice the United States would recommend to the Allies a prompt withdrawal of their troops from Russia.[25]

The Bullitt mission was to be kept secret from all of the Allies except the British, and House instructed Bullitt to confer before leaving with Philip Kerr, Lloyd George's private secretary. Kerr and Bullitt met several times and discussed unofficially possible bases of settlement in Russia. Kerr emphasized that he was expressing only his own opinion in these discussions.[26] Before his departure, Bullitt received a letter from Kerr suggesting terms of settlement generally similar to the instructions given to Bullitt by House. Kerr's letter, Bullitt testified, was based on consultations with Lloyd George and Balfour.[27]

Bullitt spent one week in Russia, where he talked with Lenin, Litvinov, and Tchicherin. The Soviets suggested armistice terms which Bullitt regarded as acceptable and asked for a "semi-official" Anglo-American guarantee that the French would respect the

[23] Churchill to Lloyd George, March 14, 1919, Churchill, *The Aftermath*, p. 180.

[24] Lansing to Bullitt, February 18, 1919, *Hearings before the Committee on Foreign Relations, United States Senate, 66th Congress, First Session, on the Treaty of Peace with Germany*, Document No. 106 (Washington: United States Government Printing Office, 1919), September 12, 1919, Bullitt Exhibit No. 9, p. 1234.

[25] *Hearings before the Senate Committee on Foreign Relations*, September 12, 1919, p. 1246.

[26] *ibid.*, pp. 1246-1247; Kerr to Sir R. Graham, July 11, 1919, E. L. Woodward and Rohan Butler, eds., *Documents on British Foreign Policy, 1919-1939*, First Series (8 Vols., London: His Majesty's Stationery Office, 1947-1958), Vol. 3, pp. 425-426.

[27] Kerr to Bullitt, February 21, 1919, *Hearings before the Senate Committee on Foreign Relations*, September 12, 1919, Bullitt Exhibit No. 16, p. 1247.

terms of an armistice.[28] From Helsinki, Bullitt sent telegrams to Wilson, Lansing, and House stating that the Bolshevik Government was firmly in control and supported by the masses and recommending that the Allies offer terms of peace to the Bolsheviks.[29] According to Bullitt, he asked House to show the telegram to Kerr for Lloyd George's information and upon Bullitt's return, House told him that Lloyd George and Balfour had been informed.[30]

Upon returning to Paris, Bullitt submitted a report to President Wilson recommending the acceptance of the Soviet peace offer as just and reasonable.[31] Bullitt also provided copies of his report and of the Soviet proposals to Philip Kerr. Lloyd George received Bullitt and questioned him closely as to conditions in Russia and the character of the Bolshevik leaders.[32] Bullitt drew up a set of proposals, based on the terms offered by the Bolshevik Government, calling for a declaration by the Allies disavowing any intervention in Russia's internal affairs and a two weeks' armistice during which all of the *de facto* governments in Russia would send representatives to a conference with the Allies. This conference would discuss peace on the basis of withdrawal of Allied forces and the retention by each Russian regime of areas then under its control, subject to the voluntary self-determination of the populations involved.[33]

The Bullitt proposals were quietly suppressed for reasons which are somewhat obscure. President Wilson at this time, early April, was greatly preoccupied with the crucial issues of the German treaty. Bullitt believed that the recent military successes of Admiral Kolchak, the anti-Bolshevik leader in Siberia, had persuaded the Allied leaders that the Bolsheviks would soon be crushed. More-

---

[28] *Hearings before the Senate Committee on Foreign Relations*, September 12, 1919, pp. 1248-1250.

[29] Bullitt to Wilson, House, and Lansing, received March 18, 1919, *Foreign Relations, 1919, Russia*, p. 83.

[30] *Hearings before the Senate Committee on Foreign Relations*, September 12, 1919, p. 1252.

[31] *Foreign Relations, 1919, Russia*, pp. 85-89; *Hearings before the Senate Committee on Foreign Relations*, September 12, 1919, Bullitt Exhibit No. 18, pp. 1253-1260.

[32] Kerr to Sir R. Graham, July 11, 1919, Woodward and Butler, eds., *Documents on British Foreign Policy, 1919-1939*, Vol. 3, p. 426; *Hearings before the Senate Committee on Foreign Relations*, September 12, 1919, pp. 1260-1261.

[33] *ibid.*, Bullitt Exhibit No. 9, pp. 1262-1263.

over, both Wilson and Lloyd George were feeling the pressures of intense anti-Bolshevik opinion from home, which would certainly have been aroused by the Bullitt proposals.[34]

Lloyd George declared to the House of Commons on April 16 that there had been no approaches from the Soviet Government. Denying knowledge of anything but the vaguest rumors as to the Bullitt mission and recommendations, Lloyd George averred that if the President had attached any importance to them, he would have brought them before the Conference, "and he certainly did not."[35] It is clear, on the basis of the evidence here cited, that Lloyd George's profession of ignorance was a deliberate falsehood. Bullitt said that members of the British delegation apologized to him and explained that Lloyd George had favored his proposals but then found that public opinion was intensely anti-Bolshevik and that Churchill and Lord Northcliffe had rigged a hostile majority in the House of Commons in case Lloyd George gave his true opinions on Russia.[36]

Whatever the reasons for the negative outcome of the Bullitt affair, it brought Anglo-American policy toward Russia once again to a dead end, while the Bolsheviks continued to consolidate their power.

III. *The Nansen Proposal of April; The Decision to Support Kolchak and the Failure of Policy in June*

President Wilson and the other heads of governments received telegrams early in April from Dr. Fridtjof Nansen, the famous Swedish Arctic explorer, suggesting the establishment of a non-political commission for the purpose of alleviating starvation in Russia. Nansen inquired as to what assistance the United States and the Allies would provide in the way of finance, shipping, and food.[37] The Nansen proposal was inspired by Herbert Hoover, the director of Allied relief operations.[38]

[34] *ibid.*, p. 1270; Arthur Walworth, *Woodrow Wilson* (2 Vols., New York, London, Toronto: Longmans, Green and Company, 1958), Vol. 2, *World Prophet*, p. 291.

[35] H.W.V. Temperley, ed., *A History of the Peace Conference of Paris* (6 Vols., London: Henry Frowde and Hodder and Stoughton, 1920-1924), Vol. 6, p. 315.

[36] *Hearings before the Senate Committee on Foreign Relations*, September 12, 1919, p. 1272.

[37] Nansen to Wilson, April 3, 1919, *Foreign Relations, 1919, Russia*, p. 102.

[38] Herbert Hoover, *The Ordeal of Woodrow Wilson* (New York, Toronto, London: McGraw-Hill Book Company, Inc., 1958), pp. 119-120.

President Wilson endorsed the Nansen proposal in the Supreme Council on April 9, suggesting that the proposed commission be composed of neutrals. Lloyd George emphasized that care would have to be taken to keep the power of distribution out of the hands of the Bolsheviks.[39] After further deliberation, the Council agreed to a reply to Nansen, drafted by Hoover, agreeing to the proposal but only on condition of a cessation of all hostilities in Russia and the suspension of all movements of troops and material.[40]

Nansen forwarded the Allied proposals to Lenin, who responded that the plan, "disfigured" by the political stipulations of the Allies, was unacceptable.[41] The Soviet Government declared in a radio reply on May 14 that it would gratefully accept relief supplies but would not cease hostilities.[42] The Council of Four considered the Soviet reply on May 20 and found it unacceptable. The Nansen proposals for relief were thereupon dropped.[43]

The collapse of all direct overtures to the Bolsheviks compelled the Supreme Council to consider the advisability of direct support of the anti-Bolshevik forces of Admiral Kolchak in Siberia and General Denikin in the Ukraine. Although Lloyd George was overheard speculating that 50,000 troops might clean that "den of vipers" out of Moscow,[44] neither Wilson nor Lloyd George seriously considered military intervention, even by volunteer forces, against the Bolsheviks. The deliberations of the Council of Four during the month of May were conditioned by the substantial military successes then being achieved by Kolchak, whose forces were advancing westward across Siberia toward Moscow.

The Council of Four agreed on the Russian clauses of the German treaty on May 2. Germany was compelled to renounce the

---

[39] Council of Four, April 9, 1919, 3:30 p.m., Paul Mantoux, *Les Délibérations du Conseil des Quatre* (2 Vols., Paris: Éditions du Centre National de la Recherche Scientifique, 1955), Vol. 1, p. 207.

[40] Wilson, Lloyd George, Clemenceau, and Orlando to Nansen, April 17, 1919, *Foreign Relations, 1919, Russia*, pp. 108-109; Hoover, *The Ordeal of Woodrow Wilson*, pp. 121-122.

[41] Soviet Note to Nansen, *circa* April 10, 1919, *Foreign Relations, 1919, Russia*, pp. 111-115.

[42] Hoover, *The Ordeal of Woodrow Wilson*, p. 123.

[43] Council of Four, May 20, 1919, 11 a.m., *Foreign Relations, 1919, The Paris Peace Conference*, Vol. 5, pp. 743-747. Concerning the Nansen proposals, see also David Hunter Miller, *My Diary at the Conference of Paris*, privately printed (21 Vols., New York: Appeal Printing Company, 1924), Vol. 7, pp. 428-462, *passim*.

[44] Stephen Bonsal, *Suitors and Suppliants* (New York: Prentice-Hall, Inc., 1946), p. 27.

Treaty of Brest-Litovsk and acknowledge the "inalienable independence" of all of the territories of the former Russian Empire. The right of Russia was reserved to obtain from Germany "the restitutions and the satisfactions based on the principles of the present treaty."[45] The settlement of Russian problems was thus all but omitted from the Treaty of Versailles.

President Wilson told the Council on May 9 that the American forces guarding the trans-Siberian railroad were encountering mounting difficulties in attempting to remain neutral between the Russian factions and that they were now confronted with the alternatives of openly assisting Kolchak or withdrawing. Lloyd George said, unhelpfully, that this strengthened his conviction that it was necessary to arrive at a policy on Russia. The President said that he had always felt that the best policy was to "clear out of Russia and leave it to the Russians to fight it out among themselves." Nevertheless, the Council agreed to delay any decision until an inquiry had been sent to Kolchak as to the democratic nature of his program.[46]

Wilson and Lloyd George were deeply concerned with Kolchak's program. They wished to know, especially, whether he would promote land distribution to the peasants and hold a free election for a constituent assembly. Wilson directed the Acting Secretary of State to dispatch a representative from the American Embassy in Tokyo to Kolchak's headquarters at Omsk with instructions to seek "official and definite assurances" that Kolchak intended to implement land reform and the election of a constituent assembly by universal suffrage, and also to report on the men influencing Kolchak and whether he was strong enough and liberal enough to control them in the "right" direction.[47]

The Council of Four undertook to assure itself of Kolchak's democratic intentions. Wilson told the Council on May 19 that he was inclined to make all further assistance to the anti-Bolshevik forces conditional upon a pledge to pursue progressive policies. Lloyd George agreed that it was important to impose conditions.[48]

[45] Council of Four, May 2, 1919, 4 p.m., *Foreign Relations, 1919, The Paris Peace Conference,* Vol. 5, pp. 421-424.

[46] Council of Four, May 9, 1919, 4 p.m., *ibid.,* pp. 528-529.

[47] Wilson to Tumulty, for Polk, May 14 and May 16, 1919, Wilson Papers, Series 8-A.

[48] Council of Four, May 19, 1919, 4 p.m., *Foreign Relations, 1919, The Paris Peace Conference,* Vol. 5, p. 725.

On May 20, the Council instructed Philip Kerr to draft a formal demand to all of the anti-Bolshevik factions for assurances that they intended to install a democratic government, all further aid being contingent on such assurances.[49]

Kerr's memorandum was approved by the Council and dispatched to Admiral Kolchak on May 26. It declared nonintervention in Russian affairs to be a "cardinal axiom" of Allied policy. Efforts to arrange a conference having failed because of the refusal of the Bolsheviks to suspend hostilities, said the letter, the Allies now declared their objective to be the restoration of peace by enabling the Russian people to resume control of their affairs through a freely elected constituent assembly. Since the Allies could not deal with the Soviets, it was affirmed, they were now disposed to assist Admiral Kolchak with arms, food, and supplies if guarantees were given that his policy was to hold free elections, establish liberties for the people, carry out land reform, and not restore class privileges. It was also stipulated that Kolchak pledge to refer boundary disputes to arbitration by the League of Nations. Finally, Russia was to join the League and accept responsibility for the financial obligations of the old regime.[50]

Kolchak promptly issued a proclamation promising the election of a constituent assembly by universal suffrage and a program of peasant land ownership, to be implemented as soon as the Bolsheviks were crushed.[51] Kolchak's formal reply to the Council of Four, received on June 5, contained all of the assurances they had demanded.[52] The Council of Four dispatched a telegram to Kolchak on June 12 indicating their approval of his reply and agreeing to extend the support proffered in their letter of May 26.[53]

The temporizing of the Peace Conference in regard to Russia seemed at last to be at an end with the decision to commit moral and material resources to the destruction of Bolshevism and the establishment of democratic government. But it was too late. No sooner had the policy of June 12 been established than the military

[49] Council of Four, May 20, 1919, 11 a.m., *ibid.*, pp. 736-737.

[50] Dispatch to Admiral Kolchak, May 26, 1919, *ibid.*, Vol. 6, pp. 73-75. See also Churchill, *The Aftermath*, pp. 182-185.

[51] American Representative at Omsk to Wilson, May 31, 1919, *Foreign Relations, 1919, The Paris Peace Conference*, Vol. 6, p. 233.

[52] Kolchak to Supreme Council, June 4, 1919, *ibid.*, pp. 321-323. See also Churchill, *The Aftermath*, pp. 185-186.

[53] Supreme Council to Kolchak, June 12, 1919, *Foreign Relations, 1919, The Paris Peace Conference*, Vol. 6, p. 356.

collapse of Kolchak's army began, and once it began, it was precipitate. By mid-June, Kolchak's military situation was deteriorating rapidly, and by the end of June, his drive on Moscow had totally collapsed. The decision of June 12 might have been effective in January. Except for Kolchak's brief successes in the spring of 1919, the period of doubt and delay had been one of steady Bolshevik consolidation and anti-Bolshevik deterioration. In the words of Winston Churchill: "The moment chosen by the Supreme Council for their declaration was almost exactly the moment when that declaration was certainly too late."[54]

IV. Further Abortive Efforts to Influence Events in Russia, July-December 1919

In the summer and autumn of 1919, the Bolsheviks continued their drive to victory in Russia while the Peace Conference continued vainly to seek means of exerting its influence. Great Britain and the United States, the latter now increasingly preoccupied with the struggle at home for ratification of the Treaty of Versailles, maintained their policy of nonintervention and, as all democratic alternatives crumbled, concurred in abandoning further efforts to influence events in Russia.

While Kolchak's situation deteriorated in Siberia and the Bolsheviks were rapidly extending their power, the Peace Conference deliberated on the question of maintaining the blockade against Soviet Russia. Henry White said on July 25 that he had received instructions from the President, who had returned home in June, that the United States could not collaborate in the blockade because it was not at war with Russia. Balfour said that, with British troops fighting at Archangel, there was a state of war *de facto* with the Bolsheviks and asked what would happen if an American vessel carrying munitions were to be sent to Russia in the face of an Allied blockade.[55] On the next day, the Council approved a telegram to President Wilson, drawn up by Balfour, which contended that in view of the *de facto* state of war in Russia the rules

---

[54] Churchill, *The Aftermath*, pp. 185-186.
[55] Council of Heads of Delegations, July 25, 1919, 3:30 p.m., *Foreign Relations, 1919, The Paris Peace Conference*, Vol. 7, pp. 265-267; Woodward and Butler, eds., *Documents on British Foreign Policy, 1919-1939*, First Series, Vol. 1, pp. 188-190.

of international law should not be rigorously enforced. The message also urged American participation in the blockade, pointing to the danger of an American "neutral" vessel entering the blockade area.[56]

The United States maintained its stand for the strict application of the international law of blockade. Frank L. Polk, now the American representative, insisted on August 29 that a neutral ship whose papers were in order could not be turned back from approaching a Russian port, although the United States would itself deny clearance papers to merchant ships bound for Russia.[57] Sir Eyre Crowe proposed on September 25 that all merchant vessels proceeding through the Gulf of Finland be turned back by the Commanders of the Allied and Associated Forces. Polk feared the creation of a dangerous precedent by the invention of a "new kind of blockade" not recognized by international law. If the Allies wanted to impose a blockade, he asserted, they should declare war on Russia. Otherwise, they should confine themselves to requesting neutrals to respect an embargo.[58] The issue was then referred to the consideration of the Drafting Committee, which advised the Council on September 29 that the proposed blockade was of dubious legality but that the Allies could take measures of blockade as sanctions under Article 16 of the Covenant of the League of Nations. Polk protested that the League and its machinery did not yet exist and that the Allies proposed to impose a pacific blockade. Crowe asked if the United States would agree to a collective request to the neutrals. Polk accepted this proposal and it was agreed that all neutral powers would be asked to impose an embargo on commerce with Soviet Russia. It was further agreed that the neutral powers would be *verbally* notified that

[56] Council of Heads of Delegations, July 26, 1919, 10:30 a.m., *Foreign Relations, 1919, The Paris Peace Conference*, Vol. 7, pp. 309, 312-314; Woodward and Butler, eds., *Documents on British Foreign Policy, 1919-1939*, First Series, Vol. 1, pp. 201-203.

[57] Council of Heads of Delegations, August 29, 1919, 11 a.m., *Foreign Relations, 1919, The Paris Peace Conference*, Vol. 8, pp. 9-10; Woodward and Butler, eds., *Documents on British Foreign Policy, 1919-1939*, First Series, Vol. 1, pp. 572-573.

[58] Council of Heads of Delegations, September 25, 1919, 10:30 a.m., *Foreign Relations, 1919, The Paris Peace Conference*, Vol. 8, pp. 345-348; Woodward and Butler, eds., *Documents on British Foreign Policy, 1919-1939*, First Series, Vol. 1, pp. 781-784.

British and French warships in the Gulf of Finland would continue to turn back merchant vessels bound for Soviet ports.[59]

Although in the autumn of 1919 both Great Britain and the United States became increasingly disposed to give up further efforts to influence events in Russia, President Wilson maintained a position of strong verbal opposition to Bolshevism. On one occasion he referred to the Bolsheviks as a "group of men more cruel than the Czar himself."[60] On another, he declared that the Russian people were being "delivered into the hands of an intolerable tyranny" under men who "maintain their power by the sword. . . ."[61]

Lloyd George took the lead in the liquidation of Allied efforts in Russia. He wrote to Churchill on September 22 that his chief concern was with reducing expenditures. ". . . I have found your mind so obsessed by Russia," he wrote, "that I felt I had good grounds for the apprehension that your great abilities, energy and courage were not devoted to the reduction of expenditures."[62] Nevertheless, the British Government warned the United States in October of the danger of a Bolshevik victory if the United States withheld further assistance from Admiral Kolchak.[63] But as reports continued to reach the Foreign Office of the disintegration of the anti-Bolshevik forces, Lloyd George gave up hope. The Bolsheviks occupied Omsk on November 15 and the Kolchak Government fled to Irkutsk. The British agent in Vladivostok reported that the Kolchak regime was moribund and that militant anti-Bolshevism was at an end in Siberia.[64] Lloyd George told Frank Polk on November 24 that Great Britain would provide no further assistance to the forces of Admiral Kolchak and General Denikin beyond supplies which had already been set aside

[59] Council of Heads of Delegations, September 29, 1919, 10:30 a.m., *Foreign Relations, 1919, The Paris Peace Conference*, Vol. 8, pp. 366-367, 438-440, 452; Woodward and Butler, eds., *Documents on British Foreign Policy, 1919-1939*, First Series, Vol. 1, pp. 824-829.

[60] Speech at Kansas City, September 6, 1919, Ray Stannard Baker and William E. Dodd, eds., *The Public Papers of Woodrow Wilson* (6 Vols., New York and London: Harper & Brothers, Publishers, 1925-1927), *War and Peace*, Vol. 2, p. 6.

[61] Speech at Billings, Montana, September 11, 1919, *ibid.*, p. 107.

[62] Lloyd George to Churchill, September 22, 1919, Owen, *Tempestuous Journey—Lloyd George: His Life and Times*, p. 519.

[63] Curzon to Grey, October 10, 1919, Woodward and Butler, eds., *Documents on British Foreign Policy, 1919-1939*, First Series, Vol. 3, p. 589.

[64] Lampson (Vladivostok) to Curzon, November 21, 1919, *ibid.*, pp. 654-655.

for them and that he thought the time had come to seek an understanding with the Bolsheviks.[65]

The State Department took a strong stand against negotiations with the Bolsheviks. Secretary of State Lansing instructed the American Ambassador in London to express to the British Government the view of the United States that it was useless to seek agreement with the Bolsheviks because their aims were hostile to all other governments and any agreement they entered would be pure opportunism. "It is my belief," said Lansing, "that if Lloyd George seeks to reach such an understanding he will incur serious moral responsibility as well as make a great tactical mistake."[66]

The Peace Conference terminated its efforts to deal with Russia in December. Lloyd George told the conference of Allied Premiers meeting in London on December 12 that all measures had failed and that Great Britain was not prepared to continue providing material assistance to the anti-Bolshevik forces. Ambassador Davis, acting as American "observer," said that he thought the United States would be unwilling to provide further aid. The Council agreed on a three-point policy, as summed up by Lord Curzon: the maintenance of a "barbed wire fence" around Russia and no further intervention; no more money and equipment to be supplied to the anti-Bolshevik forces; and the bolstering of Poland as a barrier to Russia.[67] The Council resolved on December 13 that no commitments beyond those already entered into would be made to assist the anti-Bolshevik forces. The Council defined its policy as confining the Bolsheviks "within a ring fence."[68]

Anglo-American policy toward Russia in 1919 was almost a marvel of good intentions. While the French and Italians were receptive to proposals for military intervention, British and American statesmen were determined to apply to Russia the principles of self-determination and nonintervention, even if these meant the

[65] Polk to Lansing, November 29, 1919, *Foreign Relations, 1919, Russia*, p. 126.

[66] Lansing to Davis, December 4, 1919, *ibid.*, p. 130.

[67] Council of Premiers, December 12, 1919, 11:30 a.m., *Foreign Relations, 1919, The Paris Peace Conference*, Vol. 9, pp. 849-850; Woodward and Butler, eds., *Documents on British Foreign Policy, 1919-1939*, First Series, Vol. 2, pp. 745-746.

[68] Council of Premiers, December 13, 1919, 4:30 p.m., *Foreign Relations, 1919, The Paris Peace Conference*, Vol. 9, pp. 853-857; Woodward and Butler, eds., *Documents on British Foreign Policy, 1919-1939*, First Series, Vol. 2, pp. 775-778, 782.

victory of Bolshevism. Enlightened progressives that they were, Wilson and Lloyd George recognized that Bolshevism had sprung in Russia from legitimate grievances and historic injustices. Repelled though they were by the terror and fanaticism of Bolshevism, they continued to hope that the Bolshevik leaders would prove reasonable men, with whom they could negotiate in honesty and good faith. Only when they were convinced that the Bolsheviks would deny to the Russian people the right to determine their own future did they undertake to provide moral and material support to the anti-Bolshevik factions in the hope that they would provide a democratic alternative. In the Prinkipo affair, the Bullitt mission, and in the June decision to support Admiral Kolchak, Anglo-American statesmanship demonstrated its desire to assist Russia in securing peace, democratic self-government, and an active role in the League of Nations system. It is not too much to say that the Anglo-American approach to the Russian Revolution was completely free of imperialist intent and guided by national self-interest only in its enlightened awareness that the peace and security of the democracies were threatened while the peace and security of Russia were in jeopardy.

This policy, however, whether justified or not in its own context of events and circumstances, was a total failure, for none of its objectives was achieved. Two principal reasons are suggested for this failure. First, Great Britain and the United States were almost entirely preoccupied with the problems of making peace with Germany. The Russian Revolution was hardly more than a sideshow on the diplomatic stage at Paris, and efforts to formulate an effective Russian policy were half-hearted and intermittent. This neglect is amply illustrated by the infrequency and inconclusiveness of the deliberations on Russia in the Supreme Council. While the Peace Conference temporized, events ran their fateful course in Russia, and when at last the decision to assist the anti-Bolshevik forces was made, it was too late to be effective. Secondly, Anglo-American policy was, in a sense, the victim of its own virtues. Their own adherence to the principles of self-determination and nonintervention and their own recognition of the legitimacy of the social grievances which gave rise to Bolshevism held back the English-speaking powers from the strong measures which might have defeated Bolshevism. The result of these hesitations and scruples was the establishment in Russia of a dictatorship which denied self-determination and democracy at home while becoming the implacable enemy abroad of the League of Nations system and the principles of world peace under the rule of law which were the central objectives of Anglo-American policy.

CHAPTER 6

ANGLO-AMERICAN ISSUES ARISING FROM THE "PRE-
LIMINARY PEACE," THE MILITARY CLAUSES, AND
THE DISPOSITION OF GERMAN SEA POWER

FROM mid-February to mid-March 1919, Wilson and Lloyd
George were tending to political matters at home, leaving
Colonel House and Foreign Secretary Balfour as their respective substitutes on the Supreme Council. During this period, the
first intensive efforts were made to settle specific items of the
treaty of peace with Germany. In an effort to speed up the flagging
progress of the Peace Conference, Balfour and House undertook
to hasten the conclusion of a preliminary peace containing the
military, territorial, and economic terms to be imposed upon
Germany. These events have given rise to a historical controversy
as to whether the speed-up effort was in fact a device to sidetrack
the League of Nations. When President Wilson returned to Paris,
he was greatly displeased with the efforts of Colonel House and
he brought to an end all consideration of a preliminary peace not
containing the League of Nations, thus in effect converting the
preliminary Peace Conference into a body making virtually final
decisions.

There was substantial Anglo-American accord during this period in the negotiation of the military clauses of the treaty and no
significant stresses were generated by questions of German seapower. The debate over the military terms to be imposed upon
Germany was the first of the substantive issues in which Anglo-
American liberalism and moderation conflicted with the deep
concern of France for its national security, foreshadowing the
more serious conflict over French schemes for the disposition of
the German Rhineland. The problem of the disposition of the
German fleet evoked few differences between Britain and America, the two great seapowers, since it was generally agreed that
German seapower was to be reduced to negligible proportions.
The question of whether to sink the German warships, as desired
by Great Britain and the United States, or to distribute them
among the victors, as desired by the continental Allies, was largely

[154]

settled by the Germans when they scuttled a great part of their fleet at Scapa Flow on June 21, 1919. When distribution of the remainder was decided upon, an Anglo-American squabble over proportions led to the United States receiving no warships at all. A brief but sharp controversy between Great Britain and the United States over the retention as reparations of German merchant vessels seized during the war was settled by a mutually satisfactory compromise.

I. The "Preliminary Peace" and the House-Balfour Speed-Up of the Peace Conference, February-March 1919

The conviction of the French in the winter of 1919 that Germany was attempting to evade the disarmament requirements of the Armistice by various pretexts galvanized the Peace Conference into an early effort to conclude the final military and naval terms of the treaty. The French at first pressed for more stringent terms in each renewal of the Armistice, but the United States objected to this approach. In the Council of Ten on February 7, Marshal Foch appealed for a large new surrender of weapons in the next renewal, but President Wilson strongly opposed the imposition of new terms as "not sportsmanlike."[1] It was agreed on February 10 to establish a Committee of Military and Economic Advisers under Marshal Foch to report on means of compelling German compliance with Armistice terms.[2] The Committee submitted its report on February 12, recommending that the problem be coped with by drawing up the final military and naval clauses at once and imposing them on the enemy.[3]

Wilson and Balfour strongly endorsed this proposal. Balfour offered a resolution on February 12 calling for an indefinite renewal of the Armistice and the appointment of a commission to draw up final military, naval, and air terms. President Wilson vig-

[1] Council of Ten, February 7, 1919, 3:30 p.m., Department of State, *Papers Relating to the Foreign Relations of the United States, 1919, The Paris Peace Conference* (13 Vols., Washington: United States Government Printing Office, 1942-1947), Vol. 3, pp. 896-905, hereafter referred to as *Foreign Relations*. See also André Tardieu, *The Truth about the Treaty* (Indianapolis: The Bobbs-Merrill Company, Inc., 1921), pp. 126-129.

[2] Council of Ten, February 10, 1919, 3 p.m., *Foreign Relations, 1919, The Paris Peace Conference*, Vol. 3, p. 952.

[3] *ibid.*, pp. 980-986.

orously supported the Balfour resolution and said that he was prepared to leave it to the Council to determine the military clauses
while he was absent in America. He did not wish his absence,
said the President, "to stop so important, essential and urgent work
as the preparation of a preliminary peace." Although he hoped to
return by March 13 or 15, Wilson added, he "did not wish that,
during his unavoidable absence, such questions as the territorial
question and questions of compensation should be held up."[4]

The Council accepted the Balfour resolution on February 12
and a committee of military, naval, and air advisers was constituted under the chairmanship of Marshal Foch to draw up final
military, naval, and air clauses for Germany.[5] It was agreed on
February 13 that this committee would also draw up final military,
naval, and air terms for Austria-Hungary.[6] An indefinite renewal
of the Armistice was signed by Germany and the Allied and
Associated Powers on February 16, the Allies reserving the right
to terminate it on three days' notice.[7]

House and Balfour hoped to accomplish more than the conclusion of military terms during the absence of their chiefs. They
agreed on February 9 that while Wilson and Lloyd George were
away they would attempt to launch a program for the early completion of the articles of a preliminary peace.[8] Wilson's statement
in the Council of Ten on February 12 indicated his full approval
of such a plan. Moreover, according to Colonel Bonsal, President
Wilson, in Bonsal's presence, gave House definite instructions not
to hold up the territorial and reparations questions during his
absence. House did not interpret this as authorizing him to make
definite settlements but as an invitation to press these problems

[4] Council of Ten, February 12, 1919, 11 a.m., 3 p.m., *ibid.*, pp. 972-979, 1003-
1004. See also Charles Seymour, ed., *The Intimate Papers of Colonel House* (4
Vols., Boston and New York: Houghton Mifflin Company, 1926-1928), Vol. 4,
pp. 325-330; Ray Stannard Baker, *Woodrow Wilson and World Settlement* (3
Vols., Garden City, New York: Doubleday, Page and Company, 1922), Vol. 1,
pp. 289-290.
[5] Council of Ten, February 12, 1919, 3 p.m., *Foreign Relations, 1919, The Paris
Peace Conference*, Vol. 3, p. 1009.
[6] Council of Ten, February 13, 1919, 3 p.m., *ibid.*, p. 1015.
[7] *ibid.*, Vol. 4, pp. 42-43.
[8] House Diary, February 9, 1919, Edward M. House Papers, Sterling Library,
Yale University.

to the point where they would be ready for the President's final judgment upon his return.[9]

House and Balfour, to whom Lloyd George had given full powers, thereupon set to work. Clemenceau was wounded in an attempt at assassination on February 19 and Pichon replaced him in the Council. House reported to Wilson on February 19 a plea by Marshal Foch for the early settlement of terms, including a lump sum of reparations and the detachment of the Rhineland from Germany.[10] In another cable to Wilson on the same day, House indicated that he was undertaking to hasten the work of the Conference, "so that when you return terms of preliminary peace will be ready for your [consideration]."[11] Wilson cabled back instructing House not to acquiesce in any French schemes for the Rhineland. The President indicated that he was willing to have military, naval, and air terms decided and presented to Germany promptly, but nothing more.[12] This, presumably, did not rule out the consideration of other terms before the President's return.

Balfour presented a resolution to the Council on February 22 calling for the consideration, "with all possible speed," and without prejudice to the decision of February 12 to present military terms at an early date, of other preliminary peace terms, including those relating to Germany's frontiers, the financial arrangements to be imposed upon Germany, economic relations with Germany, and breaches of the law of war. The resolution further requested the expert commissions to submit their reports by March 8. House endorsed Balfour's view of the necessity to hasten the conclusion of a preliminary peace, and Lansing expressed his preference for a preliminary peace including territorial and economic as well as military terms.[13] The Council approved the Balfour resolution,

[9] Stephen Bonsal, *Unfinished Business* (Garden City, New York: Doubleday, Doran and Company, Inc., 1944), p. 49.
[10] House to Wilson, February 19, 1919, Seymour, ed., *Intimate Papers*, Vol. 4, pp. 332-334.
[11] House to Wilson, February 19, 1919, Woodrow Wilson Papers, Library of Congress, Washington, D.C., Series 8-A.
[12] Wilson to House, February 20, 1919, Seymour, ed., *Intimate Papers*, Vol. 4, pp. 335-336.
[13] Council of Ten, February 22, 1919, 3 p.m., *Foreign Relations, 1919, The Paris Peace Conference*, Vol. 4, pp. 85-88; Baker, *Wilson and World Settlement*, Vol. 1, pp. 298-301.

substantially but not entirely as introduced, on February 24, applying it to the Austro-Hungarian, Bulgarian, and Turkish treaties as well as to the German treaty, and resolving to "proceed without delay to the consideration of preliminary peace terms" and "to press on the necessary investigations with all possible speed." The question of a separate military preliminary treaty was left undecided, depending on the report of the Foch commission.[14]

The Balfour speed-up resolution engendered a major controversy. Rumors as to its implications spread through Paris. One American observer commented in his diary that European diplomacy was in "high gear," aiming to have its ambitions drafted into the treaty before Wilson's return.[15] Ray Stannard Baker charges that the Balfour resolution was a betrayal of Wilson's plan for a preliminary military peace and that its real purpose was to provide a means for dividing up the spoils of war without reference to the League of Nations while President Wilson was away. The probable reason for this betrayal, according to Baker, was that Lloyd George, "who had politics but no principles," had found such great discontent in England over the proceedings in Paris that he had a complete change of mind as to the preliminary peace plan of February 12.[16] Baker's charge of an intrigue against Wilson's plans was published in *The New York Times* in 1922. House thereupon wrote to Balfour: ". . . you and I were moved solely by a desire to accelerate the treaty, and we were acting as much upon my initiative as your own."[17]

Balfour had the Foreign Office prepare a secret memorandum on the matter, which he sent to House in July 1922, and which he authorized House to publish in July 1927.[18] The memorandum most vigorously denied Baker's allegation of a plot, pointing out that the determination not to interfere with the preliminary peace plan of February 12, 1919, was expressed in the very terms of the resolution as submitted by Balfour to the Supreme Council on

[14] Council of Ten, February 24, 1919, 3 p.m., *Foreign Relations, 1919, The Paris Peace Conference*, Vol. 4, pp. 108-111; Seymour, ed., *Intimate Papers*, Vol. 4, pp. 336-342. See also F. G. Marston, *The Peace Conference of 1919* (London, New York, Toronto: Oxford University Press, 1944), pp. 137-145.

[15] Charles T. Thompson, *The Peace Conference Day by Day* (New York: Brentano's Publishers, 1920), p. 232.

[16] Baker, *Wilson and World Settlement*, Vol. 1, pp. 301-303.

[17] Seymour, ed., *Intimate Papers*, Vol. 4, pp. 363-364.

[18] *ibid.*, pp. 364-366.

February 22: *"Without prejudice to the decision of the Supreme War Council to present Naval, Military, and Air Conditions of Peace to Germany at an early date,* the Conference agrees that it is desirable to proceed without delay to the consideration of other Preliminary Peace Terms with Germany and to press on the necessary investigations with all possible speed."[19] The crucial "without prejudice" clause was stricken from the resolution at the instance of Secretary Lansing, the memorandum points out, who proposed the substitute clause which appeared in the resolution as passed on February 24: "The Conference agrees that it is desirable to proceed without delay to the consideration of Preliminary Peace Terms and to press on the necessary investigations with all possible speed." The purpose of this revision, Lansing explained, was to yield a text applicable to all enemy countries.[20] The speed-up resolution was passed, the Foreign Office memorandum points out, on the understanding that the question of a separate military treaty was to be left open until the Foch committee reported. Foch submitted his final report on March 17, and the question, therefore, was still open when Wilson returned to Paris on March 14.[21]

The evidence provided by the minutes of the Council of Ten for February 22, 1919, seems fully to sustain the positions taken by House and Balfour against Baker's charge. Moreover, the Balfour speed-up resolution was not contrary to Wilson's statement in the Council of Four on February 12: ". . . But he [Wilson] did not wish that, during his unavoidable absence, such questions as the territorial question and questions of compensation should be held up."[22] In his account of this session, Baker omits this statement by the President, using dots, however, to indicate the missing material.[23]

If, in fact, a preliminary peace containing the military terms, or broader terms, had been carried out, it would in all probability

[19] Council of Ten, February 22, 1919, 3 p.m., *Foreign Relations, 1919, The Paris Peace Conference*, Vol. 4, p. 85.

[20] Council of Ten, February 22, 1919, 3 p.m., *ibid.*, p. 93.

[21] The Foreign Office Memorandum of July 1922, is reproduced in Seymour, ed., *Intimate Papers*, Vol. 4, pp. 366-374. It draws on the minutes of the Supreme Council herein cited.

[22] Council of Ten, February 12, 1919, 3 p.m., *Foreign Relations, 1919, The Paris Peace Conference*, Vol. 3, p. 1004.

[23] Baker, *Wilson and World Settlement*, Vol. 1, p. 290.

have upset Wilson's plan for establishing the Covenant of the League of Nations as an integral part of the treaty, for a preliminary treaty would have required consent to ratification by the United States Senate. Wilson and his colleagues on the Supreme Council apparently failed to think this matter through. Moreover, had the Balfour speed-up resolution linked the League of Nations Commission with the territorial commissions, the phrasing would have had to be very carefully drawn in order not to imply that this work was not already well advanced, as it was. The Covenant was at the time further advanced than any other part of the Treaty.

The charge of a conspiracy to set aside the League of Nations and impose a preliminary peace containing harsh military, territorial, and economic terms can be dismissed as wholly unsupported by the evidence. When President Wilson returned to France, however, he was greatly shocked by the events which had taken place during his absence. House came aboard the "George Washington" when it docked in Brest and retired with the President for a lengthy conference. When House had left, Mrs. Wilson entered the President's cabin and found him visibly shaken. "House," he said, "has given away everything I had won before we left Paris. He has compromised on every side, and so I have to start all over again and this time it will be harder, as he has given the impression that my delegates are not in sympathy with me."[24] Thereafter began the coolness between Wilson and House which resulted ultimately in a total breach between the two old friends.

Back in Paris on March 15, the President instructed Ray Stannard Baker to issue a statement that there would be no preliminary peace with Germany excluding the Covenant of the League of Nations. The statement reaffirmed the decision of the Plenary Session of January 25 that the Covenant was to be an integral part of the treaty of peace.[25] The project for a preliminary peace containing the military terms to be imposed on the Central Powers was thus terminated. Thereafter the terms of peace determined by the Peace Conference were recognized as definitive.

[24] Edith Bolling Wilson, *My Memoir* (Indianapolis, New York: The Bobbs-Merrill Company, Inc., 1938), pp. 245-246.
[25] Baker, *Wilson and World Settlement*, Vol. 1, pp. 310-311.

II. *The Military Clauses and General Disarmament*

One of the major objectives of the English-speaking powers at Paris was to reduce the burden of national armaments through international agreements for general disarmament. This goal had been an integral part of their war aims and the reduction of national armaments to the lowest point consistent with national safety and the requirements of international peace enforcement was called for by Article 8 of the Covenant of February 14, 1919. The aim of Anglo-American diplomacy in the debate over the military clauses of the treaty was to eliminate Germany as a military threat and thereby to promote world disarmament. It achieved the former objective, as events turned out, only for the briefest time, and the latter not at all.

The Military Commission under Marshal Foch which had been established by the resolution of the Council of Ten of February 12 reported to the Supreme Council on March 3. In the course of the Commission's deliberations, General Bliss and Marshal Haig, the British representative, had stood against Foch's demand that Germany be stripped of all frontier fortifications and its army reduced to 100,000 men. Bliss had maintained that Germany, according to its population and boundaries, was entitled to an army of 400,000 and to fortifications on both eastern and western frontiers. Haig had proposed an army of 200,000 or 250,000 and fortifications on the eastern but not the western frontiers of Germany.[26] The report submitted to the Supreme Council on March 3 called for German land forces not to exceed 200,000 men and 9,000 officers and the abolition of the German air force. Army officers and noncommissioned officers were to serve as volunteers, the former for twenty-five year terms, the latter for fifteen years. Private soldiers were to be conscripted for one-year terms of service. A British dissent attached to the report called for voluntary enlistments only. An Allied Committee of Control was to supervise the execution of these terms. The report contained no mention of general disarmament.[27]

[26] Frederick Palmer, Bliss, *Peacemaker—The Life and Times of General Tasker Howard Bliss* (New York: Dodd, Mead and Company, 1934), p. 374.

[27] Council of Ten, March 3, 1919, 3 p.m., *Foreign Relations, 1919, The Paris Peace Conference*, Vol. 4, pp. 183-184; David Lloyd George, *The Truth about the Peace Treaties* (2 Vols., Victor Gollancz, Ltd., 1938), Vol. 1, pp. 589-590.

Lloyd George arrived back in Paris on March 5. In the Council meeting on the next day, he assailed the Foch report, contending that the training of 200,000 men a year would give Germany a vast trained force over a period of years. Against Foch's contention that this would be an "army of sheep," Lloyd George contended that Germany should be permitted an army no greater than Britain's.[28] The Prime Minister submitted a draft resolution on March 7 calling for military, naval, and air terms based on the principles of voluntary service, minimum terms of twelve years of service for all ranks, the limitation of the army and air force to 200,000 men, and a navy not to exceed 15,000 men. Great Britain, said Lloyd George, would never agree to German conscription or an army exceeding 200,000 men. The Prime Minister's plan was accepted by the Council and the military advisers were instructed to redraft the military clauses accordingly.[29]

On March 10, Clemenceau asserted that if Germany was to have a long-term volunteer army it should not exceed 100,000 men. General Bliss thought that internal safety required at least 140,000. Clemenceau thereupon pointed out that when British and American forces were withdrawn the burden of guarding against a German resurgence would fall to France, and he asked that that burden be lightened by acceptance of the smaller figure. Lloyd George declared himself "much impressed" with this view, and, in recognition of the fact that France was unprotected by the sea like Britain and the United States, he yielded to Clemenceau's insistence. Lansing endorsed Lloyd George's view, and the Council agreed that the German Army would be limited to 100,000 men.[30] On March 12, the Council agreed to air clauses forbidding all German military aviation.[31]

[28] Council of Ten, March 6, 1919, 3 p.m., *Foreign Relations, 1919, The Paris Peace Conference*, Vol. 4, pp. 217-219; Lloyd George, *The Truth about the Peace Treaties*, Vol. 1, pp. 590-596.

[29] Council of Ten, March 7, 1919, 3 p.m., *Foreign Relations, 1919, The Paris Peace Conference*, Vol. 4, pp. 263-265; Lloyd George, *The Truth about the Peace Treaties*, Vol. 1, pp. 597-598.

[30] Council of Ten, March 10, 1919, 3 p.m., *Foreign Relations, 1919, The Paris Peace Conference*, Vol. 4, pp. 295-299; Lloyd George, *The Truth about the Peace Treaties*, Vol. 1, pp. 599-600. See also Tardieu, *The Truth about the Treaty*, pp. 130-132.

[31] Council of Ten, March 12, 1919, 3 p.m., *Foreign Relations, 1919, The Paris Peace Conference*, Vol. 4, pp. 335-346.

President Wilson, who returned to Paris on March 14, joined the discussion on March 17. He accepted the figure of 100,000 for the German Army and the other agreements which had been reached but objected to a draft clause submitted by the military advisers requiring Germany to notify the Allies of all armaments manufacturing and orders for armaments. Lloyd George agreed that the provision would be intolerably humiliating unless the League of Nations were to require all of its members to notify each other of their armaments programs. The notification clause was dropped.[32]

Britain and the United States thus accepted military clauses which reduced the German military establishment to a negligible force but which hardly in themselves constituted a step toward world disarmament. Lloyd George and Balfour held the view that the reduction of the German Army to a police force of 100,000 imposed on the Allies a duty to set up some machinery in the treaty for general disarmament. In his Fontainebleau Memorandum of March 25, which contained a broad set of recommendations for the Peace Conference, Lloyd George included a proposal that the principal members of the League of Nations enter into an agreement for armaments limitations among themselves as well as for Germany.[33] President Wilson suggested to the Council of Four on April 26 that the military clauses would be rendered more palatable to the Germans if they were presented as preparing the way for general disarmament. The Council agreed to an introductory clause defining the military terms as having the object of "rendering possible the preparation of the general limitation of armaments of all nations. . . ."[34] German objections to the military clauses were dismissed by the Allies with another general assurance that they were designed to constitute a first step toward general disarmament.[35]

The Treaty of Versailles thus contained two general provisos for world disarmament: Article 8 of the League Covenant, which called for reduction of armaments to the lowest point consistent

[32] Council of Ten, March 17, 1919, 3 p.m., *ibid.*, pp. 357-360.
[33] Lloyd George, *The Truth about the Peace Treaties*, Vol. 1, pp. 600-601.
[34] Council of Four, April 26, 1919, 3 p.m., *Foreign Relations, 1919, The Paris Peace Conference*, Vol. 5, p. 299.
[35] Reply of the Allied and Associated Powers to the Observations of the German Delegation on the Conditions of Peace, June 16, 1919, *ibid.*, Vol. 6, p. 954.

with national safety, and the introduction to the German military clauses. Both of these provisions were extremely vague and subsequently proved ineffective. Insofar as world disarmament as well as the removal of the German military threat was an object of British and American policy at the Peace Conference, it must be admitted that the results achieved were little more than a bromide for the Anglo-American conscience.[36]

Great Britain and the United States also attempted to advance the cause of general disarmament through the military terms applied to Austria and the states of eastern Europe. Wilson and Lloyd George favored the abolition of conscription in Austria and the succession states and staunchly insisted, over French and Italian opposition, on the imposition of limitations on the military forces of the east European states.

Lloyd George raised the question of the size of the armies of the new states in the Council of Four on May 15. Fearing that the small states would be perpetually at war with each other if they were allowed great armies, Lloyd George suggested that the military advisers be directed to submit recommendations for limitations on the armies of Greece, Yugoslavia, Roumania, Czechoslovakia, and Poland. President Wilson agreed that the size of the Austrian Army could not be determined without reference to the forces of the surrounding states. The Council instructed the military advisers of the Supreme War Council to prepare recommendations accordingly, taking the German Army of 100,000 as a proportional standard.[37]

In their report, submitted on May 23, the military advisers contended that military forces for Austria and the eastern European states fixed in proportion to the German figure would leave these states with armies inadequate to maintain internal order. They recommended, therefore, substantially higher figures.[38] President Wilson was impressed with these recommendations but

[36] See Tasker Howard Bliss, "The Problem of Disarmament," *What Really Happened at Paris* (Edward Mandell House and Charles Seymour, eds., New York: Charles Scribner's Sons, 1921), pp. 370-397.

[37] Council of Four, May 15, 1919, 11 a.m., *Foreign Relations, 1919, The Paris Peace Conference*, Vol. 5, pp. 627-635; Baker, *Wilson and World Settlement*, Vol. 1, pp. 399-403.

[38] Report of the Military Representatives, May 23, 1919, *Foreign Relations, 1919, The Paris Peace Conference*, Vol. 5, pp. 885-898.

Lloyd George pleaded with his colleagues not to allow the small states to use the Great Powers as "catspaws for their miserable ambitions." Clemenceau contended that Poland and Czechoslovakia should be allowed to have military establishments large enough to serve as counterweights to Germany.[39]

The matter was discussed further in the Council on June 4. Clemenceau argued against fixing the size of the forces of any but the enemy states. Lloyd George observed acidly that he "had no doubt what the size of their forces would be if no action were taken," and President Wilson said that he fully shared Lloyd George's fears. Clemenceau then proposed that the fixing of the forces of the new states be postponed for consideration by the League in 1921. Lloyd George and Wilson demanded that the limitations be established immediately. After further debate, the Council agreed to fix the Austrian Army at 30,000 men and to hear the representatives of the eastern European states at the next meeting.[40]

Wilson presented the proposals of the military advisers on the armies of the eastern European states to their representatives on June 5. Vesnich of Yugoslavia, Venizelos of Greece, Bratiano of Roumania, Beneš of Czechoslovakia, and Paderewski of Poland all offered strong resistance to the proposed limitations. Wilson and Lloyd George explained that these limitations were not to be applied until current dangers were past, but Clemenceau supported the small states and Orlando saw merit in everyone's position.[41]

The military clauses for the Austrian treaty were adopted on June 16,[42] but the proposal to limit the armed forces of the small powers was dropped after the discussion of June 5. Thus the results of the negotiations on military terms for eastern and

[39] Council of Four, May 23, 1919, 4 p.m., *Foreign Relations, 1919, The Paris Peace Conference*, Vol. 5, pp. 904-905; Baker, *Wilson and World Settlement*, Vol. 1, pp. 398-399, 403-404.

[40] Council of Four, June 4, 1919, 5 p.m., *Foreign Relations, 1919, The Paris Peace Conference*, Vol. 6, pp. 182-183; Baker, *Wilson and World Settlement*, Vol. 1, pp. 395-398, 405.

[41] Council of Four, June 5, 1919, 4 p.m., *Foreign Relations, 1919, The Paris Peace Conference*, Vol. 6, pp. 202-209; Baker, *Wilson and World Settlement*, Vol. 1, pp. 406-407.

[42] Council of Four, June 16, 1919, 12:30 p.m., *Foreign Relations, 1919, The Paris Peace Conference*, Vol. 6, pp. 487-492.

southeastern Europe did not significantly further the Anglo-American objective of using the military clauses of the treaties as the precursor to general disarmament. Germany and Austria were disarmed, but neither the Great Powers around Germany nor the small powers adjacent to Austria were compelled to accept anything more than the vague promise of disarmament contained in the Covenant of the League of Nations.

III. *The Naval Clauses and Anglo-American Issues Arising from the Disposition of German Warships and Merchant Vessels*

Great Britain and the United States were in basic agreement that Germany should be virtually stripped of ships of war and compelled to yield much of her merchant fleet as reparations. Nevertheless squabbles—hardly quarrels—developed between the two great sea powers over the issues of the distribution of the German fleet and the retention by the United States of German merchant vessels seized at the time of the American declaration of war. The basic issue, however, was the elimination of Germany as a sea power, and this was settled to the satisfaction of both England and America.

The British Admiralty wished to eliminate every possible threat which Germany might pose to British maritime supremacy. In January 1919, the Admiralty established, among other requirements, three basic essentials for the achievement of this objective: the surrender of the entire German submarine fleet and the destruction of all submarines in construction; the surrender or destruction of all surface vessels interned in Allied and neutral ports at the time of the Armistice; and, in order to deny Germany any overseas naval bases, the retention by the Allies of all of Germany's colonies.[43] The last requirement was effectuated by the January agreements of the Council of Ten regarding mandates.[44]

The United States was at first somewhat uneasy at the prospect

---

[43] H. W. V. Temperley, ed., *A History of the Peace Conference of Paris* (6 Vols., London: Henry Frowde and Hodder and Stoughton, 1920-1924), Vol. 2, pp. 143-145.
[44] See Chapter 3, Section IV.

of unchallenged British naval predominance which would follow from total destruction of German sea power. President Wilson's naval advisers recommended in November 1918 that Germany be permitted to retain a navy of sufficient strength to exercise a restraining influence on Great Britain.[45] Wilson himself was not at first in favor of destroying the German fleet, although it is not clear that he would have had the Germans retain any significant portion of it. "It is certainly not my intention to back the Allies up in the matter of sinking German ships," he wrote to Tumulty on December 22, 1918. "I am utterly opposed to such silly extremes. . . ."[46] The President took a quite different position at the Peace Conference.

The Council of Ten on January 13, 1919, decided to require the delivery of all movable German submarines to Allied ports, and the destruction of all others, including those under construction. It was further demanded that the entire German merchant fleet be placed at the disposal of the Allies in order to augment the total world tonnage available for provisioning Europe, including Germany.[47]

The Military Commission established by the resolution of February 12 submitted draft naval clauses to the Council of Ten on March 6. The admirals proposed a German Navy limited to 15,000 officers and men, six battleships, six light cruisers, twelve destroyers, and twelve torpedo boats. Sharp limitations on naval construction were called for as well as a total prohibition on the construction of submarines until such time as it might be removed by the League of Nations. The draft terms called for the creation of an Allied Naval Commission to oversee the execution of these requirements.[48] The Council approved the naval clauses, except for certain questions which were reserved for further consideration. These included the manner of disposal of the ships to be surrendered by Germany, the total number of naval personnel to be permitted, the prohibition or limitation of the con-

[45] Memorandum by Planning Section of United States Naval Advisory Staff, November 4, 1918, Wilson Papers, Series 8-A.

[46] Wilson to Tumulty, December 22, 1918, Wilson Papers, Series 8-A.

[47] Council of Ten, January 13, 1919, 2:30 p.m., *Foreign Relations, 1919, The Paris Peace Conference*, Vol. 3, pp. 521-523.

[48] *ibid.*, Vol. 4, pp. 242-251.

struction of submarines, and the final disposition of the islands of Heligoland and Dune.[49]

The naval clauses were highly satisfactory to the British Government and Admiralty. "The truth is," exulted Lloyd George, "that we have got our way. . . . The German Navy has been handed over; the German mercantile shipping has been handed over, and the German colonies have been given up."[50]

The important issues of the disposition of the surrendered German warships and merchant vessels, however, remained to be settled, and both generated some Anglo-American controversy. Colonel House told Lloyd George at a luncheon meeting on March 6 that if Great Britain did not consent to sinking the German fleet rather than partitioning it, the result would be that the United States would undertake a great naval program and Britain and America would then be in a competitive relationship similar to that of Britain and Germany in the past.[51] According to House, he and Lloyd George and Clemenceau reached agreement in a private conference on the morning of March 7 that the German warships should be partitioned among the Allies but that the United States, Great Britain, and Japan, the three great naval powers, should sink their shares.[52] Admirals Benson, Wemyss, and du Bon were thereupon instructed to confer on the proposal that France be allowed a share of the German fleet to recoup her loss of wartime naval production, while the United States and Great Britain would arrange to sink their shares simultaneously in the middle of the Atlantic.[53]

The tentative agreements of early March seem to have been set aside, because the disposal of the German warships was discussed inconclusively in the following weeks. Secretary of the Navy Josephus Daniels, who came to Paris at the end of March, was at first willing to apportion a share of the German fleet to the continental Allies, but on March 30 he wrote to Wilson that

[49] Council of Ten, March 6, 1919, 3 p.m., *ibid.*, p. 229.
[50] *Lord Riddell's Intimate Diary of the Peace Conference and After, 1918-1923* (New York: Reynal and Hitchcock, Inc., 1934), p. 42.
[51] House Diary, March 6, 1919, Seymour, ed., *Intimate Papers*, Vol. 4, p. 356.
[52] House to Wilson, March 7, 1919, *ibid.*, p. 358.
[53] Hankey to Wemyss, March 7, 1919, David Hunter Miller, *My Diary at the Conference of Paris*, privately printed (21 Vols., New York: Appeal Printing Company, 1924), Vol. 6, p. 291.

on further thought he favored the sinking of the whole German fleet as the "most tangible evidence of faith in reduction of armaments. . . ."[54] Wilson, Lloyd George, and Clemenceau met with their naval advisers in Wilson's apartment on April 25 and were unable to agree on the disposition of the German fleet, the British and Americans contending that it should be sunk and the French arguing for distribution.[55] The issue was still unsettled when the main phase of the Peace Conference ended in June.

There was a notable difference of opinion between the United States and Great Britain over the restrictions to be imposed upon German fortification of the North Sea island of Heligoland and the Kiel Canal. In the Council of Ten on March 6, Lansing objected to the destruction of the fortifications on the islands of Heligoland and Dune on the ground that Germany should be allowed to defend her coast, but Balfour contended that the German fortifications were designed for offensive naval use and the issue was deferred. In the same discussion, Admiral Benson objected to a clause of the draft naval terms providing for the maintenance of free access to the Kiel Canal at all times for the commercial vessels and warships of all nations. Balfour defended the clause, arguing that German use of the canal for strategic purposes should be limited. It was agreed to refer the matter to the Commission on International Ports, Waterways, and Railways.[56]

Balfour argued for the demilitarization of Heligoland in the Supreme Council on April 15, contending that the German naval base on the island posed a threat to the east coast of Great Britain. Wilson agreed that some disarmament was desirable, but said that he was opposed to the destruction of installations of which peaceful use could be made for fear of giving the impression of gratuitous violence. Furthermore, Wilson pointed out, Germany was being reduced to a third-rate naval power and could hardly be regarded as a threat. Balfour maintained, nonetheless, that the

[54] Josephus Daniels, *The Wilson Era* (Chapel Hill: The University of North Carolina Press, 1946), p. 373.

[55] Baker, *Wilson and World Settlement*, Vol. 1, p. 388. See also Temperley, ed., *A History of the Peace Conference of Paris*, Vol. 2, pp. 148-149.

[56] Council of Ten, March 6, 1919, 3 p.m., *Foreign Relations, 1919, The Paris Peace Conference*, Vol. 4, pp. 224-226.

port served only naval, not commercial, purposes. In the face of Balfour's persistence, Wilson yielded, and it was agreed that the port as well as the fortifications on the island of Heligoland would be destroyed.[57]

It was agreed on April 16 that the Kiel Canal would remain under German sovereignty subject to rules authorizing free navigation by all commercial and war vessels of states at peace with Germany. President Wilson then argued against the destruction of the canal's fortifications, observing that it would be "delicate" for the United States to impose different conditions for the Kiel Canal from those which were applied to the Panama Canal. Balfour, however, with the support of Clemenceau, contended that the canal in effect doubled the naval power of Germany and insisted on the destruction of the fortifications.[58] In the meeting of April 25, Lloyd George supported Wilson and Admiral Benson in upholding the right of Germany to fortify the Kiel Canal for defensive purposes. The Council thereupon agreed to strike out the draft clause calling for destruction of the fortifications.[59]

A more significant Anglo-American controversy arose over the German merchant ships seized in American ports when the United States declared war in 1917. Britain and the Allies wanted all such ships put into a common pool and redistributed among the Allies in proportion to wartime losses, while the United States insisted upon the cession of seized vessels to the individual powers in possession.

Among the forms of payments in kind to be made by Germany as part of the reparations settlement, the subcommittee of the Commission on Reparation concerned with such payments recommended the inclusion of enemy merchant ships for the re-

[57] Council of Four, April 15, 1919, 4 p.m., Paul Mantoux, *Les Délibérations du Conseil des Quatre* (2 Vols., Paris: Éditions du Centre National de la Recherche Scientifique, 1955), Vol. 1, pp. 251-255. Mantoux does not record the *decision* of the issue at this meeting, but on April 29 Wilson recalled that it had been decided as here indicated on April 15. Council of Four, April 29, 1919, 4 p.m., *Foreign Relations, 1919, The Paris Peace Conference*, Vol. 5, p. 339.

[58] Council of Four, April 16, 1919, 11 a.m., Mantoux, *Les Délibérations du Conseil des Quatre*, Vol. 1, pp. 263-264; Baker, *Wilson and World Settlement*, Vol. 2, p. 443.

[59] Council of Four, April 25, 1919, 5:30 p.m., *Foreign Relations, 1919, The Paris Peace Conference*, Vol. 5, pp. 235-237, 243.

placement of Allied wartime losses on a ton for ton basis. The American representative on the subcommittee asked that all enemy merchant ships seized during the war be exempted from distribution as payment in kind. The British and French objected, contending that the United States would thereby acquire almost twice as many ships as she had lost.[60] The representatives were unable to agree, and the report of the subcommittee on payments in kind contained a British-drafted clause calling for the cession of enemy merchant vessels not excepting those seized during the war. The American representative appended his dissent to this report.[61]

The Council of Four readily adopted recommendations by the subcommittee for the cession of existing German merchant vessels and additional tonnage to be built by the Germans over a period of five years, but the question of the vessels seized during the war remained open. Wilson told the Council on April 23 that "it would not be tolerable to public opinion in the United States if their title to these ships was not recognized." Lloyd George replied that "there was a great difference between the value of ships to Great Britain and the United States. It was like the value of ships to a fisherman compared with ships to a swell yachtsman." Lloyd George proposed as a compromise that the United States might retain the seized ships on condition of making an appropriate payment into the reparations fund.[62]

A special agreement on shipping, implementing the compromise proposed by Lloyd George, was signed by the President and the Prime Minister on May 3. It provided that each of the Allied and Associated Governments would retain all ships captured, seized, or detained during the war, but would pay to the permanent Reparations Commission a "reasonable value" on the excess of the total value of the tonnage retained over the share

[60] Reparation Commission, Second Subcommittee, March 31, 1919, Philip Mason Burnett, *Reparation at the Paris Peace Conference from the Standpoint of the American Delegation* (2 Vols., New York: Columbia University Press, 1940), Vol. 2, pp. 724-726, Vol. 1, pp. 112-118.

[61] Reparation Commission, Second Subcommittee, April 5, 1919, *ibid.*, Vol. 2, pp. 730-734; Vol. 1, p. 119.

[62] Council of Four, April 23, 1919, 4 p.m., *Foreign Relations, 1919, The Paris Peace Conference*, Vol. 5, pp. 162-163.

which that government would have received if all German tonnage were divided in proportion to war losses.[63]

Great Britain thus largely conceded the American demands on merchant shipping. One American shipping expert noted that Great Britain had shown "proper liberality" in connection with the ship distribution since in fact she had substantially the same merchant tonnage at the end of the war as before and her relative position in world shipping was therefore much stronger than before the war.[64] Lloyd George's liberality, however, was none too gracious. He complained in the Council of Four that the United States had made a net gain in shipping while Great Britain had suffered grievous losses. President Wilson pointed out that this shipping was all the reparation that the United States would receive, but Lloyd George maintained that shipping would be more valuable than money in the postwar years, providing an enormous advantage in overseas trade, and that he could more easily justify to Parliament an American claim for war pensions than for ships.[65]

German seamen substantially solved the problem of the distribution of the German fleet when on June 21 they scuttled nine battleships, ten cruisers, and thirty destroyers interned at Scapa Flow. Clemenceau was in favor of strong reprisals against Germany, suggesting the temporary occupation of the city of Essen after the treaty was signed.[66] President Wilson averred that the German Government could not be held legally responsible for the scuttling at Scapa Flow and Lloyd George maintained that the Allies were not entitled to occupy a city left to Germany by the treaty. Lloyd George "begged" France not to occupy a German city. He would waive, he said, any British claim to two

[63] ibid., Vol. 13, pp. 845-848; Burnett, Reparation at the Paris Peace Conference, Vol. 1, pp. 1124-1126. See also Bernard M. Baruch, The Making of the Reparation and Economic Sections of the Treaty (New York and London: Harper & Brothers, Publishers, 1920), pp. 38-39.

[64] Henry M. Robinson, U.S. Shipping Board, to House, May 28, 1919, Burnett, Reparation at the Paris Peace Conference, Vol. 2, pp. 49-51.

[65] Council of Four, June 10, 1919, 11 a.m., Foreign Relations, 1919, The Paris Peace Conference, Vol. 6, pp. 276-277; Baker, Wilson and World Settlement, Vol. 2, pp. 394-395.

[66] Council of Four, June 24, 1919, 11:15 a.m., Foreign Relations, 1919, The Paris Peace Conference, Vol. 6, pp. 651-652.

battleships which had been saved and yield them to France, and the British Government would give up all claims to the destroyers which had been saved. Wilson said that any exercise of force would be an act of war, "and the whole treaty would be at an end." Clemenceau at last yielded to these importunities, and it was agreed that Germany would be told that the Admiral in charge at Scapa Flow was to be brought to trial and restitution made as far as possible.[67]

Ultimately the German Government was held responsible for the scuttling at Scapa Flow. On October 30, 1919, the Council instructed the naval advisers to draw up a plan of reparation to be paid by Germany for the sinking of the ships.[68]

The problem of disposing of the remnants of the German fleet remained to be solved in the later stage of the Peace Conference. Britain and the United States much preferred that the German ships be sunk or broken up, but the British were willing to accept an arrangement for distribution of the ships, those lost at Scapa Flow to be counted as part of the British share. The United States contended that if agreement could not be reached to sink the German warships, they should be distributed according to national *effort* in the war.[69]

The British submitted a plan in November for the breaking up of most of the German surface ships, with the proceeds therefrom to be divided up in proportion to *losses* during the war. Under this plan, Great Britain would receive 70 per cent of the proceeds, France and Italy 10 per cent each, Japan 8 per cent, and the United States 2 per cent.[70] Frank L. Polk, the American delegate, strenuously objected to the allocation of a mere 2 per cent to the United States, arguing on November 28 that wartime naval effort as well as shipping losses should be part of the criterion of

[67] Council of Four, June 25, 1919, 11 a.m., *ibid.*, pp. 657-663.

[68] Council of Heads of Delegations, October 30, 1919, 10:30 a.m., *ibid.*, Vol. 8, pp. 836-837; E. L. Woodward and Rohan Butler, eds., *Documents on British Foreign Policy, 1919-1939, First Series* (8 Vols., London: His Majesty's Stationery Office, 1947-1958), Vol. 2, p. 122.

[69] Temperley, ed., *A History of the Peace Conference of Paris*, Vol. 2, pp. 153-156.

[70] Council of Heads of Delegations, November 17, 1919, 10:30 a.m., *Foreign Relations, 1919, The Paris Peace Conference*, Vol. 9, pp. 188, 201-202; Woodward and Butler, eds., *Documents on British Foreign Policy, 1919-1939*, First Series, Vol. 2, pp. 332-333, 344-345.

compensation. The United States, said Polk, would destroy its share anyway, but it was a "question of principle" on which American opinion ran high.[71] At the next meeting, Sir Eyre Crowe inquired as to the basis of distribution desired by the United States, and Polk spoke vaguely of a "question of principle which affected the national feeling." Crowe said that "unfortunately he had a passion for clearness but he still remained confused." Distribution, Crowe asserted, should be based on a clear principle such as losses, and American losses had been less than 2 per cent. After a further sharp exchange, in which Polk asserted and Crowe denied that the British-proposed allocations were "arbitrary," Polk said that he would have to refer the matter to Washington.[72]

The German warships were disposed of with little further controversy. The Council agreed on November 29 that all recipients of German ships would be free to sink them or break them up for use of their component parts.[73] On December 2, it was decided that all German submarines, except for ten which were to be allocated to France, would be demolished under the supervision of the Naval Inter-Allied Commission.[74] The British proposal on proportions for allocation of the German surface ships was adopted by the Council on December 9, the United States reserving the question of its 2 per cent share.[75]

Formal American participation in the Peace Conference ended

[71] Council of Heads of Delegations, November 28, 1919, 10:30 a.m., *Foreign Relations, 1919, The Paris Peace Conference,* Vol. 9, pp. 345-347; Woodward and Butler, eds., *Documents on British Foreign Policy, 1919-1939,* First Series, Vol. 2, pp. 407-408.

[72] Council of Heads of Delegations, November 29, 1919, 10:30 a.m., *Foreign Relations, 1919, The Paris Peace Conference,* Vol. 9, pp. 360-362; Woodward and Butler, eds., *Documents on British Foreign Policy, 1919-1939,* First Series, Vol. 2, pp. 415-417.

[73] Council of Heads of Delegations, November 29, 1919, 10:30 a.m., *Foreign Relations, 1919, The Paris Peace Conference,* Vol. 9, p. 365; Woodward and Butler, eds., *Documents on British Foreign Policy, 1919-1939,* First Series, Vol. 2, p. 421.

[74] Council of Heads of Delegations, December 2, 1919, 10:30 a.m., *Foreign Relations, 1919, The Paris Peace Conference,* Vol. 9, pp. 436-437; Woodward and Butler, eds., *Documents on British Foreign Policy, 1919-1939,* First Series, Vol. 2, p. 472.

[75] Council of Heads of Delegations, December 9, 1919, 10:30 a.m., *Foreign Relations, 1919, The Paris Peace Conference,* Vol. 9, p. 537; Woodward and Butler, eds., *Documents on British Foreign Policy, 1919-1939,* First Series, Vol. 2, p. 516.

on December 9, 1919. Ambassador Wallace, who remained as American "observer," said on January 13, 1920, that inasmuch as the Council insisted on an American share of only 2 per cent of the German surface ships, the United States would not demand or expect to receive *any* German ships, or any compensation for the scuttling at Scapa Flow. Lord Curzon noted that the American waiver created a 2 per cent surplus, which he suggested should be divided between France and Italy. The Council agreed to this proposal.[76]

The issue of the disposition of German sea power was thus brought to an end with a flourish of Anglo-American disharmony. For reasons not easily understood, the United States elevated this minor issue over the privilege of sinking a few German ships into a matter of "principle" reflecting on the American war effort. This arid Anglo-American debate, of no great substantive importance, is of interest chiefly as an illustration of the breakdown of American participation in the Peace Conference within the much more significant context of the American return to isolation at the end of 1919.

In summary, it may be said that Great Britain and the United States shared a common outlook on the military and naval issues of the Peace Conference. The project for a preliminary peace containing the military, naval, and air clauses was abandoned by President Wilson for reasons which remain obscure, but principally, perhaps, because of fear of presenting a preliminary treaty to the Senate which did not contain the Covenant of the League of Nations. The charge of a conspiracy by Balfour and House to use the preliminary peace as a means of sidetracking the League seems fully disproved. Anglo-American diplomacy undertook to use the disarmament of the enemy as a first step toward world disarmament but in fact achieved only vague expressions of sentiment for general disarmament. Despite some differences over the distribution of German merchant vessels and warships, Britain and the United States were in full agreement in their basic objective of eliminating Germany as a sea power.

[76] Council of Foreign Ministers, January 13, 1920, 11 a.m., *Foreign Relations, 1919, The Paris Peace Conference*, Vol. 9, pp. 975-976; Woodward and Butler, eds., *Documents on British Foreign Policy, 1919-1939*, First Series, Vol. 2, p. 840. See also Temperley, ed., *A History of the Peace Conference of Paris*, Vol. 2, pp. 153-157.

CHAPTER 7

THE PRINCIPLE OF SELF-DETERMINATION IN ANGLO-AMERICAN POLICY: FRENCH SECURITY AND THE TERRITORIAL SETTLEMENT OF WESTERN EUROPE

IN the months of March and April of 1919, Anglo-American concepts of a just and stable settlement of Germany's western frontiers clashed with the determination of France to create a system of strategic security against future German aggression. The French desired specifically to detach the Rhineland from Germany and to convert it into a military vassal of France. Great Britain and the United States both opposed this design with great determination if not for precisely the same reasons. Wilson and Lloyd George were equally dedicated to the application of the principle of self-determination to Germany, the President more perhaps in deference to the moral criteria of impartial justice, the Prime Minister more perhaps in fear of the practical dangers of "another Alsace-Lorraine." Whatever their differences of motivation, Wilson and Lloyd George both acted to preserve the national integrity of Germany against the demands of French security.

The essence of the Anglo-American problem was to provide security for France by some means other than the territorial mutilation of Germany and by some instrumentality supplementary to the League of Nations, of whose untested machinery the French were skeptical. Anglo-American statesmen achieved substantial success in coping with this dilemma. Through the devices of a temporary occupation of the Rhineland, a temporary administration of the Saar by the League of Nations, and a direct Anglo-American military guarantee to France, the requirements of French security were met without doing any great or permanent wrong to the German nation. The early breakdown of the delicate machinery thus created was no part of the work of the statesmen of 1919.

[176]

I. *French Security, the Rhineland, and the Anglo-American Treaties of Guarantee, February-March 1919*

The end of World War I brought French military power to the banks of the Rhine for the first time since the wars of Napoleon. The Rhineland had been under the rule of Prussia and the German Empire since 1814 and prior to that had been French only from 1794 to 1814. While its people had then been attracted by the great reforms of the French Revolution, many Frenchmen in 1919 were inclined to forget that French traditions had long since faded in the Rhineland and that the left bank had become closely bound to the right as a result of the great industrial development of Germany. There was, in fact, little effort —and little ground—to advance an ethnic basis for the French claims. The most serious French advocates of acquisition of the left bank of the Rhine were the military, whose thoughts were of a strategic frontier and not of some illusory historical affinity. The disposition of this area of 10,000 square miles, with its great industrial complex, strategic significance, and incontestably German population of five and one-half million, became the greatest single test in the Peace Conference of the avowed Anglo-American determination to apply the principle of self-determination impartially to friends and enemies alike.[1]

Against the demand of France for the Rhine as her military frontier, Great Britain and the United States had nearly parallel views from the outset. President Wilson's opposition to the French scheme was based on its incompatibility with the self-determination of the Fourteen Points, the prospect of a new source of chronic Franco-German enmity, the economic unfeasibility of the separation of the Rhineland from Germany, and the fundamental repugnance of the scheme to the principles of justice in which the League of Nations system was to be rooted. Lloyd George's opposition was motivated by similar considerations, but especially by the danger to peace inherent in a reversal of Alsace-Lorraine

---

[1] See Charles Homer Haskins and Robert Howard Lord, *Some Problems of the Peace Conference* (Cambridge: Harvard University Press, 1920), pp. 118-132; Charles Homer Haskins, "The New Boundaries of Germany," *What Really Happened at Paris* (Edward Mandell House and Charles Seymour, eds., New York: Charles Scribner's Sons, 1921), pp. 37-42, 49-54.

and by a conviction that British interests would be ill served if Germany were placed wholly at the mercy of France. Wilson and Lloyd George fully admitted the validity of the French demand for security, but not of the methods by which France proposed to achieve it.

The French pressed their demands early and vigorously. On January 10, Marshal Foch submitted to the Supreme Council a memorandum warning against excessive faith in the League of Nations, citing the dangers of resurgent German militarism, and prescribing as a remedy the Rhine as a military barrier for France.[2] André Tardieu presented a general memorandum on February 26, prepared at the instruction of Clemenceau, calling for the fixing of Germany's western frontier at the Rhine and an allied occupation of the left bank as essential for French security. France, according to the Tardieu memorandum, did not wish to annex the left bank but desired only to establish there a "zone of safety." Such an arrangement, it was argued, would also provide Britain and America with a continental bridgehead to supplement sea power in their own security systems.[3]

Nothing definite was settled regarding the French claims during President Wilson's absence from mid-February to mid-March. The Supreme Council during this period was largely concerned with the military clauses of the treaty and territorial questions were being considered by the expert commissions. Colonel House cabled the substance of the French proposals to President Wilson on February 19 and Wilson cabled back instructing House not to acquiesce in any French schemes for the Rhineland.[4]

The French proposals, embodied in the Foch and Tardieu memoranda, were submitted for preparatory discussions to a committee of Tardieu, Philip Kerr, and Dr. Mezes, who met on March 11 and 12. Tardieu explained the proposals contained in

[2] Louis A. R. Yates, *United States and French Security, 1917-1921* (New York: Twayne Publisher, Inc., 1957), pp. 159-168; David Lloyd George, *The Truth about the Peace Treaties* (2 Vols., London: Victor Gollancz, Ltd., 1938), Vol. 1, pp. 387-389.

[3] André Tardieu, *The Truth about the Treaty* (Indianapolis: The Bobbs-Merrill Company, Inc., 1921), pp. 147-167; Yates, *United States and French Security*, pp. 177-198.

[4] House to Wilson, February 19, Wilson to House, February 20, 1919, Charles Seymour, ed., *The Intimate Papers of Colonel House* (4 Vols., Boston and New York: Houghton Mifflin Company, 1926-1928), Vol. 4, pp. 332-336.

his memorandum of February 26, becoming increasingly conscious of the "psychological barrier" between himself and his colleagues. Mezes in fact remained silent, and the debate was between Tardieu and Kerr. England, said Kerr, was opposed to a military occupation of the left bank because it would create a nationalist agitation throughout Germany and might "at the same time foster in Anglo-Saxon countries a propaganda unfavorable to the Allies, and especially to France." Kerr strongly opposed the creation of an independent left bank republic, which he thought would generate new conflicts. "If war results from these conflicts," Kerr asserted, "neither England nor her Dominions will have that deep feeling of solidarity with France which animated them in the last war." Tardieu replied that as the "sentinel of the overseas democracies," France was entitled to measures of security. "To ask us to give up occupation," Tardieu affirmed, "is like asking England and the United States to sink their fleets of battleships. We refuse."[5]

The inability of the special committee to agree threw the issue back to their chiefs. Lloyd George and Colonel House conferred privately in an anteroom at the Quai d'Orsay on March 12. The Prime Minister said that he was seriously troubled by the French demand for the Rhine frontier. He recognized, he said, that it would take time for the League of Nations to become a strong organization, and he was therefore prepared to offer a pledge of British assistance to France in case of invasion, in lieu of an occupation and the detachment of the Rhineland. Lloyd George asked if the United States would join Great Britain in such a guarantee. House said that he did not know.[6]

Lloyd George conferred secretly with Wilson on the morning of March 14, the day of the President's return, and told him of the gravity of the French situation and of his proposed military guarantee to France. The President agreed to join in the guarantee, and in a secret meeting that afternoon at the Crillon, Wilson and Lloyd George offered to Clemenceau treaties of guarantee committing

<hr>

[5] Tardieu, *The Truth about the Treaty*, pp. 172-175; Lloyd George, *The Truth about the Peace Treaties*, Vol. 1, pp. 396-398. Lloyd George believed that the American delegation was at least willing to entertain proposals for the detachment of the Rhineland, as against the resolute opposition of the British Government. *ibid.*, pp. 398-399.

[6] House Diary, March 12, 1919, Seymour, ed., *Intimate Papers*, Vol. 4, p. 360.

Great Britain and the United States to come to the assistance of France against German invasion, on condition that France give up its demands for the occupation and detachment of the Rhineland.[7] In making this significant offer, the President and the Prime Minister were proposing a revolutionary innovation in the historical relations between their nations and the continent of Europe.

Clemenceau, though perhaps more pleased with the guarantee offer than he cared to show, gave no immediate answer to Wilson and Lloyd George. On March 17, he handed to the President and the Prime Minister a note accepting the guarantee proposal only if coupled with a thirty-years' Allied occupation of the Rhineland and the complete demilitarization of Germany to a line 50 kilometers east of the Rhine, with any German violation to be regarded as an act of aggression. The note called further for the creation of an Anglo-French-American commission of inspection to oversee German compliance with these terms and also demanded that France be given the right to reoccupy German territory in the event of German violations after the end of the thirty years' occupation.[8]

Although Wilson and Lloyd George resolutely opposed the proposals contained in the French note of March 17, the French clung to their demands and their intransigence now cast an atmosphere of crisis and pessimism over the Peace Conference. "The President," wrote House in his diary on March 22, "looked worn and tired. . . . From the looks of things the crisis will soon be here."[9] Lloyd George was greatly distressed and decided to withdraw for a few days of meditation. "I am going to Fontainebleau for the week-end," he told Lord Riddell, "and mean to put in the hardest forty-eight hours' thinking I have ever done."[10] Lloyd

[7] Lloyd George, *The Truth about the Peace Treaties*, Vol. 1, p. 403; Tardieu, *The Truth about the Treaty*, pp. 176-177; Yates, *United States and French Security*, pp. 49-51. This discussion, and most of the discussions concerning the French Rhineland claims, except for those relating to the Saar, were held as private conferences among Clemenceau, Wilson, and Lloyd George, and are thus not reported in the official minutes of the Councils of Ten and Four.

[8] Clemenceau to Wilson and Lloyd George, March 17, 1919, Tardieu, *The Truth about the Treaty*, pp. 178-182; Yates, *United States and French Security*, pp. 53, 198-202. See also Paul Birdsall, *Versailles Twenty Years After* (London: George Allen and Unwin, Ltd., 1941), pp. 207-211.

[9] House Diary, March 22, 1919, Seymour, ed., *Intimate Papers*, Vol. 4, p. 389.

[10] *Lord Riddell's Intimate Diary of the Peace Conference and After, 1918-1923* (New York: Reynal and Hitchcock, Inc., 1934), p. 36.

George conferred at Fontainebleau with General Smuts, Sir Henry Wilson, Sir Maurice Hankey, and Philip Kerr and produced a document which expressed British thinking on all of the major problems awaiting settlement.[11]

The Fontainebleau Memorandum of March 25 declared that any effort to hold Germany down by harsh and unjust terms of peace would surely fail. As to the French Rhineland proposals, Lloyd George wrote: "I cannot conceive of any greater cause of future war. . . ." The Prime Minister proposed as a "guiding principle of the peace" that "as far as is humanly possible the different races should be allocated to their motherlands, and that this human criterion should have precedence over considerations of strategy or economics or communications. . . ." Until the League has established its effectiveness, it was asserted, an Anglo-American guarantee to France against aggression was essential. Outlining a broad set of proposed peace terms, Lloyd George suggested as to the Rhineland that it be demilitarized but not separated from Germany, while the Anglo-American guarantee to France would be automatically invoked if German forces crossed the Rhine without the consent of the League Council. As to Germany's western frontier, the memorandum called for German cessions to restore the French frontier of 1814, or alternately, French use of the Saar coal mines for a period of ten years.[12]

The paradoxical nature of Anglo-American relations at the Peace Conference is evidenced by the fact that Lloyd George's statesmanlike document was conceived and issued unilaterally, although it contained scarcely a clause to which President Wilson could not have wholeheartedly subscribed. Indeed, the key point of the memorandum, that injustice in the hour of triumph is the cause of future wars, was also one of the President's most cherished principles. Yet the President and the Prime Minister apparently did not even consider a joint statement of their common ideas although such a common front would certainly have strengthened the diplomatic positions of both. One possible ex-

---

[11] Lloyd George, *The Truth about the Peace Treaties*, Vol. 1, pp. 403-404.

[12] "Some Considerations for the Peace Conference before They Finally Draft Their Terms," March 25, 1919, Great Britain, Parliament, *Papers by Command*, 1922, Cmd. 1614; Lloyd George, *The Truth about the Peace Treaties*, Vol. 1, pp. 404-415. The Fontainebleau memorandum is also reproduced in Baker, *Wilson and World Settlement*, Vol. 3, pp. 449-457. Baker, however, mistakenly attributes it not to Lloyd George but to General Bliss. *ibid.*, Vol. 2, pp. 495-496, Vol. 3, p. 449.

planation for this is that Wilson and Lloyd George, while wholly in accord over the French Rhineland claims, were at this time in sharp disagreement over the reparations question.[13] A more fundamental explanation that suggests itself is the mutual temperamental alienation of the two statesmen which again and again in the course of the Peace Conference led them to strike parallel but never common diplomatic postures.

Lloyd George sent his document to Wilson and Clemenceau on March 26. Clemenceau had Tardieu, who saw the Fontainebleau Memorandum as the latest manifestation of Lloyd George's "parliamentary obsession," prepare a contentious reply, to which Lloyd George in turn responded in angry and caustic terms.[14] So far as is known, President Wilson did not specifically reply to or comment on the Fontainebleau Memorandum.[15]

The French demands and the Anglo-American counterproposals were vigorously debated in the Council of Four on March 27. President Wilson appealed for moderation, urging Clemenceau not to give Germany cause to seek revenge, while Lloyd George, with some lack of tact, recalled to Clemenceau how in 1815 Castlereagh and Wellington had restrained Prussia from destroying France. But Clemenceau was unmovable. "The Germans," he said, "are a servile people who need force to uphold an argument." France needed security, declared the Premier, and since the League of Nations did not provide military sanctions, France had to seek them elsewhere—an equivalent, in short, for the seas which protected England and America. Agreeing now to the demilitarization of Germany to a line 50 kilometers east of the Rhine as demanded in the French note of March 17, President Wilson asserted that this, coupled with the military guarantee of Great Britain and the United States, would fully satisfy the requirements of French security. Clemenceau replied that France could not be satisfied with a *temporary* military guarantee and

---

[13] See Chapter 9, Sections IV-VI.

[14] Lloyd George, *The Truth about the Peace Treaties*, Vol. 1, pp. 416-422; Tardieu, *The Truth about the Treaty*, pp. 115-118.

[15] The Wilson Papers contain a copy of the Fontainebleau Memorandum, the French response, and a personal note from Lloyd George to Wilson dated April 2 enclosing a copy of Lloyd George's reply to the Clemenceau-Tardieu letter, but no communication or commentary by the President. Woodrow Wilson Papers, Library of Congress, Washington, D.C., Series 8-A.

asked if the guarantee could not be written into the Covenant of the League. Wilson replied that provisions for a particular nation could not be put into a pact of general principles, but he assured Clemenceau that Britain and the United States would be fully prepared to come to the assistance of France against unprovoked German aggression.[16]

While Clemenceau was thus contesting the adequacy of the proffered Anglo-American guarantee, the American Commissioners were registering opposition to it. Henry White told Colonel House that he and Lansing and Bliss regarded the proposed military alliance as "extremely unfortunate" and "absolutely fatal to the success of the League of Nations."[17]

The deadlock among the heads of government gave rise to speculation that the Peace Conference might break up. "The time has not yet come," said President Wilson; "we cannot risk breaking up the Peace Conference—yet." But apparently he had begun to consider American withdrawal.[18]

The question of French security was again fruitlessly debated in the Council of Four on March 31. Clemenceau now demanded the occupation as a guarantee of reparations payments and Marshal Foch argued that the Rhine was the essential strategic frontier of all of the western powers. Without it, he averred, the Anglo-American guarantee would be inadequate, for the German generals would attempt to defeat France before Anglo-American power could be brought to bear. Wilson and Lloyd George offered vigorous but vain resistance.[19] The deadlock at this juncture seemed quite unbreakable.

[16] Council of Four, March 27, 1919, 11 a.m., 3:30 p.m., Paul Mantoux, Les Délibérations du Conseil des Quatre (2 Vols., Paris: Éditions du Centre National de La Recherche Scientifique, 1955), Vol. I, pp. 41-45, 50.
[17] Minutes of the Daily Meetings of the American Commissioners, March 27, 1919, Department of State, Papers Relating to the Foreign Relations of the United States, 1919, The Paris Peace Conference (13 Vols., Washington: United States Government Printing Office, 1942-1947), Vol. II, p. 133; hereafter referred to as Foreign Relations. See also Robert Lansing, The Peace Negotiations (Boston and New York: Houghton Mifflin Company, 1921), pp. 180-185.
[18] Baker's Diary, March 28, 1919, Baker, Wilson and World Settlement, Vol. 2, p. 40.
[19] Council of Four, March 31, 1919, 11 a.m., 3 p.m., Mantoux, Les Délibérations du Conseil des Quatre, Vol. I, pp. 89-90, 92-95.

II. *The Saar Struggle, the Crisis of April, and the League of Nations Solution*

Besides their strategic demands for the Rhine frontier and the occupation of the Rhineland, the French made special demands in regard to the heavily industrialized and coal-producing but German-populated Saar valley. The French eastern frontier of 1814 had included part of the district within France, but it had been entirely German since 1815, and its population had an unquestionable German affinity. The French, however, made a strong claim for the Saar on grounds of reparation. The German Army had despoiled and flooded the French coal mines at Lens and Valenciennes, and Great Britain and the United States readily agreed that France was entitled to restitution from the rich Saar coal fields. The problem was to give France the coal without giving her the German population.[20]

As early as February 21, a group of British and American experts had agreed that France was entitled to full ownership of the Saar coal mines. It was felt, however, that some special regime would be essential to avoid imposing French sovereignty on the Saarlanders.[21] But the Saar problem was not considered in earnest by the heads of governments until the end of March.

The Council of Four took up the Saar issue on March 28. André Tardieu appealed for the French frontier of 1814, French ownership of the mines, and a special administration for the mining and industrial areas, basing the French claims on grounds of historical affiliation and reparation. Lloyd George and Wilson readily agreed that France was entitled to economic compensation, but the President vigorously maintained that annexation by France would be a violation of the fundamental principles on which the peace was to be based. Justice, he said, required compensation to France but proper guarantees for the Saar as a whole. Clemenceau argued eloquently for annexation, contending that justice should satisfy "sentiments" as well as "abstract principles." Lloyd George

[20] See Haskins and Lord, *Some Problems of the Peace Conference,* pp. 135-146; Haskins, "The New Boundaries of Germany," *What Really Happened at Paris* (House and Seymour, eds.), pp. 56-61; Birdsall, *Versailles Twenty Years After,* pp. 224-237.

[21] David Hunter Miller, *My Diary at the Conference of Paris,* privately printed (21 Vols., New York: Appeal Printing Company, 1924), Vol. 19, pp. 59-60.

supported the President, appealing to Clemenceau not to repeat the German error of Alsace-Lorraine. The Prime Minister proposed as a compromise the creation of an autonomous Saar state. Wilson objected that it was as much a violation of self-determination to give to a population an independence that it did not want as it was to place it under an alien sovereignty.[22]

With Lloyd George favoring a separate regime, President Wilson stood alone in upholding the right of the Saarlanders to remain part of Germany. Colonel House appealed vainly to the President to avoid the "tactical error" of adhering to a position which was not supported by the British.[23] The French submitted a note on March 29 demanding ownership of the Saar mines, a special political administration, and a fifteen-year French occupation under a League of Nations mandate with a plebiscite to be held at the end of that period.[24] President Wilson rejected these proposals in the Council of Four on March 31, submitting a new plan which agreed to French ownership of the mines but again rejected the demand for a separate political administration.[25]

On April 1, Henry Wickham Steed, the British journalist, took it upon himself to attempt to mediate between Wilson and Clemenceau on the Saar issue. He proposed a French mandate over the Saar for fifteen years, to be followed by a plebiscite. France would have the use but not the ownership of the mines, but if at the end of the fifteen years the French mines were found to be irreparable, France would retain control of the Saar mines regardless of the outcome of the plebiscite. Wickham Steed sent his proposal to House, who submitted it to the President with a penciled note in the margin advising Wilson to let Wickham Steed submit the plan to Clemenceau.[26] It is difficult to understand how Wickham Steed, or House, could have supposed that this plan, which was not a compromise but almost a stiffening of the French demands, would be acceptable to President Wilson. Nevertheless, Wickham Steed

[22] Council of Four, March 28, 1919, 4 p.m., Mantoux, *Les Délibérations du Conseil des Quatre*, Vol. 1, pp. 63-74; Tardieu, *The Truth about the Treaty*, pp. 251-265.
[23] House Diary, March 28, 1919, Seymour, ed., *Intimate Papers*, Vol. 4, p. 397.
[24] Tardieu, *The Truth about the Treaty*, pp. 266-268.
[25] Council of Four, March 31, 11 a.m., Mantoux, *Les Délibérations du Conseil des Quatre*, Vol. 1, p. 89; Baker, *Wilson and World Settlement*, Vol. 2, pp. 73-74.
[26] Wickham Steed to House, April 1, 1919, Wilson Papers, Series 8-A.

reports calling at the Crillon on April 2 and being informed by Frazier that the President had flown into a terrible rage upon seeing his proposals. "Then Clemenceau is quite right," Wickham Steed told Frazier. "Your President is an utterly impossible fellow. . . ."[27]

With the French crisis seemingly insuperable, Bolshevism spreading in Germany, and widespread turmoil elsewhere in Europe, President Wilson by early April seemed almost ready to break off negotiations. Baker told the President on April 2 that he was being widely held responsible for the crisis and Wilson replied: "I know that. . . . But we've got to make peace on the principles laid down and accepted, or not make it at all."[28] On April 3, Wilson fell seriously ill with influenza and for days thereafter lay in bed while the Council of Four, with House sitting in for the President, debated fruitlessly in the next room. The British, who had agreed to a separate political administration for the Saar, provided no support for the President. Baker discussed Lloyd George's attitude with Wilson on April 7, and the President said: "Well, I suppose I shall have to stand alone."[29] Sir William Wiseman privately recommended that the President lay before the Council of Four a draft treaty of peace based strictly on the Fourteen Points and that he threaten to go home unless there were immediate action. If Wilson would offer the inducement of a deferral of all Allied war loans, Wiseman urged, the Allies would be bound to accept an "American peace."[30]

The President summoned the U.S.S. "George Washington" on April 7, authorizing the American Press Bureau to announce this publicly. The announcement had a resounding impact, shocking the French with the prospect of an American departure and the loss of the promised military guarantee.[31] Baker visited the

[27] Henry Wickham Steed, *Through Thirty Years, 1892-1922* (2 Vols., London: William Heinemann, Ltd., 1924), Vol. 2, pp. 310-313.

[28] Baker, *Wilson and World Settlement*, Vol. 2, pp. 40-41.

[29] *ibid.*, pp. 43-44.

[30] Wiseman to House, April 5, 1919, Edward M. House Papers, Sterling Library, Yale University.

[31] Baker, *Wilson and World Settlement*, Vol. 2, pp. 57-58; Yates, *United States and French Security*, pp. 59-60; Charles T. Thompson, *The Peace Conference Day by Day* (New York: Brentano's Publishers, 1920), p. 289; Thomas A. Bailey, *Woodrow Wilson and the Lost Peace* (New York: The Macmillan Company, 1944), pp. 223-224.

President on the evening of April 7 and left convinced that the summoning of the "George Washington" was not merely a diplomatic bluff. "Well, the time has come to bring this thing to a head," Baker reports the President as saying. ". . . One mass of tergiversations! I will not discuss anything with them any more."[32]

Wilson's stroke produced immediate results. The summoning of the "George Washington" had a "castor oil" effect on the French, Dr. Grayson wrote to Tumulty on April 10, generating more progress in two days than there had been in the previous two weeks.[33] The negotiations from April 8 to April 14 produced basic agreements on the Saar and Rhineland issues, essentially resolving the French crisis.

The deadlock still seemed hopeless when Wilson returned to the Council of Four on the afternoon of April 8. Lloyd George that morning had endorsed the French position on the Saar, proposing to make it an independent entity under League of Nations authority, with a French mandate and customs union, and with French ownership of the coal mines and control of the administration and foreign relations.[34] Wilson now proposed the retention of German sovereignty over the Saar and the establishment of a commission of arbitration composed of three members appointed by the League of Nations and one each by France and Germany to rule on all issues of French economic rights. In fifteen years, under the President's scheme, there would be a definitive plebiscite to settle the permanent sovereignty over the Saar. Clemenceau maintained adamantly that the economic rights of France were incompatible with German sovereignty and Lloyd George agreed that there should be a special regime.[35]

Tardieu submitted a note to the Council on the morning of April 9 which rejected the President's proposal of the previous

[32] Ray Stannard Baker, *American Chronicle* (New York: Charles Scribner's Sons, 1945), pp. 403-404.

[33] Grayson to Tumulty, April 10, 1919, Wilson Papers, Series 8-A.

[34] Council of Four, April 8, 1919, 11 a.m., *Foreign Relations, 1919, The Paris Peace Conference*, Vol. 5, pp. 60-61, 66-70; Mantoux, *Les Délibérations du Conseil des Quatre*, Vol. 1, pp. 181-183; Tardieu, *The Truth about the Treaty*, p. 271.

[35] Council of Four, April 8, 1919, 3 p.m., Mantoux, *Les Délibérations du Conseil des Quatre*, Vol. 1, pp. 193-194; Tardieu, *The Truth about the Treaty*, pp. 271-272; Baker, *Wilson and World Settlement*, Vol. 2, pp. 74-75; Seymour, ed., *Intimate Papers*, Vol. 4, p. 405.

day, insisting on a special political administration under a French mandate but agreeing to a plebiscite in fifteen years.[36] The British presented a draft plan which was in most respects the same as the Tardieu proposal.[37] Lloyd George recommended the Tardieu plan to the President as embodying a great concession and he urged the President to agree now to a special political administration for the Saar.[38]

President Wilson rejected the Anglo-French proposals but in the afternoon session of April 9 he set forth a new proposal which broke the impasse. Wilson's plan called for a fifteen-year administration of the Saar under a commission appointed by and responsible to the League of Nations. The commission, though instructed to respect local institutions, would be fully endowed with legislative and executive powers and empowered to arbitrate disputes concerning the economic rights of France. During the fifteen-year period, under this plan, German sovereignty would be *suspended* in practice while retained in theory, and at the end of it, a definitive plebiscite would be held. Lloyd George was at once converted. He now gave his enthusiastic support to President Wilson, maintaining that his plan fully met the objections of the French to the retention of German sovereignty. It was agreed that the experts would consider this proposal, and at the end of the discussion Clemenceau allowed that he foresaw agreement on the basis of Wilson's scheme.[39]

In the remaining negotiations on the Saar, Wilson and Lloyd George stood together for the President's plan. It was accepted in principle on April 10 and its details examined on April 10 and 11. At Clemenceau's insistence, it was agreed that the treaty clause would not specifically state that German sovereignty was maintained. The plan as adopted gave France full ownership of the Saar coal mines and a customs union.[40] The essence of the com-

[36] Tardieu, *The Truth about the Treaty*, pp. 272-276.

[37] Miller, *Diary*, Vol. 8, pp. 165-166.

[38] Council of Four, April 9, 1919, 11 a.m., Mantoux, *Les Délibérations du Conseil des Quatre*, Vol. 1, p. 196.

[39] Council of Four, April 9, 1919, 3:30 p.m., *ibid.*, pp. 203-207; Tardieu, *The Truth about the Treaty*, p. 276.

[40] Council of Four, April 10, 1919, 11 a.m., April 11, 1919, 11 a.m., Mantoux, *Les Délibérations du Conseil des Quatre*, Vol. 1, pp. 209-213, 224-228; Tardieu, *The Truth about the Treaty*, pp. 276-277; Seymour, ed., *Intimate Papers*, Vol. 4, pp. 405-406.

promise, which rendered the French demands compatible with President Wilson's principles, was the practical suspension but theoretical maintenance of German sovereignty.

The resolution of the Saar crisis was made possible by the prospective existence of the League of Nations. In this as in other substantive issues dealt with by the Peace Conference, the fledgling League served as a vehicle for the accommodation of seemingly irreconcilable positions. The Saar issue also illustrates the rather different motives of Wilson and Lloyd George in resisting the French program for military security. The President was preeminently concerned with the principles of justice involved and resisted the Saar and Rhineland claims of the French with equal vigor insofar as they would have placed German populations under an alien sovereignty. Lloyd George was primarily fearful of the practical consequences of the French designs for European stability and equilibrium, and this perhaps explains why he resisted the permanent detachment of the Rhineland with almost greater vigor than the President while raising no objection to French political administration of the Saar. The latter issue, apparently, did not at first seem to the Prime Minister to pose the threat of "another Alsace-Lorraine." Since one way or the other France was to acquire at least temporary domination of the Saar, Lloyd George was not disposed to quibble over the abstract question of sovereignty. He therefore readily accepted the demand for a French mandate, but when the President devised a scheme to give France economic restitution while reserving the right of the Saarlanders later to elect German nationality, Lloyd George enthusiastically accepted the President's plan as a workable synthesis of political realities and Wilsonian abstractions.[41]

III. *The Resolution of the Rhineland Crisis and the Anglo-
American Treaties of Guarantee, April 11-29; Other
Territorial Issues in Western Europe*

The settlement of the Saar crisis was followed by the resolution of the Rhineland issue and the question of French security. The

[41] For a good brief discussion of the Saar issue at the Peace Conference, see Frank M. Russell, *The Saar: Battleground and Pawn* (Stanford, California: Stanford University Press, 1951), pp. 7-17.

core of the ultimate compromise between the conflicting French and Anglo-American positions was the abandonment by France of plans for the detachment of the Rhineland from Germany in return for binding Anglo-American military commitments to France contained in the proposed treaties of guarantee.

The basis of agreement was established with relative ease. In a note handed to the French on April 12, President Wilson reaffirmed the offer of military guarantees to France while warning that these represented the "maximum of what I myself deem necessary for the safety of France, or possible on the part of the United States."[42] Clemenceau refused an Anglo-American proposal to limit the treaties of guarantee to a period of three years and it was agreed that they would be terminated when a majority of the League Council agreed that the League of Nations itself afforded sufficient protection against German aggression. Clemenceau, in turn, agreed to give up all plans for the detachment of the Rhineland from Germany, but he insisted upon the demilitarization of Germany to a line 50 kilometers east of the Rhine and on a fifteen-years' occupation, no longer demanding one of thirty years.[43]

The compromise was consummated in a conference between Clemenceau and Colonel House on April 14. Clemenceau agreed to couple the treaties of guarantee and the demilitarization of western Germany with a fifteen-year, three-stage occupation providing for partial withdrawals of occupation forces at five-year intervals depending upon German compliance with the treaty. In a meeting with House on April 15, the President, although expressing distaste for the occupation provisions, agreed to the total plan, and on the 16th House informed Clemenceau of the President's compliance.[44]

Lloyd George continued to have grave misgivings about the occupation. He was shocked by Wilson's "surrender" of April 15 and suspected that the President's agreement to the Rhineland occupation was part of a bargain with Clemenceau whereby the latter suddenly called off the hitherto sharp attacks on the Presi-

[42] Tardieu, *The Truth about the Treaty*, p. 184.
[43] *ibid.*, pp. 207-209; Yates, *United States and French Security*, pp. 59-60.
[44] Seymour, ed., *Intimate Papers*, Vol. 4, pp. 406-409; Yates, *United States and French Security*, pp. 60-61; Baker, *Wilson and World Settlement*, Vol. 2, pp. 76-83.

dent by the French press. "I did my best," writes Lloyd George, "to convince President Wilson of the mischievous possibilities of the occupation, but in vain."[45]

Lloyd George capitulated in the meeting of the Council of Four on April 22, agreeing to the fifteen-year occupation. Clemenceau handed round the draft treaty of guarantee, which he and Wilson had agreed to on April 20. President Wilson, perhaps in fear of the possible reaction in the United States to a direct alliance with England, opposed a tri-partite treaty and suggested that two separate treaties be signed, between France and the United States and between France and Great Britain. Lloyd George readily agreed to this arrangement.[46]

At French insistence, the occupation clause of the treaty was further amended on April 29 to permit a delay in the evacuation of Allied forces at the end of fifteen years if the guarantees against German aggression at that time "are not considered sufficient by the Allied and Associated Governments. . . ." This was designed to meet French fears that the United States Senate might deny its consent to the ratification of the treaty of guarantee.[47]

The agreement on the treaties of guarantee was announced at the Plenary Session of the Peace Conference on May 6.[48] At the end of the session, Wilson and Lloyd George handed letters to Clemenceau expressing their agreement to conclude the guarantee treaties with France and to submit them to their respective legislatures. Lloyd George's letter stipulated that the Anglo-French treaty "will be in similar terms to that entered into by the United States and will come into force when the latter is ratified."[49] On the day before the Plenary Session, President Wilson had commented to David Hunter Miller that "Lloyd George had slipped

[45] Lloyd George, *The Truth about the Peace Treaties*, Vol. 1, pp. 425-426.

[46] Council of Four, April 22, 1919, 11 a.m., *Foreign Relations, 1919, The Paris Peace Conference*, Vol. 5, pp. 113-114, 118; Tardieu, *The Truth about the Treaty*, pp. 186-187; Yates, *United States and French Security*, pp. 61-62.

[47] Tardieu, *The Truth about the Treaty*, pp. 210-216; Georges Clemenceau, *Grandeur and Misery of Victory* (New York: Harcourt, Brace and Company, 1930), pp. 237-239; Yates, *United States and French Security*, p. 63.

[48] Plenary Session, May 6, 1919, *Foreign Relations, 1919, The Paris Peace Conference*, Vol. 3, p. 379.

[49] Lloyd George and Balfour to Clemenceau, May 6, 1919, *Foreign Relations, 1919, The Paris Peace Conference*, Vol. 5, pp. 494-495; Wilson and Lansing to Clemenceau, May 6, 1919, *ibid.*, pp. 495-496. See also Yates, *United States and French Security*, pp. 64-68.

a paragraph into the British note about ratification by the United States and that he [the President] did not think Clemenceau had noticed it."[50]

Woodrow Wilson has been severely criticized for entering into an "entangling alliance" with France. A noted historian has contended that Wilson "probably knew" that the Senate would refuse to consider the guarantee treaty and that it was "a way the diplomatists had to get around a difficult corner."[51] The accusation that Wilson entered the treaty in bad faith is difficult to credit, not only because of Wilson's character, but because the protracted and difficult negotiations which led to the treaty of guarantee suggest a most serious *bona fide* effort to work out an acceptable commitment and certainly do not provide any evidence of bad faith. Moreover, the French, who were left "holding the bag," did not charge Wilson with bad faith. In July 1920, André Tardieu told Colonel Bonsal that he considered such charges unfounded. "I am not so sure of the good faith of Lloyd George," said Tardieu. "Why should he have made the assistance of Britain contingent upon the ratification of the pact by Washington?"[52]

President Wilson did not conceive of the guarantee pact as a conventional alliance. It was, he told the Senate on July 29, 1919, a "temporary supplement" to the treaty, not independent of the League of Nations but under it.[53] Wilson's concept of collective security assumed a world of juridically equal states and he refused to recognize an Anglo-French-American alliance as its nucleus. The guarantee treaties were, to Wilson, a significant but temporary supplement to the League designed to assuage the fears of France.

The rejection of the treaties of guarantee by the United States and Great Britain did much to destroy the possibility of a liberal development of the Versailles system. By throwing France back to the letter of the treaty in her vain quest for security, the United States and Great Britain contributed indirectly to the rise of the

---

[50] Miller's Diary, May 5, 1919, Miller, *Diary*, Vol. 1, p. 294.

[51] Samuel Flagg Bemis, *A Diplomatic History of the United States* (4th edn., New York: Henry Holt and Company, 1955), pp. 636-637.

[52] Stephen Bonsal, *Suitors and Suppliants* (New York: Prentice-Hall, Inc., 1946), p. 217.

[53] Ray Stannard Baker and William E. Dodd, eds., *The Public Papers of Woodrow Wilson* (6 Vols., New York and London: Harper & Brothers, Publishers, 1925-1927), *War and Peace*, Vol. 1, pp. 555-556.

spirit of revenge in Germany, which was further encouraged by the absence of an instrument for the automatic reformulation of the coalition which had defeated Germany in 1918.[54]

The Rhineland crisis was over by the end of April. A movement by French generals to overturn the decisions of the Peace Conference by promoting an artificial separatist movement in the Rhineland in late May and early June angered and alarmed British and American statesmen. Wilson and Lloyd George lodged strong protests with Clemenceau, who loyally took strong measures to crush the "Rhineland rebellion," which consequently ended in ignominious failure.[55]

Of all of the territorial changes which took place in 1919, none was settled with greater ease and unanimity than the restoration of Alsace-Lorraine to France. Both Great Britain and the United States had made the restitution of Alsace-Lorraine an integral part of their war aims. The Treaty of Versailles restored Alsace-Lorraine to France as of the date of the Armistice. Both Britain and the United States fully agreed with the French that a plebiscite, as requested by the Germans, would have been "insultingly illegitimate," implying that the German act of 1871 was an open question.[56]

Besides the Rhineland and Saar questions, the Peace Conference was confronted with only minor territorial problems in western Europe. Belgium demanded certain adjustments of her frontiers with Germany and the Netherlands and of her neutralized status under the treaty of 1839, and Denmark asked for restitution of part of the territory which had been forcibly taken from her by Prussia in 1864. In dealing with the Belgian and Danish territorial

[54] See Clemenceau, *Grandeur and Misery of Victory*, pp. 246-247; Denis Saurat, "How the Treaty Looks to France Today," *The Versailles Treaty and After* (Lord Riddell, C. K. Webster, Arnold J. Toynbee, Denis Saurat, et al., contributors, New York: Oxford University Press, 1935), p. 104.

[55] Baker, *Wilson and World Settlement*, Vol. 2, pp. 84-94; Clemenceau, *Grandeur and Misery of Victory*, pp. 215-233; Yates, *United States and French Security*, pp. 69-70.

[56] Haskins and Lord, *Some Problems of the Peace Conference*, pp. 75-112; Haskins, "The New Boundaries of Germany," *What Really Happened at Paris* (House and Seymour, eds.), pp. 46-48; Tardieu, *The Truth about the Treaty*, pp. 238-246; H.W.V. Temperley, ed., *A History of the Peace Conference of Paris* (6 Vols., London: Henry Frowde and Hodder and Stoughton, 1920-1924), Vol. 2, pp. 167-168.

claims, Great Britain and the United States adhered harmoniously to the principle of self-determination, refusing to transfer unwilling populations to alien control.

The Belgian claims were taken up early in the Peace Conference. The Belgian Government submitted a memorandum on January 17 calling for the release of Belgium from the obligation of neutrality imposed by the treaty of 1839 and, on grounds of strategic necessity, for the cession by Holland of Dutch territory on the left bank of the Scheldt. The memorandum further requested the cession of small German territories around Eupen and Malmédy, and asked the Allies to foster a union of Luxemburg with Belgium.[57] The Belgian Foreign Minister, Hymans, set forth these claims in the Council of Ten on February 11,[58] and on February 12 the Council established an expert commission to deal with Belgian affairs under the chairmanship of André Tardieu.[59]

The Commission for Belgian Affairs advised the revision of the treaty of 1839 to release Belgium from the obligation of neutrality and the Council agreed to this on March 8, advising the signatories to the 1839 treaty to negotiate its revision.[60]

The Belgian demand for cessions by the Netherlands encountered firm Anglo-American opposition to the extraction of territory from a friendly and neutral state. In the Council of Ten on February 26, Balfour and Lansing spoke firmly against any compulsion of Holland or, as the Belgians proposed, the compensation of Holland with German territory.[61] Hymans pressed these claims on March 31, bitterly complaining at the lack of attention to Belgian views, and Lloyd George reprimanded him sternly, threatening not to allow Hymans to appear again before the Council.[62] The Commission for Belgian Affairs recommended that the Belgian claims to the left bank of the Scheldt and Dutch Limberg be satisfied, with Holland to be compensated by German territory.[63]

[57] Miller, *Diary*, Vol. 4, pp. 426-440.

[58] Council of Ten, February 11, 1919, 3 p.m., *Foreign Relations, 1919, The Paris Peace Conference*, Vol. 3, pp. 958-969.

[59] Council of Ten, February 12, 1919, 3 p.m., *ibid.*, pp. 1006-1007.

[60] Tardieu, *The Truth about the Treaty*, pp. 218-223; Council of Ten, March 8, 1919, 3 p.m., *Foreign Relations, 1919, The Paris Peace Conference*, Vol. 4, pp. 270-271.

[61] Council of Ten, February 26, 1919, 3 p.m., *ibid.*, pp. 142-143.

[62] Council of Four, March 31, 1919, 3 p.m., Mantoux, *Les Délibérations du Conseil des Quatre*, Vol. 1, pp. 95-98.

[63] Tardieu, *The Truth about the Treaty*, pp. 222-223.

President Wilson and Balfour opposed the Commission's recommendations in the Council of Four on April 16, arguing the injustice of imposing a penalty on Germany in an issue unrelated to the war. The Council rejected any cessions of territory by Holland to Belgium or by Germany to Holland.[64]

The Belgians asked the Peace Conference to compel the cession to Belgium of the German localities of Eupen and Malmédy and the railroad connecting these two towns. The Belgians contended that they were entitled to the forests around Eupen as compensation for adjacent forests in Belgium destroyed by the German Army and that the inhabitants of Malmédy were French-speaking.[65] The Commission for Belgian Affairs recommended that these claims be met. In the Council of Four on April 16, Wilson and Balfour expressed doubts as to Belgian acquisition of the German-populated territory traversed by the railroad between Eupen and Malmédy. The Council granted to Belgium the territories demanded, stipulating, however, that in six months public registers would be opened to permit the filing of protests or expressions of consent by the transferred population.[66]

Anglo-American statesmanship treated the modest territorial claims of Denmark with the same scrupulous regard for the principle of self-determination as that applied to the French and Belgian claims. On February 21, the Danish Minister in Paris presented his country's claim to the central part of the province of Schleswig, which had been forcibly taken from Denmark by Prussia in 1864. The issue was referred to the Commission for Belgian Affairs.[67] The Commission recommended a three-stage plebiscite: by the district as a whole in the northern zone, by communes, a few weeks later, in the middle zone where the population was mixed, and by communes in the southern zone still later.[68] The Council of Four readily agreed to this plan on April 15, although the plebiscite in the German-populated south-

[64] Council of Four, April 16, 1919, 11 a.m., Mantoux, *Les Délibérations du Conseil des Quatre*, Vol. 1, pp. 262-263.
[65] Council of Four, April 4, 1919, 11 a.m., *ibid.*, p. 142.
[66] Council of Four, April 16, 1919, 11 a.m., *ibid.*, pp. 258-261.
[67] Council of Ten, February 21, 1919, 3 p.m., *Foreign Relations, 1919, The Paris Peace Conference*, Vol. 4, pp. 65-66.
[68] Haskins and Lord, *Some Problems of the Peace Conference*, pp. 43-44.

ern zone was subsequently cancelled.[69] The plebiscite, held in February 1920, resulted in the first district voting decisively for Denmark and the second for Germany.[70]

The settlement of Germany's western and northern boundaries in 1919 was one of almost exemplary moderation and justice, due, in the main, to the diplomacy of Great Britain and the United States. Germany was deprived of no territory in the west or the north which was predominantly German in population. The formidable effort of France to detach from Germany the left bank of the Rhine led the English-speaking powers to devise binding military guarantees as an alternate means of providing security to France. For both Britain and America, the treaties of guarantee constituted a revolutionary innovation in traditional foreign policies. Britain was no longer to hold her power in reserve from the continental balance and the United States was to abandon its isolation. To President Wilson, the guarantee pacts merely restated an obligation which was inherent in membership in the League of Nations, but he accepted them as a tactically appropriate device to prevent the imposition of an unjust territorial settlement on Germany. In the disposition of the Belgian and Danish territorial claims, where no strategic interests were at stake, British and American statesmen applied the principle of self-determination with the same scrupulous care that was applied to the French claims.

As the two powers with no territorial ambitions, Great Britain and the United States had a common stake in just and stable territorial settlements in Europe, and yet this identity of interest was never translated into a coordinated Anglo-American strategy. Wilson and Lloyd George acted for the most part separately in their opposition to the French claims. Had Wilson sought to form a common front with Lloyd George on the issue of the occupation of Germany, or had Lloyd George offered consistent support to the President in opposing the detachment of the

[69] Council of Four, April 15, 1919, 4 p.m., Mantoux, *Les Délibérations du Conseil des Quatre*, Vol. 1, pp. 255-256.

[70] Haskins and Lord, *Some Problems of the Peace Conference*, pp. 45-46; Haskins, "The New Boundaries of Germany," *What Really Happened at Paris* (House and Seymour, eds.), pp. 42-43; Temperley, ed., *A History of the Peace Conference of Paris*, Vol. 2, pp. 203-206.

Saar from Germany, the French would have been deprived of the opportunities for maneuver which contributed to their success in winning agreement to the fifteen-years' occupation and the suspension of German sovereignty over the Saar. Almost certainly, the common objectives of British and American diplomacy would have been more fully realized by a genuinely coordinated strategy.

IV. *Ireland: An Anglo-American Conflict Unrealized*

There were at least two reasons why the ancient oppression of Irish nationality by Great Britain could have been the genesis of a clash between Britain and the United States at the Paris Peace Conference. The first was the dedication of President Wilson to the right of all nationalities to self-realization; the second was the existence in the United States of a vociferous Irish-American pressure group demanding Presidential action to assist their former countrymen. That the issue did not erupt into an Anglo-American conflict was due to President Wilson's confidence in the ability of the League of Nations to serve as a permanent forum for the correction of injustices and to the President's sense of proportion in refusing to take up issues which were beyond the scope of the Peace Conference.

President Wilson had long been critical of Great Britain's Irish policy. Once, before the war, he told Tumulty that he had tried to impress upon Englishmen with whom he had discussed the matter that "there never could be a real comradeship between America and England until this issue is out of the way."[71] Irish-Americans hoped that Wilson would apply pressures to the British at the Peace Conference for Irish Home Rule, but the President felt that he could not overtly interfere in a British imperial matter lest such intervention arouse British opposition to his primary objectives.

The Irish question caused Wilson great embarrassment at the Peace Conference. In January, for instance, the city of Dublin offered to the President the freedom of the city, and while he felt certain that his acceptance of the honor would irritate the

[71] Joseph P. Tumulty, *Woodrow Wilson As I Know Him* (Garden City, New York, and Toronto: Doubleday, Page and Company, 1921), pp. 394-395.

British, he hardly knew on what grounds he might decline.[72] Still more embarrassing to the President was the action of Congressman Flood of Virginia, who introduced a resolution of sympathy for Irish Home Rule in the House of Representatives. Wilson asked Tumulty to explain to Flood that the resolution would disrupt relations with Great Britain and that the President's opposition to the proposed resolution was not a question of sympathy but of "international tactics."[73] Tumulty persuaded Flood to use the form of a concurrent rather than a joint resolution, obviating the need thereby for either a Presidential veto or expression of approval.[74]

Tumulty pressed Wilson while he was at home in late February and early March to take some action for the cause of Irish Home Rule. At Tumulty's urging, the President received an Irish-American delegation after his speech at the Metropolitan Opera House on March 5, but he refused to receive the extremist leader of the delegation, one Daniel F. Cohalan, thereby angering the other members.[75] "They were so insistent," he told Ray Stannard Baker after the meeting, "that I had hard work keeping my temper." The Irish problem, Wilson said to Baker, was a domestic British matter in which no foreign power could interfere, but he anticipated that the League of Nations might take it up as a probable cause of war.[76]

A group of Irish-American delegates, commissioned by a congress of Irish societies which had met in Philadelphia in February, arrived in Paris in March and set up a clamor for Irish Home Rule. Wilson received them cordially. Lloyd George agreed to receive them, then found himself too busy, and finally, under prodding from Colonel House, provided them with transportation to visit Ireland.[77] In Ireland, the group traveled about making incendiary speeches and denouncing British "atrocities," causing Lloyd George to give up his experiment in accommodation.[78]

[72] Wilson to Lansing, January 24, 1919, Wilson Papers, Series 8-A.
[73] Wilson to Tumulty, January 26, 1919, Wilson Papers, Series 8-A.
[74] Tumulty to Wilson, February 5, 1919, Wilson Papers, Series 8-A.
[75] John M. Blum, *Joe Tumulty and the Wilson Era* (Boston: Houghton Mifflin Company, 1951), pp. 176-177.
[76] Baker, *American Chronicle*, pp. 385-386.
[77] House Diary, April 21, 29, 30, 1919, House to Wilson, May 9, 1919, House Papers.
[78] Lloyd George to House, May 9, 1919, House Papers; H.C.F. Bell, *Woodrow*

The Irish-American commission returned to Paris and the chairman, Frank P. Walsh, then wrote to the Secretary of State challenging the right of Great Britain to sign the treaty on behalf of Ireland and demanding that Irish representatives be received at the Peace Conference.[79] Wilson instructed Lansing to reply to the Irish-Americans that every effort had been made to put them into friendly communication with the British but that their offensive utterances in Ireland had made it impossible to assist them further.[80] Wilson was greatly angered by the Irish-Americans. He said to Baker on May 29: "I don't know how long I shall be able to resist telling them what I think of their miserable mischiefmaking. They can see nothing except their own small interest."[81]

The President was subjected to extreme pressures from home to act for the Irish cause. The Senate adopted a resolution expressing sympathy with the aspiration of the Irish people to self-government and calling upon the American delegation to attempt to secure a hearing before the Peace Conference for Eamon de Valera, the Irish national leader.[82] Tumulty cabled an urgent appeal to the President on June 7 to act for Irish Home Rule, warning that feeling was so intense in the United States that it might seriously damage the prospects of the League of Nations.[83] Wilson promptly cabled back that through unofficial approaches to the British he had practically cleared the way for Irish representatives to come to Paris but that the conduct of the Irish-American commission in Ireland had so inflamed British public opinion that any further efforts on behalf of Ireland would be utterly futile and might create an actual breach between Britain and the United States.[84] In a stormy interview on June 11, the President bluntly told Walsh that his group had "kicked over

---

Wilson and the People (Garden City, New York: Doubleday, Doran and Company, Inc., 1945), pp. 316-319.

[79] Walsh to Lansing, May 22, 1919, Wilson Papers, Series 8-A.

[80] Wilson to Lansing, May 22, 1919, Wilson Papers, Series 8-A.

[81] Baker, *American Chronicle*, p. 435.

[82] Lansing to Wilson, June 7, 1919, Wilson Papers, Series 8-A.

[83] Tumulty to Dr. Grayson, for Wilson, June 7, 1919, Wilson Papers, Series 8-A; Tumulty, *Wilson As I Know Him*, pp. 401-402.

[84] Wilson to Tumulty, June 8, 1919, Wilson Papers, Series 8-A; Tumulty, *Wilson As I Know Him*, p. 402.

the apple cart" and thwarted Wilson's plan to get a hearing for de Valera.[85] Tumulty pleaded with the President again, warning that de Valera's impending visit to America would intensify the problem and encourage Republican exploitation of the issue.[86] Wilson replied that the League of Nations would "afford a forum not now available for bringing the opinion of the world and of the United States in particular to bear on just such problems."[87]

President Wilson thus resisted a potent domestic pressure group in order to avoid a serious collision with Great Britain over an issue which, at least legally, was a purely domestic British problem. With the cooperation of Lloyd George, Wilson attempted to achieve partial satisfaction for the Irish demands, but the excesses and indiscretions of the Irish-American delegation thwarted this effort. Wilson did not allow the Irish question to come to the surface at the Peace Conference because of the need for British support in the achievement of his primary objectives, particularly in the establishment of the League of Nations, which, he believed, would provide permanent processes for the realization of just such aspirations as those of Irish nationality.

[85] Bell, *Wilson and the People*, p. 319.
[86] Tumulty to Wilson, June 25, 1919, Wilson Papers, Series 8-A; Tumulty, *Wilson As I Know Him*, pp. 403-404.
[87] Wilson to Tumulty, June 27, 1919, *ibid.*, p. 404.

CHAPTER 8

THE PRINCIPLE OF SELF-DETERMINATION IN ANGLO-AMERICAN POLICY: TERRITORIAL PROBLEMS OF EASTERN EUROPE AND THE MIDDLE EAST

THE task of adjusting boundaries to the complicated pattern of intermixed and overlapping nationalities in eastern and southeastern Europe proved far more difficult than the drawing of boundaries in western and northern Europe where national divisions were generally clear-cut and easily identified. To the east and south of Germany, the realization of the principle of self-determination required the creation of new national units and the re-creation of nations long submerged. By contrast with France, who wished to create strategic counterweights to Germany, and Italy, who had expansionist ambitions, Great Britain and the United States attempted to redraw the map of eastern and southeastern Europe along clearly recognizable lines of nationality. For the most part, especially in dealing with the boundaries of the Austro-Hungarian succession states, Britain and America worked harmoniously through the use of expert commissions. Elsewhere, there were differences in emphasis. In the task of re-creating Poland, American statesmen were influenced by a strong sympathy for the Polish national cause while the British were fearful of future conflicts which might arise from too generous a treatment of Poland at the expense of Germany. When the new boundaries of eastern and southeastern Europe had been drawn and it was clear that the complex intermixtures of national groups had not been and could not be completely sorted out, Great Britain and the United States led the Peace Conference to impose upon the new states treaties defining minimum standards for the treatment of the national minorities within their borders.

Difficult territorial problems also arose from the sudden emergence of national states in the Arab portions of the disintegrated Ottoman Empire. There was no question of their restoration to Turkish rule. The principal issues arose from the conflicting

[201]

claims of Arab nationality and western imperial interests. The British contrived, generally, to satisfy their own strategic and economic interests in the area, while identifying themselves with the Arab cause as against French aspirations. The United States, with no material interests at stake, was primarily concerned with the application of the principle of self-determination. Palestine was a special case in which both Great Britain and the United States departed from the strict application of self-determination by established populations and strongly supported the Zionist movement for the restoration of the ancient Jewish homeland.

I. *Anglo-American Approaches to the Re-creation of Poland*

In the first years of the war Great Britain had been obliged, and perhaps inclined, to accept the Polish policy of her Russian ally. Indeed, when Colonel House discussed Poland with British officials in February 1916, Balfour had argued against an independent Polish state lest it pose a barrier to Russian assistance to the West in any future conflict with Germany.[1] The Russian Revolution removed this consideration, and Britain, and especially France, began to think of a reconstructed Poland as a counterweight to Germany. In his war aims address of January 5, 1918, Lloyd George declared that "government with the consent of the governed must be the basis of any territorial settlement in this war," and this, he wrote in his memoirs, "inferentially included both Poland and Finland."[2] President Wilson was much more explicit, calling in Point 13 of his address of January 8, 1918, for an independent Poland composed of "indisputably Polish populations," with "free and secure access to the sea. . . ."[3]

Both the United States and Great Britain went to the Peace Conference with an active interest in the reconstruction of the long submerged Polish nation, but the problem of delineating boundaries for this long-extinguished state which had no clear frontiers by either nature or history was an extremely difficult one, compounded by the fact that the Poles themselves demanded the expansive frontiers of eighteenth century Poland before the par-

[1] Louis L. Gerson, *Woodrow Wilson and the Rebirth of Poland, 1914-1920* (New Haven: Yale University Press, 1953), pp. 27-28.
[2] David Lloyd George, *The Truth about the Peace Treaties* (2 Vols., London: Victor Gollancz, Ltd., 1938), Vol. 2, p. 971.
[3] See Chapter 1, Section v.

titions. The British were acutely sensitive to the dangers of placing a large German population within Poland and it was they more than any other delegation at Paris who resisted Polish demands for extensive territories of predominantly German population. The chief objective of Britain's Polish policy was to confine Poland within frontiers which would not arouse the national wrath of Germany and Russia when they inevitably reemerged as Great Powers. Lloyd George regarded the Polish claims as "by every canon of self-determination extravagant and inadmissible."[4] American statesmen, on the other hand, were inclined to sympathize with the aspirations of the Poles, partly, perhaps, out of sentimental regard for the experiment in republican government of the old Poland. The tone of American policy was set by the chief Polish expert of the American delegation, Robert Howard Lord, who believed that the restoration of Poland represented the "triumphant righting of the greatest political wrong that Europe had witnessed, the vindication of the principles of justice in international relations, a decisive victory for the cause of universal liberty."[5]

The Peace Conference began to act on the Polish frontiers in January 1919. The American experts of the Inquiry went far to meet the Polish demands for German territory in a tentative report submitted on January 21 calling for the cession to Poland of the port city of Danzig and a corridor between Germany and East Prussia connecting it to Poland. The report admitted that Danzig was "unquestionably a German city" but defended the recommendation on grounds of economic and geographic necessity.[6] The Council of Ten first discussed the Polish question on January 22, and it was decided to send an Allied commission to Poland to investigate conditions and sentiments.[7] On January 29,

---

[4] Lloyd George, *The Truth about the Peace Treaties*, Vol. 2, p. 972.

[5] Charles Homer Haskins and Robert Howard Lord, *Some Problems of the Peace Conference* (Cambridge: Harvard University Press, 1920), p. 153.

[6] David Hunter Miller, *My Diary at the Conference of Paris*, privately printed (21 Vols., New York: Appeal Printing Company, 1924), Vol. 4, pp. 224-226. See also John Brown Mason, *The Danzig Dilemma* (Stanford University, California: Stanford University Press, 1946), pp. 42-44.

[7] Council of Ten, January 22, 1919, 11 a.m., Department of State, *Papers Relating to the Foreign Relations of the United States, 1919, The Paris Peace Conference* (13 Vols., Washington: United States Government Printing Office, 1942-1947), Vol. 3, p. 675; hereafter referred to as *Foreign Relations*.

the Polish representative, Dmowski, delivered himself of a five-hour appeal for the Polish frontiers of 1772 as the "point of departure" in the delineation of the new Poland, drawing upon strategic, historic, and ethnographic arguments in support of Poland's claims.[8] On January 31, the Council agreed to send a Commission of Control to Teschen to attempt to avoid a conflict between Poles and Czechs over that contested district.[9]

A Commission on Polish Affairs was appointed by the Council of Ten on February 12 with Jules Cambon as chairman. The American member was Isaiah Bowman and the British member was Sir William Tyrrell.[10] The chief problem of the Commission was to determine a German-Polish boundary through a region in which the populations were extremely intermingled. A special conference of the British and American experts attempted on February 21 to devise alternatives to the cession of "purely German" areas to Poland and came to an agreement in favor of the cession of Danzig and the corridor to Poland.[11] House cabled Wilson on February 23 that Clemenceau and the British and American experts favored the cession of Danzig to Poland but that the British Government itself disagreed. Wilson cabled back instructing House to make no commitments.[12] At Balfour's suggestion, it was decided on February 26 to refer the issue of Polish boundaries to the Commission on Polish Affairs with instructions to report by March 8.[13]

The Polish Commission submitted its report on March 12. It recommended that large parts of Posen and Upper Silesia be ceded to Poland, as well as the central and eastern parts of West Prussia, including Danzig and both banks of the lower Vistula, thus dividing East Prussia from Germany. The inclusion of the German city of Danzig and the German-populated district of Marienwerder

---

[8] Council of Ten, January 29, 1919, 11 a.m., and 3:30 p.m., *ibid.*, pp. 773-782; Lloyd George, *The Truth about the Peace Treaties*, Vol. 2, pp. 972-976.

[9] Council of Ten, January 31, 1919, 3 p.m., *Foreign Relations, 1919, The Paris Peace Conference*, Vol. 3, pp. 820-822.

[10] Council of Ten, February 12, 1919, 3 p.m., *ibid.*, p. 1007.

[11] Miller, *Diary*, Vol. 19, p. 85.

[12] House to Wilson, February 23, 1919, Wilson to House, February 24, 1919, Charles Seymour, ed., *The Intimate Papers of Colonel House* (4 Vols., Boston and New York: Houghton Mifflin Company, 1926-1928), Vol. 4, pp. 334-336.

[13] Council of Ten, February 26, 1919, 3 p.m., *Foreign Relations, 1919, The Paris Peace Conference*, Vol. 4, pp. 139-141.

was held essential to provide Poland with a seaport and with control of the railroad between Warsaw and Danzig. The Commission recommended a plebiscite for the Allenstein district of southern East Prussia, with its population of Protestant, Germanized Poles.[14]

The report of the Polish Commission was presented to the Council of Ten on March 19. Jules Cambon explained the inclusion of Danzig and the corridor within Poland as necessitated by economic and strategic rather than ethnographic considerations. Lloyd George assailed the report, noting that it would put over two million Germans in Poland, raising the prospect of future trouble for the Poles and, more immediately, the possibility that Germany would not sign the treaty. Lloyd George especially objected to the proposed transfer of Marienwerder, with its German majority, for the sake of giving Poland a railroad. President Wilson noted that many Poles were in fact being left in German territory and Cambon held the railroad from Warsaw to Danzig to be essential to Poland's economic life. Lloyd George countered that the creation of a *Germania Irredenta* would sow the seeds of future wars. President Wilson admitted that the inclusion of two million Germans in Poland violated the ethnographic principle, but, he pointed out, Germany had been told that Poland was to have free and secure access to the sea. Poland was being created as a new and weak state, said the President, and it was thus necessary to take into account its strategic needs. "It was a question," said Wilson, "of balancing antagonistic considerations." Lloyd George proposed that the report be reconsidered by the Commission with a view to excluding historically and ethnographically Prussian territory from Poland while still giving Poland access to the sea. Wilson asked that the Commission merely be instructed to reconsider their report in the light of the Council's discussion, and it was so agreed.[15]

[14] Miller, *Diary*, Vol. 6, pp. 350-366; Robert Howard Lord, "Poland," *What Really Happened at Paris* (Edward Mandell House and Charles Seymour, eds., New York: Charles Scribner's Sons, 1921), pp. 75-78. See also Gerson, *Wilson and the Rebirth of Poland*, pp. 126-127.

[15] Council of Ten, March 19, 1919, 3 p.m., *Foreign Relations, 1919, The Paris Peace Conference*, Vol. 4, pp. 413-419; Lloyd George, *The Truth about the Peace Treaties*, Vol. 2, pp. 981-990. See also Gerson, *Wilson and the Rebirth of Poland*, pp. 128-129; Mason, *The Danzig Dilemma*, pp. 51-54.

The difference in the positions taken by the President and the Prime Minister in the discussion of March 19 was more striking than any of their disagreements over the French Rhineland claims. Lloyd George stood alone for a decision based on the ethnographic principle, while the President joined the French in stressing strategic and economic considerations. Lloyd George believed that the Poles had a powerful hold on the American delegation, including the President, owing to the Polish vote in the United States.[16] It seems more likely that the President's pro-Polish attitude was principally the result of natural sympathy for a long suppressed nationality and, to a lesser extent, of such factors as the influence of Robert Howard Lord and the reputedly magnetic charm of Ignace Jan Paderewski, celebrated musician and Prime Minister of the Provisional Polish Government.

The Commission on Polish affairs returned its report to the Council of Ten on March 20 with a unanimous reconfirmation of its earlier proposals.[17] Lloyd George warned again of the danger of driving Germany to such desperation that she would not sign the treaty, but he accepted the recommendations of the Commission provisionally, subject to revision by the Council when their full effects were seen. The Council thereupon provisionally accepted the report.[18]

Lloyd George gave up hope for alterations in the draft clauses by the Commission on Polish Affairs. The French, he believed, were motivated only by a desire to build up Poland as a counterweight to Germany, while he considered the American Polish experts to be "fanatical pro-Poles" whose judgment was "vitiated by an invincible partisanship."[19] On March 25, Lloyd George produced his Fontainebleau Memorandum, which stated as to the Polish-German frontier: "Poland to be given a corridor to Danzig, but this to be drawn irrespective of strategic or transportation conditions so as to embrace the smallest possible number of Germans."[20]

[16] Lloyd George, *The Truth about the Peace Treaties*, Vol. 1, p. 311.

[17] Miller, *Diary*, Vol. 9, pp. 14-24; *Foreign Relations, 1919, The Paris Peace Conference*, Vol. 4, pp. 452-454.

[18] Council of Ten, March 22, 1919, 3 p.m., *ibid.*, pp. 449-450.

[19] Lloyd George, *The Truth about the Peace Treaties*, Vol. 2, pp. 990-991.

[20] Great Britain, Parliament, *Papers by Command*, 1922, *Cmd.* 1614; Lloyd George, *The Truth about the Peace Treaties*, Vol. 1, p. 413.

The Prime Minister resumed his campaign for revision of the Polish Commission's recommendations in the Council of Four on March 27. Of all of the very harsh terms to be imposed upon Germany, Lloyd George contended, that which aroused the Germans most was the prospect of losing millions of their countrymen to Poland. Lloyd George urged upon the Council that they make Danzig a free port and leave the Poles in Poland and the Germans in Germany. He reminded France that her allies had promised to come to her assistance with all their forces in the event of German aggression. "But we ought not ourselves to sow the seeds of war." President Wilson remained silent in this phase of the discussion.[21]

President Wilson at this juncture began to come over to Lloyd George's point of view. Lloyd George believed that the President had been uneasy for some time, entertaining misgivings despite the recommendations of his experts.[22] The President and the Prime Minister conferred privately and Wilson agreed that Danzig should be made a free or international city.[23]

In the Council of Four on April 1, Lloyd George urged that Danzig be made a free city with economic ties to Poland and that the district of Marienwerder, which the Polish Commission had assigned to Poland although it contained 420,000 Germans, be left to East Prussia. President Wilson endorsed Lloyd George's proposal for Danzig and the Council agreed that Danzig should be made a free city governed by a League of Nations high commission. At Wilson's suggestion, it was also agreed that a plebiscite would be held in Marienwerder and that Poland would be guaranteed free transit if the district should elect to remain in East Prussia.[24]

It has been speculated that Wilson's position on Poland was connected with his preoccupation with the Italian claim to the Adriatic port city of Fiume.[25] David Hunter Miller wrote that the President agreed to make Danzig a free city "because he did

[21] Council of Four, March 27, 1919, 11 a.m., Paul Mantoux, *Les Délibérations du Conseil des Quatre* (2 Vols., Paris: Éditions du Centre National de la Recherche Scientifique, 1955), Vol. 1, pp. 46-48.
[22] Lloyd George, *The Truth about the Peace Treaties*, Vol. 2, p. 992.
[23] Mason, *The Danzig Dilemma*, pp. 55-56.
[24] Council of Four, April 1, 1919, 4 p.m., Mantoux, *Les Délibérations du Conseil des Quatre*, Vol. 1, pp. 110-112.
[25] See Chapter 12, Section 11.

not want to give Fiume to the Italians, and if Danzig went to the Poles he would have to consent to Fiume being Italian. . . ."[26] Winston Churchill commented as follows on the President's initial reluctance to resist Polish ambitions: "Cynics pointed to the fact that Italian emigrants to America usually return to Italy without acquiring voting rights, while the Polish vote was a formidable factor in the domestic politics of the United States."[27] Aside from the fact that Churchill's "cynics" had misinformed him as to the voting habits of Italian-Americans, there would seem to be no evidence either to support or refute the alleged connection between the Polish and Italian issues. The present guess is that President Wilson was at first greatly, if not overly, impressed with the Polish claims and was then partially converted by the merit of Lloyd George's arguments.

The details of the agreements of April 1 were worked out by a special committee and presented to the Council of Four on April 9: Danzig was to be an autonomous state under the League of Nations and in a customs union with Poland; Poland was to own the connecting railroad and have free use of the port of Danzig and control of its external affairs; a plebiscite was to be held in Marienwerder under an inter-allied commission on a commune by commune basis; if Marienwerder elected to remain with East Prussia, the Vistula would be placed under the regime of international rivers; Germany was to be guaranteed free railroad transit across the Polish corridor. Paderewski thereupon entered the meeting and Wilson explained the Council's decisions to him as designed to create a viable Poland with as few enemies as possible. Paderewski did not appreciate this service and he launched forth an appeal for Danzig as the *sine qua non* for a strong Poland, rejecting also the plebiscite for Marienwerder and warning ominously that if the Poles lost faith in the Allies the door would be open for Bolshevism. Wilson and Lloyd George attempted vainly to explain the merit of their plan.[28]

Clemenceau suggested on April 12 that if Marienwerder were left to the Poles they might accept the independence of Danzig,

[26] Miller, *Diary*, Vol. 9, p. 208.

[27] Winston S. Churchill, *The Aftermath*, Vol. 4 of *The World Crisis, 1918-1928* (New York: Charles Scribner's Sons, 1929), p. 219.

[28] Council of Four, April 9, 1919, 11 a.m., Mantoux, *Les Délibérations du Conseil des Quatre*, Vol. 1, pp. 197-202.

but Lloyd George and Wilson firmly rejected this proposal. "The Poles," exclaimed Lloyd George, "are getting independence after one and a half centuries of servitude. If they cannot live without a territory of 150,000 Germans! . . ." Wilson suggested that a signed declaration be sent to Paderewski explaining that the motive of the Council was not to favor the enemies of Poland but to preserve Poland from future dangers.[29]

The Poles were compelled to accept the decisions of the Supreme Council. The changes made by the Council of Four in favor of Germany and in favor of the principle of self-determination greatly altered the plan unanimously submitted by the Commission on Polish Affairs. These alterations almost certainly would not have been made but for the initiative of Lloyd George. Wilson at first supported the claims of the Poles and the recommendations of his Polish experts in regard to Danzig and Marienwerder, then seemed to fall silent for a time, and finally gave full support to the proposals of Lloyd George. Although many Germans were placed within Poland, the intermixture of populations made this inevitable and the settlement on the whole would seem to have been an honest application of the Fourteen Points and the principle of self-determination. When these arrangements ultimately cracked, in the words of Charles Seymour, "It was not from inherent weakness or injustice but from external assault."[30]

The April settlements of the German-Polish borderlands were further liberalized in June, again under the leadership of Lloyd George, and again with the belated support of President Wilson.[31] The Treaty of Versailles did not cope with the problem of Poland's eastern frontiers. In the later stages of the Peace Conference, however, an effort was made to deal with Polish claims to Teschen in the south and Galicia in the southeast.[32]

II. Anglo-American Approaches to the Territorial Settlement of Southeastern Europe

Despite the enormous complexity of the task of drawing ethnographic boundaries between the intermixed nationalities of the

---

[29] Council of Four, April 12, 1919, 11 a.m., *ibid.*, pp. 231-232.

[30] Charles Seymour, *Geography, Justice, and Politics at the Paris Conference of 1919* (New York: The American Geographical Society, 1951), p. 21.

[31] See Chapter 13, Section III.   [32] See Chapter 14, Section V.

disintegrated Austro-Hungarian Empire, the issues involved generated no stresses in Anglo-American relations. Both Great Britain and the United States were disinterested in their approaches to this problem, wishing only to satisfy the national aspirations of the peoples concerned and thereby to erect a territorial structure that would pose no threat to the future peace of Europe. To this end, the English-speaking powers relied for the determination of the boundaries of southeastern Europe on the judgments of expert territorial commissions.

The dissolution of the Austro-Hungarian Empire was not an act of the peace makers of 1919 but a condition confronting the Peace Conference when it convened. In the final week of the war, the subject nationalities broke away from the Dual Monarchy and set up their own national governments. The nationalities were unwilling to consider remaining in some sort of federation, however desirable that might have been for purposes of political and economic stability. They demanded the fullest realization of the principle of self-determination. President Wilson, who had called in Point 10 for the "freest opportunity of autonomous development" for the subject nationalities, told the Austro-Hungarian Government in September 1918, when it asked for peace, that under changed circumstances autonomy would no longer suffice. Lloyd George had called on January 5, 1918, for "genuine self-government on true democratic principles" for the peoples of Austria-Hungary.[33] In any case, the Armistice of November 3, 1918, was not based on the Fourteen Points and the Peace Conference was thus the executor for the heirs of the Dual Monarchy: Czechoslovakia, Poland, Roumania, Yugoslavia, and the new Austria and Hungary. The Peace Conference, but especially Great Britain and the United States, relied in the main for their decisions on the recommendations of the expert commissions set up to deal with the conflicting claims of the new nationalities. The commissions were instructed to base their recommendations on considerations of economic unity, geography, and defense, as well as on the nationality of populations.[34]

[33] See Chapter 1, Section v.

[34] See Victor S. Mamatey, *The United States and East Central Europe, 1914-1918* (Princeton, New Jersey: Princeton University Press, 1957), pp. 318-384; Charles Seymour, "The End of an Empire: Remnants of Austria-Hungary," *What Really Happened at Paris* (House and Seymour, eds.), pp. 87-102; Haskins and

One of the first territorial disputes submitted to the Council of Ten was that between Roumania and Serbia, the latter now merged into the new state of Yugoslavia, over the Banat of Temesvár, a quadrangle of formerly Hungarian territory between the Danube and the Transylvania mountains. Bratiano of Roumania and Vesnitch of Serbia presented their conflicting claims to the Banat before the Council of Ten on January 31.[35] Considering the difficulty and arbitrariness of basing decisions on the statements of the parties concerned, Lloyd George recommended on the next day that an expert commission on Roumanian affairs be constituted, with two members appointed by each of the four Great Powers, to make recommendations for a just settlement. President Wilson agreed, stipulating that the experts should concern themselves only with territorial and ethnographic, and not political, considerations. The Council thereupon established the Commission on Roumanian Territorial Claims as recommended by Lloyd George.[36]

The Roumanian Commission dealt with the various territorial claims of Roumania, of which the Banat controversy was the thorniest. The Commission based its recommendations primarily on ethnographic but also on economic and strategic considerations. It awarded the eastern two-thirds of the Banat, which had a predominantly Roumanian population, to Roumania, and the western one-third, which contained a Serb plurality among a population including Roumanians, Germans, and Magyars, to Serbia. Part of the Serbian zone was awarded as necessary for the defense of Belgrade. The recommendations of the Commission were adopted without alteration by the Supreme Council.[37]

Lord, *Some Problems of the Peace Conference*, pp. 206-210; Lloyd George, *The Truth about the Peace Treaties*, Vol. 2, pp. 902-912; F. S. Marston, *The Peace Conference of 1919* (London, New York, Toronto: Oxford University Press, 1944), pp. 203-207.

[35] Council of Ten, January 31, 1919, 3 p.m., *Foreign Relations, 1919, The Paris Peace Conference*, Vol. 3, pp. 822-830.

[36] Council of Ten, February 1, 1919, 3 p.m., *ibid.*, pp. 851-855; Lloyd George, *The Truth about the Peace Treaties*, Vol. 2, pp. 953-955.

[37] Haskins and Lord, *Some Problems of the Peace Conference*, p. 240; Seymour, "The End of an Empire: Remnants of Austria-Hungary," *What Really Happened at Paris* (House and Seymour, eds.), pp. 105-107; H.W.V. Temperley, ed., *A History of the Peace Conference of Paris* (6 Vols., London: Henry Frowde and Hodder and Stoughton, 1920-1924), Vol. 4, pp. 226-230; Lloyd George, *The Truth about the Peace Treaties*, Vol. 2, p. 956.

Within the Roumanian Commission and the other expert commissions subsequently established, there developed a pattern of close and informal cooperation between the American and British members and their assistants. This pattern is well illustrated by a few excerpts from Harold Nicolson's diary:

> February 6: Went over Roumanian and Czech claims with Seymour and American geographer Major Johnson. Our views are really identical.
>
> February 7: Spent most of the day tracing Roumanian and Czech frontiers with Charles Seymour of the United States Delegation.
>
> February 8: Again work all day with the Americans.
>
> February 9: Walk down to Crillon and go over Greek claims with the Americans.[38]

The Commission on Roumanian Territorial Claims established the pattern for the disposition of subsequent claims set before the Council of Ten. Venizelos of Greece appeared before the Council on February 3 and set forth Greek claims in northern Epirus, Rhodes, the Dodecanese islands, Cyprus, Thrace, and other areas.[39] On February 4, Lloyd George proposed and the Council agreed to the establishment of an expert commission on the model of the Roumanian Commission with instructions to "reduce the questions for decision within the narrowest possible limits and make recommendations for a just settlement."[40] The Greek Commission dealt primarily with Macedonia, which it ultimately divided between Greece and Serbia in accordance with population patterns, although denying a portion to Bulgaria despite a substantial Bulgarian population.[41]

The expert commissions were utilized only in boundary problems involving small powers. When Vesnitch stated the claims of Yugoslavia on February 18, Baron Sonnino refused to permit any

[38] Harold Nicolson, *Peacemaking 1919* (Boston and New York: Houghton Mifflin Company, 1933), pp. 259-260.
[39] Council of Ten, February 3, 1919, 11 a.m., *Foreign Relations, 1919, The Paris Peace Conference*, Vol. 3, pp. 859-866.
[40] Council of Ten, February 4, 1919, 11 a.m., *ibid.*, p. 875.
[41] Haskins and Lord, *Some Problems of the Peace Conference*, pp. 263-280.

expert commission to examine or make recommendations on Italian-Yugoslav issues. Balfour explained in vain to Sonnino that the purpose of such a commission was solely to furnish the Council with facts. The Yugoslav claims were assigned to the Roumanian Commission with the stipulation that it was not to deal with questions involving Italy.[42]

The claims of Czechoslovakia were presented to the Council of Ten by Dr. Beneš on February 5. The claims were extensive: Bohemia, Moravia, Austrian Silesia, Slovakia, Teschen, and even a corridor to the Adriatic. Beneš based his claim to German Bohemia on historic, geographic, and economic affiliation and on the need for defensible western frontiers, promising full minority guarantees and an "extremely liberal regime." The Council set up a new expert commission modeled on the Roumanian Commission to consider the frontiers of Czechoslovakia. Lloyd George viewed the Czech claims to German and Magyar areas with "serious misgiving."[43]

The chief problem faced by the Czech Commission was whether to delineate the western frontier of the new state according to ethnographic divisions or along lines of historical affiliation, natural economic units, and strategically defensible boundaries. German Bohemia was the most industrialized part of the old Hapsburg Empire, with a compact German population, but tied economically to Czech agriculture, labor, and markets. The region had long been administered from Prague and had never been part of Germany, from which it was divided by mountains. The Commission decided on the economic-historic-strategic western frontier, thereby placing areas almost entirely German in population within Czechoslovakia. The new state as finally constituted had a population over one-third German, Magyar, and Ruthenian. In this one case, the Peace Conference allowed the principle of nationality to be overridden by considerations of history, economics, and defense, all of which indicated the advisability of placing the Sudeten Germans under Czech rule.[44] Although Lloyd George

[42] Council of Ten, February 18, 1919, 3 p.m., *Foreign Relations, 1919, The Paris Peace Conference*, Vol. 4, pp. 54-55.
[43] Council of Ten, February 5, 1919, 3 p.m., *ibid.*, Vol. 3, pp. 877-887; Lloyd George, *The Truth about the Peace Treaties*, Vol. 2, pp. 932-942.
[44] Haskins and Lord, *Some Problems of the Peace Conference*, pp. 213-221;

agreed without protest in the Council of Four to the inclusion of German Bohemia in Czechoslovakia, and even agreed before President Wilson's consent was formally given,[45] he later objected to the "polyglot and incoherent state of Czechoslovakia," with "hundreds of thousands of protesting Magyars and some millions of angry Germans."[46] The new Austrian Republic strongly protested the western frontiers of Czechoslovakia, conveying on June 15 a memorandum of protest by the Sudeten Germans.[47] The Allied reply rejected the protest, defending the Czech frontier on historical and economic grounds.[48]

Negotiations for a treaty of peace with the new state of Hungary were delayed until the final stages of the Peace Conference by the internal upheavals which rocked that country in 1919. A republican government set up under Count Károlyi in October 1918 was displaced by the Bolshevik regime of Béla Kun in March 1919, which in turn was overthrown in August 1919. In fact, the dismemberment of Hungary was accomplished through the settlement of the frontiers of the surrounding states, but a treaty was not presented to Hungary until January 1920.[49]

Although the French and Italians opposed any dealings with the Béla Kun regime, the United States and Great Britain urged that some contact be made with the Bolshevik government. Expressing the view that the regime had a "nationalist side," Balfour urged on March 31 that a mission be sent to Budapest. President Wilson agreed that the Béla Kun government was "probably nationalist" and saw merit in a mission to learn what the Hungarians were thinking. Lloyd George strongly endorsed this view and, at his

---

Seymour, "The End of an Empire: Remnants of Austria-Hungary," *What Really Happened at Paris* (House and Seymour, eds.), p. 105; Temperley, ed., *A History of the Peace Conference of Paris*, Vol. 4, pp. 268-277.

[45] Council of Four, April 4, 1919, 4 p.m., Mantoux, *Les Délibérations du Conseil des Quatre*, Vol. 1, p. 149.

[46] Lloyd George, *The Truth about the Peace Treaties*, Vol. 2, p. 942.

[47] Note from the Austrian Delegation to the Peace Conference, June 15, 1919, Nina Almond and Ralph Haswell Lutz, eds., *The Treaty of St. Germain* (Stanford University, California: Stanford University Press, 1935), pp. 448-460.

[48] Reply of the Allied and Associated Powers to the Austrian Delegation, September 2, 1919, *ibid.*, pp. 470-471.

[49] Haskins and Lord, *Some Problems of the Peace Conference*, pp. 231-239; Temperley, ed., *A History of the Peace Conference of Paris*, Vol. 4, pp. 415-418. See Chapter 14, Section III.

suggestion, the Council agreed to send General Smuts to Budapest on a mission of inquiry.[50]

General Smuts and his party left Paris on April 1. He received Béla Kun in his compartment on the train in Budapest and demanded Hungarian compliance with the terms of the Military Convention of November 13, 1918, in return for which Smuts would recommend the lifting of the embargo on supplies to Hungary. Béla Kun refused to withdraw Hungarian forces from contact with the Roumanian Army, insisting on the Armistice line of November 3, 1918, beyond which Roumanian forces were far advanced. The discussions failed and Smuts departed from Budapest without having left his train.[51] Smuts told Colonel Bonsal, who joined him in Vienna, that it was clear that Béla Kun would not last long and that he would advise the Peace Conference to assume a waiting attitude.[52] The Smuts mission thus came to nothing. Back in Paris, Bonsal, who had extended his tour through southeastern Europe, suggested to Smuts that a subconference of the succession states be convened in Paris. This too came to nothing.[53] The head of the American Political Mission to Austria recommended in May that French forces be sent to Hungary to remove the Bolshevik regime and establish a government with which the Peace Conference could negotiate peace,[54] but this proposal was carried no further, and the Anglo-American policy thereafter was, as Smuts suggested, to let events in Hungary take their course.

German Austria was reduced by the war and the Treaty of St. Germain to a republic of six and one-half million people. The only significant question which arose in determining its frontiers was that of the Klagenfurt basin in the valley of the Drave between Austria and Yugoslavia. Although the area was an obvious economic unity, its population was Slovene in the south and Ger-

[50] Council of Four, March 31, 1919, 3 p.m., Mantoux, Les Délibérations du Conseil des Quatre, Vol. 1, pp. 98-104.

[51] Sarah Gertrude Millin, General Smuts (2 Vols., London: Faber and Faber, Ltd., 1936), Vol. 2, pp. 200-205.

[52] Stephen Bonsal, Unfinished Business (Garden City, New York: Doubleday, Doran and Company, Inc., 1944), pp. 77-78.

[53] ibid., pp. 141-142.

[54] Minutes of the Daily Meetings of the American Commissioners, May 26, 1919, Foreign Relations, 1919, The Paris Peace Conference, Vol. 11, pp. 187-188.

man in the north.[55] The Commission on Roumanian and Yugo-slav Affairs, to which the issue was referred, recommended on April 6 that although the basin was an economic unit naturally tied to Austria, provisions should be made for the inhabitants to elect union with Yugoslavia.[56] The American experts, Clive Day, Charles Seymour, Douglas Johnson, and Colonel Miles, advised on May 27 that their survey of the Klagenfurt basin indicated that a majority of the people were for union with Austria.[57]

The Council of Four decided on May 29 to hold a plebiscite in the Klagenfurt basin.[58] President Wilson, with the support of Lloyd George, rejected a request by Yugoslavia that the plebiscite be conducted by communes on the ground that the area consti-tuted an economic unit which should not be divided.[59] On June 2, Wilson received a memorandum from Douglas Johnson advising him that the Slovene population in the southern part of the basin might prefer Yugoslavia and that the district was so predomi-nantly agricultural that its economic unity was not of overriding importance.[60] When Vesnitch pressed the Yugoslav claim on June 4, Wilson agreed to separate plebiscites in the Slovene and German zones, refusing, with the staunch support of Lloyd George, any further concessions to Yugoslavia.[61] The Council decided finally to hold a plebiscite under an inter-Allied commis-sion in the Slovene area within three months of the coming into force of the treaty, to be followed by a plebiscite in the German northern zone if the first zone went for Yugoslavia.[62]

The Allied and Associated Powers denied the contention of Dr. Renner that the Austrian Republic was a state *de novo* and not the residue of the Austro-Hungarian Empire, thus compelling Austria to receive the Treaty of St. Germain as a defeated state, sharing with Hungary the responsibilities of the Dual Monarchy.[63]

---

[55] Haskins and Lord, *Some Problems of the Peace Conference*, pp. 222-223.
[56] Almond and Lutz, eds., *The Treaty of St. Germain*, pp. 504-505.
[57] *ibid.*, pp. 505-508.
[58] Council of Four, May 29, 1919, 11 a.m., *Foreign Relations, 1919, The Paris Peace Conference*, Vol. 6, pp. 102-106.
[59] Council of Four, June 2, 1919, 4 p.m., *ibid.*, p. 138.
[60] Miller, *Diary*, Vol. 9, pp. 471-476.
[61] Council of Four, June 4, 1919, 4 p.m., *Foreign Relations, 1919, The Paris Peace Conference*, Vol. 6, pp. 173-180.
[62] Council of Four, June 21, 1919, 3:45 p.m., *ibid.*, pp. 585-586.
[63] Plenary Session, June 2, 1919, *ibid.*, Vol. 3, pp. 427-428; Seymour, "The End of an Empire: Remnants of Austria-Hungary," *What Really Happened at*

The signing of the Treaty of St. Germain on September 10, 1919, formalized the demise of the Hapsburg Empire.[64] In the process of dividing the ancient estate among its heirs, the English-speaking powers made a disinterested and generally successful effort to apportion territories impartially according to objective criteria of geography, economics, history, and, above all, the will of the peoples concerned. As illustrated by their approach to the Klagenfurt controversy, Great Britain and the United States attempted to treat the "residue" state, Austria, with the same impartiality as the successor states. After the signing at St. Germain, Dr. Renner expressed the gratitude of Austria to Great Britain and the United States for their impartiality in the peace negotiations as compared with France and Italy. Although the treaty was harsh, said Renner, it had been mitigated by England and America, to whom the new Austria now looked for friendship and assistance.[65]

III. *The Minorities Treaties*

Inevitably, the new frontiers of eastern and southeastern Europe left many national minorities within the jurisdiction of states of alien nationality. Under Anglo-American leadership, the Peace Conference agreed on measures to protect the ethnographic, religious, and linguistic minorities of Europe, imposing upon the new states and old states which were acquiring new territories the duty to respect the rights of their domestic minorities as an international obligation. Minorities treaties were drawn up for Poland, Czechoslovakia, Yugoslavia, Roumania, and Greece.[66]

The first official proposal for the protection of minorities was made by President Wilson in the Council of Four on May 1. The President called attention to reports he had received of the

---

Paris (House and Seymour, eds.), p. 109; Temperley, ed., *A History of the Peace Conference of Paris*, Vol. 4, pp. 395-401.

[64] Plenary Session, September 10, 1919, *Foreign Relations, 1919, The Paris Peace Conference*, Vol. 3, p. 432; Treaty of Peace Between the Allied and Associated Powers and Austria, St. Germain-en-Laye, September 10, 1919, Great Britain, Treaty Series No. 11 (1919); *Cmd.* 400.

[65] Albert Halstead (Vienna) to Lansing, September 15, 1919, *Foreign Relations, 1919, The Paris Peace Conference*, Vol. 12, pp. 570-573.

[66] Manley O. Hudson, "The Protection of Minorities and Natives in Transferred Territories," *What Really Happened at Paris* (House and Seymour, eds.), pp. 205-213; Temperley, ed., *A History of the Peace Conference of Paris*, Vol. 5, pp. 123-127.

mistreatment of Jews in Poland and submitted a draft of a proposed treaty between Poland and the Allied and Associated Powers for the protection of minorities. Lloyd George suggested that the new states be required to accept even wider obligations, on such matters as international commerce, telecommunication, and copyrights. The Council agreed thereupon to establish a Committee on New States and the Protection of Minorities to consider the whole range of the international obligations of new states.[67]

The Committee on New States held sixty-four meetings from May to December 1919. The British members were Headlam-Morley and Carr, the Americans, David Hunter Miller and Manley O. Hudson, and later Allen W. Dulles.[68] Miller and Headlam-Morley agreed on May 2 that the obligations of the new states should be embodied in separate treaties between each of these states and the five principal Allied and Associated Powers.[69] The Council of Four on May 3 adopted the preliminary report of the Committee on New States which called for the inclusion in the German treaty of a clause binding Poland to enter into a treaty with the five Great Powers for the protection of racial, linguistic, and religious minorities.[70] The draft treaty with Poland which was subsequently drawn up became the model for all of the minorities treaties.

The new and aggrandized states upon whom the Supreme Council decided to impose minorities obligations bitterly protested the projected treaties as intolerable incursions upon their sovereignty. Under the leadership of Bratiano of Roumania, they stated their protests in the plenary session of May 31. President Wilson assured them that the Great Powers, who, he reminded them, would bear the chief burdens for the maintenance of peace, were seeking only to eliminate elements that might disturb the peace of the world. Since their military strength would constitute

[67] Council of Four, May 1, 1919, 11 a.m., *Foreign Relations, 1919, The Paris Peace Conference*, Vol. 5, pp. 393-395, 397-399.

[68] The *procès-verbaux* of the meetings of the Committee on New States, from May 3 to December 9, 1919, with attached documents, are reproduced in Miller, *Diary*, Vol. 13; and in *La Documentation Internationale, La Paix de Versailles* (12 Vols., Paris: Les Éditions Internationales, 1929-1939), Vol. 10.

[69] Miller to Wilson, May 3, 1919, Miller, *Diary*, Vol. 9, pp. 256-260.

[70] Council of Four, May 3, 1919, 12:10 p.m., *Foreign Relations, 1919, The Paris Peace Conference*, Vol. 5, pp. 439-444; Miller, *Diary*, Vol. 9, p. 263.

the final guarantee of the peace, the President declared, the Great Powers were entitled to say to their associates: "We cannot afford to guarantee territorial settlements which we do not believe to be right, and we cannot agree to leave elements of disturbance unremoved, which we believe will disturb the peace of the world." The representatives of the small powers declared themselves moved by the President's eloquence, but their positions remained unchanged.[71]

The minorities treaty between Poland and the principal Allied and Associated Powers was signed at Versailles on June 28. Under its provisions, Poland was obligated to guarantee full protection of life and liberty to all of its inhabitants regardless of place of birth, nationality, language, race, or religion. It conferred on all inhabitants the right to Polish citizenship and guaranteed equality before the law, free use of languages, the right to private or public education, and freedom of religious institutions. Powers to maintain, enforce, and modify the treaty were entrusted to the Council of the League of Nations, with disputes as to law or fact to be referred to the Permanent Court of International Justice.[72] Treaties on the model of the Polish treaty were subsequently signed between the principal Allied and Associated Powers and Czechoslovakia, Yugoslavia, Roumania, and Greece.

IV. *Problems of Self-Determination in the Middle East*

The deliberations of the Peace Conference with respect to the Near and Middle East were conditioned by secret engagements which had been entered into by the Allied Powers during the war as well as by their declared war aims. The most important of the secret treaties was the Sykes-Picot Agreement of May 16, 1916, which committed Great Britain and France to the establishment of an independent Arab state or confederation of Arab states except for direct French control over the Syrian coast and direct British control over Mesopotamia.[73] The agreement of St. Jean de

[71] Plenary Session, May 31, 1919, *Foreign Relations, 1919, The Paris Peace Conference*, Vol. 3, pp. 395-410; Lloyd George, *The Truth about the Peace Treaties*, Vol. 2, pp. 1366-1384; Temperley, ed., *A History of the Peace Conference of Paris*, Vol. 5, pp. 128-132.
[72] Great Britain, Treaty Series No. 8 (1919); Cmd. 223.
[73] E. L. Woodward and Rohan Butler, eds., *Documents on British Foreign Policy, 1919-1939*, First Series (8 Vols., London: His Majesty's Stationery Office,

Maurienne of April 17, 1917, was designed to appease Italy with concessions in Asia Minor.[74] In his war aims address of January 5, 1918, Lloyd George declared that the Allies did not wish to deprive Turkey of areas "indisputably Turkish in population," including Constantinople, but the straits should be internationalized, he said, and Arabia, Armenia, Mesopotamia, Palestine, and Syria were entitled to a "recognition of their separate national conditions." President Wilson's Point 12 set forth the same formula: a "secure sovereignty" for the Turkish portions of the Ottoman Empire, but the straits to be open under international guarantees, and an "absolutely unmolested opportunity of autonomous development" for the non-Turkish nationalities.[75] In November 1918, the British and French Governments issued a joint declaration in regard to Turkey, which proclaimed it as their objective in the Middle East to "ensure the complete and final emancipation of all those peoples so long oppressed by the Turks, and to establish national governments and administrations which shall derive their authority from the initiative and free will of the peoples themselves." To this end, the British and French Governments promised to "encourage and assist" the establishment of native governments in Syria, Mesopotamia, and the other liberated territories.[76]

Great Britain thus entered the Peace Conference with the potentially conflicting commitments of the secret treaties on the one hand and the promises of national self-determination on the other, while the United States came to Paris with an unqualified commitment to the principle of self-determination. Britain and the United States were in full agreement, however, in looking to a system of mandates as the key to the solution of Turkish problems.

The claims of Arab nationality were raised early in the Peace Conference. On February 6, 1919, the Emir Feisal of the Hedjaz appealed to the Council of Ten for the independence of all Arab peoples, with each to have the option of selecting complete inde-

---

1947-1958), Vol. 4, pp. 241-254. See Lloyd George, *The Truth about the Peace Treaties*, Vol. 2, pp. 1022-1025. A good account of the wartime diplomacy and secret treaties regarding the Ottoman Empire, as well as of the Turkish settlement as a whole, may be found in Harry N. Howard, *The Partition of Turkey* (Norman, Oklahoma: University of Oklahoma Press, 1931), pp. 181-249.

[74] Woodward and Butler, eds., *Documents on British Foreign Policy, 1919-1939*, First Series, Vol. 4, pp. 639-643.

[75] See Chapter I, Section v.

[76] Anglo-French Declaration on Turkey, November 7, 1918, *Foreign Relations, 1919, The Paris Peace Conference*, Vol. 2, pp. 274-275.

pendence or a mandatory power of its own choice. The Emir Feisal was assisted in the presentation of his case by Colonel T. E. Lawrence, who had led the uprising of the Arabs against Turkish rule.[77]

The subsequent negotiations were marked by strong British resistance to French claims in Syria. In the Council of Ten on March 20, Lloyd George vigorously contested the demand of the French for a mandate over all of Syria rather than only the coastal region assigned to French control by the Sykes-Picot Agreement. Specifically, Lloyd George insisted that the French mandate should not include the localities of Damascus, Homs, Hama, and Aleppo, which had been promised to the Arabs as part of their independent state. Lloyd George pointed further to the fact that the conquest of Syria had been accomplished almost entirely by British Empire forces and he flatly refused to break faith with the Arabs. President Wilson, who up to this point had been silent, said that he "would now seek to establish his place in the Conference." The United States, he declared, was indifferent to the claims both of Great Britain and France and wished only for a solution based on the desires of the peoples concerned. He proposed that an inter-Allied commission be sent to Syria "to elucidate the state of opinion." Clemenceau said that the inquiry should be extended to Palestine, Mesopotamia, and Armenia as well. Wilson and Lloyd George agreed, and, at the suggestion of Lloyd George, the President undertook to draw up terms of reference for the commission.[78]

The French and British Governments hedged almost at once on the decision of March 20. The French Government refused to designate members of the Inter-Allied Commission, and the British declined to participate without the French.[79] On March 27, Lloyd George told the Council that British administrators advised delay in sending the Commission on the ground that the information that it could obtain would be inadequate. Wilson, now with

---

[77] Council of Ten, February 6, 1919, 3 p.m., *ibid.*, Vol. 3, pp. 889-894; Lloyd George, *The Truth about the Peace Treaties*, Vol. 2, pp. 1039-1044.

[78] Council of Four, March 20, 1919, 3 p.m., *Foreign Relations, 1919, The Paris Peace Conference*, Vol. 5, pp. 3-14; Lloyd George, *The Truth about the Peace Treaties*, Vol. 2, pp. 1060-1075; Ray Stannard Baker, *Woodrow Wilson and World Settlement* (3 Vols., Garden City, New York: Doubleday, Page and Company, 1922), Vol. 1, pp. 72-77.

[79] Lloyd George, *The Truth about the Peace Treaties*, Vol. 2, p. 1077; Temperley, ed., *A History of the Peace Conference of Paris*, Vol. 6, p. 148.

the support of Clemenceau, insisted that the Commission be sent.[80] Wilson told the Council on April 11 that the American commissioners were ready to depart for the Middle East and asked when the British and French commissioners would be designated. Lloyd George replied that an Anglo-French accord on Syria was necessary before the Commission could be sent. The President countered that the purpose of the Commission was to learn the will of the native populations, not to achieve Anglo-French accord.[81] Wilson instructed the Secretary of State on April 15 to sign the appointments of H. C. King and Charles R. Crane as the American commissioners to go to Syria, despite the failure of Britain and France to designate members of the Commission.[82]

The American commissioners began their work in Syria and Palestine without awaiting their British and French colleagues, who in fact were never designated. Meanwhile, the Anglo-French controversy over the extent of French control of Syria continued in the Council of Four. President Wilson protested on May 22 that he "had never been able to see by what right France and Great Britain gave this country away to anyone." Lloyd George assured Wilson that Great Britain would accept the Commission's interpretation of the will of the Arab peoples even though it remained a purely American Commission.[83] Lloyd George again refused on May 31 to designate British commissioners unless French commissioners were also appointed. Clemenceau said that he would name them as soon as British forces were replaced by French troops in Syria, but Lloyd George flatly refused to meet this condition on the ground that the presence of French troops would provoke Arab outbreaks.[84] Nevertheless, Lloyd George instructed the British commander in Syria to give every facility to the American commissioners and authorized him to state that Britain would give the "fullest weight" to their recommendations.[85]

[80] Council of Four, March 27, 1919, 3:30 p.m., Mantoux, *Les Délibérations du Conseil des Quatre*, Vol. 1, p. 49.

[81] Council of Four, April 11, 1919, *ibid.*, pp. 228-229.

[82] Wilson to Lansing, April 15, 1919, *Foreign Relations, 1919, The Paris Peace Conference*, Vol. 12, p. 748.

[83] Council of Four, May 22, 1919, 11 a.m., *ibid.*, Vol. 5, pp. 811-812; Lloyd George, *The Truth about the Peace Treaties*, Vol. 1, pp. 1077-1078.

[84] Council of Four, May 31, 1919, 5:30 p.m., *Foreign Relations, 1919, The Paris Peace Conference*, Vol. 6, pp. 132-133.

[85] Balfour to General Sir E. Allenby, May 31, 1919, *ibid.*, p. 137; Woodward

The King-Crane Commission spent the late spring and early summer studying conditions in Palestine, Syria, and Asia Minor. King and Crane reported on July 10, and affirmed in their final report, that the Syrians were strongly opposed to a French mandate and that the United States was their first choice as a mandatory power.[86] The Commission recommended a single mandate for Syria and Palestine under the United States, or, if the United States refused it, under Great Britain, who was the second choice of the Arab population.[87]

The King-Crane report was suppressed by the United States Government in the face of the patent unwillingness of both the United States and Britain to take the Syrian mandate. Lloyd George told the Council on September 15 that British troops would be withdrawn from Syria by November 1, to be replaced by French forces in the area allotted to France under the Sykes-Picot Agreement. Lloyd George suggested that if agreement as to permanent boundaries between Syria and Mesopotamia and between Syria and Palestine could not be reached among the British, French, and Arabs, the matter should be referred to an arbitrator appointed by President Wilson.[88] In the outcome, the French seized Damascus and the other areas reserved to the independent Arab state and established their mandate over all of Syria.[89]

V. *Anglo-American Attitudes and Policies toward the Zionist Program for Palestine*

Great Britain and the United States were in complete accord in supporting the movement for a Jewish national home, but not

---

and Butler, eds., *Documents on British Foreign Policy, 1919-1939*, First Series, Vol. 4, p. 259.

[86] King and Crane to American Commission to Negotiate Peace, July 10, 1919, *Foreign Relations, 1919, The Paris Peace Conference*, Vol. 12, p. 750.

[87] Report of the American Section of the International Commission on Mandates in Turkey, August 28, 1919, Syria, *ibid.*, pp. 751-799, 848-863. See also Lloyd George, *The Truth about the Peace Treaties*, Vol. 2, pp. 1079-1080; Baker, *Wilson and World Settlement*, Vol. 2, pp. 217-218.

[88] Council of Heads of Delegations, September 15, 1919, 10:30 a.m., *Foreign Relations, 1919, The Paris Peace Conference*, Vol. 8, pp. 205-206; Woodward and Butler, eds., *Documents on British Foreign Policy, 1919-1939*, First Series, Vol. 8, pp. 690-691.

[89] See Lloyd George, *The Truth about the Peace Treaties*, Vol. 2, pp. 1081-1114; Temperley, ed., *A History of the Peace Conference of Paris*, Vol. 6, pp. 148-149.

necessarily a Jewish state, in Palestine. Anglo-American cooperation in support of the movement for a Jewish national home extended beyond the official level, encompassing contacts between the British Government and private supporters of the movement in America as well as England.

Great Britain took the lead in endorsing Jewish aspirations during the war. Lloyd George became interested in the movement in 1915, when, as Minister of Munitions, he used the services of Dr. Chaim Weizmann to organize chemical works. Weizmann subsequently won the support of Balfour, Cecil, and Smuts for the Zionist cause. Moreover, the British Government was alarmed in 1916 and 1917 by the active German courting of Zionist sympathy and took fright lest the sentiments of Russian Jews and the financial resources of American Jews be enlisted in support of the Central Powers.[90] In June 1917, Balfour asked for Colonel House's views on a proposed declaration of sympathy with the Zionist cause, which, he pointed out, was under consideration by the British Cabinet in view of reports that the German Government was making great efforts to capture the Zionist movement.[91]

Balfour issued the following declaration on November 8, 1917: "His Majesty's Government view with favor the establishment in Palestine of a national home for the Jewish people, and will use their best endeavor to facilitate the achievement of this object, it being clearly understood that nothing shall be done which may prejudice the civil and religious rights of existing non-Jewish communities in Palestine, or the rights and political status enjoyed by Jews in any other country. . . ."[92] Although there was considerable sympathy for the Zionist movement in Great Britain, the issuance of the Balfour Declaration was, by Lloyd George's admission, essentially a war measure, designed to thwart the efforts of the Central Powers to win the support of world Jewry and to enlist Jewish sympathies and financial power in support of the Entente.[93] The British Government understood the term "na-

[90] Lloyd George, *The Truth about the Peace Treaties*, Vol. 2, pp. 1116-1122.
[91] Balfour to House, June 10, 1917, House Papers.
[92] James Brown Scott, ed., *Official Statements of War Aims and Peace Proposals, December 1916 to November 1918* (Washington, D.C.: Carnegie Endowment for International Peace, 1921), p. 188.
[93] Lloyd George, *The Truth about the Peace Treaties*, Vol. 2, pp. 1119-1120, 1134. See also Temperley, ed., *A History of the Peace Conference of Paris*, Vol. 6, pp. 171-173.

tional home" to mean "some form of British, American, or other protectorate. . . . It did not necessarily involve the early establishment of an independent Jewish state. . . ." A Jewish state was envisioned only if the Jews, through unrestricted immigration, became a majority in Palestine.[94] Balfour himself was motivated by more than tactical considerations in the issuance of his memorandum. Through his contacts with Weizmann, he had become a sincere advocate of Zionism.[95]

President Wilson registered warm but unofficial enthusiasm for the Zionist cause, which he understood as a movement for a Jewish national home, but not a state, in Palestine. He wrote to Rabbi Stephen S. Wise on August 31, 1918: ". . . I welcome an opportunity to express the satisfaction I have felt in the progress of the Zionist movement in the United States and in the Allied countries since the declaration by Mr. Balfour. . . ."[96] Again, on January 13, 1919, he wrote to Lord Rothschild that he was "greatly interested in the development of the plans for Palestine. I hope with all my heart," said Wilson, "that they can be given satisfactory form and permanency."[97]

The British Foreign Office submitted an official memorandum to the War Cabinet in December 1918, contending that the principle of self-determination was not in itself an adequate basis for the disposition of Palestine and that the historical and religious claims of the Jews were entitled to full consideration. The memorandum called for a British mandate on the ground of Britain's vital strategic interest in Palestine as a buffer for the Suez Canal and on the ground that both the Arabs and the Zionists would prefer Britain to any other power.[98]

Balfour acted as the champion of the Zionist cause at the Peace Conference, working closely with the American Zionists. The Zionist deputation presented its case to the Council of Ten on February 27, asking for a Jewish national home in Palestine under

[94] Lloyd George, *The Truth about the Peace Treaties*, Vol. 2, pp. 1137-1139.
[95] Blanche E. C. Dugdale, *Arthur James Balfour* (2 Vols., New York: G. P. Putnam's Sons, 1937), Vol. 2, pp. 155-171.
[96] Wilson to Rabbi Wise, August 31, 1918, Ray Stannard Baker and William E. Dodd, eds., *The Public Papers of Woodrow Wilson* (6 Vols., New York and London: Harper & Brothers, Publishers, 1925-1927), *War and Peace*, Vol. 1, p. 243.
[97] Wilson to Lord Rothschild, January 13, 1919, Wilson Papers, Series 8-A.
[98] Lloyd George, *The Truth about the Peace Treaties*, Vol. 2, pp. 1151-1154.

a British mandate.[99] The Zionist claims were not acted upon by the heads of government, but in the spring of 1919 Balfour conferred from time to time with the Zionist delegates. In a meeting on June 24 attended by Balfour, Lord Eustace Percy, Felix Frankfurter, and Justice Brandeis, Balfour agreed to several conditions for the projected mandate proposed by Brandeis. Balfour explained to the group that he had opposed sending the Inter-Allied Commission to Palestine because the Allied commitment to the Zionist cause overrode "numerical self-determination," Palestine being a unique problem that involved the wishes not of an *existing* community but of a *future* community. Balfour said that he could not see how President Wilson reconciled his belief in the principle of self-determination with his adherence to Zionism. Brandeis replied with the conjecture that Wilson too was thinking of the self-determination of a future community.[100]

The reports of the King-Crane Commission pointed out the incompatibility of the Zionist program with self-determination by existing populations. King and Crane reported to President Wilson from Jerusalem on June 20 that Moslems and Christians were united in the "most hostile attitude" toward any Jewish immigration. The Zionist program, they affirmed, could be carried out only by force of arms.[101] The final King-Crane report estimated that nine-tenths of the population of Palestine were against the entire Zionist program and recommended a "greatly reduced Zionist program" of "definitely limited" Jewish immigration, the abandonment of the project for a distinctly Jewish commonwealth, and the incorporation of Palestine and Syria into a single mandate under the United States or, alternately, Great Britain. The report questioned the feasibility of an American mandate because "the vague but large encouragement given to the Zionist aims might prove particularly embarrassing to America, on account of her large and influential Jewish population. . . ."[102]

[99] Council of Ten, February 27, 1919, 3 p.m., *Foreign Relations, 1919, The Paris Peace Conference*, Vol. 4, pp. 161-169; Lloyd George, *The Truth about the Peace Treaties*, Vol. 2, pp. 1156-1158.

[100] Memorandum by Frankfurter of an Interview in Balfour's Apartment, Paris, June 24, 1919, 4:45 p.m., Woodward and Butler, eds., *Documents on British Foreign Policy, 1919-1939*, First Series, Vol. 4, pp. 1276-1278.

[101] King and Crane to American Commission, for Wilson, June 20, 1919, *Foreign Relations, 1919, The Paris Peace Conference*, Vol. 12, p. 748.

[102] Report of the American Section of the International Commission on Mandates in Turkey, August 28, 1919, Syria, *ibid.*, pp. 792-795.

Both Great Britain, officially, and the United States, unofficially, maintained their support for the Jewish national home. At the urging of Brandeis, President Wilson instructed the American Ambassador in Paris in February 1920 to press the Conference of Ambassadors to draw "rational boundaries" for Palestine and to uphold the Balfour Declaration.[103] The British resisted French proposals to restrict the program for a Jewish national home and were accorded the mandate for Palestine at San Remo in the spring of 1920.[104]

In summary, it is clear that the principle of self-determination was the dominant, but by no means exclusive, factor in both British and American policies in the territorial settlements. The Peace Conference applied the principle of self-determination to the new and old states of eastern and southeastern Europe even to the extent of laying down conditions of minority guarantees for the acquisition of territory. Both in the determination of ethnographic frontiers and in the laying down of the requirements for the rights of national minorities, the leadership was taken by Great Britain and the United States. Lacking territorial interests of their own, the English-speaking powers had a vital interest in the justice and stability of the settlements which they were to guarantee and enforce with their military power. Except in the determination of the German-Polish frontier, where the leadership was taken by Great Britain while the United States was temporarily bemused by sympathy for the Polish national cause, Anglo-American initiative was prompt and decisive in drawing the new map of Europe according to the will of the peoples concerned, excepting only those cases in which overriding economic, strategic, and historical considerations were allowed to prevail.

Great Britain and the United States championed the cause of national self-determination in the Middle East with almost equal vigor but decidedly less success than in eastern Europe. Although the British did not join in the American effort to secure objective information as to the wishes of the Arab peoples, they were quite prepared to accept the findings of the American experts and to

---

[103] Sir G. Grahame, British Ambassador in Paris, to Earl Curzon, February 10, 1920, Woodward and Butler, eds., *Documents on British Foreign Policy, 1919-1939*, First Series, Vol. 4, p. 634.
[104] Lloyd George, *The Truth about the Peace Treaties*, Vol. 2, pp. 1184-1201.

award mandates in accordance with Arab wishes. Only in the case of Palestine did the English-speaking powers depart from a settlement based on self-determination, and here the United States enthusiastically followed the leadership of Britain in promoting the historic claims of the Zionists for a Jewish national home in Palestine.

The major conclusion to be drawn for the last two chapters is that the criteria by which the territorial settlements were determined in 1919, with admittedly significant exceptions, were for the first time in a general peace congress not those of power, equilibrium, and strategic and material interest, but agreed principles of impartial justice, and that Anglo-American diplomacy was the dominant and decisive factor which led to this striking victory of broad principles over narrow interests. It may well be questioned whether the principle of national self-determination, which guided Anglo-American policy in 1919, was the best and wisest principle which could have been applied, whether indeed it was not a fundamental derogation from and contradiction to the international principles of the League of Nations. But both nationalism and internationalism, however paradoxically, were dominant forces in the world in 1919, and Great Britain and the United States guided them both to their fullest historical realization.

CHAPTER 9

THE CONFLICT OF BRITISH AND AMERICAN POLICIES IN THE REPARATIONS SETTLEMENT

O N no issue at the Peace Conference did British and American policies conflict more directly and more fundamentally than on the question of reparations. American policy was generally quite clear: to require, in compliance with the Pre-Armistice Agreement, the payment by Germany of a manageable fixed sum within a defined period of time for damages specifically done to the civilian populations of Allied countries and their property. Of the major powers, the United States was certainly the only disinterested party in its approach to the reparations issue. Its own claims were insignificant and it was generally free of pressures from public opinion. British policy, on the other hand, was ill defined. There were two conflicting sets of opinions within the British delegation, one disposed to moderation, the other disposed to extract vast and undefined sums from the enemy. Lloyd George, plagued by his campaign promises of December 1918, or at least by those of his associates, for huge reparations payments, attempted to reconcile the two sets of views within his delegation, but when decisions had to be made, the pressures of British public and parliamentary opinion drove the Prime Minister to take his position for large or undefined sums.

The negotiations over reparations took the form of a series of contests between the United States on the one side and Great Britain and the continental Allies on the other, with the latter usually successful. The United States won its initial point in securing the elimination of war costs as a demand to be made upon Germany, but the European Allies subsequently succeeded in eliminating the fixed sum and the time limit, and in securing the inclusion of pensions and separation allowances as a category of damages. Although the British position on reparations was in some instances more moderate than that of France or Italy, it was in others more severe, and it marked the most significant instance of the Peace Conference in which Great Britain pursued

[229]

interests much more nearly parallel to those of the continental Allies than to those of the United States.

I. *British and American Positions on Reparations Prior to and at the Outset of the Peace Conference*

Pre-Conference utterances and instruments indicated a moderate and limited reparations settlement. In his war aims speech of January 5, 1918, Lloyd George called for the political and economic restoration of the invaded countries and for "reparations for injuries done in violation of international law." Lloyd George did not then require a war indemnity. President Wilson, in his speech of January 8, 1918, required the restoration of Belgium in Point 7, of the invaded portions of France in Point 8, and of Roumania, Serbia, and Montenegro in Point 11. None of the Fourteen Points dealt with reparations as such.[1] The Pre-Armistice Agreement required compensation by Germany for "all damage done to the civilian populations of the Allies and their property by the aggression of Germany by land, by sea and from the air."[2] This was Germany's contractual obligation, which by any reasonable interpretation could not be taken to encompass the war costs of the Allied Powers.

In the period between the Armistice and the Peace Conference, both the United States and Great Britain began to prepare their positions on reparations. In November, Colonel House appointed Brigadier General C. H. McKinstrey of the Army Engineers to lead a staff in investigating damages in the field in France and Belgium for purposes of formulating accurate estimates.[3] John Maynard Keynes of the British Treasury was engaged in November in the preparation of a report estimating German capacity to pay at no more than $10 billion.[4] Keynes told the American

---

[1] See Chapter 1, Section v.

[2] See Chapter 2, Section ii.

[3] House to Wilson, November 23, 1918, Department of State, *Papers Relating to the Foreign Relations of the United States, 1919, The Paris Peace Conference* (13 Vols., Washington: United States Government Printing Office, 1942-1947), Vol. 2, p. 576; hereafter referred to as *Foreign Relations*; Bernard M. Baruch, *The Making of the Reparation and Economic Sections of the Treaty* (New York and London: Harper & Brothers, Publishers, 1920), pp. 18, 47.

[4] Philip Mason Burnett, *Reparation at the Paris Peace Conference from the Standpoint of the American Delegation* (2 Vols., New York: Columbia University Press, 1940), Vol. 1, pp. 10-11. The present chapter relies heavily on this

Treasury expert Norman Davis that Great Britain would restrict its own claims to damages for tonnage illegally destroyed by the enemy and would seek to restrict all excessive demands for indemnity.[5]

British policy underwent a marked change in December 1918. The Inter-Allied Conference in London agreed on December 2 to set up a Commission on Reparations and Indemnities to study German capacity to pay indemnities. Colonel House asked that the term "indemnity" be struck out.[6] Sir William Wiseman told David Hunter Miller that the Allied leaders had agreed on a policy of large indemnities, because "that question has become politically here of great importance."[7] In the December election campaign, Lloyd George and his supporters at first reflected the moderate views of the Treasury, but in the course of the campaign their demands, especially those of subordinate candidates of the Coalition, became very severe. While Lloyd George himself tended to avoid the reparations issue in the campaign, he also avoided mention of Great Britain's obligations under the Pre-Armistice Agreement.[8] A special committee of politicians and financiers appointed by Lloyd George to study Germany's capacity to pay, whose membership included Prime Minister Hughes of Australia and Lord Cunliffe, the former Governor of the Bank of England, reported that there was no reason to suppose that the enemy could not sustain annual payments of $6 billion as interest on a total capital sum of $120 billion.[9]

While the British were thus expanding their claims for reparation and indemnity, American experts adhered to a strict construc-

---

source, which, although lacking some of the documentation subsequently published in *The Paris Peace Conference* volumes of *Papers Relating to the Foreign Relations of the United States* and in Paul Mantoux's *Les Délibérations du Conseil des Quatre*, remains the best single collection of documents on the reparations settlement of 1919.

[5] Davis to Auchincloss, received by Miller November 29, 1918, David Hunter Miller, *My Diary at the Conference of Paris*, privately printed (21 Vols., New York: Appeal Printing Company, 1924), Vol. 2, pp. 135-136; Burnett, *Reparation at the Paris Peace Conference*, Vol. 1, p. 425.

[6] See Chapter 2, Section IV.

[7] Miller to House, December 3, 1918, Miller, *Diary*, Vol. 1, pp. 25-27; Burnett, *Reparation at the Paris Peace Conference*, Vol. 1, pp. 432-434.

[8] See Chapter 2, Section V.

[9] Burnett, *Reparation at the Paris Peace Conference*, Vol. 1, pp. 429-430. See also David Lloyd George, *The Truth about Reparations and War Debts* (Garden City, New York: Doubleday, Doran and Company, Inc., 1932), p. 11.

tion of the Pre-Armistice Agreement. Allyn A. Young, the head of the Division of Economics of the Inquiry, submitted a proposed reparations policy on December 28 which called for the use of reparations receipts only for the repair of actual damages to civilians and their property, "in order to make it clear beyond question that an indemnity is *compensatory* rather than *punitive*."[10]

It was clear, by the time the Peace Conference convened, that British and American statesmen were not in agreement as to the quantity and character of reparations authorized by the Pre-Armistice Agreement. As the Peace Conference got underway, it became clear, too, that Britain and the continental Allies were motivated in their reparations policies far more by political fear of disappointing public expectations than by reasoned economic assessments of Germany's position. British moderates were increasingly compelled to rely on American leadership in the reparations question.

II. *The Commission on the Reparation of Damage: Conflict over War Costs, February 3-21*

Lloyd George proposed to the Council of Ten on January 22 that a commission be appointed to examine and report on the amount of "reparation and indemnity" which the enemy should and could pay and the form of payment. President Wilson asked that the word "indemnity" be struck out and Lloyd George agreed, provided that the word "reparations" was taken "in its widest terms."[11] The Council approved Lloyd George's draft terms for the commission on the next day,[12] and the Commission on the Reparation of Damage was constituted by the plenary Conference on January 25. The Commission was to have three members appointed by each of the five Great Powers and two each by Belgium, Greece, Poland, Roumania, and Serbia. Portuguese and Czech representatives were subsequently added to the Commission. Its defined function was to examine and report on the amount of

[10] "A Suggestion for American Policy with Respect to Indemnities," December 28, 1918, Burnett, *Reparation at the Paris Peace Conference*, Vol. 1, pp. 474-475.

[11] Council of Ten, January 22, 1919, 3 p.m., *Foreign Relations, 1919, The Paris Peace Conference*, Vol. 3, p. 682.

[12] Council of Ten, January 23, 1919, 10:30 a.m., *ibid.*, pp. 698-699.

reparation to be asked by the Allies, the capacity of Germany to pay, and the method, form, and time of payments.[13]

The Commission on the Reparation of Damage convened on February 3. The American representatives were Vance C. Mc-Cormick, chairman of the War Trade Board, Bernard M. Baruch, chairman of the War Industries Board, and Norman H. Davis, the United States Treasury representative in London. Thomas W. Lamont served as alternate and John Foster Dulles as legal adviser. The British representatives were Prime Minister Hughes of Australia, Lord Cunliffe, and Lord Sumner, an eminent judge. Louis-Lucien Klotz, the French Minister of Finance, was elected chairman, and three subcommittees were established: on evaluation, capacity, and guarantees.[14]

The plenary Commission, in attempting to determine what was to be included in the category of damages to civilians and their property, fell into a debate over war costs. The British representatives led the argument that war costs should be regarded as part of the burden of civilian damages. From the outset, the attitude of Hughes, Sumner, and Cunliffe augured ill for the prospects of Anglo-American harmony. Davis reported that Cunliffe was talking of a total reparations figure of $120 billion, Hughes of $100 billion.[15]

Each delegation submitted a memorandum on the principles of liability on February 10. The British memorandum asserted that the Allies had an "absolute right to demand the whole cost of the war." The continental powers also demanded integral reparations. The American memorandum enunciated four "principles of reparation," in close adherence to the Pre-Armistice Agreement, calling for compensation for illegal acts, restitution of invaded territories, compensations for damages to civilian property, and compensations for personal damages to civilians.[16]

---

[13] Plenary Session, January 25, 1919, *ibid.*, pp. 199-202.

[14] Burnett, *Reparation at the Paris Peace Conference*, Vol. 1, pp. 18-19. See, generally, Thomas William Lamont, "Reparations," *What Really Happened at Paris* (Edward Mandell House and Charles Seymour, eds., New York: Charles Scribner's Sons, 1921), pp. 259-290.

[15] Miller's Diary, February 3, 1919, Miller, *Diary*, Vol. 1, p. 107.

[16] Reparation Commission, February 10, 1919, Burnett, *Reparation at the Paris Peace Conference*, Vol. 2, pp. 298-307; Baruch, *The Making of the Reparation and Economic Sections of the Treaty*, pp. 19-20.

The debate on war costs reflected the conflict of the memoranda. Prime Minister Hughes was the most articulate advocate of war costs, asserting before the Reparation Commission on February 10 that the tax burden imposed upon the peoples of the Allied countries for the conduct of the war was properly to be regarded as damage to civilians, indeed that Wilsonian justice required the payment of war costs. "There is absolutely no distinction," proclaimed Hughes, "on any ground of logic, or justice, between a claim for restoration of devastated areas and a claim for general compensation. Every argument which establishes the one establishes the other. If the one is just, the other is equally just."[17] Norman Davis told his American colleagues that Hughes represented the viewpoint of those English politicians who "had been forced to dwell on the question of tremendous reparations as a campaign measure," but that "the Treasury officials of England felt much as we did in this matter."[18]

John Foster Dulles presented the American point of view before the Commission on February 13. While the United States appreciated the enormity of the crimes of the enemy, said Dulles, the American memorandum limited reparations claims "because the United States did not consider itself free." Arguing that the Pre-Armistice Agreement constituted a binding contract, Dulles said that "an act must be illegal, and not only unjust or cruel, in order to establish the right to reparation." Lord Sumner challenged the binding nature of the Pre-Armistice Agreement. No text of international law, he asserted, denied a victor the right to exact war costs, and in any case, said Sumner, the agreement of November 1918 only furnished bases of discussion which defined but did not restrict the rights of the victors.[19]

In subsequent discussions, Dulles continued to insist that the November instruments were contractual and binding. Moreover, he pointed out on February 14, there was mounting evidence of a limited German capacity, and if war costs were included as a

[17] Reparation Commission, February 10, 1919, Burnett, *Reparation at the Paris Peace Conference*, Vol, 2, pp. 298-307; Baruch, *The Making of the Reparation and Economic Sections of the Treaty*, pp. 19-20.

[18] Minutes of the Daily Meetings of the American Commissioners, February 11, 1919, *Foreign Relations, 1919, The Paris Peace Conference*, Vol. 11, p. 31.

[19] Reparation Commission, February 13, 1919, Burnett, *Reparation at the Paris Peace Conference*, Vol. 1, pp. 564-569, Vol. 2, pp. 309-312; Baruch, *The Making of the Reparation and Economic Sections of the Treaty*, pp. 289-297.

category of compensation to be taken from a limited capacity, the result would be to enhance the shares of Great Britain and the United States. If war costs were excluded, said Dulles, France and Belgium, having suffered the greatest civilian damages, would receive the largest share. The French and Belgians began to be impressed with the "play of the percentages" which Dulles called to their attention and both presently turned against the inclusion of war costs. Hughes, however, was not impressed by Dulles' appeal. The Pre-Armistice Agreement, he asserted, was based not only on the Fourteen Points but on the principles of *justice* contained in the President's subsequent addresses, and, he declared: "It is just that war costs be borne by the aggressor."[20] Dulles reasserted his position at the meeting of February 19, and the Commission decided to submit to the Supreme Council the question of the compatibility of war costs with the Pre-Armistice Agreement.[21]

Dulles drafted a clause for the treaty on February 21 calling for German responsibility for war costs in *theory*, to be renounced because of the limitations of German capacity to pay.[22] This laid the basis for Article 231 of the Treaty of Versailles and enabled the Allies to yield their demand for war costs and still appease public opinion. President Wilson sent a radio message from the U.S.S. "George Washington" instructing the American delegation that it was "bound in honor to decline to agree to war costs in the reparations demanded," and that it should dissent publicly if necessary.[23] Thus fortified, the American delegates, at an informal conference, secured from Lloyd George, Clemenceau, and Orlando an agreement to give up the demand for war costs.[24]

Although Hughes continued his fulminations for a time, the Allies in fact ceased to press their demand for war costs in the

[20] Reparation Commission, February 14, 1919, Burnett, *Reparation at the Paris Peace Conference*, Vol. 1, pp. 570-575, Vol. 2, pp. 298-319; Baruch, *The Making of the Reparation and Economic Sections of the Treaty*, pp. 21-22; André Tardieu, *The Truth about the Treaty* (Indianapolis: The Bobbs-Merrill Company, Inc., 1921), p. 292.

[21] Reparation Commission, February 19, 1919, Burnett, *Reparation at the Paris Peace Conference*, Vol. 1, pp. 616-617, Vol. 2, pp. 335-338; Baruch, *The Making of the Reparation and Economic Sections of the Treaty*, pp. 323-337.

[22] First Dulles Draft, February 21, 1919, Burnett, *Reparation at the Paris Peace Conference*, Vol. 1, pp. 600-604.

[23] Wilson to Lansing, February 24, 1919, *ibid.*, pp. 613-614.

[24] Baruch, *The Making of the Reparation and Economic Sections of the Treaty*, p. 26.

first week in March. Three reasons have been suggested for the Allied acceptance of the American position: the "play of the percentages," which persuaded France and Belgium that their share would be maximized by the confinement of reparations to the category of civilian damages; the formula of theoretical responsibility invented by Dulles to enable the Allies to escape the pressure of public opinion; and, finally, the absolute refusal of President Wilson to yield to a proposal which was clearly incompatible with his principles as embodied in the Pre-Armistice Agreement. The United States thus won the first round in its conflict with Great Britain over reparations. It was a clear and significant victory of principle, but subsequent developments were to render it Pyrrhic in practice.

III. *The Struggle for a Fixed Sum in the First and Second Subcommittees of the Commission on Reparation of Damage*

The central objective of American policy was to secure the inclusion in the peace treaty of a reasonable fixed sum of reparations. In its first stages, the struggle to secure the fixed sum was conducted in the First Subcommittee of the Reparation Commission, which was concerned with the evaluation of damages suffered by the Allies, and in the Second Subcommittee, the function of which was to assess German capacity to pay.

Although the British and American positions on the valuation of damages were far from harmonious, Lord Sumner, the chairman of the First Subcommittee, lent substantial support to the American member, Vance C. McCormick, in the latter's insistence that damage claims be stated in figures. McCormick readily agreed with the other members that a complete assessment of damages could not be made for at least two years, having been so advised by General McKinstrey, who had been surveying the devastated regions of France and Belgium. McCormick and Sumner conceded that only approximate claims could be set, but Lebrun of France and Van den Heuvel of Belgium led all the other members of the Subcommittee in refusing even to discuss figures. The only thorough estimates available were those which had been prepared by General McKinstrey, who estimated total civilian damages as being between $15 and $25 billion, figures which were clearly unacceptable to Allied public opinion. Lord Sumner strongly supported McCormick in urging that at least estimates be submitted, perhaps because British losses, mostly marine, could be easily assessed, but more probably because Great Britain had no intention of confining her claims to civilian damage and was thus not constrained by the McKinstrey estimate.[25]

Being unable to discuss damage figures, the First Subcommittee turned its attention to the examination of damage categories and methods of evaluation. Each delegation submitted a memorandum on the categories it would claim and its methods of evaluation, on the basis of which the secretariat drew up summary tabulations.[26] Lord Sumner found fault with some of the categories submitted as "too vague" and "excessive" and urged moderation on the delegations.[27] On March 8, the Subcommittee adopted general principles of valuation submitted by Sumner and designed to restrain vague and excessive claims.[28] On March 31, the Subcommittee adopted its final report, listing categories of damage, without figures, and methods of evaluation. Dulles suggested that the words "for which reparation may be asked" be stricken from the title of the report, pointing out that the American delegation regarded the tabulation as summarizing the kinds of damages that had occurred without determining whether in fact they were all proper claims. Sumner dismissed this complaint as "quite irregular" and the report was adopted as a basis of claims, with Dulles reserving his point.[29] The report on categories of damage, adopted by the plenary Commission on April 7, included, with the concurrence of Dulles, pensions and separation allowances as an approved category of claims.[30]

[25] Burnett, *Reparation at the Paris Peace Conference*, Vol. 1, pp. 32-35. See also Baruch, *The Making of the Reparation and Economic Sections of the Treaty*, pp. 46-53; David Lloyd George, *The Truth about the Peace Treaties* (2 Vols., London: Victor Gollancz, Ltd., 1938), Vol. 1, p. 490.

[26] Burnett, *Reparation at the Paris Peace Conference*, Vol. 1, pp. 37-38, Vol. 2, pp. 387-434.

[27] Reparation Commission, First Subcommittee, February 28, 1919, *ibid.*, Vol. 2, pp. 438-439.

[28] Reparation Commission, First Subcommittee, March 8, 1919, *ibid.*, pp. 450-452.

[29] Reparation Commission, First Subcommittee, March 31, 1919, *ibid.*, Vol. 1, p. 46, Vol. 2, pp. 575-579.

[30] Reparation Commission, April 7, 1919, *ibid.*, Vol. 2, pp. 358-371. See Section v below.

The United States also failed to secure agreement on a fixed sum in the Second Subcommittee on German capacity to pay. Lord Cunliffe was the chairman of the Second Subcommittee and Thomas William Lamont, a financial expert of the United States Treasury, was the American member.[31] The Subcommittee readily agreed on German cash payments of $5 billion to be paid within two years.[32] In the discussion of overall German capacity for long-term payments, the debate in the Second Subcommittee was clearly based on political bargaining rather than economic assessments, and there was a huge gap between the proposals of Cunliffe and Lamont. On February 21, Cunliffe proposed a figure of $120 billion. He did not cite specific sources of revenue from which this sum might be derived but expressed reliance on such imponderables as German industriousness and economies resulting from the reduction of military costs. The American experts had calculated German capacity at from $15 billion to $25 billion, but since such figures were manifestly unacceptable to Britain and France, Lamont proposed a sum of $30 billion, one-half of which, in order to mitigate the transfer problem, would be payable in marks.[33]

With the gap between Cunliffe's figure of $120 billion and the American figure of $30 billion seemingly unbridgeable, the delegates commissioned a special committee of Lamont, Cunliffe, and Loucheur to negotiate for agreement.[34] In hard bargaining sessions, Loucheur came down to $40 billion and Cunliffe agreed to consider $47.5 billion. Then, according to Lamont, Cunliffe and Sumner "put their heads together, went off the deep end, and refused to compromise at all." Loucheur was quite conciliatory and the responsibility for the failure of these negotiations, in Lamont's view, lay entirely with Cunliffe.[35]

[31] See Lamont, "Reparations," *What Really Happened at Paris* (House and Seymour, eds.), pp. 275-277.

[32] Reparation Commission, Second Subcommittee, February 17-20, 1919, Burnett, *Reparation at the Paris Peace Conference*, Vol. 1, pp. 47-48, Vol. 2, pp. 594-621.

[33] Reparation Commission, Second Subcommittee, February 21, 1919, *ibid.*, Vol. 1, pp. 48-49, Vol. 2, pp. 621-624; Baruch, *The Making of the Reparation and Economic Sections of the Treaty*, p. 27.

[34] Reparation Commission, Second Subcommittee, February 24, 1919, Burnett, *Reparation at the Paris Peace Conference*, Vol. 1, pp. 49-50, Vol. 2, p. 632.

[35] Lamont, "Reparation," *What Really Happened at Paris* (House and Seymour, eds.), p. 277.

Direct negotiations for a fixed sum through the determination of German capacity to pay had by early March failed as completely as the attempt to fix the sum through the evaluation of damages. Having successfully eliminated war costs, the United States failed, largely because of British intransigence, to translate that victory into a limited and defined reparations obligation. In delivering the report of the Second Subcommittee, Cunliffe informed the plenary Commission that it had proved impossible to agree on a fixed sum.[36] Had John Maynard Keynes been a member of the Reparation Commission, it is quite possible that Sumner and Cunliffe would have had to pay close attention to his views as a representative of the British Treasury. Keynes's own analysis of German capacity to pay led him to the conclusion that an over-all reparations sum of $40 billion, or even $25 billion, was "not within the limits of reasonable possibility."[37] When the issue of the fixed sum was taken up by the Supreme Council, however, it was the views of Sumner and Cunliffe, and not of Keynes, which influenced Lloyd George, bringing him into direct collision with President Wilson.

The reparations issue was essentially a political question from the British point of view and it was the unwillingness, or inability, of the British to deal with it in terms of economic possibilities and contractual obligations that generated an increasing strain in Anglo-American relations. At a private luncheon with Colonel House on March 6, Lloyd George quite frankly conceded that Germany could not be expected to pay reparations of the size demanded by Britain and France. But, he explained, he wanted a large sum even if Germany could not pay and it had to be reduced later. It was a political matter, said Lloyd George, in which he did not wish to allow the Conservatives to "throw him."[38]

[36] Reparation Commission, April 8, 1919, Burnett, *Reparation at the Paris Peace Conference*, Vol. 2, p. 373. See also Tardieu, *The Truth about the Treaty*, pp. 302-308.

[37] John Maynard Keynes, *The Economic Consequences of the Peace* (New York: Harcourt, Brace and Howe, 1920), p. 202; R. F. Harrod, *The Life of John Maynard Keynes* (London: Macmillan and Company, Ltd., 1951), pp. 236-237.

[38] House Diary, March 6, 1919, Edward M. House Papers, Sterling Library, Yale University.

IV. *The Struggle for a Fixed Sum in the Council of Four*

The failure of the Commission on Reparation of Damage to agree on figures for compensation returned the issue to the Supreme Council. On March 10, Lloyd George, Clemenceau, and House commissioned a special committee of three experts to negotiate anew for agreement on a reparations figure. The experts, Norman H. Davis, Edwin S. Montagu, and Louis Loucheur, met in secret. The three experts agreed on a report which paralleled the position taken by Lamont in the Second Subcommittee, calling for $30 billion as an absolute maximum of reparations, half of which was to be payable in marks. Davis made these recommendations in a private meeting with Lloyd George, Clemenceau, and House in the latter's apartment at the Crillon on March 15. Lloyd George and Clemenceau, according to Davis, were finally persuaded, and Davis left this meeting with the conviction that a tacit agreement had been reached to work out a solution along the line proposed by the experts.[39]

The apparent agreement of March 15 proved illusory. Davis and Loucheur met privately with Wilson, Lloyd George, and Clemenceau on March 18. Montagu had been called home for personal reasons and Lord Sumner and Keynes attended as the British experts. Sumner put forth an argument for heavy reparations, and, according to Davis, President Wilson told Lloyd George he "thought we had reached an agreement in the previous meeting as to substantially what would be done," and the Prime Minister replied that he "did not believe that we had. . . ."[40]

The British, French, and American experts continued their efforts to reach agreement, attempting to devise a flexible schedule of maximum and minimum reparations payments. Between March 19 and March 24, the Anglo-American experts worked out five drafts of reparations clauses, each providing for flexibility of

[39] Conversations between Davis and Burnett, October 18-19, 1938. Burnett, *Reparation at the Paris Peace Conference*, Vol. 1, pp. 53-56. The report of Davis, Montagu, and Loucheur is reproduced *ibid*., pp. 689-692, and in Ray Stannard Baker, *Woodrow Wilson and World Settlement* (3 Vols., Garden City, New York: Doubleday, Page and Company, 1922), Vol. 3, pp. 376-379. See also Baruch, *The Making of the Reparation and Economic Sections of the Treaty*, p. 26.

[40] Davis, Peace Conference Notes, July 5, 1919, Burnett, *Reparation at the Paris Peace Conference*, Vol. 1, p. 56. See also Lloyd George, *The Truth about the Peace Treaties*, Vol. 1, pp. 502-506.

payments by giving the permanent reparations commission limited power to suspend or cancel payments. But the experts, now including both Sumner and Cunliffe for Britain, were unable to agree on figures.[41] Lloyd George told Lamont and Davis on March 22 that he would readily agree to a figure of $25 billion if they could win the agreement of Cunliffe and Sumner, without which he feared that he would be "crucified" at home.[42] Davis advised President Wilson on March 25 that the experts would be unable to submit a unanimous report. "We have agreed substantially upon the form for the peace treaty and upon the plan for its execution," Davis reported, "but we have been unable to arrive at any agreement with Lords Sumner and Cunliffe . . . because these two gentlemen still stand upon their original estimate of 11 billion pounds."[43]

In his Fontainebleau Memorandum of March 25, Lloyd George was vague on reparations, saying that "the duration for the payments of reparation ought to disappear if possible with the generation which made the war," and that "Germany should pay an annual sum for a stated number of years," the amount "to be agreed among the Allied and Associated Powers."[44] The British, French, and American experts submitted proposed figures on March 25: the British figure was Sumner's $55 billion, the French $31 billion to $47 billion, the American $25 billion to $35 billion.[45] In the Council of Four on the same day, President Wilson warned of the danger of setting reparations beyond the reduced capacity of a Germany deprived of much of its territory and resources. Lloyd George replied that he could not forget public opinion and proposed the inclusion of pensions to the families of soldiers killed and incapacitated as a category of reparation.[46]

[41] Burnett, *Reparation at the Paris Peace Conference*, Vol. 1, pp. 56-58, Vol. 2, pp. 699-707; Miller, *Diary*, Vol. 7, pp. 147-151.

[42] House Diary, March 24, 1919, House Papers.

[43] Davis to Wilson, March 25, 1919, Baker, *Wilson and World Settlement*, Vol. 3, pp. 383-385; Burnett, *Reparation at the Paris Peace Conference*, pp. 711-712.

[44] Great Britain, Parliament, *Papers By Command*, 1922, Cmd. 1614; Lloyd George, *The Truth about the Peace Treaties*, Vol. 1, p. 415.

[45] Davis, Strauss, and Lamont to Wilson, March 25, 1919, Baker, *Wilson and World Settlement*, Vol. 3, pp. 385-396; Burnett, *Reparation at the Paris Peace Conference*, Vol. 1, pp. 713-719.

[46] Council of Four, March 25, 1919, 11 a.m., Paul Mantoux, *Les Délibérations du Conseil des Quatre* (2 Vols., Paris: Éditions du Centre National de la Recherche Scientifique, 1955), Vol. 1, pp. 15-16.

Lloyd George struck a different posture on March 26, now contesting the reparations figures proposed by both the French and British experts. Pointing to the danger of a German refusal to sign the treaty, Lloyd George averred that it would be as hard for him as for Clemenceau to dispel "the illusions which prevail on the subject of reparations," but that both should serve their countries as best they could. If he were defeated for failing to do the impossible, he declared, his successor would be able to do no better, and he was convinced that the Germans would not sign the provisions as contemplated. The statesmen, he urged, should stand up to their domestic oppositions. President Wilson replied with enthusiasm: "I cannot fail to express my admiration for the spirit which manifests itself in Mr. Lloyd George's words. There is nothing more honorable than to be driven from power because one was right." If reasonable proposals were made and explained, said the President, not a parliament in the world would be able to blame the statesmen for their decisions. Clemenceau then proposed that the experts be asked to devise a plan setting maximum and minimum *annual* payments but not designating a total sum, but President Wilson insisted that the treaty should contain either a total sum or a time limit. Lloyd George averred that he saw no use in reconvening the experts. His own, he said, were unmovable. When he warned Sumner of the danger of Bolshevism if too much were demanded, said Lloyd George, Sumner had replied: "In that case the Germans will cut their own throats; I would like nothing better."[47]

The French Finance Minister, Klotz, proposed in the meeting of March 28 that no final sum be stated in the treaty but that reparations figures be set for only a year or two while a commission calculated the total damages and then set a final figure. Lloyd George found this a most satisfactory proposal. At this point, John Maynard Keynes was brought into the discussion, and he proposed that Germany be confronted in the treaty with a total bill representing the sum of damages, but that the amount actually to be paid be settled later on the basis of final determinations as to Germany's capacity to pay. Wilson vigorously objected to the Klotz plan as a dangerous proposal asking Germany to open an unlimited credit to the Allies. Keynes's proposal, said

[47] Council of Four, March 26, 1919, 11 a.m., *ibid.*, pp. 25-31.

Wilson, was quite different, in that it would tell Germany what she owed and leave for later decision only the question of what Germany could in fact pay. Lloyd George professed to believe that the two plans were reconcilable, but in any case he favored the Klotz proposal for telling Germany only what the categories of damage were and leaving the figure to be determined by a commission. The Klotz plan, said Lloyd George, whose resolve of the 26th had apparently faded, would provide the means to avoid discussions in their parliaments and would dispel the differences within the Council. Reiterating that Klotz's proposal was not really different from that of Keynes, Lloyd George suggested that any differences within the proposed commission be arbitrated by an appointee of the President of the United States. President Wilson said that he must reserve judgment on the plan.[48]

President Wilson offered some further resistance to the proposals of March 28, but the issue was essentially resolved on that date against the inclusion of a sum of reparations in the treaty. The decisive factor in the defeat of the fixed sum was undoubtedly the final position taken by Lloyd George. After showing some inclination to accept a moderate figure, as in the discussion with the experts on March 15 and in the Council of Four on March 26, Lloyd George ended his vacillations by coming down on the side of the French plan, leaving President Wilson isolated. Throughout the debate on the fixed sum, there had been two views within the British delegation, the extremist position of Lords Sumner and Cunliffe, and the moderate position of the Treasury as represented by Keynes. In his tergiversations of policy Lloyd George made it plain that his own inclinations were for the moderate view, but the pressures of British public and parliamentary opinion brought him finally to the side of improvisation as an easy escape from the pressures exerted by the extremists. In later years, Lloyd George adhered to his view that the decision against the fixed sum was, in the face of the passions of public opinion, a wise one, leaving the determination to the "cooler light of reason and of practical experience. . . ."[49]

[48] Council of Four, March 28, 1919, 11 a.m., *ibid.*, pp. 58-62. See also Tardieu, *The Truth about the Treaty*, pp. 295-297.

[49] Lloyd George, *The Truth about Reparations and War Debts*, p. 29.

Had President Wilson been able and willing to connect a cancellation or mitigation of inter-Allied war debts with the question of a fixed sum of reparations, it is altogether possible that the latter could have been achieved. Sir William Wiseman urged that a deferral of all war loans, to be paid "if and when" the Allies were able, would constitute the great inducement that would end all British opposition to a moderate reparations settlement and make Wilson the "absolute master" of the situation.[50] But such an inducement was rejected by Wilson and his advisers, and if attempted, it almost certainly would have been repudiated by Congress and American public opinion.[51]

V. *The Anglo-American Controversy over Pensions*

The defeat of the fixed sum did not in itself satisfy British interests. It was necessary then to establish within the contractual basis of German liability a category of reparations which would provide compensations for the financial losses suffered by Great Britain in the war as against the personal and property losses suffered by France and Belgium. The category chosen to serve this end was that of military pensions and separation allowances.

Lord Sumner read a paper to the American experts on March 27 claiming that pensions were properly to be regarded as civilian damages and not as war costs.[52] President Wilson pronounced Sumner's memorandum "very legalistic" and, according to Lamont, threw it out "almost with contempt."[53] Lloyd George believed that pensions were a legitimate category of financial obligations to civilians incurred by the Allied Governments and was evidently concerned that, without this category, the British share of reparations would be insignificant although Great Britain's aggregate wartime expenditures were the greatest of all of the Allied Powers.[54] The French supported the British demand for

[50] Wiseman to House, April 5, 1919, House Papers.
[51] See Thomas A. Bailey, *Woodrow Wilson and the Lost Peace* (New York: The Macmillan Company, 1944), pp. 246-247; Lloyd George, *The Truth about Reparations and War Debts*, pp. 100-105.
[52] Burnett, *Reparation at the Pairs Peace Conference*, Vol. 1, pp. 719-725.
[53] Lamont to Burnett, June 25, 1934, *ibid.*, p. 63.
[54] Lloyd George, *The Truth about the Peace Treaties*, Vol. 1, pp. 491-492.

pensions, probably because they favored any proposal which might raise the total bill.[55]

General Smuts, whom Wilson greatly admired, was prevailed upon by Lloyd George to try his hand at persuading the President to accept pensions. On March 31, Smuts produced a paper which presented a closely reasoned argument for the compatibility of pensions and separation allowances with the Allied reservation on civilian damages in the Pre-Armistice Agreement.[56] The Germans, argued Smuts, had bound themselves to pay compensation for all damages to civilians and their property, wherever and however arising, as long as they were the result of German aggression. Taking the hypothetical case of a French shopkeeper wounded as a soldier and permanently disabled, Smuts reasoned that the disability allowances paid to him after his discharge and the pension paid to his wife were in fact compensations by the French Government for civilian damages. The "plain, common-sense construction" of the Allied reservation in the Pre-Armistice Agreement, Smuts contended, entirely justified the conclusion that "damage done to the civilian populations of the Allies and their property" included "all war pensions and separation allowances."[57]

In a meeting with his financial experts on April 1, President Wilson said that he was "very much impressed" with General Smuts's memorandum. The experts contended unanimously that the Smuts proposal was contrary to the Pre-Armistice Agreement, that all the logic was against it. "Logic! Logic!" exclaimed the President. "I don't give a damn for logic. I am going to include pensions!"[58]

Wilson's decision of April 1 was widely condemned as an unwarrantable surrender. Keynes, for instance, thought it "perhaps the most decisive moment in the disintegration of the President's moral position and the clouding of his mind. . . ."[59] The

[55] Baker, *Wilson and World Settlement*, Vol. 2, p. 383; Tardieu, *The Truth about the Treaty*, pp. 291-292.

[56] See Chapter 2, Section 11.

[57] Baruch, *The Making of the Reparation and Economic Sections of the Treaty*, pp. 29-32; Burnett, *Reparation at the Paris Peace Conference*, Vol. 1, pp. 773-775; Lloyd George, *The Truth about the Peace Treaties*, Vol. 1, pp. 495-496.

[58] Lamont, "Reparations," *What Really Happened at Paris* (House and Seymour, eds.), p. 272; Memorandum by Dulles, April 1, 1919, Burnett, *Reparation at the Paris Peace Conference*, Vol. 1, pp. 775-776.

[59] Keynes, *The Economic Consequences of the Peace*, pp. 52-53.

American experts, on the other hand, although greatly disappointed, believed that the inclusion of pensions, in view of the limited capacity of Germany to pay, would only alter the apportionment and not the sum of reparations.[60]

Whatever the responsibility of President Wilson for the inclusion of pensions, General Smuts was certainly no less responsible. It was undoubtedly the influence and prestige of Smuts, with whom Wilson shared so deep a community of thought regarding the League of Nations, that persuaded the President to overrule his experts in the decision of April 1. Long afterwards, Smuts said that if he had known that so much would hang on his opinion, he would not so readily have given it. Both Wilson and Smuts, however, were almost certainly convinced at the time that they were making a decision as to the distribution of a fixed sum and not as to the size of that sum.[61]

VI. *Article 231 of the Treaty: the "War Guilt" Clause*

The success of the United States in persuading the Allies to give up their demand for war costs was due in part to the possibilities for appeasing Allied public opinion opened up by the Dulles formula for a statement of theoretical enemy responsibility for integral reparation.[62] Lloyd George revived this formula in a draft of the reparations clauses submitted to the Council of Four on March 29.[63] President Wilson objected that the very assertion of the right to war costs was a violation of the Pre-Armistice Agreement and proposed a simple statement to the effect that Allied losses were so great that Germany would not be able to compensate for them in their entirety. Lloyd George agreed to omit a positive assertion of the right to war costs but insisted that that right could not be renounced although Germany's obligations in fact would be explicitly confined to material possibilities. Lloyd George demanded that the treaty contained some indication of the enemy's incapacity to pay all he owed, in order to justify the British and

---

[60] Baruch, *The Making of the Reparation and Economic Sections of the Treaty*, p. 29.

[61] Sarah Gertrude Millin, *General Smuts* (2 Vols., London: Faber and Faber, Ltd., 1936), Vol. 2, pp. 219-225; J. C. Smuts, *Jan Christian Smuts* (New York: William Morrow and Company, Inc., 1952), p. 207.

[62] See Section II above.

[63] Burnett, *Reparation at the Paris Peace Conference*, Vol. 1, pp. 754-756.

French Governments before public opinion for their renunciation of war costs.[64] With the full support of Clemenceau and Klotz, Lloyd George insisted again on March 31 on the political necessity of the treaty containing some indication that the limitation of reparations was a voluntary renunciation of Allied rights. President Wilson saw new dangers in this formula.[65]

The drafting of appropriate clauses for the treaty was turned over to the financial experts. Klotz, Loucheur, and Montagu demanded a positive statement of the right of the Allies to integral reparation, while Lamont and Dulles proposed instead to express the Allied right obliquely by an affirmation of enemy responsibility. On April 2, the experts agreed to clauses along the lines suggested by Lamont and Dulles. As adopted by the experts, the clauses read that the Allies "affirm the responsibility of the enemy for causing all the loss and damage" suffered by the Allies "as consequence of the war imposed upon them by the aggression of the enemy states," but that since the Allies "recognize that the financial resources of the enemy are not unlimited . . . they judge that it will be impracticable for the enemy states to make complete reparation for all such loss and damage."[66]

These clauses were further refined by the Council of Four on April 5. Lloyd George and Clemenceau insisted that the clauses contain a German acceptance as well as an Allied affirmation of responsibility. Lloyd George found the simple affirmation "hardly adequate to meet the political situation, either British or French." House and Davis questioned the compatibility with the Pre-Armistice Agreement of an explicit German acceptance of responsibility, but they yielded. "The American delegation has no special interest in the first article," said Davis. "In drafting it we have attempted to meet the views of Great Britain and France."[67] The clause adopted on April 5, with some subsequent alterations

---

[64] Council of Four, March 29, 1919, 4 p.m., Mantoux, *Les Délibérations du Conseil des Quatre*, Vol. 1, pp. 83-84; Tardieu, *The Truth about the Treaty*, p. 292.

[65] Council of Four, March 31, 1919, 11 a.m., Mantoux, *Les Délibérations du Conseil des Quatre*, Vol. 1, pp. 85-86.

[66] Burnett, *Reparation at the Paris Peace Conference*, Vol. 1, pp. 777-785; Baker, *Wilson and World Settlement*, Vol. 3, pp. 397-398.

[67] Council of Four, April 5, 1919, 11 a.m., *Foreign Relations, 1919, The Paris Peace Conference*, Vol. 5, pp. 21-22; Burnett, *Reparation at the Paris Peace Conference*, Vol. 1, pp. 825-826.

of wording, became Article 231 of the Treaty of Versailles, which read: "The Allied and Associated Governments affirm and Germany accepts the responsibility of Germany and her allies for causing all the loss and damage to which the Allied and Associated Governments and their nationals have been subjected as a consequence of the war imposed upon them by the aggression of Germany and her allies." Article 232 stated that "the Allied and Associated Governments recognize that the resources of Germany are not adequate . . . to make complete reparation for all such loss and damage."[68]

Germany bitterly protested Article 231 as basing her reparations liability on an accusation of the sole responsibility of the Central Powers for the war. The "war guilt" clause became a major focus of German agitation against the Treaty of Versailles during the interwar years. In fact, Article 231 had no financial consequences whatever, because Article 232 clearly confined German liability to civilian damages. The significance of Article 231 lies not in its implications but in its *origins*. It was carefully designed as a compromise between the American determination to comply with the Pre-Armistice Agreement by excluding war costs and the desire of Lloyd George and Clemenceau to appease public opinion by a declaration of at least theoretical German liability for integral reparation.[69]

VII. *The Struggle for a Time Limit*

The defeat of American efforts to secure a statement in the treaty of a fixed sum of reparations made it all the more important, from the American point of view, to limit Germany's obligation by a time limit on payments. In pursuing this objective, American policy once again ran against the fears of Lloyd George and Clemenceau as to public opinion, and once again the American proposals were defeated.

[68] Great Britain, Treaty Series No. 4 (1919), *Treaty of Peace between the Allied and Associated Powers and Germany; Cmd.* 153, pp. 101-102.

[69] See Keynes, *The Economic Consequences of the Peace*, pp. 152-153; Étienne Mantoux, *The Carthaginian Peace* (New York: Charles Scribner's Sons, 1952), pp. 100-101; Paul Birdsall, *Versailles Twenty Years After* (London: George Allen and Unwin, Ltd., 1941), pp. 253-255; H.W.V. Temperley, ed., *A History of the Peace Conference of Paris* (6 Vols., London: Henry Frowde and Hodder and Stoughton, 1920-1924), Vol. 2, pp. 43-47, 73-77.

In his Fontainebleau Memorandum of March 25, Lloyd George had asserted that "the duration for the payments of reparation ought to disappear if possible with the generation which made the war." In his draft reparations clauses of March 29, however, Lloyd George proposed to leave the amount, *time*, and manner of reparations payments to be determined by a permanent reparations commission.[70] A draft submitted by the Anglo-American experts on April 1 provided for a time limit of thirty years on an amount to be determined by the permanent commission by May 1, 1921, but also said that the enemy was to compensate for damages "at whatever cost to themselves."[71]

The question of a time limit was debated and settled in the Council of Four on April 5. President Wilson at this time was ill and House and Davis spoke for the United States. Klotz objected to the time limit of thirty years in the Anglo-American draft of April 1, and Lloyd George assured him that this was merely an "expression of opinion" and that the document of April 1 did not limit reparations payments to thirty years if the agreed sum had not by then been paid. Davis contested Lloyd George's interpretation, affirming that the British experts "had made it quite clear that the document did so limit it." Lloyd George and Sumner insisted that the British position was that Germany ought to pay within thirty years, but that if she could not do so, the commission should have the right to extend the time of payment. Davis said that when President Wilson had agreed to pensions, he had counted on a thirty-year time limit so that the pensions would affect only the distribution and not the amount which Germany would pay. Moreover, said Davis, if the period of payment exceeded thirty years, the accumulation of interest charges would make total payment impossible.[72]

Colonel House broke the impasse. "Everyone," he said, "was agreed that if the Germans could not pay in thirty years, then they must pay the amount in forty years." He "did not understand, therefore, what the discussion was all about." Clemenceau ex-

[70] Burnett, *Reparation at the Paris Peace Conference*, Vol. 1, pp. 754-756; Lloyd George, *The Truth about the Peace Treaties*, Vol. 1, pp. 501-502.

[71] Burnett, *Reparation at the Paris Peace Conference*, Vol. 1, pp. 779-780.

[72] Council of Four, April 5, 1919, 11 a.m., *Foreign Relations, 1919, The Paris Peace Conference*, Vol. 5, pp. 22-24; Burnett, *Reparation at the Paris Peace Conference*, Vol. 1, pp. 826-829.

plained to House that the issue was whether the permanent commission was to determine in 1921 only what Germany could pay in thirty years, or what the total amount was that she had to pay. Lloyd George then rehearsed the arguments against fixing a thirty-year time limit. It would be impossible, he said, to assess German capacity until Germany had recovered economically from the war. He would agree to a period of thirty years "under normal conditions," but, he declared, the *next* thirty years would not be normal. House suggested that the clauses be drafted as suggested by Lloyd George and Sumner and that nothing should be said about the thirty-year limit.[73]

Colonel House, who seems not to have understood the significance of his concession, thus surrendered a major principle of American reparations policy. When President Wilson had given up the struggle for a fixed sum, the next logical line of defense for a reparations settlement based on the Pre-Armistice Agreement was to limit German payments by a time limit. With the President absent from the Council, House agreed in effect that the permanent Reparations Commission would only compute a total bill and enforce payments without reference to any limitations of amount or time. The rejection of the time limit, moreover, insofar as it opened the way to increasing the total amount to be paid by Germany, meant the financial effectuation of pensions, for with the removal of limitations on payments, the pensions ceased to be, as Wilson had intended, merely a matter of distribution of a given sum and became an additional category of compensation to be calculated by the Reparations Commission. The vagaries of British policy were no less striking than those of American policy under Colonel House. As on previous issues, there were two voices within the British delegation, that of the experts, who had agreed

[73] Council of Four, April 5, 1919, 11 a.m., *Foreign Relations, 1919, The Paris Peace Conference*, Vol. 5, pp. 25-27. According to the somewhat different minutes reproduced by Burnett, House said, upon hearing Clemenceau's argument against the time limit: "It seems to me that M. Clemenceau's conclusion is very close to the American proposal." Burnett, *Reparation at the Paris Peace Conference*, Vol. 1, p. 823. At the end of the discussion, according to Burnett's minutes, Davis commented on the agreement which had been reached: "This is a complete departure from the principles upon which we have been working for three months." *ibid.*, p. 833. See also Baker, *Wilson and World Settlement*, Vol. 2, pp. 379-380; Charles Seymour, ed., *The Intimate Papers of Colonel House* (4 Vols., Boston and New York: Houghton Mifflin Company, 1926-1928), Vol. 4, pp. 398-400.

to a time limit, and that of Lloyd George, abetted by Lord Sumner, who through vacillation and sophistry finally brought British policy to a position of unqualified opposition to the time limit. Only the French had a clear and consistent policy, and they secured their desire, the partial restoration in practice of the war costs which they had yielded in principle. It remained to determine the powers of the Permanent Reparations Commission, which, depending on how they were defined and utilized, could still effectuate, or finally nullify, the American policy of confining reparations to at least the spirit of the Pre-Armistice Agreement.

VIII. *The Anglo-American Controversy over the Powers of the Permanent Reparations Commission*

The debate on the powers of the Reparations Commission was opened in the Council of Four on April 7. The experts presented a clause, drawn up in accordance with the decision of April 5, stating that the Commission would present a total bill to Germany by May 1, 1921, along with a schedule for payments within thirty years, but that if Germany should fail to meet these payments, then the Commission, or the Allied and Associated Governments acting through the Commission, would determine payment in subsequent years or other means of settlement. Klotz asked whether, under the last provision, the Allied and Associated Governments would have to be unanimous in instructing the Commission, and whether a deferral of payments by the Commission would require a unanimous vote. Clemenceau considered unanimity essential and Lloyd George and Orlando concurred. It was agreed that any deferral of payments would require a unanimous vote, House reserving the opinion of the President.[74] Wilson agreed tacitly to the unanimity requirement, despite the fact that it would narrow the possibility of a flexible enforcement policy.[75]

Despite the very substantial victories which Lloyd George had won on the issues of the fixed sum and the time limit, his Coalition majority in the House of Commons became restive at the failure of the Peace Conference explicitly to require war costs. On April 8, Lloyd George received a telegram signed by 370 members of the

[74] Council of Four, April 7, 1919, 4 p.m., *Foreign Relations, 1919, The Paris Peace Conference*, Vol. 5, pp. 46-47.
[75] Burnett, *Reparation at the Paris Peace Conference*, Vol. 1, p. 81.

House of Commons expressing the "greatest anxiety" at the "persistent reports from Paris that the British delegates, instead of formulating the complete financial claim of the Empire, are merely considering what amount can be exacted from the enemy. . . . Our constituents, (said the telegram) have always expected —and still expect—that the first action of the peace delegates would be, as you repeatedly stated in your election speeches, to present the bill in full, to make Germany acknowledge the debt, and then to discuss ways and means of obtaining payment." The Members of Parliament asked the Prime Minister for renewed assurances that he had not departed from his "original intention." Lloyd George returned to London the following week and explained his policy to Parliament on April 16, emphasizing that he had pointed to the limitations of German capacity in the campaign and explaining the agreements reached in the Supreme Council. The House gave him a strong vote of confidence in his conduct of the negotiations.[76]

In fact, Lloyd George had secured virtually all that the House of Commons desired. The decisions of April 5 in regard to the time limit and of April 7 in regard to deferrals of payments made it clear that the Reparations Commission would not have the power to alter payments, once determined, in accordance with German capacity, but was merely to determine a total sum by adding up the demands of the Allies in the accepted categories and to enforce payments of this sum by Germany. In the Council of Four on April 10, President Wilson formally agreed that unanimity of the Reparations Commission was essential for the cancellation of any part of the enemy debt.[77]

A significant issue arose from the plan of the experts for a German bond issue on the world market designed to "materialize" the German debt through private investment. President Wilson insisted that the Reparations Commission would have to agree unanimously to the amount of such a bond issue, while Lloyd George and Clemenceau favored a majority decision. Lloyd George said that a requirement of unanimity could hold up the

[76] Lloyd George, *The Truth about the Peace Treaties*, Vol. 1, pp. 563-566; Frank Owen, *Tempestuous Journey—Lloyd George: His Life and Times* (London: Hutchinson and Company, Ltd., 1954), pp. 539-543.

[77] Council of Four, April 10, 1919, 4 p.m., *Foreign Relations, 1919, The Paris Peace Conference*, Vol. 5, p. 72.

work of the Commission indefinitely and would be "fatal to the whole scheme." The object of the bond issue, Wilson countered, was collateral for borrowing, much of which would be in the United States, and because an extravagant bond issue would upset Germany's credit, the United States insisted, as a condition of its participation on the Reparations Commission, on the safeguard of unanimity as to the amount of the bond issue.[78]

The outcome was a compromise defining the minimum of German bond issues in the treaty and requiring unanimous votes of the Commission for additional issues. The Council agreed on April 12 to a plan submitted by Lord Sumner for minimum German bond issues of $25 billion, consisting of an immediate issue of $5 billion, an issue of $10 billion after the signing of the treaty, and an additional issue of $10 billion at such time as the Reparations Commission should consider appropriate.[79] On April 23, Lloyd George proposed that the decision on the third and any subsequent bond issues be by a majority of the Reparations Commission. Wilson, now with French support, insisted on unanimity, and Lloyd George yielded.[80] This meant that beyond the first two bond issues, amounting to $15 billion, any subsequent issues considered by the Reparations Commission would be subject to the veto of the United States.

This arrangement gave rise to a postwar controversy between David Hunter Miller and John Maynard Keynes as to whether the limitation on *bond issues* in fact constituted a limitation on *payments* by Germany. Keynes argued that the German debt existed apart from the bond issues and was not confined to payment through the issuance of bonds and that, because of the requirement of unanimity for deferral or cancellation of payments, the total debt could only be *reduced* by unanimous vote of the Reparations Commission. Moreover, argued Keynes, the requirements for compound interest on the German debt meant that Germany "in effect engaged herself to hand over to the Allies the whole of her surplus productivity in perpetuity."[81] In an article in

---

[78] Council of Four, April 10, 1919, 4 p.m., *ibid.*, pp. 76-77.

[79] Council of Four, April 12, 1919, Mantoux, *Les Délibérations du Conseil des Quatre*, Vol. 1, p. 236.

[80] Council of Four, April 23, 1919, 4 p.m., *Foreign Relations, 1919, The Paris Peace Conference*, Vol. 5, p. 157.

[81] Keynes, *The Economic Consequences of the Peace*, pp. 165-168.

the *New York Evening Post* on February 6, 1920, David Hunter Miller contended that the German debt had to be distinguished from the payments prescribed in the treaty and that "the payment is *solely* by means of bonds." Since no bonds could be issued beyond $15 billion without the unanimous consent of the Reparations Commission, Miller argued, German payments could not exceed $15 billion without the consent of the United States.[82]

If the Miller view was correct, the decision of the Council of Four requiring unanimity of the Reparations Commission to increase the bond issues beyond $15 billion was a great diplomatic victory for the United States. Norman Davis agreed with Miller's interpretation of the bonding provisions, but the other financial experts shared the Keynes view, that the debt and the obligation to pay it existed independently of the bond issues, that the bonds were simply a means by which creditor governments could discount payments in advance.[83] There is no evidence that Great Britain and France consciously granted the power of veto to the United States as claimed by Miller and Davis. After fighting the United States to defeat on the fixed sum in various forms, Lloyd George and Clemenceau granted the bond veto in the Council of Four on April 23, 1919, with little resistance. It is extremely unlikely that they intended thereby to give the United States the power to limit German reparations payments singlehandedly. It seems clear, therefore, that Britain and France did not intend the bond issues to be regarded as the sole form of German payments. It is also possible, however, that, through judicious use of its own vast financial strength, the United States might as a member of the Reparations Commission have been able to enforce limitations on German payments in practice.[84]

A minor Anglo-American issue arose over the question of reparations and German taxation levels. In the Council of Four on April 23, Lord Sumner urged that the Reparations Commission

[82] David Hunter Miller, "Vital Point in Peace Treaty Misstated by John M. Keynes," *The Evening Post* (New York), February 6, 1920, p. 10, columns 5-6.
[83] See Burnett, *Reparation at the Paris Peace Conference*, Vol 1, p. 87; Tardieu, *The Truth about the Treaty*, pp. 313-315.
[84] See Burnett, *Reparation at the Paris Peace Conference*, Vol. 1, pp. 88-90; Temperley, ed., *A History of the Peace Conference of Paris*, Vol. 2, pp. 79-82; Birdsall, *Versailles Twenty Years After*, pp. 262-263.

should be forbidden to relieve Germany of any payments until German taxes had been raised at least to the level of the most heavily taxed state represented on the Reparations Commission. Wilson objected to the proposal and Lloyd George yielded, agreeing to a general provision that, in estimating German capacity, the Commission would satisfy itself that Germany was as heavily taxed as any state represented on the Commission.[85] Since cancellation of payments in any case required a unanimous vote of the Commission, Great Britain in fact retained the power to enforce Sumner's demand.

The question of guarantees to enforce German payments was one on which Great Britain stood with the United States in opposition to the direct controls and harsh sanctions demanded by the French. The issue had been considered inconclusively in the Third Subcommittee of the Commission on Reparation of Damage, of which Prime Minister Hughes was chairman and Bernard Baruch vice-chairman. Hughes and Baruch objected to a French scheme of controls including a tax on German exports and also objected to military occupation as a sanction against default.[86] In the Council of Four on April 23, President Wilson raised objections to a report of the experts suggesting six specific economic sanctions to be applied in the event of German default. The President secured the agreement of the Council to a simple formula calling for "economic or financial prohibitions and reprisals, and in general such other measures as the respective Governments may determine to be necessary in the premises."[87] Although Great Britain and the United States almost certainly intended the "other measures" of Wilson's formula to mean only economic measures, France referred to this clause in 1923 in justification of its military occupation of the Ruhr.[88]

The United States thus secured certain measures in the constitution of the permanent Reparations Commission to regulate the discharge of the German debt although losing the fixed sum.

[85] Council of Four, April 23, 1919, 4 p.m., *Foreign Relations, 1919, The Paris Peace Conference*, Vol. 5, pp. 159-161.

[86] Reparation Commission, Third Subcommittee, March 11 and 13, 1919, Burnett, *Reparation at the Paris Peace Conference*, Vol. 2, pp. 772-783.

[87] Council of Four, April 23, 1919, 4 p.m., *Foreign Relations, 1919, The Paris Peace Conference*, Vol. 5, p. 161.

[88] See Tardieu, *The Truth about the Treaty*, pp. 329-332.

President Wilson and his experts came to regard the Reparations Commission as the instrument through which a moderate reparations policy could still be secured. Lloyd George believed that Britain and the United States, acting in concert on the Reparations Commission, could have enforced moderation, but the withdrawal of the United States completely altered the balance of the Commission, leaving it to the control of France and Belgium. "The whole reparations scheme," Lloyd George concluded, "was thus wrecked by the defection of America."[89]

IX. The Allocation of Reparations Payments and the Belgian Demand for Priority; Austria-Hungary and the Succession States

The question of how reparations receipts would be apportioned among the Allied states was essentially an Anglo-French-Belgian issue in which the United States, with no claims of its own, played a mediatorial role. On March 26, Lloyd George proposed a simple apportionment of 50 per cent for France and 30 per cent for Great Britain in order to avoid belaboring "disagreeable details" as to actual losses.[90] In a simultaneous meeting of the experts, Loucheur demanded a ratio of 56 per cent for France and 25 per cent for Britain, while Sumner held out for Lloyd George's proposal of 50 per cent for France and 30 per cent for Britain. Norman Davis suggested several compromise ratios, settling on a proposed 55 per cent for France and 28 per cent for Britain.[91] After further fruitless negotiations among the statesmen and experts in which American efforts at conciliation failed to reconcile Anglo-French differences, Wilson, Lloyd George, and Clemenceau signed a memorandum on May 1 providing that each nation's reparations receipts would be based on the ratio of its aggregate claims, as accepted by the Reparations Commission by May 1, 1921, to the aggregate claims of all.[92]

[89] Lloyd George, *The Truth about the Peace Treaties*, Vol. 1, pp. 512-513. See also Lloyd George, *The Truth about Reparations and War Debts*, p. 26.

[90] Council of Four, March 26, 1919, 3:30 p.m., Mantoux, *Les Délibérations du Conseil des Quatre*, Vol. 1, pp. 35-36.

[91] Council of Experts, March 26, 1919, 3:30 p.m., *ibid.*, pp. 37-40.

[92] Burnett, *Reparation at the Paris Peace Conference*, Vol. 1, p. 1110. See also Baker, *Wilson and World Settlement*, Vol. 2, pp. 387-388.

Belgium was treated as a special case. The United States, which had successfully opposed war costs for the other Allies, upheld the right of Belgium to receive compensation for her total war expenditures, while Great Britain, who had gone to war in 1914 because of the violation of Belgian neutrality, resisted the Belgian demands. The United States based its position on the full liability of Germany, which Germany herself had recognized, for the violation of Belgian neutrality.[93] In the Council of Four on April 5, Lloyd George contested a recommendation by John Foster Dulles for the payment by Germany of Belgian war costs. "It is England and France," said Lloyd George, "who have actually paid Belgium's war costs."[94] On April 29, Belgian Foreign Minister Hymans demanded the inclusion in the reparations clauses of provisions for German payment of Belgium's war costs, a substantial Belgian priority in the first reparations receipts, and a general stipulation for the full discharge of Belgian reparations within ten years. Unless her demands were met, Hymans threatened, Belgium might refuse to sign the treaty. Wilson, by now impatient with the truculence of Hymans' demands, reminded Belgium that the Pre-Armistice Agreement confined reparations to civilian damages.[95]

The Council finally agreed to a Belgian priority in reparations receipts and, in effect, to the payment of Belgian war costs. Loucheur suggested on May 2 that Belgium receive 15 per cent of the first $500 million paid by Germany. Wilson said that the sum was "hardly worth contesting," but Lloyd George still maintained that Belgium should receive no special treatment.[96] On May 3, it was agreed that a special bond issue would be required of Germany to the value of the total sum which Belgium had borrowed from the Allies as a result of the violation of her neutrality. Germany would thus be directly liable to the Allies for the Belgian war debts, a virtual satisfaction of Belgium's demand for war costs.[97] Lloyd George ultimately yielded on the Belgian de-

[93] See Lamont, "Reparations," *What Really Happened at Paris* (House and Seymour, eds.), pp. 279-281. See also Chancellor Bethmann Hollweg's speech to the Reichstag on August 4, 1914, in Burnett, *Reparation at the Paris Peace Conference*, Vol. I, p. 354.
[94] Council of Four, April 5, 1919, 4 p.m., *Foreign Relations, 1919, The Paris Peace Conference*, Vol. 5, p. 32.
[95] Council of Four, April 29, 1919, 4:30 p.m., *ibid.*, pp. 344-351.
[96] Council of Four, May 2, 1919, 4 p.m., *ibid.*, p. 419.
[97] Council of Four, May 3, 1919, 12:30 p.m., *ibid.*, pp. 447-448; Lamont,

mand for priority, and on June 24, an Agreement on Priority in Reparations for Belgium was signed giving Belgium a priority of 2.5 billion gold francs out of the first cash payments made by Germany.[98]

The reparations clauses of the treaties with Austria and Hungary were closely modeled on the German treaty although it was acknowledged that these diminished states could not make complete reparation.[99] As to the succession states, President Wilson objected to proposals that they be required to share the reparations burden. Lloyd George disagreed, pointing out that nationals of the new states had fought against the Allies and that these states were receiving substantial territories. "Why," asked Lloyd George, "should they get their freedom without paying for it?" Wilson was brought to agree with Lloyd George "in principle" but expressed fear that a heavy reparations burden on the succession states would damage the credit structure of Europe.[100] In the face of objections on the part of the new states to the payment of "reparations," Wilson suggested a "contribution towards the cost of their own liberation."[101] It was agreed on June 23 that the new states would pay as a contribution to the cost of their own liberation a sum equal to 20 per cent of the portion of the bonded Austro-Hungarian war debt as of October 27, 1918, apportioned to the territory which each had acquired from Austria-Hungary on the same principle as the prewar debt. These amounts were to be balanced against the reparations claims of the new states.[102] This arrangement was embodied in a special inter-Allied agreement signed on September 10 and modified on December 9, 1919.[103]

The negotiations on reparations represent a low point of Anglo-American relations at the Peace Conference. The conflict of Amer-

---

"Reparations," *What Really Happened at Paris* (House and Seymour, eds.), pp. 281-282.

[98] *Foreign Relations, 1919, The Paris Peace Conference*, Vol. 13, pp. 849-850.

[99] See Temperley, ed., *A History of the Peace Conference of Paris*, Vol. 5, pp. 3-11.

[100] Council of Four, May 22, 1919, 4:15 p.m., *Foreign Relations, 1919, The Paris Peace Conference*, Vol. 5, pp. 830-831.

[101] Council of Four, May 27, 1919, 11:45 a.m., *ibid.*, Vol. 6, pp. 65-66.

[102] Council of Four, June 23, 1919, 4:30 p.m., *ibid.*, p. 640.

[103] Great Britain, Treaty Series No. 14 (1919); *Cmd.* 458; Treaty Series No. 7 (1920); *Cmd.* 637.

ican and British policies issued essentially from the strict adherence
of President Wilson and his advisers to the Pre-Armistice Agreement as against the British effort, resulting from the pressures of
public and parliamentary opinion, to commit a vast sum of reparations upon Germany. For the most part, British policy was successful. Although war costs as such were renounced, the defeat of the
fixed sum and of the time limit, and the construction of the permanent Reparations Commission with rigidly constrained powers,
amounted to a substantial victory for British and continental policies. Whether, had the United States taken part as a member of the
Reparations Commission, she could have brought the other members of the Commission to accept an application of the terms in
closer conformity with the spirit of the Pre-Armistice Agreement,
is problematical, but this seems not unlikely. It is even more likely
that if the United States had been willing to abate the war debts
of the Allies, a much more reasonable set of reparations provisions
might have been secured, but this was not considered practical
by Wilson at the time.

CHAPTER 10

PROBLEMS OF IMMEDIATE AND
LONG-RANGE ECONOMIC COOPERATION

T HERE was a marked divergence of British and American policies in regard to proposals for post-war economic cooperation among the Allied and Associated Powers. The British
were generally inclined to utilize the organs of wartime cooperation as instruments for an international approach to the problems
of economic readjustment, while the United States was disposed
to disband the instrumentalities of international control as rapidly
as possible. In approaching the immediate problems of relief and
food supplies for Europe, the United States rejected proposals for
control of the relief program by an international agency, but took
the lead, with British support, in supplying relief goods to the
continent, refusing to use such supplies as a weapon of political
pressure on the enemy. It was in the area of proposals for long-
term economic cooperation that British and American policies
were most at variance. British proposals for permanent measures
of economic and financial cooperation were firmly rejected by the
United States. In their reluctance to undertake economic commitments, American statesmen maintained a basic faith in the automatic healing processes of a free international economy.

I. Anglo-American Approaches to Problems of Relief
and the Blockade of Germany

At the end of World War I, millions of people in the liberated
and enemy states faced the immediate prospect of famine in the
wake of a general breakdown of production and facilities of distribution. With a prepared surplus of some 20 million tons of food
and textiles, the United States was virtually the only possible
source of urgently needed supplies. The problem of relief was
greatly complicated, however, by an acute world shortage of shipping, by the illiquidity of the needy countries, by the continuing
blockade against the enemy countries, and by the rising threat of
anarchy and Bolshevism in eastern and central Europe. American
policy in these circumstances called for the removal of the block-

ade, contributions by all surplus countries to a pool of relief supplies, the utilization of two million tons of enemy shipping confined in neutral and enemy ports, the extension of credit to the liberated states, the revival of the instruments of production and distribution, and the wide distribution of a temporary but substantial flow of relief supplies.[1]

The British were strongly disposed to utilize the organs of wartime cooperation to cope with the problems of relief and economic readjustment, but the United States was almost vehement in its opposition. In October 1918, the Foreign Office submitted a scheme to the Imperial War Cabinet proposing the continued use of such organs as the Allied Food Council and the Allied Maritime Transport Council. On October 30, Joseph C. Cotton, the American representative on the Allied Food Council, cabled Herbert Hoover, the director of the American Food Administration, that the British and French intended to propose that food supplies, raw materials, and other commodities going to Europe be channeled through existing Allied organs.[2] With the approval of President Wilson, Hoover cabled back that the United States "will not agree to any program that even looks like inter-Allied control of our economic resources after peace."[3] Because of the total lack of sympathy on the part of the United States, British proposals for the continued use of the wartime agencies came to nothing and these agencies were rapidly disbanded after the Armistice of November 11, 1918.[4]

Although refusing to place the relief program under international auspices, President Wilson undertook to secure Allied cooperation in a coordinated program of relief under an American

[1] Herbert Hoover, "The Economic Administration during the Armistice," *What Really Happened at Paris* (Edward Mandell House and Charles Seymour, eds., New York: Charles Scribner's Sons, 1921), pp. 336-343.

[2] Ambassador Sharp (Paris) to Lansing (from Cotton for Hoover), October 30, 1918, Department of State, *Papers Relating to the Foreign Relations of the United States, 1918*, Supplement 1, *The World War* (2 Vols., Washington: United States Government Printing Office, 1933), Vol. 1, pp. 614-616; hereafter referred to as *Foreign Relations*.

[3] Lansing to House (from Hoover for Cotton), November 8, 1918, *ibid.*, pp. 616-617; Herbert Hoover, *The Ordeal of Woodrow Wilson* (New York, Toronto, London: McGraw-Hill Book Company, Inc., 1958), pp. 91-93.

[4] Alfred Zimmern, *The League of Nations and the Rule of Law, 1918-1935* (2nd edn., London: Macmillan and Company, Ltd., 1945), pp. 151-156; Howard P. Whidden, Jr., "Why Allied Unity Failed in 1918-1919," *Foreign Policy Reports*, Vol. 18, No. 23 (February 15, 1943), pp. 303-305; J. A. Salter, *Allied Shipping Control* (Oxford: The Clarendon Press, 1921), pp. 216-222.

director. He asked Hoover to go to Europe and arrange such a program with the Allies. Hoover met with Allied representatives in London on November 22, and they suggested that the relief program be placed under the direction of an inter-Allied board. Hoover flatly rejected this proposal and insisted on an organization under the Supreme War Council with a single American director. Hoover believed that the Allied proposal rested on a desire to use reconstruction and relief for purposes of "pressure and empire."[5]

Failing to secure Allied agreement to his proposals, Hoover went to Paris and laid the situation before Colonel House, who then undertook to win British assent to the American plan. House cabled the President on November 27 that the British Treasury was prepared to participate in the American plan to the extent of goods furnished from the British Empire. The chief problem, House said, was to devise a plan which "will not antagonize the Allies and particularly Great Britain and at the same time permit single American leadership in relief to the civilian populations of Europe."[6] At Wilson's instruction, House wrote to Balfour on December 1 outlining the President's food relief plan. Explaining the "political necessity of American control over American resources," House proposed the appointment of Hoover as Director-General of Relief, who would in that capacity be responsible to the Supreme War Council.[7] In a conference in London on December 10, Hoover yielded to Allied opposition to the Supreme War Council as the directing body of the relief program and agreed to a council of the four principal Allied and Associated Governments. The Allies conceded that the administration might be under an American Director-General.[8]

Details of the proposed council were worked out while the United States Food Administration went ahead with relief operations on its own. Hoover proceeded to build an extensive organiza-

[5] Hoover, *The Ordeal of Woodrow Wilson*, pp. 93-95.

[6] House to Wilson, November 27, 1918, *Foreign Relations, 1919, The Paris Peace Conference* (13 Vols., Washington: United States Government Printing Office, 1942-1947), Vol. 2, p. 639; Hoover, *The Ordeal of Woodrow Wilson*, pp. 95-96.

[7] House to Balfour, December 1, 1918, *Foreign Relations, 1919, The Paris Peace Conference*, Vol. 2, pp. 647-648; Hoover, *The Ordeal of Woodrow Wilson*, pp. 96-99.

[8] Memorandum of Conference in London, December 10, 1918, *Foreign Relations, 1919, The Paris Peace Conference*, Vol. 2, pp. 649-651.

tion covering thirty-two countries, recruiting over 4,000 personnel from the American armed forces in Europe.[9] The United States formally accepted the Allied plan of a relief council composed of American, British, French, and Italian representatives and President Wilson promptly appointed Hoover and Norman Davis to the policy-making council, designated the Inter-Allied Supreme Council for Supply and Relief. On January 4, Wilson selected Hoover as Director-General.[10] The British Government designated Lord Reading, British Ambassador to Washington, and Sir John Beale, Chairman of the Wheat Executive in London, as its members of the Relief Council, which convened in Paris for the first time on January 11.[11] The Supreme Council for Supply and Relief, although based on a compromise of American and Allied views, was, with its American Director-General, much closer to the American concept of a loosely coordinated relief organization under American leadership than to the British concept of an organic international agency.

The independent Relief Council was short-lived. On February 8, the Council of Ten adopted a resolution introduced by President Wilson for the creation of a Supreme Economic Council, to absorb or supersede existing organs, for purposes of dealing during the Armistice period with such immediate problems as finance, food, blockade control, shipping, and raw materials.[12] Although it became a genuine coordinating agency, the Supreme Economic Council did not exercise the powers over materials and distribution which the wartime agencies had enjoyed. Existing agencies were incorporated, the Supply and Relief Council becoming the Food and Relief Section of the Supreme Economic Council. The bulk of the work of the new agency fell to Hoover's Food Section, which concentrated on supplying food and reconstruction relief to eastern Europe. The burden fell mainly to the United States, but Great Britain also made major contributions of goods and services.[13]

[9] Hoover, *The Ordeal of Woodrow Wilson*, pp. 90, 99, 101.

[10] *ibid.*, p. 101; Ray Stannard Baker, *Woodrow Wilson and World Settlement* (3 Vols., Garden City, New York: Doubleday, Page and Company, 1922), Vol. 2, p. 322.

[11] Auchincloss to the Acting Secretary of State, January 12, 1919, *Foreign Relations, 1919, The Paris Peace Conference*, Vol. 2, p. 718.

[12] Council of Ten, February 8, 1919, 3 p.m., *ibid.*, Vol. 3, pp. 934-935.

[13] H.W.V. Temperley, ed., *A History of the Peace Conference of Paris* (6 Vols.,

A major conflict arose among the Allied and Associated Powers over the question of relaxing the blockade and supplying food to Germany. On this issue, Great Britain and the United States consistently favored a liberal policy of providing urgently needed supplies to Germany. On January 13, the Council of Ten accepted a recommendation by the Relief Council that, on condition of the German merchant fleet's being placed at the disposal of the Associated Governments under the next renewal of the Armistice, they would "permit Germany to import a prescribed quantity of foodstuffs, so limited as not to interfere in any way with the priority of supply which must be assured to Allied, liberated, and neutral countries." It was further prescribed as a "condition precedent to any supply," that "satisfactory arrangements" be made by Germany for payment.[14]

Because the relief grants authorized by the American Congress and the British Parliament excluded Germany, supplies could be purchased by Germany only through the use of liquid assets, which the French demanded as immediate reparations payments. The Germans, moreover, refused to deliver their merchant fleet until a definite program of food supplies was arranged. On March 6, the Armistice Commission at Spa reported the breakdown of negotiations for the delivery of the German merchant fleet. The result was the maintenance of the blockade against Germany, which Hoover considered a "most insensate, wicked action." The British members of the Supreme Economic Council generally shared Hoover's view and pressed for the lifting of the blockade.[15]

Hoover and Lord Robert Cecil agreed early in March on a plan for stipulated quantities of food to be supplied to Germany upon the surrender of the German merchant ships. Lloyd George summoned Hoover on March 7 and General Plumer, the commander of the British Army of Occupation, described shocking conditions of starvation in Germany. Lloyd George asked Hoover why no food was being sent. Hoover became angry and recited to Lloyd George instances of British obstruction. Lloyd George, according

London: Henry Frowde and Hodder and Stoughton, 1920-1924), Vol. 1, pp. 296-300; Baker, *Wilson and World Settlement*, Vol. 2, pp. 341-342.

[14] Council of Ten, January 13, 1919, 2:30 p.m., *Foreign Relations, 1919, The Paris Peace Conference*, Vol. 3, pp. 521-523.

[15] Hoover, *The Ordeal of Woodrow Wilson*, pp. 157-163; Baker, *Wilson and World Settlement*, Vol. 2, p. 347.

to Hoover's account, was impressed and asked Hoover to repeat his statement before the Council of Ten. Because he thought himself regarded as a "fanatic" on the matter of the blockade, Hoover prevailed upon Cecil, who was the chief British member of the Supreme Economic Council, to make a formal statement to the Council of Ten.[16]

Lloyd George was greatly aroused when the issue was taken up in the Council of Ten on March 8. Cecil reported the breakdown of the negotiations at Spa, and, on behalf of the Supreme Economic Council, recommended that Germany be informed that as soon as she handed over her merchant fleet, which she was bound to do by the Armistice renewal of January 16, the Allies would undertake to supply Germany with food. Hoover urged that the German demand be met for a guarantee of food supplies until the next harvest. Lloyd George declared himself "rather staggered" by an assertion of Marshal Foch that the Allies ought not to part with so great a weapon for applying pressure to Germany and urged "with all his might" that steps be taken to revictualize Germany. The Prime Minister declared that the Allies were bound by honor and by the Armistice to provision Germany and that starvation in Germany raised the threat of revolution and Bolshevism. Clemenceau maintained that the Armistice contained no promise of provisions and that the Germans were using the threat of Bolshevism as a bogey with which to blackmail the Allies. Lloyd George then read a telegram which he had received from General Plumer regarding starvation in Germany and proposed that an ultimatum be delivered to Germany demanding immediate surrender of the merchant ships with a promise that the Allies would provide food and supplies. It was agreed that Admiral Wemyss would deliver such an ultimatum. Klotz raised objections to Germany's paying for provisions in gold. Lloyd George rebuked Klotz rather sharply and Colonel House expressed his agreement with Lloyd George.[17]

[16] Hoover, *The Ordeal of Woodrow Wilson*, pp. 164-165.

[17] Council of Ten, March 8, 1919, 3 p.m., *Foreign Relations, 1919, The Paris Peace Conference*, Vol. 4, pp. 274-292; Baker, *Wilson and World Settlement*, Vol. 2, pp. 347-349; Hoover, *The Ordeal of Woodrow Wilson*, pp. 166-170; David Lloyd George, *The Truth about the Peace Treaties* (2 Vols., London: Victor Gollancz, Ltd., 1938), Vol. 1, pp. 293-306.

The Allied food representatives, with Admiral Wemyss presiding, met with the Germans at Brussels on March 13-14 and reached agreement on a stipulated monthly flow of supplies to Germany, German payment in acceptable foreign securities, and the surrender of the German merchant fleet. No credits were allowed to Germany and, in practice, the Finance Section of the Supreme Economic Council found gold to be the only acceptable means of payment.[18]

Within ten days, Hoover's organization, with British and neutral assistance, moved 200,000 tons of food into Germany, but the American and British members of the Supreme Economic Council continued to press for further relaxation of the blockade. Over French opposition, the American, British, and Italian representatives on the Supreme Economic Council agreed on April 23 to recommend the termination of almost all restrictions on trade with the neutrals and the authorization of each of the Allied states to permit their nationals to trade with Germany.[19] Cecil appealed directly to President Wilson for the immediate suspension of the blockade.[20] On May 5, however, Cecil was obliged to report to the Supreme Economic Council that the Council of Four preferred to take no further action for the present on the suspension of the blockade.[21] On May 14, Hoover lodged a strong protest with the President against proposals for the reinforcement of the blockade in the event of a German refusal to sign the treaty.[22]

Zealous though he was in the performance of his duties, Hoover looked to an early termination of the relief program and its machinery of operation. In a memorandum on general food policy, dated May 31, 1919, he averred that the continuation of assistance beyond the 1919 harvest would undermine the initiative and self-reliance of the liberated and enemy states. Thereafter, Hoover urged, these states should rely on themselves for pur-

[18] Temperley, ed., *A History of the Peace Conference of Paris*, Vol. 1, pp. 313-317; Hoover, *The Ordeal of Woodrow Wilson*, pp. 170-171.
[19] Supreme Economic Council, April 23, 1919, 10 a.m., *Foreign Relations, 1919, The Paris Peace Conference*, Vol. 10, pp. 213-215.
[20] Cecil to Wilson, April 27, 1919, Woodrow Wilson Papers, Library of Congress, Washington, D.C., Series 8-A.
[21] Supreme Economic Council, May 5, 1919, 10 a.m., *Foreign Relations, 1919, The Paris Peace Conference*, Vol. 10, pp. 229-230.
[22] Hoover to Wilson, May 14, 1919, Hoover, *The Ordeal of Woodrow Wilson*, pp. 230-231.

chases, transport, and administration, with Allied assistance confined to financial support.[23]

British and American approaches to the problems of relief and the blockade, both matters of immediate economic necessity, were thus essentially parallel. Both nations pressed for a relatively liberal treatment of the enemy and both recoiled from proposals for the exploitation of Germany's urgent economic needs as a means of applying political pressure. The American economic policy, however, was designed merely to cope with an emergency situation, and when the British came up with proposals for long-range economic cooperation, American statesmen rejected these out of hand in favor of a return to international economic individualism.

II. *American Rejection of British Proposals for Measures of Postwar Economic Cooperation*

The Peace Conference accomplished almost nothing in the way of contractual provision for the removal or reduction of economic barriers and the establishment of equality of trade conditions, as called for in President Wilson's Point 3. An Economic Commission was established to consider measures for the removal of trade barriers and commercial discrimination. The British and American representatives, who wished only to abolish discriminatory tariffs, resisted French and Italian proposals for a general ban on import and export duties on raw materials except against Germany. In the end, the whole issue of general commercial agreements was left to the League of Nations.[24]

From the outset of the Peace Conference, the British took a vigorous lead in the advocacy of concerted international measures for the promotion of general economic recovery and financial stabilization, while American statesmen tended to suspect all such proposals as devices for the entanglement of the United

[23] Memorandum by Hoover, May 31, 1919, Supreme Economic Council, *Foreign Relations, 1919, The Paris Peace Conference*, Vol. 10, pp. 342-343.

[24] See Baker, *Wilson and World Settlement*, Vol. 2, pp. 411-428; Temperley, ed., *A History of the Peace Conference of Paris*, Vol. 5, pp. 53-71; Bernard M. Baruch, *The Drafting of the Reparation and Economic Sections of the Treaty* (New York and London: Harper & Brothers, Publishers, 1920), pp. 80-89; Allyn Abbott Young, "The Economic Settlement," *What Really Happened at Paris* (House and Seymour, eds.), pp. 291-318.

States in the economic problems of Europe. Norman Davis warned President Wilson of what seemed to him to be a concerted movement to interlock American resources with the tangled financial problems of Europe under the "cloak" of proposals for stabilizing international exchange, pooling raw materials, and guaranteeing German reparations payments. The United States should entertain only specific requests for assistance, Davis averred, because participation in any general arrangements would amount to providing Europe with a "blank check."[25] Wilson replied that he was well aware of this effort on the part of the Allies and on guard against it. He urged Davis to alert Bernard Baruch and the American Treasury officials to the Allied schemes.[26]

The British representatives on the Supreme Economic Council submitted a proposal on April 5 for a comprehensive Allied policy, beyond relief, for the stabilization of currencies, transport, capital and raw materials, plants and machinery. The chief problem, said the British, was to provide working capital, a task which was too great for private enterprise to undertake alone.[27] Colonel House proposed the creation of a special commission of inquiry and turned the matter over to Bernard Baruch, who thereupon wrote a letter to Lord Robert Cecil condemning the principle of government interference in economic matters. "The salvation of the world," wrote Baruch, "must rest upon the initiative of individuals."[28] In his reply, Cecil vigorously challenged the American point of view: "You think that without question the economic situation can be solved by individual initiative. It may be so, though my own opinion is to the contrary. . . . It may be that the result of the inquiry will show that without American assistance on a large scale, nothing can be done, and it may also be that America will decline to give that assistance. If she intends to take that attitude, forgive me for

[25] Davis to Wilson, February 2, 1919, Wilson Papers, Series 8-A.
[26] Wilson to Davis, February 7, 1919, Wilson Papers, Series 8-A.
[27] Note submitted to the Supreme Economic Council by the British representatives, April 5, 1919, *Foreign Relations, 1919, The Paris Peace Conference,* Vol. 10, pp. 110-113.
[28] Baruch to Cecil, April 12, 1919, Baker, *Wilson and World Settlement,* Vol. 3, pp. 332-334.

saying that she ought to take it quite openly, and before the face of the world."[29]

Despite the negative attitude of the United States, the British Government continued to consider schemes for concerted economic measures. John Maynard Keynes, who in March had urged his Government to press the United States for a total cancellation of all inter-Allied debts,[30] devised a cooperative financial plan in April, which amounted to a sort of Marshall Plan, albeit on a smaller scale. The plan called for a German bond issue of $5 billion and lesser bond issues by the other enemy states and liberated states, all to be guaranteed by Allied and neutral powers. The German bonds would be received by the Allied and Associated Powers on account of reparations, and—the core of the plan—the bonds would be "accepted at their par value plus accrued interest in payment of all indebtedness between any of the Allied and Associated Governments."[31] The plan would have disposed of international debts as a hindrance to trade but its essence was that the United States would be left bearing the ultimate burden of Germany's direct indebtedness.

Lloyd George forwarded the Keynes plan to President Wilson on April 23 with an attached letter which recommended the scheme as a bold and urgent solution for the desperate financial conditions of Europe. While the United Kingdom was in no such straits as the continental nations, Lloyd George pointed out, its chief financial problem being the payment of its debt to the United States, neither was it in a position to assist the European states on anything approaching the scale required. The financial restoration of Europe, Lloyd George affirmed, was far too great a problem for private enterprise alone, requiring a program of worldwide cooperation. The Keynes plan, he said, would meet this need, ameliorating the problems of international indebted-

[29] Cecil to Baruch, April 14, 1919, Baker, *Wilson and World Settlement*, Vol. 3, pp. 334-335.

[30] Keynes, Secret Memorandum, March 1919, "The Treatment of Inter-Ally Debt Arising out of the War." Sir William Wiseman Papers, Sterling Library, Yale University.

[31] John Maynard Keynes, "Scheme for the Rehabilitation of European Credit and for Financing Relief and Reconstruction," April 1919, Baker, *Wilson and World Settlement*, Vol. 3, pp. 341-343; Philip Mason Burnett, *Reparation at the Paris Peace Conference from the Standpoint of the American Delegation* (2 Vols., New York: Columbia University Press, 1940), Vol. 1, pp. 1011-1013.

ness by permitting the enemy bonds to be converted into purchasing power for reconstruction, and, incidentally, greatly promoting the foreign trade of both Great Britain and the United States.[32]

President Wilson referred the Keynes scheme to his Committee of Economic Advisers, who rejected it, among other reasons because a German bond issue of $5 billion had already been authorized for purposes of immediate reparations payments.[33] President Wilson thereupon replied to Lloyd George that the American financial advisers found Keynes's proposal unsound, that Congress would almost certainly deny him authority to place an American guarantee upon bonds of European origin, and that, in any case, the United States Treasury adhered to the view that credits should be secured through private channels. The President contended that the reparations clauses took away Germany's working capital and that the United States was now being asked to make good this deficiency. "How," asked Wilson, "can anyone expect America to turn over to Germany in any considerable measure new working capital to take the place of that which the European nations have determined to take from her?"[34]

Wilson's rejection of the Keynes plan ultimately evoked strong British reactions. Keynes wrote to Philip Kerr that it was "surely impossible for the Americans to disclaim responsibility for the peace treaty to which, wisely or not, they have put their name equally with the other governments. . . ."[35] In a strongly worded letter, Lloyd George reminded the President that he had never objected to the initial German bond issue of $5 billion on which he now based his rejection of the Keynes scheme. Aware as he was of the difficulties faced by Germany, the Prime Minister averred, he was far more concerned with the intolerable burdens imposed upon the Allies by Germany. Citing the staggering costs of the war to Great Britain, her huge foreign debt, and the un-

[32] Lloyd George to Wilson, April 23, 1919, Baker, *Wilson and World Settlement*, Vol. 3, pp. 336-341; Burnett, *Reparation at the Paris Peace Conference*, Vol. 1, pp. 1014-1019.

[33] Hoover, *The Ordeal of Woodrow Wilson*, p. 148. See Chapter 9, Section VIII.

[34] Wilson to Lloyd George, May 5, 1919, Baker, *Wilson and World Settlement*, Vol. 3, pp. 344-346; Burnett, *Reparation at the Paris Peace Conference*, Vol. 1, pp. 1127-1129.

[35] R. F. Harrod, *The Life of John Maynard Keynes* (London: Macmillan and Company Ltd., 1951), p. 247.

likelihood that she would ever recover the vast sums owned to her by the continental Allies, Lloyd George contended that Britain was quite unable to provide the assistance needed. "The responsibility for the reconstruction of the world," he wrote, "therefore depends in an exceptional measure upon the United States. . . ." Britain would help if she could, Lloyd George concluded. "As she cannot, the responsibility must rest principally on the shoulders of the United States."[36]

Despite the President's rejection of the Keynes proposal, the British continued to press for some sort of financial scheme. The question came up on May 9 at a joint conference of the heads of governments and their chief delegates to the Supreme Economic Council. Cecil argued that the mere provision of food was quite useless, that a plan should be devised to make raw materials available and provide credit for the continental states. At President Wilson's suggestion, a resolution was adopted establishing a committee of economic advisers to submit recommendations on measures to assist nations in need of food, raw materials, and credit.[37] Wilson asked Davis and Lamont to suggest measures acceptable to the United States, and on May 15, they recommended that while credits should be extended as far as possible through the normal channels of private enterprise, the United States Government might extend some supplementary credits for reconstruction purposes.[38] The report of the committee of experts appointed on May 9 was never really considered. The Council of Four set it aside on June 6 in the face of urgent problems requiring settlement for the completion of the treaty.[39]

There was thus no serious consideration by the Peace Conference of the broader problems of economic reconstruction. The Allies had overridden the United States in denying a fixed sum of reparations and in draining Germany's liquid capital. The United States now refused to consider a program that would require the United States Government to provide working capital. Even with a sound and moderate reparations prospect, it may be

[36] Lloyd George to Wilson, June 26, 1919, Wilson Papers, Series 8-A.
[37] Council of Four, May 9, 1919, 10:30 a.m., *Foreign Relations, 1919, The Paris Peace Conference*, Vol. 5, pp. 521-524; Baker, *Wilson and World Settlement*, Vol. 2, pp. 359-360.
[38] *ibid.*, Vol. 3, pp. 352-362.
[39] Council of Four, June 6, 1919, 4 p.m., *Foreign Relations, 1919, The Paris Peace Conference*, Vol. 6, p. 223.

doubted whether private initiative could have sufficed at the out-set, although it might have contributed much, granted govern-mental interest and some minimum guarantees. As it was, neither one nor the other eventuated in the first critical years of peace.

The question of continued inter-Allied economic cooperation evoked an Anglo-American conflict of views in the Supreme Eco-nomic Council. Cecil submitted a British memorandum on June 10 calling for the continued operation of the Supreme Economic Council during the economic transition period after the signing of the peace. The American delegates contended that they were purely "war officials" and that the Council had been constituted solely to deal with transitory measures during the Armistice.[40] On June 13, the American economic advisers urged Wilson to reject a proposal by Lloyd George for inter-Allied measures to control food purchases in order to keep prices down.[41] The British delegates on the Supreme Economic Council submitted another memorandum on June 20 calling for the continuation of the Council after the ratification of the treaty under the direction of the Council of the League of Nations. The French members submitted a memorandum in similar vein.[42] In a note prepared by Herbert Hoover, the American representatives on June 27 de-clared themselves in "entire disagreement" with many of the propositions of the British memorandum of June 20. So far as the United States was concerned, they said, all existing economic arrangements would end with the signing of the peace, and they themselves would thereafter cease to participate in all existing agencies "except in the sheer sense of liquidation at the earliest possible moment."[43]

Cecil presented to the Council of Four on June 28 the British case for the establishment of permanent machinery of economic cooperation under the League, proposing also that the Supreme Economic Council be authorized to establish some temporary means of economic consultation until the permanent instruments were formed. With the reluctant acquiescence of President Wilson,

[40] Supreme Economic Council, June 10, 1919, 3:30 p.m., *ibid.*, Vol. 10, pp. 346, 355-356.
[41] Hoover, *The Ordeal of Woodrow Wilson*, p. 149.
[42] *Foreign Relations, 1919, The Paris Peace Conference*, Vol. 10, pp. 414-424.
[43] *ibid.*, pp. 434-435.

the Council of Four adopted a resolution calling for consultation "in some form" until the issue could be dealt with by the Council of the League. The Supreme Economic Council was to consider the means of such consultation.[44]

In accordance with the resolution of the Council of Four, the Supreme Economic Council on June 30 appointed a Committee on Policy to prepare recommendations for continued economic consultation.[45] The Committee on Policy submitted its recommendations on July 10, calling for the creation of an International Economic Council to meet periodically in one or another of the Allied capitals.[46]

The United States, probably because of the mounting difficulties being encountered by the treaty at home, rapidly abandoned the half-hearted agreement of June 28 to engage in continued economic consultations. Henry White told the Supreme Council on July 28 that the United States was "quite unwilling to sanction the continuance of the Supreme Economic Council," while Balfour pressed for an expansion of its functions.[47] The American representatives attended the meeting of the Supreme Economic Council for the last time on August 2. At this meeting, the British delegates announced the agreement of their Government to the recommendations of the Committee on Policy and proposed that the first meeting of the International Economic Council be held in Washington. It was agreed that a Permanent Committee under the new Council would be established in London.[48] Frank Polk, the head of the remaining American delegation in Paris, advised Secretary Lansing on September 13 that he and Hoover were opposed to American participation in the new International Economic Council. Polk also recommended that the United States officially terminate its representation on the Supreme Economic Council. The Acting Secretary of State re-

---

[44] Council of Four, June 28, 1919, 11 a.m., *ibid.*, Vol. 6, pp. 741-743.

[45] Supreme Economic Council, June 30, 1919, 10 a.m., *ibid.*, Vol. 10, p. 431.

[46] Supreme Economic Council, July 10, 1919, 4:30 p.m., *ibid.*, pp. 450-451.

[47] Council of Heads of Delegations, July 28, 1919, 10:30 a.m., *ibid.*, Vol. 7, pp. 343-344; E. L. Woodward and Rohan Butler, eds., *Documents on British Foreign Policy, 1919-1939*, First Series (8 Vols., London: His Majesty's Stationery Office, 1947-1958), Vol. 1, pp. 217-218.

[48] Supreme Economic Council, August 2, 1919, 10:30 a.m., *Foreign Relations, 1919, The Paris Peace Conference*, Vol. 10, p. 499.

plied favorably to Polk's proposal.[49] The names of the members of the Permanent Committee of the new International Economic Council were announced in the Supreme Economic Council on September 20. It was noted that no American appointee had been designated.[50]

The defection of the United States resulted in Great Britain herself drawing back from her hitherto ardent advocacy of measures for international economic cooperation. When, on November 23, the French representatives raised the question of the future of the Supreme Economic Council, the British delegates said that Great Britain preferred not to be committed to any definite plans for the future of the Council. "The British Government," they declared, "would have to take into careful consideration current political events in the United States and the position of Great Britain in relation to these events."[51]

As the leading economic and financial powers, the United States and Great Britain in 1919 could have formulated and effected an international program for economic recovery. The British took a vigorous lead in advocating such a program, but of necessity the United States, with its preponderant economic power, would have had to supply most of the economic assistance needed by the war-shattered nations of Europe. The United States provided supplies on a large scale to alleviate immediate hardships in Europe, and Britain contributed substantially to this cause also. Further, these two powers pressed for the relaxation of the blockade against the enemy states. But in the area of a long-range international program for economic and financial recovery the United States flatly rejected British proposals. Keynes has suggested that a positive Anglo-American economic program might have consisted of the cancellation of inter-Allied debts, the limitation of German reparations payments to $10 billion, British renunciation of her share in favor of the new states, and a

[49] Polk to Lansing, September 13, 1919, Phillips to Polk, September 16, 1919, *ibid.*, Vol. 1, pp. 8-9.
[50] Supreme Economic Council, September 20, 1919, 10 a.m., *ibid.*, Vol. 10, pp. 559-560. See also Temperley, ed., *A History of the Peace Conference of Paris*, Vol. 1, pp. 326-333.
[51] Supreme Economic Council, November 23, 1919, 11 a.m., *Foreign Relations, 1919, The Paris Peace Conference*, Vol. 10, p. 624.

guarantee by all parties to the treaty of a portion of the German obligations in order to provide a basis of credit. Such a program, Keynes wrote, would have involved an appeal to American generosity, which he thought both fair and practicable.[52]

The United States refused even to consider such a program. For this refusal, four reasons are suggested: first, President Wilson conceived of a new world order primarily in political terms and was only incidentally concerned with its economic aspects; secondly, the isolationist tradition of America and its increasing grip on congressional and public opinion during the Peace Conference made any participation in permanent international economic arrangements politically unthinkable for the American statesmen at Paris; thirdly, the American statesmen and economic advisers were wedded in their own thinking to traditional concepts of unregulated *laissez faire* economy; and finally, President Wilson and his advisers were convinced that the proposals for long-range international economic and financial recovery were in great measure devised by Great Britain and the continental Allies in order to extricate themselves, at the expense of the United States, from the consequences of an unreasonable reparations settlement which they had forced on the enemy over staunch American resistance.

III. *Subsidiary Problems: Freedom of Transit and International Cables*

The Commission on the International Regime of Ports, Waterways, and Railways consisted of fifteen members, including Henry White and David Hunter Miller for the United States, with Manley O. Hudson as alternate, and Arthur L. Sifton and Sir Hubert Llewellyn Smith for Great Britain. The British members of the Commission were especially interested in arranging a general convention on freedom of transit among the parties to the treaty. The French, on the other hand, wished only to impose unreciprocal rights of free transit on German rivers and canals. The American members rejected both the French and British proposals, preferring to state general principles while leaving specific free transit arrangements for case by case negotiation.

[52] John Maynard Keynes, *The Economic Consequences of the Peace* (New York: Harcourt, Brace and Howe, 1920), pp. 147-148.

White, Miller, and Hudson firmly resisted the British proposal for a general convention and especially resisted its application to North American waterways.[53]

The British presented their proposed general convention on freedom of transit to the first subcommittee of the Commission on Ports, Waterways, and Railways in February. Miller secured an amendment which virtually exempted from the application of the proposed convention all international rivers crossing only two riparian states, thereby excluding North American rivers. Miller, White, and Hudson further rejected any application of the freedom of transit convention to interoceanic canals.[54] The American delegates quite frankly undertook to nullify piecemeal the very concept of a general convention. Miller records that he and Hudson attached amendments to the draft convention "which pretty well cut it to pieces."[55] Miller, White, and Hudson finally told Llewellyn Smith that the project for a general convention should be left for consideration by the League of Nations.[56]

The outcome of the Anglo-American differences on the proposed freedom of transit convention was the adoption of a plan applying the principle of free transit unreciprocally to international rivers traversing the territory of the enemy states and calling for a conference at an unspecified future date on the general principles of freedom of transit.[57] The report of the Commission on Ports, Waterways, and Railways was adopted, with minor alterations, by the Council of Four on April 26. It was agreed that the Commission would continue its deliberations on a future general convention.[58]

[53] Temperley, ed., *A History of the Peace Conference of Paris*, Vol. 2, pp. 94-97; Baker, *Wilson and World Settlement*, Vol. 2, pp. 429-432; Allan Nevins, *Henry White: Thirty Years of American Diplomacy* (New York and London: Harper & Brothers, Publishers, 1930), pp. 440-441.

[54] David Hunter Miller, *My Diary at the Conference of Paris*, privately printed (21 Vols., New York: Appeal Printing Company, 1924), Vol. 1, pp. 126-127, 139-140.

[55] Miller's Diary, February 28, 1919, *ibid.*, p. 145.

[56] Miller's Diary, March 2, 1919, *ibid.*, p. 146.

[57] Report of the Commission on Ports, Waterways, and Railways, April 7, 1919, Miller, *Diary*, Vol. 2, pp. 12-42. See also Baker, *Wilson and World Settlement*, Vol. 2, pp. 433-434.

[58] Council of Four, April 26, 1919, 11 a.m., *Foreign Relations, 1919, The Paris Peace Conference*, Vol. 5, pp. 251-252.

The British then pressed for the conclusion of a general convention on freedom of transit simultaneously with the signing of the treaty of peace. White and Miller recommended to President Wilson that consideration of a general convention be deferred to a future international conference.[59] In the Council of Four on June 7, Lloyd George conveyed a request by Sir Hubert Llewellyn Smith that a general convention be designed at once and President Wilson agreed to discuss the matter with Henry White.[60] The hopes of the British were finally dashed by American opposition. On July 1, the American representatives remaining in Paris informed the Commission on Ports, Waterways, and Railways that the United States was not prepared to consider any general convention on transit or waterways and believed that the matter should be left to the consideration of the League of Nations.[61]

Only in the matter of international cables did the United States favor a cooperative plan of international control, and in this instance the British departed from their general enthusiasm for international arrangements, favoring the retention of captured German cables by the states in possession, which meant, for the most part, by Great Britain. The American communications expert, Walter S. Rogers, submitted a memorandum to President Wilson on February 12 calling for the internationalization of principal cables under the League of Nations and League-supervised provisions for nondiscrimination in the use of nationally owned overseas communications facilities.[62]

Wilson and Lansing questioned the legality of Allied expropriation of the German cables. In the Council of Ten on March 24, Balfour argued that the Allies had the same right to appropriate cables as ships captured at sea, while Lansing, who favored restoration of the captured cables to Germany, contended that the

[59] White and Miller to Wilson, May 8, 1919, Miller, *Diary*, Vol. 9, pp. 323-324. See also Temperley, ed., *A History of the Peace Conference of Paris*, Vol. 2, pp. 104-105.
[60] Council of Four, June 7, 1919, 11 a.m., *Foreign Relations, 1919, The Paris Peace Conference*, Vol. 6, pp. 235-236.
[61] Baker, *Wilson and World Settlement*, Vol. 2, p. 436; Temperley, ed., *A History of the Peace Conference of Paris*, Vol. 2, p. 105.
[62] Baker, *Wilson and World Settlement*, Vol. 3, pp. 427-442.

seizure of cables was not legally analogous to the seizure of ships, and President Wilson agreed, pointing out that the United States had always opposed the capture of private property at sea. The Council agreed that Germany might at her own expense restore cables cut by the Allies.[63]

In subsequent discussions, President Wilson turned away from Lansing's policy of restoration of the German cables and advocated international control. The President especially expressed anxiety at the prospect of Japanese control of the island of Yap, where all major Pacific cables converged, including those between the United States and the Philippines. Wilson asked that the island of Yap be internationalized.[64] The President proposed in the Council of Four on May 1 that the enemy cables be turned over to the Allied and Associated Powers as trustees, to manage them under the terms of an international convention.[65] Wilson submitted a resolution to this effect on the next day, but Lloyd George objected that the kind of international control envisioned by the President would make it impossible to cut enemy cables in time of war. Under pressure from Lloyd George, the President abandoned his proposal for joint operation by the Allies and agreed that all German cables should be surrendered and left to the operation of those in possession, but that an international congress should convene to make recommendations for the establishment of a new system on a "fair and equitable basis."[66]

The British thus won their essential point for national retention of captured enemy cables. The disposition of the German cables was the one issue, however minor, on which the United States favored a genuinely international solution, and it is ironic that the American approach was thwarted by the British, who on so many more important matters looked to international solu-

[63] Council of Ten, March 24, 1919, 4 p.m., *Foreign Relations, 1919, The Paris Peace Conference*, Vol. 4, pp. 460-470.

[64] Council of Four, April 15, 1919, 11 a.m., Paul Mantoux, *Les Délibérations du Conseil des Quatre* (2 Vols., Paris: Éditions du Centre National de la Recherche Scientifique, 1955), Vol. 1, p. 249; Council of Four, April 18, 1919, 11 a.m., *ibid.*, pp. 275-276.

[65] Council of Four, May 1, 1919, 4 p.m., *Foreign Relations, 1919, The Paris Peace Conference*, Vol. 4, pp. 485-486.

[66] Council of Four, May 2, 1919, 5 p.m., *ibid.*, pp. 493-500. See also Baker, *Wilson and World Settlement*, Vol. 2, pp. 481-483.

tions. For the much greater part, however, it was the British who put forth the most positive proposals at the Peace Conference for international instruments of cooperation in matters of economics, finance, and transport, and it was the opposition of the United States which was the chief factor in thwarting these proposals.

CHAPTER 11

THE REVISION OF THE COVENANT AND ANGLO-AMERICAN NAVAL RIVALRY: THE BIRTH OF THE INTERNATIONAL LABOR ORGANIZATION: THE TRIAL OF THE KAISER

O N no issue at the Peace Conference was there as profound a unity of purpose between Great Britain and the United States as in the drafting of the Covenant of the League of Nations. In March and April of 1919, however, this harmony was temporarily but severely jarred by the introduction of an extraneous issue. President Wilson returned to Paris in March compelled by domestic political pressures to secure certain amendments to the Covenant, the foremost of which was a specific reservation of the Monroe Doctrine. Although Great Britain had no objection to this, and in fact had a historic stake in the principle of the Monroe Doctrine, Lloyd George undertook to exploit the President's domestic embarrassment for purposes of securing an Anglo-American agreement on naval armaments. The injection of the delicate and potentially explosive naval issue set off a brief but acrimonious controversy between the English-speaking powers. Once an accommodation had been reached on the naval issue, Great Britain dropped her artificial opposition to the Monroe Doctrine and the Covenant was completed and adopted by the Peace Conference in an atmosphere of Anglo-American unity as close as that which had prevailed in February.

Anglo-American leadership also launched in the spring of 1919 a fruitful experiment in functional international organization with the creation of the International Labor Organization. Such differences as occurred between Britain and the United States in the drafting of its Charter issued from certain incompatibilities between British concepts of a genuinely authoritative labor organization and the constitutional structure of the United States, but more fundamentally, from the socialist orientation of the British labor movement as against the nineteenth century liberal traditions of organized labor in America.

I. *President Wilson's Proposed Amendments to the Covenant and British Reactions*

President Wilson returned to Paris in mid-March beset by pressures from America for certain alterations in the Covenant. He was thus compelled at the most critical juncture of the Peace Conference to ask for concessions which his colleagues well knew were essential to his political position at home and which, therefore, they were not disposed to grant without a diplomatic price. The President was convinced, however, and not without reason, that congressional opposition to the Covenant did not accurately reflect American public opinion. Tumulty assured him on March 16 that despite the intensification of Republican opposition there was a strong drift in favor of the League on the part of public opinion. "You can afford to go to any length," Tumulty cabled, in insisting upon the incorporation of the Covenant into the treaty. "There is no doubt of your success here and abroad."[1] A poll of all American daily newspapers published on April 5, 1919, by the *Literary Digest* revealed that newspapers representing a circulation of almost 10 million were in favor of the League of Nations and papers representing almost 7 million additional readers were conditionally in favor of the League, while those in opposition represented a circulation of just over 4 million.[2] In a speech at the Metropolitan Opera House on the eve of his return to France, President Wilson asserted his conviction that the overwhelming majority of the American people were in favor of the League. He threw down the gauntlet to the opposition, declaring that "when the treaty comes back, gentlemen on this side will find the Covenant not only in it, but so many threads of the treaty tied to the Covenant that you cannot dissect the Covenant from the treaty without destroying the whole vital structure." "I have heard nothing," said the President, "except, 'Will it not be dangerous for us to help the world?' It would be fatal for us not to help it."[3]

[1] Tumulty to Wilson, March 16, 1919, Woodrow Wilson Papers, Library of Congress, Washington, D.C., Series 8-A.

[2] Thomas A. Bailey, *Woodrow Wilson and the Lost Peace* (New York: The Macmillan Company, 1944), pp. 203-204.

[3] Speech at Metropolitan Opera House, New York, March 4, 1919, Ray Stannard Baker and William E. Dodd, eds., *The Public Papers of Woodrow Wilson*

In fact, Wilson was a good deal more deferential to the opposition than he appeared to be. Early in March he rejected a proposal by House, which was supported by Cecil and Balfour, for converting the League Commission at once into a kind of provisional executive council of the permanent organization, on the ground that such a step would unduly antagonize the anti-League forces at home.[4] Moreover, the President accepted the changes proposed by the friends of the Covenant in America, not only in substance, but generally in the very language in which they were proposed. Wilson agreed to press for three amendments urged by Senator Hitchcock, the Democratic leader in the Senate, and by former President Taft: a stipulation in the Covenant that it would in no way infringe upon the Monroe Doctrine, a reservation of domestic questions, and a provision for withdrawal from the League of Nations. Taft cabled Wilson on March 18 that the "Monroe Doctrine reservation alone would probably carry the treaty, but others would make it certain."[5]

The British at first were inclined to assist President Wilson in securing his proposed amendments to the Covenant.[6] The British Government kept a close watch, through the agency of Sir William Wiseman, on political developments in the United States in the spring of 1919. Wiseman counseled a policy of accommodation to the President's domestic pressures while carefully avoiding any appearance of British policy seeming to be influenced by American internal politics.[7] Wiseman told David Hunter Miller on March 11 that Lord Eustace Percy had prepared a confidential paper advising Cecil to make a statement of proposed amend-

---

(6 Vols., New York and London: Harper & Brothers, Publishers, 1925-1927), *War and Peace*, Vol. 1, pp. 444-451.

[4] House to Wilson, February 28, 1919, Wilson to House, March 3, 1919, Wilson Papers, Series 8-A.

[5] David Hunter Miller, *The Drafting of the Covenant* (2 Vols., New York, London: G. P. Putnam's Sons, 1928), Vol. 1, pp. 276-277; Ray Stannard Baker, *Woodrow Wilson and World Settlement* (3 Vols., Garden City, New York: Doubleday, Page and Company, 1922), Vol. 1, pp. 324-331.

[6] A good brief discussion of the revision of the Covenant in March-April, 1919, is contained in Dana Frank Fleming, *The United States and the League of Nations, 1918-1920* (New York and London: G. P. Putnam's Sons, 1932), pp. 172-204.

[7] Wiseman to Cecil, March 11, 1919, Sir William Wiseman Papers, Sterling Library, Yale University. The Wiseman Papers contain numerous assessments of the domestic political temper in the United States during this period.

ments to the Covenant designed specifically to appease the Republicans in the United States.[8]

At a dinner meeting with Cecil, House, and Miller on March 18, Wilson outlined the American objections to the Covenant of February 14 and his proposed amendments, and Cecil presented a number of amendments favored by the British Government. Cecil agreed to a provision allowing a nation to withdraw from the League of Nations after giving two years' notice and to a specific reservation of domestic questions. The Monroe Doctrine amendment was temporarily set aside, largely for fear that its inclusion would compel the acceptance of a parallel Asian doctrine for Japan.[9] In his account of the meeting of March 18, Cecil writes that he saw little objection to the amendments proposed by Wilson and that Britain was "quite ready to go almost any distance to secure the two-thirds majority in the Senate needed for ratification." As each amendment was considered, according to Cecil, if he and House recommended it as improving the Covenant, Wilson readily accepted it, but if they suggested it as a concession to Senate feelings, the President was "up in arms."[10] The changes agreed to on March 18 by Wilson and Cecil were incorporated into a new text of the Covenant.[11]

A wide variety of proposed alterations were discussed in the League of Nations Commission in the latter part of March, but the negotiations proceeded in an atmosphere quite different from that of the February meetings. The awkward position in which the President had been placed by the United States Senate was fully appreciated by the British and French, and it was at this time, apparently, that Lloyd George determined to extract an agreement on naval armaments from the United States before he would accept an amendment on the Monroe Doctrine. If any one man was responsible for the ultimate success of these negotiations, it was Lord Robert Cecil.

[8] David Hunter Miller, *My Diary at the Conference of Paris*, privately printed (21 Vols., New York: Appeal Printing Company, 1924), Vol. 1, pp. 162-163.
[9] Miller, *The Drafting of the Covenant*, Vol. 1, pp. 283-296; Charles Seymour, ed., *The Intimate Papers of Colonel House* (4 Vols., Boston and New York: Houghton Mifflin Company, 1926-1928), Vol. 4, pp. 411-412.
[10] Viscount Cecil, *A Great Experiment* (New York: Oxford University Press, 1941), pp. 82-83.
[11] Miller, *The Drafting of the Covenant*, Vol. 2, pp. 580-591.

A number of significant amendments were adopted by the League Commission with little or no controversy. On March 22, the Commission adopted two amendments proposed by Cecil, one authorizing the Executive Council to increase its membership with the approval of a majority of the Body of Delegates, the other specifically requiring unanimity of all present for decisions by both the Executive Council and the Body of Delegates. Both of these had been agreed to by President Wilson in the meeting of March 18.[12] On March 24, Wilson and Cecil overrode a demand by Léon Bourgeois that the Council and its permanent advisory commission on military affairs be empowered, in anticipation of danger, to make military preparations for the coordination of national forces.[13] Article 10 of the final Covenant, the mutual guarantee of political independence and territorial integrity, was formally adopted on March 24, President Wilson indicating that he would submit an amendment to it later (on the Monroe Doctrine). President Wilson submitted an amendment to Article 15, which dealt with Council action in regard to international disputes, excluding questions "solely within the domestic jurisdiction of member states." The amendment was accepted without dispute and, with the other amendments adopted, referred to the Drafting Commission.[14]

The adoption of Article 10 on March 24 without dissent had been preceded by a significant debate on its implications within the British Empire delegation. On March 13, Sir Robert Borden had submitted a memorandum expressing the view of Canada that Article 10 should be "struck out or materially amended" on the ground that it required the members of the League to recognize all existing territorial delimitations as permanently "just and expedient." "There may be national aspirations," Borden contended, "to which the provisions of the peace treaty will not do justice and which cannot be permanently suppressed."[15] Although Canada voiced no formal protest at the time of the adoption of

[12] League of Nations Commission, Eleventh Meeting, March 22, 1919, 3 p.m., *ibid.*, pp. 338-339, Vol. I, pp. 310-321.

[13] See Chapter 4, Section VI.

[14] League of Nations Commission, Twelfth Meeting, March 24, 1919, 8:30 p.m., Miller, *The Drafting of the Covenant*, Vol. 2, pp. 344-350, Vol. I, pp. 322-335. See also Stephen Bonsal, *Unfinished Business* (Garden City, New York: Doubleday, Doran and Company, Inc., 1944), pp. 150-153, 185-186.

[15] Miller, *Diary*, Vol. 7, pp. 220-239.

Article 10, Borden told the British Empire delegation on April 21 that he regarded it as throwing an unfair burden on countries which derived the least benefit from it and that it would be Canadian policy to seek alteration of Article 10 later.[16]

A number of important amendments, including the provision for withdrawal from the League, were adopted by the Commission on March 26. Cecil proposed and the Commission accepted an amendment to Article 18, the mandates article, indicating that a mandate could be conferred only on states "who are willing to accept it." Wilson had expressed his desire for such an amendment in his conference with Cecil on March 18. The President then submitted his proposed amendment on withdrawal from the League, which read: "After the expiration of ten years from the ratification of the Treaty of Peace, of which this Covenant forms a part, any State member of the League may, after giving one year's notice of its intention, withdraw from the League, provided all its international obligations and all its obligations under this Covenant shall have been fulfilled at the time of its withdrawal." Wilson said that he "thought that if the League were successful it would be morally impossible for a state to withdraw." Larnaude objected to the withdrawal amendment, but Cecil came to the President's assistance, asserting that "it was foolish to suppose that any treaty could be permanent." Cecil preferred, however, a period of fifteen or twenty years before a state could withdraw, or, if the period were less than twenty years, a requirement of two years' notice. Orlando suggested and Wilson agreed to the abandonment of any minimum time and a general stipulation of two years' notice before withdrawal. Wilson said that he "did not entertain the smallest fear that any state would take advantage of the proposed clause. Any state which did so would become an outlaw." The President frankly admitted that his proposal was a concession to "existing prejudices" and that he feared that the Senate would reject the League without it. The amendment, which became part of Article 1 of the final Covenant, was adopted as follows: "Any State a member of the League may, after giving two years' notice of its intention, withdraw from the League, provided all its in-

---

[16] G. P. de T. Glazebrook, *Canada at the Paris Peace Conference* (London, Toronto, New York: Oxford University Press, 1942), pp. 67-71.

ternational obligations and all its obligations under this Covenant shall have been fulfilled at the time of its withdrawal."[17]
Quite clearly, the President pressed for the withdrawal amendment with the utmost reluctance. Cecil did not like it either, but
he accepted it as a necessary concession to "existing prejudices"
and gave the President effective, if not decisive, support in securing its adoption over French opposition.

While the American amendments to the Covenant in regard
to domestic jurisdiction and withdrawal from the League were
thus secured in the League Commission with relative ease, the
most important amendment, that concerning the Monroe Doctrine, was held up by Anglo-American negotiations for a mutually
acceptable clause. Each side drew up proposed clauses which
proved unacceptable to the other. On March 26, Cecil told Miller
that he personally objected to a singling out of the Monroe Doctrine except by way of reference, but that in any case it was out
of his hands because Lloyd George had expressed vigorous opposition to the Monroe Doctrine amendment as too great a concession to the United States and as a regional arrangement
inappropriate for inclusion in the Covenant. The only thing to be
done, said Cecil, was to leave Wilson and Lloyd George to discuss
the matter directly.[18]

Lloyd George made little effort to conceal the fact that his
opposition to the Monroe Doctrine was a bargaining play to
secure from the United States an agreement on naval building.
House, Balfour, and Cecil in fact reached agreement on a draft
clause on the Monroe Doctrine for inclusion in the Covenant,
but Lloyd George rejected it, and Cecil told House on March 27
that Lloyd George now maintained that he would neither agree
to the inclusion of the Covenant in the treaty nor even sign it
until the United States had come to terms on a naval agreement.[19] Whether Lloyd George was really prepared to deliver
on these grave threats may well be questioned, but there can be
no doubt as to the great importance which he attached to the

[17] League of Nations Commission, Thirteenth Meeting, March 26, 1919, 8:30
p.m., Miller, *The Drafting of the Covenant*, Vol. 2, pp. 355-360. See also Bonsal,
Unfinished Business, p. 209.

[18] Miller, *The Drafting of the Covenant*, Vol. 1, pp. 297-298, 336-337.

[19] House Diary, March 27, 1919, Edward M. House Papers, Sterling Library,
Yale University.

question of American sea power and the threat which it posed to the supremacy of the Grand Fleet.

II. *Anglo-American Naval Issues and the Monroe Doctrine Amendment*

Before relating how British objections to the Monroe Doctrine amendment were overcome, it is necessary to review the background of latent naval rivalry between Great Britain and the United States which Lloyd George interjected into the discussion of the American amendments to the Covenant.

The First World War destroyed the strategic unity of the world which had prevailed under the aegis of the *Pax Britannica*. Although the war left Great Britain with a preponderance of sea power over the continental states greater than at any time since 1815, this very condition threatened to project the United States into a bitter and futile naval race with Britain. Many American observers regarded British sea power as a great potential threat to American security, reinforced by Britain's alliance with Japan. The problem in 1918-1919 was incipient rather than acute, depending on whether the two great sea powers would come to regard each other's navies as threats or assets to their security.[20]

In the winter of 1918-1919, the United States Navy was quantitatively inferior to that of Great Britain, but on the basis of naval building in progress, the United States was forging ahead while Britain was standing still, and the prospect was for Anglo-American naval parity within five or six years.[21] British policy was, therefore, to preserve the naval *status quo*. Immediately after the Armistice, Secretary of the Navy Daniels, with the President's approval, recommended to Congress that the three-year naval building program in progress at the end of the war be continued.[22] In his annual message to Congress on December 2, 1918, President Wilson said that he took it for granted that the naval program would be continued. "It would be clearly unwise," he said, "for us to attempt to adjust our programs to a future world

[20] Harold and Margaret Sprout, *Toward a New Order of Sea Power* (2nd edn., Princeton: Princeton University Press, 1946), pp. 34-41.
[21] *ibid.*, pp. 51-54.
[22] Josephus Daniels, *The Wilson Era* (Chapel Hill: The University of North Carolina Press, 1946), p. 368.

policy as yet undetermined."[23] Daniels maintained that it would be "improper" for the United States to contribute any less than the "greatest other power" to a League of Nations naval force, but if the Peace Conference failed, the United States would need the greatest navy in the world.[24]

It is quite possible that President Wilson's motive in advocating a great naval expansion was to have a club to wield over Britain and the Allies pending their acceptance of his peace program. Wilson advised Admiral Benson on January 27, 1919, that the three-year naval building program was "necessary for the accomplishment of our objects here," but that he would be quite willing to have a proviso in the legislation for holding up the building program if the Peace Conference reached a disarmament agreement.[25] Whatever its motive, the American naval building program was regarded as a threat to the security of the British Empire by Englishmen who could not conceive that the limited overseas interests of the United States could require the greatest fleet in the world. The British Admiralty were convinced that the League of Nations, as an untested instrument, was no substitute in the foreseeable future for the supremacy of the British fleet.[26]

The issue was further complicated by the uncertainty of the British as to American intentions in regard to the freedom of the seas. The question had been evaded in the pre-Armistice negotiations by a British agreement to *discuss* it,[27] but it was by no means certain that the United States would not bring it up again at the Peace Conference. The American Ambassador in London reported in December 1918, hyperbolically perhaps, that the question of the freedom of the seas was the sole source of anxiety in Britain over the impending peace negotiations.[28] Although he

[23] Wilson's Annual Message to Congress, December 2, 1918, Baker and Dodd, eds., *Public Papers, War and Peace*, Vol. 1, p. 318.
[24] Daniels to Wilson, January 4, 1919, Wilson Papers, Series 8-A.
[25] Gilbert F. Close (Confidential Secretary to Wilson), to Benson, January 27, 1919, Wilson Papers, Series 8-A.
[26] Arthur Sweetser, "Naval Policy and the Peace Conference," *Sea Power*, Vol. 6 (February 1919), pp. 77-78; H.W.V. Temperley, ed., *A History of the Peace Conference of Paris* (6 Vols., London: Henry Frowde and Hodder and Stoughton, 1920-1924), Vol. 2, p. 147.
[27] See Chapter 2, Section II.
[28] Davis to the Acting Secretary of State, December 19, 1918, Department of State, *Papers Relating to the Foreign Relations of the United States, 1919, The*

expressed deep distrust of British sea power during the voyage to France in December,[29] in an interview for *The Times* of London on December 20, Wilson paid glowing tribute to the Grand Fleet, declaring that he fully understood the "special international questions which arise from the fact of Britain's peculiar position as an island empire."[30]

British fears over the freedom of the seas turned out to be wholly unfounded. The issue dissolved in Wilson's broadening concept of a universal League without neutrals, and therefore, without controversies over neutral rights. In a memorandum written in December 1918, David Hunter Miller pointed out that in a war between the League of Nations and other powers, "every weapon would have to be available to the League and the commerce of the belligerents opposed to the League would have to be cut off absolutely as far as sea power could do it, regardless of the interests of neutrals if there were any such." It followed that any revision of the rules of capture, contraband, and visit and search, once the League were established, would be a "matter of only academic importance."[31] The freedom of the seas was never discussed at the Peace Conference, for reasons which President Wilson later made perfectly clear in describing a "practical joke" on himself: "One of the principles I went to Paris most insisting on was the freedom of the seas. Now, the freedom of the seas means the definition of the right of neutrals to use the seas when other nations are at war, but under the League of Nations there are no neutrals, and, therefore, what I have called the practical joke on myself was that by the very thing that I was advocating it became unnecessary to define freedom of the seas. All nations . . . being comrades and partners in a common cause, we all have an equal right to use the seas."[32]

Paris Peace Conference (13 Vols., Washington: United States Government Printing Office, 1942-1947), Vol. 1, pp. 413-414; hereafter referred to as *Foreign Relations*.

[29] See Chapter 2, Section IV.

[30] Charles T. Thomson, *The Peace Conference Day by Day* (New York: Brentano's Publishers, 1920), p. 42.

[31] Memorandum by Miller, December 13, 1918, "The Relation of Sea Power to a League of Nations," Miller, *Diary*, Vol. 2, pp. 262-264.

[32] Speech at San Diego, September 19, 1919, Baker and Dodd, eds., *Public Papers, War and Peace*, Vol. 2, p. 294.

Although grateful that the United States did not bring up the issue of freedom of the seas, the British remained highly alarmed at the apparent American bid for naval superiority. For some twenty years they had taken Anglo-American naval accord for granted, and they now could not understand the strategic necessity for the United States, with no such overseas life lines to protect as their own, to build the world's greatest fleet.[33] Specifically, Lloyd George desired an American endorsement of the special British naval position and the abandonment of the American naval building program then in progress.

At the end of March 1919, Secretary of the Navy Josephus Daniels arrived in Paris to find the British and American naval advisers, Admirals Wemyss and Benson, engaged in an acrimonious "naval battle of Paris." Wemyss asked Benson to recommend to President Wilson a fixed Anglo-American naval ratio, conceding primacy to Great Britain, and the abandonment of the naval program already authorized by Congress. Benson maintained that the United States would never be satisfied with a fleet second to that of Great Britain. Secretary Daniels found it necessary to intervene "to restore the urbanities" between the quarreling Admirals.[34]

Daniels then engaged in conversations with Walter Long, the First Lord of the Admiralty. Long told Daniels that Lloyd George would withdraw his support of the League of Nations if the United States persisted in its naval program. Long said that it was intolerable that Britain should have suffered "tremendous losses . . . in men, money, and ships, and in addition become a second rate sea power. . . ." Daniels replied that the United States wanted parity not supremacy, that the American Government believed that the "peace of the world demanded equality of naval strength" between Britain and the United States. Daniels said that the United States would agree to naval reductions only when the League was a going concern and then on the basis of parity with Great Britain.[35]

[33] Forrest Davis, *The Atlantic System* (New York: Reynal and Hitchcock, 1941), pp. 266-267.
[34] Daniels, *The Wilson Era*, pp. 367-369; Davis, *The Atlantic System*, pp. 262-263; Sprout, *Toward a New Order of Sea Power*, pp. 64-65.
[35] Daniels, *The Wilson Era*, pp. 371-372; Sprout, *Toward a New Order of Sea Power*, pp. 65-66; Davis, *The Atlantic System*, p. 263.

At the suggestion of President Wilson, Secretary Daniels took up the naval question in a breakfast meeting with Lloyd George and Long. Lloyd George told Daniels that Britain had stopped building cruisers, "and you ought to stop work on your cruisers and dreadnaughts if you really believe in the League of Nations." Daniels said that the United States could not cease building until permanent peace was assured and asked if Lloyd George conditioned his support of the League on America's giving up its naval program. Lloyd George replied, "Of course not, but it would be a mere piece of rhetoric if you continue to build." Daniels explained that the United States was committed to the protection of such widely separated countries that it needed a fleet greater than Britain's. "That," said Lloyd George, "is preposterous. You are a self-contained republic with no large empire." The discussion ended in as great, if less heated, an impasse as that between the Admirals.[36] After some further fruitless negotiations, both Daniels and Long left Paris early in April with the deadlock unbroken. Daniels reported to Wilson that it was unlikely that he and Long could ever reach an agreement satisfactory to Lloyd George because of the latter's demand that the United States cease building capital ships.[37]

Meanwhile, more fruitful negotiations had got underway between Cecil and House, who in late March and early April were closeted daily in quest of a naval "understanding." In a letter to Colonel House on April 8, Cecil, while forcefully asserting the determination of Great Britain to maintain her naval supremacy, argued the inconsistency of American naval aspirations with the principles of the League of Nations: "I think you will believe me when I say that I am passionately desirous of Anglo-American friendship, and a convinced believer in its existence and durability, but I must freely admit that if I were British Minister of the Navy and I saw that British naval safety were being threatened, even by America, I should have to recommend to my fellow countrymen to spend their last shilling in bringing our fleet up to the point which I was advised was necessary for their safety." Cecil asked for assurances that the United States would abandon or modify its

[36] Daniels, *The Wilson Era,* pp. 375-380.
[37] Daniels to Wilson, April 7, 1919, Wilson Papers, Series 8-A.

naval building program and agree to year-to-year naval consultations with Great Britain.[38]

On the same day, House wrote a letter to Lloyd George. Referring to his previous inquiries as to the Prime Minister's attitude on the Monroe Doctrine amendment, House wrote: ". . . you told me as you have told me before that you could not consent without first coming to an agreement with the United States regarding our naval building program. I cannot see what connection the two matters have. . . . I understand that no one but you has raised any objection to our proposal, and I hope, my dear Prime Minister, that you will not further insist upon the point you have raised."[39]

On April 9, after consultation with President Wilson, House replied to Cecil's letter of the 8th that the United States would readily "abandon or modify" that part of its naval program which had not yet been legislated and that it was also prepared to engage in year-to-year naval consultations with Great Britain.[40]

House conferred with Cecil on the morning of April 10 and told him that the naval program already *enacted* would be completed but assured Cecil that the United States entertained no idea of naval competition with Great Britain. House told Cecil that the President would consider a postponement of work on ships already authorized but not yet in construction and would also consider a suspension of the supplementary three-year naval program then before Congress. Cecil said that House's letter of the 9th was not satisfactory to Lloyd George and House replied that the United States would bargain no further on the Monroe Doctrine amendment and the naval-building program but would present its draft amendment to the League Commission that evening. "We would like your support," said House, "but of course you can oppose us if you see fit." Cecil was impressed and very upset, according to House, and said that he was disposed to quit the whole thing.[41]

---

[38] Cecil to House, April 8, 1919, Seymour, ed., *Intimate Papers*, Vol. 4, pp. 418-420; Miller, *The Drafting of the Covenant*, Vol. 1, pp. 419-420.

[39] House to Lloyd George, April 8, 1919, *ibid.*, pp. 420-421. This letter quite probably was not seen by Lloyd George. It was received by Miller along with a note from Wiseman to House indicating that he had withheld the letter from the Prime Minister. See also Bonsal, *Unfinished Business*, pp. 201-202.

[40] House to Cecil, April 9, 1919, Seymour, ed., *Intimate Papers*, Vol. 4, pp. 420-421.

[41] House Diary, April 10, 1919, House Papers; Miller, *The Drafting of the Covenant*, Vol. 1, p. 425.

The issue now moved rapidly toward resolution. Miller conferred with Cecil later in the day and Cecil expressed the view that *if* the Monroe Doctrine amendment went into the Covenant, it should go at the end as a separate article and not under Article 10 as proposed by President Wilson. Miller reported this conversation back to House and while they were talking, a note came in from Cecil.[42] The note, which apparently was based on consultation with Lloyd George following Cecil's morning conversation with House, tacitly accepted House's assurances of the morning meeting. Thanking House for his letter of April 9, Cecil said that he anticipated Anglo-American cooperation in the exchange of information on naval programs. "You will not forget in this connection," Cecil asked, "the recognition by the President of Great Britain's special position as to sea power?"[43]

The "naval battle of Paris" was thus terminated by the informal agreements of April 10. Admiral Benson continued the struggle for an American Navy as great as that of Great Britain, but in May, President Wilson withdrew the Administration's support for the supplementary naval program of 1918.[44] It seems quite clear that in making a naval agreement the condition of British support of the Monroe Doctrine, Lord Robert Cecil was acting as a loyal but most reluctant agent of the Prime Minister. Cecil does not discuss the naval issue in *A Great Experiment*, except to observe that the question of American naval policy was the only issue relating to the League of Nations on which he and Lloyd George had disagreed.[45]

The "naval battle of Paris" was based on false premises on both sides. On the British side, it rested on unwarrantable fears that American parity or superiority on the seas would pose a threat to the security of the British Empire, and even more, perhaps, on chauvinistic pride in the supremacy of the Grand Fleet as the key symbol of imperial grandeur. On the American side, the naval issue rested on an equally unwarrantable fear that British mastery of the seas posed a threat to American security, when in fact for

[42] *ibid.*, pp. 426-427.
[43] Cecil to House, April 10, 1919, Seymour, ed., *Intimate Papers*, Vol. 4, p. 423.
[44] Sprout, *Toward a New Order of Sea Power*, pp. 71, 82-83; Davis, *The Atlantic System*, pp. 264-265.
[45] Cecil, *A Great Experiment*, p. 68.

a hundred years British maritime power had posed little or no danger to the United States and perhaps even served as a protective barrier between the United States and the power struggles of Europe.

If the threat of a great American naval program was designed as a club to compel British adherence to Wilson's peace program, then it was indeed a stuffed club. For the most part, Great Britain shared to the fullest the objectives of the American peace program—on the League, on disarmament, on the principle of self-determination. Where Great Britain opposed that program, as on reparations, there is certainly no evidence that British opposition was modified by the threat of American naval competition. The only British position which was altered by the modification of the American naval program was Lloyd George's opposition to the Monroe Doctrine amendment to the Covenant, opposition which would not have existed but for the American naval building program.

Anglo-American sea power might have formed the nucleus of world organization, the guarantor of the principles of the League of Nations. With no conflicting strategic interests of their own and with a common interest in a world order under the rule of law, Great Britain and the United States might have used their preponderant naval and economic power as the heart of the League system. But the very concept of a special alliance within the League community was pure anathema to Woodrow Wilson, and it was to take another generation of world conflict before Americans and Englishmen were prepared to recognize that an Anglo-American alliance, far from being a derogation from the principle of collective security under a world rule of law, could, by its own example, buttress and inspire a system of world collective security.

III. *The Acceptance of the Monroe Doctrine Amendment and the Adoption of the Covenant*

Although the *de facto* Anglo-American naval accommodation reached on April 10 removed the basis of British objections to a Monroe Doctrine clause, President Wilson went to the meeting of the League of Nations Commission that evening with no certainty that the British would support his amendment.[46] Before the issue was brought up, Wilson joined Cecil in advocating Geneva rather than Brussels as the seat of the League, because, as Cecil put it, "impartiality and not the preservation of the glorious memories of the war was the object of the League."[47]

President Wilson then submitted his proposed amendment to Article 10: "Nothing in this Covenant shall be deemed to affect the validity of international engagements such as treaties of arbitration or regional understandings like the Monroe Doctrine for securing the maintenance of peace." Cecil said at once that he "did not wish to oppose the amendment but to explain its meaning." "The amendment had been inserted," he said, "in order to quiet doubts, and to calm misunderstandings. It did not make the substance of the Doctrine more or less valid. He understood this amendment to say what he believed to be implicit in the Covenant, what he believed to be true—that there was nothing in the Monroe Doctrine which conflicted with the Covenant, and therefore nothing in the Covenant which interfered with international understandings like the Monroe Doctrine." Wilson assured the Commission that the Monroe Doctrine would not prevent action by the League in American affairs. The Covenant was, in fact, the "highest tribute to the Monroe Doctrine. It adopted the principle of the Monroe Doctrine as a world doctrine."[48]

Larnaude objected most strenuously. He thought the proposed amendment, dealing with only one country, to be out of harmony with the rest of the Covenant, and he feared that it might be interpreted "to mean that the United States could not participate in any settlement of European affairs decided upon by the League." Wilson assured Larnaude that if the Monroe Doctrine were ever interpreted in a manner prejudicial to world peace, the "League of Nations would be there to deal with it. . . ." Cecil explained that the amendment "simply proposed to emphasize an implicit principle: that the validity of the Monroe Doctrine was not affected by anything in the Covenant. The amendment

[46] Seymour, ed., *Intimate Papers*, Vol. 4, p. 416.

[47] League of Nations Commission, Fourteenth Meeting, April 10, 1919, 8 p.m., Miller, *The Drafting of the Covenant*, Vol. 2, pp. 365-368.

[48] League of Nations Commission, Fourteenth Meeting, April 10, 1919, 8 p.m., *ibid.*, pp. 369-370.

did not give validity to anything which did not already possess validity." Cecil did, however, agree with the French that it would be a "very unfortunate thing" to state the Monroe Doctrine singly. Larnaude and Bourgeois remained unconvinced and Wilson attempted in vain to allay their fear that the amendment would somehow release the United States from its obligations under the Covenant.[49]

Cecil thought that French anxieties might be assuaged if the amendment were not attached to Article 10, the article of greatest importance for the security of France, but to Article 20.[50] Wilson agreed to Cecil's proposal. Larnaude insisted on a definition of the Monroe Doctrine, asserting that his principal concern was "to have an obligation imposed on America to take part in European affairs." Wilson proceeded to explain the Monroe Doctrine as a barrier to absolutism in the Americas, of which the Covenant was a "logical extension." Was the United States, Wilson asked, to be "penalized for her early adoption of this policy"? Cecil asserted that Larnaude was "clearly wrong in his interpretation of the way in which the Monroe Doctrine had been applied." It "had never in a single instance been applied to American policy with regard to American participation in Europe, but always with regard to European participation in American affairs. When American statesmen or international lawyers made objections to the interference of America in European affairs, they never did so on the basis of the Monroe Doctrine, but always on the basis of Washington's farewell address." The French at last dropped their objections, which were probably only a captious bargaining device, and Wilson's Monroe Doctrine clause was adopted by the Commission as an amendment to Article 20.[51]

Cecil lent full support to President Wilson once again in the meeting of April 11 when Larnaude proposed a substitute word-

[49] League of Nations Commission, Fourteenth Meeting, April 10, 1919, 8 p.m., *ibid.*, pp. 371-373.

[50] Article 20, under the working text of the Covenant of April 5, stated the principle that the Covenant superseded all previous and inconsistent obligations. *ibid.*, p. 679.

[51] League of Nations Commission, Fourteenth Meeting, April 10, 1919, 8 p.m., *ibid.*, pp. 373-374. See also, in connection with this meeting: *ibid.*, Vol. 1, pp. 439-452; Seymour, ed., *Intimate Papers*, Vol. 4, pp. 423-427; Bonsal, *Unfinished Business*, p. 203; Baker, *Wilson and World Settlement*, Vol. 1, pp. 332-339.

ing for the Monroe Doctrine amendment, as follows: "International understandings intended to assure the maintenance of peace such as treaties of arbitration, are not considered as incompatible with the provisions of this Covenant. Likewise with regard to understandings or doctrines pertaining to certain regions, such as the Monroe Doctrine, in so far as they do not in any way prevent the signatory States from executing their obligations under this Covenant." President Wilson objected to this text on the ground that it would "create the impression that there was an incompatibility between the Monroe Doctrine and the obligations of the Covenant and that an unwarranted suspicion would thus be cast upon the Doctrine." Cecil questioned whether the French text "would be likely to satisfy the criticisms and the fears which had arisen in the United States." Expanding on his understanding of the Monroe Doctrine, Cecil declared that its "sole object" was "to prevent any European power from acquiring any influence, territory, or political supremacy on the American continent. The idea that the Monroe Doctrine would prevent the Executive Council, in the execution of an unanimous decision, from acting in Europe, America, Africa, or Asia, was a perversion of the Monroe Doctrine, and citizens of the United States would be the first to disclaim it." After some further acrimonious debate, President Wilson declared Larnaude's proposal not adopted. The Monroe Doctrine amendment, as adopted on April 10, became part of Article 21 of the final Covenant.[52]

All of the principal objections to the Covenant which had been urged on President Wilson by American public and congressional opinion were thus secured by April 11. The success of President Wilson in securing the American amendments to the Covenant was in very great measure due to Cecil's acute sensitivity to the importance of appeasing Senatorial sentiment. Cecil had participated with the greatest reluctance in Lloyd George's unprincipled effort to bargain over the Monroe Doctrine, and when Lloyd George was at last appeased by the informal naval agreements of April 10, Cecil supported President Wilson in the meetings of the League Commission on April 10 and 11 with such

[52] League of Nations Commission, Fifteenth Meeting, April 11, 1919, 8:30 p.m., Miller, *The Drafting of the Covenant*, Vol. 2, pp. 381-384. See also Seymour, ed., *Intimate Papers*, Vol. 4, pp. 427-428; Bonsal, *Unfinished Business*, pp. 198-201.

vigor and eloquence as to suggest an act of apology for the naval imbroglio.

The League of Nations Commission completed its work on April 11, but one final Anglo-American issue arose before the formal adoption of the Covenant by the Peace Conference. The British Dominions took alarm at the wording of Article 4, which said that the Council would consist of the five Great Powers, "together with Representatives of four other *States* which are Members of the League."[53] Since the Dominions were not regarded as "States," it appeared that they would not be eligible for membership on the Council. On April 21, Cecil's secretary wrote to Miller urging the substitution of the term "Members of the League" for "States" in all relevant places. Miller took up the matter with House, who contended that the change could not be made without a meeting of the League Commission and that, in any case, he did not think the Dominions should be eligible for membership on the Council. Miller wrote a reply to Cecil on April 22 expressing the view that it was "the intention of the Commission to exclude the Dominions and colonies from such representation." Cecil thereupon circulated a memorandum among the members of the League Commission asking that any who objected to his proposed changes ask President Wilson to convene the League Commission.[54]

Prime Minister Borden of Canada conferred with President Wilson on the matter on May 1 and the President agreed that the Dominions should be eligible under Article 4 for membership on the League Council.[55] In a meeting at President Wilson's residence on May 6, Wilson, Lloyd George, and Clemenceau signed a memorandum to Borden expressing their "entire concurrence" in the view that the Dominions were eligible for membership on the Council.[56]

The "six votes of the British Empire" in the League of Nations

[53] Text of April 21, Miller, *The Drafting of the Covenant*, Vol. 2, p. 684.
[54] *ibid.*, Vol. 1, pp. 477-482; Bonsal, *Unfinished Business*, p. 204.
[55] Borden to Lloyd George, May 2, 1919, Henry Borden, ed., *Robert Laird Borden: His Memoirs* (2 Vols., New York: The Macmillan Company, 1938), Vol. 2, p. 947.
[56] Miller, *The Drafting of the Covenant*, Vol. 1, pp. 489-490; Bonsal, *Unfinished Business*, p. 205.

became one of the critical issues in the debate over the ratification of the treaty in the United States. The requirement of unanimity for decisions in both the Council and the Assembly made the "six votes" quite meaningless, but the issue became a key factor in the Senate's rejection of the treaty. President Wilson pointed out in a speech on September 12, 1919, that in both the Assembly and the Council, the one vote of the United States constituted an "absolute veto." "As we can always veto," said the President, "always offset with one vote the British six votes, I must say that I look with perfect philosophy upon the difference in number."[57]

The Covenant was formally adopted by the Peace Conference in its Plenary Session of April 28. President Wilson made a speech explaining the alterations in the text of February 14, and on the President's nomination, Sir Eric Drummond was selected as Secretary-General of the League. President Wilson's motion for the adoption of the Covenant was carried unanimously.[58] As House left the Plenary Session with Colonel Bonsal, they were joined by General Smuts, who said to House: "The peace treaty may fade into oblivion—and that would be, I sometimes think, a merciful dispensation of a kind Providence—but the Covenant will stand— as sure as fate. It must and shall succeed because there is no other way to salvage the future of civilization."[59]

The completed Covenant was almost entirely an embodiment of Anglo-American ideas and it marked the highest achievement of Anglo-American cooperation at the Peace Conference. The Anglo-American concept of the League was ably expressed in a statement for the press which the British delegation released on April 28. The League, said the British statement, was not a superstate but a "solemn agreement between sovereign states," which "must continue to depend on the free consent, in the last resort, of its component states. . . ." If nations should continue to be bellicose, the statement affirmed, "no instrument or machinery will restrain them." The Covenant accepts the "political facts of the present,"

[57] Speech at Spokane, Washington, September 12, 1919, Baker and Dodd, eds., *Public Papers, War and Peace*, Vol. 2, pp. 160-161.
[58] Plenary Session, April 28, 1919, *Foreign Relations, 1919, The Paris Peace Conference*, Vol. 3, pp. 286-315.
[59] Bonsal, *Unfinished Business*, p. 214.

while trying to "encourage an indefinite development in accordance with the ideas of the future."[60]

Besides the community of ideas and purpose which inspired the British and American delegations in the drafting of the Covenant, Anglo-American harmony was furthered by the spiritual union of its two chief architects, President Wilson and Lord Robert Cecil. The President wrote a gracious tribute to Cecil in a letter of May 2, 1919: "I feel, as I am sure all the other members of the commission feel, that the laboring oar fell to you and that it is chiefly due to you that the Covenant has come out of the confusion of debate in its original integrity. May I not express my own personal admiration of the work you did and my own sense of obligation?"[61] Cecil replied that it had been a "great honor" to work with the President "in so great a cause." The Covenant, said Cecil, was still a "skeleton," a "dead body unless a spirit can be infused into it. For that we must look under God to the peoples of the world and especially to those of America and England."[62]

The completed Covenant consisted of elements both evolutionary and revolutionary, of which the former were essentially British in origin and the latter American. The British contributed a reconstruction of the experience of the Concert of Europe and its breakdown in 1914, of which the chief elements were the provisions, contained in Article 11, for mobilizing a "hue and cry" against war as a matter of universal concern and the provisions, contained in Articles 12 to 16, for obligatory consultations before resort to war, procedures of peaceful settlement, and a system of graduated sanctions. The chief American contribution was the potentially revolutionary principle of Article 10: a world system of collective security based on a universalization of the principle of the Monroe Doctrine and firmly rooted in the rule of law.[63]

IV. *The Japanese Proposal for a Racial Equality Clause in the Covenant*

As the first non-white nation in the modern era to attend a general peace congress as a Great Power, Japan brought to Paris

[60] Miller, *Diary*, Vol. 18, p. 50.
[61] Wilson to Cecil, May 2, 1919, Wilson Papers, Series 8-A; Cecil, *A Great Experiment*, p. 100.
[62] Cecil to Wilson, May 4, 1919, Wilson Papers, Series 8-A.
[63] See Alfred Zimmern, *The League of Nations and the Rule of Law, 1918-1935* (2nd edn., London: Macmillan and Company, Ltd., 1945), p. 271.

as one of her principal desiderata a proposal for the inclusion in the Covenant of the League of Nations of a clause upholding the principle of equality of races. This demand seems to have been a sincere objective in itself, secondary to but not merely a bargaining lever for Japan's imperialist aspirations in China and the Pacific. It was aimed at such discriminatory practices as the law forbidding alien land ownership in California, but even more, perhaps, at the theory of white supremacy implicit in the British imperial system. The United States was at first inclined to be sympathetic to the racial equality clause but both Great Britain and the United States were driven ultimately to oppose it by pressures generated from within the British Empire. The debate over the racial equality clause and its final rejection constitutes a strand in the evolution of the Covenant which reflects little credit on either British or American statesmanship.

Although in the end President Wilson joined with the British to kill the racial equality clause, the United States was not at the outset hostile to the Japanese proposal. Colonel House conferred with Baron Makino and Viscount Chinda on February 4 and advised them to draft two resolutions, "one which they desired, and another which they would be willing to accept in lieu of the one they prefer." The Japanese brought House the two drafts on the next day. House conferred on them with Wilson, who found the alternate draft acceptable with minor alterations.[64] The Japanese, however, considered the clause offered by the President to be too weak, and House decided to "place them 'on the backs' of the British," because "every solution which the Japanese and I have proposed Hughes of the British delegation objects to."[65] Balfour and Cecil told Makino and Chinda that the subject of race was outside of the frame of reference of the League and should not even be discussed.[66] Balfour told House and Miller on February 9 that the doctrine that all men were created equal was an eighteenth century idea which he did not believe to be true.[67] Chinda reported to House on February 12 that he could get nothing definite from the British and that he intended, therefore, to submit a more

[64] Seymour, ed., *Intimate Papers*, Vol. 4, pp. 309-310.
[65] House Diary, February 9, 1919, *ibid.*, p. 313.
[66] Letter from a Japanese correspondent to Fifield, March 15, 1951, Russell H. Fifield, *Woodrow Wilson and the Far East* (New York: Thomas Y. Crowell Company, 1952), p. 160.
[67] Miller, *Diary*, Vol. 1, p. 116.

drastic resolution to the League of Nations Commission, which, although it would be rejected, would serve to satisfy Japanese public opinion.[68]

The Japanese racial equality clause was submitted to the League Commission on February 13. It read: "The equality of nations being a basic principle of the League of Nations, the High Contracting Parties agree to accord, as soon as possible, to all alien nationals of states members of the League equal and just treatment in every respect, making no distinction, either in law or in fact, on account of their race or nationality." Lord Robert Cecil observed that racial equality was a "question which had raised extremely serious problems within the British Empire." Although he recognized the "nobility of thought" which inspired the Japanese proposal, he urged that its consideration be deferred. The Commission agreed that, for the present, it was better not to allude to race or religion.[69]

The racial question was revived when the League of Nations Commission reconvened in March and April. During March, Baron Makino and Viscount Chinda solicited support from the British and American delegations. They conferred with Prime Minister Hughes on March 14 and, on March 18, Cecil told Wilson, House, and Miller that "they were getting on very well with him."[70] But Hughes declined to meet them again, and on March 19, Cecil came out against the Japanese proposal.[71] Hughes was by far the most vehement opponent of the racial equality clause. Colonel Bonsal recorded in his diary on March 16 that Hughes "morning, noon, and night bellows at poor Lloyd George that if race equality is recognized in the preamble or any of the articles of the Covenant, he and his people will leave the Conference bag and baggage."[72]

The Dominion Prime Ministers conferred with the Japanese in Borden's apartment on March 25 on the current Japanese draft, which called for "equal and just treatment to be accorded to all

[68] House Diary, February 12, 1919, Seymour, ed., *Intimate Papers*, Vol. 4, p. 313.

[69] League of Nations Commission, February 13, 1919, 3:30 p.m., Miller, *The Drafting of the Covenant*, Vol. 2, pp. 323-325, Vol. 1, p. 183.

[70] Miller, *Diary*, Vol. 1, p. 295.

[71] Fifield, *Wilson and the Far East*, pp. 162-163.

[72] Stephen Bonsal, *Suitors and Suppliants* (New York: Prentice-Hall, Inc., 1946), p. 229.

alien nationals of states members of the League." Botha and Massey agreed to support the clause if the term "equal" were taken out, but the Japanese would not agree to this, and Hughes would not consent to anything.[73] On March 29, Smuts, who had attempted on behalf of the Japanese to mediate with Hughes, conferred with Makino in Colonel Bonsal's room and told him that Hughes had threatened to make an inflammatory speech in the Plenary Conference. ". . . I must warn you," Smuts told Makino, "that if you persist in your motion, for which I have much sympathy, and if Hughes of Australia opposes it, as he undoubtedly will, I shall have to fall in line and vote with the Dominions, like a 'good Indian.' "[74] Colonel House took the same view, fearing that an inflammatory speech by Hughes would create a storm in the western part of the United States as well as in the Dominions. "I told Makino frankly," he wrote in his diary on March 29, "that while we would agree to the pallid formula they desired, yet unless Hughes promised not to make trouble we would be against putting it in. . . . I urged Makino to let the matter drop for the moment."[75] Further efforts by Borden and Smuts to find a compromise ended in failure.

Baron Makino asked the League of Nations Commission on April 11 to add to the preamble of the Covenant, as one of the means of promoting international cooperation, peace, and security, the clause: "by the endorsement of the principle of the equality of nations and the just treatment of their nationals."[76] Prior to the meeting, President Wilson had been disposed to accept the amendment, but House urged him to "stay with the British, which he did."[77] Cecil said that he could not vote for the amendment although he was personally in favor of it. "The British Government realized the importance of the racial question," he said, "but its solution could not be attempted by the Commission without encroaching upon the sovereignty of states members of the League.

[73] Borden, ed., *Borden's Memoirs*, Vol. 2, p. 926.

[74] Bonsal, *Unfinished Business*, pp. 169-170; Roy Watson Curry, *Woodrow Wilson and Far Eastern Policy, 1913-1921* (New York: Bookman Associates, 1957), p. 255.

[75] House Diary, March 29, 1919, Seymour, ed., *Intimate Papers*, Vol. 4, p. 415.

[76] League of Nations Commission, April 11, 1919, 8:30 p.m., Miller, *The Drafting of the Covenant*, Vol. 2, pp. 387-389.

[77] Seymour, ed., *Intimate Papers*, Vol. 4, p. 428.

. . ."[78] Miller recorded in his diary that "Cecil acted as though he was in a very difficult position, and after making his statement sat silent with eyes fixed on the table."[79] The Japanese amendment was strongly endorsed by the French and other delegations. President Wilson said that he "felt that the greatest difficulty lay in controversies which would be bound to take place outside the Commission over the Japanese proposal, and that in order to avoid these discussions it would perhaps be wise not to insert such a provision in the preamble. . . ." Makino asked for a vote. Eleven out of the seventeen members of the Commission voted for the Japanese amendment and no negative vote was taken. President Wilson declared that since the vote was not unanimous the amendment was not adopted.[80]

It was thus British and American opposition which killed the racial equality amendment. The opposition of the British was manifestly due to Hughes's warning of an uproar in the Dominions. President Wilson, greatly fearing an outburst of hostile opinion in the western part of the United States, also submitted to the threats of Hughes, although he otherwise favored the Japanese amendment. The Japanese accepted defeat on the race issue, but they stood firm on their imperialist demands in China, and here, as will be seen, Great Britain and the United States yielded to the Japanese substantially all that they desired.[81]

V. *The Drafting of the Charter of the International Labor Organization*

Of the few surviving elements of the peace settlement of 1919, none has proved more useful and stable an instrument than the modest experiment in functional international organization of the International Labor Office and Conference. Although the British and American labor representatives brought different concepts of

---

[78] League of Nations Commission, April 11, 1919, 8:30 p.m., Miller, *The Drafting of the Covenant*, Vol. 2, p. 389.

[79] Miller's Diary, April 11, 1919, Miller, *Diary*, Vol. 1, p. 245.

[80] League of Nations Commission, April 11, 1919, 8:30 p.m., Miller, *The Drafting of the Covenant*, Vol. 2, pp. 390-392, Vol. 1, pp. 461-464; Fifield, *Wilson and the Far East*, pp. 165-169; Bonsal, *Unfinished Business*, pp. 192-198; Baker, *Wilson and World Settlement*, Vol. 2, pp. 237-240; A. Whitney Griswold, *The Far Eastern Policy of the United States* (New York: Harcourt, Brace and Company, 1938), pp. 251-252.

[81] See Chapter 12, Section IV.

the role of organized labor to the drafting of the Charter of the International Labor Organization, they collaborated successfully and the final product was a synthesis of British and American ideas.

No serious preparations for the labor clauses of the treaty were made in the United States, where labor legislation was regarded as a state rather than federal function. American labor leaders were in any case more interested in having the treaty stipulate a "bill of rights" for labor than in the creation of a permanent organization.[82] In England, on the other hand, most elaborate preparations were made by the Intelligence Division of the Ministry of Labor, where only scant attention was given to a "labor charter" and the focus of interest was on the creation of a permanent organization, representing workers and employers as well as governments, to establish international labor standards.[83]

During January 1919, the British and American labor representatives and experts engaged in frequent consultations regarding the British proposals for a permanent organization. A pattern of especially close cooperation developed between James T. Shotwell of the American delegation and Edward J. Phelan of the British Ministry of Labor.[84] On January 21, Shotwell submitted a memorandum to the American delegation calling for provisions in the treaty for the regulation and protection of the labor of children, women, and aliens, and for a periodic international labor conference and a labor bureau under the League of Nations. On the same day, the British delegation submitted to the Peace Conference a fully developed scheme for the proposed labor organization.[85]

[82] Leifur Magnusson, "American Preparations," *The Origins of the International Labor Organization* (James T. Shotwell, ed., 2 Vols., New York: Columbia University Press, 1934), Vol. 1, pp. 97-99; Proposals of the American Federation of Labor to the Inter-Allied Labor and Socialist Conference, September 1918, *ibid.*, Vol. 2, pp. 75-76.

[83] Edward J. Phelan, "British Preparations," *ibid.*, Vol. 1, pp. 107-110; Memorandum prepared by Phelan, January 15-20, 1919, *ibid.*, Vol. 2, pp. 117-125. See also David Lloyd George, *The Truth about the Peace Treaties* (2 Vols., London: Victor Gollancz, Ltd., 1938), Vol. 1, pp. 643-652.

[84] Phelan, "British Preparations," *The Origins of the International Labor Organization* (Shotwell, ed.), Vol. 1, pp. 114-121; James T. Shotwell, *At the Paris Peace Conference* (New York: The Macmillan Company, 1937), pp. 107-124.

[85] Shotwell, ed., *The Origins of the International Labor Organization*, Vol. 2, pp. 134-140.

The Council of Ten agreed on January 23 to submit to the plenary conference a proposal to establish a commission to "enquire into the conditions of employment from the international aspect, and to consider the international means necessary to secure common action on matters affecting conditions of employment and to recommend the form of a permanent agency to continue such enquiry in cooperation with and under the direction of the League of Nations."[86] In accordance with this recommendation, the Plenary Session on January 25 constituted the Commission on International Labor Legislation.[87]

The Labor Commission convened on February 1 and its deliberations continued until March 24.[88] The American representatives on the Commission were Samuel Gompers, President of the American Federation of Labor, and Henry M. Robinson, a California banker. The British representatives were George N. Barnes, the representative of the Labour Party in the British War Cabinet, and Edward J. Phelan. Gompers was chosen as Chairman. American cooperation in the drafting of the labor clauses was conditioned by the traditional distrust of the American labor movement for legislation as an instrument for the advancement of their objectives and by the Gompers philosophy of labor-management "voluntarism" and freedom from state interference.[89] Gompers, in fact, regarded the socialists on the Labor Commission as not being true representatives of labor. ". . . much of the time," he wrote, "I found myself in the position of being the sole representative of trade-union thought."[90]

Gompers clashed with the British representatives at the outset over the proposal in the British plan that each member state in the permanent organization appoint two government representa-

[86] Council of Ten, January 23, 1919, 10:30 a.m., *Foreign Relations, 1919, The Paris Peace Conference*, Vol. 3, p. 697.

[87] Plenary Session, January 25, 1919, *ibid.*, p. 200.

[88] The minutes of the meetings of Commission on International Labor Legislation are reproduced as Document 34 in Shotwell, ed., *The Origins of the International Labor Organization*, Vol. 2, pp. 149-322.

[89] Samuel McCune Lindsay, "The Problem of American Cooperation," *ibid.*, Vol. 1, pp. 331-332. See also Lloyd George, *The Truth about the Peace Treaties*, Vol. 1, pp. 653-654.

[90] Samuel Gompers, "The Labor Clauses of the Treaty," *What Really Happened at Paris* (Edward Mandell House and Charles Seymour, eds., New York: Charles Scribner's Sons, 1921), pp. 320-321.

tives as well as one each for labor and management. To Gompers, this meant that in each delegation labor might be outvoted three to one. Unlike the British and European socialists, Gompers neither anticipated nor desired labor control of governments. The British plan, however, was carried over Gompers' objections.[91]

A more serious controversy arose in the latter part of February over the British plan for enacting labor legislation by treaties, which the member states would be bound to submit to their legislatures. Gompers and Robinson pointed out that under the Constitution of the United States legislation governing labor was beyond the federal authority, being among the powers reserved to the states.[92] On February 27, Barnes submitted a plan for federal governments to submit the conventions of the labor organization to their state or provincial legislatures to adhere to separately. Robinson objected to this on the ground that the states would be unrepresented in the drafting of the conventions. Gompers and Robinson proposed that the British plan of labor legislation by treaties be abandoned and that the organization confine itself to recommendations to the member states. The Commission rejected this proposal.[93] Barnes regarded the American proposals as designed to reduce the International Labor Organization to an agency for the issuance of pious declarations.[94]

The Labor Commission adjourned on February 28 to allow the delegates to consult their governments and experts. During this period, the British representatives consulted with Shotwell in regard to the American constitutional problem. In a special subcommittee, Shotwell, who now served as technical adviser to the Commission, and Sir Malcolm Delevingue worked out a plan which became the basis of a compromise on the problem of treaty adoption by federal states. The Commission agreed on March 19 that the International Labor Organization would adopt both recommendations and conventions for labor legislation, but

[91] *ibid.*, p. 322; Shotwell, *At the Paris Peace Conference*, pp. 168-169.
[92] Labor Commission, February 20, 1919, Shotwell, ed., *The Origins of the International Labor Organization*, Vol. 2, pp. 181-185; Shotwell, *At the Paris Peace Conference*, pp. 186-188.
[93] Labor Commission, February 27, 1919, Shotwell, ed., *The Origins of the International Labor Organization*, Vol. 2, pp. 198-207.
[94] Phelan, "Commission on International Labor Legislation," *ibid.*, Vol. 1, p. 157.

that federal states might regard all enactments as recommendations.[95]

Once the British scheme for the International Labor Organization had been adopted with the accommodation for federal states, attention was directed to the American proposal for a labor charter, or bill of rights. A proposed charter of nineteen points prepared by a special subcommittee had been presented to the Labor Commission on March 15. Gompers strongly endorsed it but Barnes took the view that such a charter was not appropriate for inclusion in the peace treaty and should be left to the consideration of the permanent organization. With Barnes leading the opposition to the charter, the Commission reduced the nineteen points to nine.[96] The Labor Commission unanimously adopted its final report for the Peace Conference on March 24.[97]

Barnes presented the report and recommendations of the Commission on International Labor Legislation to the Plenary Session on April 11. He explained the draft constitution of the International Labor Organization and asked for the insertion in the treaty of resolutions for its formulation. Speeches of approval were made, President Wilson expressing the "entire concurrence" of American labor in "this admirable document." The report of the Labor Commission and the draft convention creating the International Labor Organization were unanimously adopted.[98]

By accident or design, the proceedings of the Plenary Session were conducted with such dispatch that the nine points of the proposed labor charter, so dear to Gompers, were not taken up. With Gompers gone, Barnes, although not in sympathy with the proposed charter, felt obliged to secure its acceptance. During April, Barnes, Robinson, and Shotwell attempted to renegotiate the nine points of the labor charter. Barnes was loyal to the absent Gompers, defending against British objections his favorite

[95] Labor Commission, March 19, 1919, Shotwell, ed., *ibid.*, Vol. 2, pp. 285-298; Shotwell, *At the Paris Peace Conference*, pp. 194-206, 216-217.

[96] Labor Commission, March 15, 1919, Shotwell, ed., *The Origins of the International Labor Organization*, Vol. 2, pp. 247-255; Shotwell, *At the Paris Peace Conference*, pp. 220-226.

[97] Shotwell, ed., *The Origins of the International Labor Organization*, Vol. 2, pp. 368-378.

[98] Plenary Session, April 11, 1919, *Foreign Relations, 1919, The Paris Peace Conference*, Vol. 3, pp. 241-260.

principle, which stated that labor was not to be regarded as a "commodity or article of commerce."[99] A series of conferences among Barnes, Balfour, Robinson, and the Dominion Prime Ministers culminated in a general meeting on April 27 at the residence of Sir Robert Borden at which agreement was reached on a redraft of the nine points prepared by Borden. The original Gompers clause emerged as a proposition "that labor should not be *regarded merely* as a commodity or article of commerce."[100]

In the Plenary Session of April 28, after the adoption of the Covenant of the League, Barnes, as a gesture of loyalty to Gompers, submitted the original nine principles of the proposed labor charter. Borden then presented the redraft of the previous day, which was adopted unanimously.[101]

Gompers was greatly displeased by the mutilation of his labor charter. Wilson asked Tumulty to tell him that the redraft of April 28 was the "best that could be got out of a maze of contending interests. . . ." Tumulty replied that Gompers considered himself "sold out" and might even throw the American Federation of Labor against the League of Nations.[102]

As in the case of the Council of the League of Nations, the United States temporarily resisted the demand of the Dominions for eligibility to be represented on the governing body of the International Labor Organization. In a meeting with Robinson on April 29, Borden protested the stipulation in Article 7 of the Charter that no member, together with its colonies and dominions, self-governing or not, could nominate more than one member of the governing body. Robinson said that public opinion in the United States prevented him from acceding to Borden's desire to alter this provision.[103] Although President Wilson was, in Borden's view, "obstinate as a mule" on the issue of Dominion representation on the governing body, he yielded in the meeting

[99] Shotwell, *At the Paris Peace Conference*, pp. 257-266; Phelan, "Labor Proposals before the Peace Conference," *The Origins of the International Labor Organization* (Shotwell, ed.), Vol. 1, pp. 212-213.

[100] *ibid.*, pp. 213-216; Borden, ed., *Borden's Memoirs*, Vol. 2, pp. 943-944.

[101] Plenary Session, April 28, 1919, *Foreign Relations, 1919, The Paris Peace Conference*, Vol. 3, pp. 316-319. See also Gompers, "The Labor Clauses of the Treaty," *What Really Happened at Paris* (House and Seymour, eds.), pp. 323-324.

[102] Wilson to Tumulty, May 3, 1919, Tumulty to Wilson, May 16, 1919, Wilson Papers, Series 8-A.

[103] Borden, ed., *Borden's Memoirs*, Vol. 2, pp. 945-946, 950-951.

with Lloyd George and Clemenceau on May 6. In the memorandum which the three sent to Borden on that day regarding Dominion representation on the League Council, they agreed also to strike Article 7 from the Charter of the International Labor Organization.[104]

In a cable to Gompers on June 20, Wilson expressed the view that the "problems of the chief British colonies and dominions are much more like our own than like Great Britain's so that their representation will be a source of strength to our point rather than an embarrassment."[105] Gompers, who in due course recovered from his pique of May 1919, found in later years that the Dominions "were more often with the United States than with England, and that they were more often with progress than against it."[106]

Although the British and American labor representatives brought sharply divergent concepts to the framing of the International Labor Organization, they compromised their differences in an atmosphere of reasonable and constructive cooperation. The organization created was in great measure a synthesis of the Fabian socialist principle of government action to promote the well-being of labor and the nineteenth century voluntarist traditions of the American labor movement. Lloyd George regarded the creation of the International Labor Organization as one of the most valuable achievements of the Peace Conference,[107] and President Wilson referred to the labor clauses as a "Magna Charta, a great guarantee for labor," providing that labor "shall have the counsels of the world devoted to the discussion of its conditions and of its betterment. . . ."[108] The International Labor Organization has survived as a significant experiment in functional international organization, its objective being the elimination of social injustice, an approach in depth

[104] ibid., pp. 952-961; Glazebrook, Canada at the Paris Peace Conference, pp. 78-80. See Section III above.

[105] Wilson to Gompers, June 20, 1919, Shotwell, ed., The Origins of the International Labor Organization, Vol. 2, pp. 441-443.

[106] Gompers, "The Labor Clauses of the Treaty," What Really Happened at Paris (House and Seymour, eds.), p. 334.

[107] Lloyd George, The Truth about the Peace Treaties, Vol. 1, pp. 671-673.

[108] Speech at Des Moines, September 6, 1919, Baker and Dodd, eds., Public Papers, War and Peace, Vol. 2, p. 17.

to the promotion of peace by an attack on one of the principal causes of war.

VI. *Anglo-American Differences in Regard to the Proposed Trial of the Kaiser*

Quite naturally, the British, who had been involved in World War I from its outset and whose losses in blood and treasure far exceeded those of the United States, entertained fewer scruples than did the American statesmen at Paris in regard to the almost unprecedented proposal to bring the head of the enemy state to personal account for the authorship of the war. The trial of the Kaiser was first proposed in Great Britain at a meeting of the Imperial War Cabinet on November 20, 1918, at which Lord Curzon demanded the trial of William II as the "arch-criminal of the world." Lloyd George agreed to the proposal and referred the matter to the Law Officers of the Crown, who on November 28 presented a unanimous recommendation to the Cabinet for the prosecution of the Kaiser by an international tribunal of the Allied nations for such specific violations of international law as the invasion of Belgium and the practice of unrestricted submarine warfare. The Imperial War Cabinet unanimously adopted the report of the Law Officers and resolved that, "so far as the British Government have the power, the ex-Kaiser should be held personally responsible for his crimes against international law."[109] The proposal to bring the Kaiser to trial, even to "hang the Kaiser," became a key factor in the electoral campaign of December 1918, with the result that the British delegation came to Paris as much committed on this issue as it was to the extraction of astronomical reparations.[110]

The American attitude was more dispassionate, taking careful account of the dubious legal foundations of the proposal to bring the Kaiser to trial. In a memorandum drawn up at the outset of the Peace Conference, the American legal advisers, David Hunter Miller and James Brown Scott, pointed out that the heads of states and governments who acted to cause the war were not in 1914 personally accountable under international law

[109] Lloyd George, *The Truth about the Peace Treaties*, Vol. 1, pp. 93-114.
[110] See Chapter 2, Section v.

for the political acts of their governments. To create a retroactive criminal responsibility, it was asserted, would be contrary to international law and the law of civilized states. The memorandum held that only acts contrary to international law committed by individuals in the war were subject to criminal prosecution.[111]

The Plenary Session of January 25 created a Commission on Responsibilities to inquire into and report on the responsibility of the authors of the war.[112] Secretary Lansing, as president of the Commission, opposed a trial of the Kaiser and recommended that the Peace Conference instead issue a devastating moral indictment of William II. The British and French and other members of the Commission demanded the extradition of the Kaiser from Holland and his trial by an international tribunal.[113] Lansing told the American Commissioners on March 5 that while the United States favored the prosecution of specific violations of the law of war by military tribunals, the British demanded the establishment of a tribunal of all of the Allied Powers to prosecute the Kaiser and all other alleged war criminals. Lansing said that the French and Italians had tried unsuccessfully to bring about an Anglo-American compromise and that he thought that the British were "not very sincere" in their desire to bring the Kaiser to trial but "merely felt that they had to urge this measure because of a political pledge."[114] In its final report of March 29, the Commission on Responsibilities overrode Lansing's objections and adopted the British proposals for the constitution of an Allied tribunal to try the Kaiser and other individuals, for compelling Germany to yield persons and evidence, and for representations to the Netherlands to extradite the Kaiser.[115]

[111] Memorandum submitted by Miller and Scott (*circa*) January 18, 1919, Miller, *Diary*, Vol. 3, pp. 456-457.
[112] Plenary Session, January 25, 1919, *Foreign Relations, 1919, The Paris Peace Conference*, Vol. 3, pp. 199-200.
[113] The minutes of the Commission on Responsibilities and its three subcommittees have been published only in French, in La Documentation Internationale, *La Paix de Versailles* (12 Vols., Paris: Les Éditions Internationales, 1929-1939), Vol. 3.
[114] Minutes of the Daily Meetings of the American Commissioners, March 5, 1919, *Foreign Relations, 1919, The Paris Peace Conference*, Vol. 11, pp. 93-94.
[115] La Documentation Internationale, *La Paix de Versailles*, Vol. 3, pp. 457-482.

Lloyd George raised the question of responsibilities in the Council of Four on April 2, strongly endorsing the report of the Commission. President Wilson questioned the right of the Allies to constitute a tribunal composed solely of belligerents. He thought it would set a dangerous precedent. Hitherto, said the President, responsibility for international crimes had been collective, and it would not be just to establish individual responsibility *ex post facto*. Lloyd George insisted on the absolute right of the Allies to bring the guilty to justice, suggesting that the tribunal could be constituted under the League of Nations. Wilson recommended that the trials at least be delayed until the passions of war had subsided, but Lloyd George, with the support of Clemenceau, countered that if the League of Nations was to be a success, it should demonstrate at the outset its ability to punish crimes.[116]

Wilson offered some further resistance but in the end yielded. In the discussion of April 8, the President rehearsed the doubts of Lansing as to the legality of putting individuals to trial for acts committed during the war under military orders. Wilson proposed that the Allies confine themselves to some measure for dishonoring the former Kaiser, but Lloyd George insisted that he should be held criminally responsible at least for the violation of the neutrality of Belgium. Wilson would agree only to trials by military tribunals for specific violations of the law of war, and he also maintained that there was no legal means of compelling the Netherlands to yield the Kaiser. Lloyd George suggested that Holland should be denied admittance to the League if she refused to hand over the Kaiser. Clemenceau fully supported Lloyd George in this discussion.[117] On April 9, President Wilson, rather suddenly, yielded to the views of his colleagues, proposing trials by military tribunals of individuals accused of violations of the law of war and the trial of William II by a tribunal of five judges, one appointed by each of the principal Allied and Associated Powers, for a supreme offense against international morality and the sanctity of treaties.[118]

[116] Council of Four, April 2, 1919, 4 p.m., Paul Mantoux, *Les Délibérations du Conseil des Quatre* (2 Vols., Paris: Éditions du Centre National de la Recherche Scientifique, 1955), Vol. I, pp. 120-124.

[117] Council of Four, April 8, 1919, 3 p.m., *ibid.*, pp. 184-192.

[118] Council of Four, April 9, 1919, 11 a.m., *ibid.*, p. 195.

Wilson's proposals of April 9 became the basis of the clauses inserted in Treaty of Versailles.[119]

The President thereafter entertained no doubts about the proposed trial of the Kaiser. On June 25, he said that some "demand" would soon have to be made to Holland to deliver the Kaiser and that Holland was "morally obliged" to comply. It was agreed that Lansing would draft a communication to the Dutch Government.[120] The Council on the next day approved a draft by Lansing calling upon the Netherlands to deliver the Kaiser for prosecution "for a supreme offense against international morality and the sanctity of treaties." It was emphasized that the charges being brought were judicial and not political.[121] On June 28, the Council of Four rejected an offer by the former Chancellor Bethmann Hollweg to submit himself for trial in place of William II.[122]

The Netherlands rejected repeated appeals by the Peace Conference to deliver William II for trial on the ground that this would violate traditional state practices of political asylum and hospitality. On January 16, 1920, the Council of Allied Prime Ministers dispatched a final futile appeal to the Queen of Holland and the dubious project thus came to an end.[123] It had been primarily of British sponsorship and might have generated a serious Anglo-American controversy if President Wilson had not abandoned his initial scruples as to the legality of this first experiment in twentieth century war criminality.

[119] See James Brown Scott, "The Trial of the Kaiser," *What Really Happened at Paris* (House and Seymour, eds.), pp. 232-256.

[120] Council of Four, June 25, 1919, 4 p.m., *Foreign Relations, 1919, The Paris Peace Conference*, Vol. 6, p. 677.

[121] Council of Four, June 26, 1919, 11 a.m., *ibid.*, pp. 699-700, 705-706.

[122] Council of Four, June 28, 1919, 5 p.m., *ibid.*, pp. 751-752.

[123] Council of Premiers, January 16, 1920, 4 p.m., *ibid.*, Vol. 9, pp. 886-888; E. L. Woodward and Rohan Butler, eds., *Documents on British Foreign Policy, 1919-1939*, First Series (8 Vols., London: His Majesty's Stationery Office, 1947-1958), Vol. 2, pp. 911-913.

CHAPTER 12

AMERICAN PRINCIPLES VERSUS BRITISH TREATY OBLIGATIONS: THE TERRITORIAL CLAIMS OF ITALY AND JAPAN

Two basic factors conditioned Anglo-American relations in the diplomacy of the Italian claims in the Adriatic. The first was a basic agreement on the principle of self-determination, which meant the opposition of both nations to the Italian demand for the port city of Fiume. The second was a secondary conflict deriving from the absolute refusal of Britain to violate its treaty obligations to Italy as against the absolute refusal of President Wilson to accept any solution of the Italian claims which did not rest on the consent of the peoples concerned. The result was a protracted and acrimonious controversy over an issue which in itself was of minor significance. On this issue perhaps above all others, President Wilson took an unyielding stand on the principle of self-determination. Lloyd George, caught between his policy of Anglo-American entente and the obligations which Britain had incurred as the price of Italian participation in the war, dedicated himself to the conciliation of the conflict between Italy and the United States. In the long and frustrating negotiations, Lloyd George jumped from one proposal to another, in quest of any solution which would satisfy both the United States and Italy. The Fiume controversy did not involve a primary clash of British and American interests, but a derivative conflict between Wilsonian principles and British treaty obligations.

Anglo-American relations in the diplomacy of the Japanese claims at Paris were conditioned by the same kind of conflicting commitments as those involved in the Italian claims. In regard to the central issue of the Chinese province of Shantung, the dedication of the United States to the principle of self-determination came into conflict with a wartime engagement which committed Great Britain to support the claims of Japan. By contrast with Italy in the Fiume controversy, however, Japan had an almost unassailable legal case and, as a greater power than Italy, posed a more serious threat to the success of the League of Nations if her desires were not met. In the end, the United States yielded to Japan on the Shantung question but salvaged agreements which promised ultimate justice to China. As in the Fiume controversy, the Far Eastern problem did not involve a direct conflict of British and American interests, but rather a secondary conflict deriving from the treaty commitments of Great Britain to her Japanese ally as against the intense distrust of the United States for Japanese aspirations in China and the Pacific.

I. *The Origins of the Adriatic Issue and Its Emergence at the Peace Conference*

Early in 1915, the British Foreign Office entered into negotiations with the Italian Ambassador in London, the Marquis Imperiali, to explore the conditions under which Italy might be brought into the war against the Central Powers. The Italian territorial demands went far beyond the limits of *Italia Irrendenta*, but with conditions on the eastern front growing steadily worse and the British and French armies hard pressed in the west, the British Government was not disposed to entertain scruples over ethnographic frontiers. "War," as Lloyd George put it, "plays havoc with the refinements of conscience."[1] The Treaty of London, signed on April 26, 1915, guaranteed the acquisition by Italy of Trieste and the Trentino, of the German Tyrol and Slavic Istria and Dalmatia, except for Fiume, which was assigned to Croatia, and Valona in Albania. Italy was also to receive the Dodecanese islands, an equal share of Asia Minor if it were partitioned, a share in any war indemnity, and an immediate British loan of 50 million pounds. The treaty was signed by France, Russia, Great Britain, and Italy.[2] Balfour explained to President Wilson early in 1918 that the Treaty of London was the result of the intense anxiety of the Allies to get Italy into the war, "and of the use to which that anxiety was put by the Italian negotiators. But a treaty is a treaty: and we . . . are bound to uphold it in letter and in spirit."[3]

[1] David Lloyd George, *The Truth about the Peace Treaties* (2 Vols., London: Victor Gollancz, Ltd., 1938), Vol. 2, pp. 762-765.

[2] Great Britain, Parliament, *Papers by Command*, Miscellaneous No. 7 (1920), *Cmd.* 671; Edward Parkes, ed., *British and Foreign State Papers, 1919* (London: His Majesty's Stationery Office, 1922), pp. 973-977. See also Lloyd George, *The Truth about the Peace Treaties*, Vol. 2, pp. 765-767.

[3] Balfour to Wilson, January 31, 1918, Edward M. House Papers, Sterling Library, Yale University.

President Wilson's Point 9 called for a readjustment of Italian frontiers "along clearly recognizable lines of nationality," a principle with which the strategic frontiers of the Treaty of London were clearly incompatible. An Italian effort in the pre-Armistice conference of October-November 1918 to attach a written reservation to Point 9 was brushed aside on the ground that the Pre-Armistice Agreement did not apply to Austria-Hungary.[4] President Wilson conceded on April 20, 1919, that he "fully realized that Italy was not bound by the Fourteen Points in making peace with Austria."[5] Although the legal claim of Italy on Britain and France under the Treaty of London was thus unquestioned, the view of the British Foreign Office at the end of the war was that the breakup of Austria-Hungary had rendered the Treaty of London obsolete in terms of Italy's strategic needs. It was agreed by the Imperial War Cabinet, however, that while every effort should be made to persuade Italy to reduce her claims, Great Britain was bound to honor the terms of the treaty if Italy so required.[6]

Early in the Peace Conference, President Wilson yielded to Italy without controversy the Brenner Pass frontier with Austria. He accepted it as the best possible strategic frontier for Italy in the north although it included within Italy some 250,000 Germans of the South Tyrol. It had been promised to Italy by the Treaty of London, and by yielding this pocket of Germans to Italy, Wilson not only accepted a violation of Point 9 but lost a bargaining point for the Fiume issue. To the Italians at least, he seemed to accept the Treaty of London.[7] The decision was attributable to the President's lack of knowledge at the time of the ethnography of the South Tyrol. "I am sorry for that decision," he told Ray Stannard Baker on May 28, 1919. "I was

[4] See Chapter 2, Section 11.
[5] Council of Four, April 20, 1919, 10 a.m., Department of State, *Papers Relating to the Foreign Relations of the United States, 1919, The Paris Peace Conference* (13 Vols., Washington: United States Government Printing Office, 1942-1947), Vol. 5, p. 98; hereafter referred to as *Foreign Relations*.
[6] Lloyd George, *The Truth about the Peace Treaties*, Vol. 2, pp. 791-794.
[7] Douglas William Johnson, "Fiume and the Adriatic Problem," *What Really Happened at Paris* (Edward Mandell House and Charles Seymour, eds., New York: Charles Scribner's Sons, 1921), pp. 112-118; Charles Homer Haskins and Robert Howard Lord, *Some Problems of the Peace Conference* (Cambridge: Harvard University Press, 1920), pp. 224-225; Thomas A. Bailey, *Woodrow Wilson and the Lost Peace* (New York: The Macmillan Company, 1944), pp. 252-256.

ignorant of the situation when the decision was made."[8] The President told Charles Seymour that his approval of the Brenner frontier was based on "insufficient study."[9]

The port of Fiume, a city of 50,000 of which a majority were Italian, but with an overwhelmingly Croatian hinterland, was assigned by the Treaty of London to Croatia. Fiume had long been the principal Adriatic outlet for Austria-Hungary and was desired by the new state of Yugoslavia as the only good port on its Adriatic littoral. Italian annexation of Fiume and its surrounding territories would have meant the inclusion of 500,000 Yugoslavs within Italy. The American experts found these people overwhelmingly opposed to Italian annexation and in their report of January 21 concluded that Italy had no valid claim to the Fiume territory on the basis of nationality, history, or economic or strategic necessity. The American experts proposed a frontier along the crest of the mountain barrier between the natural hinterlands of Trieste on the west and Fiume on the east. Even this line was based on strategic and economic rather than ethnographic considerations, for it still assigned some 300,000 Yugoslavs to Italian sovereignty. Italy, however, adamantly demanded a frontier which would include Fiume within her territory. The American experts, with British and French support, unanimously advised President Wilson that the Italian claims were without justification.[10]

President Wilson saw in the Fiume issue an unambiguous conflict between Italian ambitions and the principles for which America had gone to war. Lloyd George and Clemenceau regarded the issue as of secondary importance, and while they opposed Italian acquisition of Fiume, they were not unalterably opposed to it as part of a broader compromise. Colonel House shared this view. But the President was unbending, treating the issue, what-

[8] Ray Stannard Baker, *American Chronicle* (New York: Charles Scribner's Sons, 1945), p. 433.
[9] Charles Seymour, ed., *The Intimate Papers of Colonel House* (4 Vols., Boston and New York: Houghton Mifflin Company, 1926-1928), Vol. 4, p. 435, n.2.
[10] Report of the American Experts on Italian Claims, January 21, 1919, Ray Stannard Baker, *Woodrow Wilson and World Settlement* (3 Vols., Garden City, New York: Doubleday, Page and Company, 1922), Vol. 3, pp. 259-262; Memorandum of March 18, 1919, by four American experts, *ibid.*, pp. 263-265; Johnson, "Fiume and the Adriatic Problem," *What Really Happened at Paris* (House and Seymour, eds.), pp. 120-137; Haskins and Lord, *Some Problems of the Peace Conference*, pp. 256-260.

ever its intrinsic importance, as a supreme test of principle. As the fruitless negotiations proceeded, Lloyd George became vastly annoyed by the President's intransigence. "He worked himself to such a pitch of indignation," wrote Lloyd George in his memoirs, "that for some time he concentrated his thoughts and his energies upon this comparatively trivial incident to the exclusion of vastly more important subjects which were still awaiting decision."[11]

II. *The Climax of the Fiume Controversy, April 3-24: President Wilson's Position and British Efforts at Conciliation*

In the month of April, with the great controversies over the Rhineland and German reparations disposed of, the Italian claims dominated the proceedings of the Council of Four. President Wilson made one great concession, an offer to establish Fiume as a free international port, but he would not under any circumstances consider Italian annexation, in part perhaps as a reaction to the concessions which had been exacted from him on more important issues. Lloyd George generally supported the President on Fiume while casting about for almost any arrangement which would conciliate both Italian nationalism and Wilsonian principles. The Prime Minister was inflexible only in his determination to honor the Treaty of London if Italy so required.[12]

In the Council of Four on April 3, Wilson and Lloyd George submitted to Premier Orlando a proposal to make Fiume a free city, detached from both Italy and Yugoslavia but serving as a port for the entire surrounding hinterland. Orlando found this proposal unacceptable.[13] Five of the President's chief experts submitted a memorandum on April 4 asserting that "it is unwise to make Fiume a free city," but if it should be, the amplest economic rights should be assured to the Yugoslavs.[14] Wilson

---

[11] Lloyd George, *The Truth about the Peace Treaties*, Vol. 2, p. 809.

[12] See René Albrecht-Carrié, *Italy at the Paris Peace Conference* (New York: Columbia University Press, 1938), pp. 114-152.

[13] Council of Four, April 3, 1919, 11 a.m., Paul Mantoux, *Les Délibérations du Conseil des Quatre* (2 Vols., Paris: Éditions du Centre National de la Recherche Scientifique), Vol. 1, pp. 129-131. See also Seymour, ed., *The Intimate Papers of Colonel House*, Vol. 4, pp. 441-442.

[14] Baker, *Wilson and World Settlement*, Vol. 3, pp. 266-271; Albrecht-Carrié, *Italy at the Paris Peace Conference*, pp. 440-442.

adhered to the free city proposal, and on April 13, he suggested that Orlando meet with him the next day in a private "tête-à-tête." Lloyd George declared himself "ready to accept in advance any solution on which President Wilson and Signor Orlando agree."[15] The private meeting between Orlando and Wilson on April 14 was unsuccessful and in a memorandum issued that day the President set forth his determination to stand on the Fourteen Points in the Austrian treaty while reasserting the proposal to make Fiume an autonomous international port.[16] Wilson's experts advised him on April 17 that the only just solution was to make Fiume an integral part of Yugoslavia. "If Italy gets even nominal sovereignty over Fiume as the price of supporting the League of Nations," they averred, "she has brought the League down to her level. It becomes a coalition to maintain an unjust settlement."[17] Wilson told his American associates on April 18 that Italy "could not have Fiume with his consent and that he would not recognize the Treaty of London."[18]

The basic positions of both the United States and Great Britain in regard to the Italian claims were set forth with great clarity in the discussion in the Council of Four on April 19. President Wilson declared that "it was not reasonable . . . to have one basis of peace with Germany and another set of principles for the peace with Austria-Hungary, Bulgaria, and Turkey." The nations, said Wilson, were trying "to make peace on an entirely new basis and to establish a new order of international relations. At every point the question had to be asked whether the lines of the settlement would square with the new order." He acceded to Italy's demand for her "natural" borders, including Trieste and the Istrian peninsula. But to give Fiume to Italy, said the President, "would be absolutely inconsistent with the new order of international relations." As to Italy's strategic need for Dalmatia, Wilson asserted that it had been rendered obsolete by the new system of the League of Nations. Clemenceau pointed out that while Britain and France were bound by the Treaty of London to support Italy's Dalmatian claims, they were not

[15] Council of Four, April 13, 1919, 6 p.m., Mantoux, *Les Délibérations du Conseil des Quatre*, Vol. I, pp. 244-245.
[16] Baker, *Wilson and World Settlement*, Vol. 3, pp. 274-277; Albrecht-Carrié, *Italy at the Paris Peace Conference*, pp. 445-447.
[17] Baker, *Wilson and World Settlement*, Vol. 3, pp. 278-280.
[18] *ibid.*, Vol. 2, p. 154.

so bound as to Fiume. Italy, said Clemenceau, could not uphold one part of that treaty and repudiate another. Lloyd George endorsed the views of Clemenceau. He acknowledged the "strength of President Wilson's arguments," but, he averred, "if we felt scruples about the Italian claims, they should have been expressed before Italy lost half a million gallant lives." Lloyd George said that Great Britain "stood by the treaty, but she stood by the whole of the treaty." To give Fiume to Italy, said Lloyd George, would violate the Treaty of London and break faith with Serbia. President Wilson asserted that a settlement based on the Treaty of London "would draw the United States of America into an impossible situation."[19]

Orlando told the Council of Four on April 20 that if Fiume were denied to Italy the Italian people would be aroused to the most violent explosion. But, he said, if the Peace Conference guaranteed to Italy all of her rights under the Treaty of London, he would not be obliged to break the Alliance. Wilson declared the Italian position "incredible." He admitted that Italy was not legally bound by the Fourteen Points as to Austria, but he refused to make peace with Germany on one set of principles and with Austria on another. The Italian attitude, he repeated, was "incredible." Lloyd George "regretted that the Supreme Council found itself confronted with the most difficult situation that had faced it since the beginning of the Conference." Lloyd George suggested a separate meeting of the parties to the Treaty of London, "to consider President Wilson's grave decision." But if Italy refused to modify her stand, Lloyd George warned, he was "bound to take his stand by his bond."[20]

The British, French, and Italian Premiers and Foreign Ministers conferred on the morning of April 21. Lloyd George warned that it would be a grave thing indeed if the United States refused to sign the Austrian treaty. He feared that the populations of eastern Europe would be encouraged to agitation in the belief that the

[19] Council of Four, April 19, 1919, 11 a.m., *Foreign Relations, 1919, The Paris Peace Conference*, Vol. 5, pp. 84-93; Lloyd George, *The Truth about the Peace Treaties*, Vol. 2, pp. 812-818; Baker, *Wilson and World Settlement*, Vol. 2, pp. 156-164.

[20] Council of Four, April 20, 1919, 10 a.m., *Foreign Relations, 1919, The Paris Peace Conference*, Vol. 5, pp. 95-100; Lloyd George, *The Truth about the Peace Treaties*, Vol. 2, pp. 820-822.

United States was behind them and that Europe could not recover economically "if the United States does not put oil in the machine." He said that President Wilson had come closer to European views than had been thought possible on such issues as reparations and the Saar and that if at all possible, therefore, concessions should be made to the President in regard to the Italian claims. But under any circumstances, Lloyd George maintained, Great Britain would honor the Treaty of London if Italy required it. Orlando and Sonnino were unmovable, warning of revolution in Italy if Wilson's views were allowed to prevail. "In that case," said Lloyd George, "I see no hope. For, on Fiume, I am in agreement with President Wilson. The pact of London I uphold absolutely. But the pact of London stated that Fiume would be given to the Serbs. . . . We can no more break our word to them than to you." Clemenceau endorsed the views of Lloyd George, but the Italians remained intransigent and the meeting ended without agreement.[21]

In the afternoon meeting of the Supreme Council of April 21, President Wilson indicated that he might issue a public statement on the Italian claims. Lloyd George and Clemenceau appealed to him not to do so, warning that a public declaration would make it impossible for Italy to recede from her demands, and the President agreed not to publish a statement "immediately."[22] Orlando was absent from the Council on the next day and the President again proposed to publish a statement, contending that after the initial inflammation the Italian people would see that it was better to cooperate with the United States than to stand on the Treaty of London. Lloyd George prevailed upon Wilson to delay once again while he conferred privately with Orlando on the free city proposal.[23] Lloyd George reported the failure of this effort to Wilson and Clemenceau on the morning of April 23 and Wilson

[21] Conference of British, French, and Italian Premiers and Foreign Ministers, April 21, 1919, 10 a.m., Mantoux, *Les Délibérations du Conseil des Quatre*, Vol. 1, pp. 300-306; Lloyd George, *The Truth about the Peace Treaties*, Vol. 2, pp. 822-825.
[22] Council of Four, April 21, 1919, 4 p.m., *Foreign Relations, 1919, The Paris Peace Conference*, Vol. 5, p. 109.
[23] Council of Four, April 22, 1919, 4 p.m., *ibid.*, pp. 136-137; Lloyd George, *The Truth about the Peace Treaties*, Vol. 2, pp. 825-827.

[322]

declared that he would publish his statement that evening. Lloyd George then presented a communication, drafted by Balfour, which he and Clemenceau proposed to send to Orlando.[24]

The Lloyd George-Clemenceau letter, handed to Orlando on the next day, expressed regret at Italy's severance from the Allies. It asserted that the conditions which had given rise to the Treaty of London in 1915 were, by November 1918, "profoundly changed," and that a lasting peace required boundaries resting on the consent of the populations concerned. As to Fiume, the two Premiers affirmed: "The Pact of 1915 is against the Italian contention; and so also, it seems to us, are justice and policy." The letter concluded with an appeal to Italy not to break with her Allies.[25]

President Wilson released his public statement on the evening of April 23 and it appeared in the Paris papers on the morning of the 24th. Since the signing of the Treaty of London, the statement declared, "the whole face of circumstances has been altered." Other powers had entered the war with no knowledge of the existence of that treaty and Austria-Hungary no longer existed. The peace with Germany, said the President, was based on certain principles, and "principles of another kind" could not be applied to Austria and the Balkan states. If the agreed principles of the peace were to be adhered to, Fiume could not be assigned to Italy. Along with the other Great Powers, the statement affirmed, Italy had become "one of the chief trustees of the new order," and in addition had achieved her natural frontiers. "It is within her choice to be surrounded by friends; to exhibit to the newly liberated peoples across the Adriatic that noblest quality of greatness, magnanimity, friendly generosity, the preference of justice over interest." America, the President explained, having initiated the peace, was under the "compulsion" to square every decision with the principles on which it had been made.[26]

---

[24] Council of Four, April 23, 1919, 11 a.m., *Foreign Relations, 1919, The Paris Peace Conference*, Vol. 5, pp. 149-150.

[25] Memorandum by Lloyd George and Clemenceau, April 23, 1919, "Fiume and the Peace Settlement," *ibid.*, pp. 223-227; Lloyd George, *The Truth about the Peace Treaties*, Vol. 2, pp. 829-836; Baker, *Wilson and World Settlement*, Vol. 3, pp. 281-286.

[26] "Statement of President Wilson regarding the Disposition of Fiume," April 23, 1919, Baker, *Wilson and World Settlement*, Vol. 3, pp. 287-290; Albrecht-Carrié, *Italy at the Paris Peace Conference*, pp. 498-500; Lloyd George, *The Truth about the Peace Treaties*, Vol. 2, pp. 837-840.

President Wilson's pronouncement evoked a storm of Italian reaction. Orlando replied on April 24 with a rebuke to President Wilson for appealing to the Italian people over the head of their government—a procedure, he protested, "which, until now, has been used only against enemy governments. . . ." Orlando adamantly maintained that the aspirations of Italy were solidly based on "reason and justice" and that the principle of self-determination established the right of Italy to both Fiume and the Dalmatian coast.[27]

Lloyd George told Wilson and Clemenceau on the morning of April 24 that he had already conferred with Orlando since the President issued his statement and that the Italian Premier had intimated his desire for a statement by Lloyd George and Clemenceau requesting him not to leave the Peace Conference. Wilson objected to this proposal, observing that there was a growing impression that the United States was divided from the Allies. Wilson said that he would be pleased, however, if Orlando would delay his departure, and it was agreed that Lloyd George would convey such a request to Orlando.[28]

Orlando acceded to Lloyd George's appeal, and the four heads of government met late in the afternoon of April 24 at Lloyd George's residence. Orlando told his colleagues that Wilson's statement had made it necessary for him to return to Rome to establish his position before Parliament. Wilson explained that his statement had not been meant as an appeal over Orlando's head but was designed to clarify his position as reported in the French and Italian press. Lloyd George appealed to Orlando to accept the free city proposal for Fiume in return for concessions on Italy's claims in Dalmatia. Wilson said that he accepted the free city plan but must reserve judgment on any concessions regarding Dalmatia. Various compromise proposals were explored without result, and Lloyd George finally complained that he was "in his usual disagreeable role of trying to effect a conciliation when both

[27] Statement by Orlando, April 24, 1919, Baker, *Wilson and World Settlement*, Vol. 3, pp. 291-295; Albrecht-Carrié, *Italy at the Paris Peace Conference*, pp. 501-504; Lloyd George, *The Truth about the Peace Treaties*, Vol. 2, pp. 840-845.

[28] Council of Four, April 24, 1919, 11 a.m., *Foreign Relations, 1919, The Paris Peace Conference*, Vol. 5, pp. 202-203; Lloyd George, *The Truth about the Peace Treaties*, Vol. 2, p. 846.

sides were inclined to refute him." Wilson rejected the idea of the Council's formulating a proposal for Orlando to present to the Italian Parliament. He thought that Orlando should explain to his Parliament that "Great Britain and France were bound by the pact and the United States by principles," and should ask for general authority to make the best settlement he could. Lloyd George insisted that a compromise should be reached then and there. Wilson said that he would agree to anything that was consistent with his principles but had no proposals to make. Lloyd George began a petulant comment on the President's refusal to entertain concrete proposals when Orlando announced that he must leave to catch his train. As Orlando departed, Maurice Hankey handed him the letter which Lloyd George and Clemenceau had drawn up the previous day.[29]

Wilson's public appeal of April 23 was generally but by no means universally deplored by British opinion. The *London Morning Post* called it "wild-west diplomacy."[30] But British liberal opinion was enthusiastic. Harold Nicolson wrote in his diary on April 27 that if Wilson "sticks to his guns, all will be well. We are overjoyed."[31] A group of British labor leaders sent a telegram of congratulation to the President and one to Lloyd George urging him to support Wilson.[32] Such support, however, was scattered and Lloyd George and Clemenceau seemed content to let Wilson bear in isolation the onus for the Italian explosion. In the sessions of the Supreme Council during the absence of the Italians, President Wilson found himself increasingly isolated from the British and French, while Lloyd George grew increasingly irritated with the President's lofty intransigence.

[29] Council of Four, April 24, 1919, 4 p.m., *Foreign Relations, 1919, The Paris Peace Conference*, Vol. 5, pp. 210-222; Lloyd George, *The Truth about the Peace Treaties*, Vol. 2, pp. 847-855. See also Baker, *Wilson and World Settlement*, Vol. 2, pp. 172-174; Stephen Bonsal, *Suitors and Suppliants* (New York: Prentice-Hall, Inc., 1946), pp. 112-113.

[30] Quoted in Arthur Walworth, *Woodrow Wilson* (2 Vols., New York, London, Toronto: Longmans, Green and Company, 1958), Vol. 2, *World Prophet*, p. 311, n.10.

[31] Nicolson's Diary, April 27, 1919, Harold Nicolson, *Peacemaking 1919* (Boston and New York: Houghton Mifflin Company, 1933), p. 317.

[32] Carl F. Brand, "The Attitude of British Labor toward President Wilson during the Peace Conference," *The American Historical Review*, Vol. 42, No. 2 (January 1937), p. 249.

III. *Further Abortive Efforts to Settle the Fiume Controversy, May 2-June 28*

Clemenceau joined Wilson on May 2 in urging Lloyd George to agree to the publication of the letter that the two Premiers had handed to Orlando on the day of his departure. Wilson said that it had been understood in the discussion of April 23 that Lloyd George and Clemenceau were to publish something on the morning after Wilson issued his own statement. The President complained that the Anglo-French silence created the impression that the United States stood alone. Lloyd George said that he feared publication would drive the Italians to remain away, proposing that "the first thing was to patch up an arrangement with Italy if it could be patched up honorably." Wilson protested that the United States was "left in isolation" and insisted on the necessity for publication of the Lloyd George-Clemenceau letter, but the Prime Minister maintained that such action might lead to the fall of the Orlando Government and its replacement by an extreme nationalist cabinet.[33]

Wilson's reference to an understanding on April 23 for the publication of the Lloyd George-Clemenceau letter is not substantiated by the minutes of the Council for that day.[34] Ray Stannard Baker accepts the view that the President was led by the British and French to expect public support for his statement.[35] Colonel Bonsal records that House sent him on April 28 to Lloyd George's residence to inquire as to when public support would be given and that Lloyd George's secretaries implied that the Prime Minister had made such a promise but had decided not to honor it.[36] On the other hand, Maurice Hankey, who kept the English minutes, wrote to Arthur Walworth in 1953: "If there was any understanding, which I do not think there was, it must have been reached informally outside of the formal conversations."[37] It may

[33] Council of Four, May 2, 1919, 11 a.m., *Foreign Relations, 1919, The Paris Peace Conference*, Vol. 5, pp. 407-412; Lloyd George, *The Truth about the Peace Treaties*, Vol. 2, pp. 859-862; Baker, *Wilson and World Settlement*, Vol. 2, pp. 176-177.

[34] Council of Four, April 23, 1919, 11 a.m., *Foreign Relations, 1919, The Paris Peace Conference*, Vol. 5, pp. 149-150.

[35] Baker, *Wilson and World Settlement*, Vol. 2, p. 166.

[36] Bonsal, *Suitors and Suppliants*, pp. 110-111.

[37] Hankey to Walworth, December 24, 1953, Walworth, *Wilson*, Vol. 2, *World Prophet*, p. 311, n.9.

be that Lloyd George decided, when the Italians left Paris, to abandon a commitment to present a united front with Wilson against the Italians, but the evidence is inconclusive and it remains uncertain whether such a commitment was in fact made.

Lloyd George and Clemenceau on the morning of May 3 each offered drafts of a proposed message to Italy, the latter warning that Italy's absence from the presentation of the treaty of peace to Germany would constitute a violation of the provision of the Treaty of London against a separate peace by any of its signatories. Wilson refused to be a party to any invitation to Italy to return based on the Treaty of London. Such a communication, he said, would make the isolation of the United States more serious than ever. The President appealed again for the publication of the Lloyd George-Clemenceau letter of April 23, warning of a rift with the United States if it were not: "The effect of this would be that the United States' opinion would say: 'We will get out of this.'" Lloyd George replied that he now found it necessary to speak "very frankly." "It must not be forgotten," he affirmed, "that there was a growing feeling that Europe was being bullied by the United States of America." A rift, he warned, would "put an end to the League of Nations." Wilson demanded that Italy be shown that Britain, France, and the United States were united. Lloyd George replied that "in fact they were not completely united," owing to the commitment of Britain and France to the Treaty of London. The President asserted that the letter of April 23 demonstrated that the three were united "in judgment" if not "in position," but Lloyd George saw "no use being united in judgment when a decision was wanted." After some further recriminations over the merits and morals of the Treaty of London, Lloyd George declared: "If there must be a break, a break with Italy would be bad enough but not a disaster; a break with the United States would be a disaster." Nonetheless, Lloyd George still withheld his consent from the renewed appeal of both Wilson and Clemenceau for the publication of the letter of April 23.[38]

In the afternoon meeting of May 3, Lloyd George reported a heated interview with the Marquis Imperiali, who had accused

[38] Council of Four, May 3, 1919, 10 a.m., *Foreign Relations, 1919, The Paris Peace Conference*, Vol. 5, pp. 428-436; Lloyd George, *The Truth about the Peace Treaties*, Vol. 2, pp. 863-867; Baker, *Wilson and World Settlement*, Vol. 2, p. 179.

Britain and France of breaking the Treaty of London. Lloyd George said that he had replied: "Do you expect us to declare war on the United States?" Lloyd George had warned the Marquis, he said, that if the Italians did not attend the presentation of the treaty of peace to Germany, Britain and France would regard themselves as free of the Treaty of London, and that the Italians were "under an entire delusion" if they thought they could have Fiume. President Wilson said that no offer should be made to Italy, contending that the Italian refusal to yield Fiume in itself liberated Britain and France from the Treaty of London.[39] Although no communication was sent to the Italians, word was received on May 5 that Orlando and Sonnino were returning in time for the presentation of the treaty to Germany.[40]

When the Italians returned, Lloyd George's efforts to "patch up an arrangement" took a new turn. He now proposed to buy off the Italian demand for Fiume by major concessions to Italian ambitions in Asia Minor. Reports had been received of mounting Italian military activities in Asia Minor, including the dispatch of seven battleships to Smyrna and agitation inciting the Turks against Greeks in the Smyrna area.[41] Lloyd George at first proposed strong measures against the Italians in Asia Minor, winning the consent of Wilson and Clemenceau on May 6 to the dispatch of Greek forces to occupy the Smyrna region.[42] It was agreed on May 11 and 12 that an Anglo-French fleet would be dispatched to Smyrna and landing parties put ashore to supplement the Greek forces and that the Italians would be permitted to land no greater forces than either the British or French.[43]

[39] Council of Four, May 3, 1919, 4 p.m., *Foreign Relations, 1919, The Paris Peace Conference*, Vol. 5, pp. 452-457; Lloyd George, *The Truth about the Peace Treaties*, Vol. 2, pp. 869-870.

[40] Council of Four, May 5, 1919, 11 a.m., *Foreign Relations, 1919, The Paris Peace Conference*, Vol. 5, p. 465.

[41] Council of Four, May 2, 1919, 11 a.m., *ibid.*, pp. 412-413; Council of Four, May 5, 1919, 11 a.m., *ibid.*, pp. 465-468; Lloyd George, *The Truth about the Peace Treaties*, Vol. 2, pp. 871-872.

[42] Council of Four, May 6, 1919, 11 a.m., *Foreign Relations, 1919, The Paris Peace Conference*, Vol. 5, pp. 483-484.

[43] Council of Four, May 11, 1919, 12 noon, Mantoux, *Les Délibérations du Conseil des Quatre*, Vol. 2, pp. 40-44; Baker, *Wilson and World Settlement*, Vol. 2, pp. 192-194; Council of Four, May 12, 1919, 3:30 p.m., *Foreign Relations, 1919, The Paris Peace Conference*, Vol. 5, pp. 577-578.

President Wilson submitted a new plan on May 13, prepared by his experts, calling for plebiscites in Dalmatia and Fiume, with Italy, if she won the latter, to build port facilities for Yugoslavia at the Dalmatian town of Buccari. Lloyd George, however, now set forth a whole new concept of the Italian case. The attitude of the Italians, he said, sprang from a feeling of being treated as less than a first-class power. Their national pride had been hurt at not being asked to assist in the tutelage of backward peoples. Could not Italy, asked Lloyd George, play such a role in Asia Minor? He felt that "the whole frame of mind of the Italian representatives would change if the questions could be discussed as a whole." Specifically, he proposed that the United States be given mandates for Armenia and Constantinople, France for northern Anatolia, and Italy for southern Anatolia, with the Smyrna region to be annexed by Greece. Italy might also be given a role in Somaliland. President Wilson was not ill-disposed toward this plan, favoring only a larger area to be annexed by Greece than proposed by Lloyd George.[44] On May 14, Lloyd George presented a comprehensive plan for the partition of Turkey along the lines of his proposals of the previous day. It was agreed that Italy would be offered a mandate for southern Anatolia.[45]

Lloyd George abandoned his grand design for appeasing Italy in Asia Minor as rapidly as he had conceived it. On the morning of May 17, Lloyd George presented a memorandum on Italy and Asia Minor. The new British plan, drawn up by Balfour, rejected the mandates scheme of May 13 and called for a unified independent Turkey with a special economic sphere of influence for Italy in southern Anatolia. Balfour admitted candidly that the scheme was a bad one, "but the whole plan is primarily devised in order to do something to satisfy Italian appetites. . . ." "From an administrative point of view," Balfour asserted, "the scheme would no doubt be much better if the Italians played no part in it. I freely admit it—but I submit that the argument is irrelevant. The Italians must somehow be mollified, and the only question is

[44] Council of Four, May 13, 1919, 4 p.m., *ibid.*, pp. 579-587; Lloyd George, *The Truth about the Peace Treaties,* Vol. 2, pp. 873-876; Baker, *Wilson and World Settlement,* Vol. 2, pp. 185-191.

[45] Council of Four, May 14, 1919, 4 p.m., *Foreign Relations, 1919, The Paris Peace Conference,* Vol. 5, pp. 614-623.

how to mollify them at the smallest cost to mankind."[46] Lloyd George contended, in support of the Balfour proposals, that the entire Moslem world would be aroused if Turkey were partitioned.[47] Lloyd George brought a delegation of Indian Moslems to the afternoon session on May 17, including the Aga Khan, who appealed for the territorial integrity of Turkey.[48]

Thus pressed by the Moslems within the British Empire delegation, Lloyd George now reversed tactics altogether and undertook to buy the Italians out of Asia Minor by yielding on Fiume. He reported to the Supreme Council on May 19 a conversation with Orlando of the previous day, in which Lloyd George had rejected a demand for an Italian mandate over the whole of Anatolia. "At last," Lloyd George related, Orlando "let out that he really did not care a scrap about Asia Minor if he could get Fiume." "At the risk of appearing to vacillate," Lloyd George said, he "would like to reconsider the provisional decision already taken." Because of the attitude of the Moslem world, he thought that the Italians should be out of Asia Minor altogether. President Wilson observed that he "did not in the least mind vacillating, provided the solution reached was the right one." Wilson agreed that the sovereignty of Turkey should be preserved, but that question, he noted, brought back the problem of Fiume. Lloyd George then declared that "if the Italians could be got out of Asia Minor altogether it would . . . be worth giving them something they were specially concerned in, even if it involved the Allies swallowing their words." President Wilson replied that he "hoped that Mr. Lloyd George would not press this point of view." Wilson said that he was "bound to adhere to his principle that no peoples should be handed over to another rule without their consent." But Lloyd George pressed his new proposal with renewed vigor. "After all," he declared, "Fiume was a town with an Italian

[46] Memorandum by Balfour, May 16, 1919, "The Problem of Italy and Turkey in Anatolia," *Foreign Relations, 1919, The Paris Peace Conference*, Vol. 5, pp. 669-672; Baker, *Wilson and World Settlement*, Vol. 3, pp. 303-307; Albrecht-Carrié, *Italy at the Paris Peace Conference*, pp. 526-529.

[47] Council of Four, May 17, 11 a.m., *Foreign Relations, 1919, The Paris Peace Conference*, Vol. 5, p. 669.

[48] Council of Four, May 17, 1919, 4:15 p.m., *ibid.*, pp. 688-701; Baker, *Wilson and World Settlement*, Vol. 2, p. 198.

flavor and an Italian name." He felt sure that if the Italians built another harbor for the Yugoslavs, they would consent to give up Fiume. Lloyd George stressed again the importance of getting the Italians out of Asia Minor.[49]

Lloyd George submitted a new memorandum on May 21 calling for the establishment of Italian sovereignty over Fiume on condition that Italy first constructed a port for Yugoslavia, warning again of the effects which the partition of Turkey would have upon the Moslem world. Wilson said that he saw "certain inconsistencies" in Lloyd George's proposed application of the principle of consent of peoples to Turkey but not to Yugoslavia. Wilson favored the maintenance of Fiume as a free port until Italy built port facilities for Yugoslavia at Buccari. Then there might be *plebiscites* in Fiume and Dalmatia.[50]

In late May and during the month of June, nothing further was heard of Asia Minor in connection with the Italian claims, but despite the continued efforts of Lloyd George, the deadlock between the Italian demand for Fiume and Wilson's defense of the principle of self-determination remained unbroken. On May 26, Orlando asserted that if agreement could not be reached he would stand on the Treaty of London, and Wilson observed that the Council was "getting into a cul-de-sac." If Italy insisted on the Treaty of London, he said, "she would strike at the roots of the new system and undermine the new order."[51] On May 28, the Council considered a plan submitted by Colonel House and André Tardieu to establish a free state of Fiume and its surrounding territories under the League of Nations, with a plebiscite to be held in fifteen years.[52] Wilson agreed to this proposal on condition that it was acceptable to Yugoslavia.[53] Having received qualified Yugoslav acceptance, Wilson handed Orlando a memo-

[49] Council of Four, May 19, 1919, 11:30 a.m., *Foreign Relations, 1919, The Paris Peace Conference*, Vol. 5, pp. 707-711; Baker, *Wilson and World Settlement*, Vol. 2, pp. 199-201.

[50] Council of Four, May 21, 1919, 11 a.m., *Foreign Relations, 1919, The Paris Peace Conference*, Vol. 5, pp. 756-759, 769-770.

[51] Council of Four, May 26, 1919, 4:15 p.m., *ibid.*, Vol. 6, pp. 47-49; Lloyd George, *The Truth about the Peace Treaties*, Vol. 2, pp. 879-881.

[52] Council of Four, May 28, 1919, 11 a.m., *Foreign Relations, 1919, The Paris Peace Conference*, Vol. 6, pp. 78-81.

[53] Council of Four, May 28, 1919, 4 p.m., *ibid.*, p. 90.

randum on June 7 on behalf of Lloyd George, Clemenceau, and himself, calling for a free state of Fiume and its surrounding territories. The free state was to be self-governing under the superintendence of a commission of the League of Nations, and there was to be a plebiscite in five years.[54] Wilson represented this plan as the extreme concession of the United States to the difficulties imposed upon Great Britain and France by the Treaty of London. Orlando found it unacceptable.[55]

Owing to its failure to secure Fiume, the Orlando Government fell on June 21. President Wilson on June 26 called the attention of the Council to the fact that the new Nitti Government was continuing to land troops in Asia Minor and asserted that Italy was threatening to "place herself outside the law." Lloyd George agreed that the policy of the Italian Government was "madness."[56] In their final meeting on June 28, Wilson, Lloyd George, and Clemenceau agreed to send memoranda to the new Italian delegation remonstrating against Italy's policies and demanding a total resurvey of the Italian claims.[57]

The futile negotiations concerning the Italian claims were continued through the final stages of the Peace Conference.[58] The major negotiations, during April and May, were marked by an almost total absence of common Anglo-American policy, a disharmony which cannot be explained solely by the commitment of Great Britain under the Treaty of London, for on the central issue, Fiume, Britain was under no obligation to Italy. The differences in the American and British approaches lay, fundamentally, in the altogether different degrees of importance which Wilson and Lloyd George attached to the disposition of Fiume. To the President, it represented an unambiguous test of the agreed principles of the peace, an issue on which, after many compromises on more important questions, he chose to take an uncompromising stand. The President was as flexible as his principles would allow, agreeing to a free city status for Fiume and even to Italian annexation if a plebiscite so decided. To Lloyd

[54] "Memorandum as to a Suggested Basis for Settlement of the Adriatic Question," June 7, 1919, *ibid.*, pp. 249-251.
[55] Council of Four, June 7, 1919, 4 p.m., *ibid.*, pp. 244-245.
[56] Council of Four, June 26, 1919, 4 p.m., *ibid.*, pp. 712-714.
[57] Council of Four, June 28, 1919, 6 p.m., *ibid.*, pp. 759-762.
[58] See Chapter 14, Section II.

George, on the other hand, Fiume was vexatious, trivial, and expendable. He was opposed to Italian annexation of Fiume on principle, but the principle involved was far from his supreme concern. Lloyd George was concerned to avoid a break with the Italians, to appease the pressures within the British Empire in regard to Turkey, and, above all, to find almost any solution which would not alienate the United States.

IV. *The Shantung Controversy*

In 1898, Germany forced upon China a convention leasing the area surrounding Kiaochow Bay in the province of Shantung to German administration for ninety-nine years and giving Germany special railroad and mining rights in the rest of Shantung. On August 15, 1914, Japan delivered an ultimatum to Germany demanding the unconditional transfer of the leased territory to Japan, with a view to its ultimate restoration to China. Upon the expiration of this ultimatum on August 23, 1914, Japan declared war on Germany and rapidly occupied Kiaochow and the Shantung railway. On January 18, 1915, Japan presented its Twenty-One Demands to China, which required Chinese consent in advance to any ultimate arrangement between Japan and Germany regarding the German rights in Shantung and which contained other provisions for the recognition of preeminent Japanese interests in Manchuria and northern China. The United States protested the incursions upon Chinese sovereignty in the Twenty-One Demands and unsuccessfully asked the European Entente Powers to join in representations to Japan.[59] In a treaty with Japan signed on May 25, 1915, China consented in advance to any arrangements which Japan might make with Germany concerning the disposition of the German rights in Shantung.[60]

In February 1917, it will be recalled, formal agreements were concluded between Japan and Britain, France and Russia which bound the European Allies to support at the Peace Conference Japanese claims to the German rights in Shantung and to the Ger-

[59] Russell H. Fifield, *Woodrow Wilson and the Far East* (New York: Thomas Y. Crowell Company, 1952), pp. 3-48.

[60] Edward Parkes, ed., *British and Foreign State Papers, 1916* (London: His Majesty's Stationery Office, 1920), pp. 791-792. Ratifications of this treaty were exchanged at Tokyo on June 8, 1915.

man islands of the North Pacific.[61] Lloyd George explained these agreements quite frankly on grounds of military necessity. He told the Council of Four on April 22, 1919, that in January 1917 Britain had urgently requested Japanese naval support in the Mediterranean, that Japan had made her assistance contingent upon these arrangements, and that the Allies, being hard pressed, had therefore agreed.[62]

The Japanese Government sent Viscount Ishii on a special mission to Washington in June 1917 for the purpose of securing some American recognition of the special position of Japan in relation to China. President Wilson and Secretary Lansing refused to recognize Japanese interests in China as paramount, and in the resulting Lansing-Ishii agreement, embodied in an exchange of notes on November 2, 1917, the United States recognized that Japan had "special interests" in China based on territorial propinquity and the two Governments denied any purpose to infringe upon the independence or territorial integrity of China and agreed to uphold the policy of the "open door," declaring also their opposition to the acquisition by any government of special rights which would affect Chinese independence or territorial integrity.[63] The Lansing-Ishii agreement had little effect on Japanese policy in China. On September 24, 1918, secret notes were exchanged between China and Japan conceding various Japanese privileges in Shantung, including police functions, joint Sino-Japanese management of the Kiaochow-Tsinan railroad, and concessions for new railroads to be built by Japan in Manchuria and Mongolia as well as in Shantung.[64] Japan thus came to the Peace Conference fortified in her demands by valid international legal engagements as well as by her position as the dominant military power of the Far East. Moreover, Japan was in possession of Shantung.

In contrast to the strong legal case of Japan, China came to the

[61] See Chapter 3, Section v.

[62] Council of Four, April 22, 1919, 4:30 p.m., *Foreign Relations, 1919, The Paris Peace Conference*, Vol. 5, p. 139.

[63] Carnegie Endowment for International Peace, John V. A. MacMurray, ed., *Treaties and Agreements with and Concerning China, 1894-1919* (2 Vols., New York: Oxford University Press, 1921), Vol. 2, pp. 1394-1396. See Fifield, *Wilson and the Far East*, pp. 79-84; Roy Watson Curry, *Woodrow Wilson and Far Eastern Policy, 1913-1921* (New York: Bookman Associates, 1957), pp. 176-179.

[64] MacMurray, ed., *Treaties and Agreements with and Concerning China, 1894-1919*, Vol. 2, pp. 1445-1446. See Fifield, *Wilson and the Far East*, pp. 109-119.

Peace Conference with a strong political and moral case for the restoration of Shantung. The greatest asset of the Chinese was the sympathy and support of the United States, while Great Britain and France were legally bound to support Japan. Chinese strategy was to proclaim the justice of their case while depending upon President Wilson to insure its success.[65] The Japanese presented their claims to the Council of Ten on January 27, demanding the unconditional cession of Kiaochow and all German rights in Shantung.[66] V. K. Wellington Koo presented China's case to the Council of Ten on the next day, asking for the direct restoration to China of the leased territory of Kiaochow and all other German rights in Shantung.[67]

The Shantung question was not taken up seriously by the Supreme Council until mid-April. On April 15, President Wilson declared his sympathy for the Chinese claim for direct restitution. Balfour reminded the President that Great Britain was committed to support Japan and, in any case, he saw no objection to the German rights being ceded to Japan, who would then hand them over to China. It was, Balfour said, a matter of "national pride."[68] Wilson suggested on April 18 that Britain, France, and the United States could more readily counsel generosity to Japan if they renounced their own zones of influence in China. Lloyd George thought that such renunciation would be acceptable to British opinion provided that the policy of the "open door" was maintained.[69]

The critical period in the Shantung negotiations was April 21 to April 30. In these debates, President Wilson was motivated by his deep sympathy for China's claim to Shantung, while Lloyd George was guided by the obligations of Great Britain under the secret agreements of February 1917, and by the broader obligations of the Anglo-Japanese Alliance of 1902.

Wilson conferred with Baron Makino and Viscount Chinda on the morning of April 21 and reported to Lloyd George and

[65] See *ibid.*, pp. 174-194; Ge-Zay Wood, *The Shantung Question* (New York and Chicago: Fleming H. Revell Company, 1922), pp. 102-149.

[66] Council of Ten, January 27, 1919, 3 p.m., *Foreign Relations, 1919, The Paris Peace Conference*, Vol. 3, pp. 738-740.

[67] Council of Ten, January 28, 1919, 11 a.m., *ibid.*, pp. 754-757.

[68] Council of Four, April 15, 1919, 11 a.m., Mantoux, *Les Délibérations du Conseil des Quatre*, Vol. 1, p. 250.

[69] Council of Four, April 18, 1919, 11 a.m., *ibid.*, pp. 273-274.

Clemenceau that he had proposed that "all claims in the Pacific be ceded to the Allied and Associated Powers as trustees, leaving them to make fair and just dispositions." Wilson said that the Japanese had been "very stiff" about this proposal and had insisted that the powers yield the German rights in Shantung to Japan and trust her to yield them in turn to China. Lloyd George suggested that Kiaochow be ceded to the League of Nations, but Wilson thought that the Japanese would be "too proud" to accept a League solution but might consent to give up their spheres in China if all other powers would do so.[70]

Baron Makino, in the Council on the morning of April 22, stressed the legal obligations of China under the 1915 and 1918 treaties, arguing that China's declaration of war on Germany did not legally abrogate the German lease. Lloyd George noted that Britain had a "definite engagement with Japan," but suggested that the disposition of Shantung, like the assignment of mandates, be deferred and that the treaty merely stipulate Germany's renunciation of her rights in Shantung. Viscount Chinda refused to consider a postponement and threatened not to sign the treaty if Japanese wishes were not met. President Wilson observed that, "as has happened in many instances, he was the only one present whose judgment was entirely independent. His colleagues were both bound by treaties, although perhaps he might be entitled to question whether Great Britain and Japan had been justified in handing round the islands of the Pacific. This, however, was a private opinion." The President said that he feared that Japan, by standing on the treaties, was "thinking more of her rights than of her duties to China." He recommended that Kiaochow be ceded to the Allied and Associated Powers as trustees to advise on how the treaties could best be carried out. Although he "did not wish to interfere with treaties," Wilson averred, "there were cases he felt where treaties ought not to have been entered into." The Japanese were unmoved by the President's appeal.[71]

In the afternoon session of April 22, Lloyd George explained

[70] Council of Four, April 21, 1919, 4 p.m., *Foreign Relations, 1919, The Paris Peace Conference*, Vol. 5, pp. 109-111; Baker, *Wilson and World Settlement*, Vol. 2, pp. 247-249.

[71] Council of Four, April 22, 1919, 11:30 a.m., *Foreign Relations, 1919, The Paris Peace Conference*, Vol. 5, pp. 125-133; Baker, *Wilson and World Settlement*, Vol. 2, pp. 249-252; Seymour, ed., *Intimate Papers*, Vol. 4, pp. 450-451.

how military necessity had compelled Great Britain to accept the obligation to support the Japanese claims, and President Wilson conceded that Britain, France, Japan, and China were all bound to honor their treaty engagements, "because the war had largely been fought for the purpose of showing that treaties could not be violated." The President said that there were doubts as to the validity of the Sino-Japanese agreements, but none as to the British and French engagements. Lloyd George lectured Wellington Koo that it would ill serve China "to regard treaties as von Bethmann Hollweg had regarded them, as mere scraps of paper to be turned down when they were not wanted." Surprisingly, President Wilson allowed at the end of the discussion that the British and French agreements with Japan were "instruments for the salvation of China."[72]

Beset by the pressure of the other events, the President began to yield. The Fiume crisis was at its climax; the Belgians were disaffected; and the presentation of the treaty to Germany was imminent. Wilson genuinely feared for the League of Nations if the Japanese were thwarted in their demands. "They are not bluffers," he told Baker, "and they will go home unless we give them what they should not have."[73] In a conference on the evening of April 22 with Baker and E. T. Williams, the American Technical Adviser on Far Eastern Affairs, Wilson said that the war "had been one in a large measure to enforce respect for treaties and that while there were some treaties that were unconscionable in character, it was a question whether these too ought not to be enforced." Williams asked if the President included treaties exacted by force.[74]

As between the alternatives of Japanese acquisition of German rights, to which Britain and France were committed by the agreements of 1917, and the execution of the Sino-Japanese treaties of 1915 and 1918, a committee of British, French, and American

[72] Council of Four, April 22, 1919, 4:30 p.m., *Foreign Relations, 1919, The Paris Peace Conference*, Vol. 5, pp. 139-147; Baker, *Wilson and World Settlement*, Vol. 2, pp. 253-257.

[73] *ibid.*, p. 258.

[74] Testimony by Williams, August 22, 1919, *Hearings before the Committee on Foreign Relations, United States Senate, 66th Congress, First Session, on the Treaty of Peace with Germany*, Document No. 106 (Washington: United States Government Printing Office, 1919), pp. 621-622.

experts, in a report to the Council of Four on April 24, recommended the former as the lesser incursion on Chinese sovereignty.[75] Williams, however, the American member of the committee, wrote a separate letter to the President urging the rejection of both alternatives.[76] The Council of Four received a Chinese statement on April 25 which declared both alternatives unacceptable. Wilson asked Lloyd George and Clemenceau if they were "bound to transfer Kiaochow and Shantung to Japan," and Lloyd George replied that they were, but that "we should like to talk over the terms on which Japan would hand them back to China." Wilson noted that the Japanese had indicated a willingness to discuss a general renunciation of "unusual rights" in China. Lloyd George replied that Britain "could not allow other nations to cooperate in the Yangtze Kiang. . . ." "The reason we could not do so," he said, "was because we should have to allow the Japanese in." It was agreed that the Japanese would be sounded as to their attitude before they came to the Council again.[77]

At the President's request, Secretary Lansing conferred with Viscount Chinda on April 26. The meeting was unsuccessful as Chinda told Lansing flatly that the Japanese delegates were instructed not to sign the treaty if the German rights were not transferred to Japan.[78] Balfour conferred with Makino and Chinda on April 26 and 27 and reached agreements which he submitted in a memorandum to the Council of Four on April 27. Balfour reported that the Japanese denied any intention of expanding the rights which Germany had exercised in Shantung and that they intended, moreover, to restore Chinese military and civil control in the leased territory, retaining only the right to guard the Shantung railway with Japanese troops during a brief transition period. The Japanese, said Balfour, wished to retain only economic rights, and even these would not exclude the commerce of other powers.[79]

---

[75] Report of Jean Gout, E. T. Williams, and Ronald Macleay, April 24, 1919, *Foreign Relations, 1919, The Paris Peace Conference*, Vol. 5, pp. 227-228.

[76] Williams to Wilson, April 24, 1919, Fifield, *Wilson and the Far East*, pp. 258-260.

[77] Council of Four, April 25, 1919, 6:30 p.m., *Foreign Relations, 1919, The Paris Peace Conference*, Vol. 5, pp. 245-250; Baker, *Wilson and World Settlement*, Vol. 2, pp. 259-260.

[78] *ibid.*, pp. 260-261; Fifield, *Wilson and the Far East*, pp. 264-265.

[79] Memorandum by Balfour, April 27, 1919, *Foreign Relations, 1919, The Paris Peace Conference*, Vol. 5, pp. 324-325; Baker, *Wilson and World Settlement*, Vol.

Lloyd George told the Council of Four on the morning of April 28 that the Japanese had agreed to the stipulations of the Balfour memorandum. President Wilson observed that while he did not consider these terms sufficiently explicit, they showed a more promising attitude on the part of the Japanese. Wilson said that there was nothing on which American public opinion was more firm "than on this question that China should not be oppressed by Japan." American opinion, he said, expected him to take the same line for Japan that he had taken for Italy. Balfour entered the Council at this point and reported that the Japanese demanded an immediate decision. Wilson said that he "could not possibly abandon China," but if the Japanese would reduce their claims to the German economic rights only, he would regard such terms as an improvement for China. Balfour assured the President that this was what the Japanese proposed. Wilson thereupon made his critical decision. He said that "if the Japanese would concede all military rights and make their agreement a purely economic one, he would agree to what they desired." It was agreed that Baron Makino would be invited to attend the meeting of the Council on the next day.[80] Wilson thus yielded under the pressures generated by the decision against Japan in regard to the racial clause in the Covenant, the Anglo-French commitments of 1917, the Sino-Japanese treaties of 1915 and 1918, and, most of all, the real threat of the Japanese to refuse to sign the treaty and thereby do perhaps mortal damage to the Covenant of the League of Nations.

Despite Wilson's concession in the morning session of the Council of Four, Lloyd George took Colonel House aside after the Plenary Session on April 28 and asked him to try to get the President "in a more amenable frame of mind." Lloyd George said that he and Balfour thought that Wilson was unfair to the Japanese, whose demands, in his view, were no worse than those of the other Allies.[81] House wrote to Wilson on April 29 urging

---

3, pp. 311-312. See also Blanche E. C. Dugdale, *Arthur James Balfour* (2 Vols., New York: G. P. Putnam's Sons, 1937), Vol. 2, p. 332.

[80] Council of Four, April 28, 1919, 11 a.m., *Foreign Relations, 1919, The Paris Peace Conference*, Vol. 5, pp. 316-318. See also Bonsal, *Suitors and Suppliants*, p. 237.

[81] House Diary, April 28, 1919, Seymour, ed., *Intimate Papers*, Vol. 4, pp. 451-452.

him to accept the assurances which Makino had given to Balfour: ". . . we had best clean up a lot of old rubbish with the least friction and let the League of Nations and the new era do the rest."[82] General Bliss wrote to Wilson on the same day, on behalf of Lansing, Henry White, and himself, urging the President not to "abandon the democracy of China to the domination of the Prussianized militarism of Japan."[83]

The meeting of the Council on April 29 was marked by a sharp exchange between Wilson and the Japanese as to the details of the Japanese rights to be exercised in Shantung, with the British supporting the President. Wilson and Balfour challenged the Japanese contention that their joint ownership of the Shantung railway with the Chinese would confer the right of extraterritoriality, and, with it, the right to police the railroad with Japanese troops. Balfour attempted to conciliate, asserting that the broad issue of restoring Chinese sovereignty was settled and that the remaining issues were only as to "temporary and transitional arrangements." But Lloyd George joined Wilson in opposing the policing of the railroad by Japanese troops.[84]

The Japanese conferred that evening and Balfour continued his mediation. The Japanese announced their formula for Shantung on April 30 and it was accepted by the Council of Four:

> The policy of Japan is to hand back the Shantung peninsula in full sovereignty to China retaining only the economic privileges granted to Germany and the right to establish a settlement under the usual conditions at Tsingtao.
>
> The owners of the railway will use special police only to ensure security for traffic. They will be used for no other purpose.
>
> The police force will consist of Chinese, and such Japanese instructors as the directors of the railway may select will be appointed by the Chinese Government.

[82] House to Wilson, April 29, 1919, *ibid.*, p. 454.

[83] Bliss to Wilson, April 29, 1919, Frederick Palmer, *Bliss, Peacemaker—The Life and Letters of General Tasker Howard Bliss* (New York: Dodd, Mead and Company, 1934), p. 393.

[84] Council of Four, April 29, 1919, 11 a.m., *Foreign Relations, 1919, The Paris Peace Conference*, Vol. 5, pp. 327-335.

The clause agreed upon for insertion in the Treaty of Versailles provided only for the unconditional surrender to Japan of all German rights in Shantung. President Wilson said that the Japanese representatives proposed to make public their declaration of policy by means of an interview. He "supposed he was at liberty to use the part of the declaration that most concerned him as he understood it." Baron Makino emphasized that no impression should be given that the declaration was anything but a voluntary expression of its policy on the part of the Japanese Government.[85]

Wilson told Baker that the settlement of April 30 was the "best that could be had out of a dirty past. . . ." "The only hope," he said, was "to keep the world together, get the League of Nations with Japan in it and then try to secure justice for the Chinese not only as regarding Japan but England, France, Russia, all of whom had concessions in China."[86] The President cabled a statement to Tumulty on April 30: "The Japanese-Chinese matter has been settled in a way which seems to me as satisfactory as could be got out of the tangle of treaties in which China herself was involved. . . . I regard the assurances given by Japan as very satisfactory in view of the complicated circumstances."[87]

The Chinese regarded themselves as betrayed by the Shantung decision. The Chinese representative formally protested the Shantung clause at the Plenary Session of May 6.[88] Paul S. Reinsch, the American Minister to China, resigned his post on June 7 with a protest against the Shantung settlement and a call for firm Anglo-American resistance to Japanese militarism.[89] The Council of Four received notification from the Chinese delegation on June 25 that they would sign the treaty with a reservation as to the Shantung clauses. Wilson thought that if it were merely a

[85] Council of Four, April 30, 1919, 12:30 p.m., *ibid.*, pp. 363-365, 367; Baker, *Wilson and World Settlement*, Vol. 2, pp. 263-265. See also Fifield, *Wilson and the Far East*, pp. 277-282; Curry, *Wilson and Far Eastern Policy*, p. 278.

[86] Baker, *Wilson and World Settlement*, Vol. 2, p. 266.

[87] Wilson to Tumulty, April 30, 1919, Ray Stannard Baker and William E. Dodd, eds., *The Public Papers of Woodrow Wilson* (6 Vols., New York and London: Harper & Brothers, Publishers, 1925-1927), *War and Peace*, Vol. 1, pp. 474-475; Joseph P. Tumulty, *Woodrow Wilson As I Know Him* (Garden City, New York, and Toronto: Doubleday, Page and Company, 1921), pp. 390-391.

[88] Plenary Session, May 6, 1919, *Foreign Relations, 1919, The Paris Peace Conference*, Vol. 3, p. 383.

[89] Fifield, *Wilson and the Far East*, p. 321.

"protest," they were entitled to make it.[90] The Council decided, however, that the Chinese might be permitted to protest only after signing the treaty.[91] The result was that China refused to sign the treaty and issued a statement to the press blaming the Four for her inability to sign and submitting her case to the "impartial judgment of the world."[92]

The chief factor in Wilson's acceptance of a solution of the Shantung controversy which clearly displeased him was the absence of British and French support for his defense of the rights and interests of China. While the French regarded Shantung as a "side show" and took little interest in its disposition, the British were deeply committed to support Japan, not only by the engagement of 1917, but by Japan's broader moral claim, deriving from the Anglo-Japanese Alliance of 1902 and from the naval assistance which Japan had provided during the war. Legally, politically, and morally, the British commitment to Japan was more binding than the obligation to Italy under the Treaty of London.[93]

Confronted with British opposition more intense than in the case of the Italian claims, the legal strength of the Japanese case, the fact of Japanese possession, and the danger that Japan would seriously damage the prospects of the League of Nations if her demands were denied, President Wilson had extremely limited diplomatic leverage in dealing with the Shantung affair. Although the outcry against the Shantung agreement was one of the principal factors in the defeat of the treaty by the United States Senate, the settlement was a substantial achievement for the President in the face of the Anglo-French obligations to Japan. "It was reached," Wilson told the Senate Committee on Foreign Relations, "because we thought it was the best that could be got, in view of the definite engagements of Great Britain and France, and the necessity of a unanimous decision. . . ."[94] Moreover, the Shantung

[90] Council of Four, June 25, 1919, 4 p.m., *Foreign Relations, 1919, The Paris Peace Conference*, Vol. 6, pp. 674-675.

[91] Council of Four, June 26, 1919, 4 p.m., *ibid.*, p. 710.

[92] Fifield, *Wilson and the Far East*, p. 332.

[93] *ibid.*, pp. 290-292.

[94] *Report of the Conference between Members of the Senate Committee on Foreign Relations and the President of the United States, at the White House, August 19, 1919, Treaty of Peace with Germany*, 66th Congress, First Session, Senate, Document No. 76 (Washington: United States Government Printing Office, 1919), p. 32.

settlement did not deny justice to China but deferred it. "Japan," the President pointed out in September 1919, "is under solemn promise to forego all sovereign rights in the province of Shantung and to retain only what private corporations have elsewhere in China. . . ."[95] It would seem, therefore, that the Shantung settlement was not a great miscarriage of justice as it has been so often described. It was, however, far short of the genuine satisfaction of Anglo-American as well as Chinese interests that might have been achieved if Great Britain had been able and willing to join the United States in a common stand against Japanese ambitions.

Both the Fiume and Shantung controversies set Great Britain and the United States largely against each other on issues in which their own unfettered interests would have united them against claims which clearly violated the principle of self-determination and, therefore, their own professed objectives. The wartime engagements which bound Britain to Italy and Japan to that extent separated her from the United States, with the result that both Italy and Japan had diplomatic leverage toward the realization of their expansionist aspirations which they could not possibly have exercised in the face of an Anglo-American entente.

[95] Speech at San Francisco, September 17, 1919, Baker and Dodd, eds., *Public Papers, War and Peace*, Vol. 2, p. 223.

CHAPTER 13

THE ANGLO-AMERICAN REACTION AGAINST
THE DRAFT TREATY AND LLOYD GEORGE'S
PROPOSALS FOR REVISION, MAY 7-JUNE 28

IN the weeks following the presentation of the draft treaty of peace to Germany early in May, members of the British and American delegations entertained second thoughts as to the wisdom and justice of many of the decisions which had been reached during the months of arduous negotiation. Among the British, these doubts reached the proportions of a rebellion against some of the most significant and painfully negotiated decisions of the Peace Conference. The draft treaty was criticized on grounds of both principle and expediency. There were those who regarded its provisions as constituting a Carthaginian peace, while others pointed to the danger that Germany would not sign, thereby necessitating an invasion and occupation of Germany by the rapidly shrinking Allied Armies. The latter considerations finally impelled Lloyd George, after the German counterproposals had been received, to make proposals for major alterations in the terms of peace. The result was a new crisis within the Peace Conference, in which President Wilson yielded with marked reluctance to the importunities of Lloyd George although the latter's proposals for liberalization of the peace terms were in great measure propositions for which the President had contended unsuccessfully in the earlier deliberations. The negotiations of early June placed Wilson and Lloyd George for the most part on the same side of each issue while revealing fundamental differences in the basic concepts with which the two leaders approached the problems of the peace. The result of the June rebellion was the incorporation of a few important concessions to Germany in the Treaty of Versailles.

I. The Presentation of the Draft Treaty and
Anglo-American Reactions, May 7-31

Clemenceau presented the draft treaty of peace to the German delegates in a ceremony in the Trianon Palace at Versailles on

May 7, stipulating that there were to be no oral negotiations but that the Germans might submit written observations for the consideration of the Allied and Associated Powers. The German Foreign Minister, Count Brockdorff-Rantzau, offended the proprieties by remaining seated while he delivered a sullen and defiant speech. "We cherish no illusions," he declared, "as to the extent of our defeat—the degree of our impotence. We know that the might of German arms is broken." Brockdorff-Rantzau vehemently denied the sole guilt of Germany for the war: ". . . such an admission on my lips would be a lie," and appealed to the principles of President Wilson as Germany's only ally.[1] Both Wilson and Lloyd George were offended by Brockdorff-Rantzau's speech and demeanor. "The Germans are really a stupid people," Wilson commented to Lord Riddell after the session. "They always do the wrong thing. . . ." "Those insolent Germans made me very angry yesterday," Lloyd George commented at golf on the next day. "I don't know when I have been more angry. . . ."[2]

While the Germans prepared their counterproposals in the weeks that followed, certain members of the British and American delegations began to register protests against what seemed to them the extreme harshness of the treaty as a whole. The "remorse complex" became especially pronounced among the British. Herbert Hoover, having received a copy of the treaty, encountered General Smuts and John Maynard Keynes early on the morning of May 7 walking in the streets of Paris: "It flashed through all our minds why each was walking about at that time of morning. Each was greatly disturbed. We agreed that the consequences of many parts of the proposed treaty would ultimately bring destruction. We also agreed that we would do what we could among our

[1] Plenary Session, May 7, 1919, Department of State, *Papers Relating to the Foreign Relations of the United States, 1919, The Paris Peace Conference* (13 Vols., Washington: United States Government Printing Office, 1942-1947), Vol. 3, pp. 415-420; hereafter referred to as *Foreign Relations*; David Lloyd George, *The Truth about the Peace Treaties* (2 Vols., London: Victor Gollancz, Ltd., 1938), Vol. 1, pp. 675-682; Ray Stannard Baker, *Woodrow Wilson and World Settlement* (3 Vols., Garden City, New York: Doubleday, Page and Company, 1922), Vol. 2, pp. 500-505. A good description of the work of the German delegation at the Peace Conference is contained in Alma Luckau's documentary history, *The German Delegation at the Paris Peace Conference* (New York: Columbia University Press, 1941), pp. 54-91.

[2] *Lord Riddell's Intimate Diary of the Peace Conference and After, 1918-1923* (New York: Reynal and Hitchcock, Inc., 1934), pp. 74, 76.

own nationals to point out the dangers. . . ."[3] In a memorandum written on May 8, Secretary of State Lansing expressed profound dissatisfaction with the treaty, describing even the League of Nations as an instrument for the suppression of the vanquished.[4] John Maynard Keynes suffered extreme emotional distress over the draft treaty of peace. He wrote to his wife on May 14: "I've never been so miserable as for the last two or three weeks; the peace is outrageous and impossible and can bring nothing but misfortune behind it. . . . Certainly if I was (*sic*) in the Germans' place I'd rather die than sign such a peace."[5] William C. Bullitt, perhaps disgruntled by the failure of the President to pay more respectful attention to his proposals on Russia,[6] submitted an impertinent letter to President Wilson on May 17 announcing his resignation as attaché to the American Commission: ". . . our government has consented now to deliver the suffering peoples of the world to new oppressions, subjections and dismemberments—a new century of war. . . . I am sorry that you did not fight our fight to the finish and that you had so little faith in the millions of men, like myself, in every nation who had faith in you."[7]

Harold Nicolson wrote to an unnamed correspondent on May 28: "I have been working like a little beaver to prevent the Austrian treaty from being as rotten as the German. The more I read the latter the sicker it makes me. . . . If I were the Germans I shouldn't sign for a moment."[8]

Among the former supporters of President Wilson who turned against him after the presentation of the treaty were the radicals of the British labor movement. In an article published in the *Labour Leader* on May 22, Philip Snowden of the Independent Labour Party denounced Wilson as a "broken reed . . . utterly discredited . . . the weakest and most incompetent person whom

[3] Herbert Hoover, *The Ordeal of Woodrow Wilson* (New York, Toronto, London: McGraw-Hill Book Company, Inc., 1958), p. 234.

[4] Robert Lansing, *The Peace Negotiations* (Boston and New York: Houghton Mifflin Company, 1921), pp. 272-274.

[5] Keynes to Mrs. Keynes, May 14, 1919, R. F. Harrod, *The Life of John Maynard Keynes* (London: Macmillan and Company, Ltd., 1951), p. 249.

[6] See Chapter 5, Section 11.

[7] Bullitt to Wilson, May 17, 1919, *Foreign Relations, 1919, The Paris Peace Conference*, Vol. 11, pp. 573-574.

[8] Harold Nicolson, *Peacemaking 1919* (Boston and New York: Houghton Mifflin Company, 1933), p. 350.

a malignant fate ever entrusted with the power to interfere in human affairs."[9]

Sir William Wiseman was also disturbed by the completed draft treaty. ". . . I am afraid, as it stands," he wrote to House on June 4 "it will not produce a lasting settlement." The peoples of the world were counting on a peace based on President Wilson's principles, Wiseman observed. "The world will hold him responsible if the treaty is found to be based on other principles."[10]

Among the leading figures of the Peace Conference, the most articulate dissenter from the draft treaty was General Smuts. He told House on May 16 that he and General Botha had almost decided not to sign the treaty unless liberal revisions were granted to Germany.[11] Smuts told a meeting of the British Empire delegation that he considered the treaty "such as to make future peace and goodwill in Europe unlikely. . . ." Under its terms, he declared, ". . . the fires will be kept burning and the pot will be kept boiling until it again boils over, either in a new war, or in the breakdown of the European system under the onslaught of social and industrial anarchy. . . ." Smuts appealed for revision of the clauses covering the occupation, reparations, the Saar, Germany's eastern frontiers, and the military and air terms.[12]

Smuts wrote to President Wilson on May 14: "The more I have studied the peace treaty as a whole, the more I dislike it. . . . Under this treaty Europe will know no peace; and the undertaking to defend Europe against aggression may at any time bring the British Empire into the fire. . . . I pray you will use your power and influence to make the final treaty a more moderate and reasonable document. . . ."[13]

In his reply to General Smuts, the President revealed his fundamental view that the principal criterion of the peace should be not

[9] Carl F. Brand, "The Attitude of British Labor toward President Wilson during the Peace Conference," *The American Historical Review*, Vol. 42, No. 2 (January 1937), pp. 251-252.

[10] Wiseman to House, June 4, 1919, Edward M. House Papers, Sterling Library, Yale University.

[11] House Diary, May 16, 1919, Charles Seymour, ed., *The Intimate Papers of Colonel House* (4 Vols., Boston and New York: Houghton Mifflin Company, 1926-1928), Vol. 4, pp. 466-467.

[12] Sarah Gertrude Millin, *General Smuts* (2 Vols., London: Faber and Faber, Ltd., 1936), Vol. 2, pp. 230-231.

[13] Smuts to Wilson, May 14, 1919, *ibid.*, pp. 231-232.

its harshness or liberality but its *justice*: ". . . The treaty is undoubtedly very severe indeed. I have of course had an opportunity to go over each part of it, as it was adopted, and I must say that though in many respects harsh, I do not think that it is on the whole unjust in the circumstances, much as I should have liked certain features altered. . . . I feel the terrible responsibility of the whole business, but inevitably my thought goes back to the very great offense against civilization which the German state committed and the necessity for making it evident once and for all that such things can lead only to the most severe punishment. . . ."[14]

Smuts fairly bombarded the President with his appeals. He wrote to Wilson again on May 22 calling for sweeping alterations in the clauses of the treaty relating to reparations and the eastern and western frontiers of Germany and calling for oral discussions with the Germans. Smuts appealed for a "Wilson peace" which "should not be capable of moral repudiation by the German people hereafter. . . ."[15]

The main effect of the Anglo-American criticisms of the draft treaty was not on President Wilson but on Lloyd George, who went into a panic lest the Germans refuse to sign the treaty. Wilson told Ray Stannard Baker that Lloyd George was in a "perfect funk."[16] In the Council of Four on May 29, Lloyd George declared that the whole question of the occupation of the Rhineland ought to be reconsidered, because, he averred, it "had been agreed to too readily." Despite objections on the part of Clemenceau, it was agreed that a commission would be constituted to rewrite the draft convention on the occupation of the Rhineland so as to guarantee minimum interference with the German civil administration.[17]

The formal German counterproposals were submitted to the Peace Conference on May 29. In this lengthy document, among many other proposals, the Germans protested the occupation and asked that all of the signatories to the treaty abolish conscription

[14] Wilson to Smuts, May 16, 1919, Woodrow Wilson Papers, Library of Congress, Washington, D.C., Series 8-A; Millin, *General Smuts*, Vol. 2, pp. 232-233.

[15] Smuts to Wilson, May 22, 1919, Baker, *Wilson and World Settlement*, Vol. 3, pp. 458-465.

[16] Baker, *Wilson and World Settlement*, Vol. 2, p. 109.

[17] Council of Four, May 29, 1919, 11 a.m., *Foreign Relations, 1919, The Paris Peace Conference*, Vol. 6, pp. 109-110.

and reduce their forces to the same degree as was required of Germany; asked for immediate admission to the League of Nations and the appointment of Germany as mandatory for her former colonies; called for a plebiscite in Alsace-Lorraine and vehemently protested the Saar and Danzig settlements and the cession of Upper Silesia to Poland; submitted elaborate counterproposals in regard to reparations, objecting especially to the powers of the Reparations Commission, and offering to pay $25 billion, without interest, on condition of major concessions in other provisions of the treaty; asked for oral negotiations and called for a neutral inquiry into the responsibility for the war.[18]

The receipt of the German counterproposals was followed by a renewed effort on the part of the British and American critics of the draft treaty to bring about major alterations of its terms. Herbert Hoover arranged a meeting among Smuts, Keynes, Vance McCormick, and himself, in the hope that McCormick, whom Hoover believed to have great influence on the President, would press Wilson to support major changes in the draft treaty.[19] Smuts wrote to Wilson on May 30 renewing his earlier criticisms of the treaty and calling again for a "Wilson peace," expressing the view that the Germans "make out a good case in regard to a number of provisions."[20] The President replied to Smuts that the Council of Four was quite willing to restudy its earlier conclusions.[21] Hoover and Norman Davis visited Wilson and urged him to take maximum advantage of the British recantation.[22] In a conversation with the President on the evening of May 31, Ray Stannard Baker commented that the reparations clauses were unworkable, and Wilson replied: "I told Lloyd George and Clemenceau as much when we had it under discussion, but there was no changing them." Baker pointed out that Lloyd George now wished to make changes. "Yes," said the President, "he is hearing from his own liberals."[23]

[18] "Observations of the German Delegation on the Conditions of Peace," May 29, 1919, *ibid.*, pp. 795-901; Luckau, *The German Delegation at the Paris Peace Conference*, pp. 302-406.

[19] Hoover, *The Ordeal of Woodrow Wilson*, p. 239.

[20] Smuts to Wilson, May 30, 1919, Baker, *Wilson and World Settlement*, Vol. 3, pp. 466-468.

[21] Wilson to Smuts, May 31, 1919, Wilson Papers, Series 8-A.

[22] Hoover, *The Ordeal of Woodrow Wilson*, p. 243.

[23] Ray Stannard Baker, *American Chronicle* (New York: Charles Scribner's Sons, 1945), pp. 439-440.

II. *Lloyd George's Proposals for Revision and the Meetings of the British and American Delegations, June 1-3*

Under the pressures of the British critics of the draft treaty and after close study of the German counterproposals and consultations with his experts, Lloyd George undertook, in the first days of June, to formulate specific proposals for revision. He rejected the German denial of war guilt, having "not one wavering doubt as to the culpability of the Central Powers," and remained convinced that the case for stripping Germany of her colonies was overwhelming. He decided, however, that the German-Polish frontier settlement should be altered, and especially that there ought to be a plebiscite in Upper Silesia. He thought that Germany should be given time to examine damages and then make a definite reparations offer to the Allies. Lloyd George found the German plea for general disarmament "irrefutable" and thought that the Allies should make definite pledges on this matter.[24]

The British Empire delegation met on June 1 and 2 to consider the reply to be made to the German counterproposals. Lloyd George submitted two questions to the delegates: (1) Should any concessions be made, or should the British Empire stand on the draft treaty? (2) If concessions were to be made, should they be communicated in writing or negotiated face to face with the Germans? All of the British delegates indicated that they favored some concessions, and two days of discussion followed as to what these ought to be.[25]

Smuts led off with a severe criticism of the treaty, contending its incompatibility with the Fourteen Points. He opposed the military occupation as "quite unnecessary" and favored the admission of Germany to the League of Nations as soon as the treaty was signed. Smuts said that Poland was an "historic failure" and that her frontiers should be reconsidered. He called also for a fixed sum of reparations. Balfour replied to Smuts, averring that "it was only necessary to read the Fourteen Points to see that they were incapable of being treated in that strictly legal manner." Balfour, and all of the delegates, agreed that the settlement of the Polish-German frontier was unsatisfactory. Balfour also thought that the

[24] Lloyd George, *The Truth about the Peace Treaties*, Vol. 1, pp. 684-688.
[25] *ibid.*, pp. 688-691.

length of the occupation and the number of troops involved should be reduced, but he defended the reparations clauses. Lloyd George recommended a plebiscite in Upper Silesia as the most urgently needed change. He defended the Saar settlement as a necessary compromise and contended that Germany could not be admitted to the League at once but that her entry need not be delayed longer than a year. Lloyd George also defended the reparations clauses, asserting that it was impossible for the present to determine either German capacity or the cost of repairing the devastated regions. He agreed that the occupation should be reduced. Would the delegation support him, the Prime Minister asked, in refusing British troops to advance to Berlin and in refusing to maintain the blockade of Germany if concessions were refused? The delegates expressed strong support for Lloyd George's proposals.[26]

The meeting of the British Empire delegation was terminated on June 2 with the adoption of a resolution defining the concessions which the Prime Minister would press on the Council of Four. It was agreed that: the eastern frontiers of Germany should be revised with areas of predominantly German population to be assigned to Germany and plebiscites to be held in Upper Silesia and other doubtful areas; Germany should be promised early admission to the League on condition that she make an honest effort to meet her obligations; the number of troops in occupation of the Rhineland and the length of the occupation should be reduced as much as possible; a fixed sum of reparations should be sought, either by Germany's undertaking to pay the whole cost of restoration and paying a fixed sum at an early date, or by allowing Germany to make a cash offer, or an offer of cash and kind, within three months of the signing of the treaty, with the stipulation that if the German offer were not acceptable, the reparations clauses would stand as originally drawn up. The delegation further agreed that if the Council of Four rejected these proposals, Lloyd George might refuse to allow the British Army to participate in an invasion of Germany and the British Navy to maintain the blockade.[27]

Lloyd George was by no means prepared to go as far as Smuts in overhauling the draft treaty. He struck back at Smuts's criti-

[26] *ibid.*, pp. 691-714.　　　　　　　　　　[27] *ibid.*, pp. 718-720.

cisms with a sardonic inquiry as to whether Smuts was prepared to give up pensions as a category of reparations and the Union's claim to German Southwest Africa.[28] Smuts replied with another eloquent appeal for sweeping revisions of the treaty, which, he said, "breathes a poisonous spirit of revenge. . . ." "In this great business," Smuts wrote, "Southwest Africa is as dust compared to the burdens now hanging over the civilized world." But he did not offer to give it up.[29]

On the afternoon of June 2, Lloyd George submitted to the Council of Four the proposals for revision of the draft treaty which the British delegation had agreed upon. He said that the British Empire delegation was unanimous in refusing to invade Germany and reimpose the blockade if their proposals were rejected. British public opinion, said Lloyd George, "wanted to get peace and was not so much concerned about the precise terms." President Wilson asserted that Lloyd George's proposals were of such importance that he wished to consult the American delegates and experts. At the President's request, the meeting scheduled for the next morning was canceled to allow Wilson and Clemenceau to confer with their advisers. Clemenceau objected most strenuously to the British proposals, contending that they created a "very grave" situation. Lloyd George said that if the French refused concessions on the occupation, he "would have no alternative but to go home and put the whole matter before his Parliament." France, he said, should have chosen between the occupation of the Rhineland and the Anglo-American treaties of guarantee. Asked by Wilson for further definition of his reparations proposals, Lloyd George explained his scheme and expressed his recently acquired view that "there was something in the contention that Germany should not be presented with an unknown liability." "The difficulty," he declared, "was that they did not know what they had to pay."[30]

President Wilson conferred with the American commissioners and technical advisers on the morning of June 3. The President

[28] Lloyd George to Smuts, June 3, 1919, Millin, *General Smuts*, Vol. 2, pp. 241-242.

[29] Smuts to Lloyd George, June 4, 1919, *ibid.*, pp. 243-245.

[30] Council of Four, June 2, 1919, 4 p.m., *Foreign Relations, 1919, The Paris Peace Conference*, Vol. 6, pp. 139-146. See also André Tardieu, *The Truth about the Treaty* (Indianapolis: The Bobbs-Merrill Company, Inc., 1921), pp. 195-198.

opened the discussion with an account of the British proposals in regard to the eastern frontiers of Germany, reparations, the occupation, and German admission to the League. The reparations question was discussed first. Norman Davis, Thomas William Lamont, Bernard Baruch, and Vance McCormick all felt that the British proposals provided an opportunity to revive the fixed sum. President Wilson recalled the failure of earlier efforts to reach agreement on a fixed sum, and Lamont observed that "Mr. Lloyd George kicked over the traces; but now he has come back to the fold." "Now the joke of it is," said Wilson, "that Lord Sumner was one of those who contributed to the unanimous counsel of the British the other day, and he takes a different position now."[31]

President Wilson turned to the other British proposals. As to Germany's eastern frontiers, Robert Howard Lord said that only very minor changes, if any, were warranted. A fair plebiscite for Upper Silesia, he contended, would be won by Poland, but he doubted that a fair plebiscite was possible, owing to the domination of the Polish masses by German capitalists and landowners. As to the occupation of the Rhineland, Wilson observed that the problem was not so much military as one of French public opinion. General Bliss argued for a substantial reduction of the occupation and its immediate termination upon Germany's entering the League. The President thought that the issue would "solve itself" when Germany was admitted to the League. Secretary Lansing asked if it were possible to fix the time of German admittance to the League, and Wilson replied: "I don't honestly think it is. I think it is necessary that we should know that the change in government and the governmental method in Germany is genuine and permanent. We don't know either of them yet."[32]

[31] "Stenographic Report of Meeting between the President, the Commissioners, and the Technical Advisers of the American Commission to Negotiate Peace," Hotel Crillon, June 3, 1919, 11 a.m., *Foreign Relations, 1919, The Paris Peace Conference*, Vol. 11, pp. 198-205; Philip Mason Burnett, *Reparation at the Paris Peace Conference from the Standpoint of the American Delegation* (2 Vols., New York: Columbia University Press, 1940), Vol. 2, pp. 110-117; Baker, *Wilson and World Settlement*, Vol. 3, pp. 470-481.

[32] Meeting of the American Delegates, June 3, 1919, 11 a.m., *Foreign Relations, 1919, The Paris Peace Conference*, Vol. 11, pp. 205-215; Baker, *Wilson and World Settlement*, Vol. 3, pp. 481-494.

The discussion turned to general considerations of the justice and expediency of the proposed concessions to Germany. The President said that the question chiefly in his mind was: "Where have they shown that the arrangements of the treaty are essentially unjust?" and not: "Where have they shown merely that they are hard?" For, said Wilson, "they are hard—but the Germans earned that." "I have no desire to soften the treaty," the President affirmed, "but I have a very sincere desire to alter those portions of it that are shown to be unjust, or which are shown to be contrary to the principles which we ourselves have laid down." Herbert Hoover thought that the expediency of inducing Germany to sign the treaty should be the primary consideration in regard to the proposed revisions, "because the weighing of justice and injustice in these times is pretty difficult." "Well," said Wilson, "I don't want to seem to be unreasonable, but my feeling is this: that we ought not, with the object of getting it signed, make changes in the treaty, if we think that it embodies what we are contending for; that the time to consider all these questions was when we were writing the treaty, and it makes me a little tired for people to come and say now that they are afraid the Germans won't sign, and their fear is based upon things that they insisted upon at the time of the writing of the treaty; that makes me very sick. . . . These people that overrode our judgment and wrote things into the treaty that are now the stumbling blocks, are falling all over themselves to remove these stumbling blocks. Now, if they ought not to have been there, I say, remove them, but I say do not remove them merely for the fact of having the treaty signed."[33]

The President's ire was clearly directed against the British. "Here is a British group," he declared, "made up of every kind of British opinion, from Winston Churchill to Fisher. From the unreasonable to the reasonable, all the way around, they are all unanimous, if you please, in their funk. Now that makes me very tired. They ought to have been rational to begin with and then they would not have needed to have funked at the end. They ought to have done the rational things, I admit, and it is

---

[33] Meeting of the American Delegates, June 3, 1919, 11 a.m., *Foreign Relations, 1919, The Paris Peace Conference*, Vol. 11, pp. 218-222; Baker, *Wilson and World Settlement*, Vol. 3, pp. 498-503.

not very gracious for me to remind them—though I have done so with as much grace as I could command." "They say that they do not quite understand why you permitted them to do that," said Davis. "I would be perfectly willing to take the responsibility if the result is good," the President affirmed. "But though we did not keep them from putting irrational things in the treaty, we got very serious modifications out of them. If we had written the treaty the way they wanted it, the Germans would have gone home the minute they read it."[34]

Wilson's candid remarks to the American delegates evidence quite clearly the fundamental differences between himself and Lloyd George not only with respect to the British proposals for revision of the draft treaty but also in the basic approaches of the two statesmen to the entire peace settlement. Lloyd George was governed by considerations of practicality and expediency, above all, in this instance, by his desire to induce Germany to sign the treaty without a renewal of hostilities. The President, on the other hand, was prepared to risk the dangers and inconveniences of a German refusal to sign, nor was he interested in moderation or liberality as such. His objective was justice, or, more accurately, an approach in this world toward a concept of absolute and transcendental justice, and, in his own conception, he was bound to its service not by choice but by compulsion.

The depth of this conviction was never clearer than in a speech which he had delivered on Memorial Day at the Suresnes Cemetery, in which he said: ". . . If I may speak a personal word, I beg you to realize the compulsion that I myself feel that I am under. By the Constitution of our great country I was the commander-in-chief of these men. I advised the Congress to declare that a state of war existed. I sent these lads over here to die. Shall I—can I—ever speak a word of counsel which is inconsistent with the assurances I gave them when they came over? It is inconceivable. There is something better, if possible, that a man can give than his life, and that is his living spirit to a service that is not easy, to resist counsels that are hard to resist, and to stand against purposes that are difficult to stand against, and to say,

[34] Meeting of the American Delegates, June 3, 1919, 11 a.m., *Foreign Relations, 1919, The Paris Peace Conference*, Vol. 11, p. 222, Baker, *Wilson and World Settlement*, Vol. 3, pp. 503-504.

'Here stand I, consecrated in spirit to the men who were once my comrades and who are now gone, and who have left me under eternal bonds of fidelity.' "[35]

In the first two weeks of June, the British proposals were debated in the Council of Four. In the service of practical necessity, Lloyd George appealed for concessions to the Germans, and, in the service of principle, Wilson came reluctantly to agree with the Prime Minister. But the basic distrust remained between the two statesmen with their radically different motives. A few days after the meeting of the American delegates, Herbert Hoover appealed to President Wilson to make common cause with Lloyd George, and the President replied sharply: "Lloyd George will not stand up against Clemenceau despite what he says."[36]

III. *The Debate in the Council of Four on Lloyd George's Proposals for Revision of the Draft Treaty, June 3-16; The Allied Reply to the German Counterproposals and the Signing of the Treaty, June 16-28*

The deliberations of the Council of Four in the first two weeks of June were concerned with the four categories of revisions proposed by Lloyd George: the German-Polish border, the reparations settlement, the admission of Germany to the League of Nations, and the duration and conditions of the Allied occupation of the Rhineland.

Lloyd George opened the discussion of the German-Polish frontiers on the afternoon of June 3 with his proposal for a plebiscite in Upper Silesia. Wilson reported Lord's contention that the region was dominated by a few German capitalists and landed magnates who would thwart a free expression of the will of the people. Lloyd George replied that an Allied occupation would be necessary to prevent intimidation of the people. His understanding of self-determination, he said, was "that of the people themselves, and not that of experts like Mr. Lord."

[35] Speech at Suresnes Cemetery, May 30, 1919, Ray Stannard Baker and William E. Dodd, eds., *The Public Papers of Woodrow Wilson* (6 Vols., New York and London: Harper & Brothers, Publishers, 1925-1927), *War and Peace*, Vol. 1, p. 507.
[36] Hoover, *The Ordeal of Woodrow Wilson*, p. 248.

Lloyd George declared himself to be "simply standing by President Wilson's Fourteen Points and fighting them through." Wilson replied that he was fully in favor of a plebiscite if there were assurances of a free vote, and, rather heatedly, that he "could not allow Mr. Lloyd George to suggest that he himself was not in favor of self-determination." Lloyd George explained that his concern with Upper Silesia was motivated by a strong desire to avoid the necessity of Allied forces marching on Berlin, which, he feared, would be another "Moscow campaign." Wilson said that he was "less concerned with the question of whether Germany would or would not sign than with ensuring that the arrangements in the treaty of peace were sound and just." Lloyd George replied that he was "ready to make any concession that was fair and just, particularly if it would give the Germans an inducement to sign." Clemenceau vigorously opposed a plebiscite in Upper Silesia, and Wilson noted that it was not required by Point 13.[37] Nevertheless, Wilson agreed to a plebiscite to be conducted under the supervision of an inter-Allied commission, and the Council agreed that the draft treaty would be amended to provide for a plebiscite in the portion of Upper Silesia which had been transferred to Poland.[38]

A sharp exchange took place on the morning of June 5 between Lloyd George and Paderewski of Poland. Paderewski bitterly protested the plebiscite decision, contending that it violated promises made to Poland and that it would destroy the faith of the Polish people in the Allies. Lloyd George bluntly accused Poland of ingratitude and imperialist designs. ". . . not only has she no gratitude," fulminated the Prime Minister, "but she says she has lost faith in the people who have won her freedom." ". . . it fills me with despair," he declared, "the way in which I have seen small nations, before they have hardly leaped into the light of freedom, beginning to oppress other races than their own."[39]

[37] See Chapter 1, Section v.
[38] Council of Four, June 3, 1919, 4 p.m., *Foreign Relations, 1919, The Paris Peace Conference*, Vol. 6, pp. 149-155, 186-187; Lloyd George, *The Truth about the Peace Treaties*, Vol. 1, pp. 720-723. See also Louis L. Gerson, *Woodrow Wilson and the Rebirth of Poland, 1914-1920* (New Haven: Yale University Press, 1953), pp. 132-133.
[39] Council of Four, June 5, 1919, 11:30 a.m., *Foreign Relations, 1919, The Paris Peace Conference*, Vol. 6, pp. 191-198; Lloyd George, *The Truth about the Peace Treaties*, Vol. 2, pp. 992-1000. See also Gerson, *Wilson and the Rebirth of Poland*, pp. 133-137.

The British and American critics of the draft treaty were impressed with Lloyd George's stand and puzzled by Wilson's apparent reticence. Harold Nicolson, for instance, recorded in his diary on June 5: ". . . Cannot understand Wilson. Here is a chance of improving the thing and he won't take it. Lloyd George, however, is fighting like a little terrier all by himself."[40]

President Wilson gave increasing support to Lloyd George but showed no real enthusiasm for the plebiscite in Upper Silesia. On June 11, he reiterated that the plebiscite was not necessary in principle under Point 13. The Allies, he said, while refusing all sacrifices on their own part, were throwing upon Poland the burden of appeasing Germany. Lloyd George reaffirmed his threat that he would not order British soldiers to fight if the Germans broke with the Peace Conference over the plebiscite.[41] A special committee on Germany's eastern frontiers, which had been constituted on June 3, reported on June 11 that the Poles in Upper Silesia were not free to form their own opinions and recommended, therefore, that the plebiscite be delayed. The American member, Lord, and the French and Italian members, urged a delay of one or two years, while the British member, Headlam-Morley, thought that the plebiscite could be held sooner.[42] President Wilson proposed that the plebiscite be delayed as recommended by the majority of the committee, and the Council agreed. It was further agreed to place Upper Silesia temporarily under the administration of a four-member inter-Allied commission.[43] Wilson explained the plebiscite decision to Paderewski on June 14 as designed to deny Germany any excuse for disturbing the peace. Paderewski pronounced it a "very serious blow to Poland," and Lloyd George joined the President in attempting to assuage the Polish leader's distress. After Paderewski left, the Council decided that the plebiscite would be held within six to eighteen months of the establishment of the commission, rather than one or two years as at first agreed.[44]

---

[40] Nicolson's Diary, June 5, 1919, Nicolson, *Peacemaking 1919*, p. 358.

[41] Council of Four, June 11, 1919, 4 p.m., *Foreign Relations, 1919, The Paris Peace Conference*, Vol. 6, pp. 303-304.

[42] Council of Four, June 11, 1919, 5 p.m., *ibid.*, pp. 311-313.

[43] Council of Four, June 11, 1919, 5:45 p.m. *ibid.*, pp. 316-317.

[44] Council of Four, June 14, 1919, 4:45 p.m., *ibid.*, pp. 450-452; Lloyd George, *The Truth about the Peace Treaties*, Vol. 1, pp. 722-723.

Starting from an attitude of marked reluctance, Wilson came finally to full support of Lloyd George in regard to the Polish-German frontier. Henry White exercised considerable influence in bringing the President to this stand. In 1923, Wilson said to White's daughter: "But for your father I should have never known the truth about Upper Silesia; the French and the Poles had entirely misled me."[45]

The British proposals in regard to reparations gave rise to a renewed American effort to secure agreement on a fixed sum. In a memorandum submitted on June 3, Bernard Baruch pointed to the financial advantages of a fixed sum to all of the Allied states.[46] Wilson raised the issue in the Council of Four on the afternoon of June 3, but Lloyd George maintained that "every possible way of arriving at a fixed sum had been attempted, but it had not been found possible." He described his two alternative schemes: a German contract to make full restoration of the devastated areas within a certain time, with a fixed sum to cover all other items, including pensions; or, a German offer within three months of the signing of the treaty of a lump sum in settlement of all reparations claims, with the stipulation that if this were not acceptable to the Allies the original clauses of the treaty would stand. The Council constituted a special committee of Lloyd George, Baruch, and Loucheur to examine the Prime Minister's proposals.[47]

Wilson and his experts continued to press for the determination of a fixed sum of reparations for inclusion in the treaty. Baruch and Lamont conferred with Lloyd George on June 7, appealing to him to reconsider the fixed sum, but he continued to press his own proposals, contending that any fixed sum to which the Allies might agree would be too high for the Germans to accept.[48] "Any figures that would not frighten them," Lloyd George

[45] Allan Nevins, *Henry White: Thirty Years of American Diplomacy* (New York and London: Harper & Brothers, Publishers, 1930), pp. 422-423.

[46] Bernard M. Baruch, *The Making of the Reparation and Economic Sections of the Treaty* (New York and London: Harper & Brothers, Publishers, 1920), pp. 66-69.

[47] Council of Four, June 3, 1919, 4 p.m., *Foreign Relations, 1919, The Paris Peace Conference*, Vol. 6, pp. 156-157; Lloyd George, *The Truth about the Peace Treaties*, Vol. 1, pp. 723-724.

[48] Council of Four, June 7, 1919, 4 p.m., *Foreign Relations, 1919, The Paris Peace Conference*, Vol. 6, p. 240; Burnett, *Reparation at the Paris Peace Conference*, Vol. 1, p. 137.

told the Council on June 9, "would be below the figure with which he and M. Clemenceau could face their peoples in the present state of public opinion." President Wilson said that he was "perfectly willing to stand by the treaty provided that it were explained to the Germans, but he had understood that the British and French Governments were desirous of making some concessions as a possible inducement to the Germans to sign." "If we must make concessions," he said, "then he was in favor of perfectly definite concessions."[49] Wilson then read a proposal submitted by the American experts calling for a fixed sum of $25 billion and assurances to Germany of a certain amount of working capital.[50] Lloyd George said that he liked the "crust and the seasoning but not the meat" of the American proposal. Wilson agreed to omit the fixed sum from the treaty.[51]

Lloyd George's reparations proposals were adopted by the Council of Four. Wilson said on June 10 that the American proposals had been offered only in a spirit of cooperation and that if they were not acceptable they could be withdrawn. Lloyd George declared that he fully agreed with the "spirit" of the American proposals but that all that was needed to induce Germany to sign the treaty was "some general assurance."[52] On June 11, the Council agreed on its reply to the German counter-proposals regarding reparations. Although the first of Lloyd George's alternate plans was dropped at the insistence of Clemenceau, the reply included the offer to allow Germany to submit within four months a lump sum proposal or "any practicable plan" for the restitution of damages, with the Allies to reply to any German plan within two months of its submission.[53]

Lloyd George's vague proposal for the early admission of Germany to the League of Nations was readily accepted by Presi-

[49] Council of Four, June 9, 1919, 11:45 a.m., *Foreign Relations, 1919, The Paris Peace Conference*, Vol. 6, pp. 262-263; Baker, *Wilson and World Settlement*, Vol. 2, p. 406.

[50] "United States Project for Reply to German Counter-Proposals," *Foreign Relations, 1919, The Paris Peace Conference*, Vol. 6, pp. 267-271.

[51] Council of Four, June 9, 1919, 11:45 a.m., *ibid.*, p. 264.

[52] Council of Four, June 10, 1919, 11 a.m., *ibid.*, pp. 278-279.

[53] Council of Four, June 11, 1919, 11 a.m., *ibid.*, pp. 290-300; "Reply to German Counterproposals," *ibid.*, pp. 305-310. See also Baruch, *The Making of the Reparation and Economic Sections of the Treaty*, pp. 70-72; Burnett, *Reparation at the Paris Peace Conference*, Vol. 1, pp. 137-139; Baker, *Wilson and World Settlement*, Vol. 2, pp. 407-408.

dent Wilson. Wilson favored a "general assurance" to Germany of her admission to the League as soon as the Allies were convinced that the changes in her Government were sincere. It was so agreed.[54] The final reply to Germany in regard to the League, adopted on June 12, informed Germany that her immediate admittance was not justified but that if she acted sincerely to meet her obligations under the treaty, she would be admitted to the League "in the near future."[55]

The United States was in essential sympathy with Lloyd George's proposal for the mitigation of the terms of the occupation. Clemenceau appealed to the Council on June 12 to make no changes in the Rhineland settlement, but Lloyd George maintained that Parliament might refuse to accept both the treaty of guarantee and a long occupation of the Rhineland. Clemenceau asserted that a reduction of the period of occupation was impossible.[56] The commission established on May 29 to rewrite the draft convention on the occupation of the Rhineland submitted recommendations which were adopted by the Council on June 13.[57] The concessions adopted were embodied in a declaration on the occupation of the Rhineland signed by Wilson, Lloyd George, and Clemenceau on June 16. The declaration promised that if before the end of the projected fifteen-year occupation Germany has given proof of her good will and satisfactory guarantees to assure the fulfillment of her obligations, the Allied and Associated Powers "will be ready to come to an agreement between themselves for the earlier termination of the period of occupation." The declaration promised further that as soon as Germany fulfilled the disarmament clauses of the treaty, the annual charge to Germany for the cost of the occupation would not exceed $60 million.[58]

[54] Council of Four, June 3, 1919, 4 p.m., *Foreign Relations, 1919, The Paris Peace Conference*, Vol. 6, pp. 157-158. See also Baker, *Wilson and World Settlement*, Vol. 2, pp. 515-516.

[55] Council of Four, June 12, 1919, 11 a.m., *Foreign Relations, 1919, The Paris Peace Conference*, Vol. 6, p. 327; "The League of Nations—Reply to German Proposals," *ibid.*, pp. 341-342. See also Lloyd George, *The Truth about the Peace Treaties*, Vol. 1, p. 725.

[56] Council of Four, June 12, 1919, 11 a.m., *Foreign Relations, 1919, The Paris Peace Conference*, Vol. 6, pp. 328-329.

[57] Council of Four, June 13, 1919, 12 noon, *ibid.*, pp. 377-379.

[58] Council of Four, June 16, 1919, 6:45 p.m., *ibid.*, p. 521. "Declaration by the Governments of the United States of America, Great Britain and France in

The Anglo-American rebellion against the draft treaty thus came to an end with modest alterations of the treaty in regard to reparations, German admission to the League, and the Rhineland occupation, and with a major alteration in regard to Germany's eastern frontier. The episode illustrates once again the failure of Great Britain and the United States to coordinate strategy in promoting common objectives. Some of the changes advocated by Lloyd George in May and June had been advocated by President Wilson earlier in the Peace Conference and defeated. In June, Wilson thought it too late to make major changes although he lent rather grudging support to Lloyd George. On the crucial issue of reparations, the President did seriously probe Lloyd George's intentions but found him unwilling to go beyond "general assurances" that might induce the Germans to sign the treaty. The British were puzzled by the tepidness of Wilson's support, failing, apparently, to understand the mentality which made the President feel bound to his covenants with Clemenceau, however reluctantly entered, just as he felt bound to his covenants with the enemy under the Pre-Armistice Agreement. Wilson, moreover, felt a profound disgust with the motivations of pure expediency which underlay the British proposals for revision, a sentiment which he revealed without a trace of ambiguity in his conference with the American delegates on June 3. When motives are set aside, however, and consequences considered, it seems quite clear that Lloyd George, and not Wilson, was the principal champion of a settlement both just and expedient in regard to the occupation of the Rhineland and the German-Polish borderlands.

The comprehensive reply of the Allied and Associated Powers to the German counterproposals was delivered on June 16. The reply upheld the compatibility of the draft treaty with the Fourteen Points and, except for the alterations discussed above, granted only minor concessions to Germany.[59] Wilson and Lloyd George

---

Regard to the Occupation of the Rhine Provinces," *ibid.*, p. 522; Great Britain, Parliament, *Papers by Command, Cmd.* 240. See also Lloyd George, *The Truth about the Peace Treaties*, Vol. 1, pp. 726-727.

[59] "Reply of the Allied and Associated Powers to the Observations of the German Delegation on the Conditions of Peace," June 16, 1919, *Foreign Rela-*

concurred in refusing any further concessions to Germany. The German Government dispatched a note to the Supreme Council on June 22 declaring their acceptance of the treaty except for the "war guilt" clause and the demand for handing over persons for trial.[60] The Council of Four immediately replied that the time for discussion was past and demanded an unequivocal decision on the part of Germany to sign or not.[61] The Germans, "yielding to overwhelming force," accepted the treaty unconditionally on June 23.[62]

The treaty of peace was signed on June 28 in a terse ceremony in the Hall of Mirrors in the palace at Versailles. Along with the Treaty of Versailles were signed the British and American treaties of guarantee with France, the agreement with regard to the military occupation of the Rhineland, and the minorities treaty with Poland.[63]

The treaty was a work of compromise and synthesis of the sharply different hopes, fears, and ambitions of a great coalition of nations, and as such, it was completely satisfactory to none of the statesmen. But both the British Prime Minister and the American President were able to contemplate the completed treaty with some satisfaction and with great hope. "Where it is not perfect," Lloyd George reported to the House of Commons, "I look forward to the organization of the League of Nations to remedy, to repair, and to redress."[64] President Wilson looked upon the treaty as a just settlement of accounts, but, much more,

---

tions, 1919, The Paris Peace Conference, Vol. 6, pp. 926-996; Luckau, *The German Delegation at the Paris Peace Conference,* pp. 411-472. See also H.W.V. Temperley, ed., *A History of the Peace Conference of Paris* (6 Vols., London: Henry Frowde and Hodder and Stoughton, 1920-1924), Vol. 2, pp. 246-254.

[60] German Note of June 22, *Foreign Relations, 1919, The Paris Peace Conference,* Vol. 6, pp. 609-611; Luckau, *The German Delegation at the Paris Peace Conference,* pp. 478-481.

[61] Council of Four, June 22, 1919, 7:15 p.m., *Foreign Relations, 1919, The Paris Peace Conference,* Vol. 6, pp. 605-606. Allied Note of June 22, *ibid.,* p. 612; Luckau, *The German Delegation at the Paris Peace Conference,* p. 481.

[62] German Note of June 23, *Foreign Relations, 1919, The Paris Peace Conference,* Vol. 6, p. 644; Luckau, *The German Delegation at the Paris Peace Conference,* p. 482.

[63] Plenary Session, June 28, 1919, *Foreign Relations, 1919, The Paris Peace Conference,* Vol. 3, pp. 422-423. Treaty of Peace between the Allied and Associated Powers and Germany, Versailles, June 28, 1919, Great Britain, Treaty Series No. 4 (1919); *Cmd.* 153.

[64] Lloyd George, *The Truth about the Peace Treaties,* Vol. 1, p. 734.

as an instrument for the achievement of a new order of international relations. He cabled to Tumulty on June 28 a statement for the American people: "The treaty of peace has been signed. If it is ratified and acted upon in full and sincere execution of its terms, it will furnish the charter for a new order of affairs in the world. It is a severe treaty in the duties and penalties it imposes upon Germany, but it is severe only because great wrongs done by Germany are to be righted and repaired. . . . And it is much more than a treaty of peace with Germany. . . . It ends, once for all, an old and intolerable order. . . . It associates the free governments of the world in a permanent league in which they are pledged to use their united power to maintain peace by maintaining right and justice. It makes international law a reality supported by imperative sanctions. . . . There is ground here for deep satisfaction, universal reassurance, and confident hope."[65]

President Wilson left Paris on the evening of June 28. Lloyd George, owing to a recent illness, was not among the dignitaries who saw Wilson off at the railroad station but he called at the Crillon before the President's departure and said to him: "You have done more than any one man to bring about further cordial relations between England and the United States. You have brought the two countries closer together than any other individual in history."[66]

[65] Wilson to Tumulty, June 28, 1919, Baker and Dodd, eds., *Public Papers, War and Peace*, Vol. 1, pp. 523-524; *Foreign Relations, 1919, The Paris Peace Conference*, Vol. 11, pp. 604-605.

[66] Rear Admiral Cary T. Grayson, *Woodrow Wilson* (New York: Holt, Rinehart and Winston, 1960), p. 89; Grasty to *The New York Times*, June 29, 1919, quoted in Joseph P. Tumulty, *Woodrow Wilson As I Know Him* (Garden City, New York, and Toronto: Doubleday, Page and Company, 1921), p. 533.

CHAPTER 14

THE BREAKDOWN OF ANGLO-AMERICAN COOPERATION IN THE FINAL STAGES OF THE PEACE CONFERENCE: PROBLEMS OF ASIA MINOR, THE ADRIATIC AND EASTERN EUROPE

I N the months following the departure of the heads of government, the continuing Peace Conference was primarily concerned with the Turkish treaty, the still unsettled problem of Italian claims in the Adriatic, and political and territorial conflicts in southeastern Europe. The principal decisions regarding the disposition of the shattered Ottoman Empire were still to be made when the heads of government dispersed on June 28, 1919. Between January and June, the Peace Conference had considered the problems arising from the emergence of national states in the Arab portions of the disintegrated Empire, but the principal Anglo-American issues in the negotiation of the Turkish treaty were connected with the disposition of Armenia and Constantinople. These were dealt with in the final stages of the Peace Conference under the shadow of the retreat of the United States to isolation. British policy was to build the Turkish settlement around American mandates over Armenia and the territories surrounding the straits, and the long delay in the formulation of the Turkish treaty was due to the protracted indecision of the United States in regard to the mandates. British efforts to persuade the United States to accept mandatory responsibility were finally defeated by the victory of isolationism in America.

As in the case of the Turkish settlement, Anglo-American relations in dealing with the continuing Fiume controversy and the tangled problems of self-determination among the ambitious new states of eastern Europe were primarily conditioned by the withdrawal of the United States to isolation. In the nagging issue of Fiume, Britain's treaty commitment to Italy versus rigid American adherence to the principle of self-determination, complicated now by the withdrawal of the United States, generated mounting Anglo-American disharmony and mutual recrimination. As to the remaining problems of southeastern Europe:

the United States, in its sympathy for the new Poland, supported dubious Polish claims to Eastern Galicia while Great Britain resisted them; in the case of Bulgaria, the United States adhered to the nationality principle in advocating Bulgarian territorial interests in Thrace against Greek claims which were supported by the British; in regard to Hungary, the English-speaking powers stood together in opposition to Roumanian encroachments.

I. *The Question of American Mandates for Constantinople and Armenia*

The fundamental issues in regard to Asia Minor were considered only intermittently and incidentally by the heads of government during the main stage of the Peace Conference.[1] The Council of Four did agree on the claims of Greece in Asia Minor in the course of the abortive negotiations in May in connection with Italian military activities and political ambitions in Turkey. The Council agreed on May 6, it will be recalled, to the dispatch of Greek forces to Smyrna.[2] The American members of the Territorial Commission on Greek Affairs had opposed the establishment of any Greek sovereignty in Asia Minor, while the British and French members had supported the claim of Venizelos for Greek annexation of Smyrna.[3] Wilson, however, overrode his experts and gave his full support to the annexation by Greece of the Smyrna district.[4] The Council adopted a resolution on May 14 providing for the cession of the district of Smyrna and the Dodecanese islands to Greece in full sovereignty.[5] Lloyd George took the lead in championing the Greek claims in Asia Minor,

[1] Good brief accounts of the Turkish settlement may be found in Harry N. Howard, *The Partition of Turkey* (Norman, Oklahoma: University of Oklahoma Press, 1931), pp. 217-249, and William Linn Westermann, "The Armenian Problem and the Disruption of Turkey," *What Really Happened at Paris* (Edward Mandell House and Charles Seymour, eds., New York: Charles Scribner's Sons, 1921), pp. 176-203.

[2] See Chapter 12, Section III.

[3] Westermann, "The Armenian Problem and the Disruption of Turkey," *What Really Happened at Paris* (House and Seymour, eds.), pp. 193-194.

[4] Council of Four, May 13, 1919, 4 p.m., Department of State, *Papers Relating to the Foreign Relations of the United States, 1919, The Paris Peace Conference* (13 Vols., Washington: United States Government Printing Office, 1942-1947), Vol. 5, pp. 584-586; hereafter referred to as *Foreign Relations*.

[5] Council of Four, May 14, 1919, 4 p.m., *ibid.*, pp. 614-616, 622-623.

possibly in the hope that Greek military domination of Turkey, backed by British sea power, would guarantee British ascendency over the straits. Wilson seems to have supported the Greek case solely because of the Greek population of the Smyrna region.[6]

The Ottoman delegation which presented itself at Paris in June appealed for the maintenance of the territorial integrity of the Ottoman Empire on the basis of President Wilson's principles.[7] The Council dismissed the Turkish plea with contempt, and, on June 21, gave its approval to a reply drafted by Balfour, which rejected the Turkish plea with a slashing attack on the tyranny and cruelty of the Ottoman Government. The Council, said the letter, "wishes well to the Turkish people, and admires their excellent qualities. But they cannot admit that among these qualities are to be counted capacity to rule over alien races." President Wilson subscribed to this reply "with great satisfaction."[8] Lloyd George suggested on June 25 that a "short, sharp peace," to "put Turkey out of her misery," be formulated while the Turkish delegation was still in Paris.[9] On the next day, however, Wilson suggested that the Turkish delegation be sent home. "They had exhibited complete absence of common sense," he said, "and a total misunderstanding of the West." Lloyd George agreed that "this was Turkish diplomacy."[10] The Council decided on June 27 that further consideration of the Turkish treaty would be deferred until it was known whether the United States would accept mandates for Armenia and Constantinople.[11]

British policy in regard to Asia Minor centered in the hope that the United States could be persuaded to accept mandatory authority over the long-suppressed Armenian nation and over the territories adjacent to the Turkish straits. The question of

[6] See Arnold J. Toynbee, *The Western Question in Greece and Turkey* (Boston and New York: Houghton Mifflin Company, 1922), pp. 73-74, 87.

[7] Council of Four, June 17, 1919, 11 a.m., *Foreign Relations, 1919, The Paris Peace Conference*, Vol. 6, pp. 509-512.

[8] Draft Reply to the Turks, June 21, *ibid.*, pp. 577-580; Council of Four, June 21, 1919, 4 p.m., *ibid.*, p. 576. See also David Lloyd George, *The Truth about the Peace Treaties* (2 Vols., London: Victor Gollancz, Ltd., 1938), Vol. 2, pp. 1001-1014.

[9] Council of Four, June 25, 1919, 4 p.m., *Foreign Relations, 1919, The Paris Peace Conference*, Vol. 6, pp. 675-678.

[10] Council of Four, June 26, 1919, 4 p.m., *ibid.*, p. 711.

[11] Council of Four, June 27, 1919, 4 p.m., *ibid.*, p. 729.

American mandates had been raised on January 11, 1919, at a meeting attended by David Hunter Miller, Lord Robert Cecil, Colonel Lawrence, and other British officials, and, according to Miller, there was unanimous sentiment among the British present that the United States should take mandates for Constantinople and Armenia.[12] Lloyd George regarded the United States as the only Great Power which could be entrusted with the straits mandate because of its immunity from European rivalries.[13]

From January to June, the question of American mandates was discussed intermittently. The Armenian delegation on February 26 presented its case for a unified independent state under the protective mandate of a Great Power.[14] Sir William Wiseman inquired discreetly of Colonel Bonsal on March 3 as to when the President might bring up the Armenian question for settlement and received an evasive answer.[15] President Wilson, apparently unwilling to raise a new controversial issue at a time when he already faced great difficulties both in Paris and at home, rejected as "premature and unwise" proposals that he launch a campaign to "educate" the American people for acceptance of an Armenian mandate.[16] On May 14, Lloyd George submitted a draft resolution to the Council of Four calling for American mandates over Armenia and the straits territories, and President Wilson agreed to accept them subject to the approval of the Senate, which he said he could not guarantee.[17] Lloyd George submitted much broader proposals in a memorandum on May 21, calling for an American mandate for all of Anatolia as well as Armenia and the straits.[18] Lloyd George contended that some

[12] David Hunter Miller, *My Diary at the Conference of Paris*, privately printed (21 Vols., New York: Appeal Printing Company, 1924), Vol. 1, p. 74. See also Howard, *The Partition of Turkey*, pp. 231-232.

[13] Lloyd George, *The Truth about the Peace Treaties*, Vol. 2, pp. 1259-1260.

[14] Council of Ten, February 26, 1919, 3 p.m., *Foreign Relations, 1919, The Paris Peace Conference*, Vol. 4, pp. 147-157.

[15] Stephen Bonsal, *Suitors and Suppliants* (New York: Prentice-Hall, Inc., 1946), pp. 191-192.

[16] Wilson to Polk, March 12, 1919, Woodrow Wilson Papers, Library of Congress, Washington, D.C., Series 8-A.

[17] Council of Four, May 14, 1919, 4 p.m., *Foreign Relations, 1919, The Paris Peace Conference*, Vol. 5, pp. 614, 622. See also Lloyd George, *The Truth about the Peace Treaties*, Vol. 2, pp. 1263-1265.

[18] Memorandum by Lloyd George, May 21, 1919, *Foreign Relations, 1919, The Paris Peace Conference*, Vol. 5, p. 770.

control over Turkey was essential and that the United States was more acceptable to Moslems than either Britain or France. If the United States rejected the mandate for Anatolia, Lloyd George proposed, it should be left to the Turks with no mandatory authority. Wilson said that the United States could not accept a mandate for all of Asia Minor. The French, he feared, would feel that Britain had brought the United States in in order to get France out. The President suggested that the issue be deferred.[19] Balfour drew up a memorandum on June 26 calling for an immediate settlement of the main outlines of the Turkish treaty, with the United States to be accorded the mandates for Armenia and the straits territories but the bulk of Anatolia to be left as an independent Turkish state.[20] On June 27, Wilson said that he personally favored acceptance of the mandates for Constantinople and Armenia, but that it was for the American people to decide.[21]

The prospects of American acceptance of the mandates began to dim at once as the Senate took up consideration of the Treaty of Versailles. Henry White reported to the Council on July 18 that President Wilson had informed him that there would be a "very considerable" delay in the decision of the United States as to the mandates. Balfour agreed to postpone the decision of the Council.[22] Lord Curzon inquired on August 15 of Lindsay, the British Chargé in Washington, as to the prospects of American acceptance of the mandates. Lindsay replied that acceptance seemed "most unlikely." Public opinion was unformed, he reported, "but I confidently anticipate it will be hostile."[23] Late in August, the British Government expressed its desire to withdraw British troops from Armenia and asked the United States, as the probable mandatory power, to finance the maintenance of the British forces until they could be replaced by American

[19] Council of Four, May 21, 1919, 11 a.m., *ibid.*, pp. 756-766.

[20] Memorandum by Balfour, June 26, 1919, Edward M. House Papers, Sterling Library, Yale University.

[21] Charles T. Thompson, *The Peace Conference Day by Day* (New York: Brentano's Publishers, 1920), p. 406.

[22] Council of Heads of Delegations, July 18, 1919, 10 a.m., *Foreign Relations, 1919, The Paris Peace Conference*, Vol. 7, p. 193; E. L. Woodward and Rohan Butler, eds., *Documents on British Foreign Policy, 1919-1939*, First Series (8 Vols., London: His Majesty's Stationery Office, 1947-1958), Vol. 1, pp. 131-132.

[23] Curzon to Lindsay, August 15, 1919, Lindsay to Curzon, August 16, 1919, *ibid.*, Vol. 4, p. 730.

troops.[24] Secretary of State Lansing replied that no funds were available to finance the British forces and appealed to Great Britain to maintain military control in Armenia. Lansing explained that any appeal to Congress for funds would antagonize the Senate and further complicate the situation in regard to the German treaty.[25]

The American delay in regard to the mandates continued to hold up the Turkish treaty in the autumn of 1919. Lloyd George told the Council on September 15 that the treaty could not be drawn up until the American reply on the mandates was received. Polk said that the position of the United States might be clear by the end of October. Lloyd George thought this view "rather sanguine."[26] Wilson, according to Lloyd George, put the Allies in an "impossible position" as to the Turkish treaty. "We were in despair," he wrote in his memoirs, "as to what action we could take without risking a breach with America."[27] Lord Grey, who was now special British Ambassador in Washington, reported on October 10 that American acceptance of the mandates, since the President's illness, seemed "altogether out of the question."[28] Curzon cabled Grey on October 18 that the American delay was already producing "lamentable consequences" and might "gravely imperil chances of peace with Turkey."[29] Admiral Sir J. M. deRobeck reported to the British Government from Constantinople on November 18 that the delay in making peace was having disastrous effects. The Turks were no longer cowed, he reported, and Mustafa Kemal's nationalists were growing rapidly in strength.[30] Grey reported on November 23 that an American decision had still not been reached and recommended that negotiations on the Turkish treaty be begun.[31]

[24] Ambassador Davis to Lansing, August 20, 1919, *Foreign Relations, 1919, The Paris Peace Conference*, Vol. 2, pp. 832-833.

[25] Lansing to Davis, August 23, 1919, *ibid.*, p. 834.

[26] Council of Heads of Delegations, September 15, 1919, 10:30 a.m., *ibid.*, Vol. 8, p. 203; Woodward and Butler, eds., *Documents on British Foreign Policy, 1919-1939*, First Series, Vol. 1, pp. 688-689.

[27] Lloyd George, *The Truth about the Peace Treaties*, Vol. 2, pp. 1266-1267.

[28] Grey to Curzon, October 10, 1919, Woodward and Butler, eds., *Documents on British Foreign Policy, 1919-1939*, First Series, Vol. 4, pp. 797-798, n.3.

[29] Curzon to Grey, October 18, 1919, *ibid.*, pp. 826-896.

[30] deRobeck to Curzon, November 18, 1919, *ibid.*, pp. 895-896.

[31] Grey to Curzon, November 23, 1919, *ibid.*, p. 901.

The Allies began to look for an alternate solution in the late autumn. Lloyd George told Frank Polk on November 24 that he assumed that the United States would not accept the mandates, for which he expressed keen regret, since it was the "only real solution."[32] In a conference with Lloyd George in London on December 11, Clemenceau proposed the abandonment of mandates for Asia Minor. Lloyd George agreed, but he insisted that Constantinople and the straits be internationalized, perhaps under a neutral international commission, with the Sultan remaining at Constantinople "in a sort of Vatican." Clemenceau observed that it was "quite bad enough to have one Pope in the West," but that some sort of international authority to guide the Turkish Government was necessary. He opposed having the President of the United States nominate the head of such an authority, because he was "too far away" and because "America had forced a peace system on the Allies with which she now refused to agree."[33]

As the Allied leaders proceeded with the Turkish treaty in 1920, problems arose as to the relationship of the United States to the continuing Peace Conference, and harsh feelings developed on both sides. At Lord Curzon's suggestion, the Foreign Ministers agreed on January 21, 1920, to communicate to Washington their desire for an American plenipotentiary to attend the forthcoming meeting of Premiers in London, along with a warning that Turkish problems could no longer be delayed.[34] The United States rejected the invitation to participate in the Turkish negotiations, and the Allied leaders began their deliberations in London on February 12 with only an American observer present.[35] Lloyd George opened the discussion on February 12 with the observation that the long delay in negotiation of a Turkish

[32] Polk to Lansing, November 29, 1919, *Foreign Relations, 1919, The Paris Peace Conference*, Vol. 11, pp. 675-676.

[33] Council on Premiers, December 11, 1919, 3 p.m., Woodward and Butler, ed., *Documents on British Foreign Policy, 1919-1939*, First Series, Vol. 2, pp. 727-731.

[34] Council of Foreign Ministers, January 21, 1920, 11 a.m., *Foreign Relations, 1919, The Paris Peace Conference*, Vol. 9, pp. 1008-1009; Woodward and Butler, eds., *Documents on British Foreign Policy, 1919-1939*, First Series, Vol. 2, pp. 965-967.

[35] The minutes of the London Conference of February 12-April 10, 1920, were published for the first time in 1958, in Woodward and Butler, eds., *Documents on British Foreign Policy, 1919-1939*, First Series, Vol. 7.

settlement was not the fault of the Peace Conference but was due to the fact that President Wilson had led them to believe that after his return to America he could give an early answer on whether the United States would accept mandates. Since no answer was yet forthcoming, said Lloyd George, "it was right for the other powers concerned to bring the matter to a conclusion."[36] Lord Curzon expressed the view on February 27 that the United States, since it completely disassociated itself from the proceedings, could not be asked to sign the Turkish treaty. It was agreed, however, that a copy of the completed treaty would be sent to the United States with an invitation to decide for itself whether it wished to sign.[37]

As the Peace Conference encountered increasing difficulties with the rising force of Turkish nationalism, Lloyd George gave vent to increasing ire at the President's continuing flow of counsel to the Peace Conference coupled with the absolute refusal of the United States to share in the responsibility for dealing with Turkey. In a discussion on March 5 of measures to be taken in the wake of massacres of Armenians in Cilicia by the Turkish nationalists, Lloyd George noted that the Conference had received "endless telegrams from the United States asking why nothing was done to help Armenia," and suggested that it might not be amiss to invite the Americans to join in measures to assist their "special protégés." "The Americans," declared the Prime Minister, "had always taken a very exalted position and had lectured us severely on our inaction. They appeared to assume responsibility for the sole guardianship of the Ten Commandments and for the Sermon on the Mount; yet, when it came to a practical question of assistance and responsibility, they absolutely refused to accept these." Lloyd George suggested that a telegram be sent asking the United States to participate in measures to assist Armenians. He was "quite certain that the Americans would do nothing, but their refusal to assist would make it far easier for us in the future to deal with them." It was agreed that Lord Curzon would convey such a request to Ambassador Davis.[38]

[36] First London Conference, February 12, 1920, 11 a.m., *ibid.*, pp. 1-2; Lloyd George, *The Truth about the Peace Treaties*, Vol. 2, pp. 1267-1268.
[37] First London Conference, February 27, 1920, 6 p.m., Woodward and Butler, eds., *Documents on British Foreign Policy, 1919-1939*, First Series, Vol. 7, p. 278.
[38] First London Conference, March 5, 1919, 3 p.m., *ibid.*, pp. 428-430.

In his memoirs, Lloyd George reaches unmatched heights of wrath in discussing the relationship of the United States to the Turkish negotiations in the winter and spring of 1920. President Wilson, he fulminates, "who dreamed of a Turkish settlement based on liberty and the wishes of the inhabitants, was confined to his sickroom—a broken and baffled prophet unable to put up any further fight for his faith."[39] As to the American attitude toward the brutalization of the Armenians by the Turkish nationalists: "It was becoming more and more apparent that their idea was that their righteous anger should be vindicated by, and at the expense in blood and treasure of, the nations who had already suffered most in the war and who were exhausted by the sacrifices they had endured in the struggle."[40]

Despite their disillusionment, the Allied leaders continued to approach the United States for assistance in the Turkish settlement. The Conference decided on March 12 to appeal to the Council of the League of Nations to accept responsibility for the future protection of Armenia.[41] The French Ambassador asked Acting Secretary of State Polk on March 12 whether any American participation in the negotiations on Turkey could be expected.[42] Frank Colby, the new Secretary of State, replied on March 24 that the President considered American participation inadvisable but that, because the United States was "profoundly interested in the future peace of the world," he thought that the views of the United States on the Turkish treaty should be frankly expressed. The United States was opposed, said Colby, to the retention of Turkish rule at Constantinople and favored the "most liberal treatment for Armenia." The note expressed the confidence of the United States Government that the powers would "be animated by a spirit of fairness and of a scrupulous regard for the interests of the vanquished, victor and neutral alike."[43] Lloyd George regarded this message, following upon the Senate's rejection of the Treaty of

---

[39] Lloyd George, *The Truth about the Peace Treaties*, Vol. 2, p. 1285.
[40] *ibid.*, pp. 1294-1295.
[41] First London Conference, March 12, 1920, 11:30 a.m., Woodward and Butler, eds., *Documents on British Foreign Policy, 1919-1939*, First Series, Vol. 7, pp. 477-479.
[42] Jusserand to Polk, March 12, 1920, *Foreign Relations, 1920* (3 Vols., Washington: United States Government Printing Office, 1935-1936), Vol. 3, pp. 748-750.
[43] Colby to Jusserand, March 24, 1920, *ibid.*, pp. 750-753.

Versailles on March 19, as a new pinnacle of American pontificating and presumptuousness. Noting that the message contained not one indication of American support, Lloyd George asserts in his memoirs that if Wilson had "even sent us privately a message of sympathy for the predicament in which we had been placed by the backsliding of American politicians, we should have felt grateful. But that was not in his obdurate and self-centered nature."[44]

The Allies continued their deliberations on the Turkish treaty at San Remo in April. Lloyd George took the position that because of the defection of the United States it would be impossible to constitute a large Armenia capable of supporting and defending itself.[45] Before making a definite decision, however, the Conference decided to make a final appeal to the United States. In a note drafted by Lord Curzon and conveyed through the American Ambassador to Italy on April 27, the Allies declared that they had long regarded the United States alone as "qualified alike by its sympathies and material resources" to undertake the mandate for Armenia on behalf of humanity. The Council thus made a "definite appeal to the United States Government to accept the mandate for Armenia." Regardless of the answer on the mandate, the Allies asked the President to arbitrate several boundary problems between Armenia and Turkey, and regardless of both the mandate and the arbitration, the United States was asked to provide volunteer forces or military assistance for the defense of Armenia and, even more urgently, an American loan to set Armenia on her feet.[46]

In the following months, the United States liquidated its last connections with the settlement of Turkey. President Wilson readily agreed to arbitrate the Turkish-Armenian boundaries and his word was conveyed to the Allied Powers on November 24, 1920.[47] The President appealed to Congress on May 24 to accept the mandate: "In response to the invitation of the Council at San Remo, I urgently advise and request that the Congress grant the

[44] Lloyd George, *The Truth about the Peace Treaties*, Vol. 2, pp. 1300-1301.
[45] *ibid.*, pp. 1302-1324.
[46] Ambassador Johnson (San Remo) to Colby, April 27, 1920, *Foreign Relations, 1920*, Vol. 3, pp. 779-783; Lloyd George, *The Truth about the Peace Treaties*, Vol. 2, pp. 1325-1333.
[47] Colby to Ambassador Wallace (Paris), May 17, 1920, *Foreign Relations, 1920*, Vol. 3, p. 783; Colby to Wallace, November 24, 1920, *ibid.*, pp. 789-804.

Executive power to accept for the United States a mandate for Armenia."[48] On November 30, President Wilson reported to the League Council that the Senate had rejected the invitation to accept the Armenian mandate. As to the request for military assistance and credits the President replied: "I am without authorization to offer or employ military forces of the United States in any project for the relief of Armenia, and any material contributions would require the authorization of the Congress which is not now in session and whose action I could not forecast." The President offered his personal good offices to end the attacks on the Armenian people.[49]

Armenia, under the Treaty of Sèvres, was recognized as a free and independent state, and Constantinople was left to the sovereignty of Turkey.[50] President Wilson's arbitral award was not carried out and the Armenian state was presently overrun by the Turkish nationalists under Mustafa Kemal.

Anglo-American relations in the context of the Turkish settlement were conditioned above all by the American withdrawal to isolation in late 1919 and 1920. The hope of the British to build the peace around American mandates over Constantinople and Armenia was dashed by the United States Senate. The British placed the blame for the fatal delay in the Turkish negotiations on the United States, and Lloyd George gave vent to bitter recriminations when the United States resigned all responsibility but continued to provide gratuitous counsel to the Allied statesmen. Lloyd George's charges were not unprovoked, but, in their recklessness, the simple distinction was not made between the President, who made every effort to fulfill the responsibilities which he had accepted for the United States, and the Senate, which denied him the authority to do so. Anglo-American har-

[48] Message to Congress, May 24, 1920, Ray Stannard Baker and William E. Dodd, eds., *The Public Papers of Woodrow Wilson* (6 Vols., New York and London: Harper & Brothers, Publishers, 1925-1927), *War and Peace*, Vol. 2, p. 489.

[49] Wilson to the President of the Council of the League of Nations (Hymans), November 30, 1920, *Foreign Relations, 1920*, Vol. 3, pp. 804-805.

[50] Treaty of Peace between the Allied and Associated Powers and Turkey, Sèvres, August 10, 1920, Great Britain, Treaty Series No. 11 (1920); *Papers by Command, Cmd.* 964.

mony in the Turkish settlement became one of the many victims of the headlong flight of the United States from international responsibility.

II. *Anglo-American Diplomacy and the Continuing Fiume Controversy*

Despite formidable expenditures of time and diplomatic energy, the Supreme Council had failed by the end of June to approach even bases of agreement on the Italian claims in the Adriatic, and the heads of government had left Paris with a demand for a total resurvey of the Italian claims.[51] The fruitless negotiations continued through the summer and autumn, still conditioned by the Anglo-French commitments under the Treaty of London and the American stand on principle against Italian annexation of Fiume. Asked on July 3 for new proposals on the Adriatic, Tittoni, the new Italian Foreign Minister, only reiterated familiar Italian views on the Treaty of London and the requirements of Italian public opinion.[52] The negotiations were stalled in July by the outbreak of riots in which Italian nationalists attacked the British and French troops of the nominally inter-Allied military establishment in Fiume. A commission of investigation sent to Fiume by the Supreme Council recommended that real inter-Allied control be established, but on September 12, the extreme nationalist D'Annunzio seized control of the city and the Allied troops were compelled to withdraw.[53]

New proposals for compromise were put forth in September. Lloyd George and Clemenceau sent a new plan to President Wilson on September 10, based on concessions offered by Tittoni. The plan called for a substantial reduction of the Italian claims in Dalmatia under the Treaty of London and for the establishment of an independent buffer state of Fiume and its surrounding territory, or, alternately, Italian annexation of the city of Fiume, Yugoslav annexation of the remainder of the buffer state area, and the placing of the port facilities of Fiume under the super-

[51] See Chapter 12, Section III.

[52] Council of Heads of Delegations, July 3, 1919, 2:30 p.m., *Foreign Relations, 1919, The Paris Peace Conference*, Vol. 7, p. 18.

[53] H.W.V. Temperley, ed., *A History of the Peace Conference of Paris* (6 Vols., London: Henry Frowde and Hodder and Stoughton, 1920-1924), Vol. 4, pp. 307-309.

vision of the League of Nations.[54] Clemenceau endorsed the latter alternative before the Council on the morning of September 15. Lloyd George said that he "would agree to anything which was acceptable both to President Wilson and the Italians." "The question," he believed, "was not one which ought to split the nations in two. It was really too trivial."[55] In the afternoon session on the same day, Polk expressed his conviction that President Wilson would not find the new proposal acceptable.[56] Polk's conviction was only partially confirmed by a telegram which he received from Wilson on September 22. The President agreed to the buffer state as proposed by Lloyd George and Clemenceau but flatly rejected Italian sovereignty over Fiume in any form.[57]

The compromise proposals of September were wrecked by new outbursts of nationalist feeling in Italy. The British Foreign Office received reports from Rome that the Government was powerless and that the Italian Army and people were solidly for D'Annunzio.[58] In a private conversation with Sir Eyre Crowe on September 30, Polk urged that Britain and France join the United States in a representation to Italy warning that the annexation of Fiume would mean a break with the three powers. Polk said that President Wilson felt so strongly on the matter that he was even considering sending American troops back to Europe, or at least an American naval squadron to the Adriatic. Polk further urged that Britain reinforce her naval squadron in the Adriatic.[59] The Foreign Office replied cautiously to the Polk proposals, asserting that a joint declaration would be considered but that naval cooperation with the United States could only be decided upon by the Admiralty after a policy had been determined in Paris.[60]

[54] Lloyd George and Clemenceau to Wilson, September 10, 1919, Woodward and Butler, eds., Documents on British Foreign Policy, 1919-1939, First Series, Vol. 4, pp. 123-125.

[55] Council of Heads of Delegations, September 15, 1919, 10:30 a.m., Foreign Relations, 1919, The Paris Peace Conference, Vol. 8, pp. 214-215; Woodward and Butler, eds., Documents on British Foreign Policy, 1919-1939, First Series, Vol. 1, p. 699.

[56] Council of Heads of Delegations, September 15, 1919, 4 p.m., Foreign Relations, 1919, The Paris Peace Conference, Vol. 8, p. 224; Woodward and Butler, eds., Documents on British Foreign Policy, 1919-1939, First Series, Vol. 1, p. 706.

[57] Wilson to Polk, September 22, 1919, ibid., Vol. 4, p. 125.

[58] Mr. Kennard (Rome) to Curzon. September 24, 1919, ibid., p. 75; Sir R. Rodd (Rome) to Curzon, September 29, 1919, ibid., pp. 83-86.

[59] Crowe to Curzon, September 30, 1919, ibid., pp. 90-92.

[60] Curzon to Crowe, October 4, 1919, ibid., p. 100.

The impasse continued through the autumn, with the British Government attempting to mediate between the positions of Italy and the United States. Lloyd George instructed Lord Grey, then in Washington, to press President Wilson for concessions to Premier Nitti, lest his Government be overwhelmed by the extremists.[61] Sir Eyre Crowe was much more inclined to align British policy with that of the United States. In a communication to Lord Curzon on November 3, he expressed the view that Britain was "under some obligation to the United States Government" because of Wilson's efforts to extricate Britain from the obligations of the Treaty of London. Crowe said that it would be "deplorable" for Britain to abandon the United States in the Fiume issue. "The British and American delegations," he affirmed, "have consistently stood together in resisting these Italian maneuvers."[62] Philip Kerr replied to Crowe with a private letter that most clearly expressed the policy of the British Government: ". . . I am not sure that you fully understand the Prime Minister's attitude on the Adriatic question. . . . He feels that both sides . . . have now been driven to take their stand on what are in themselves points of minor importance. . . . I don't think he would entirely agree with the view expressed in your despatch of November 3. . . . The British attitude has always been that it has considered itself bound by treaty to Italy. It did its best to persuade Italy to abandon its claims, but it has always admitted that it was bound by these obligations and could not, therefore, definitely side with the United States. Its position, therefore, was that of a mediator bound to one side but whose sympathies were engaged with the other. . . ."[63]

The British, French, and American delegates agreed on a joint memorandum to Italy on December 9, which represented to the United States a final offer of compromise on the Adriatic. The memorandum rejected the latest Italian demand for a free city of Fiume coupled with Italian annexation of an Adriatic coastal strip connecting Italy with Fiume and proposed the establishment of a free state of Fiume encompassing the city and its surrounding territory. The free state would be under the authority of the League

[61] Curzon to Grey, from Lloyd George, October 31, 1919, *ibid.*, pp. 150-151.
[62] Crowe to Curzon, November 3, 1919, *ibid.*, pp. 156-158.
[63] Kerr to Crowe, November 14, 1919, *ibid.*, pp. 182-183.

and its future would be left to the League, President Wilson's earlier demand for an eventual plebiscite now being dropped as a concession to Italy. Concessions were made also to the Italian demands in Dalmatia and the Adriatic islands, and Italy was conceded the mandate for Albania.[64]

The proposal of December 9 was quickly abandoned by all concerned except the United States. In a memorandum to Lloyd George on January 6, 1920, Nitti demanded fulfillment of the Treaty of London, and, while agreeing to the proposed free state of Fiume, insisted that the city itself must be constituted as a *corpus separatum* within the free state and that Italy must annex the coastal strip connecting Italian territory with Fiume.[65] In a memorandum submitted to the conference of Allied Premiers on January 9, Lloyd George and Clemenceau abandoned the plan of December 9 and conceded the Italian demand for Fiume as a *corpus separatum*.[66] After further negotiations with Nitti, Lloyd George and Clemenceau on January 14 handed revised proposals to Trumbitch of Yugoslavia for abolishing the free state but establishing Fiume as a *corpus separatum* under the League of Nations with its port facilities available to both Italy and Yugoslavia. Italy was to have the connecting coastal strip and the Albanian mandate.[67] The Yugoslav reply, received on January 20, accepted the proposal only with certain qualifications.[68] Nitti declared in the meeting of the Premiers on January 20 that he could make no further concessions and was departing at once for Rome.[69]

The United States reacted with intense displeasure to the Anglo-French abandonment of the joint memorandum of December 9. Lansing instructed Ambassador Wallace to protest to the British

[64] Memorandum by Clemenceau, Polk, and Crowe, December 9, 1919, Great Britain, Parliament, *Papers by Command, Cmd.* 586, 1920, Miscellaneous No. 2, "Correspondence Relating to the Adriatic Question," Doc. 1; Edward Parkes, ed., *British and Foreign State Papers, 1920* (London: His Majesty's Stationery Office, 1923), pp. 807-816.

[65] Nitti to Lloyd George, January 6, 1920, *ibid.*, pp. 819-820.

[66] Council of Premiers, January 9, 1920, 12:15 p.m., *Foreign Relations, 1919, The Paris Peace Conference,* Vol. 9, pp. 859-862.

[67] Lloyd George and Clemenceau to Trumbitch, January 14, 1920, Parkes, ed., *State Papers, 1920,* pp. 833-834.

[68] Trumbitch to Lloyd George and Clemenceau, January 20, 1920, *Foreign Relations, 1919, The Paris Peace Conference,* Vol. 9, pp. 943-951.

[69] Council of Premiers, January 20, 1920, 6:30 p.m., *ibid.*, pp. 934-935; Woodward and Butler, eds., *Documents on British Foreign Policy, 1919-1939,* First Series, Vol. 2, pp. 950-951.

and French their handling of Italian problems without ascertaining the views of the United States and to point out the unacceptability to President Wilson of their latest proposals on Fiume.[70] Lloyd George and Clemenceau handed their reply to Ambassador Davis in London on January 22. It denied any Anglo-French intention of settling the Fiume controversy without consulting the United States and contended that the proposals of January 14 retained "practically every important point of the joint memorandum of December 9, 1919." Moreover, averred the two Premiers, in the absence of an American plenipotentiary, Britain and France had no choice but to proceed with the search for a solution.[71]

President Wilson reacted with a letter to the British and French Governments on February 10 which condemned the Allied conduct of the Adriatic negotiations as an abnegation of the agreed principles of the peace. Declaring the Allied proposals of January 14 unacceptable, the President asserted that they "profoundly altered" the memorandum of December 9 and opened the way to Italian domination of Fiume. Wilson denounced the entire scheme as a "positive denial of the principles for which America entered the war." The Adriatic issue, he declared, "raises the fundamental question as to whether the American Government can on any terms cooperate with its European associates in the great work of maintaining the peace of the world by removing the primary causes of war." ". . . if, in a word," the President continued, "the old order of things which brought so many evils on the world is still to prevail, then the time is not yet come when this Government can enter a concert of powers, the very existence of which must depend upon a new spirit and a new order." If it does not appear feasible to secure acceptance of the concessions offered in the memorandum of December 9, Wilson threatened, then he "must take under serious consideration the withdrawal of the treaty with Germany and the agreement between the United States and France of the 28th June, 1919, which are now before the Senate and permitting the terms of the European settlement

[70] Lansing to Wallace, January 19, 1920, *Foreign Relations, 1919, The Paris Peace Conference*, Vol. 9, pp. 999-1000.

[71] Lloyd George and Clemenceau to Davis, January 22, 1920, Parkes, ed., *State Papers, 1920*, pp. 838-840.

to be individually established and enforced by the Associated Governments."[72]

The President's note, against the background of the political situation in America, was more than Lloyd George could bear. He pronounced it a "most pompous, dictatorial document."[73] In the Council on February 14, Lord Curzon suggested a reply to Wilson explaining the January compromise proposals and warning that if he maintained his objections to them the Allies would fall back on the Treaty of London. Lloyd George said that the Conference wished to know whether Yugoslavia preferred the compromise offer or the Treaty of London, "and not which of the two President Wilson preferred." The Prime Minister was opposed to delaying a positive proposal to Trumbitch "simply because President Wilson did not agree."[74] The Council again discussed a reply to Wilson on February 16, and Curzon said that Ambassador Davis and Lord Grey advised a most courteous reply, "in view of the President's present irritability."[75] Lloyd George and Millerand, the new French Premier, dispatched a note to the United States on February 17 which contested President Wilson's view of the Anglo-French proposals of January 14 and expressed the hope that the United States would "reconsider its attitude." If the United States maintained its position, the Prime Ministers said, Britain and France would not insist on their proposals but would be forced to revert to the Treaty of London. Britain and France, said the note, were "reluctant to believe" that their proposed changes in the memorandum of December 9 could "constitute in themselves a justification for a withdrawal from all further cooperation with them in the attempt to adjust peaceably the world's affairs." Lloyd George and Millerand declared themselves "deeply concerned that the United States should even contemplate the action to which they refer" and expressed the hope that the

[72] Wilson's Note of February 10, 1920, *ibid.*, pp. 843-846. See also Temperley, ed., *A History of the Peace Conference of Paris*, Vol. 4, pp. 322-324.

[73] *Lord Riddell's Intimate Diary of the Peace Conference and After, 1918-1923* (New York: Reynal and Hitchcock, Inc., 1934), p. 169.

[74] First London Conference, February 14, 1920, 4 p.m., Woodward and Butler, eds., *Documents on British Foreign Policy, 1919-1939*, First Series, Vol. 7, pp. 51-53.

[75] First London Conference, February 16, 1920, 5:15 p.m., *ibid.*, pp. 72-76.

United States would not, because of the Adriatic, "wreck the whole machinery" of the treaties.[76]

In subsequent communications, both Wilson and the Allies adopted a more moderate tone. In a reply dated February 24, President Wilson reasserted the American position but suggested that Italy and Yugoslavia enter into direct negotiations, agreeing to endorse any arrangement accepted by both. If the direct negotiations should fail, Wilson suggested, Italy and Yugoslavia should accept the decision of Britain, France, and the United States.[77] Wilson's reply was discussed by the Allied Premiers on the afternoon of February 25, and Lloyd George noted that while the tone was much more moderate, it contained the "same unalterable determination as far as fundamentals were concerned." Lloyd George questioned the value of Italian-Yugoslav negotiations "at a time when the Yugoslavs thought the Allied Governments were still crouching at the crack of President Wilson's whip. . . ."[78] Nevertheless, Lloyd George and Millerand dispatched a memorandum to the United States on February 26 welcoming the President's suggestion and proposing that the United States, Britain, and France issue a joint invitation to Italy and Yugoslavia to negotiate directly, with the stipulation that if they failed the three powers would again consider the issue.[79]

Once again, the approach to a unified policy ended in failure. In a note to the Allied leaders on March 4, President Wilson refused to withdraw the memorandum of December 9 in conjunction with an invitation to Italy and Yugoslavia to enter negotiations.[80] Lloyd George declared to the Council on March 8 that Wilson's position made it possible for the Yugoslavs to refuse to compromise and the Marquis Imperiali asserted that the Presi-

[76] Reply of Lloyd George and Millerand to Wilson, February 17, 1920, *Cmd.* 586, Doc. 2; Parkes, ed., *State Papers, 1920,* pp. 846-852. See also Lloyd George, *The Truth about the Peace Treaties,* Vol. 2, pp. 896-897.

[77] American Reply to Lloyd George and Millerand, February 24, 1920, *Cmd.* 586, Doc. 14; Parkes, ed., *State Papers, 1920,* pp. 853-857; Baker and Dodd, eds., *Public Papers, War and Peace,* Vol. 2, pp. 469-475.

[78] First London Conference, February 25, 1920, 4 p.m., Woodward and Butler, eds., *Documents on British Foreign Policy, 1919-1939,* First Series, Vol. 7, p. 252.

[79] Reply of Lloyd George and Millerand to the United States, February 26, 1920, Parkes, ed., *State Papers, 1920,* pp. 857-859.

[80] Wilson to Lloyd George and Millerand, March 4, 1920, Baker and Dodd, eds., *Public Papers, War and Peace,* Vol. 2, pp. 476-479.

dent's attitude made negotiations between Italy and Yugoslavia impossible. Lloyd George proposed that the entire issue be brought to a head by conveying the correspondence between the Allies and the United States to Italy and Yugoslavia with an explanation that Britain and France had done their best to find a solution and had failed and now stood on the Treaty of London.[81] The Council agreed on March 15 that no further reply would be made to President Wilson.[82]

Thus ended the protracted Fiume controversy in general failure. Greatly discouraged by the fall of President Wilson and the Democratic Party in the election of 1920, the Yugoslavs signed the Treaty of Rapallo with Italy on November 12, 1920, under which Italy achieved most of her demands. Fiume was constituted as a *corpus separatum* within a Free State of Fiume and Italy was conceded a connecting coastal strip giving her contiguity to Fiume.[83] The breakdown of Anglo-American amity in the final stages of the Fiume crisis may be attributed to underlying hostility on both sides resulting from the American withdrawal from the peace settlement. President Wilson, beset by the pressure of events at home, grew testy and pontifical in his messages of counsel to the Allied leaders. Lloyd George, on the other hand, was irritated in the extreme at what he considered the presumptuousness of American pronouncements on the issue since the United States had resigned all responsibility for it. He failed, however, as in the Turkish negotiations, to show any regard for the fact that it was the Senate, and not the President, which had repudiated the responsibility of the United States. Moreover, Wilson seems to have become even more deeply convinced of the sanctity of the principle at stake in the Fiume controversy, while Lloyd George, who never regarded Fiume as a very significant question, became more than ever persuaded of its triviality. Thus it came about that Great Britain and the United States ended in a relationship of mutual anger and disgust over an issue of secondary importance in itself

[81] First London Conference, March 8, 1920, 12:15 p.m., Woodward and Butler, eds., *Documents on British Foreign Policy, 1919-1939*, First Series, Vol. 7, pp. 436-437.

[82] First London Conference, March 15, 1920, 12:45 p.m., *ibid.*, pp. 501-502.

[83] *Cmd.*, 1238; Parkes, ed., *State Papers, 1920*, pp. 1087-1092. See Temperley, ed., *A History of the Peace Conference of Paris*, Vol. 4, pp. 327-333.

and one which in no way involved a direct conflict of interests between the two English-speaking powers.

III. Questions of Self-Determination in Regard to Eastern Galicia, Thrace, Hungary, and Roumania

As in the case of the Polish-German boundary, Great Britain was the principal opponent of Polish claims in Eastern Galicia, while the United States demonstrated the same tenderness for Poland which it had displayed in the early negotiations over Danzig and Upper Silesia. Western Galicia was an area overwhelmingly Polish in population, but Eastern Galicia had a substantial majority of Ruthenians. Hostilities between Poles and Ruthenians had begun with the collapse of Austria-Hungary, and by June 1919, Polish forces were in complete occupation of Eastern Galicia.[84] The Council of Foreign Ministers on June 25 endorsed the Polish occupation and authorized the Poles to set up a civil government, but reserved the right of the principal Allied and Associated Powers to take measures for the self-determination of Eastern Galicia.[85]

The Council deliberated on the disposition of Eastern Galicia in the autumn of 1919. Sir Eyre Crowe on September 19 urged the separation of Eastern Galicia from Poland, noting that its Ruthenian majority might wish eventually to associate with Russia or the Ukraine.[86] But on September 25, Frank Polk, with French and Italian support, submitted a memorandum calling for the attachment of Eastern Galicia to Poland under League of Nations oversight, with provision for an eventual plebiscite.[87] The British

[84] See *ibid.*, Vol. 6, pp. 246-283; Louis L. Gerson, *Woodrow Wilson and the Rebirth of Poland, 1914-1920* (New Haven: Yale University Press, 1953), pp. 119-120; Charles Homer Haskins and Robert Howard Lord, *Some Problems of the Peace Conference* (Cambridge: Harvard University Press, 1920), pp. 189-192.

[85] Council of Foreign Ministers, June 25, 1919, 3 p.m., *Foreign Relations, 1919, The Paris Peace Conference*, Vol. 4, pp. 854-855; Woodward and Butler, eds., *Documents on British Foreign Policy, 1919-1939*, First Series, Vol. 3, pp. 857-858.

[86] Council of Heads of Delegations, September 19, 1919, 11 a.m., *Foreign Relations, 1919, The Paris Peace Conference*, Vol. 8, p. 272; Woodward and Butler, eds., *Documents on British Foreign Policy, 1919-1939*, First Series, Vol. 1, p. 735.

[87] Council of Heads of Delegations, September 25, 1919, 10:30 a.m., *Foreign Relations, 1919, The Paris Peace Conference*, Vol. 8, pp. 349, 368-370; Woodward and Butler, eds., *Documents on British Foreign Policy, 1919-1939*, First Series, Vol. 1, pp. 784, 787-788.

Government took a firm position against Polish annexation of Eastern Galicia but proposed a Polish mandate of ten years and subsequent reconsideration of the disposition of the territory by the League of Nations.[88] In the meeting of the Council on November 7, Crowe argued against the final union of Eastern Galicia with Poland but agreed to a fifteen-year Polish mandate. Polk said that the British proposal would leave Eastern Galicia in ferment and Poland in uncertainty, adding that it was difficult to see where the territory could go except to Poland. The issue was referred to the Polish Commission.[89] The Polish Commission recommended a Polish mandate of twenty-five years, at the end of which period the League of Nations would have full authority to revise the status of Eastern Galicia.[90] Although Crowe preferred a ten-year mandate and Polk an indefinite mandate, the recommendation of the Polish Commission was adopted by the Council as a satisfactory compromise.[91]

The question then arose as to whether the revision of the status of Eastern Galicia at the end of the mandate period would be by majority or unanimous vote of the League Council. The American, French, Italian, and Japanese members of the Polish Commission proposed to vest full powers in a majority to maintain or modify the status of Eastern Galicia, while the British member insisted upon unanimity.[92] Henry White argued before the Council on November 21 against any one power exercising a veto as to the disposition of Eastern Galicia, but Crowe maintained the British insistence upon unanimity. The impasse was compromised, or evaded, by a simple agreement that the League Council would have full powers to revise, maintain, or modify the status of

[88] Curzon to Crowe, October 13, 1919, *ibid.*, Vol. 3, pp. 895-896; Curzon to Crowe, October 24, 1919, *ibid.*, p. 897.

[89] Council of Heads of Delegations, November 7, 1919, 10:30 a.m., *Foreign Relations, 1919, The Paris Peace Conference*, Vol. 9, pp. 20-21; Woodward and Butler, eds., *Documents on British Foreign Policy, 1919-1939*, First Series, Vol. 2, pp. 218-219.

[90] Report of Polish Commission, November 11, 1919, *Foreign Relations, 1919, The Paris Peace Conference*, Vol. 9, pp. 115-117; Woodward and Butler, eds., *Documents on British Foreign Policy, 1919-1939*, First Series, Vol. 2, pp. 283-285.

[91] Council of Heads of Delegations, November 11, 1919, 10:30 a.m., *Foreign Relations, 1919, The Paris Peace Conference*, Vol. 9, pp. 100-101; Woodward and Butler, eds., *Documents on British Foreign Policy, 1919-1939*, First Series, Vol. 2, pp. 280-281.

[92] Report of the Polish Commission, November 20, 1919, *Foreign Relations, 1919, The Paris Peace Conference*, Vol. 9, pp. 271-272.

Eastern Galicia at the end of twenty-five years, with no mention of whether its decision would be by majority or unanimous vote.[93]

The agreement on Eastern Galicia was stillborn. In the wake of vigorous protests by the Polish Government, the decision for the twenty-five year mandate was suspended on December 22, the British acquiescing with the greatest reluctance.[94] The Peace Conference took no further action on Eastern Galicia, thereby leaving unchallenged its conquest by Poland.[95] In this debate, as in the deliberations in the spring of 1919 on the Polish-German frontier, the British took an isolated stand for the strict implementation of the principle of self-determination, while the United States again displayed a curious solicitude for Polish ambitions and a seeming indifference to the principle which it so rigorously upheld in the case of the Italian claims in the Adriatic.

The dispute between Poland and Czechoslovakia over the coal-producing district of Teschen produced no special problems for Anglo-American diplomacy. Both Wilson and Lloyd George in April 1919, expressed sympathy for the Polish claim on the ground that the majority of the population of Teschen was Polish. Lloyd George, however, emphasized that Czechoslovakia should have some rights in regard to the coal produced in the district, on which Czech industries had long been dependent.[96] An Inter-Allied Commission on Teschen arranged direct negotiations between the Czechs and Poles, who conferred in Cracow in the summer but broke up in disagreement on July 29.[97] Beneš presented the Czech

[93] Council of Heads of Delegations, November 21, 1919, 10:30 a.m., *ibid.*, pp. 285-286, 293-295; Woodward and Butler, eds., *Documents on British Foreign Policy, 1919-1939*, First Series, Vol. 2, pp. 377-378, 383-384. See also Titus Komarnicki, *The Rebirth of the Polish Republic* (London, Melbourne, Toronto: William Heinemann, Ltd., 1957), pp. 388-389.

[94] Council of Heads of Delegations, December 22, 1919, 10:30 a.m., *Foreign Relations, 1919, The Paris Peace Conference*, Vol. 9, p. 626; Woodward and Butler, eds., *Documents on British Foreign Policy, 1919-1939*, First Series, Vol. 2, p. 585; Komarnicki, *The Rebirth of the Polish Republic*, pp. 389-390.

[95] See Haskins and Lord, *Some Problems of the Peace Conference*, pp. 193-196; Temperley, ed., *A History of the Peace Conference of Paris*, Vol. 6, pp. 272-274.

[96] Council of Four, April 12, 11 a.m., Paul Mantoux, *Les Délibérations du Conseil des Quatre* (2 Vols., Paris: Éditions du Centre National de la Recherche Scientifique, 1955), Vol. 1, p. 232.

[97] Colonel Pakenham Walsh, President of the Inter-Allied Commission on Teschen, to Balfour, August 1, 1919, Woodward and Butler, eds., *Documents on British Foreign Policy, 1919-1939*, First Series, Vol. 6, p. 116.

claim to Teschen to the Council on September 4, stressing the historic and economic affiliation of the district with Czechoslovakia.[98] The Polish case, based on the ethnography of the district, was presented on the next day.[99] The Council agreed on September 11, without controversy and with Polish and Czech assent, to hold a plebiscite in Teschen and the attached districts under Allied supervision.[100]

A rather sharp controversy developed between Great Britain and the United States in the summer of 1919 over the disposition of Western Thrace, with Britain supporting the claim of Greece and the United States acting as champion of the ethnographic and economic interests of the enemy state of Bulgaria. Henry White reported to President Wilson on July 18 that the American experts unanimously opposed Greek annexation of Western Thrace. The British showed some annoyance with the American attitude because they felt that the United States, which had not been at war with Bulgaria, had no right to play a major role in the settlement of Bulgarian issues. Wilson, however, instructed White to stand on the recommendations of the American experts.[101] In the Council on July 31, White argued against the detachment of Western Thrace from Bulgaria on grounds of self-determination and the need of Bulgaria for an Aegean outlet. Balfour, with French support, contested White's view, emphasizing the role which Bulgaria had played in prolonging the war.[102]

[98] Council of Heads of Delegations, September 4, 1919, 11 a.m., *Foreign Relations, 1919, The Paris Peace Conference*, Vol. 8, pp. 102-106; Woodward and Butler, eds., *Documents on British Foreign Policy, 1919-1939*, First Series, Vol. 1, pp. 624-628.

[99] Council of Heads of Delegations, September 5, 1919, 11 a.m., *Foreign Relations, 1919, The Paris Peace Conference*, Vol. 8, pp. 118-124; Woodward and Butler, eds., *Documents on British Foreign Policy, 1919-1939*, First Series, Vol. 1, pp. 635-640.

[100] Council of Heads of Delegations, September 11, 1919, 11 a.m., *Foreign Relations, 1919, The Paris Peace Conference*, Vol. 8, pp. 185, 194-198; Woodward and Butler, eds., *Documents on British Foreign Policy, 1919-1939*, First Series, Vol. 1, pp. 674, 682-685.

[101] Allan Nevins, *Henry White: Thirty Years of American Diplomacy* (New York and London: Harper & Brothers, Publishers, 1930), pp. 470-471. See also Haskins and Lord, *Some Problems of the Peace Conference*, pp. 281-285.

[102] Council of Heads of Delegations, July 31, 1919, 3:30 p.m., *Foreign Relations, 1919, The Paris Peace Conference*, Vol. 7, pp. 434-439; Woodward and Butler, eds., *Documents on British Foreign Policy, 1919-1939*, First Series, Vol. 1, pp. 258-263.

Rejecting the majority report of the Commission on Greek Affairs, which endorsed the Greek claims, Frank Polk cited to the Council on August 7 census figures showing the population of Western Thrace in 1914 to have consisted of some 100,000 Bulgarians and only 30,000 Greeks. Expressing regret at his inability to support the wishes of Venizelos, Polk said that he "had no desire to favor the Bulgarians but it was not always advantageous to give even a good boy all he wanted." He was, he said, under clear instructions from President Wilson not to hand over a large Bulgarian population to Greece.[103]

Efforts to reach a compromise led to a tentative agreement to place Eastern and Western Thrace within an international state of Constantinople, but the United States differed with the Allies over its size, insisting that northwestern Thrace be left to Bulgaria.[104] President Wilson instructed Polk late in August that the United States would sign and guarantee the Bulgarian treaty only if it were based on the self-determination of peoples. The President insisted upon the international state, which Venizelos vigorously opposed, with a guarantee to Bulgaria of free passage across the territory of the international state and free use of the port of Dedeagatch on the Aegean.[105] Clemenceau asserted on September 1 that if the President adhered to his position a settlement would not be possible, but Balfour devised a formula of evasion for inclusion in the Bulgarian treaty. Although he felt that President Wilson "had not given sufficient consideration to the position of M. Venizelos," Balfour proposed that the southern frontier of Bulgaria be drawn as proposed by Wilson but that the disputed territory simply be ceded to the Allied and Associated Powers for their ultimate disposition.[106] The proposal was adopted

[103] Council of Heads of Delegations, August 7, 1919, 3:30 p.m., *Foreign Relations, 1919, The Paris Peace Conference*, Vol. 7, pp. 609-610; Woodward and Butler, eds., *Documents on British Foreign Policy, 1919-1939*, First Series, Vol. 1, pp. 362-363.

[104] Council of Heads of Delegations, August 12, 1919, 3:30 p.m., *Foreign Relations, 1919, The Paris Peace Conference*, Vol. 7, p. 671; Woodward and Butler, eds., *Documents on British Foreign Policy, 1919-1939*, First Series, Vol. 1, pp. 399-400.

[105] Lansing to Polk, August 28, 1919, *Foreign Relations, 1919, The Paris Peace Conference*, Vol. 8, pp. 50-51; Woodward and Butler, eds., *Documents on British Foreign Policy, 1919-1939*, First Series, Vol. 1, pp. 594-595.

[106] Council of Heads of Delegations, September 1, 1919, 11 a.m., *Foreign Relations, 1919, The Paris Peace Conference*, Vol. 8, pp. 35-37; Woodward and

by the Council on September 2.[107] The treaty of peace was presented to the Bulgarians on September 19 and signed at Neuilly on November 27.[108]

The Greco-Bulgarian territorial problem was disposed of in the course of the negotiations on the Turkish treaty in the spring of 1920. In his message to the First London Conference of March 24, 1920, Wilson contended, on ethnographic grounds, that the northern part of Eastern Thrace, including Adrianople, should be left to Bulgaria.[109] Lord Curzon challenged the American contention as based on false ethnographic data and produced statistics indicating that both Greeks and Moslems outnumbered Bulgarians in the area of Adrianople.[110] The Supreme Council dispatched a note from San Remo on April 27 informing the United States Government that it had been decided to award all of Eastern Thrace, outside of Constantinople, to Greece, thereby abandoning altogether the proposed international state.[111] When the treaty of peace with Turkey was signed on August 10, 1920, a separate treaty was concluded between Greece and the Allies which awarded all of Thrace to Greece, conceding to Bulgaria the right of free transit to the Aegean and the use of the port of Dedeagatch.[112]

The differences between the United States and Great Britain in regard to the Bulgarian rights in Western and Eastern Thrace represent another instance of the determination of the United States to treat the enemy states with the same impartial justice

---

Butler, eds., *Documents on British Foreign Policy, 1919-1939*, First Series, Vol. I, pp. 589-591.

[107] Council of Heads of Delegations, September 2, 1919, 11 a.m., *Foreign Relations, 1919, The Paris Peace Conference*, Vol. 8, pp. 55, 63-67; Woodward and Butler, eds., *Documents on British Foreign Policy, 1919-1939*, First Series, Vol. I, pp. 597, 603-604.

[108] Plenary Session, September 19, 1919, *Foreign Relations, 1919, The Paris Peace Conference*, Vol. 3, pp. 436-441; Plenary Session, November 27, 1919, *ibid.*, pp. 442-444. Treaty of Peace between the Allied and Associated Powers and Bulgaria, Neuilly-sur-Seine, November 27, 1919, Great Britain, Treaty Series No. 5 (1920); *Cmd.* 522.

[109] Colby to Jusserand, March 24, 1919, *Foreign Relations, 1920*, Vol. 3, p. 751; Lloyd George, *The Truth about the Peace Treaties*, Vol. 2, p. 1298.

[110] First London Conference, March 30, 1919, 4:30 p.m., Woodward and Butler, eds., *Documents on British Foreign Policy, 1919-1939*, First Series, Vol. 7, pp. 680-681.

[111] Ambassador Johnson to Colby, April 27, 1920, *Foreign Relations, 1920*, Vol. 3, p. 755.

[112] Treaty between the Allied and Associated Powers and Greece Relative to Thrace, Sèvres, August 10, 1920, Great Britain, Treaty Series, No. 13 (1920); *Cmd.* 1236.

as the Allied states, in order to secure a peace settlement which the United States could guarantee. Great Britain, in the Bulgarian settlement, seems to have been motivated at least in part by a desire to punish Bulgaria and reward Greece for their respective roles in the war.

Great Britain and the United States pursued a generally common policy in regard to the making of peace with Hungary. The dismemberment of Hungary was in fact determined by the settlement of the frontiers of the surrounding states, but the actual negotiation of a treaty was delayed first by the tenure of power of Béla Kun's Bolshevik regime until August 1919, and then by the Roumanian occupation of Hungary.[113] Britain and the United States stood firmly together in demanding Roumanian withdrawal from Hungary before the conclusion of a treaty of peace.

Anglo-American efforts to compel the withdrawal of Roumanian forces met with Roumanian defiance and only lukewarm support from the French and Italians. Balfour and Polk directed the attention of the Council on September 2 to expropriations of Hungarian property by the Roumanian forces and their refusal to withdraw.[114] Balfour submitted a draft ultimatum on September 4 demanding Roumanian withdrawal from Hungary and acceptance of the decisions of the Peace Conference. The Council approved the ultimatum and commissioned the British diplomat, Sir George Clerk, to deliver it to Bucharest.[115] On September 15, Lloyd George and Polk complained of reports from Bucharest that the French and Italian Ministers were actively encouraging the Roumanians to believe that only Britain and the United States were hostile to their policy in Hungary.[116]

The Clerk mission to Bucharest proved inconclusive. Clerk arrived in Bucharest on September 11 and extracted a promise from

[113] See Chapter 8, Section II.

[114] Council of Heads of Delegations, September 2, 1919, 11 a.m., *Foreign Relations, 1919, The Paris Peace Conference*, Vol. 8, pp. 57-60; Woodward and Butler, eds., *Documents on British Foreign Policy, 1919-1939*, First Series, Vol. 1, pp. 598-601.

[115] Council of Heads of Delegations, September 4, 1919, 11 a.m., *Foreign Relations, 1919, The Paris Peace Conference*, Vol. 8, pp. 101, 111-114; Woodward and Butler, eds., *Documents on British Foreign Policy, 1919-1939*, First Series, Vol. 1, pp. 623, 630-632.

[116] Council of Heads of Delegations, September 15, 1919, 4 p.m., *Foreign Relations, 1919, The Paris Peace Conference*, Vol. 8, p. 227; Woodward and Butler, eds., *Documents on British Foreign Policy, 1919-1939*, First Series, Vol. 1, pp. 709-710.

Bratiano that Roumanian forces would be withdrawn from Hungary.[117] The British Minister in Bucharest, however, reported that the French were encouraging Roumanian defiance of Great Britain and the United States.[118] Clerk returned to Paris early in October and recommended to the Council that the Allies make clear to Roumania their absolute determination to enforce the decisions of the Peace Conference in regard to Roumania's frontier with Hungary and other aspects of the Hungarian treaty.[119] The Council dispatched a note to the Roumanian Government on October 11 to the effect of the Clerk recommendations.[120]

Attention was then directed toward efforts to bolster a Hungarian Government which could maintain order and negotiate peace. The Council on October 16 commissioned Clerk to go as its agent on a mission to Budapest for the purpose of communicating with the Hungarian political parties.[121] Clerk reported from Budapest on October 25 that the political situation in Hungary was confused and that no stable government could be formed until the Roumanian forces had been evacuated.[122]

The crisis was ended in the course of November and early December. Roumanian forces were withdrawn from Budapest early in November and, on November 15, the Council dispatched an ultimatum to the Roumanian Government demanding complete withdrawal of Roumanian forces from Hungary and compliance with certain other requirements of the Council on the threat of a severance of relations between Roumania and the Peace

[117] Clerk to Supreme Council, September 16, 1919, *Foreign Relations, 1919, The Paris Peace Conference*, Vol. 8, pp. 333-335; Woodward and Butler, eds., *Documents on British Foreign Policy, 1919-1939*, First Series, Vol. 1, pp. 772-774.

[118] Rattigan to Curzon, September 18, 1919, *ibid.*, Vol. 6, p. 243.

[119] Council of Heads of Delegations, October 10, 1919, 10:30 a.m., *Foreign Relations, 1919, The Paris Peace Conference*, Vol. 8, pp. 539, 550-561; Woodward and Butler, eds., *Documents on British Foreign Policy, 1919-1939*, First Series, Vol. 1, pp. 884, 892-908. Clerk's written report on his mission to Bucharest, dated October 7, 1919, is also reproduced in Francis Déak, *Hungary at the Paris Peace Conference* (New York: Columbia University Press, 1942), pp. 503-512.

[120] Supreme Council to the Roumanian Government, October 11, 1919, *Foreign Relations, 1919, The Paris Peace Conference*, Vol. 8, pp. 583-586; Woodward and Butler, eds., *Documents on British Foreign Policy, 1919-1939*, First Series, Vol. 1, pp. 916-919; Déak, *Hungary at the Paris Peace Conference*, pp. 517-520.

[121] Council of Heads of Delegations, October 16, 1919, 10:30 a.m., *Foreign Relations, 1919, The Paris Peace Conference*, Vol. 8, p. 675; Woodward and Butler, eds., *Documents on British Foreign Policy, 1919-1939*, First Series, Vol. 2, pp. 5-7.

[122] Clerk to Crowe, October 25, 1919, *ibid.*, Vol. 6, p. 310.

Conference.[123] After some further attempts at evasion, the Rou-manian Government gave assurances of its compliance with the Allied demands.[124] The Council agreed on December 1 to invite the Hungarian Government to send representatives to Neuilly.[125] The draft treaty was communicated to the Hungarian Govern-ment in January, and Count Apponyi appeared before the Council of Allied Premiers on January 16 and eloquently protested the terms of peace.[126]

The United States took little part in the subsequent negotiations regarding Hungary. In March, the United States protested altera-tions in the draft treaty made by the Allies without consulting Washington, but Lord Curzon contended that the United States had no right to protest in view of the fact that it had been invited to participate in the negotiations and had refused. The Council rejected the American protest.[127] The Treaty of Peace with Hungary was signed at Trianon on June 4, 1920.[128]

Anglo-American diplomacy made an honest effort in the sum-mer and autumn of 1919 to secure conditions of justice for the negotiation of the Hungarian treaty. Britain and the United States led the Peace Conference in thwarting the effort of Roumania, an ally, to impose *de facto* terms of peace on defeated Hungary. Implicit in the Anglo-American policy of compelling Roumanian withdrawal from Hungarian territory and of assisting Hungary to constitute a stable government before the conclusion of peace was the Wilsonian principle of impartial justice to enemies as well as Allies.

[123] Supreme Council to the Roumanian Government, November 15, 1919, *Foreign Relations, 1919, The Paris Peace Conference*, Vol. 9, pp. 182-184.

[124] Rattigan to Crowe, December 6, 1919, Woodward and Butler, eds., *Documents on British Foreign Policy, 1919-1939*, First Series, Vol. 6, p. 496.

[125] Council of Heads of Delegations, December 1, 1919, 10:30 a.m., *Foreign Relations, 1919, The Paris Peace Conference*, Vol. 9, p. 388; Woodward and Butler, eds., *Documents on British Foreign Policy, 1919-1939*, First Series, Vol. 2, p. 438.

[126] Council of Premiers, January 16, 1920, 2:30 p.m., *Foreign Relations, 1919, The Paris Peace Conference*, Vol. 9, pp. 872-884; Woodward and Butler, eds., *Documents on British Foreign Policy, 1919-1939*, First Series, Vol. 2, pp. 900-910. See also Lloyd George, *The Truth about the Peace Treaties*, Vol. 2, pp. 962-970.

[127] First London Conference, March 25, 1920, 4 p.m., Woodward and Butler, eds., *Documents on British Foreign Policy, 1919-1939*, First Series, Vol. 7, pp. 635-638.

[128] Treaty of Peace between the Allied and Associated Powers and Hungary, Trianon, June 4, 1920, Great Britain, Treaty Series No. 10 (1920); *Cmd.* 896.

CHAPTER 15

EPILOGUE AND CONCLUSIONS

I. *Epilogue: Great Britain and the Struggle for Treaty Ratification in the United States*

T HE British Government kept anxious watch in the summer and autumn of 1919 on President Wilson's struggle for ratification of the Treaty of Versailles. It tried scrupulously to avoid any word or act which might worsen the chances of the treaty and engaged in a delicate and unsuccessful effort to help it along toward ratification. The latter task was assigned, or fell, to Viscount Grey of Falladon, who had tried and failed, for lack of machinery for the maintenance of peace, to prevent the outbreak of war in 1914, and who now undertook to do what little he could to save the newly created machinery of peace from repudiation by its own chief engineer.[1]

President Wilson defined the stakes of the ratification struggle in his presentation of the treaty to the Senate and in his September speaking tour. In his address to the Senate on July 10, the President described the League of Nations as the "main object of the peace, as the only thing that could complete it or make it worth while." "Dare we reject it," he asked, "and break the heart of the world?" "There can be no question," he said, "of our ceasing to be a world power. The only question is whether we can refuse the moral leadership that is offered us, whether we shall accept or reject the confidence of the world."[2] And if that leadership and that confidence were rejected: ". . . then," said Wilson, "if we must stand apart and be the hostile rivals of the rest of the world, then we must do something else. We must be physically ready for

[1] The present discussion is based primarily on the correspondence between Viscount Grey and the British Foreign Office during the period of Grey's special mission to Washington from August to December of 1919. This correspondence is published in E. L. Woodward and Rohan Butler, eds., *Documents on British Foreign Policy, 1919-1939*, First Series (8 Vols., London: His Majesty's Stationery Office, 1947-1958), Vol. 5, pp. 980-1065.

[2] Address to Senate, July 10, 1919, Ray Stannard Baker and William E. Dodd, eds., *The Public Papers of Woodrow Wilson* (6 Vols., New York and London: Harper and Brothers Publisher, 1925-1927), *War and Peace*, Vol. 1, pp. 548, 551.

anything that comes. We must have a great standing army. We must see to it that every man in America is trained to arms. . . ."[3]

The British Government began at once, as the debate on the treaty was launched, to take the pulse of the American body politic. Sir William Wiseman cabled the British Ambassador in Paris on July 2 that the public attitude in America was one of "grudging recognition" that the future peace of the world depended upon Anglo-American cooperation.[4] On July 5, Wiseman provided his Government with a detailed and perceptive summary of the nature of the Republican objections to the treaty and the state of party politics and public opinion in America.[5]

It was announced to the House of Commons on August 13 that, pending the appointment of a permanent Ambassador to the United States, Lord Grey "has consented to go on a mission to Washington to deal especially with questions arising out of the peace."[6] President Wilson wrote House that he was "delighted" at Lord Grey's appointment and looked forward "with great pleasure to being associated with him."[7] The purpose of Grey's mission, as defined by his instructions from the Foreign Office, was to deal with three issues: Anglo-American cooperation in the League of Nations, the question of naval armaments, and the Irish problem.[8] Although during his three months in the United States Grey became deeply preoccupied with the question of the ratification of the treaty, there is no evidence that his mission was specifically *intended* to influence internal American politics.

The correspondence between Grey and the Foreign Office in early October reflected mounting British concern with the debate in the Senate and with the President's illness. On October 4, Grey reported that the prospect was for ratification of the treaty

[3] Speech at St. Louis, September 5, 1919, *ibid.*, p. 638.

[4] Wiseman to Derby, July 2, 1919, Woodward and Butler, eds., *Documents on British Foreign Policy, 1919-1939*, First Series, Vol. 5, p. 984.

[5] "Notes on the Political Situation in America," July 5, 1919, Sir William Wiseman Papers, Sterling Library, Yale University.

[6] Statement by Bonar Law in the House of Commons, August 13, 1919, Woodward and Butler, eds., *Documents on British Foreign Policy, 1919-1939*, First Series, Vol. 5, pp. 985-986.

[7] Wilson to House, August 15, 1919, Edward M. House Papers, Sterling Library, Yale University.

[8] Curzon to Grey, September 9, 1919, Woodward and Butler, eds., *Documents on British Foreign Policy, 1919-1939*, First Series, Vol. 5, pp. 997-1000.

with mild reservations.[9] In another dispatch on the same day, Grey warned that Wilson was opposed to even mild reservations and that "nothing should therefore be said to give impression such reservations would be acceptable or even unobjectionable to His Majesty's Government."[10] Curzon made frequent inquiries as to the President's health. "The whole British nation," he cabled Grey on October 6, "is watching with intense anxiety and concern the illness of the President, whose life is of such importance not merely to his own country but to mankind. . . ."[11]

The Senate debate focused for a time on the question of the voting power of Great Britain and the Dominions in the League of Nations Assembly. Grey attempted to persuade the Foreign Office to make a statement that would provide the American Administration with an argument against the clamor over the "six British votes." On October 11, Grey requested permission to state publicly that in any dispute involving Great Britain or one of the Dominions none of the members of the British Empire would cast a vote.[12] Curzon endorsed this interpretation of the voting rights of the British Empire but forbade a public declaration on the ground that it would be dangerous to make such a statement without having consulted the Dominions.[13] Grey reported on November 6 that the Secretary of State had, in strictest secrecy, asked his opinion on the Senate reservations and that he had told Lansing why no public statement on the six votes could be made, adding: "I hope he was more impressed by this reason than I was."[14]

Sir Robert Borden conferred with Grey in New York and agreed on the need for a public statement that none of the British Empire votes in the League Assembly would be used in a dispute to which any member was a party. Grey cabled to Curzon: "Sir Robert Borden feels and I entirely agree that complete failure of treaty in Senate followed by a separate peace between United States and Germany would be a calamity and that nothing, however slight the chance, should be omitted which might help to

---

[9] Grey to Curzon, October 4, 1919, *ibid.*, p. 1003.
[10] Grey to Curzon, October 4, 1919, *ibid.*, p. 1004.
[11] Curzon to Grey, October 6, 1919, *ibid.*, p. 1005.
[12] Grey to Curzon, October 11, 1919, *ibid.*, pp. 1008-1009.
[13] Curzon to Grey, October 24, 1919, *ibid.*, p. 1012.
[14] Grey to Curzon, November 6, 1919, *ibid.*, pp. 1017-1018.

avert it."[15] Curzon replied that a public statement was out of the question because General Smuts and Prime Minister Hughes had been consulted and had registered strong opposition.[16] Smuts himself regarded the Senate reservations as quite tolerable, and he strongly urged the British Government to take some measures to assuage American fears, but *not* with regard to the voting rights of the Dominions in the League Assembly.[17] In a cable to Curzon on December 11, Grey maintained that Smuts greatly underestimated the damage which the Senate reservations would inflict on the Covenant but that, on the other hand, it was quite impossible for the United States to accept the right of six British countries to vote in a dispute between the United States and Canada.[18]

As the prospects of Senate consent to the ratification of the treaty dimmed in November, Grey maintained hope that some compromise would still be worked out. He counseled his Government on November 17 to say nothing which would enable the American opponents of the treaty to blame the British Government for its demise.[19] Despite the three hostile votes in the Senate on November 19, Grey cabled Curzon on November 23 that some compromise on the fourteen Lodge reservations could probably be reached if Wilson would "take new departure of admitting that Senate majority leaders must be consulted about policy."[20] Sir William Tyrrell reported from New York on November 24 that he was consulting with Colonel House on a possible compromise. "The Colonel seems hopeful about compromise being arrived at by Senate factions," he cabled, "and we are at work on a scheme, though personally I dread the obstinacy of President."[21]

Despite these hopes of compromise on the part of its representatives, the British Government took a grave view of the Senate reservations. Lloyd George's private secretary passed along

[15] Grey to Curzon, November 14, 1919, *ibid.*, pp. 1021-1022.
[16] Curzon to Grey, November 18, 1919, *ibid.*, p. 1023.
[17] Smuts to Lloyd George, November 29, 1919, *ibid.*, pp. 1056-1057.
[18] Grey to Curzon, December 11, 1919, *ibid.*, pp. 1059-1060.
[19] Grey to Curzon, November 17, 1919, *ibid.*, p. 1022.
[20] Grey to Curzon, November 23, 1919, *ibid.*, p. 852.
[21] Mr. Watson (for Tyrrell) to Curzon (for Wiseman), November 24, 1919, *ibid.*, p. 1035.

a warning early in November that "His Majesty's Government do not think they will be able to accept any American reservations whatever."[22] Both Grey and the French Ambassador, in a private interview with Senator Hitchcock, the Democratic leader in the Senate, expressed the belief that their countries would reject a treaty amended in accordance with the Lodge reservations.[23] In a memorandum of observations sent to Grey on November 27, Curzon contended that the total effect of the reservations would be to put the United States on a special footing in relation to the League which might lead to the breakdown of the Covenant. Britain, said Curzon, could not accept the responsibilities of the mutual guarantee of political independence and territorial integrity under Article 10 if the United States were free of it.[24] Curzon forwarded another proposal on November 27, which Philip Kerr had suggested to Frank Polk, calling for the United States to accept the treaty without reservations, but to give immediate notice of withdrawal from the League in two years if American objections were not met in that period. This scheme, Curzon recommended, would allow the Democrats and Republicans to settle the issue in the election of 1920 and, moreover, would give all nations an opportunity to suggest amendments to the Covenant on the basis of a year or two of experience. Curzon instructed Grey to make whatever use of this proposal he thought wise.[25] Grey, apparently, made no use of it.

Grey abandoned hope for the success of his mission early in December. He conferred with House on December 5 and told him that he was sailing for England on January 2. Grey said that he felt it important that he be in London to try to persuade

[22] Tyrrell (for Kerr) to Wiseman, November 12, 1919, Wiseman to House, November 12 (or 20?), 1919, Wiseman Papers.

[23] So Hitchcock reported to President Wilson in a private meeting on November 17, 1919, at which Dr. Grayson was present. Rear Admiral Cary T. Grayson, *Woodrow Wilson* (New York: Holt, Rinehart and Winston, 1960), p. 104.

[24] Curzon to Grey, November 27, 1919, Woodward and Butler, eds., *Documents on British Foreign Policy, 1919-1939*, First Series, Vol. 5, pp. 1040-1042. The Senate reservation as to Article 10 provided that the United States would assume no obligation to enforce it except by act or resolution of Congress in each particular case. Ruhl J. Bartlett, ed., *The Record of American Diplomacy* (3rd edn., New York: Alfred A. Knopf, 1954), p. 471.

[25] Curzon to Grey, November 27, 1919, Woodward and Butler, eds., *Documents on British Foreign Policy, 1919-1939*, First Series, Vol. 5, pp. 1042-1043.

the British Government to accept the treaty with the inevitable American reservations, if indeed it was ratified at all. Moreover, Grey pointed out, the President had not and apparently would not receive him and it was of little value to confer with Lansing who himself had not seen the President for over three months.[26] Grey advised the Foreign Office in a secret message dated December 6 that the prospects of his ever seeing the President were remote, that "there is no one with whom I can discuss anything effectively in Washington," and that he wished, therefore, to end his mission.[27] On December 11, Grey reported that the Secretary of State had shown no surprise upon learning of his impending departure: "He said situation here was very disappointing and one in which foreign governments could only do harm if they attempted to influence it."[28] In the wake of this warning from Grey as to the danger of foreign intervention, Lloyd George persuaded Clemenceau on December 13 to suppress a proposed Anglo-French declaration accepting most of the Lodge reservations.[29] Grey expressed the fear on December 24 that the American opposition to the treaty would focus on the "six British votes" and would therefore take an increasingly anti-British tone.[30]

Grey returned to England for "consultations," persuaded that neither he nor any other foreigner, with whatever friendly intent, could influence the outcome of the debate in America. On January 31, 1920, Grey published a letter in *The Times* of London, entitled "America and the Treaty." Denying any breach of faith on the part of the United States, Grey explained the Senate reservations as rooted in traditional American foreign policy. For the Senate to accept the Covenant of the League, Grey wrote, would mean a "plunge into something which its historical advice and tradition have hitherto positively disapproved." Nevertheless, he contended, the success of the League depended on American adherence, and while Great Britain could not yield on the separate representation of the Dominions in the

[26] House Diary, December 5, 1919, House Papers.
[27] Grey to Curzon, "Personal and Secret," December 6, 1919, Woodward and Butler, eds., *Documents on British Foreign Policy, 1919-1939*, First Series, Vol. 5, p. 1055.
[28] Grey to Curzon, December 11, 1919, *ibid.*, p. 1059.
[29] Council of Premiers, December 13, 1919, 11 a.m., *ibid.*, Vol. 2, pp. 753-754.
[30] Grey to Curzon, December 24, 1919, *ibid.*, Vol. 5, p. 1064.

League Assembly, most of the reservations were reasonable and worth accepting in order to win American cooperation. "Without the United States," Grey concluded, "the present League of Nations may become little better than a League of Allies for armed self-defense against a revival of Prussian militarism . . . predominantly a European and not a world organization."[31]

It has been contended by Thomas A. Bailey that the Grey letter of January 31, 1920, smashed Wilson's argument that the Allies would not accept the Senate reservations.[32] The Grey-Curzon correspondence of the autumn of 1919 does not substantiate this conclusion. These dispatches, notably Grey's dispatch to Curzon of December 11 and Curzon's cable message to Grey of November 27, as well as Grey's warning to Senator Hitchcock of British opposition to the Lodge reservations, make it clear that at that time, at least, both Grey and the British Foreign Office took a very grave view of the Senate reservations. Moreover, the Grey-Curzon correspondence reveals that British opposition focused on what were perhaps the two reservations most insistently demanded by the American opponents of the treaty, those relating to the "six British votes" in the League Assembly and to Article 10 of the Covenant. Grey's letter of January 31, 1920, represents, it would seem, a *change* in Grey's attitude toward the Senate reservations since his sojourn in Washington— a change of attitude quite possibly motivated by a desire on Grey's part to persuade the British Government to accept the reservations, however distasteful, rather than to leave the United States outside of the treaty altogether. Bailey, however, is probably quite right in asserting that the *effect* of the Grey letter was to strengthen the Lodge faction in the United States Senate and to weaken President Wilson and the Democrats.[33]

The Grey mission to Washington was a sorry epilogue to the Anglo-American relationship at the Peace Conference, demonstrating the anxiety and futility of effort felt by the British Government in the face of the retirement of the United States from

[31] Grey's Letter to *The Times*, January 31, 1920, H.W.V. Temperley, ed., *A History of the Peace Conference of Paris* (6 Vols., London: Henry Frowde and Hodder and Stoughton, 1920-1924), Vol. 6, pp. 419-420.

[32] Thomas A. Bailey, *Woodrow Wilson and the Great Betrayal* (New York: The Macmillan Company, 1947), p. 238.

[33] *ibid.*, p. 242.

international responsibility. Although the Grey mission was conceived as an effort to deal with Anglo-American issues relating to sea power, the Irish question, and the functioning of the League of Nations, it became in fact an honest but, inevitably, an ineffectual effort to assist the cause of treaty ratification in the United States. The failure of the Grey mission was, as Grey wrote to Charles Seymour in 1928, an "inevitable but only a very minor detail in what amounted to a political catastrophe."[34]

In the winter of 1919-1920, an unofficial but very potent British contribution to the repudiation of the treaty in America was made in the form of John Maynard Keynes's *The Economic Consequences of the Peace*. Keynes resigned his post in Paris in June 1919. Back in London, he wrote to General Smuts urging "revelation" and "protestation" of the treaty of peace. Smuts replied with a suggestion that Keynes write an account of the economic and financial clauses of the treaty, their meaning and their probable consequences.[35] The *Economic Consequences of the Peace* was published in December 1919, and it soon became a best seller in England and America.[36]

Instead of the reasoned account of the meaning and consequences of the economic settlement suggested by Smuts, Keynes's work was a polemic against the "Carthaginian Peace."[37] President Wilson was characterized as an antiquated theologian, with "no plan, no scheme, no constructive ideas whatever for clothing with the flesh of life the commandments which he had thundered from the White House." "There can seldom have been a statesman of the first rank," railed Keynes, who had neither attended the meetings of the Supreme Council nor had access to its minutes, "more incompetent than the President in the agilities of the Council chamber." Keynes pictured the President as artless, slow-minded, and bewildered in negotiating with his European col-

[34] Grey to Seymour, July 4, 1928, Charles Seymour, ed., *The Intimate Papers of Colonel House* (4 Vols., Boston and New York: Houghton Mifflin Company, 1926-1928), Vol. 4, p. 500.
[35] Sarah Gertrude Millin, *General Smuts* (2 Vols., London: Faber and Faber, Ltd., 1936), Vol. 2, pp. 255-256.
[36] See Étienne Mantoux, *The Carthaginian Peace* (New York: Charles Scribner's Sons, 1952), pp. 4-5.
[37] See John Maynard Keynes, *The Economic Consequences of the Peace* (New York: Harcourt, Brace and Howe, 1920), pp. 36-37.

leagues.[38] In the end, wrote Keynes, Clemenceau secured what he wished, while Lloyd George found that, after the months of compromise, "it was harder to de-bamboozle this old Presbyterian than it had been to bamboozle him. . . ."[39] As to the reparations clauses, Keynes denounced them as the realization of a policy of "reducing Germany to servitude for a generation, of degrading the lives of millions of human beings, and of depriving a whole nation of happiness. . . ."[40]

Keynes's work appeared in the United States in January 1920, where it enjoyed a phenomenal sale and was seized upon with enthusiasm by the enemies of the President and the League. Senator Borah read lengthy extracts from the book in the Senate on February 10, 1920.[41] "When I encouraged Keynes to write that book," said Smuts long afterwards, "I knew his views about the statesmen at Paris. But I did not expect a personal note in his book, I did not expect him to turn Wilson into a figure of fun."[42] Keynes's book, said Smuts, "helped to finish Wilson, and it strengthened the Americans against the League."[43] Keynes's polemic became itself a *cause* of the crumbling of the peace. It allowed Germany to blame the treaty for her economic chaos in the postwar years and, above all, it put a powerful weapon into the hands of the American isolationists.[44]

II. *Conclusions*

There are two fundamental conclusions to be drawn from the present study. The first is that in the negotiation of the peace settlement of 1919 there was a fundamental community of purpose and interest between the United States and the British Empire but that this basic unity, although often expressed in parallel and even identical policies, was almost never translated into a common strategy for the attainment of common objectives. The second general conclusion is a value judgment, unproved and unprovable. It is that, with certain exceptions, Britain and the United States were responsible for the most enlightened,

[38] *ibid.*, pp. 42-44.   [39] *ibid.*, pp. 54-55.   [40] *ibid.*, p. 225.
[41] Mantoux, *The Carthaginian Peace*, pp. 9-10.
[42] Millin, *General Smuts*, Vol. 2, p. 174.
[43] *ibid.*, p. 257.
[44] Herbert Feis, "Keynes in Retrospect," *Foreign Affairs*, Vol. 29, No. 4 (July 1951), p. 567.

most progressive, and most moral features of the treaties of peace.

There were only three sets of issues connected with the peace settlement which involved direct and fundamental conflicts between the United States and the British Empire, those relating to sea power, colonies and mandates, and the reparations and economic settlements.

As to the first of these, the conflict was incipient rather than acute. If any issue bore the potentialities of Anglo-American conflict, it was that of freedom of the seas, for which the United States had twice gone to war. But while it produced a heated Anglo-American controversy in the pre-Armistice negotiations, it was never mentioned at the Peace Conference because Wilson's concept of a new order of world law under the aegis of the League of Nations rendered obsolete the very concept of neutrality and neutral rights. The other aspect of Anglo-American controversy over sea power was the alarm felt by the British at the prospect of an American Navy equal or superior to the Grand Fleet, but this issue too was readily disposed of, by the informal naval agreement of April 10, 1919. It seems quite likely that neither Great Britain nor the United States was as deeply concerned with this problem as each appeared to be during the "naval battle of Paris," for it received only incidental attention from the heads of the two Governments, and the issue itself was belied by a century of experience during which each of the English-speaking powers had found the sea power of the other complementary to its own in maintaining the security of the Atlantic area.

The Anglo-American controversy over colonies and mandates was one between the United States and the British Empire as a whole. It was not a clear-cut conflict between American adherence to the principle of international trusteeship in the colonial settlement on the one hand and the imperialism of the British Dominions on the other, for the mandates idea was as much British as American in origin, and what the British countries proposed were certain exceptions to its application. These exceptions, however, represented to President Wilson an abnegation in detail, and there resulted a major clash between the President and the imperial Prime Ministers. The conflict was brief and decisive and, coming at the beginning of the Peace Conference, it did not complicate Anglo-American cooperation on other issues. It ended in a compromise that gave the Dominions the substance of their desires while preserving intact the principle of international trusteeship.

The most significant conflict of British and American policies at the Peace Conference was in the reparations settlement, but even here the issue was by no means a clear-cut one between American moderation and British vindictiveness. The reparations policy of the United States was clear and consistent: a fixed sum based on the capacity of the enemy to pay and limited to the categories of compensation authorized by the Pre-Armistice Agreement. British policy, on the other hand, was confused and vacillating. Bound by the irresponsible promises of the electoral campaign of December 1918, Lloyd George attempted to straddle the views of the moderates and the extremists within the British delegation and usually came down on the side of the latter. Reparations posed one of the few major instances of the Peace Conference in which British diplomacy led solid Allied opposition to the United States. The one major inducement with which the United States might have secured a reparations settlement to its liking would have been an abatement of Allied debts to the United States, but this was probably a political impossibility in 1919 and it was given no serious consideration.

Great Britain and the United States were also at fundamental odds over proposals for long-range postwar economic cooperation. Britain, the second-greatest economic and financial power, put forth constructive proposals for an international program of industrial and commercial recovery, but these proposals were rejected out of hand by the United States, the greatest economic and financial power, because of their political unfeasibility, because of the continuing dedication of the American economic advisers to nineteenth century concepts of economic individualism, and because of the indifference of President Wilson to the economic aspects of a program for permanent peace.

Certain issues of the Peace Conference involved secondary, or derivative, conflicts between British and American policies, notably the controversies over the Italian and the Japanese claims. In both of these, Great Britain was compelled by wartime engagements to oppose the stand of the United States on the principle of self-determination. The British commitments to Italy and Japan were undertaken quite frankly, and, in the present view, justifiably, as measures of military necessity. The result was that Britain was compelled to take stands against the United States on issues in which there was no direct conflict of interests between the English-speaking powers, and in which, but for the wartime engagements, the two nations quite probably would have stood together. In the case of the Italian claims, the Anglo-American dispute was unnecessarily protracted and acrimonious, because of a stiff unwillingness on the part of President Wilson to sympathize with, or even tolerate, the position in which the British found themselves, and because of an equally unwarrantable attitude of contempt on the part of Lloyd George for the principles which dictated the American position.

Anglo-American cooperation at the Peace Conference achieved its fullest fruition in the territorial settlement of Europe and in the area of international organization.

There was a natural harmony of interests between Britain and America in regard to the boundary settlements of Europe. Neither had material interests of its own at stake but both nations had a vital interest in lasting peace, and both undertook to serve this interest by drawing boundary lines which they hoped would be durable because they were based on the self-determination of nationalities, or, where exceptions were made, on natural economic units. There were differences in emphasis between Britain and the United States in their approaches to the European territorial settlement. The British put up stronger resistance to French schemes for the Rhineland, the United States to the French program for the Saar. The British firmly opposed Polish incursions on German national territory while the Americans for a time displayed excessive tenderness for the ambitions of the reborn Polish state. But these differences were only of emphasis, and in the territorial settlement as a whole, Anglo-American diplomacy led the Peace Conference, especially through the use of expert commissions, in drawing the best ethnographic map which Europe has ever had, before or since.

The highest achievement of Anglo-American cooperation was the Covenant of the League of Nations. The Covenant drew its chief inspiration from the long experience of the Anglo-American polities with ordered societies under the rule of law. The immediate origins of the Covenant were the ideas and proposals of official and unofficial advocates of international organization in England and America. Before the Peace Conference convened, a pattern of close and fruitful consultation had developed between the British and American supporters of a league for peace, and the Covenant was drawn up at Paris in a milieu of close Anglo-American collaboration. The personal unity of spirit and purpose between President Wilson and Lord Robert Cecil was an especially fortunate aspect of the drafting of the Covenant. The final Covenant was preeminently an Anglo-American document, based on Anglo-American principles of voluntarism and equal justice under law.

Cooperation and conflict between the United States and Great Britain at the Peace Conference were to a very substantial degree conditioned by the interactions of personalities. Regardless of common interests and objectives, the possibility of a unified Anglo-American approach to the problems of the peace was precluded by the mutual alienation of temperaments between Wilson and Lloyd George. Wilson's leadership represents perhaps the most complete synthesis of national power with moral purpose in the modern history of the West. In his dedication to the service of transcendent values, Wilson was a leader for whom compromise, concession, and accommodation were confined to a limited spectrum. Being under "eternal bonds of fidelity" to the men whom he had sent to fight and die for the achievement of a peace of justice, the President was not a free agent but a man bound to fight for the realization of his principles in every aspect of the peace settlement. Lloyd George, on the other hand, was a pragmatist—humane, moderate, and sensible—with all of the pragmatist's distrust for abstraction and solutions untested by experience. He was a democratic politician of the twentieth century—sensitive to criticism and with an enormous respect for the power of public opinion. He was endlessly flexible in his approaches to problems, guided only by the pragmatic instinct to avoid extremes.

In the course of the Peace Conference, Wilson and Lloyd George displayed the best and worst characteristics, respectively, of the Christian moralist and the pragmatic opportunist. In such tasks as the enunciation of war aims and the drafting of the Covenant, Wilson demonstrated massive integrity and the power to inspire. In such issues as the Fiume crisis and the June rebellion of the British against the draft treaty, the President displayed the arrogant side of his nature—a disposition to patronize, to pontificate, and to condemn the sins of his colleagues. Lloyd George was at his best in dealing with issues that lent themselves to compromise—such as the mandates controversy, the French Rhineland claims, and the German-Polish borderlands. In matters involving moral, as distinguished from legal, obligation, the Prime Minister descended at times to shabbiness. This seems especially true of his approach to reparations, in which he surrendered his own instinct for moderation to the jingoistic demands of public and parliamentary opinion, and of his blatant blackmail of the United States in regard to the unconnected issues of Anglo-American naval rivalry and the Monroe Doctrine amendment to the Covenant. The conclusion to be drawn is that between two such statesmen as Wilson and Lloyd George there could be no community of spirit and conviction, and that, while on most issues the two English-speaking democracies found themselves in natural alignment, the character of leadership was such that the Anglo-American relationship was at best an entente without a directorate.

Among the other personalities of the Peace Conference, several played special roles in the Anglo-American relationship. The most impressive of these, in the present view, was Lord Robert Cecil, who, as a man of both good sense and moral conviction, was a natural link between British and American diplomacy. In matters in which Cecil played a major role, notably the drafting of the Covenant, Anglo-American relations were at their best. There was, next, Colonel House, who, though at times a faltering advocate of Wilsonian policies and principles, enjoyed a special relationship of mutual confidence with the British Government. House was successful on a number of occasions in forging Anglo-American amity out of situations of conflict, as in the pre-Armistice negotiations and in the naval conversations of April. Sir William Wiseman must be mentioned as a special figure in Anglo-American relations because of his role as confidant to Colonel House, and, to a lesser degree, to President

Wilson. Wiseman alone came near to transcending nationality of outlook—his point of view was preeminently "Anglo-American."

Three of the Dominion leaders played significant roles in Anglo-American relations. Sir Robert Borden of Canada, representing a country whose basic interests depended upon a good understanding between the United States and the British Empire, was a natural and effective conciliator of Anglo-American issues. General Smuts of South Africa played a prominent but not altogether constructive role in Anglo-American relations. He was disposed to public pronouncements of moral grandeur and was a sincere advocate of a new order of world affairs under the aegis of the League of Nations, and he enjoyed, consequently, the fullest confidence of President Wilson. But where his own professed principles conflicted with the material interests of the Union of South Africa, as in the mandates controversy and in the question of pensions as a category of reparations, Smuts unfailingly devised reasoned arguments for the satisfaction of the latter. Smuts's view of the peace settlement as a whole was by no means the same as Wilson's. Where the President favored a peace of "impartial justice," regardless of the harshness or liberality of any of its particulars, Smuts was an advocate of generosity as such, and the final treaty, which to the President represented a charter for a new era, seemed to Smuts, except for the Covenant, a vehicle of revenge which he hoped to see dismantled as rapidly as possible. Prime Minister Hughes of Australia was the bête noire of Anglo-American relations at the Peace Conference. A noisome demagogue, he fought against the mandates principle, killed the racial equality clause proposed by Japan, and earned the contempt of both British and American statesmen.

The British Foreign Secretary, Arthur James Balfour, though a supporter of Anglo-American understanding, played no special role in British relations with the United States. The American Secretary of State, Robert Lansing, was a minor figure at the Peace Conference, as were Henry White and General Bliss.

The year 1919 was the high-water mark of democracy in world history. The victory of the democratic states was complete and was virtually theirs alone, unshared with great autocratic powers.

As the foremost democratic powers, the United States and the British Empire, with a preponderance of world power, were in a position to make and enforce a democratic peace. They had not only their moment of supreme opportunity, but, in Woodrow Wilson, a leader who recognized that opportunity. And yet, somehow, the great opportunity was lost—but not at the Paris Peace Conference. Whatever the defects of the particulars of the treaties, the settlement as a whole was a reasonable embodiment of the Fourteen Points, and, more broadly, of the democratic principles of Anglo-American society. In the Covenant of the League of Nations, the British and American statesmen of 1919 left to their successors an instrument with permanent processes for the ordering of international affairs and for the redress of international grievances, an instrument rooted in the ancient Anglo-Saxon concept of equal justice under the law. The loss of the opportunity which so briefly presented itself to the democratic world was the work not of the statesmen of 1919 but of their successors, who lost it completely. Because of the legal repudiation of the Versailles system by the United States and its moral repudiation by Great Britain, only the worst particulars of the treaties were enforced, while the best were stillborn.

The proportions of the tragedy are vastly heightened when it is recognized that the opportunity of 1919 was not to be repeated. By 1945, Anglo-American statesmen were ready to retrieve the fatal errors of the interwar years, but those errors had permitted the spawning of powerful new totalitarian forces whose share in the victory of 1945 precluded the kind of democratic peace settlement envisioned by Woodrow Wilson. The mistakes of the past can often be identified, but they cannot always be retrieved.

NOTES ON SOURCES

Among the published collections of documents relating to the Paris Peace Conference, the most complete is the set published by the Department of State, *Papers Relating to the Foreign Relations of the United States, 1919, The Paris Peace Conference* (13 Vols., Washington: United States Government Printing Office, 1942-1947). These volumes are the official American record of the Peace Conference. The documents contained in them are drawn from the files of the Department of State and the American Commission to Negotiate Peace, as well as from the private papers of Wilson, House, Lansing, Miller, and other participants in the Peace Conference. The most important documents contained in these volumes are undoubtedly the official minutes of the Councils of Ten and Four. These are the English minutes of Sir Maurice Hankey, there having been no separate American minutes kept except for a brief period. The volumes contain also a substantial collection of relevant correspondence.

The most valuable addition of recent years to the documentary record of the Peace Conference is Paul Mantoux's *Les Délibérations du Conseil des Quatre* (2 Vols., Paris: Éditions du Centre National de la Recherche Scientifique, 1955). Mantoux was the official interpreter for the Council of Four and the documents contained in these volumes are not *procès-verbaux* but Mantoux's personal notes, dictated daily. For the most part, these notes recapitulate Hankey's more extensive minutes, and they do not have relevant documents appended to the record of each meeting, as in *Foreign Relations*. Their principal value is as the only documentary account of the proceedings of the Council of Four from March 24 to April 19, during which period no minutes were kept and Mantoux was the only one present besides the heads of government.

David Hunter Miller's *My Diary at the Conference of Paris*, privately printed (21 Vols., New York: Appeal Printing Company, 1924) is an exceedingly rich and varied collection. Volume 1 contains Miller's personal diary, and subsequent volumes contain letters and papers on various subjects, but especially on the League of Nations and the reparations question. Certain sets of *procès-verbaux*, not readily found elsewhere, are included, notably those of the Commissions on New States and Ports, Waterways, and Railways.

The richest collection of documents relating to the final stages of the Peace Conference, that is, after June 28, 1919, is contained in the selection from the British archives edited by E. L. Woodward and

Rohan Butler, *Documents on British Foreign Policy, 1919-1939*, First Series (8 Vols., London: His Majesty's Stationery Office, 1947-1958). Besides the minutes of the Council of Heads of Delegations, which appear in *Foreign Relations*, these volumes include extensive selections of Foreign Office correspondence and papers relating to the Peace Conference. Volumes 7 and 8 contain the *procès-verbaux*, here published for the first time, of the London and San Remo conferences of the spring of 1920. This first series was edited by Rohan Butler, who was given complete freedom to study and select documents from the Foreign Office archives.

Several collections of private papers are indispensable in the study of the Peace Conference for enrichment of detail if not for basic facts and trends: The Peace Conference Series (Series 8) of the Woodrow Wilson Papers in the Library of Congress is a vast collection of letters, memoranda, and documents providing rich insights into the President's thoughts and feelings on a plethora of subjects, major and trivial. Within the Peace Conference collection, the seventy boxes of papers in Series 8-A, containing the major correspondence and other papers acquired by Wilson between December 1918, and July 1919, are the most useful to the student. Series 8-B contains routine correspondence and papers, and Series 8-C contains documents such as *procès-verbaux* of meetings of the Councils of Ten and Four, reports of commissions, etc., which are now largely available in published collections.

Equally valuable is the admirably organized and maintained Edward M. House Collection at Yale University. These papers include the full House diary and House's rich correspondence with virtually every major figure, as well as a good many minor ones, at the Peace Conference. The diary and the correspondence with Sir William Wiseman are especially useful sources of information on Anglo-American relations. The Sir William Wiseman Papers, maintained as an allied collection, contain many duplicates of papers found in the House Collection and include very little on the Peace Conference itself, but they are an enormously valuable source of information on Anglo-American wartime relations and on the British view of American affairs during the entire period of the war and the Peace Conference.

The greatest documentary gap encountered by the student of the Peace Conference is that left by the still closed British archives for the main period of the Peace Conference, that is, prior to June 28, 1919. The only British documentation currently available is the sparse selection of *Command Papers* and the equally sparse selection of Peace Conference documents contained in *British and Foreign State Papers, 1919* (London: His Majesty's Stationery Office, 1922).

Several other American collections are of some value to the student of the Peace Conference. *The Public Papers of Woodrow Wilson*, edited by Ray Stannard Baker and William E. Dodd (New York and London: Harper & Brothers, Publishers, 1925-1927), is the most complete collection of Wilson's messages, addresses, and other public papers. The last two volumes, titled *War and Peace*, cover the Peace Conference period. Wilson's speeches during his western tour of September 1919, reproduced in *War and Peace*, Vol. 2, contain many useful expressions of the President's views on particular aspects of the Covenant and the Treaty of Versailles. Of some interest for the student of the Peace Conference is the testimony in the summer of 1919 of President Wilson and other members of the American peace delegation reproduced in Hearings before the Committee on Foreign Relations, United States Senate, 66th Congress, First Session, on the *Treaty of Peace with Germany* (Washington: United States Government Printing Office, 1919). These statements, however, are of very limited value because of the extremely partisan conduct of the hearings, in which witnesses hostile to the treaty were allowed to speak freely while those supporting it were subjected to frequent interruption and senatorial badgering.

A number of valuable documentary histories have been published for the Carnegie Endowment for International Peace in a series titled *The Paris Peace Conference: History and Documents*. The most valuable of these is Philip Mason Burnett's *Reparation at the Paris Peace Conference from the Standpoint of the American Delegation* (2 Vols., New York: Columbia University Press, 1940), which, although lacking in the important documentation published since 1940, remains the most complete collection of American documents concerning the reparations question. The carefully organized documents are supplemented by an excellent brief narrative of the reparations settlement. Other useful volumes in the Carnegie series, containing both narrative and relevant documents available at their time of publication, are: Alma Luckau's *The German Delegation at the Paris Peace Conference* (New York: Columbia University Press, 1941); René Albrecht-Carrié's *Italy at the Paris Peace Conference* (New York: Columbia University Press, 1938); Francis Déak's *Hungary at the Paris Peace Conference* (New York: Columbia University Press, 1942); and James T. Shotwell's *The Origins of the International Labor Organization* (2 Vols., New York: Columbia University Press, 1934). The Carnegie series includes a most convenient collection of statements on war aims, edited by James Brown Scott, under the title, *Official Statements of War Aims and Peace Proposals, December 1916 to November 1918* (Washington: Carnegie Endowment for International Peace, 1921). The publications of the Hoover War Library include a valuable documentary history of the Austrian treaty, edited by Nina Almond and Ralph Haswell Lutz, *The Treaty of St. Germain* (Stanford University, California: Stanford University Press, 1935).

Among the memoirs of participants in the Peace Conference, quite the most interesting, exhaustive, and provocative are those of David Lloyd George, the English edition of which is titled *The Truth about the Peace Treaties* (2 Vols., London: Victor Gollancz, Ltd., 1938). Lloyd George provides a thorough account of almost every aspect of the Peace Conference (except for the drafting of the Covenant and the Far Eastern settlement), drawing on the minutes of the Councils of Ten and Four, which were still secret at the time of his writing, personal interviews, letters, and impressions. Lloyd George's account of *events*, especially of the deliberations of the Supreme Council, is generally factual and complete, rarely distorted or *ex parte*. Even Lloyd George's defense of his role in the electoral campaign of December 1918, an extremely sensitive issue, faithfully sets forth all relevant facts. In the area of *impressions* and *commentary*, however, Lloyd George is frequently intemperate, malicious, and, by all reasonable standards, inaccurate. In his very brief discussion of the drafting of the Covenant, for instance, Lloyd George sets forth the extraordinary proposition that the Covenant was primarily an Anglo-French creation which in the absence of President Wilson would scarcely have been weakened in a single particular. (Vol. 1, pp. 278, 281-282, 636-642.)

Next in importance to the memoirs of Lloyd George is the selection from the House Papers, edited with a connecting narrative by Charles Seymour, *The Intimate Papers of Colonel House* (4 Vols., Boston and New York: Houghton Mifflin Company, 1926-1928). The fourth volume of this work contains letters between Colonel House and President Wilson and others and excerpts from House's diary between June 1918 and November 1919. The selections richly illustrate, and perhaps to some extent exaggerate, the role of Colonel House in the formulation and execution of American policy and are especially interesting in the present context for their illustration of House's close relations with various officials of the British Government.

Among other first-hand accounts, André Tardieu's *The Truth about the Treaty* (Indianapolis: The Bobbs-Merrill Company, Inc., 1921) is an excellent rendering of the French point of view, with a number of illuminating comments on French attitudes toward the United

States and Great Britain at the Peace Conference. Viscount Cecil's *A Great Experiment* (New York: Oxford University Press, 1941) is a valuable source of information on Cecil's deep dedication to the league of nations idea, and is especially interesting in its account of Cecil's close working relations with President Wilson and Colonel House in the drafting of the Covenant. Bernard M. Baruch's *The Making of the Reparation and Economic Sections of the Treaty* (New York and London: Harper & Brothers, Publishers, 1920) is a first-hand account useful primarily for the insights it provides into the dedication of the American economic experts to a moderate reparations settlement and their negative attitude toward proposals for long-range international economic cooperation. *Robert Laird Borden: His Memoirs* (2 Vols., New York: The Macmillan Company, 1938), edited by Henry Borden, contains extracts from the letters and diary of the Canadian Prime Minister which are a useful source of information on the special problems of the Dominions and on the preeminent concern of Canada with Anglo-American amity. The most recent personal contribution is Herbert Hoover's *The Ordeal of Woodrow Wilson* (New York, Toronto, London: McGraw-Hill Book Company, Inc., 1958). The title is misleading in that Hoover is primarily concerned with those aspects of the Peace Conference, e.g. food and relief, in which he was personally involved, about which the account is most illuminating. On the broader aspects of the Peace Conference, except for his discussion of a few personal interviews with various officials, Hoover relies on the standard sources. Stephen Bonsal's *Unfinished Business* (Garden City, New York: Doubleday, Doran and Company, Inc., 1944) is the most useful of the personal diaries of lesser figures at the Peace Conference. Bonsal was officially an adviser on Balkan affairs, but his more interesting comments derive from his position as an intimate to Colonel House and, occasionally, to President Wilson, and as interpreter for the League of Nations Commission. Bonsal is especially helpful in his discussions of the personal relations between Wilson and Cecil and other members of the League Commission.

David Hunter Miller's *The Drafting of the Covenant* (2 Vols., New York, London: G. P. Putnam's Sons, 1928) is the definitive work on the League of Nations at the Paris Peace Conference, from the Phillimore Report of March 1918 to the Covenant as embodied in the Treaty of Versailles. Containing both narrative and exhaustive documentation, the work is a painstaking account of the evolution of the Covenant through many drafts and informal negotiations, in most of which Miller was personally involved. Among the documents is a reproduction of the entire *procès-verbaux* of the League of Nations Commission, amplified by corresponding narrative. The student is left with no doubt, after study of this work, as to the preeminently Anglo-American origins of the Covenant.

Ray Stannard Baker's *Woodrow Wilson and World Settlement* (3 Vols., Garden City, New York: Doubleday, Page and Company, 1922), the first major contribution to the historiography of the Peace Conference, remains one of the most useful, primarily because of the documents reproduced in Volume 3, some of which are not conveniently available elsewhere. Although Baker had complete access to the secret minutes of the Councils of Ten and Four and to the personal papers of President Wilson, his narrative contains a number of factual errors, attributable to the unavailability at the time of his writing of other vital documentation. The principal defect of Baker's work, however, for which it has been much criticized, is its narrowly partisan outlook, which views the entire Peace Conference as a struggle between the "new" and the "old," between Wilsonian moralism and European trickery and *realpolitik*. In order to uphold his preconceptions, Baker resorts at times to *ex parte* use of evidence which was certainly at his disposal.

The most exhaustive general history of the Peace Conference is the work edited by H.W.V. Temperley, *A History of the Peace Conference of Paris* (London: Henry Frowde and Hodder and Stoughton, 1920-1924), published under the auspices of the British Institute of International Affairs. Among the contributors to these volumes are many British and a number of American participants in the Peace Conference. Much of the substance is arid analysis of principles and legalities, and, lacking access to *procès-verbaux* and other documentation, the work fails to provide a running account of the negotiations. Temperley's *History* is perhaps a good starting point for Peace Conference research but as a general study it is largely obsolete. The best short history of the Peace Conference is still Paul Birdsall's *Versailles Twenty Years After* (London: George Allen and Unwin, Ltd., 1941), but a new monograph could profit greatly from additions of documentation and perspective since 1939.

A number of monographs, most of them published since the Second World War, have provided valuable accounts of specific phases of the peace settlement of 1919. Louis A. R. Yates's *United States and French Security, 1917-1921* (New York: Twayne Publishers, Inc., 1957) is a carefully documented account of the negotiation of the British and American treaties of guarantee with France. Russell H. Fifield's *Woodrow Wilson and the Far East* (New York: Thomas Y. Crowell Company, 1952) is a definitive study of the Shantung question and related issues involving Japan at the Peace Conference. Louis L. Gerson's *Woodrow Wilson and the Rebirth of Poland, 1914-1920* (New Haven: Yale University Press, 1953) contains a succinct and well-documented discussion of the settlement of the Polish-German frontier. Of special value in the area of Anglo-American cooperation during the war and in preparation for the Peace Conference is Sir Arthur Willert's *The Road to Safety* (London: Derek Verschoyle, Ltd., 1952). Alfred Zimmern's *The League of Nations and the Rule of Law, 1918-1935* (2nd edn., London: Macmillan and Company, Ltd., 1939) contains an extremely good analysis of the Covenant and, particularly, of the contributions of Great Britain and the United States to its character. The negotiation of the Pre-Armistice Agreement and the Anglo-American controversy over freedom of the seas, as well as the broader negotiations leading to the Armistice itself, are reviewed with admirable scholarship and style in Harry R. Rudin's *Armistice, 1918* (New Haven: Yale University Press, 1944).

The best of the biographies of Woodrow Wilson in its discussion of the Peace Conference period is Arthur Walworth's *Woodrow Wilson* (2 Vols., New York, London, Toronto: Longmans, Green and Company, 1958), awarded the Pulitzer Prize for biography in 1958. Volume 2, *World Prophet*, is a richly documented and eminently readable account of the President's role at the Peace Conference, although the image of Wilson as a "prophet" is perhaps overworked. Another good recent biography, fundamentally sympathetic to Wilson but reasonably critical, is the brief work of Silas Bent McKinley, *Woodrow Wilson* (New York: Frederick A. Praeger, 1957).

Thomas Jones's *Lloyd George* (Cambridge, Massachusetts: Harvard University Press, 1951) contains an account of Lloyd George's role in the Peace Conference which is generally impartial but not to the exclusion of judicious criticism. A number of biographical works on Lloyd George are marred by excessive partisanship. The discussion of the Peace Conference, for instance, in Frank Owen's *Tempestuous Journey—Lloyd George: His Life and Times* (London: Hutchinson and Company, Ltd., 1954) is well documented, but the account is sometimes *ex parte* and almost joyously anti-Wilson.

Two other biographies are worthy of mention for excellence of scholarship and style. Sarah Gertrude Millin's *General Smuts* (2 Vols., London: Faber and Faber, Ltd., 1936) looks deeply and sympathetically into Smuts's character and provides rich information on his role at the Peace Conference and on his unique relationship with President Wilson. Blanche E. C. Dugdale's *Arthur James Balfour* (2 Vols., New York: G. P. Putnam's Sons, 1937) is sympathetic but not apologetic in its discussion of the British Foreign Secretary's role in the making of the peace.

BIBLIOGRAPHY

Published Documentary Sources

Baker, Ray Stannard and Dodd, William E., eds., *The Public Papers of Woodrow Wilson* (6 Vols., New York and London: Harper & Brothers, Publishers, 1925-1927).

Bartlett, Ruhl J., ed., *The Record of American Diplomacy* (3rd edn., New York: Alfred A. Knopf, 1954).

British and Foreign State Papers, 1916, 1917-1918, 1919, 1920 (Parkes, Edward, ed., London: His Majesty's Stationery Office, 1920-1923).

Carnegie Endowment for International Peace, *Official Statements of War Aims and Peace Proposals, December 1916 to November 1918* (Scott, James Brown, ed., Washington, D.C.: Carnegie Endowment for International Peace, 1921).

――――, *Treaties and Agreements With and Concerning China, 1894-1919* (MacMurray, John V. A., ed., 2 Vols., New York: Oxford University Press, 1921).

――――, *The Treaties of Peace, 1919-1923* (2 Vols., New York: Carnegie Endowment for International Peace, 1924).

Department of State, *Papers Relating to the Foreign Relations of the United States, 1916*, Supplement, *The World War* (Washington: United States Government Printing Office, 1929).

――――, *Papers Relating to the Foreign Relations of the United States, 1917*, Supplement 1, *The World War* (Washington: United States Government Printing Office, 1931).

――――, *Papers Relating to the Foreign Relations of the United States, 1918*, Supplement 1, *The World War* (2 Vols., Washington: United States Government Printing Office, 1933).

――――, *Papers Relating to the Foreign Relations of the United States, 1918, Russia* (3 Vols., Washington: United States Government Printing Office, 1931-1932).

――――, *Papers Relating to the Foreign Relations of the United States, 1919* (2 Vols., Washington: United States Government Printing Office, 1934).

――――, *Papers Relating to the Foreign Relations of the United States, 1919, The Paris Peace Conference* (13 Vols., Washington: United States Government Printing Office, 1942-1947).

――――, *Papers Relating to the Foreign Relations of the United States, 1919, Russia* (Washington: United States Government Printing Office, 1937).

[417]

Department of State, *Papers Relating to the Foreign Relations of the United States, 1920* (3 Vols., Washington: United States Government Printing Office, 1935-1936).

———, *Papers Relating to the Foreign Relations of the United States, The Lansing Papers, 1914-1920* (2 Vols., Washington: United States Government Printing Office, 1939-1940).

Dickinson, G. Lowes, ed., *Documents and Statements Relating to Peace Proposals and War Aims* (December 1916-November 1918) (London: George Allen and Unwin, Ltd., 1919).

La Documentation Internationale, *La Paix de Versailles* (12 Vols., Paris: Les Éditions Internationales, 1929-1939).

Great Britain, Parliament, *Papers by Command*, 1917-1920.

Great Britain, *Treaty Series, 1917-1919, 1920.*

Mantoux, Paul, *Les Délibérations du Conseil des Quatre* (2 Vols., Paris: Éditions du Centre National de la Recherche Scientifique, 1955).

Miller, David Hunter, *My Diary at the Conference of Paris*, privately printed (21 Vols., New York: Appeal Printing Company, 1924).

Moon, Thomas Parker, ed., *The Principal Declarations Respecting Terms of Peace by President Wilson and by the Secretary of State* (Paris: American Commission to Negotiate Peace, Section of Territorial, Economic and Political Intelligence, February 10, 1919).

United States Senate, *Hearings before the Committee on Foreign Relations, United States Senate, 66th Congress, First Session, on the Treaty of Peace with Germany*, Document No. 106 (Washington: United States Government Printing Office, 1919).

———, *Report of the Conference between Members of the Senate Committee on Foreign Relations and the President of the United States, at the White House, August 19, 1919, Treaty of Peace with Germany*, 66th Congress, First Session, Senate, Document No. 76 (Washington: United States Government Printing Office, 1919).

———, *Treaties, Conventions, International Acts, Protocols, and Agreements between the United States of America and Other Powers, 1910-1923* (Washington: United States Government Printing Office, 1923).

United States Treaties, *Treaty Series*, 600-667, February 1914-April 1923.

Woodward, E. L. and Butler, Rohan, eds., *Documents on British Foreign Policy, 1919-1939*, First Series (8 Vols., London: His Majesty's Stationery Office, 1947-1958).

Unpublished Documentary Sources

American Commission to Negotiate Peace, Paris, 1918-1919 (Official Records of the Department of State), National Archives, Washington, D.C.

Edward M. House Papers, Sterling Library, Yale University.

Sir William Wiseman Papers, Sterling Library, Yale University.

William H. Buckler Papers, Sterling Library, Yale University.

Woodrow Wilson Papers, Library of Congress, Washington, D.C.

Memoirs and Diaries

Baker, Ray Stannard, *American Chronicle* (New York: Charles Scribner's Sons, 1945).

Balfour, Arthur James, *Retrospect* (Boston and New York: Houghton Mifflin Company, 1930).

Bandholtz, Major General Harry Hill, U.S.A., *An Undiplomatic Diary* (New York: Columbia University Press, 1933).

Baruch, Bernard M., *The Making of the Reparation and Economic Sections of the Treaty* (New York and London: Harper & Brothers, Publishers, 1920).

Bonsal, Stephen, *Suitors and Suppliants* (New York: Prentice-Hall, Inc., 1946).

——, *Unfinished Business* (Garden City, New York: Doubleday, Doran and Company, Inc., 1944).

Borden, Henry, ed., *Robert Laird Borden: His Memoirs* (2 Vols., New York: The Macmillan Company, 1938).

Callwell, Major General Sir C. E., *Field Marshal Sir Henry Wilson* (2 Vols., London, Toronto, Melbourne, Sydney: Cassell and Company, Ltd., 1927).

Cecil, Viscount, *A Great Experiment* (New York: Oxford University Press, 1941).

Grayson, Rear Admiral Cary T., *Woodrow Wilson* (New York: Holt, Rinehart and Winston, 1960).

Lloyd George, David, *The Truth about Reparations and War Debts* (Garden City, New York: Doubleday, Doran and Company, Inc., 1932).

——, *The Truth about the Peace Treaties* (2 Vols., London: Victor Gollancz, Ltd., 1938).

——, *War Memoirs of David Lloyd George* (6 Vols., Boston: Little, Brown and Company, 1933-1937).

Riddell, Lord George, *Lord Riddell's Intimate Diary of the Peace Conference and After, 1918-1923* (New York: Reynal and Hitchcock, Inc., 1934).

Seymour, Charles, ed., *The Intimate Papers of Colonel House* (4 Vols., Boston and New York: Houghton Mifflin Company, 1926-1928).

Tardieu, André, *The Truth about the Treaty* (Indianapolis: The Bobbs-Merrill Company, Inc., 1921).

Wickham Steed, Henry, *Through Thirty Years*, 1892-1922 (2 Vols., London: William Heinemann, Ltd., 1924).

Wilson, Edith Bolling, *My Memoir* (Indianapolis, New York: The Bobbs-Merrill Company, Inc., 1938).

General Historical Works

Allen, H. C., *Great Britain and the United States* (New York: St Martin's Press, Inc., 1955).

Bemis, Samuel Flagg, *A Diplomatic History of the United States* (4th edn., New York: Henry Holt and Company, 1955).

Carr, Edward Hallett, *The Twenty Years' Crisis, 1919-1939* (London: Macmillan and Company, Ltd., 1956).

Churchill, Winston S., *The Aftermath*, Vol. 4 of *The World Crisis, 1918-1928* (New York: Charles Scribner's Sons, 1929).

Fish, Carl Russell, Angell, Sir Norman, Hussey, Rear Admiral Charles L., *The United States and Great Britain* (Chicago: University of Chicago Press, 1932).

Holborn, Hajo, *The Political Collapse of Europe* (New York: Alfred A. Knopf, 1951).

Kennan, George F., *American Diplomacy, 1900-1950* (Chicago: University of Chicago Press, 1951).

Mowat, R. B., *The American Entente* (London: Edward Arnold and Company, 1939).

——, *A History of European Diplomacy, 1914-1925* (London: Edward Arnold and Company, 1927).

Soward, F. H., *Twenty-Five Troubled Years, 1918-1943* (London, New York, Toronto: Oxford University Press, 1944).

General Works on the Paris Peace Conference

Bailey, Thomas A., *Woodrow Wilson and the Lost Peace* (New York: The Macmillan Company, 1944).

Baker, Ray Stannard, *What Wilson Did at Paris* (Garden City, New York: Doubleday, Page and Company, 1919).

———, *Woodrow Wilson and World Settlement* (3 Vols., Garden City, New York: Doubleday, Page and Company, 1922).

Bartlett, Vernon, *Behind the Scenes at the Peace Conference* (London: George Allen and Unwin, Ltd., n.d. [probably 1919]).

Bass, John Foster, *The Peace Tangle* (New York: The Macmillan Company, 1920).

Beadon, Colonel R. H., *Some Memories of the Peace Conference* (London: Lincoln Williams, 1933).

Birdsall, Paul, *Versailles Twenty Years After* (London: George Allen and Unwin, Ltd., 1941).

Burlingame, Roger, and Stevens, Alden, *Victory without Peace* (New York: Harcourt, Brace and Company, 1944).

Clemenceau, Georges, *Grandeur and Misery of Victory* (New York: Harcourt, Brace and Company, 1930).

Dillon, Dr. E. J., *The Inside Story of the Peace Conference* (New York and London: Harper & Brothers, Publishers, 1920).

Hansen, Harry, *The Adventures of the Fourteen Points* (New York: The Century Company, 1919).

Haskins, Charles Homer, and Lord, Robert Howard, *Some Problems of the Peace Conference* (Cambridge: Harvard University Press, 1920).

Hoover, Herbert, *America's First Crusade* (New York: Charles Scribner's Sons, 1942).

House, Edward Mandell, and Seymour, Charles, eds., *What Really Happened at Paris* (New York: Charles Scribner's Sons, 1921).

Lansing, Robert, *The Big Four and Others of the Peace Conference* (Boston and New York: Houghton Mifflin Company, 1921).

———, *The Peace Negotiations* (Boston and New York: Houghton Mifflin Company, 1921).

Marston, F. S., *The Peace Conference of 1919* (London, New York, Toronto: Oxford University Press, 1944).

Nicolson, Harold, *Peacemaking 1919* (Boston and New York: Houghton Mifflin Company, 1933).

Nitti, Francesco, *The Wreck of Europe* (Indianapolis: The Bobbs-Merrill Company, Inc., 1922).

Nowak, Karl Friedrich, *Versailles* (London: Victor Gollancz, Ltd., 1928).

Riddell, Lord, et al., *The Treaty of Versailles and After* (New York: Oxford University Press, 1935).

Shotwell, James T., *At the Paris Peace Conference* (New York: The Macmillan Company, 1937).

Temperley, H.W.V., ed., *A History of the Peace Conference of Paris* (6 Vols., London: Henry Frowde and Hodder and Stoughton, 1920-1924).

Thompson, Charles T., *The Peace Conference Day by Day* (New York: Brentano's Publishers, 1920).

Monographs Relating to Specific Aspects of the Paris Peace Conference

Albrecht-Carrié, René, *Italy at the Paris Peace Conference* (New York: Columbia University Press, 1938).

Almond, Nina, and Lutz, Ralph Haswell, eds., *The Treaty of St. Germain* (Stanford University: Stanford University Press, 1935).

Beer, George Louis, *African Questions at the Paris Peace Conference* (New York: The Macmillan Company, 1923).

Briggs, Mitchell Pirie, *George D. Herron and the European Settlement* (Stanford University: Stanford University Press, 1932).

Burnett, Philip Mason, *Reparation at the Paris Peace Conference from the Standpoint of the American Delegation* (2 Vols., New York: Columbia University Press, 1940).

Creel, George, *The War, The World and Wilson* (New York and London: Harper & Brothers, Publishers, 1920).

Curry, Roy Watson, *Woodrow Wilson and Far Eastern Policy, 1913-1921* (New York: Bookman Associates, 1957).

Déak, Francis, *Hungary at the Paris Peace Conference* (New York: Columbia University Press, 1942).

Fifield, Russell H., *Woodrow Wilson and the Far East* (New York: Thomas Y. Crowell Company, 1952).

Gerson, Louis L., *Woodrow Wilson and the Rebirth of Poland, 1914-1920* (New Haven: Yale University Press, 1953).

Glazebrook, G. P. de T., *Canada at the Paris Peace Conference* (London, Toronto, New York: Oxford University Press, 1942).

Hills, Warren, *Lex Talionis* (Baltimore: Fleet-McGinley Company, 1922).

Howard, Harry N., *The Partition of Turkey* (Norman: University of Oklahoma Press, 1931).

Keynes, John Maynard, *The Economic Consequences of the Peace* (New York: Harcourt, Brace and Howe, 1920).

Komarnicki, Titus, *Rebirth of the Polish Republic* (London, Melbourne, Toronto: William Heinemann, Ltd., 1957).

Luckau, Alma, *The German Delegation at the Paris Peace Conference* (New York: Columbia University Press, 1941).

Mantoux, Étienne, *The Carthaginian Peace* (New York: Charles Scribner's Sons, 1952).

Marburg, Theodore, and Flack, Horace E., eds., *Taft Papers on League of Nations* (New York: The Macmillan Company, 1920).

Martel, René, *The Eastern Frontiers of Germany* (London: Williams and Norgate, Ltd., 1930).

Mason, John Brown, *The Danzig Dilemma* (Stanford University: Stanford University Press, 1946).

McCallum, R. B., *Public Opinion and the Last Peace* (London, New York, Toronto: Oxford University Press, 1944).

Miller, David Hunter, *The Drafting of the Covenant* (2 Vols., New York, London: G. P. Putnam's Sons, 1928).

Noble, George Bernard, *Policies and Opinions at Paris, 1919* (New York: The Macmillan Company, 1935).

Russell, Frank M., *The Saar: Battleground and Pawn* (Stanford University: Stanford University Press, 1951).

Seymour, Charles, *Geography, Justice, and Politics at the Paris Conference of 1919* (New York: The American Geographical Society, 1951).

Shotwell, James T., ed., *The Origins of the International Labor Organization* (2 Vols., New York: Columbia University Press, 1934).

Wilson, Florence, *The Origins of the League Covenant* (London: The Hogarth Press, 1928).

Wood, Ge-Zay, *The Shantung Question* (New York and Chicago: Fleming H. Revell Company, 1922).

Yates, Louis A. R., *United States and French Security, 1917-1921* (New York: Twayne Publishers, Inc., 1957).

Other Monographic Studies

Bailey, Thomas A., *Woodrow Wilson and the Great Betrayal* (New York: The Macmillan Company, 1947).

Bartlett, Ruhl J., *The League to Enforce Peace* (Chapel Hill: The University of North Carolina Press, 1944).

Beveridge, Sir William, *The Price of Peace* (London: The Pilot Press, 1945).

Bloomfield, Lincoln P., *Evolution or Revolution* (Cambridge: Harvard University Press, 1957).

Cocks, Frederick Seymour, *The Secret Treaties and Understandings* (London: Union of Democratic Control, 1918).

Daniels, Josephus, *The Wilson Era* (Chapel Hill: The University of North Carolina Press, 1946).

Davis, Forrest, *The Atlantic System* (New York: Reynal and Hitchcock, 1941).

Eagleton, Clyde, *International Government* (revised edn., New York: The Ronald Press Company, 1948).

Fleming, Dana Frank, *The United States and the League of Nations, 1918-1920* (New York and London: G. P. Putnam's Sons, 1932).

Forster, Kent, *The Failures of Peace* (Washington: American Council on Public Affairs, 1941).

Gottleib, W. W., *Studies in Secret Diplomacy during the First World War* (London: George Allen and Unwin, Ltd., 1957).

Griswold, A. Whitney, *The Far Eastern Policy of the United States* (New York: Harcourt, Brace and Company, 1938).

Hankey, Lord Maurice, *Diplomacy by Conference* (London: Ernest Benn, Ltd., 1946).

Herron, George D., *The Defeat in the Victory* (London: Cecil Palmer, 1921).

Holt, W. Stull, *Treaties Defeated by the Senate* (Baltimore: The Johns Hopkins Press, 1933).

Kennedy, A. L., *Old Diplomacy and New* (London: John Murray, 1922).

Kenworthy, Lt. Commander J. M., and Young, George, *Freedom of the Seas* (London: Hutchinson and Company, Ltd., n.d. [probably 1927]).

Latané, John H., ed., *Development of the League of Nations Idea* (2 Vols., New York: The Macmillan Company, 1932).

Lippmann, Walter, *The Political Scene* (New York: Henry Holt and Company, 1919).

——, *United States Foreign Policy: Shield of the Republic* (Boston: Little, Brown and Company, 1943).

Lyddon, Colonel W. G., *British War Missions to the United States, 1914-1918* (London, New York, Toronto: Oxford University Press, 1938).

Mamatey, Victor S., *The United States and East Central Europe, 1914-1918* (Princeton: Princeton University Press, 1957).

Martin, Laurence W., *Peace without Victory* (New Haven: Yale University Press, 1958).

Osgood, Robert Endicott, *Ideals and Self-Interest in America's Foreign Relations* (Chicago: The University of Chicago Press, 1953).

Rappard, William E., *The Quest for Peace* (Cambridge: Harvard University Press, 1940).

Rappaport, Armin, *The British Press and Wilsonian Neutrality* (Stanford University: Stanford University Press, 1951).

Rudin, Harry R., *Armistice, 1918* (New Haven: Yale University Press, 1944).

Salter, J. A., *Allied Shipping Control* (Oxford: The Clarendon Press, 1921).

Seymour, Charles, *American Diplomacy during the World War* (Baltimore: The Johns Hopkins Press, 1934).

Sprout, Harold and Margaret, *Toward a New Order of Sea Power* (2nd edn., Princeton: Princeton University Press, 1946).

Stone, Julius, *Legal Controls of International Conflict* (New York: Rinehart and Company, Inc., Publishers, 1954).

Toynbee, Arnold J., *The Western Question in Greece and Turkey* (Boston and New York: Houghton Mifflin Company, 1922).

Walters, F. P., *A History of the League of Nations* (2 Vols., London, New York, Toronto: Oxford University Press, 1952).

Willert, Sir Arthur, *The Road to Safety* (London: Derek Verschoyle, Ltd., 1952).

Willis, Irene Cooper, *England's Holy War* (New York: Alfred A. Knopf, 1928).

Willson, Beckles, *America's Ambassadors to England (1785-1928)* (London: John Murray, 1928).

————, *Friendly Relations (1791-1930)* (Boston: Little, Brown and Company, 1934).

Winkler, Henry R., *The League of Nations Movement in Great Britain, 1914-1919* (New Brunswick: Rutgers University Press, 1952).

Zimmern, Alfred, *The League of Nations and the Rule of Law, 1918-1935* (2nd. edn., London: Macmillan and Company, Ltd., 1945).

Biographies and Other Books on Woodrow Wilson

Baker, Ray Stannard, *Woodrow Wilson: Life and Letters* (8 Vols., Garden City, New York: Doubleday, Doran and Company, Inc., 1927-1939).

Bell, H. C. F., *Woodrow Wilson and the People* (Garden City, New York: Doubleday, Doran and Company, Inc., 1945).

Blum, John Morton, *Woodrow Wilson and the Politics of Morality* (Boston, Toronto: Little, Brown and Company, 1956).

Buehrig, Edward H., *Woodrow Wilson and the Balance of Power* (Bloomington: Indiana University Press, 1955).

Cranston, Ruth, *The Story of Woodrow Wilson* (New York: Simon and Schuster, 1945).

George, Alexander L., and George, Juliette L., *Woodrow Wilson and Colonel House* (New York: The John Day Company, 1956).

Hoover, Herbert, *The Ordeal of Woodrow Wilson* (New York, Toronto, London: McGraw-Hill Book Company, Inc., 1958).

Link, Arthur S., *Wilson the Diplomatist* (Baltimore: The Johns Hopkins Press, 1957).

McKinley, Silas Bent, *Woodrow Wilson* (New York: Frederick A. Praeger, 1957).

Notter, Harley, *The Origins of the Foreign Policy of Woodrow Wilson* (Baltimore: The Johns Hopkins Press, 1937).

Tumulty, Joseph P., *Woodrow Wilson As I Know Him* (Garden City, New York and Toronto: Doubleday, Page and Company, 1921).

Walworth, Arthur, *Woodrow Wilson* (2 Vols., New York, London, Toronto: Longmans, Green and Company, 1958).

Publications in Connection with the Woodrow Wilson Centennial Celebration, 1956

Alsop, Em Bowles, ed., *The Greatness of Woodrow Wilson, 1856-1956* (New York and Toronto: Rinehart and Company, Inc., 1956).

Buehrig, Edward H., ed., *Woodrow Wilson's Foreign Policy in Perspective* (Bloomington: Indiana University Press, 1957).

Confluence, Vol. 5, No. 3 (Autumn 1956); Vol. 5, No. 4 (Winter 1957): *Woodrow Wilson and the Problems of Liberalism*.

Latham, Earl, ed., for the American Political Science Association, *The Philosophy and Policies of Woodrow Wilson* (Chicago: The University of Chicago Press, 1958).

The University of Chicago in cooperation with the Woodrow Wilson Foundation, Lectures and Seminar at the University of Chicago, January 30-February 3, 1956, in Celebration of the *Centennial of Woodrow Wilson, 1856-1956*, Central Theme: *Freedom for Man: A World Safe for Mankind*.

The Virginia Quarterly Review, Woodrow Wilson, 1856-1924, Centennial Number, Vol. 32, No. 4 (Autumn 1956).

Woodrow Wilson Centennial, Final Report of the Woodrow Wilson Centennial Celebration Commission (Washington, 1956).

Biographies of David Lloyd George

Jones, Thomas, *Lloyd George* (Cambridge: Harvard University Press, 1951).

Owen, Frank, *Tempestuous Journey—Lloyd George: His Life and Times* (London: Hutchinson and Company, Ltd., 1954).

Thomson, Malcolm, *David Lloyd George* (London: Hutchinson and Company, Ltd., n.d.).

Other Biographies

Blum, John M., *Joe Tumulty and the Wilson Era* (Boston: Houghton Mifflin Company, 1951).

Dugdale, Blanche E. C., *Arthur James Balfour* (2 Vols., New York: G. P. Putnam's Sons, 1937).

Gwynn, Stephen, ed., *The Letters and Friendships of Sir Cecil Spring-Rice* (2 Vols., Boston and New York: Houghton Mifflin Company, 1929).

Harrod, R. F., *The Life of John Maynard Keynes* (London: Macmillan and Company, Ltd., 1951).

Hendrick, Burton J., *The Life and Letters of Walter H. Page* (3 Vols., Garden City, New York: Doubleday, Page and Company, 1922-1925).

Millin, Sarah Gertrude, *General Smuts* (2 Vols., London: Faber and Faber, Ltd., 1936).

Nevins, Allan, *Henry White: Thirty Years of American Diplomacy* (New York and London: Harper & Brothers, Publishers, 1930).

Palmer, Frederick, *Bliss, Peacemaker—The Life and Letters of General Tasker Howard Bliss* (New York: Dodd, Mead and Company, 1934).

Rodd, Sir James Rennell, *Social and Diplomatic Memories, 1902-1919*, Third Series (London: Edward Arnold and Company, 1925).

Smuts, J. C., *Jan Christian Smuts* (New York: William Morrow and Company, Inc., 1952).

Articles, Addresses, and Pamphlets

Bowman, Isaiah, "The Strategy of Territorial Decisions," *Foreign Affairs* (January 1946), Vol. 24, No. 2, pp. 177-194.

Brand, Carl F., "The Attitude of British Labor Toward President Wilson during the Peace Conference," *The American Historical Review*, Vol. XLII, No. 2 (January 1937), pp. 244-255.

Cecil, Lord Robert, *The League of Nations, Its Moral Basis*, The Essex Hall Lecture, 1923, Pamphlet, 32 pp., Christianity and World Problems: No. 4 (New York: George H. Doran Company, 1924).

———, *The New Outlook* (London: George Allen and Unwin, Ltd., 1919).

Cramer, Frederick H., "Who Won World War I?" *Current History*, Vol. 12, No. 65 (January 1947), pp. 8-19.

Feis, Herbert, "Keynes in Retrospect," *Foreign Affairs*, Vol. 29, No. 4 (July 1951), pp. 564-577.

Fraser, Sir John Foster, "What Europe Thinks of Woodrow Wilson," *Current Opinion*, Vol. LXVII, No. 1 (July 1919), pp. 16-18.

Gardiner, A. G., "The Prospects of Anglo-American Friendship," *Foreign Affairs*, Vol. 5, No. 1 (October 1926), pp. 6-17.

Gathorne-Hardy, G. M., *The Fourteen Points and the Treaty of Versailles, Pamphlets on World Affairs*, No. 6 (New York: Farrar and Rinehart, Inc., 1939).

Gooch, G. P., "British War Aims, 1914-1919," *The Quarterly Review*, No. 556, Vol. 280 (April 1943), pp. 168-179.

Haas, Ernest B., "The Reconciliation of Conflicting Colonial Policy Aims: Acceptance of the League of Nations Mandate System," *International Organization*, Vol. VI, No. 4 (November 1952), pp. 521-536.

Harrison, Austin, "The Americanization of the Treaty," *The English Review* (December 1919), pp. 565-573.

Miller, David Hunter, "Vital Point in Peace Treaty Misstated by John M. Keynes," *The Evening Post* (New York) (February 6, 1920), p. 10, columns 5-6.

Seymour, Charles, "Versailles in Perspective," *The Making of Modern Europe*, Book 2: *Waterloo to the Atomic Age* (Ausubel, Herman, ed., New York: The Dryden Press, 1951), pp. 992-1006.

———, "War-Time Relations of America and Great Britain," *The Atlantic Monthly*, Vol. 133, No. 5 (May 1924), pp. 669-677.

Sweetser, Arthur, "Naval Policy and the Peace Conference," *Sea Power*, Vol. VI (February 1919), pp. 77-78.

Whidden, Howard P., Jr., "Why Allied Unity Failed in 1918-1919," *Foreign Policy Reports*, Vol. XVIII, No. 23 (February 15, 1943), published by the Foreign Policy Association.

Woodrow Wilson Foundation, First Annual Dinner of Award in Honor of The Right Honorable Viscount Cecil of Chelwood, the Recipient on the Occasion of Woodrow Wilson's Birthday (Sunday, December 28, 1924), Grand Ballroom, Hotel Astor, New York City. Text of *Addresses* by Norman H. Davis and Viscount Cecil.

Wright, Quincy, "Woodrow Wilson and the League of Nations," *Social Research*, Vol. 24, No. 1 (Spring 1957), pp. 65-86.

Bibliographical Guides

Almond, Nina, and Lutz, Ralph H., *An Introduction to a Bibliography of the Paris Peace Conference* (Stanford University, California: Stanford University Press, 1935).

Bemis, Samuel Flagg, and Griffin, Grace Gardner, *Guide to the Diplomatic History of the United States, 1775-1921* (Washington: United States Government Printing Office, 1935).

Turnbull, Laura Shearer, *Woodrow Wilson: A Selected Bibliography of His Published Writings, Addresses, and Public Papers* (Princeton: Princeton University Press, 1948).